D1171753

James Joyce
The Citizen and the Artist

JAMES JOYCE

The Citizen and the Artist

C. H. PEAKE

STANFORD UNIVERSITY PRESS

Stanford, California 1977

Stanford University Press
Stanford, California
© 1977 by C. H. Peake
Originating publisher: Edward Arnold Ltd, London, 1977
Stanford edition printed in the U.S.A.
ISBN 0-8047-0914-9
LC 76-47985

Contents

Acknowledgements

The Publishers' thanks are due to the following for permission to use copyright material:
Hugh Kenner and Chatto and Windus Ltd for an extract from Hugh Kenner, *Dublin's Joyce*; Oxford University Press for extracts from Richard Ellmann, *James Joyce* (© Oxford University Press 1959); The Bodley Head and Random House Inc. for extracts from James Joyce, *Ulysses* (© 1914, 1918 by Margaret Caroline Anderson and renewed 1942, 1946 by Nora James Joyce); Faber and Faber Ltd and The Viking Press Inc. for extracts from *Letters of James Joyce*, vol. I, edited by Stuart Gilbert (1957) and vol. II, edited by Richard Ellmann (1966), from Stuart Gilbert, *James Joyce's 'Ulysses'* (1930; revised edition 1952) and from *The Critical Writings of James Joyce*, edited by Ellsworth Mason and Richard Ellmann (1959); Jonathan Cape Ltd and The Society of Authors for extracts from James Joyce, *Stephen Hero*, edited with Introduction by Theodore Spencer, revised edition with additional material and Foreword by John J. Slocum and Herbert Cahoon; Jonathan Cape Ltd, The Society of Authors and The Viking Press for extracts from James Joyce, *A Portrait of the Artist as a Young Man*, definitive text corrected from the Dublin holograph by Chester G. Anderson, edited by Richard Ellmann (1968), and from James Joyce, *Dubliners*, edited by Robert Scholes (1967).

Preface

All of Joyce's books, like Thomas Mann's, fit into the
broadening dialectical pattern of Künstler *versus* Bürger.   Harry Levin

This book began as a series of intercollegiate lectures given at Birkbeck College, University of London, in 1963, and, although little of the original material remains unchanged, some of the book's general characteristics derive from its origin. The lecture audience consisted for the most part of interested readers rather than specialists; the book is primarily addressed to a similar audience, and, although I hope it has new emphases, views and interpretations of interest to the specialist, I have not left out materials or steps in the argument merely because he would already know them. The existence of the dialectical pattern referred to by Professor Levin is beyond dispute; but it seemed to me that its complexities and ramifications, shaping not only Joyce's themes but every aspect of his work, had not been fully explored, and that such an exploration would throw light on much that was supposedly obscure or the product of irresponsible virtuosity. I have, therefore, stressed the developing continuity of Joyce's methods as well as of his vision, and have considered most thoroughly those parts of his writings (such as the later chapters of *Ulysses*) which have caused most difficulty for new readers and most controversy among critics. The lectures were not planned to treat of *Finnegans Wake*, and to discuss that book in detail would require more space and more assurance of full understanding than I possess; yet, certainly, the best approach to it is by way of the earlier works, and I have therefore outlined, in the concluding chapter, some of the ways in which *Finnegans Wake* relates to, develops and modifies, in content and manner, the central citizen/artist polarity.

I am well aware of the need to trust the tale not the teller, but, wherever possible, I have used Joyce's own comments, theorizings and schemes as approaches to his writing and as means of ordering my discussions, because I found nothing else that showed as sure a sense of the nature and fundamental structure of the books. For all their imperfections, inaccuracies, limitations, obscurities and vaguenesses, they have provided the basic vocabulary of Joyce commentary and criticism, although, in some of their more speculative and dubious aspects, they may have encouraged the critical tendency to concentrate on surface intricacies regardless of their function, to devise improbable ingenuities, and to provide symbolic systems supposedly necessary to decode the works and reveal their true significance and beauty. There are notable exceptions among the critics, but 'symbolic' and far-fetched criticism continues to dominate, and to flourish on Joyce's works as on the works of no other writer, familiarizing readers with kinds of evidence and argument that would not be accepted in other contexts and establishing an eccentric orthodoxy: many unlikely and wild interpretations of particular stories or passages are now treated as recognized truths, and repeated unchallenged in book after book, article after article. For all their intricacies, Joyc's writings survive and will continue to survive because they possess the traditional literary values, articulating a profound, extensive and coherent vision of life by methods adapted and developed from the traditional methods of the novelist.

When I have consciously taken a suggestion from another critic, or where a point, similar to one I have made, has been made elsewhere, I have acknowledged the debt or the coincidence of opinion in the notes. But unconscious debts are always more numerous and substantial than conscious ones. Ideas that originated in other men's minds enter one's own and are modified and given different applications, until one forgets that they did not spring up unaided. There is no way of recognizing and acknowledging this kind of influence. I can only make a general acknowledgement to those critics and scholars whose work has contributed to my understanding and enjoyment of Joyce's books – especially to Robert M. Adams, Chester G. Anderson, J. S. Atherton, Warren Beck, Frank Budgen, Anthony Burgess, Richard Ellmann, Stuart Gilbert, S. L. Goldberg, Clive Hart, David Hayman, Phillip F. Herring, Stanislaus Joyce, Richard M. Kain, Hugh Kenner, Harry Levin, A. Walton Litz, Ellsworth Mason, Michael Mason, Father W. T. Moon, Joseph Prescott, Robert Scholes, William B. Schutte, W. B. Stanford, Erwin R. Steinberg, Stanley Sultan, and, although I distrust the mode of symbolic interpretation of which they are the most distinguished exponents, to Marvin Magalaner and William York Tindall.

I have not supplied a bibliography. A list of the works most frequently referred to is given under 'Abbreviations'; a fuller list would repeat what is already available in Robert H. Deming's *A Bibliography of James Joyce* (Kansas University Press 1964) and, more selectively, in *The New Cambridge Bibliography of English Literature*, Volume 4: *1900–1950*, edited by I. R. Willison (Cambridge University Press 1972). These lists go up to the end of 1961 and the end of 1969 respectively, and are supplemented by the annual bibliographies in the *James Joyce Quarterly*.

Abbreviations

Page references in the text are to the following editions:

(D —)   *Dubliners*, the corrected text with an explanatory note by Robert Scholes (London, Jonathan Cape 1967).

(SH —)   *Stephen Hero*, edited with an introduction by Theodore Spencer, revised edition with additional material and a foreword by John J. Slocum and Herbert Cahoon (Jonathan Cape 1956).

(P —)   *A Portrait of the Artist as a Young Man*, the definitive text corrected from the Dublin holograph by Chester G. Anderson and edited by Richard Ellmann (Jonathan Cape 1968).

(U —/—)   *Ulysses* (London, John Lane, The Bodley Head 1937, reprinted 1941),
          and
          Ulysses (The Bodley Head 1960).

(FW —)   *Finnegans Wake* (London, Faber and Faber 1939).

In the notes the following abbreviations are used for works and editions referred to several times:

Adams	Robert Martin Adams, *Surface and Symbol: The Consistency of James Joyce's 'Ulysses'* (London, Oxford University Press 1962)
Allusions	Weldon Thornton. *Allusions in 'Ulysses': An Annotated List* (Chapel Hill, North Carolina University Press 1968)
Approaches	Thomas F. Staley and Bernard Benstock (eds.), *Approaches to 'Ulysses': Ten Essays* (Pittsburgh University Press 1970)
Bonnerot	Louis Bonnerot (ed.), *'Ulysses' Cinquante Ans Après: Témoignages Franco–Anglais sur le Chef D'Œuvre de James Joyce* (Paris, Didier 1974)
Budgen	Frank Budgen, *James Joyce and the Making of 'Ulysses', and other writings*, with an introduction by Clive Hart (London, Oxford University Press 1972 edn) (originally published in 1934)
CH	Robert H. Deming (ed.), *James Joyce: The Critical Heritage*, vol. I, 1902–1927; vol. II, 1928–1941 (London, Routledge and Kegan Paul 1970)
CW	Ellsworth Mason and Richard Ellmann (eds), *The Critical Writings of James Joyce* (London, Faber and Faber 1959)
Diary–SJ	George H. Healey (ed.), *The Complete Dublin Diary of Stanislaus Joyce* (Ithaca, Cornell University Press 1971)
Ellmann–JJ	Richard Ellmann, *James Joyce* (London, Oxford University Press 1959)
Ellmann–Ulysses	Richard Ellmann, *Ulysses on the Liffey* (London, Faber and Faber 1972)
Gilbert	Stuart Gilbert, *James Joyce's 'Ulysses'* (London, Faber and Faber, 1952 edn) (originally published in 1930)
Givens	Seon Givens (ed.), *James Joyce: Two Decades of Criticism*,

	with a new introduction (New York, Vanguard Press, 1963 edn) (originally published in 1948)
Goldberg	S. L. Goldberg, *The Classical Temper: A Study of James Joyce's 'Ulysses'* (London, Chatto and Windus 1961)
Gorman	Herbert Gorman, *James Joyce: A Definitive Biography* (London, John Lane, The Bodley Head 1941)
Hart and Hayman	Clive Hart and David Hayman (eds.), *James Joyce's 'Ulysses': Critical Essays* (Berkeley and Los Angeles, California University Press 1974)
Hart–Dubliners	Clive Hart (ed.), *James Joyce's 'Dubliners': Critical Essays* (London, Faber and Faber 1969)
Hart–Ulysses	Clive Hart, *James Joyce's 'Ulysses'* (Sydney University Press 1968)
JJM2	Marvin Magalaner (ed.), *A James Joyce Miscellany: Second Series* (Carbondale, Southern Illinois University Press 1959)
JJM3	Marvin Magalaner (ed.), *A James Joyce Miscellany: Third Series* (Carbondale, Southern Illinois University Press 1962)
JJQ	*The James Joyce Quarterly* (Tulsa University Press 1963—)
Kain	Richard M. Kain, *Fabulous Voyager: James Joyce's 'Ulysses'* (Chicago University Press 1947)
Kenner	Hugh Kenner, *Dublin's Joyce* (London, Chatto and Windus 1955)
Letters, I	Stuart Gilbert (ed.), *Letters of James Joyce* (London, Faber and Faber 1957)
Letters, II *Letters, III*	Richard Ellman (ed.), *Letters of James Joyce*, vols II and III (London, Faber and Faber 1966)
Levin	Harry Levin, *James Joyce: A Critical Introduction* (London, Faber and Faber, 1944 edn) (originally published in 1941)
Litz	A. Walton Litz, *The Art of James Joyce: Method and Design in 'Ulysses' and 'Finnegans Wake'* (London, Oxford University Press 1961)
Magalaner and Kain	Marvin Magalaner and Richard M. Kain, *Joyce: The Man, the Work, the Reputation* (London, Calder 1957) (originally published in 1956)
MBK	Stanislaus Joyce, *My Brother's Keeper*, edited with an introduction by Richard Ellmann, with a preface by T. S. Eliot (London, Faber and Faber 1958)
New Light	Fritz Senn (ed.), *New Light on Joyce from the Dublin Symposium* (Bloomington, Indiana University Press 1972)
Noon	William T. Noon, SJ, *Joyce and Aquinas* (New Haven, Conn., Yale University Press 1957)
Notesheets	Phillip F. Herring (ed.), *Joyce's 'Ulysses' Notesheets in the British Museum* (Charlottesville, Virginia University Press 1972)
Steinberg	Erwin R. Steinberg, *The Stream of Consciousness and Beyond in 'Ulysses'* (Pittsburgh University Press 1973)
Sultan	Stanley Sultan, *The Argument of 'Ulysses'* (Columbus, Ohio State University Press 1964)
Tindall–RG	William York Tindall, *A Reader's Guide to James Joyce* (London, Thames and Hudson 1959)
Workshop	Robert Scholes and Richard M. Kain (eds.), *The Workshop of Daedalus: James Joyce and the Raw Materials for 'A Portrait of the Artist as a Young Man'* (Evanston, Northwestern University Press 1965)

James Joyce
The Citizen and the Artist

Chapter 1 *Dubliners*

The scheme

In October 1905, when Joyce was twenty-three, he wrote from Trieste to the English publisher, Grant Richards, offering a collection of twelve short stories to be called *Dubliners*. To support his plea for early publication, he claimed that no writer had yet 'presented Dublin to the world', and concluded with a sentence which implied some native rottenness in Ireland:

> From time to time I see in publishers' lists announcements of books on Irish subjects, so that I think people might be willing to pay for the special odour of corruption which, I hope, floats over my stories.[1]

He could hardly have foreseen that keen-nosed printers and publishers would locate the corruption in a few vulgar adjectives and such expressions as 'changed the position of her legs often', and that consequently the publication of his book, so far from being early, would be delayed until June 1914.

The first report of the printer's objections drew from Joyce, besides protests, a statement of what he had tried to do:

> My intention was to write a chapter of the moral history of my country and I chose Dublin for the scene because that city seemed to me the centre of paralysis. I have tried to present it to the indifferent public under four of its aspects: childhood, adolescence, maturity and public life. The stories are arranged in this order. I have written it for the most part in a style of scrupulous meanness and with the conviction that he is a very bold man who dares to alter in the presentment, still more to deform, whatever he has seen and heard.[2]

After further pressure he submitted to a few minor alterations, but still fought to preserve his original scheme:

> The points on which I have not yielded are the points which rivet the book together. If I eliminate them what becomes of the chapter of the moral history of my country? I fight to retain them because I believe that in composing my chapter of moral history in exactly the way I have composed it I have taken the first step towards the spiritual liberation of my country.

[1] *Letters* II, 122–3.   [2] *Ibid.*, 134.

Though this belief, he said, might be a 'genial illusion', nevertheless it had served him 'in the office of a candlestick during the writing of the book'.[3]

As characteristic of the young Joyce as the confidence, ambition and lofty moral purpose is the thoroughness of his design. The subject is Dublin, a great European capital not previously presented in literature; the theme, the moral paralysis of Ireland; the purpose, to further the spiritual liberation of that country; the form, a collection of stories riveted together; the structure, a progress from childhood to maturity and public life; the pervading atmosphere, 'the special odour of corruption'; the style, one of 'scrupulous meanness'. Add to this that the beginner had already outlined in his notebooks an aesthetic theory which his work should exemplify, and already he appears, in intention at least, a peculiarly systematic and deliberate artist, believing in artistic forethought and conscious devising, practising what he called 'the classical tradition of my art',[4] and possessing a notion of the social role of the artist worthy of Shelley.

But how could moral paralysis be adequately diagnosed, or a chapter of the moral history of a country contained in a dozen stories, many of them only a few pages long? Could the varied and involved life of a modern city be even sketched, much less evaluated, in so small a compass? If variety were achieved, would it not necessarily be at the expense of cohesion, of the projected formal unity of stories riveted together in a single 'chapter'? Such problems have engrossed the most mature and dedicated of artists, and, like other victims of 'the fascination of what's difficult',[5] Joyce has been accused of an obsession with the mechanics of his art. But the accusation misses the point: it is the intensity of the imaginative pressure, the profundity of the intuition, the complexity of the moral vision which produce the technical problems, as it is the urgency of the creative purpose which supplies the energy and patience to search for and discover the technical solutions. The specific solutions which a writer discovers depend on his peculiar temperament and bent, if only because these determine the way in which he frames his problems. Joyce's predilection, evident in all his work, was for the construction of an elaborate framework of patterns, systems and schemes of relationship, as though he felt that the fertility of his imagination was both disciplined and encouraged by a firm and carefully prepared structure.[6] Certainly it was in such a structure that he found a solution to some of the problems raised by his ambitious intentions – though it might be truer to say that intentions, problems and solutions evolved together.

The elementary organization was the simple succession of 'childhood, adolescence, maturity and public life':

---

[3] *Letters* I, 62–3. [4] *Ibid.*, 60.
[5] This expression is the first line of a poem by Yeats, but Joyce knew the fascination. He told Stanislaus that, although he thought *Dubliners* 'indisputably well done . . . I am not rewarded by any feeling of having overcome difficulties' (*Letters* II, 99).
[6] Cf. 'For the imagination has the quality of a fluid, and it must be held firmly, lest it become vague, and delicately, that it may lose none of its magical powers' (review of Ibsen's *Catilina*, *CW*, 101).

The order of the stories is as follows. *The Sisters, An Encounter* and another story [*Araby*] which are stories of my childhood: *The Boarding-House, After the Race* and *Eveline,* which are stories of adolescence: *The Clay* [sic], *Counterparts* and *A Painful Case* which are stories of mature life; *Ivy Day in the Committee Room, A Mother* and the last story of the book [*Grace*] which are stories of public life in Dublin.[7]

For Joyce, 'adolescence' did not refer to a physical stage, but to a state of spiritual immaturity: Jimmy Doyle may be twenty-six, Bob Doran thirty-four or thirty-five, Lenehan thirty, but having failed to reach adulthood they remain adolescents. The original scheme thus consisted of four sections of three stories each, but as soon as he had sent his book to the publisher Joyce saw the possibility of a pattern more functional and more intricate, though equally symmetrical. He warned Richards that two more stories were needed to complete the design, and within a few months had sent 'Two Gallants' and 'A Little Cloud', which introduced new relationships requiring changes in the order of the stories in the two central groups.

The childhood section remained unchanged in number and order, presenting the onset of moral paralysis through the frustration of the boy's increasingly conscious desires to escape from the humdrum of Dublin life. In 'The Sisters', Dublin offers to the developing soul two equally stunting and stupefying ways of life; in 'An Encounter' it undermines the spirit of adventure; in 'Araby' it devalues love and romance. In each story, the child, as well as being frustrated by his environment, is progressively corrupted by it as its values impose themselves on him, until at the end of the third story he is revealed to himself in his corrupted state.

The stories of adolescence now numbered four, formed, by a rearrangement of the original order, into two pairs. In 'Eveline' a timid and simple-minded young girl, and in 'After the Race' a nervous and simple-minded young man long for what they call 'life', and are defeated by the inhibiting fears and prejudices which the city has planted in them. The next two stories retain the male/female contrast but concern central figures who appear not inhibited but unscrupulous, parasitical or predatory: in 'Two Gallants' a male predator and his parasite prey on a woman, and in 'The Boarding House' two women, similarly cooperating, prey on a man. Yet underlying the contrasts within and between the pairs are the same moral disabilities.

The new story added to the maturity group also demanded a re-ordering and a pairing of the stories into two of married life and two of celibacy. Chandler in 'A Little Cloud' clings to the belief that his responsibilities as a family man, coupled with his shyness, stand in the way of his ambition to be a poet: on the other hand, Farrington of 'Counterparts' is a brutal and irresponsible husband and father, yet as deeply disappointed, thwarted, humiliated as Chandler. In Dublin 'marriage has many pains, but celibacy has no pleasures', for Mr Duffy in 'A Painful Case' steers clear of all emotional ties only to find that his life is barren, while Maria, the old maid

[7] *Letters* II, 111.

of 'Clay', longing vainly for such ties, is, as it were, living a posthumous existence.

Completing the pattern are the three stories of public life, involving the three centres of civic activity: politics, reduced in 'Ivy Day in the Committee Room' to mercenary triviality and lip-service; art, represented in 'A Mother' by a petty squabble between part-time entertainers; and religion, exposed in 'Grace' as a respectable disguise for the service of Mammon.

This simplification of the content of the stories does at least bring out the central pattern of organization round the theme of paralysis, a pattern worth emphasizing, for it is, as far as I know, an original way of composing a collection of short stories and the reason why the stories are so much more powerful and significant in their context than when plucked out by anthologists. But besides giving extra point to each story through its relationship to the other stories of the group and to the book as a whole, the systematic arrangement suggests that all the chief aspects of Dublin life are covered, permits the metaphor of moral paralysis to emerge implicitly as the common thematic centre of the varied lives examined, and creates the basis of an aesthetic coherence and unity extremely rare in collections of short stories.

Many other relationships rivet the stories together in subsidiary aspects of theme and subject matter. The first story, showing the child's experience of Dublin religion, is related to the last (i.e. 'Grace' – 'The Dead' was a later addition), where the adult attitude towards religion and its role in public life is critically viewed. The political squalor exhibited in its public manifestations in 'Ivy Day in the Committee Room' is briefly seen from a personal viewpoint in Mr Duffy's political dabblings in 'A Painful Case'. 'Eveline' is linked not only to 'After the Race', but also, as a presentation of a debilitated desire for romance, to 'Araby', and, as a portrait of a woman defeated in life by a helpless submission to family, to 'Clay'. The dream of life 'abroad' operates in 'A Little Cloud' as well as in 'Eveline' and 'After the Race', and, less conspicuously, in 'The Sisters' and 'An Encounter'. Domineering and scheming motherhood unites Mrs Mooney of 'The Boarding-House' and Mrs Kearney of 'A Mother'. 'A Painful Case' very properly concludes the stories of individual lives because Mr Duffy carefully avoids all the snares into which his fellow-citizens fall, and yet through his Pharisaical avoidance of involvement becomes the purest specimen of the moral paralytic. The unity of the book is also sustained by a network of similarity and contrast in image, symbol and formal treatment, and by the recurring elements of the Dublin scene – the shabby streets, the shallow nationalism, and the pathetic dependence on alcohol (in nearly every story drinking or intoxication is somehow involved).

Although these patternings and relationships help create a structural unity and show the pervasiveness of the disease through the apparent variety of Dublin life, they were no more than a partial solution to Joyce's problems. In particular he needed to find some way of avoiding monotony and repetitiveness in a series of related studies of the same disease. To show more or less identical signs in different people and in different situations would not be enough: moral paralysis is not the measles. There would have to be diverse actions, finely discriminated symptoms and manifestations, distinct and appropriate techniques of presentation, distinct and appropriate styles. Consequently, one is more conscious of the differences between the stories in *Dubliners* than of their similarities, and the focusing of such varied stories on a single thematic centre diagnoses the moral disease and illustrates its diffusion throughout the city much more effectively than could the parallelisms of a homogeneous collection. Whether the story, like 'Counterparts' or 'A Painful Case', approximates to tragedy, or, like 'Grace', is near farce; whether the overall tone is satirical, as in 'Ivy Day in the Committee Room', or pathetic, as in 'Eveline' and 'Clay'; whether the presentation is in the mode of social comedy, as in 'After the Race' and 'A Mother', or savage and squalid, like 'Two Gallants' – the same sickness appears, and the variations of all kinds contribute to its identification and to recognition of the extent of its contagion.

Similarly, even within the groups, there are elements of resemblance and of variation. First-person narrative distinguishes the stories of childhood: the stories of adolescence share an ironic detachment; the mature are explored more deeply and emotionally; and there is more comedy, as well as a greater dispersal of interest, in the stories of public life. But, on the other hand, every story has an individual character, and a distinctive style (or styles), which makes Joyce's reference to 'a style of scrupulous meanness' puzzling. The context of this phrase was Joyce's resistance to the printer's complaints about certain expressions in his book, and it seems possible that he was merely insisting that the words and phrases objected to were such as might be heard every day in the streets of Dublin; he may have had in mind the commonplace language of the stories rather than their style in the full sense.[8] This is to reject what seems the natural sense of the phrase, but the apparently natural sense is inapplicable to *Dubliners*. 'A style' is even more misleading than 'scrupulous meanness', for *Dubliners* has no one style, any more than *Ulysses* has, and many of the invented styles of the later work are foreshadowed in less extreme form in the short stories.

The simple stylistic distinction between direct and indirect speech is used to mark out the basic structure of 'The Sisters', and in other stories this same distinction is part of the story's total meaning: for instance, in 'Ivy Day in the Committee Room', with a single significant exception, everything is in direct speech, to present Joyce's vision of Dublin politics, whereas in 'A Painful Case' (this time with two important exceptions)

---

[8] Joyce's review of the poems of William Rooney (*CW*, 84–7) offers a clue to the meaning of 'scrupulous meanness'. Joyce complains that 'the writing is so careless, and is yet so studiously mean', and says of a quoted stanza, written in commonplace poetical diction, 'Here the writer has not devised, he has merely accepted, mean expressions.' The expressions (e.g. 'the sheltering hills', 'the fiercest-hearted of Erin's daughters') are 'mean' in being stock phrases. Stanislaus Joyce says that he wrote to his brother at the time suggesting 'that studious (that is, careful) meanness can become a positive virtue', and he supposes that Joyce recalled this observation when writing to Grant Richards (*MBK*, 204). If so, Joyce would have been claiming that he had used, for the most part, stock materials, but with a great deal of care.

direct speech is carefully avoided, to present the inturned life of Mr Duffy. But the use of such minor differentiations of style is a comparatively inconspicuous, though not unimportant, aspect of the brilliant and varied handling of diction and rhythm throughout. 'Araby' opens with a sensuous evocation of the children chasing through the streets and lanes in the dusk, and other brief passages of description are equally rich and vivid. The opening paragraph of 'Two Gallants', for instance, with its use of alliteration, assonance, echoings, repetitions to suggest an underlying enervation, is as careful and in its way as economical as anything in the *Portrait* or *Ulysses*.

More important than such set-pieces is the use of style to characterize and evaluate. In 'Clay', what we learn about Maria in the opening paragraphs is not so much what is stated as what the style expresses:

> Maria was a very, very small person indeed but she had a very long nose and a very long chin. She talked a little through her nose, always soothingly: *Yes, my dear*, and *No, my dear*. . . .
> . . . She used to have such a bad opinion of Protestants but now she thought they were very nice people, a little quiet and serious, but still very nice people to live with. (*D* 110–11)

What is central to the story here is not Maria's reaction to Protestants but the way in which we are told about her. The repetitions, the simple repetitive syntax carry the weight of meaning, and, although they may also suggest the way Maria talked, their prime function is to create an image of what it was to be Maria. Basically the same device is used in *Ulysses* to present Gerty MacDowell: in each case a style is specially devised to verbalize the essence of a woman, and, simultaneously, to comment on her. In 'The Boarding House' Jack Mooney hardly appears, but his coarse and brutal presence has to be felt in the background; a few slangy sentences economically create a verbal equivalent for him. Equally the array of clichés expressing Mrs Mooney's sense of outrage betrays the falsity and only partial self-deception of her mood:

> To begin with she had all the weight of social opinion on her side: she was an outraged mother. She had allowed him to live beneath her roof, assuming that he was a man of honour, and he had simply abused her hospitality. He was thirty-four or thirty-five years of age, so that youth could not be pleaded as his excuse; nor could ignorance be his excuse since he was a man who had seen something of the world. He had simply taken advantage of Polly's youth and inexperience: that was evident. (*D* 69–70)

The strung-out clichés characterize Mrs Mooney, and provide all the psychological and moral commentary that is necessary. Again this use of style is extremely important in *Ulysses*, particularly in the 'Cyclops' and the 'Eumaeus' chapters.

The variety of styles is equalled by the variety of uses made of them. The circling obsessive manner of the pervert's conversation in 'An Encounter' is at once described and reflected, as is the flamboyant romanticism of the boy in 'Araby'. There is propriety of style, but Joyce often goes beyond propriety towards pastiche and parody, and makes style the medium for conveying the heart of his meaning. Thus there is no need for authorial commentary to balance Mr Chandler's admiration of the great journalist, Ignatius Gallaher, because the way in which Gallaher's conversation is reported sufficiently exposes his pompous vulgarity:

> Ignatius Gallaher puffed thoughtfully at his cigar and then, in a calm historian's tone, he proceeded to sketch for his friend some pictures of the corruption which was rife abroad. He summarized the vices of many capitals and seemed inclined to award the palm to Berlin. . . . He spared neither rank nor caste. He revealed many of the secrets of religious houses on the Continent and described some of the practices which were fashionable in high society and ended by telling, with details, a story about an English duchess – a story which he knew to be true.   (*D* 85)

This is not merely reported speech – Gallaher did not say that 'he spared neither rank nor caste' – but the smug journalese fixes and evaluates him. Similarly, though more sympathetically, the style by itself is sufficient to enable us to estimate the nature and potentiality of Little Chandler's poetic aspirations:

> He tried to weigh his soul to see if it was a poet's soul. Melancholy was the dominant note of his temperament, he thought, but it was a melancholy tempered by recurrences of faith and resignation and simple joy. If he could give expression to it in a book of poems perhaps men would listen. He would never be popular: he saw that. He could not sway the crowd but he might appeal to a little circle of kindred minds. The English critics, perhaps, would recognize him as one of the Celtic school by reason of the melancholy tone of his poems; besides that, he would put in allusions.   (*D* 80)

The two men are differentiated and judged by the styles in which they are presented.

It is difficult to refer to the style of a single story, let alone 'a style of scrupulous meanness' in the whole collection, for within one story Joyce may have varied his styles to evoke atmospheres and scenes, to present fundamental character, to make an implied moral or intellectual comment, and to shape the total structure. Had it not been for that unlucky phrase in the letter to Richards it seems unlikely that the stylistic variety and virtuosity of the short stories could so often have gone unrecognized.

The management of the styles reflects the character of the book as a whole, its precise and economical combining of diverse materials (diversified, that is, within a certain range) into a compact unity. The nature of the unity is difficult to define because so many factors contribute to it – the overall scheme; the common theme of moral paralysis; the manner, consistently detached but embracing many shades and varieties of detachment; the links of imagery and phrasing; and the force of Joyce's conviction that, beneath the differences of personality and circumstance, his fellow-citizens shared generic traits:

> . . . on account of many circumstances which I cannot detail here, the expression 'Dubliner' seems to me to have some meaning and I doubt whether the

same can be said for such words as 'Londoner' and 'Parisian' both of which have been used by writers as titles.[9]

This formal unity in diversity has an unstrained appropriateness to the nature of a city, at least of a city such as Dublin was about 1900. The stories are of particular people in particular situations; the book composes a moral portrait of a particular city: and, although both are in some way expressive of the lives of all men and all cities, the universality is, as it were, a by-product of the book's particularities.

This is characteristic of most good fiction and would not need emphasizing if so much criticism of *Dubliners* did not make an entirely different emphasis – on mythical and symbolic significances. The objection to these interpretations is not that they are too ingenious or too subtle, but that they spread over stories of rich and delicately articulated meaning a coarse membrane of symbolic and archetypal platitudes, or substitute for the author's finely-formed progeny the sooterkins aborted by the critic. Indeed, it is sometimes suggested that the stories would be of little account were it not for the deeper levels plumbed by symbolic analysis;[10] and, in pursuit of such revelations, the simple facts of the stories are often ignored, misconstrued or even invented; such symbols as are present, like the dying fire in 'Ivy Day in the Committee Room', are exaggerated, distorted and bent to fit some archetypal scheme (usually a simplified derivative from *Ulysses* or *Finnegans Wake*); and arguments are offered which would not be acceptable in dissertations on the Number of the Beast or the Baconian theory. Scientific proof cannot be required of critical interpreters, but it does not follow that free association can pass for literary analysis.

Each story is itself a symbol (in that it represents more than is made explicit, and is not reducible to simple statements) more complex and significant than any symbol it may contain, and in the creation of that greater symbol what is said and done is as important as – usually more important than – what can be identified as symbolic objects or motifs. The apprehension and examination of symbols within a story is part of a critic's task, but it is a part which should be handled with special caution. The symbol-mania which afflicts so many critics of *Dubliners* neglects the whole for the part, and also inflates the part until it deforms or destroys the whole.

Joyce uses symbols in all his works, but, like all other elements, they are subordinated and contributory to the integrated and articulated aesthetic

[9] *Letters* II, 122.
[10] For instance, Marvin Magalaner complains that 'too few have seen the trouble that Joyce took to give more than a surface meaning to his seemingly transparent, harmless stories' (*Magalaner and Kain*, 75). I suspect that few readers have found the stories transparent, and Joyce's contemporaries certainly did not think them 'harmless'. The same critic speaks of 'the fragile narrative' of 'An Encounter' (75) and the 'otherwise trivial narrative' of 'Clay' (71). Similarly, William York Tindall thinks that, if it were not for the symbols he claims to find in them, 'Clay' 'has little point beyond the exhibition of pointlessness' (*Tindall-RG*, 29), and 'A Mother' little to offer beyond a funny story (37–8).

image.[11] In fact, in Stephen Dedalus's account of his aesthetic theory (a theory much in Joyce's mind while he was writing *Dubliners*) he specifically dismisses any general symbolism.[12] Considering Aquinas's term, *claritas* ('that supreme quality of beauty, the clear radiance of the esthetic image'), Stephen says he was for a long time baffled by it:

> It would lead you to believe that he had in mind symbolism or idealism, the supreme quality of beauty being a light from some other world, the idea of which the matter is but the shadow, the reality of which it is but the symbol. I thought he might mean that *claritas* is the artistic discovery and representation of the divine purpose in anything or a force of generalization which would make the esthetic image a universal one, make it outshine its proper conditions. But that is literary talk. (*P* 217)

In *Stephen Hero*, when Stephen says that 'the clock of the Ballast Office was capable of an epiphany', he certainly does not mean that it could become a symbol of something else; he means that, at the right moment, its own essential nature could be wholly, intensely and instantly apprehended as though brought into 'exact focus':

> By an epiphany he meant a sudden spiritual manifestation, whether in the vulgarity of speech or of gesture or in a memorable phase of the mind itself. He believed that it was for the man of letters to record these epiphanies with extreme care, seeing that they themselves are the most delicate and evanescent of moments....
> ... First we recognize that the object is *one* integral thing, then we recognize that it is an organized composite structure, a *thing* in fact: finally, when the relation of the parts is exquisite, when the parts are adjusted to the special point, we recognize that it is *that* thing which it is. Its soul, its whatness, leaps to us from the vestment of its appearance. The soul of the commonest object, the structure of which is so adjusted, seems to us radiant. The object achieves its epiphany. (*SH* 216–18)

There could hardly be a more emphatic assertion that an epiphany was an apprehension of the thing's or person's unique particularity,[13] and not a symbol of something else. Of course, this uniqueness would have wider

[11] Irene Hendry [Chayes] suggests that Joyce's conception of a symbol approximates to that of the medieval Church: 'a symbol has a specific function to perform in a given situation, and, when that function has been performed, nothing prevents the use of the symbol again in a totally different context' ('Joyce's Epiphanies', *Sewanee Review* LIV (1946), 449–67; reprinted in *Givens*, 45).

[12] Cf. 'Stephen specifically rejects in so many words any aesthetic based on symbolism' (Anthony Cronin, *A Question of Modernity* (London, Secker and Warburg 1966), 66).

[13] Stanislaus Joyce gives a similar account of his brother's 'epiphanies', though in less romantic terms. He refers to them as 'manifestations or revelations', and says that they were 'in the beginning ironical observations of slips, and little errors and gestures – mere straws in the wind – by which people betrayed the very things they were most careful to conceal.... The revelation and importance of the subconscious had caught his interest. The epiphanies became more frequently subjective and included dreams which he considered in some way revelatory.... And I could see what he was driving at: the significance of unreflecting admissions and unregarded trifles, delicately weighed, in assaying states of mind for what is basic in them' (*MBK*, 134–7).

reference: the epiphany of the Ballast Office Clock would include apprehensions of the forces that made it precisely what it was and of the general or urban functions it served, and thus would illuminate the nature of all clocks or of all 'Dublin's street furniture'. But this is a very different matter from seeing it as a symbol. Similarly, the image of the paralysed priest in 'The Sisters', besides being an attempt to express the essence of the man's life and nature, is a point in which certain aspects of the Irish priesthood are focused; and the story of the truancy in 'An Encounter', besides conveying an intense apprehension of a particular experience, crystallizes one kind of childhood dream and frustration. In the stories, it is the particularities of the individual life or situation which are intensely illuminated and reflect light around them; in the symbolic interpretations the assumption is that the particularities must be translated into abstractions before their significance can be understood.

The stories of *Dubliners* are not themselves epiphanies[14] (though they include moments of epiphany for the reader and for some characters) because epiphanies are, by definition, 'the most delicate and evanescent of moments'. The moments which Joyce recorded had to be given an environment – in this case a narrative environment – if they were to be apprehended by a reader:

> the artist who could disentangle the subtle soul of the image from its mesh of defining circumstances most exactly and re-embody it in artistic circumstances chosen as the most exact for it in its new office, he was the supreme artist. (*SH* 82)

The stories are the chosen and exact circumstances in which the apprehended quintessences of Dublin life were re-embodied. Nevertheless, they resemble epiphanies in the mode of their operation, in that they focus the essence of a human life or situation in one specific incident, and attempt to define the meaning of 'the expression Dubliner' through an interrelated collection of such specific incidents.[15]

It does not follow that *Dubliners* is merely a practical exemplification of the esthetic theories boldly asserted by Stephen, although both stories

---

[14] Joyce's own term for the stories was 'epicleti' (*Letters* I, 55). Peter K. Garrett says that the correct plural is '*epicleses*', *epiclesis* being 'the ritual invocation asking the Holy Ghost to transform the host into the body and blood of Christ' ('Introduction' to *Twentieth Century Interpretations of 'Dubliners'* (Englewood Cliffs, NJ, Prentice-Hall 1968), 11, n. 17).

[15] None of Joyce's surviving 'epiyhanies' (see *Workshop*, 11–51) were used in *Dubliners*, though many were used in *Stephen Hero* and the *Portrait* and a few in *Ulysses*. However, as Warren Beck has suggested, there are moments of revelation in *Dubliners* corresponding to both kinds of 'epiphany' recorded by Joyce: 'as there are in Joyce's early experimental fragments two kinds of epiphany, the naturalistic-objective and the subjective-psychological, so too with *Dubliners*. In some stories the habit-ridden characters may exemplify chiefly their own unresponsiveness, and since for them self-knowledge is largely paralyzed, any epiphany must accrete in the reader's recognitions. In other stories, characters themselves experience a crisis of emotion under stress of a further realization, which they demonstrate' (*Joyce's 'Dubliners': Substance, Vision and Art* (Durham, NC, Duke University Press, 1969), 23).

and theories developed during the same period of Joyce's life. But the manner of the book is illuminated by the theories, and the content confirms Joyce's account of it in his letters: it depends on the exact presentation of essential particularities, and offers a coherent, critical, realistic image of Dublin as seen by an author unwilling 'to alter in the presentment, still more to deform, whatever he has seen and heard'. For the young man in Dublin and Trieste, there were two ways of discovering and asserting his own nature – the examination of his own past and of the forces which had shaped him, and the establishment of his own attitudes towards the world about him. His vision of the nature of the artist and his vision of the nature of the city were two aspects of the one being, but, at this point in his career, they are sharply differentiated in manner as well as content. There are no artists among the Dubliners (Chandler hardly qualifies), and Stephen's development is towards escape from the city and denial of the ties which bind him to its citizens. As Joyce matured, the division became less sharp, but to read into *Dubliners* a fragmentary and incoherent Odyssey[16] or symbolic searches for spiritual aid is to blur the course of his development. In *Dubliners*, the subject is a city afflicted with moral paralysis: the artist is present only in the judging eye which looks upon the disease at 'its deadly work'.

Childhood

When *Dubliners* was referred to as a collection of sketches, it was presumably because some of the stories seemed at first glance inconclusive as narratives and unclimactic in form. 'The Sisters', especially, is often discussed as though it presented a situation rather than a process – as though the incidents, such as they are, were designed merely to display the symbol of the paralysed priest. In fact, there is a double process: on the one hand, the boy's response to the priest's death makes him aware of complexities in his own nature which he had not suspected and cannot understand, and, on the other, the initial exposure of the Dublin sickness develops through the conversations. All that happens is that the boy learns of the death of the priest who has been teaching him, and, with his aunt, visits the dead priest's house, where he views the body, and hears from one of the priest's sisters of the accident which led to her brother's breakdown and consequent paralysis. Considered simply in terms of its action, the story would seem to be about an imaginative boy's encounter with death: considered as a symbolic sketch, it is dominated by the figure of the dead priest, representing apparently the state of the Irish Church. But the technique of presentation, while not suppressing either of these implications, emphasizes a different aspect of the narrator's experience. By the use of the elementary stylistic distinction between direct and indirect speech (a distinction used frequently

[16] See Richard Levin and Charles Shattuck, 'First Flight to Ithaca: A New Reading of Joyce's *Dubliners*', *Accent* IV (1944), 75–99; reprinted in *Givens*, 47–94.

and for varied purposes in *Dubliners*) the story is shaped into three parts.

After an introductory paragraph, where the word 'paralysis' is introduced, there follows a conversation in direct speech between the boy's uncle and that 'tiresome old red-nosed imbecile' Mr Cotter, a conversation in which the boy, though present, hardly speaks. Here, by implication, the priest seems to represent the world of the intellect, an alternative to the materialist and mundane family. Then comes a long middle section telling of the boy's dream on the night of the priest's death, his observation the next morning of the notice on the door of the dead man's house, his memories of the priest and of their relationship, and his visit with his aunt to view the body. The account of the relationship begins to raise some doubts about the priest as a representative of the spirit and the intellect. Throughout this middle section direct speech is avoided. Finally, in the priest's home, his sister Eliza and the boy's aunt chat; again direct speech is used, and again the boy is present but silent. This conversation reveals the fear-ridden and frustrated life that lies behind the old priest's teaching and his paralysis. The pattern stresses the importance of the two conversations, the first chiefly between two men hostile to the priest and his influence, the second between two women sympathetic to him. The conversations exemplify the alternative modes of life Dublin has to offer the boy. The two men recommend a mindless physical existence: the boy should 'run about and play with young lads of his own age', 'learn to box his corner', take exercise and cold baths. The conversation of the two women epiphanizes the spiritual life to which the boy has been introduced.

By his anger at old Cotter's stupidities the boy seems to have made his choice between the alternatives, but in dreams he feels himself alarmingly pursued by the priest's heavy grey face, and, next day, when passing the priest's door, is surprised

> at discovering in myself a sensation of freedom as if I had been freed from something by his death. I wondered at this for, as my uncle had said the night before, he had taught me a great deal. (*D* 11)

No direct explanation is given of this reaction which occasions the boy's surprise and wonder; instead, the echoing of the uncle's remark introduces a summary of the 'great deal' which the priest had imparted to his protégé – consisting principally of Latin pronunciation, stories about the catacombs and Napoleon, the meaning of Church ceremonies and vestments, and the consideration of difficult theological questions. The boy had been told of the intricacy and mystery of Church institutions, which till then had seemed simple, and had been impressed with the terrible burden of the priest's duties:

> I was not surprised when he told me that the fathers of the Church had written books as thick as the *Post Office Directory* and as closely printed as the law notices in the newspaper, elucidating all these intricate questions. (*D* 11–12)

In addition, he had been taught to patter through the responses of the Mass. His memories give the essence of the mental and spiritual life opened before him. Not surprisingly, he had been so stupefied by this régime that in answer to the priest's questions he 'could make no answer or only a very foolish and halting one', as though his state of mind was akin to the priest's paralysis, and resulted from similar pressures.[17] Although the boy cannot understand why the priest's death seemed a liberation, the reason for it is clear: the repetition of the phrase 'a great deal' now seems ironic, and there is further irony in the boy's dream, when in order to escape the priest's pursuing face he draws the blankets over his head and tries to think of Christmas, as though fleeing from the fears engendered by the incomprehensible and oppressive rituals of the religion expounded by the priest to the simple and joyous origins of that religion.[18]

The priest's breaking-point was, significantly, no sin or spiritual lapse, but an accidental breach of ritual. The sister's comment is an epiphany of her tabu-ridden religiosity and of the spiritual life into which the boy has been initiated:

> - It was that chalice he broke. . . . That was the beginning of it. Of course, they say it was all right, that it contained nothing, I mean. But still. . . . They say it was the boy's fault. (*D* 17)

Eliza's soul crawls rather than shines forth in her implied conviction that, if by chance the chalice had contained something, it would not have been all right. This is another side of Dublin religion, for Eliza represents a religiose, submissive, superstitious and ignorant laity, as her brother represents a priesthood obsessed with ritual and theological refinements. The empty chalice, the cause of the breakdown, reminds one that the dead priest's hands are 'loosely retaining a chalice', an object mentioned again at the end of the story:

> I knew that the old priest was lying still in his coffin as we had seen him, solemn and truculent in death, an idle chalice on his breast. (*D* 17)

The breaking of the chalice was a breach of ritual: the emptiness of the chalice, each time it is referred to, symbolizes a ritual from which all spiritual content has been emptied. Only the forms remain, the objects of superstitious fears; religion, like the old priest himself, is paralysed. Perhaps this is what is being suggested by the boy's notion that the word 'paralysis' sounded 'like the name of some maleficent and sinful being', and by his dream:

[17] In view of what we are told of the priest's instruction, I cannot understand those accounts of the story which talk of 'a boy's deprivation of spiritual guidance and support, through the death of his friend the priest Father Flynn' (Brewster Ghiselin, 'The Unity of Joyce's *Dubliners*', *Accent* XVI (1956), 75–88, and 196–213; reprinted in *Twentieth Century Interpretations of 'Dubliners'*, ed. Peter K. Garrett (Englewood Cliffs, NJ. Prentice-Hall 1968), 69–70).

[18] A similar ironic comparison between the spirit of Christmas and the usual attitudes of the Church occurs in *Stephen Hero*. When Mr Heffernan, defending the Church, says 'We have received a commandment of charity', Stephen replies, 'I hear so, . . . at Christmas' (*SH* 249).

But then I remembered that it had died of paralysis and I felt that I too was smiling feebly as if to absolve the simoniac of his sin.   (*D* 9)

Paralysis and simony are associated in the boy's mind only by the strangeness of the words, but there is some dim apprehension of a causal link between the sin and the disease. In what sense has the priest been guilty of simony? It is probable that, to the boy, simony, as he has learnt of it in the Catechism, is a characteristically priestly sin, and, as Father Flynn is a failed priest, the child supposes that he must have committed simony and been punished with paralysis. Yet just as paralysis serves as a metaphor for the state of the Irish Church, and, in the book as a whole, for the moral condition of the Dubliners, so, too, simony may relate to the transference of veneration and devotion from the spiritual aspects of religion to the material ceremonies and their ritual objects – specifically the chalice –, and to the materialism of the Dubliners which, in all the stories, but most directly in 'Grace', is seen as a kind of simony and as one of the main causes of paralysis.[19] (In fact, it seems to me that the three words, 'paralysis', 'simony', and 'gnomon', which are mysteriously sounded in the first paragraph, refer more importantly to the collection as a whole than to 'The Sisters' in particular. As 'paralysis' provides the metaphor for the spiritual condition of the Dubliners, and 'simony' the metaphor for the spiritual offence which has produced that condition, so 'gnomon', in the sense of a pointer 'which by its shadow indicates the time of day', is a metaphor for the indirect and suggestive method of the stories which indicates that paralysed and moribund condition.)[20] The notion of some maleficence associated with Church rituals recurs in the *Portrait*, when Stephen speaks of his fear of 'a malevolent reality' behind the communion services and of 'the chemical action' in his soul which a false act of homage would induce (*P* 247). It is a similar 'chemical action' in the soul which has broken the old priest and oppressed the boy; as the latter tries to escape in his dream by thinking of Christmas, so the priest has longed to revisit the scenes of his childhood, before he took up his intolerable burden. There is a further

[19] In *Stephen Hero*, Stephen refers to 'diplomatic' marriages as simony ('surely what they call the temple of the Holy Ghost should not be bargained for!'), and compares his own situation as a poet expecting reward from the public: 'I do not swear to love, honour and obey the public until my dying day.' He thinks that 'Simony is monstrous because it revolts our notion of what is humanly possible' (*SH* 206–7). This would seem to imply that the mere taking of priestly vows is a form of simony. A more ordinary form of it is suggested by the priests, who, in the passage immediately following, are seen trying to win Stephen over by offering to free him from 'the entanglement of merely material considerations' (*SH* 208–9).

[20] This interpretation of 'gnomon' is not what the word means 'in the Euclid', where it means 'that part of a parallelogram which remains after a similar parallelogram is taken away from one of its corners' (*SOED*). To the boy, the significance of the word (like 'paralysis' and 'simony') is in its strangeness rather than in its denotation. However, Gerhard Friedrich points out that the two meanings of the word are not inconsistent, and may both be relevant ('The Gnomonic Clue to James Joyce's *Dubliners*', *Modern Language Notes LXII* (1957), 421–4). Since in a geometrical gnomon the whole parallelogram is implicit though not visible, it may suggest Joyce's technique of making a part imply a much larger whole.

irony in the contrast between Eliza's attitudes to her brother's condition at the time of his breakdown, and to his appearance in death. The corpse lies solemn, grey and truculent, but she declares that 'He had a beautiful death', and made 'a beautiful corpse': on the other hand, it was when the priest was found 'wide-awake and laughing-like softly to himself' that something wrong was suspected. Eliza repeats the phrase in the last sentences of the story, so that it stands as a conspicuous epiphany:

> – Wide-awake and laughing-like to himself. . . . So then, of course, when they saw that, that made them think that there was something gone wrong with him. . . . (*D* 17)

The spiritual life offered to the boy seems to be one in which grimness and death are beautiful, and laughter indicative of 'something gone wrong'. However, this is to harden and make explicit what operates as suggestion; and the same can be said of a number of plausible interpretations of details. Thus when the boy, just after describing the priest's educational regime, tries to recall his dream, it is all very hazy:

> I remembered that I had noticed long velvet curtains and a swinging lamp of antique fashion. I felt that I had been very far away, in some land where the customs were strange – in Persia, I thought. (*D* 12)

This could be a reflection of his inner sense of Dublin religion as a kind of mysterious magical ritual, as though the priest's death has released him from a world 'where the customs were strange'; yet also, and more probably in view of the part played by the East in other stories, the dream suggests the boy's desire for escape from the world in which he finds himself. The word 'Araby' later was to 'cast an Eastern enchantment' over him (*D* 32), and Chandler contrasts unfavourably his wife's ladylike eyes with the 'dark Oriental eyes' of Jewesses. These references are no more specifically Oriental than the Turkish Delight which Mrs Kearney eats in large quantities 'to console her romantic desires' (*D* 153); they are crude symbols of the exotic for those oppressed by diurnal drabness.

Such minor aspects of the story thicken the atmosphere and relate suggestively rather than literally to the central drift, but that drift is marked out precisely and clearly enough. A small stylistic differentiation outlines the three-part structure; the structure underlines the two contrasting conversations and the two views of life they represent; this contrast raises the question, 'Why did the boy feel liberated?', and round these central materials are placed the irony about Christmas, the epiphanic remarks of Eliza, and the images of the paralysed priest and the empty chalice. The two conversations are as significantly alike as they are contrasting: in each the boy sits silent while his elders exchange their superstitious platitudes. Both what pretends to be the world of the intellect and the spirit and what claims to be the world of healthy activity are paralysing influences.[21] By

---

[21] Cf. 'individual initiative is paralysed by the influence and admonitions of the church' ('Ireland, Island of Saints and Sages', *CW*, 171).

placing the word 'paralysis' so prominently, and presenting the priest's sickness so emphatically in his first story, Joyce puts in the reader's mind the appropriate metaphor for the moral and spiritual state of Ireland, and the character of the whole book is a drawing near to and a close examination of the disease at 'its deadly work'.

'The Sisters' illustrates the careful interrelating of parts in the *Dubliners* stories. What happens, what is said, and the form of presentation, always constitute a clear significance, enriched and coloured by style, symbols, images, epiphanies; there is no need to invent esoteric mysteries. This is certainly true of 'An Encounter' where the refinements of criticism have discovered elaborate archetypal myths. What the story is explicitly about is the boy's longing for an escape from a routine environment into adventurous activity, and the frustration of his desire partly through the nature of that environment and partly through his own inner weakness. Again there is a three-part structure: first, the awakening in the boy of 'a spirit of unruliness' and a longing for adventure, which eventually demands more than the sensations stimulated by reading and 'the mimic warfare' of children's games; then, the truancy, which gradually palls until the two boys are bored and jaded; and, finally, the real and alarming encounter with the pervert.

In the opening section the narrator's substitutes for adventure are found disappointing even by his timid soul. Always on the losing side in siege and battle, and frightened by the fierceness of Joe Dillon, he has banded together with the others fearfully, as one of 'the reluctant Indians who were afraid to seem studious or lacking in robustness', so that even these mock-adventures are motivated by cowardice. The Wild West books, too, contained adventures 'remote from [his] nature'; their recommendation was that 'at least, they opened doors of escape.' Thus from the beginning he is vainly seeking escape in pursuits alien to him, and afraid to be different from the others, although by culture, constitution and temperament he *is* different. He is torn between his nature and his desire to conform.

His submissiveness to the dominant figures about him is again shown at school, when Father Butler's sneer at *The Apache Chief* 'paled much of the glory of the Wild West for me'; but, away from school, he still hungers for 'wild sensations': 'I wanted real adventures to happen to myself'. Because he believes that such adventures 'must be sought abroad', he joins in the plan to play truant. Yet the escape into adventure never materializes, initially through the discrepancies in culture and temperament between him and Mahony, the very differences he has been trying to conceal. The docks temporarily revive the boys' interest as, watching the ships, they dream of travelling, but the narrator's confused notion associating sailors and adventure with green eyes is found not to tally with the facts when he observes the crew of the three-master. From this point even the illusion of adventure fades. They tire of watching the discharging of the ship: the bright day turns sultry: they wander through squalid streets sedulously eating musty biscuits; despite the brief chase of a cat by Mahony (unaccompanied), they are bored, and finally their projected visit to the Pigeon House is abandoned:

The sun went in behind some clouds and left us to our jaded thoughts and the crumbs of our provisions. (*D* 23–4)

The story would not have been without completeness had it ended there, having traced the slow dimming of the boy's desire for adventure through the workings of impulses which make him seek escape in activities foreign to his nature and, at the same time, restrain him from any full participation. The same divided self produces, on the one hand, his thirst for adventure stories and, on the other, his response to Father Butler's contempt for 'such stuff'. The embryonic moral paralysis grows in the divided nature; in other stories (notably 'Eveline', 'After the Race', 'The Boarding House', 'A Little Cloud' and 'The Dead') a similar immobility derives from similar uncertainty. The encounter with the pervert concentrates the implications of the story in a single incident which evokes in the boy a brief and shaming self-awareness. The narrator, who in the company of other boys was afraid of seeming studious, pretends to have read every book the pervert mentions; he does this in order to distinguish himself from Mahony, and is anxious that his superiority should be recognized:

> Of course, [the man] said, there were some of Lord Lytton's works which boys couldn't read. Mahony asked why couldn't boys read them – a question which agitated and pained me because I was afraid the man would think I was as stupid as Mahony. (*D* 25)

Set against this fear of being thought stupid, which leads to an implicit alliance against Mahony, there is a growing fear of the pervert, from which Mahony is entirely free. Although Mahony is apparently unaffected by the old man's obsessed, circling remarks about his liking for young girls, the narrator, while regarding these views as liberal and reasonable, dislikes the words in the man's mouth and wonders why the man shivers. The boy listens without raising his eyes; he neither looks up nor speaks when Mahony remarks on what the 'queer old josser' is doing; he suggests they adopt false names, and is considering whether or not to go away when the man returns. He is overwhelmed by unidentified fears, whereas Mahony, untouched, runs off to chase the cat again. The extraordinary change in the character of the man's obsessive talk, from his liberal attitude about sweethearts to his declaration that he would whip any boy he found talking to girls or having a sweetheart, presumably indicates that the spectacle on which Mahony remarked was an act of masturbation, releasing the excitement built up by the talk, but there is also the suggestion that in the presence of Mahony, who had claimed three 'totties', the old man was trying to ingratiate himself by a generous attitude, while, in Mahony's absence, he wants to win over the narrator by denouncing boys who, like Mahony, were rough and went with girls. There is, too, a barely concealed threat in his observation to the boy who has denied having a sweetheart that 'if a boy had a girl for a sweetheart and told lies about it then he would give him such a whipping as no boy ever got in this world'; yet his voice 'grew almost affectionate and seemed to plead with me that I should understand him.' The irony is that this alarming appeal is a recognition of common ground which the boy has earlier invited; but now, through the monologue, the boy, save for an involuntary glance of surprise, is afraid to look up. At last his fear of the old man overcomes his fear of disapproval, and he stands up, his heart beating, pretending to be calm. The note of 'forced bravery' in his call to Mahony, and the feeling of guilt ('And I was penitent; for in my heart I had always despised him a little') repeat his pretence of robustness in the Indian games and his prick of conscience at seeing Leo Dillon exposed to Father Butler's scorn, but the sense of guilt is also a partial and immature self-revelation.

The whole story thus relates to 'The Sisters' in its presentation of a sensitive and imaginative boy nervously hesitating between the rough games of the other boys and the pseudo-culture represented by Father Butler and the pervert, with his enthusiasm for Moore, Scott and Lytton. The bewildered stupidity of the narrator of the first story as the old priest revealed the awful mysteries of the Church is recalled in the boy's silent panic as he listens to the secretive voice of the pervert, talking 'as if he were unfolding some elaborate mystery'; while the pervert's apparent plea for understanding recalls the dream-figure of the priest trying to confess. I am not suggesting that the second story is designed to parallel the first; but rather that the second is a step further into paralysis and into consciousness of paralysis. In both stories the boy moves uncertainly between two worlds, two ways of life, to neither of which he belongs although each of them demands from him some kind of submission; but whereas in 'The Sisters' his resentment against Mr Cotter and his sense of liberation on the death of the priest show that he has not as yet been broken in, in 'An Encounter' he has already submitted fearfully, on the one hand to the 'rough' boys and on the other to the sterile adult life represented by Father Butler and the pervert.

There are sudden but unemphatic illuminations: the boy's unspoken answer to the pervert – 'I was going to reply indignantly that we were not National School boys to be *whipped* as he called it' – exposes how deeply he is committed to conformity by its echo of Father Butler's cheap sneer at National School boys; and his half-formed association of the adventurous life with green eyes finds a sinister fulfilment when he is listening to the pervert enthusing about 'a nice warm whipping':

> I was surprised at this sentiment and involuntarily glanced up at his face. As I did so I met the gaze of a pair of bottle-green eyes peering at me from under a twitching forehead. (*D* 27)

Partly this implies that the alarming encounter is all the adventure that Dublin holds out to the boy, but it may also suggest that this is, in effect, his adventure, an adventure which frightens him back into conformity. The Dublin disease has already eaten into him, and he hurriedly retreats into the welcome safety of the familiar. Adventure and escape for him, as for the adult characters of the later stories, can never be more than dreams, not merely because of a squalid environment but because of the weaknesses developed in the soul. The pathos of the situation lies in the incompatibility between his dreams and his true self, and in his occasional glimpses of his own feebleness; Mahony, a simple boy, is untroubled by the routine, because for him the routine safety-valves – using slang, playing at Indians, chasing animals and other children, riding in a train – are sufficient. Mahony is unconscious of his condition: the narrator is sensitive enough to feel it and hate it, but is fixed by his fears – fear of being thought studious and fear of being thought stupid, fear of mimic adventure and fear of real adventure, fear above all of loss of approval through not behaving in the way expected of him.[22]

The glimpse of self-knowledge in the last sentence of 'An Encounter' prepares for the bitterness of the self-revelation at the end of 'Araby'. Once again the structure is basically tripartite: an evocation of the childish experience of a dingy environment, the romantic attachment to the girl, and finally the visit to the *Araby* bazaar – but this time the whole story builds up to the passionate and rhetorical last sentence where the boy's sudden insight into himself marks the end of childhood.

The brief opening colours the commonplace scene with the emotions and sense-awareness of childhood. The 'imperturbable faces' of the houses, the musty enclosed air of the littered rooms, the rusty bicycle-pump, the children playing during the dark winter evenings like a separate race from 'the rough tribes from the cottages', and hiding from the adults who would call them indoors – all belong to the shared world of childhood, imaginatively separate from the 'real' world of the adults. The sight of Mangan's sister, outlined against the light of the door as she calls her brother in for tea, plucks the boy out of this energetic, sensuous, hidden childishness, and puts him in an equally secret, but unshared and secretive, isolation. The religious intensity of his love elevates the diction, the imagery, the rhythm of the sentences: all become high-flown and romantic: 'her name was like a summons to all my foolish blood'; in the flaring gas-light of the streets, jostled by the noisy crowds, 'I imagined that I bore my chalice safely through a throng of foes':

> Her name sprang to my lips at moments in strange prayers and praises which I myself did not understand. My eyes were often full of tears (I could not tell why) and at times a flood from my heart seemed to pour itself out into my bosom. I thought little of the future. I did not know whether I would ever speak to her or not or, if I spoke to her, how I could tell her of my confused adoration. But my body was like a harp and her words and gestures were like fingers running upon the wires. (*D* 31)

In the silent house he even adopts the posture of prayer:

> I pressed the palms of my hands together until they trembled, murmuring: *O love! O love!* many times. (*D* 31)

---

[22] There is so much emphasis on the narrator's timidity that S. L. Goldberg's reference to his 'unruly, romantic, adventurous spirit' (*Joyce* (London, Oliver and Boyd 1962), 37–8) seems to place quite the wrong emphasis, and his assertion that the boy's 'courage wins him his freedom' is to me incomprehensible in terms of what happens in the story.

Through the brief conversation with the girl about the bazaar and his promise to bring her something from it, the name 'Araby' becomes a symbol for his passion, filling him with a hatred of the tedious life of school. As the crowds in the street now seem to him alien, the school, representing 'the serious work of life', seems 'child's play, ugly monotonous child's play'.

But the elevated style and imagery do not show that this passion is, as one critic puts it, 'an almost spiritual love'.[23] Certainly Joyce seems to be recalling the *Vita Nuova*, as in 'Grace' (written at about the same time as 'Araby') he recalled the *Divina Commedia*; but in both stories the Dantean reference is ironic. For despite all the spiritualizing diction and imagery, Joyce insists on the sensuous, physical origin of the boy's emotions. Apart from 'a few casual words' he has never spoken to the girl: it is 'her figure defined by the light' which at first captivates him as he watches her: 'Her dress swung as she moved her body and the soft rope of her hair tossed from side to side.' When she speaks to him about the bazaar his attention is fixed on 'the white curve of her neck', her hair, her hand, and 'the white border of a petticoat, just visible as she stood at ease'. So vividly does this physical image fill his imagination that later, looking at her dark house, he stands for an hour

> seeing nothing but the brown-clad figure cast by my imagination, touched discreetly by the lamplight at the curved neck, at the hand upon the railings and at the border below the dress. (*D* 33)

It is his blood which responds to the mention of her name, his body which responds to her words and gestures like a harp. The extravagance of his imagination converts the physical response into a pseudo-spiritual love just as it derives from the name of a bazaar 'an Eastern enchantment'. The coarse contrast of the reality – his uncle's belated and drunken homecoming, the delay at the station, the passage of the deserted train among 'ruinous houses', and finally the half-closed bazaar where he hears the inane flirtation of the salesgirl with the young men – leads to a disillusion affecting his feelings for Mangan's sister as well as his dreams of Araby:

> Gazing up into the darkness I saw myself as a creature driven and derided by vanity; and my eyes burned with anguish and anger. (*D* 36)

This is the kind of epiphany which in *Stephen Hero* is called 'a sudden spiritual manifestation . . . in a memorable phase of the mind itself' – a boyish equivalent of Gabriel Conroy's humiliation in 'The Dead'. As in the presence of Father Flynn the boy had been silent or halting, as before the pervert he was silent and unable to look up, so, although he regularly sees and follows the girl, he never speaks to her, does not know whether he would ever speak to her, and when she does address him briefly is at first too confused to answer. The timidity and inhibitions coexist with the dreams of adventure and romance; and the gulf between what is desired and what is dared, the first beyond possibility and the second far short of it, is characteristic of the Dublin disease. The point of the story is not the

---

[23] *Magalaner and Kain*, 78.

accident of the boy's late arrival at the bazaar and consequent disappoint-ment, but the whole course of his fantasy and his rejection of 'the serious work of life', which disrupt his personality and bring eventually a percep-tion of the vanity of his self-inflating dreams.

The three stories of childhood exist in lively and coherent thematic relationship; they are held together by the varied tripartite structures and the common central figure, as well as by such minor ties as the boy's thrice-repeated state of tongue-tied fear. Moreover, only these stories are told in the first person, because in this way Joyce can represent the child's growing self-consciousness, in the first story surprised to find in himself feelings he cannot explain or understand, in the second beginning to be conscious of his difference from the other boys and occasionally shamed by his alter-nating contempt for and dependence on them, and, in the third breaking free from the child's world only to achieve a devastating self-revelation. The narrative mode enables the closing in of the environment to be experi-enced from the inside as the boy's hopes and dreams of a fuller life and more intense experience are cramped and mortified. The dreams of escape in subsequent stories are doomed from the start because the characters are already paralysed: in the boy the creeping paralysis spreads as the frustra-tions of the environment impel him to dream-escapes and consequently to further and more withering frustrations.

Adolescence

Compared with the stories of childhood, those of adolescence or immaturity are, with one exception, less subtly conceived, less complexly presented, more conventional in character, and, although brilliantly executed, make their point more obviously. 'Eveline', in particular, the story of a girl long-ing to escape from a wretched life but frightened by the opportunity when it comes, is almost a demonstration. The imaginative strength of the story is in the use of the girl's physical immobility as a visual metaphor for her pre-dicament. The first two sentences fix her attitude:

> She sat at the window watching the evening invade the avenue. Her head was leaned against the window curtains and in her nostrils was the odour of dusty cretonne. (*D* 37)

Thus she remains, thinking and sentimentalizing about her past and present existence and dreaming of a life of happiness she will share with her sweet-heart in South America, until, towards the end, the opening sentences are recalled:

> Her time was running out but she continued to sit by the window, leaning her head against the window curtain, inhaling the odour of dusty cretonne. (*D* 41)

The exact verbal echoes underline her motionlessness – until the sudden panic when she recalls her mother's 'life of commonplace sacrifices closing in final craziness':

> She stood up in a sudden impulse of terror. Escape! She must escape! Frank would save her. He would give her life, perhaps love, too. But she wanted to live. Why should she be unhappy? (*D* 41-2)

This sudden movement does not erase, in the total image of the girl, the prolonged vision of her motionless vigil, thinking of her home and family, and of 'the coloured print of the promises made to Blessed Margaret Mary Alacoque' (a saint in whom self-torture produced paralysis and whose life was given over to self-mortification), and reviewing all the familiar objects and memories of her domestic prison. The brief conclusion, when, despite Frank's appeals, she is 'passive, like a helpless animal', is inevitable. The long unstirring, indecisive sitting while evening deepens and time runs out is emblematic of the theme of the story and of the collection.

The irony of the story is rather obvious and 'literary', perhaps because it plays, not without pity, round the traditional and particularly Victorian theme of a girl torn between love and duty who finally makes the heroic sacrifice of happiness at the call of home and religion. But Joyce conscientiously demolishes sentimentality. Eveline is hardly a girl in love: marriage for her means that 'people would treat her with respect then', and her affection for Frank is far from passionate: 'First of all it had been an excitement for her to have a fellow and then she had begun to like him.' The love is casually tacked on as a secondary condition in her vision of their future ('He would give her life, perhaps love, too') and, when finally he goes, 'her eyes gave him no sign of love or farewell or recognition.'[24] She seems as incapable of love as of movement, and, as no overpowering passion is drawing her away, so the dutifulness which holds her back is drab and half hearted. Her life is spent between the job she would not be sorry to leave and keeping house for a father who frightens her with his threats of violence and who will give her little money for housekeeping. Nevertheless, she persuades herself that her father will miss her, and recalls two trivial occasions when he had been 'very nice'. Even the memory of her promise to her mother 'to keep the home together as long as she could' is marred by the vision of the mother's pitiful life and final craziness. For all her prayers 'to God to direct her, to show her what was her duty', there is no real fight between love and duty inside Eveline: these are merely the conventional disguises for a feebler struggle between conflicting fears.

Explicitly it is fear of sharing her mother's fate that makes her long for escape, for life, for happiness. But even more powerful is the fear of change:

> Perhaps she would never see again those familiar objects from which she had never dreamed of being divided.
> ... In her home anyway she had shelter and food; she had those whom she had known all her life about her. (*D* 38)

---

[24] Clive Hart observes that 'Dublin has so paralysed Eveline's emotions that she is unable to love, can think of herself and her situation only by means of a series of tawdry clichés' ('Eveline', *Hart–Dubliners*, 51).

The fear of the unknown finally conquers, and makes her imagine Frank, who till now has seemed a saviour, as one who is luring her to her destruction:

> All the seas of the world tumbled about her heart. He was drawing her into them: he would drown her. (*D* 42)

The contesting fears elicit from her a cry of anguish, but paralyse her. She is a victim of those idols whom Stephen Dedalus declares he will not serve – home, Fatherland and Church – and, unlike him, cannot say, 'I do not fear . . . to leave whatever I have to leave' (*P* 251). The paralysis of the will, the undermining of the soul, which Joyce consistently presents in terms of a longing to escape or a nostalgic inflation of the past coupled with an inability to act, is perhaps most simply and straightforwardly presented in 'Eveline' and, although the thematic point is rather blatantly evident, the nature of the fears which immobilize the girl are sensitively explored and the superficial disguises of love and duty are stripped off to show the real inner forces which will prevent her from ever achieving 'life'.

Jimmy Doyle, in 'After the Race', is also concerned with 'life', though for him it is to be something to be seen. He had been sent to Cambridge 'to see a little life', and during the party on board the yacht he feels that 'this was seeing life, at least'. Unlike Eveline, however, whose poverty and family are encumbrances, Jimmy has money, the support of his father, and foreign friends. The world seems open to him and yet he, too, at the end of the story, is defeated in spirit. The story is about money and the first paragraph establishes the theme, as the racing cars speed towards Dublin:

> through this channel of poverty and inaction the Continent sped its wealth and industry. Now and again the clumps of people raised the cheer of the gratefully oppressed. Their sympathy, however, was for the blue cars – the cars of their friends, the French. (*D* 44)

This extends the paralysis into social and economic fields; the poor, inactive Irish are pictured as so feeble-spirited that they cheer their oppressors, perhaps represented by the English cars, although the context suggests rather that Joyce is thinking of the poor as victims of the rich.[25]

Jimmy Doyle's difference from the other young men who hilariously fill Ségouin's car is marked from the beginning. 'Ségouin was in good humour', 'Riviére was in good humour', 'Villona was in good humour': Jimmy, however, 'was too excited to be genuinely happy.' The nature of this excitement is analysed. Behind Jimmy stands his father, who had abandoned Nationalism as he became a prosperous 'merchant prince' through police contracts. Like his father, Jimmy has learnt what to value: at university 'he had money and he was popular', and now he is pleased with Ségouin's company since the latter 'had seen so much of the world

---

[25] Cf. Joyce's complaint that *Sinn Féin* 'is educating the people of Ireland on the old pap of racial hatred whereas anyone can see that if the Irish question exists, it exists for the Irish proletariat chiefly' (*Letters* II, 167).

and was reputed to own some of the biggest hotels in France.' All Jimmy's evaluations, like his father's, are similarly determined by cash values:

> Such a person (as his father agreed) was well worth knowing, even if he had not been the charming companion he was. Villona was entertaining also – a brilliant pianist – but, unfortunately, very poor. (*D* 45–6)

The implications of the phrase 'worth knowing' are economic, and Jimmy's excitement is defined in terms of its origins: 'Rapid motion through space elates one; so does notoriety; so does the possession of money' (*D* 46). Jimmy has been seen publicly mixing with these Continentals, and 'as to money – he really had a great sum under his control.' It might not seem much to Ségouin, but Jimmy has inherited from his father 'solid instincts' and knew 'with what difficulty it had been got together'. Previously his bills had been kept to 'the limits of reasonable recklessness': he has a keen perception of 'the labour latent in money'; and it is 'a serious thing for him' that he is about to invest the greater part of his money in Ségouin's business. 'Reasonable recklessness' sums up the struggle in Jimmy between the desire for a wild life and financial prudence, and his feverish mood is directly related to the conflict between this prudence and his hopes of making money from a prospective investment which has his father's backing. Even the car in which they are riding has to be priced ('Jimmy set out to translate into days' work that lordly car in which he sat') and Jimmy himself is similarly valued by his father who, seeing his son's gentlemanly appearance in evening dress, 'may have felt even commercially satisfied at having secured for his son qualities often unpurchasable.'

I have emphasized the repeated monetary reference of this story,[26] because without recognition of the way Joyce dwells on money, it is hard to perceive what lies beneath Jimmy's final mood. For it is his sober sense of the importance of money that prevents him from enjoying his escape into 'life'. He joins in the superficial gaiety, but when the card-playing begins his customary respect for money reasserts itself. While the other men are 'flinging themselves boldly into the adventure', Jimmy is conscious that he is losing and grows confused about his cards and his IOUs; once again money excites him, though now not the possession, but the loss of it. His excitement is always uneasy, and leaves the hangover of the closing paragraph:

> He knew that he would regret in the morning but at present he was glad of the rest, glad of the dark stupor that would cover up his folly. He leaned his elbows on the table and rested his head between his hands, counting the beats of his temples. The cabin door opened and he saw the Hungarian standing in a shaft of grey light:
> – Daybreak, gentlemen! (*D* 51)

It is the grey dawn of his usual life, where the consciousness of the cash-values will return in full strength to reproach him for the recklessness of his

---

[26] Zack Bowen points out that 'the word *money* is used nine times in the first four pages of the story, as well as a liberal sprinkling of such terms as *rich*, *wealth*, *sum*, etc.' ('After the Race', *Hart–Dubliners*, 57–8).

temporary fling at what he thinks of as life. Like the boy in 'An Encounter', like Little Chandler in 'A Little Cloud', Jimmy cannot abandon himself even to an inadequate and foolish dream; he is hamstrung by an inbred absorption in money.

Despite the insistence on the financial prudence inhibiting Jimmy's pleasures, 'After the Race' is a less direct and explicit story than 'Eveline', though few, I imagine, would rank it high among the stories in *Dubliners*, mainly because Jimmy Doyle and his companions are, by Joyce's standards, not fully realized. Certainly the next story, 'Two Gallants', is a far richer invention. Both 'Eveline' and 'After the Race' are given a denser texture by the ambiguity of the author's attitude towards the central figures, where critical irony is qualified by pity. But in 'Two Gallants' this ambiguity is more extreme and disturbing, for Lenehan is the most contemptible figure presented by Joyce, and also the most pitiable. The situation of Corley and his parasite preying on the servant girl is a more vicious conception than the stupidities of the earlier stories, and Lenehan's unscrupulous sycophancy drags him even lower than the brutal Corley; yet from the beginning, mixed with the contempt, there is an element of pity. Lenehan, ingratiatingly flattering Corley and adopting an expression of amused interest and a youthful manner, is prematurely aged; he is a boon companion but isolated: 'his adroitness and eloquence had always prevented his friends from forming any general policy against him.' He is said to be insensitive to discourtesy but the strain of his sycophantic role and his parasitic dependence is apparent, even before Corley leaves him and the surface gaiety is discarded. He is listless and morose in the crowd, tired of the need to amuse. Even the passing relief which comes to him when he has had his wretched meal of peas and ginger-beer produces only flabby daydreams to succeed his despair:

> In his imagination he beheld the pair of lovers walking along some dark road; he heard Corley's voice in deep energetic gallantries and saw again the leer of the young woman's mouth. This vision made him feel keenly his own poverty of purse and spirit. He was tired of knocking about, of pulling the devil by the tail, of shifts and intrigues. He would be thirty-one in November. Would he never get a good job? Would he never have a home of his own? He thought how pleasant it would be to have a warm fire to sit by and a good dinner to sit down to. He had walked the streets long enough with friends and with girls. He knew what those friends were worth: he knew the girls too. Experience had embittered his heart against the world. But all hope had not left him. He felt better after having eaten than he had felt before, less weary of his life, less vanquished in spirit. He might yet be able to settle down in some snug corner and live happily if he could only come across some good simple-minded girl with a little of the ready. (*D* 62)

When Lenehan envies Corley he sinks beneath the level of contempt; when he looks at his own way of life and despises it, he rises above his smug ally. The very nature of his vision of blissful escape is symptomatic of his inability to overcome his moral disabilities: he is tired of being a parasite, but even his dream of comfort, with a girl possessed of enough money for him to live off her and sufficiently simple-minded to allow him to do so, is parasitical.

Because we are taken into Lenehan's mind and not into Corley's, the latter remains an unsympathetic figure, crude, conceited, grotesque, animal, and his attitude to women, coupled with his air of a 'conqueror', makes him so repellent a figure that even the mercenary Lenehan has a note of mockery in his voice when he calls this brute 'a gay Lothario'. The heart of the story is in Lenehan's nature and predicament, for if, like Corley, he had been seen only from outside, the whole emotional interplay of pity and contempt, and the complexity of mood that makes every humiliating submission arouse greater sympathy as well as greater scorn would have been lost. The desperate state of Lenehan's mind is finally revealed when, taunted by Corley's silence about the success of the scheme, his anxiety gives way to bafflement 'and a note of menace pierced through his voice'. That all this anxiety and wretchedness is about a paltry plan to cadge a sovereign from a servant-girl defines the depths of Lenehan's 'poverty of purse and spirit'.

Except in the stories of public life, where Joyce is not primarily concerned with private misery, the satire is tempered with pity, the pity controlled and prevented from corrupting to sentimentality by the satire, and on this depends the emotional density of the stories. From the start the love-hate relationship that existed between Joyce and his fellow-Dubliners was already present and manifest. Both pity and contempt are strongly present in the last of the stories of immaturity, 'The Boarding-House', though here, as in 'Eveline', the stock anecdote (the trapping into marriage of a feeble young man) limits Joyce's exploration of character. Although Mrs Mooney and Bob Doran are drawn sharply enough, they are closer to caricatures than is, say, Lenehan. But the conventional story is enriched by the social implications of an unholy alliance between the forces of religion and society and those of hypocritical immorality. The priest tells Bob Doran he must marry the girl; his Catholic employer will, he fears (and Mrs Mooney counts on it), sack him, and, besides, Mrs Mooney, who has connived at the whole affair, is able to depend on 'all the weight of social opinion'. Joyce darkens the picture with other touches: Mrs Mooney, the ostentatiously respectable, churchgoing, butcher's daughter, who 'dealt with moral problems as a cleaver deals with meat', is referred to by her lodgers as '*The Madam*', and her house is 'beginning to get a certain fame'. (These suggestions are expanded and fulfilled in *Ulysses*, where Bob Doran appears as a drunken wreck, while the behaviour of his wife and mother-in-law is common gossip: in *Finnegans Wake* the matter is summed up, in the paragraph which runs over all the titles of the *Dubliners* stories, by the modification 'boardelhouse' – *FW* 186). Of all the characters in the book, Mrs Mooney is the one against whom Joyce shows most animus. Her energetic determination, the cunning and firmness with which she runs the house, her petty frugality, her policy with regard to her daughter, and her calculations about Bob's situation are manifestations of a greedy egotism approaching malevolence. Her own wretched marriage makes an ironic background for her determination to get her daughter married off. Respectability is the screen behind which Mrs Mooney operates, a screen which she keeps up even in her own thoughts, though a sudden change in style betrays her inner vulgarity, as the cliché-ridden thoughts which conclude that 'for her only one reparation could make up for the loss of her daughter's honour: marriage' abruptly switch to more practical considerations and a coarser vocabulary:

> She knew he had a good screw for one thing and she suspected he had a bit of stuff put by. (*D* 70)

Mrs Mooney's dominant personality may hide the importance of her daughter's part. Polly relies on her mother's intimidation to get her what she wants, as Lenehan depends on Corley's conquering manner. Polly is no mere tool in her mother's hand. Her appearance, 'like a little perverse madonna', exactly corresponds to the mixture in her behaviour of innocence and ruthlessness. She understands her mother's silent complicity, and her distraught performance in Doran's bedroom is as well calculated to force his hand as her earlier appearance there had been to seduce him. Once he has gone from the room, she is quite unperturbed and waits patiently, almost cheerfully. It is significant and ominous that though her thoughts turn to 'hopes and visions of the future', these apparently do not specifically include marriage to Doran, for it is not until her mother calls her to come downstairs to receive Doran's proposal that 'she remembered what she had been waiting for.' For her, as for her mother, marriage is merely the attainment of a social position, and if her slyness is less repellent than her mother's moral coercion it is perhaps only because she is less thoroughly exposed.

For both women, words are a means of concealment, and, consequently, Joyce makes repeated ironic use of the 'market-place' meanings of words to express the debasement of the things they stand for (as in 'Two Gallants' the word 'friends' is used). The word 'frank', for instance, is repeated and then shown to be indistinguishable from 'deceitful':

> Things were as she had suspected: she had been frank in her questions and Polly had been frank in her answers. Both had been somewhat awkward, of course. She had been made awkward by her not wishing to receive the news in too cavalier a fashion or to seem to have connived and Polly had been made awkward not merely because allusions of that kind always made her awkward but also because she did not wish it to be thought that in her wise innocence she had divined the intention behind her mother's tolerance. (*D* 69)

Equally ironic is the reference to Bob Doran, just after he has been longing to escape to another country, as 'the lover'.

Despite the obvious reversal of the sex of predators and prey, the penetration into Bob Doran's state of mind prevents 'The Boarding-House' from being too barely parallel in its general scheme to 'Two Gallants'. There might have been less sympathy to spare for Lenehan if the feelings of the 'slavey' had been explored: here, such pity as is available goes to the victim, though, in accordance with the book's general theme, Bob is as much at the mercy of his own feebleness as of the two women. He is as subservient to appearances and respectability as Mrs Mooney herself, and the landlady well realizes this: 'She did not think he would face publicity.' The embarrassment of confession and the fear of his affair being talked about dominate his mind. The endemic poverty of spirit is Bob's downfall – fear of losing the position his diligence had earned, fear of his family's scorn, fear of being 'had' and of being laughed at, fear of confronting 'the implacable faces of his employer and of the Madam', and fear of the threatening brother. Bob's helplessness, inability to shave, misting glasses make him pitiable, but essentially he is caught because of his unquestioning acceptance of the nets which trap him: it is his 'sense of honour' which over-rules his instinct for celibacy and tells him that 'reparation must be made for such a sin.' (Unknowingly he uses the very catchwords which Mrs Mooney called on to exalt her self-righteousness.) Conformity paralyses him; respectability is the cloak of his pusillanimity as it is of the Mooneys' ruthlessness.

In the four stories of immaturity Joyce traces the various symptoms of paralysis – in the poor and oppressed, in the well-to-do and 'free', in the parasite, predator and victim – with insight and understanding, though the cutting ironies in the treatment of Jimmy Doyle, Mrs Mooney and Bob Doran lack the psychological complexity of the vision of Lenehan's wretchedness. Excepting 'Two Gallants', these stories, without being grossly didactic or bluntly over-simplified, have something of the flavour of 'moral tales': they are good of their kind, but the kind does not give the fullest scope for Joyce's subtlety in apprehension of human nature and behaviour, or for his gift of perceiving in the common events of daily life an aesthetic shape and a meaning. Yet a collection of short stories, thematically unified, requires some variety of plot and treatment, and the acerbity of 'The Boarding-House' and the wry simplicity of 'Eveline' interact sharply and effectively with the resonant suggestiveness of the stories of childhood and 'Two Gallants'. The pathos of the child's predicament needed to be balanced by the more acid detachment with which Joyce regarded those who had failed to grow up, and the dominant theme had to develop from the frustrations of childhood to the exchange of the spiritual values of love and friendship for respectability, material security, status and money – the sin of simony for which the Dubliners pay with moral paralysis.

Maturity

The stories of maturity present contrasts of manner as marked as those in the stories of childhood and of adolescence. 'Counterparts' is direct and energetic; 'Clay' works almost entirely by implication. The latter may seem more characteristically Joycean, but the robustness in the handling of 'Counterparts' is an expression of the subject itself, as the paler and more delicate tones of 'Clay' and 'A Little Cloud' reflect the personalities of Maria and Little Chandler. Joyce is ranging not only over typical Dublin situations, but also over the social and cultural levels of the city. As Eveline and Jimmy Doyle are linked in a frustrated desire for life and contrasted in social and financial position, so, although both Chandler and Farrington are men who feel shackled in marriage, their stories belong in the one case to the intellectual life of Dublin, such as it is, and in the other to the amusements of the bar-flies. The same contrast is later made in *Ulysses* between, on the one hand, the groups in the newspaper office and the National Library, and, on the other, those in Davy Byrne's and Barney Kiernan's. In 'A Little Cloud', as in *Ulysses*, Dublin's literary culture is represented by journalism and the fringes of the Celtic twilight, and in both works Ignatius Gallaher figures as the great journalist; Farrington's first port of call after pawning his watch is Davy Byrne's and there he meets, as does Bloom in *Ulysses*, Nosey Flynn and Paddy Leonard, the regulars.

The comedy of 'A Little Cloud' lies in the contests in Chandler's soul between admiration and envy of his friend, between the melancholy sensitivity on which he prides himself and the assertive vulgarity which fascinates him. The end, when he is repelled by the cold and ladylike prettiness of his wife and the prim and pretty furniture of his house, seeing them as foreign to his poetic soul, recalls the opening description of Little Chandler with his small white hands, frail frame, quiet voice, refined manners, carefully-tended hair, discreet perfume, and perfect nails and teeth. Chandler's longing to escape from prim prettiness is a longing to escape from his own nature, and even his cultivated melancholy is a self-indulgent retreat from life, which is immediately humbled before the coarse temptations represented by Gallaher. The invitation to Corless's fills him with 'a present joy'; 'he knew the value of the name.' He flushes with pride when he remembers Gallaher's bold light-heartedness, and, in this reflected glory, 'for the first time in his life he felt himself superior to the people he passed.' This survives his perception of Gallaher's vulgarity: he still finds 'the old personal charm':

> And, after all, Gallaher had lived, he had seen the world. Little Chandler looked at his friend enviously. (*D* 84)

Similarly Lenehan envied Corley whom he scorned. Again, the paralysis of Dublin manifests itself in an inability to affirm one's own nature. Chandler's questions about the immorality of foreign cities betray a secret hankering after the gaudy and vulgar, and the influence of the drinks and of Gallaher's stories upsets 'the equipoise of his sensitive nature'. The attempt 'to assert his manhood' against his patronizing companion by declaring that Gallaher will marry one day leads him only to self-betrayal, when by his repetition of Gallaher's phrase he shows that he too feels that in marrying he had put his 'head in the sack', and the humiliation is completed by Gallaher's boast that when he marries it will be to some rich woman, a German or Jewess. The course of Chandler's mood from admiring joy to envious depression is carefully plotted from the early references to Gallaher's 'travelled air' and 'fearless accent' to the perception of something unpleasing in the accent and gaudy in the manner; from the recognition of Gallaher's talent as 'a brilliant figure on the London Press' to a depreciation of 'tawdry journalism'; from the belief that Gallaher 'had deserved to win' to a feeling that his success was somehow unjust; from an affectionate pride in Gallaher's friendship to a realization that he, Chandler, was being patronized. The hesitations, waverings, contradictions in Chandler's changing mood are beautifully caught in the worn but unobtrusive poeticisms of the style, and do not make him entirely ridiculous, for, however absurd his poetic ambitions may be, he is a sensitive person compared to Gallaher, though his sensitivity and cultural aspirations are spread over an underlying acceptance of the Dublin ideas of life and success; their prime function is to conceal from himself his failure. His ambivalent attitude to his native city and his country colours everything; he dreams of being a poet with the distinctive Celtic note of melancholy, but chiefly to impress the English critics; he thinks it a pity his name is not 'more Irish-looking' and seems excited when Gallaher speaks of the French liking for Irishmen, and yet feels that 'you could do nothing in Dublin.' His comparison of the cold eyes of his wife with those of the passionate and voluptuous Jewesses Gallaher had spoken of, the resentment against his life and the desire to 'escape from his little house', his recognition that marriage has made him 'a prisoner for life', all stem from his fear that it is 'too late for him to try to live bravely like Gallaher.' However shoddy Gallaher's life may be, it seems exciting and desirable compared to his own insipid delusions. Even the poem which begins to replace 'dull resentment' with his familiar self-deceiving melancholy is conventional Byronic sentimentality, covering the reality of his domination by his sharp-tongued wife with a feeble vision of a lamentation over a dead woman. The choice of poem does not indicate that Chandler wishes his wife were dead, but it does suggest that he would relish the situation of being a grief-stricken mourner. Poetry of this kind is for him an anaesthetic, for repetition of it produces a soothing sadness and the dream of writing it provides the imagined possibility of flight from Dublin: 'If he could only write a book and get it published, that might open the way for him.' The interruption of the crying baby destroys even the escape of illusion, and, by forcing him back into his envy of Gallaher's freedom, re-awakens his resentment. The uncharacteristic violence with which the quiet and delicate Mr Chandler shouts 'Stop!' into the baby's face is a measure of his frustration, and marks the extreme of his revolt. The subsequent shame and remorse demonstrate that the balance, disturbed by the meeting with Gallaher, is restored; Little Chandler has temporarily purged himself of the longing for a wild life by the one rebellious act of shouting at the baby.

For all the mockery of his melancholy, this is one of the most melancholy stories in the book; sympathy for Chandler's predicament balances the sharp satire of Dublin's literary life, perhaps because one feels that in Chandler there are signs of decency and sensitivity, subdued by feebleness of spirit: even the shout at the baby, trivial, pathetic, momentary, comically inadequate as it is, is one of the few gestures against paralysis in the book. (Some critics have thought, plausibly enough, that the title of the story is a reference to the 'little cloud out of the sea, like a man's hand' in the *First*

Book of Kings (xviii, 44).[27] But the biblical cloud is the forerunner of the rain which comes to end the famine in Israel, and one can make this apply to Joyce's story only by taking it as an irony, and a rather clumsy one at that. I think it more likely that the title refers to the transient resentment and outburst – no more than a small and passing cloud over Chandler's resigned 'equipoise'.)

Chandler feels imprisoned by his ties as husband and father; Farrington, his opposite number in 'Counterparts', is conscious of no such responsibilities. Both men are clerks, both find their work tiresome, both long for a freer, less drab life, but while Chandler is small and delicate, a mild and gentle dreamer, Farrington is tall and bulky, a man of savagery and violence.[28] 'The equipoise of [Chandler's] sensitive nature' is the antithesis of Farrington's explosive state: 'the barometer of his emotional nature was set for a spell of riot.' Chandler is remorseful for having shouted at his baby son; Farrington beats his son viciously and without mercy.

As the title suggests, there is something diagrammatic about 'Counterparts'; Farrington is abused and threatened for his inefficiency by Mr Alleyne and forced to apologize for his unpremeditated witticism, and, in turn, threatens and beats his son, forcing out of him an abject plea to be let off. The parallel between Alleyne and Farrington is maintained during the pub-crawl: as the former is disappointed in his attempt to impress Miss Delacour, and is humiliated when he tries to triumph over Farrington, so Farrington is embittered by his inability to get the woman he sees in Mulligan's and humiliated by Withers in the trial of strength. Joyce avoids a mechanical symmetry mainly by the gradual development in Farrington of a murderous rage and violence against the world. Nowhere else in his work (not even in the noisy and threatening old Citizen of *Ulysses*) does Joyce approximate to the character of Farrington, a man with 'a hanging face', wine-dark complexion and bulging eyes, like a tormented bull. The impulse to murder is felt as he looks at Alleyne's bent egg-like head 'gauging its fragility', and later, when he realizes he cannot finish his copying in time, his mood is one of undirected, indiscriminate destructiveness:

> He felt strong enough to clear out the whole office single-handed. His body ached to do something, to rush out and revel in violence. All the indignities of his life enraged him. (*D* 100)

The connection between his violent temperament and his need for alcohol is soon established ('A spasm of rage gripped his throat for a few moments and then passed, leaving after it a sharp sensation of thirst'), and his longing for the gaslight and noise of the bars is a desire to escape from 'the dark damp night'. Thus when he arrives home 'full of smouldering

---

[27] E.g. *Tindall–RG*, 26–7.
[28] Robert Scholes remarks perceptively on the stylistic device of repeatedly referring to Farrington, in simple declarative sentences, as 'the man': 'Calling him "The man" emphasizes both his dullness and his plain brutal masculinity. And the repetitious sentence pattern drums into our heads the dull round of the man's workaday existence which has certainly helped to brutalize him' ('Counterparts', *Hart–Dubliners*, 97).

anger and revengefulness', feeling thirsty again and not even drunk, to find the place in darkness and the fire out, the destructive energy which he has been restraining with difficulty all evening has to explode. This is what makes the last incident so savage: it is not merely a father beating his son but the unchaining of a murderous anger which has been boiling up throughout the story. The closing sentences of the story are boldly placed:

> – O, pa! he cried. Don't beat me, pa! And I'll . . . I'll say a *Hail Mary* for you. . . . I'll say a *Hail Mary* for you, pa, if you don't beat me. . . . I'll say a *Hail Mary*. . . . (*D* 109)

The boy's terrified plea for mercy comes near to melodrama, besides risking a shift of attention from Farrington's own wretched state to the pitiable terror of his son, but the pathos is soured by the irony that, in a world inhabited by savages like Farrington, the child has been led to believe that the oppressor can be bought off by a promise of a prayer. This is an epiphany not only of the boy and his father but of the *mores* of their society, where drunkenness and savagery co-exist with religious practices reduced to a kind of witchcraft.[29] The almost over-pathetic, almost tear-jerking, close to a harsh story is the point to which everything has been moving: the vengeful frustrated world of Farrington, with its animal escapes and satisfactions, is the essential context, the 'artistic circumstances', in which a boy's thrice-repeated promise of a prayer is an epiphany of a society.

Of all the stories 'Clay' has the most individual style, serving both as an expression of Maria's personality and as a means of creating a pervading irony. Maria is the only central character in *Dubliners* who appears satisfied with her lot. Yet this is mere appearance: her insistence that everything is 'nice' hides fundamental frustration. She recalls Joe often saying, 'Mamma is mamma, but Maria is my proper mother' because the maternal role is one she would like to have played; but the fact is that she is not a 'proper mother'. Her suppressed disappointment occasionally peeps out; when Lizzie Fleming says that 'Maria was sure to get the ring' (the promise of marriage) in the Hallow Eve games, Maria laughs and says she does not want 'any ring or man either', and yet, in laughing, her eyes sparkle 'with disappointed shyness'. Her denial and her later self-congratulation on being independent are part of her concealment, from herself and others, of her disappointment, but any careless remark can penetrate the screen. When the shop-girl impatiently asks if she wants to buy wedding-cake, Maria blushes, and she allows the drunken gentleman on the train to assume that the bag contains things for her children, favouring him 'with demure nods and hems'. Her epiphany comes when she is called upon to sing *I Dreamt that I Dwelt in Marble Halls*. Despite her poverty and her humble position in the laundry, she sings of marble halls, vassals and serfs, riches and a high ancestral name, but when she comes to the second verse, she sings the first

---

[29] Stanislaus Joyce, recording the incident in his uncle's family which suggested this climax, wrote in his diary, 'Such appalling cowardice on both sides nearly made me ill' (*Diary–SJ*, 37–8).

one over again. As Hugh Kenner has pointed out, 'the song should have gone on to treat of marriage':[30]

> I dreamt that suitors sought my hand;
> That knights upon bended knee,
> And with vows no maiden's heart could withstand,
> They pledg'd their faith to me.
> And I dreamt that one of that noble host
> Came forth my hand to claim.
> But I also dreamt which pleas'd me most,
> That you lov'd me still the same.

Maria's instinctive avoidance of the painful spot is a silent epiphany, while the concluding sentence of the story is an epiphany 'in the vulgarity of speech' of the man who speaks of Maria as his 'proper mother' but nevertheless allows her to live in servitude and confinement: he is sentimentally moved by her quavering song,

> and his eyes filled up so much with tears that he could not find what he was looking for and in the end he had to ask his wife to tell him where the corkscrew was. (*D* 118)

Maria is a less melancholy figure than Little Chandler, but only because she has more successfully subjugated her dreams and surrendered her spirit. I find the attempts to trace in Maria the Blessed Virgin, a witch or the Poor Old Woman quite unconvincing, contributing nothing to the story and demanding further tortuous explanation; yet the title 'Clay' is itself clearly symbolic. The original title of the story was 'Hallow Eve', which points in much the same direction. Hallow Eve is the time when ghosts walk, and spirits rise from the ground, and Maria's visit to the Donnellys' is indeed like the brief return of a ghost. The title 'Clay' points even more directly to Maria's death, though what the clay in the saucer symbolizes for her is not real death, but a return to the place to which she has been removed out of the circulation of life. To this extent 'Clay' foreshadows the replacement of paralysis as the metaphor for Dublin life by the image of living death which is fully registered in 'The Dead'. Maria's existence is in the past: outside her place of interment she is incompetent and at a loss. Her instinct in declining Joe's offer that she should come and live with him ('she would have felt herself in the way') was right: she no longer belongs in the world where the family has broken up and Joe and his brother will never speak to each other again; she has no real part to play, even as 'a veritable peacemaker'.

The sterility of Maria is paralleled by that of Mr Duffy in 'A Painful Case', though his self-conceit is set against her humility, and his voluntary choice of celibacy contrasted to her involuntary deprivation; she is excluded from life, he excludes himself. Mr Duffy has not succumbed to his environment, but rejected it. He lives at Chapelizod,

[30]*Kenner*, 58.

because he wished to live as far as possible from the city of which he was a citizen and because he found all the other suburbs of Dublin mean, modern and pretentious. (*D* 119)

His uncarpeted and pictureless room is furnished with a minimum of functional furniture; his books are arranged 'according to bulk'; the papers in his desk are neat and tidy: 'Mr Duffy abhorred anything which betokened physical or mental disorder'. He is detached, even from his own body, is inclined to watch himself dubiously, and invents brief impersonal sentences about himself. Above all Mr Duffy is determined to avoid the pitfalls into which the characters of all the other stories have fallen. Paying no heed to 'the conventions which regulate the civic life', he will not submit tamely to accepted moral standards ('He allowed himself to think that in certain circumstances he would rob his bank'); in all things he preserves his intellectual pride. His refusal to allow the free play of his mind to be hampered by conventional material or emotional bonds saves him from the follies of his fellow-citizens. Even when Mrs Sinico's casual remark at the concert leads to a relationship, his rectitude, his 'distaste for underhand ways', makes him insist that they meet at her house. The relationship is intellectual; nevertheless, this is the first adventure in a life which has been 'an adventureless tale' and Mrs Sinico's 'fervent nature' has its effect on him:

> Her companionship was like a warm soil about an exotic. . . . This union exalted him, wore away the rough edges of his character, emotionalized his mental life. (*D* 123-4)

Ironically, Mrs Sinico's affectionate solicitude only nourishes the growth of his egotism, while the same exaltation which lifts him higher above her draws her into a more passionate attachment: the image of the warm soil feeding the exotic plant which grows above and away from it has the right connotations. He thinks that 'in her eyes he would ascend to an angelical stature' and expatiates on 'the soul's incurable loneliness'. He listens to the sound of his own voice: 'We cannot give ourselves, it said: we are our own.' The consequence is that when, moved by his words, Mrs Sinico presses his hand passionately to her cheek, he is both surprised and disillusioned, and quickly breaks off the relationship, telling her that 'every bond . . . is a bond to sorrow.'

Inevitably the news of her death four years later, as a result of an accident while drunk, merely produces a revulsion in Mr Duffy's superior soul, to think that he had ever revealed 'what he held sacred' to a woman capable of such a squalid vice and such a vulgar death, and he congratulates himself on having broken with one who was 'unfit to live'. But even Mr Duffy's inhuman egotism cannot sustain this attitude. From self-approval he moves to self-defence as he tries to assure himself that 'he had done what seemed to him best', and the picture of her loneliness shows him his own: 'His life would be lonely too until he, too, died, ceased to exist, became a memory – if anyone remembered him.' Now, in the darkness of the park, instead of hearing his own voice, he seems to feel her hand, to hear her voice asking, 'Why had he withheld life from her? Why had he sentenced her to death?'

He feels 'his moral nature falling to pieces'. The final irony is that his epiphanic self-revelation comes from seeing lovers lying in the shadow of the park wall:

> Those venal and furtive loves filled him with despair. He gnawed the rectitude of his life; he felt that he had been outcast from life's feast. One human being had seemed to love him and he had denied her life and happiness: he had sentenced her to ignominy, a death of shame. He knew that the prostrate creatures down by the wall were watching him and wished him gone. No one wanted him; he was outcast from life's feast. (*D* 130–31)

The nature of this revelation is beautifully judged: the upright and incorruptible man, who had refused to meet Mrs Sinico 'stealthily', now feels inferior to and rejected by the 'prostrate creatures' enjoying their 'venal and furtive' sexual encounters. But despite his sense of deprivation, the terms in which he refers to the lovers indicate that there is no fundamental change in his way of regarding human relationships, and we are not, I think, intended to take his devastating experience as promising a transformation of Mr Duffy. It arises from his memory of Mrs Sinico, and from his intense feeling of her presence with him in the darkness, but this presence is like that of the train, the noise of which seems to reiterate her name. As it passes from sight and hearing so he begins 'to doubt the reality of what memory told him':

> He could not feel her near him in the darkness nor her voice touch his ear. He waited for some minutes listening. He could hear nothing: the night was perfectly silent. He listened again: perfectly silent. He felt that he was alone. (*D* 131)

The epiphany is a transient perception of what is lacking in the cold, dark, silent world of his isolation.

The technique of presentation is exactly devised: Mr Duffy's egocentricity is reflected in an inward-turned, self-regarding style which avoids all direct speech,[31] save for two brief but important exceptions: the first is the casual remark with which Mrs Sinico, seated next to Mr Duffy at a concert, breaks into his self-centred existence, and the second consists of the few words describing the moment of the death which, temporarily at least, shatters his self-approval:

> A juror—You saw the lady fall?
> Witness—Yes. (*D* 127)

The effectiveness and point of this technique is increased by the contrast with the next story where an entirely opposite verbal strategy is used.

'A Painful Case' is, structurally and thematically, one of the most important stories in the book. It has, of course, a particular relationship with 'Clay' as another view of celibacy, and, as the last of the stories of maturity, the portrait of a man who has not really lived at all has a special poignancy. But also this last story of private life affects our understanding

---

[31] This has a special appropriateness for the story of a man given to composing 'in his mind from time to time a short sentence about himself containing a subject in the third person and a predicate in the past tense' (*D* 120).

of all the stories which precede it and of the three stories of public life which follow. For Mr Duffy is a man who has carefully preserved himself from all the follies which have been the downfall of the other Dubliners. Unlike the sisters in the first story he is attached to no Church or creed; unlike the boy in 'An Encounter' he is satisfied with a life like 'an adventureless tale'; he does not hanker after the romantic as does the boy in 'Araby'; he is not, like Eveline, bound by family ties, nor attracted, like Jimmy Doyle, to the society of 'gilded youth'; he despises such 'venal and furtive' affairs as are presented in 'Two Gallants' and 'The Boarding House', and could neither be trapped into marriage like Bob Doran nor shamed by his own poverty of spirit like Lenehan; he scorns the Irish literary world of which Chandler dreams, and abhors the disorder and drunkenness of which Farrington is a victim; and, unlike Maria, his celibacy is voluntary. Equally his contempt for the timorous materialism of Irish politics looks ahead to 'Ivy Day in the Committee Room', his reference to a city where the arts are entrusted to impresarios foreshadows the musical world of 'A Mother', and, unlike the men in 'Grace', he lives 'his spiritual life without any communion with others.' Mr Duffy's rejections include all the central follies, all the private and social forces which contribute to the paralysis of his fellow-citizens, and thus his story comes to have a special centrality and significance. For in Mr Duffy's scrupulous avoidance of all the traps – religion, family ties, love, friendship, marriage, politics, art and the rest – he avoids, as well, life itself. Joyce does not reject these modes of experience. In Dublin they are all corrupt or decaying, but, though none of them provides a way of escape, neither does Mr Duffy's Pharisaical lifting of his skirts to avoid contamination by the muck of the city. The irony is that the only two figures in the book who have presented to them opportunities to escape from their paralysed condition, Eveline and Mr Duffy, miss, through spiritual timidity, the chances which love offers to them, Eveline submitting feebly to false emotional ties, Mr Duffy frightened by the possibility of forming such a 'bond to sorrow'.

Thus, 'A Painful Case' besides rounding off the stories of private life serves, too, as a transition to the world of public life, where the theme of paralysis is treated not in relation to the particular problems of individuals but as manifested in the corporate life of the city. Moreover, this story, with its vision of the ultimate barrenness of the superior soul who painstakingly sterilizes all his human contacts, points directly ahead to one of the controlling themes of the later work. In a sense Mr Duffy makes the same error that Stephen makes in the *Portrait* (the error from which he is to be rescued by Bloom), the difference being that for the young artist the mistake is a necessary portal of discovery, whereas for Mr Duffy it is a final withdrawal into a dead end.

Public life

The transition from the stories of maturity to those of public life is marked by a technical contrast, for whereas in 'A Painful Case', with two meaningful exceptions, direct speech is avoided and the whole drama enclosed in Mr Duffy's mind, in 'Ivy Day in the Committee Room' there is (with a single exception) no reported speech at all, nor (again with a single exception) do we ever enter the characters' minds. We are told only what these scroungers and hangers-on did, how they looked, and, in direct speech, what they said. The combined effects of these two techniques, one a matter of style and the other of point of view, are multiple and significant. Most obviously, they detach the reader from the scene as though he were present merely as an observer; more importantly they suggest the atmosphere of gregarious superficiality and inanity, as though nothing goes on beneath the surface behaviour; finally, they are formally relevant, on the one hand preparing for the ironic climax of the verses on Parnell's death, which are also given verbatim and without authorial comment, and, on the other, marking the beginning of the 'public life' section of the book by excluding the personal thoughts and feelings of the characters. Both the exceptions reinforce these effects, and both involve Mr Crofton, the outsider in the group, expressing his priggish withholding of himself. On the only occasion when we are taken into a character's mind, it is to find nothing there:

> He was silent for two reasons. The first reason, sufficient in itself, was that he had nothing to say; the second reason was that he considered his companions beneath him. (*D* 146)

Similarly his refusal to associate fully with the others is brought out by the last sentence, the first sentence in reported speech, when, after the others have received enthusiastically the Parnell poem, 'Mr Crofton said that it was a very fine piece of writing.'

From beginning to end the story is one of unprincipled meanness of mind, petty backbiting, and mercenary calculations of the most trivial kind. The men gathered in the Committee Room are, with the exception of Joe Hynes, employed to canvass on behalf of Mr Richard J. Tierney, but they show no confidence in or devotion to their candidate. Mr O'Connor, for instance, has spent much of the day sitting by the fire, and is now chiefly occupied with the question of how soon he will be paid. Mr Henchy, obviously in some position of authority, presumably as agent, calls the candidate, for whom he has been canvassing, a 'mean little shoeboy of hell', refers to his 'little pigs' eyes', blasts his soul, tells about Tricky Dicky's disreputable father, and suggests the candidate is engaged in some murky financial arrangements with the City Fathers. It is true that when the bottles of stout arrive Mr Henchy's view of his candidate improves slightly ('Ah, well, he's not so bad after all. He's as good as his word, anyhow . . . He means well, you know, in his own tinpot way'), but hardly to match the picture which he had presented to the electorate of Mr Tierney as '*a respectable man . . . in favour of whatever will benefit this country . . . a prominent and respected citizen.*' This is politics totally devoid of political thought, principle or concern – politics for a few bob and some free beer. Even Joe Hynes with his ivy leaf in his lapel, his defence of the working-class candidate, his poem on Parnell and his contempt for Tierney is present only in the hope of a free drink.

The only political issue raised is whether the Dublin Coporation should present a loyal address on the visit of King Edward VII. Joe Hynes asserts that the other candidate, Mr Cogan, would not vote for such an address: Mr O'Connor is sure that the Nationalist, Mr Tierney, will also refuse to support it, but as soon as Hynes queries this, Mr O'Connor concedes the point and returns to more important matters:

> —By God! perhaps you're right, Joe, said Mr O'Connor. Anyway, I wish he'd turn up with the spondulics. (*D* 136)

Mr Henchy is in no doubt about it: Mr Tierney, Nationalist or not, will support the address of welcome because the King's visit 'will mean an influx of money into this country.' He rudely brushes aside the question of what Parnell would have done and recommends the King as 'a jolly fine decent fellow . . . an ordinary knockabout like you and me . . . a bit of a rake . . . a good sportsman.' He cannot understand Mr Lyons's objection that having rejected Parnell for immorality it would be strange to welcome King Edward. On this anniversary of his death Parnell is merely a name to pay lip-service to and sentimentalize over, but, as soon as his views are raised, they are dismissed: '—Parnell, said Mr Henchy, is dead.' The old man's comment when, early in the story, Joe Hynes observes that if Parnell were alive there would be no talk of an address of welcome implies the truth about the present state of Dublin politics:

> —Musha, God be with them times! . . . There was some life in it then. (*D* 136)

There is certainly none now. In this context of feeble hypocrisy, double-dealing and petty greed, Joe Hynes's poem 'The Death of Parnell' has a touch of naive sincerity, despite its laboured rhetoric, and makes a curiously complicated impression. Joe Hynes, though a scrounger, has some genuine feeling for the '*Uncrowned King*', and his poem combines maudlin and real grief in a way which is both ludicrous and moving. Yet the applause and Mr Henchy's admiration for the poem show no awareness that in this committee-room Parnell has been betrayed again, and even Mr Crofton, who belongs to the anti-Parnell Conservative party (though now he is dead the party respects him 'because he was a gentleman'), feels free to admit that the poem was 'a very fine piece of writing'.

Joyce never shook off his own childhood attachment to Parnell, and this story, with its symbolic dying fire, shows Irish politics without Parnell as paralysed, if not dead. The sentiment for the past, though kept under control by the critical view taken of the two men who most present it, Hynes and Old Jack, blends with the satire: apart from 'The Dead', this is the only story which suggests the city's longing for its own past. But satire and sentiment are mingled with Joyce's comic view of the civic life of Dublin: he sees it as squalid but funny. Mr Henchy is a comically un-principled, mercenary, two-faced politician, energetic and mischievous like a morality Vice, but Joyce seems still too angry about the Parnell affair to laugh very heartily at the corruptions and betrayals of the committee-room, and the bitter tang is only partly mollified by the extraordinary device of placing at the end of the story the poem about Parnell. As Stanislaus Joyce remarked, it 'strikes a faint note of pathos and saves the story from being cynical.'[32] The whole story is so beautifully managed, with everything adjusted to the total composition – the style, the point of view, the symbolic dying fire, the dank evening, the drab scene, the entirely convincing dialogue – that one can easily understand Joyce's preference for it.

According to Stanislaus, of the stories in *Dubliners*, only 'An Encounter' and 'A Mother' were based on personal experience;[33] though, in another sense, every story in the book was clearly based on such experience. Yet 'A Mother' seems one of the least autobiographical of the stories, largely because Joyce confines himself for the most part to the point of view of Mrs Kearney. This seems a strange tactic, as it tends to localize the centre of interest in Mrs Kearney's personal situation rather than in the public life of the city, and the story, as a result, lacks something of the icy detachment of 'Ivy Day in the Committee Room'. The justification may be that the spectacle of Dublin's musical life is more ridiculous than pernicious, more to be laughed at than to be lashed, and the full comedy can be realized only by perceiving that the city's artistic affairs are a pallid reflection of the petty concerns of private life. The Celtic twilight appeared to Joyce, even when a student, as an association of feeble cultural pretensions with posturing and parochial nationalism; through Mrs Kearney he is able to present them as an insubstantial froth on the surface of a life motivated by respectability and money – a froth quickly dissipated when the underlying preoccupations are disturbed.

The brief biography of Mrs Kearney is thus directly relevant. As a young girl she is admired for her ladylike manners and accomplishments, but, after 'trying to console her romantic desires by eating a great deal of Turkish Delight in secret', she marries a middle-aged bootmaker who is 'sober, thrifty and pious':

> After the first year of married life Mrs Kearney perceived that such a man would wear better than a romantic person but she never put her own romantic ideas away. (*D* 153–4)

In this Jane Austenish way, Joyce presents a woman shrewdly aware of the sober values of respectability and financial stability, and reserving her romantic inclinations as a secret luxury. The Irish Revival and her daughter's musical talents allow her to indulge her taste inexpensively; she is happy to give her attention to the proper organization of the *Eire Abu* Society's

[32] *MBK*, 206.
[33] *MBK*, 79. J. S. Atherton has questioned Stanislaus Joyce's statement on the grounds that many of the stories relate to incidents or relationships in the Joyce family ('The Joyce of *Dubliners*', *James Joyce Today: Essays on the Major Works*, ed. Thomas F. Staley (Bloomington, Indiana University Press 1966), 39). But Stanislaus is talking of first-hand experience of the incidents used.

concert, and even to buy some material to improve her daughter's stage-appearance:

> It cost a pretty penny; but there are occasions when a little expense is justifiable.   (*D* 156)

The expression indicates the strict limits within which her romanticism is allowed to override her financial prudence: it is reminiscent of Jimmy Doyle's 'limits of reasonable recklessness'. But just as the young men from whom she had hoped for romance proved to be ordinary, so the reality behind the artistic and nationalist dream proves to be disillusioning. The *artistes* are poor, the small audience gets smaller, and Mrs Kearney begins to regret the money she has spent. Then the Friday night concert is cancelled, and Mrs Kearney returns from romance to the solid realities. She insists that the original contract still holds and that therefore her daughter must be paid for four concerts, and, getting little satisfaction, is tempted to mimic sarcastically Mr Fitzpatrick's accent:

> But she knew that it would not be ladylike to do that: so she was silent.   (*D* 158)

Already she is tempted, by the threat to her financial dues, to strip off her respectable demeanour as well as her illusions, and the abandonment of these last is signalled by the fact that she takes her husband, whom she respects 'as something large, secure and fixed' to the Saturday night concert. For this, all the real talent has been reserved to give 'the music-loving public' a treat. The quality of this talent is exemplified by the bass, Mr Duggan, a hall-porter's son who has become 'a first-rate *artiste*' – that is to say, he substituted one night for an opera singer in the part of the King in *Maritana*, and was well received by the gallery –

> but, unfortunately, he marred the good impression by wiping his nose in his gloved hand once or twice out of thoughtlessness.   (*D* 160)

The humour here is like that of the remark about Mrs Kearney's resort to Turkish Delight, or the descriptions of Madam Glynn, the ageing soprano who looked 'as if she had been resurrected from an old stage-wardrobe', and of Mr O'Madden Burke, who found the room where the drinks were 'by instinct', and whose 'magniloquent western name was the moral umbrella upon which he balanced the fine problem of his finances.' All of these are in the manner of social comedy and have a tone distinct from anything else in *Dubliners*. Clearly 'scrupulous meanness' has no relevance to this precisely humorous style, which gives the whole story its characteristic flavour.

In Mrs Kearney, money finally outweighs social etiquette. Forgetting her former avoidance of unladylike behaviour, she mockingly imitates Mr Holohan:

> —I thought you were a lady, said Mr Holohan, walking away from her abruptly.
> After that Mrs Kearney's conduct was condemned on all hands: everyone approved of what the committee had done.   (*D* 168)

After the Kearneys' departure, Mr Holohan paces the room: '—That's a nice lady! he said. O, she's a nice lady!' Very properly in a social comedy the catastrophe is a breach of polite manners. Nationalism and music are forgotten when Mrs Kearney fears that two of the promised eight guineas – she insists on reputable guineas, cannot be fobbed off with commonplace pounds – will not be forthcoming, and her passion leads her into social error, for what unites everyone against her is not a lack of loyalty to the movement or a mercenary attitude towards art, but a piece of unladylike behaviour. Thus the story establishes the values which are truly respected by Dublin cultural society. If, as Mr Duffy thought, Dublin had 'entrusted . . . its fine arts to impresarios', 'A Mother' shows us the kind of impresarios in charge: the muddle-headed Mr Holohan, who is most congenially engaged with Mrs Kearney's decanter or in taking the newspaper man away for a drink, and Mrs Kearney, who indulges her romanticism only to the point where it challenges her sense of what really matters – money, however small the amount involved.

The comedy of 'Grace' is nearer farce, although as the centre of interest shifts, first from Tom Kernan to his circle of friends and their attitude towards religion, and then to the priest, the tone changes from the charitable spirit of the *Inferno* section, to the laughing satire of Kernan's *Purgatorio*, and finally to the contemptuous satire of the *Paradiso* in the priest's sermon.[34] This suggests an inverted *Divine Comedy* in keeping with the irony of the title. For the word 'grace' occurs only three times in the story, and the first two occurrences have sardonic reference to the last. We are told of the commercial traveller, Mr Kernan, that he was never seen in the city without silk hat and gaiters: 'By grace of these two articles of clothing, he said, a man could always pass muster.' This is the only kind of grace with which the Dubliners are concerned: Tom Kernan's fall is not spiritual, but a fall from social respectability, symbolized by his filth-smeared clothes and the dinged silk hat which has rolled away from him, and his ascent is back into the fold of respectable business men as he sits in the church with his 'rehabilitated' hat on his knee. (The symbolic equivalence of 'grace' and 'silk hat' is confirmed by Mrs Kernan's memory of her husband at their wedding carrying 'a silk hat gracefully balanced upon his other arm', and by the attention paid to the welfare of their hats by Kernan and the other gentlemen in church.) The second reference to grace, again identified with the commercial value of social approval, concerns the 'modest grocer', Mr Fogarty, who believed that his manners would ingratiate him with housewives: 'He bore himself with a certain grace, complimented little children and spoke with a neat enunciation.' Both of these occurrences of the word

---

[34] Joyce's use of the three-part scheme of the *Divine Comedy* was first suggested by Stanislaus Joyce ('Ricordi di James Joyce', *Letteratura* V (3) (1941), 23–35; translated in *Hudson Review* II (4) (1950), 487–514), and treated more fully by Stuart Gilbert (in *Writers of Today*, ed. Denys Val Baker (London, Sidgwick and Jackson 1946), 43–57; reprinted in *Givens*, 450–68), and by Stanislaus Joyce (in 'The Background to *Dubliners*', *Listener* LI (1954), 526–7).

look forward to its use by the priest in the penultimate sentence of the sermon which concludes the story. The priest chooses for his text,

> *For the children of this world are wiser in their generation than the children of light. Wherefore make unto yourselves friends out of the mammon of iniquity so that when you die they may receive you into everlasting dwellings.* (D 197)

He does not relate this text to its context or indicate in any way that this is Christ's ironic comment at the end of the parable of the unjust steward (*Luke* xvi, 8–9), a comment which ends with the declaration 'Ye cannot serve God and mammon.' Instead, after observing that it is a difficult text to interpret properly, a text which might seem 'at variance with the lofty morality elsewhere preached by Jesus Christ', he offers the extraordinary gloss that it seems

> specially adapted for the guidance of those whose lot it was to lead the life of the world and who yet wished to lead that life not in the manner of worldlings. It was a text for business men and professional men. (D 197)

Christ, he says, with his understanding of human nature, realized that the religious life was not for all men, and that 'by far the vast majority were forced to live in the world and, to a certain extent, for the world.' Without the New Testament context, the reader may miss the full force of this epiphany: Father Purdon is arguing that most men not only can, but must, 'to a certain extent' serve God and mammon. He adds that, in the text, Christ is 'setting before them as exemplars in the religious life those very worshippers of Mammon who were of all men the least solicitous in matters religious.' Taking his cue from this, Father Purdon, having reassured the congregation that he has no terrifying purpose but speaks as 'a man of the world', introduces his business metaphor: he wishes his hearers to examine the books of their spiritual life to see whether they tallied with conscience. If they find their spiritual accounts in good order, they should say so; if there were some discrepancies they should admit them:

> *Well, I have looked into my accounts. I find this wrong and this wrong. But, with God's grace, I will rectify this and this. I will set right my accounts.* (D 198)

The irony of this is crushing. To appeal to this congregation to model their spiritual affairs on their conduct of their financial affairs is ludicrous: Mr Kernan is socially declining and in debt to Fogarty, Mr Power has inexplicable debts, Mr Cunningham's wife has pawned the furniture six times, M'Coy borrows without repaying, Mr Fogarty has already failed once in business, and among the company in church are Harford the moneylender, Grimes the pawnbroker and 'poor O'Carroll . . . who had been at one time a considerable commercial figure.' That these men conduct their spiritual accounts on the same principle as their business affairs seems only too likely. In his determination to make friends out of the mammon of iniquity the priest illustrates rather than interprets the parable of the unjust steward called by his master to give an account of his stewardship. The steward, certain of losing his job ('I cannot dig; to beg I am ashamed'), decides to insure against dismissal by making friends with his master's debtors – 'that, when I am put out of the stewardship, they may receive me into their houses', and, summoning the debtors, he considerably reduces the debt of each of them. The lord commends the man's shrewdness, and there follows the comment given in the text. This is precisely the wisdom of the priest. The spiritual debtors who appear in the church know what to expect from the priest ('He won't be too hard on us') and from the Jesuit Order ('The Jesuits cater for the upper classes'), and they get what they expect. What being 'straight and manly with God' means to them has already been exposed:

> —So we're going to wash the pot together, said Mr Cunningham.
> A thought seemed to strike him. He turned suddenly to the invalid and said:
> - Do you know what, Tom, has just occurred to me ? You might join in and we'd have a four-handed reel.   (*D* 184)

The metaphor comically places the mood in which the men approach what Mr Cunningham airily calls 'just a little . . . spiritual matter', and when Mrs Kernan acidly pities the clergyman who will have to listen to her husband's confession, the latter leaves his attitude in no doubt:

> —If he doesn't like it, he said bluntly, he can . . . do the other thing. I'll just tell him my little tale of woe. I'm not such a bad fellow—   (*D* 194)

Mr Kernan will not find much amiss when he looks into his spiritual accounts, nor will Father Purdon's 'friendly talk' inflame the consciences of his hearers. Indeed the presentation of the sermon in reported speech, after the garrulous exchanges round Kernan's bedside, is expressive of the absence of any real impact: Mr Kernan may have 'presented an attentive face', but the words indicate the depth of his attention. The priest's worldly wisdom, like that of the steward, is commended in the praise of his order:

> If you want a thing well done and no flies about it you go to a Jesuit. They're the boyos have influence.   (*D* 184-5)

The same point about the Jesuits is made in the *Portrait* when Stephen thinks that they 'had earned the name of worldlings at the hands not of the unworldly only but of the worldly also for having pleaded, during all their history, at the bar of God's justice for the souls of the lax and the lukewarm and the prudent' (*P* 195). As always, compromising religion disgusts Joyce. The squalid accident of the first section is relieved by the Good Samaritanism of the young man in the cycling-suit and Mr Power: the friendly help held out in the second section is benevolent though less substantial, and the blandly ignorant and stupid conversational exchanges are good-naturedly ridiculed: but in Father Purdon's smug and ingratiating address there is something nauseating, a flavour of corruption, strengthened for the few readers who recognized the contemptuous allusion in the name. Purdon Street was in the brothel quarter of Dublin, and is named in the 'Circe' chapter of *Ulysses*. Stanislaus Joyce, who pointed out this allusion, also recorded the fact that his brother had attended a sermon on the doctrine of grace 'and had come away angry and disgusted at the inadequacy of the exposition':

He said the preacher had not even tried to know what he was talking about, but assumed that anything was good enough for his listeners. It angered him that such shoddy stuff should pass for spiritual guidance.[35]

Some of that anger can be felt beneath the surface of 'Grace', which exposes the role played by religion in Dublin's public life, as the first story, 'The Sisters', exposes its role in the formation of the individual.

In the stories of public life, anger and laughter are mixed more plainly than in the earlier stories, if only because there is no longer the qualifying pathos of individual wretchedness. The poverty of spirit displayed in politics, culture and religion might have seemed pitiful had there been a little more of the feeble sincerity of the Parnell poem, but everywhere a smear of bonhomie and patriotism conceals a shallow corruption. Hypocrisy is hardly the word for the public behaviour of the Dubliners, for they are as self-deluded as deceitful, but the overall appearance of trivial falseness makes these three stories the most consistently satirical of the collection.

In Joyce's original scheme there was thus a progression in attitude, from the sympathetic presentation of childhood to the detached satire of public life, matching the progress of the disease: the frustrated and intimidated boy is succeeded by the adolescents deprived through internal weakness and paralysis of the escape they dream of, by the adults fettered even more securely in family and habit, and finally by the general infection of the corporate life of the citizens for whom the only saving grace is social acceptance and respectability. In the book, as originally planned, there was little to balance the general repudiation of all that Dublin stood for and prized, and this has sometimes led to the objection that *Dubliners* is negative in spirit. But there is nothing negative – except by way of gesture – in the exposure and repudiation of the forces in society which stunt the growth and stifle the free existence of men and women in their personal and social lives. If *Dubliners* truthfully uncovers what is wrong, the author is under no moral or literary obligation to declare what is right, other than by the general implications of his criticism. That he was aware from the beginning that mere contempt for and hostile withdrawal from life was no answer is apparent in 'A Painful Case', for Mr Duffy is the most wretchedly paralysed of all the Dubliners, and in many of the stories sympathy and pity modify the satire. Although Joyce later decided he had done insufficient justice to his city and his country, this belief, whether right or wrong, did not prevent him from publishing the stories: he merely added to them. Even the deeper understanding shown in *Ulysses* does not in any way invalidate the short stories; the picture of the city is at least as critical as in *Dubliners*. It is only if one supposes that there was or is available a complete, entirely just, omniscient view of a city or a country, or indeed of life itself, that one can accuse the view implicit in *Dubliners* of being negative. If, on the other hand, one believes that in this, as in everything else, there are opposed, but equally valid, viewpoints, necessary to each other and potentially valuable only insofar as they retain their integrity, then the attitude expressed in

[35] *MBK*, 225.

Dubliners is not so much negative as limited. Yet it is no more limited than the pervasive attitude of the *Portrait*. Within their own clearly defined positions both books speak truthfully and consistently: they complement each other. That Joyce came to see that the opposites, without surrendering their integrity, without coalescing into a neutral state, had to come into relationship and interact is not in any sense a rejection of the earlier books in which the seeming incompatibles were bluntly and unequivocally defined.

'The Dead'

To emphasize the coherence and direction of Joyce's original plan, I have so far ignored, save for a few passing references, what is certainly the finest story in the book. 'The Dead' is different in kind from the rest: it is on a different scale (roughly twice as long as the longest of its predecessors and about eight times as long as some of them), it was written about a year after the others had been finished, and it originated in a different and almost contrary impulse. While printers and publishers were still delaying over his manuscript, Joyce wrote to his brother Stanislaus:

> Sometimes thinking of Ireland it seems to me that I have been unnecessarily harsh. I have reproduced (in *Dubliners* at least) none of the attraction of the city for I have never felt at my ease in any city since I left it except in Paris. I have not reproduced its ingenuous insularity and its hospitality. The latter 'virtue' so far as I can see does not exist elsewhere in Europe. I have not been just to its beauty: for it is more beautiful naturally in my opinion than what I have seen of England, Switzerland, France, Austria or Italy. And yet I know how useless these reflections are. For were I to rewrite the book as G.R. suggests 'in another sense' (where the hell does he get the meaningless phrases he uses) I am sure I should find again what you call the Holy Ghost sitting in the ink-bottle and the perverse devil of my literary conscience sitting on the hump of my pen. And after all *Two Gallants* – with the Sunday crowds and the harp in Kildare Street and Lenehan – is an Irish landscape.[36]

Joyce's affection for the city is more evident in the stories than he implies: the passage in 'Two Gallants' is not the only brief evocation of a Dublin landscape or scene, and several stories are expressive of 'ingenuous insularity'; but the story which he decided to add does emphasize those qualities to which Joyce felt he had not done justice, without weakening the severity of his criticism. The dominant image becomes that of a city moribund rather than paralysed; while Dublin hospitality is represented by the annual dance given by the Misses Morkan and praised in Gabriel Conroy's after-dinner speech, the deadness of the city and its inhabitants is chiefly perceived through the relationship between Gabriel and his wife. Thus the private and the public worlds of *Dubliners* here unite and interact, so that even the hospitality appears eventually to Gabriel as a spectral survival from a livelier past, while it is the music of the party which sets

[36] *Letters* II, 166.

in motion the process by which the emptiness of the Conroy marriage is revealed.

Poetic imagery and symbol are more prevailing and assertive than in the earlier stories. The snow falls steadily and symbolically throughout, and Joyce untypically underlines one symbolic scene, when Gabriel Conroy, waiting for his wife at the food of the stairs, sees her standing near the top, listening to a man's voice coming from a nearby room:

> He stood still in the gloom of the hall, trying to catch the air that the voice was singing and gazing up at his wife. There was grace and mystery in her attitude as if she were a symbol of something. He asked himself what is a woman standing on the stairs in the shadow, listening to distant music, a symbol of. If he were a painter he would paint her in that attitude. Her blue felt hat would show off the bronze of her hair against the darkness and the dark panels of her skirt would show off the light ones. *Distant Music* he would call the picture if he were a painter.   (*D* 240)

This explicit pointing to a symbol is not an unaccustomed clumsiness in Joyce, but an aspect of Gabriel's mood – a mood of sentimental poeticizing reflected also in the laboured and pawky style. To choose such an absurd medium for what is vital to the story is typical of Joyce's ironic indirection: he had paid homage to Parnell in a piece of posturing hack-verse; he later expounded his aesthetic theories through the mouth of a pretentious undergraduate; and later still the love which lifts Leopold Bloom above the level of his fellow-citizens is expressed ludicrously and incoherently in a pub-argument. The self-conscious artiness of Gabriel Conroy is used to establish the central '*Distant Music*' symbol of 'The Dead', as well as to suggest the first movements of Gabriel's sentimental-sensuous feeling for his wife.

Once the symbol has been established and labelled, Joyce repeats and extends it, first in a fuller account of the music which has frozen Gretta Conroy on the stairs:

> The song seemed to be in the old Irish tonality and the singer seemed uncertain both of his words and of his voice. The voice, made plaintive by distance and by the singer's hoarseness, faintly illuminated the cadence of the air with words expressing grief:
>> *O, the rain falls on my heavy locks*
>> *And the dew wets my skin,*
>> *My babe lies cold . . .*   (*D* 240)

These sentences faintly sketch what will later be filled in and particularized – the nature and origin of Gretta's immobility, an emotional climate of plaintive grief, a figure standing in the rain, death. Distance in time as well as space is suggested by the mention of 'the old Irish tonality', and the half-forgotten words. Yet, Gabriel's response to the experience which has transfixed his wife is to feel, when he sees her eyes shining, 'a sudden tide of joy'. As they walk home his emotional awareness of her intensifies, and the symbol recurs, this time to express his mood:

> A wave of yet more tender joy escaped from his heart and went coursing in warm flood along his arteries. Like the tender fire of stars moments of their

life together, that no one knew of or would ever know of, broke upon and illumined his memory. He longed to recall to her those moments, to make her forget the years of their dull existence together and remember only their moments of ecstasy. For the years, he felt, had not quenched his soul or hers. Their children, his writing, her household cares had not quenched all their souls' tender fire. In one letter that he had written to her then he had said: *Why is it that words like these seem to me so dull and cold? Is it because there is no word tender enough to be your name?*

Like distant music these words that he had written years before were borne towards him from the past. He longed to be alone with her.

(D 244-5)

The ironies are manifold. The words 'distant music' are now specifically related to a distance in time, but whereas, in relation to Gretta, they have been associated with grief, wetness, cold and death, for Gabriel, they are associated with warmth, fire, moments of ecstasy and tender physical contact. The mention of 'moments . . . that no one knew of' incidentally prepares for the revelation of the great moment in Gretta's life which she had so long kept secret, a revelation which will obliterate all the memories in which Gabriel is fondly indulging.

Music, heat and physical desire become even more intensely associated when Gretta leans on her husband's arm:

after the kindling again of so many memories, the first touch of her body, musical and strange and perfumed, sent through him a keen pang of lust.

(D 246)

The word 'lust', intruding on the vague romanticism, is precisely judged: through the link of the musical image it fixes the equivalence between Gabriel's reminiscential sentimentality and the physical excitement burning in his veins, and foreshadows the moment of self-revelation when Gabriel, having heard the story of Michael Furey, who used to sing the song which had called up the symbol of '*Distant Music*', and of whom Gretta can say simply, 'I think he died for me', suddenly recognizes his idealizing sentimentality for what it is. Thus in the symbol, so awkwardly introduced, and variously developed with reference to husband and wife, all the central motifs of Gabriel's situation are focused.

But it is equally relevant to, indeed springs from, the more general theme developed in the party scenes. The party itself with its dances, performances and songs is a survival, and it is not accidental that the two old ladies and their niece are all teachers and performers of music. Music is a basic metaphor: young women laugh 'in musical echo'; Gabriel thinks of Browning's poetry as '*thought-tormented music*', and imagines the people outside, excluded from the party, as 'standing in the snow on the quay outside, gazing up at the lighted windows and listening to the waltz music.' This last fancy is itself a figure for a world where distant music represents a lost realm of light and warmth, and, in Gabriel's after-dinner speech, music is even more clearly placed at the very heart of the theme of nostalgia for a past when things were better. The superiority of the past to the present is a recurring topic, from Lily's bitter comment – 'The men that is now is only

all palaver and what they can get out of you' – to the rhetorical flourish
Gabriel plans to use in his speech:

> *Ladies and Gentlemen, the generation which is now on the wane among us may
> have had its faults but for my part I think it had certain qualities of hospitality,
> of humour, of humanity, which the new and very serious and hypereducated
> generation that is growing up around us seems to me to lack.* (D 219)

Here, of course, Gabriel is merely praising his aunts in order to score off
Miss Ivors, but the topic is treated with more conviction by others and
given a gradually deepening musical colouring. Aunt Kate complains about
the new order in church choirs, and the conversation at the supper-table
centres on the decay of singing. Mr Browne recalls the great Italian singers
of the past:

> Those were the days, he said, when there was something like singing to be
> heard in Dublin. . . . Why did they never play the grand old operas now, he
> asked, *Dinorah, Lucrezia Borgia*? Because they could not get the voices to
> sing them: that was why. (D 227)

These remarks bring the general nostalgia into a specifically musical scheme
of reference, and, in Gabriel's speech, the whole dream of the past is linked
to music:

> But we are living in a sceptical and, if I may use the phrase, a thought-
> tormented age: and sometimes I fear that this new generation, educated or
> hypereducated as it is, will lack those qualities of humanity, of hospitality,
> of kindly humour which belonged to an older day. Listening to-night to the
> names of all those great singers of the past it seemed to me, I must confess,
> that we were living in a less spacious age. Those days might, without exag-
> geration, be called spacious days: and if they are gone beyond recall let us
> hope, at least, that in gatherings such as this we shall still speak of them with
> pride and affection, still cherish in our hearts the memory of those dead and
> gone great ones whose fame the world will not willingly let die. (D 232)

As Gabriel's laboured poeticizings are, a little later, called on to introduce
the central symbol of '*Distant Music*', so here his insincere rhetoric (for he
has already doctored his speech to suit an audience whose 'grade of culture
differed from his' and economically transformed his phrase about Browning's '*thought-tormented music*' into 'a thought-tormented age') is employed
to clinch the definition of the city's condition in terms of music and the
singers of the past. Thus the musical images and allusions connect the
public and private aspects of the story: the central actions, the central
themes and emotions, are all given musical expression to create the story's
peculiar plaintiveness, like a song 'in the old Irish tonality'.

At the same time, there is a sustained irony. Nostalgia is mingled with
insincerity. The readymade syntax and phrases of the after-dinner orator
betray the falseness of Gabriel's speech even if we did not remember his
earlier outburst – 'I'm sick of my own country, sick of it!' – or his thoughts
about his aunts being 'only two ignorant old women'. He wobbles uncertainly between sentimental affection and contempt. But his praise of
Irish hospitality is a parody of the letter in which Joyce expressed his

consciousness of having failed to do justice to this quality, while, as Richard Ellmann has remarked, the fragment of an old love-letter which Gabriel recalls, employs phrases which Joyce had addressed to his wife,[37] and Gretta's romantic attachment to her dead sweetheart, Michael Furey, is based on a similar episode in the life of Nora Joyce, which caused some marital disquiet. Some critics have suggested that Conroy is a portrait of Joyce as he feared he might have become had he stayed in Dublin; perhaps it would be truer to say that Conroy is a representation of Joyce as he was – that is, when he was not an artist. The ability to recognize in himself in- compatible selves, each with its own kind of self-deception, vanity, triviality and false emotions was part of Joyce's gift. He did not spare himself in the *Portrait* or in *Ulysses*, and in *Finnegans Wake* is everywhere and everyone, not only that 'low sham', Shem the Penman, but also Shaun the Post, and all the other figures which compose the one complex personality of 'Here Comes Everybody'. In the letter to Stanislaus, Joyce seems conscious of his divided selves – of the part of him hankering after Dublin and desiring to do justice to its attractions and virtues, and of that part of him which was his literary conscience and lay in wait in ink-bottle and on pen. In 'The Dead' he allowed the former to operate, but only under the severe control of the latter. He could no more deny the validity of that part of him which was nostalgic for Dublin, wrote sentimental and lascivious love-letters, became jealous of his wife's dead lover, than he could reject the self which saw, with detachment and even hostility, his native city, regarded sardonic- ally the lover's pose, and insisted, like Richard Rowan, that marriage should be free of imposed bonds. In 'The Dead' the opposed selves are not separately incarnated, but the story is seen through the eyes of Gabriel Conroy, who, in turn, is seen through the cool gaze of the artist, the two uniting in Gabriel's vision of himself, comparable to the boy's experience in 'Araby', but deeper and more shattering:

> A shameful consciousness of his own person assailed him. He saw himself as a ludicrous figure, acting as a pennyboy for his aunts, a nervous well-meaning sentimentalist, orating to vulgarians and idealizing his own clownish lusts, the pitiable fatuous fellow he had caught a glimpse of in the mirror. (*D* 251)

This is not the whole truth about Gabriel; it is Shaun seen by Shem; the severely self-critical eye is as much part of Gabriel as the figure it condemns. The emotional richness of 'The Dead' is a product of such interplay – Gabriel's love and hatred of his city and its people, his sentimental tender- ness and crude physical appetite for his wife, his desire to impress and his scorn for those whom he wishes to impress, his conceit and self-contempt, and, permeating all these, the author's detached yet sympathetic presenta- tion of him. The irony, that the mood in Gretta which stirs and inflames Gabriel's love for her is a rejection of the whole of their life together, is not merely a local effect but an image of the general irony that in Ireland the shadowy dead are more vital than the living.

The fiery stars of the moments of ecstasy which Gabriel had longed to

[37] *Ellmann–JJ*, 255.

recall to his wife are extinguished by the memory of a death: compared with the dead boy, Gabriel is a shadow, and even Gretta's face, now she has aged, is 'no longer the face for which Michael Furey had braved death.' The dead, the vital past, still lived in the experience of Dubliners: Mr Browne could be moved by the memory of the singers of bygone days as Gretta was by the memory of Michael Furey, and from this the closing image of Dublin as a city of the spiritually dead, briefly lit up by the memories of the physically dead, develops. Such life as there is resembles distant music – whether of Gretta's dream of romance, or Gabriel's memories of past joys, or the echo of a tradition of hospitality. But the romance is preserved only because the boy died; Gabriel's attempt to recapture for the present his past excitement inevitably fails: Aunt Julia will die 'very soon', and join the shades of her father and his horse. Dublin is a city living only in its past.

The intuition of some mysterious threat to his existence had come to Gabriel when he heard Gretta say, 'I think he died for me', and he had felt terrified as though 'some impalpable and vindictive being was coming against him, gathering forces against him in its vague world.' Now his perception begins to become clearer as he prepares for sleep: 'One by one they were all becoming shades. Better pass boldly into that other world, in the full glory of some passion, than fade and wither dismally with age.' The metaphor of paralysis, which had suggested 'some maleficent and sinful being' in 'The Sisters', is being replaced by that of death, present in life as 'some impalpable and vindictive being', a development from the suggestions of premature death in 'Clay', and of a past when 'there was some life in it' in 'Ivy Day in the Committee Room'. Gabriel's vision is of a world where all that really lives is the memory of the past, where all the activities of the 'living' are as shadowy and purposeless as those of the dead:

> His soul had approached that region where dwell the vast hosts of the dead. He was conscious of, but could not apprehend, their wayward and flickering existence. His own identity was fading out into a grey impalpable world: the solid world itself which these dead had one time reared and lived in was dissolving and dwindling. (*D* 255)

The famous closing cadence which follows has been much praised and not infrequently abused for its calculated verbal music, although the alert functionalism of the style throughout the book should make one hesitate before supposing that Joyce has suddenly gone dreamy-eyed. The manner is highly rhetorical, with a profusion of soft alliteration and assonance, repetitions and inverted repetitions, parallel constructions – in fact with a whole repertoire of hushed and narcotic verbal effects. But this is not merely a purple passage; it is the close of a complex story and plainly related in every line to that story. It echoes confusedly Gabriel's experiences during the evening. 'The time had come' has been suggested by words his wife has used – 'when it came to the time'; 'his journey westward' recalls the trip to the west of Ireland which Miss Ivors has tried to persuade Gabriel to join; Mary Jane has mentioned that according to the newspapers 'the snow is general all over Ireland'; in his after-dinner speech he has spoken of the living and the dead, and his last thoughts were of the dead boy and himself; his wife has named to him the place where Michael Furey was buried; and 'their last end' is a phrase picked up from Mary Jane's account of the monks who slept in coffins 'to remind them of their last end'. At the literal level, then, the paragraph suggests the melting together of Gabriel's thoughts and memories as his consciousness dissolves into sleep. The reference to a 'journey westward' must be metaphorical, for Gabriel has made it plain to Miss Ivors that he has no intention of undertaking such a journey. Yet Gabriel does not merely think that it is time to set out on this journey: he does set out on it in this paragraph as his mind traverses the snow-covered country towards the Shannon and Oughterard. In Irish mythology the journey westward was to the Isles of the Blessed or of the Dead, the mythical islands out in the Atlantic sometimes identified with the Aran Isles. Miss Ivor's trip is to be to the Aran Isles literally, but it is for her a symbolic journey, expressing the backward-looking nationalism and language revivalism which Gabriel has rejected. For Gabriel's mind, losing consciousness, the journey westward is an acquiescent drift towards 'that region where dwell the vast hosts of the dead.' In refusing Miss Ivors he has refused to join in the past-seeking death-wish which seems to him to dominate his contemporaries in Ireland: but his self-confidence has been shattered, and now, in his submission to the figure of the dead Michael Furey, his recognition that all are becoming shades, his loss of a sense of identity, he, too, in his own way, is acquiescing in death, the common burial of all the living and the dead.[38]

The suggestions of William York Tindall and Richard Ellmann that, at the end, Gabriel is, as it were, turning to the realities of life seem to me alien to the mood of the story. Tindall recognizes that 'going west means dying', but, on the grounds that the love between Gretta and Michael Furey represents the reality which Gabriel has not experienced, argues that the closing paragraph offers two meanings, 'for Gabriel, facing reality at last, goes westward to encounter life and death.'[39] Ellmann contends that, although 'the cliché runs that journeys westward are towards death', in the story the west is 'the place where life had been lived simply and passionately'; he sees Gabriel's final half-conscious thoughts as 'a concession, a relinquishment', but takes this as 'a silent tribute' to 'a part of the country and a way of life that are most Irish. Ireland is shown to be stronger, more intense than he.'[40] This is to romanticize the West, very much as

---

[38] In *Ulysses*, westward motion again symbolizes the inevitable movement towards death (*U* 44/60).

[39] *Tindall–RG*, 46.

[40] *Ellmann–JJ*, 258–9. Some critics go much farther than either Tindall or Ellmann. J. Mitchell Morse, for instance, says, 'The story seems to me Joyce's most optimistic work; and beyond the story is Gabriel's journey westward, during which he is to redeem himself by dying for others. He is to become a Christ figure' (*The Sympathetic Alien: James Joyce and Catholicism* (New York University Press 1959), 110). One difficulty about accepting these 'affirming' interpretations of the last paragraph is that the language makes plain that the supposed visionary is dropping off to sleep.

Miss Ivors did, and to read into the Michael Furey–Gretta relationship far more than is realized in the story. The emphasis placed by the story is that the relationship belongs to the dead and to the past, and was preserved by Furey's death before the glory of passion had faded and withered with age. The real point of Gabriel's acquiescence is that as a result of his wife's story he has given up the dream of reviving his marriage, of making Gretta forget 'the years of their dull existence together': he has had to recognize that, contrary to his earlier excited conviction, the years have 'quenched all their souls' tender fire.' He accepts nonentity ('His own identity was fading out into a grey impalpable world') and the drift towards death, and if he (temporarily perhaps) submits to Ireland, it is not to a living primitivism but to a cold lifelessness. The story is, however, complicated by the snow which, falling almost throughout, takes on more and more symbolic force. Ellmann remarks:

> It does not seem that the snow can be death, as so many have said, for it falls on living and dead alike, and for death to fall on the dead is a simple redundancy of which Joyce would not have been guilty.

In consequence, he sees the snow as representing 'mutuality', the necessary connection of the dead and the living, 'a sense that none has his being alone', and the whole story as presenting Joyce's 'lyrical, melancholy acceptance of all that life and death offer.'[41] But this argument too easily dismisses the idea of 'snow' as a kind of death. No-one would suggest that the snow represents physical death, and, if it represents slow spiritual fading-away, then it can represent this as properly with regard to the dead as to the living. The life is dying in those like Gabriel who are technically alive, but it is also slowly dying in the memories of the past. Even the memory of Michael Furey has been only temporarily resuscitated by a song. The snow, falling alike on Dublin and on the graves, is like the drift of time, slowly obliterating the past, so that both the living and the dead are finally 'dissolving and dwindling' into non-existence, awaiting 'the descent of their last end' as they pass not only from human existence but also from human memory. Gabriel had tried to fend off this symbolic drift: as his solicitude for his wife's health has caused him to buy her goloshes to fend off the real snow, so in his plan to recall to her their moments of ecstasy he has hoped to wipe away their dull years of marriage and restore a pristine, burning passion. But this can no more be recaptured than can Gretta's beauty as a girl. The party, too, with its traditions is, as Gabriel hints in his speech, an attempt to hold back the passage of time; the nostalgia it arouses contributes to Gabriel's mood, as he becomes animated and sexually excited by the appearance of his wife. Like old Patrick Morkan's horse, so indoctrinated to walking in circles to drive his master's mill that when harnessed for a drive he walked round and round the statue of William III, Gabriel has been so accustomed to the routine of Dublin hospitality that, despite his

[41] *Ellmann-JJ*, 260–61.

initial cynicism, he succumbs to its influence. It is true that the cold air outside the heated rooms suggests the bracing, stimulating life which Gabriel misses at the party and feels as he follows Gretta through the street, and there is a similar suggestion when Gabriel, preparing for the love scene, which will be as though they had 'run away together with wild and radiant hearts to a new adventure', refuses a candle, so that the only illumination is the light from the street. But it is all illusory: while Gabriel looks out from the party and thinks of the pure air outside, he imagines people standing in the snow fascinated by the light and the music: the light which penetrates the hotel bedroom is 'ghostly'; and, so far from enjoying an invigorating walk, he wraps himself up against the elements and seizes the first opportunity of taking a cab. Earlier, he has exclaimed that Gretta, if she were allowed to, would walk home in the snow: obviously for him walks in the snow are merely to be contemplated.

The snow, the cold, and the darkness contribute importantly to the story's significance, but by suggestion and not as a kind of code: they contribute to the general bearing, and influence and reinforce the image of Dublin as a moribund city, where warmth and romance belong only to the memory of the dead who are buried, and the potentiality of life is avoided by the living–dead who still inhabit a ghost world. Neither the snow nor Gabriel's meditations express any mutuality between the living and the dead; the image is consistently of a people who have allowed their lives to be annexed by the dead.

So far from presenting a 'lyrical, melancholy acceptance of all that life and death offer', 'The Dead' fulfils the image of paralysis with which *Dubliners* begins. Joyce's notion of life was hostile to melancholy acceptance. In *Stephen Hero* he wrote of Ireland under 'the plague of Catholicism':

They obscured the sun. Contempt of human nature, weakness, nervous tremblings, fear of day and joy, distrust of man and life, hemiplegia of the will, beset the body burdened and disaffected in its members by its black tyrannous lice. Exultation of the mind before joyful beauty, exultation of the body in free confederate labours, every natural impulse towards health and wisdom and happiness had been corroded by the pest of these vermin. . . . He, at least, though living at the farthest remove from the centre of European culture, marooned on an island in the ocean, though inheriting a will broken by doubt and a soul the steadfastness of whose hate became as weak as water in siren arms, would live his own life according to what he recognised as the voice of a new humanity, active, unafraid and unashamed. (*SH* 198–9)

There, despite the rhetoric, one can see the Ibsenish positives that Joyce had to offer: not a feeble acquiescence but an eager, active, affirming life. The closing paragraph of 'The Dead' does not present in Gabriel a vision of reconciliation but of swooning surrender, and everything in it contributes to that conclusion. So far from being a loosely emotive purple passage, it is a precise, sympathetic but critical evocation of resignation to spiritual death – shaped by echoes of and allusions to the conversations which have left their mark on Gabriel's mind, and suggesting by sound, syntax and image the dull melancholia, the death-in-life, which is creeping all over Ireland.[42]

'The Dead' is in every way an astonishing achievement for a man still in his twenties, and not the least astonishing thing is that it should have been tacked on so successfully to an already complete work of art. Joyce's original scheme of fourteen stories composed with tight artistic economy a complex symmetrical structure: it would seem artistic suicide to add a story of different proportions, on a different scale, with a different central image and a different tone. Yet perhaps it is because of these obvious differences that 'The Dead' does not disrupt the original scheme. Its size and scope enable it to stand by itself, supplementing the other stories rather than being numbered among them. Public and private life are drawn together as the personal predicament of the Conroys is related to the public sociability and nostalgia of Dublin: the element of pity and sympathy in the earlier stories is greatly deepened and enriched until it dominates in the plaintive music of the last paragraph. New aspects of Dublin life are introduced without destroying the original vision and, instead of fusing with the other stories, 'The Dead' serves as an epilogue, qualifying the book as a whole by a modifying retrospection.

Set against the differences are numerous resemblances: the two old sisters suggest the first story; Gabriel's dream of 'a new adventure' and his shocking self-revelation are adult reflections of 'An Encounter' and 'Araby'; the regret for a time when there was some life in it and the political argument with Miss Ivors echo 'Ivy Day', as the musical and nationalist background echoes 'A Mother'; Aunt Julia's song, 'Arrayed for the Bridal' is as inappropriate as Maria's in 'Clay'; Lily's complaint of men only interested in 'what they can get out of you' recalls Corley and Lenehan, and there are many similar and varied links, mostly faint, like the mention of Kathleen Kearney, but all helping to hold 'The Dead' into the book, almost as a new dimension or a new angle of vision, fuller, more responsive, more understanding, with a more general view of public life and a deeper penetration into the soul of the individual Dubliner.

In 'The Dead', the methods of the preceding stories were complexly combined; and all the literary devices and techniques which Joyce invented or adapted or borrowed for *Dubliners* were developed, refined, extended in his later work. The method of allowing the theme to emerge by revealing its track through a series of apparently unimportant incidents; the thoroughgoing adaptation of form and manner of presentation to the particular theme, incident or person; the modifications of style, not merely for the sake of propriety but to express something far in excess of what is overtly

[42] Florence A. Walzl summarizes the various interpretations of 'The Dead' and draws an interesting conclusion: 'The context in which "The Dead" is read affects interpretations of the story. For the reader who approaches "The Dead" by way of the preceding fourteen stories of frustration, inaction, and moral paralysis, this story is likely to seem a completion of these motifs, and Gabriel's epiphany a recognition that he is a dead member of a dead society. But when "The Dead" is read as a short story unrelated to *Dubliners*, the effect is different: the story seems one of spiritual development and the final vision a redemption' ('Gabriel and Michael: The Conclusion of "The Dead" ', *JJQ* IV (1) (1966), 17).

stated; the enrichment of meaning with epiphanies and symbolic objects, settings and even poses; the use of allusions to other literature; the interaction of satire and sympathy through a shift of perspective or tone – all these were carried further and found their fullest and most adventurous development in *Ulysses*.

Chapter 2 *A Portrait of the Artist as a Young Man*

Stephen Hero

In January 1904 Joyce wrote an autobiographical paper entitled 'A Portrait of the Artist',[1] and, when it was rejected by the editors of the Irish periodical *Dana*, decided to expand the material into a novel. By 10 February he had written the first chapter of the book (now called, at his brother's suggestion, *Stephen Hero*[2]), and in March 1906, when Grant Richards, apparently not content with the difficulties he was experiencing over *Dubliners* or perhaps hoping for something less controversial, suggested that Joyce might try his hand at 'a novel in some sense autobiographical', Joyce replied that he had already written nearly a thousand pages of such a novel and calculated that 'these twenty-five chapters, about half of the book, run to 150,000 words.'[3]

Thus the writing of *Stephen Hero* was contemporaneous with the writing of *Dubliners*; the City and the Artist were from the beginning together occupying Joyce's mind. If *Stephen Hero* seems much less mature and controlled than *Dubliners*, this must be due partly to the problems any young author faces when he tries to regard with detachment his own personality and the development in which he is still involved, and partly to the fact that *Stephen Hero* is not only a fragment (perhaps less than a quarter of the novel as planned) but a fragment never revised for publication. Allowing for its unpolished and fragmentary state, it is a remarkable achievement for a writer in his early twenties. What Joyce said of *Chamber Music* can be said of *Stephen Hero*: 'it is a young man's book. I felt like that.'[4] In the *Portrait* a mature artist looks back over his own youth, from a particular viewpoint, perceiving what was significant to his development as artist, estimating what was vital and what was transitory in that development, and viewing his early self with a purposeful irony. *Stephen Hero*, although not without irony, is closer to the original experience, and the detachment is not consistently maintained.

The signs of unrevised work are frequent. Characters drift in and out to little apparent purpose; passages of youthful smartness or rhetoric crop up

---

[1] First published in *Yale Review* XLIX (1960), 355–69; reprinted in *Workshop*, 60–68.

[2] *Diary–SJ*, 12. [3] *Letters* II, 131–2. [4] *Letters* II, 219.

in chapters otherwise restrained and accurate in style; conversations are sometimes in a skeletal condition, nearer to cross-examination than talk; and the links between episodes are often perfunctory or laboured. Yet these do not create an impression of formless or hasty work; they seem rather to be blemishes in the handling of a novel which has been carefully thought out in regard to both theme and manner. The general scheme of the fragment is like that of the last chapter of the *Portrait*: it shows Stephen developing his aesthetic theories and his commitment to art, while detaching himself from his family and friends, abandoning the pursuit of romantic love, recognizing Irish nationalism to be an absurd and irrelevant game, and turning in revulsion from the Catholic Church and, in particular, from the Jesuits. All of these matters are treated in more detail and with more explicit emphasis than in the *Portrait*, and have more separate interest and shape in their own right. Whereas in the *Portrait* they are merged in the total image of the embryo artist's struggling development, here they are presented rather as distinct but interwoven strands in the development of an individual character. Similarly the people with whom Stephen is involved (in particular his mother and father, his brother Maurice, and Emma Clery) are much more fully realized than in the *Portrait*, and even passing acquaintances, like Wells, are sharply delineated. Stephen himself is a less cold and withdrawn figure, and is frequently associated with comedy, from the straightfaced humour of Maurice which makes Stephen, on one occasion, explode in laughter, to the unconscious absurdity of his pursuit of Emma with the proposal that they spend a night of love together and then part forever.[5] He is more in need of the interest and approval of others, more insistent on his humanity:

> Life is now – this is life: if I postpone it I may never live. To walk nobly on the surface of the earth, to express oneself without pretence, to acknowledge one's own humanity! (*SH* 147)

He feels impulses of pity for others and, although he resists the emotion, recognizes it as a sign of ripeness in himself, and, with the help of Ibsen, overcomes the temptation to regard his inner life and his environment as inevitably alien to each other. He is recognizably the same person as the figure in the *Portrait*, but the emphasis is different. This is particularly obvious in the extended treatment of the illness, death and burial of Stephen's sister, Isabel, the one major action which is completed in the fragment.

From the moment when Isabel returns from the convent because of her delicate health, her situation as a child drained of life and individuality is movingly developed. Her father regards her as a hindrance, while Stephen, to whom she is 'almost a stranger', uses her illness as an occasion for 'a few leagues of theory on the subject of the tyranny of home.' Her submissiveness and his notion of her future if she lived, 'a Catholic wife of limited intelligence and of pious docility', make him, despite his anger and com-

---

[5] At the time, Joyce was well satisfied with his handling of this episode and told Stanislaus that he considered it 'a remarkable piece of writing' (*Letters* II, 93).

miseration, feel that her case is hopeless and beyond his help. He attempts no mental or spiritual contact with her, and feels no 'natural, unreasoning affection'; he consciously resists feelings of pity. For all that, the disquiet in the young man's mind, his inability to escape some feeling of responsibility, is shadowed in his attempts to convince himself that his sister is in no great danger:

> He told Cranly she was probably growing too fast; many girls were delicate at that age. He confessed that the subject tired him a little.   (*SH* 132)

His resistance is only increased by his mother's attempt to persuade him to pray on her behalf for Isabel. Isabel's real condition is mentioned almost in passing, when we learn of the mother's difficulties in furnishing the delicacies ordered by the doctor, in dealing with creditors and her husband, and in 'attending on her dying daughter'. Earlier in the book Stephen, moved to an impulse of pity for Wells, saw it as a sign of ripeness and maturity. A similar impulse now begins to stir as he tries indirectly to encourage the girl to 'Live! live!'

The brief death-bed scene painfully contrasts the reality of the dying child with the play-acting of the parents, fixed in their habitual roles. The comic irony of the maudlin father's pressing champagne on a child whose presence in the house he had felt as yet another economic burden, and tearfully urging everyone to cheer her up, is matched by the ironic pathos of the mother's comforting the child, who had had such a miserable homecoming from the convent, with the promise ' "You are going home, dear, now" '; the parents are as incapable of honestly facing the situation as had been the priest ('Leave it to God: He knows best') and the doctor, who said 'while there was life there was hope.'

Isabel epitomizes in the story the death-in-life of those who submit to the social and religious pressures of Dublin; she is an acquiescent but frightened victim, representative of the moribundity from which Stephen is trying to escape but compelling from him an unwilling concern. In his immediate response to his sister's death, Stephen exhibits both a new sympathy and a renewed determination to persist in the egoistic claim to live by his own standards, the value of which he had been doubting just prior to Isabel's death.

The funeral is as economically and pointedly presented as the death-bed scene (which was presumably why so much of it was salvaged and used later), and, in the incident when the mourners stop at a pub for a drink, Stephen's double mood is sharply defined when he orders a pint, ignoring his father's gaze, 'feeling too cold-hearted to be abashed', but tasting, as he drinks, 'the savour of the bitter clay of the graveyard sharp in his throat.' His resentful sympathy for the dead girl is deepened and roughened by the formal sympathy of friends of the family, 'always uttered in the same listless unconvincing monotone', and by McCann's polite regret:

> Stephen released his hand gradually and said:
> —O, she was very young . . . a girl.
> McCann released his hand at the same rate of release, and said:

—Still . . . it hurts.
The acme of unconvincingness seemed to Stephen to have been reached at that moment. (*SH* 174)

Despite the incompleteness of the fragment, one can see the episode's functional importance, bending Stephen from his stiff, initial resolve not to interfere, arousing his sympathy, and strengthening his determination to serve no longer the forces which had prevented Isabel from living. While, in *Dubliners,* Joyce was presenting his vision of the city's paralysis, in *Stephen Hero* he was tracing the process by which he had arrived at that vision, and the Isabel story shows the emergence of the blend of pity and bitterness evident in the planning and handling of the short-stories.

It is hard to understand how a young writer, having created this poignant image of the wasting of life in Dublin, could have discarded it completely in revision. It was not that Joyce thought nothing in the Isabel story worth preserving, because some passages, eliminated from the *Portrait,* were preserved and used in *Ulysses.* In *Stephen Hero,* Stephen sees two mourners at the gates of Glasnevin Cemetery:

A girl, one hand catching the woman's skirt, ran a pace in advance. The girl's face was the face of a fish, discoloured and oblique-eyed; the woman's face was square and pinched, the face of a bargainer. The girl, her mouth distorted, looked up at the woman to see if it was time to cry: the woman, settling a flat bonnet, hurried on towards the mortuary chapel. (*SH* 172)

Bloom sees the same pair at Glasnevin:

Mourners came out through the gates: woman and a girl. Leanjawed harpy, hard woman at a bargain, her bonnet awry. Girl's face stained with dirt and tears, holding the woman's arm looking up at her for a sign to cry. Fish's face, bloodless and livid. (*U* 93/127)

The image is not contemptuous: it is a bitter epiphany[6] of the failure of grief to lend any nobility to features unchangeably shaped by the pettiness and squalor of life, and thus an emblem of the behaviour of the mourners at the funerals of both Isabel and Paddy Dignam. Dignam's funeral has other borrowings from Isabel's: the 'great toad-like belly' and 'croaking voice' of the priest, the server 'piping responses at intervals', the sobs of Simon Dedalus, and the friend who takes his arm consolingly, Stephen's reflections about 'the claims of water and fire to be the last homes of dead bodies' – all these, although left out of the *Portrait* with the rest of the Isabel story, were sufficiently to Joyce's taste to be used in *Ulysses.* The only likely explanation is that the *Portrait* was conceived not simply as a condensation of *Stephen Hero* but as a work of different intention, and organized on a principle which demanded the exclusion of materials Joyce liked well enough to save and use later.

Certainly *Stephen Hero* did not appear formless to its author while he

---

[6] It is indeed an 'epiphany'. The *Stephen Hero* version is not importantly changed from the original form in *Workshop,* 31. According to Stanislaus Joyce, his brother had observed this pair of mourners on the occasion of their mother's funeral (*MBK,* 231).

was writing it. A reply to some criticisms from Stanislaus implies that Joyce had a clear formal scheme in mind:

> Mrs Riordan who has left the house in Bray returns you have forgotten, to the Xmas dinner-table in Dublin. The immateriality of Isabel is intended. The effect of the prose piece 'The spell of arms' is to mark the precise point between boyhood (pueritia) and adolescence (adulescentia) – 17 years. Is it possible you remark no change?. . . . Your criticism of the two aposopeias [sic] is quite just but I think full dress is not always necessary. Stephen's change of mind is not effected by that sight as you seem to think, but it is that small event so regarded which expresses the change. His first skin falls. [7]

Later he insisted on the necessity for the novel's length ('It would be easy for me to do short novels if I chose but what I want to wear away in this novel cannot be worn away except by constant dropping') and mentioned the note of voluntary exile 'on which I propose to bring my novel to a close.' [8] These remarks, though they give only vague hints of the design of *Stephen Hero*, could hardly have been made by a writer without a significant form in mind, although that form certainly differed from the tighter and more intricate organization of the *Portrait*.

Stanislaus Joyce gives an account of the original scheme:

> In Dublin when he set to work on the first draft of the novel, the idea he had in mind was that a man's character, like his body, develops from an embryo with constant traits. The accentuation of those traits, their reactions to hereditary influences and environment, were the main psychological lines he intended to follow, and, in fact, the purpose of the novel as originally planned. [9]

While that scheme of the interaction between what is constant and what is developing remains a formal principle of the *Portrait*, it does so with the important limitation that in that book the subject is not 'a man's character' but specifically an artist's nature. Moreover, there appears to have been a change in the proposed conclusion of the autobiographical novel. Stanislaus's account suggests that the original conclusion was to present the completion of development and the attainment of maturity. But, while the novel was being written, Joyce's life had taken a new course, which required a different conclusion. Richard Ellmann writes:

> Finally, he announced to Stanislaus on February 28 [1905] that he interpreted his own condition as that of an exile: 'I have come to accept my present situation as a voluntary exile – is it not so? This seems to me important both because I am likely to generate out of it a sufficiently personal future to satisfy Curran's heart and also because it supplies me with the note on which I propose to bring my novel to a close.' His departure from Dublin with Nora would give the book its conclusion. [10]

[7] *Letters* II, 79.   [8] *Letters* II, 83 and 84.   [9] *MBK*, 39.
[10] *Ellmann–JJ*, 201. The motive for the voluntary exile was probably to have been supplied by the projected 'Tower episode', reserved instead for *Ulysses*. See *Ellman–JJ*, 214.

Thus the novel would end with an event which had not occurred when he began writing it. It is easy to see why. The relationship with Nora and the choice of voluntary exile now represented for Joyce the attainment of his maturity. He could no longer see the ambitious young man who had begun the novel as a mature figure. Later letters to Nora dwell on the importance to his development of the meeting with her:

> Do you know what a pearl is and what an opal is? My soul when you came sauntering to me first through those sweet summer evenings was beautiful but with the pale passionless beauty of a pearl. Your love has passed through me and now I feel my mind something like an opal, that is, full of strange uncertain hues and colours, of warm lights and quick shadows and of broken music.[11]

Through the romantic diction, one can see Joyce's recognition of the change from the refined poeticism of *Chamber Music* to the richer texture of his fiction. Nora was not, he told her, the girl 'fashioned into a curious grave beauty by the culture of generations before her' for whom he had written *Chamber Music*, but the beauty of Nora's soul outshone the young man's vision of the verses: 'There was something in you higher than anything I had put into them':[12]

> *Everything* that is noble and exalted and deep and true and moving in what I write comes, I believe, from you. O take me into your soul of souls and then I will become indeed the poet of my race.[13]

Nora, he said, 'made me a man.'[14]

With such a change in his conception of what had matured him, Joyce could hardly accept the *Stephen Hero* image of the artist heroically making himself, trusting in 'that ineradicable egoism which he was afterwards to call redeemer' (*SH* 39). He now believed that the completion of his development required some kind of transformation through a relationship with a spirit very different from his own, and it would be impossible to tack such a relationship on to the story of Stephen's redemption through egoism. The turning-point in his attaining maturity as a man and an artist would have to be postponed to a later book (set, characteristically, on 16 June 1904, the date of his first rendezvous with Nora), and *Stephen Hero* would have to be reshaped to emphasize only the achievement of 'passionless' isolation: the pearl had to be formed before it could be transmuted into an opal. This, at least, seems to me the most likely explanation for the elimination of many of the best elements in *Stephen Hero*, especially those which show Stephen in a less cold, more sympathetic light: the Isabel story had to be removed, and the humorous intimacy with Maurice; Emma Clery had to be reduced to a shadowy figure formed by romantic and erotic fantasies; and the theory of the epiphany, with its implication of a vital contact between the artist and the life about him, had to be omitted in favour of a fuller exposition of applied Aquinas. Instead of ending, as planned, with the voluntary exile of

---

[11] *Letters* II, 237. [12] *Ibid.* [13] *Letters* II, 248.
[14] *Letters* II, 233. Cf. Bertha's claim in *Exiles* (Act III): 'I made him a man.'

1904,[15] the revised novel would end with the immature and unsuccessful flight to the Continent in 1902. The title, too, was changed to *A Portrait of the Artist as a Young Man*, and, as Frank Budgen conjectured, hearing Joyce underlining with his voice the last four words of the title, 'the emphasis may have indicated that he who wrote the book is no longer that young man, that through time and experience he has become a different person.'[16]

There is a limit to legitimate criticism of *Stephen Hero*, because it is an unrevised fragment of a work about whose unifying formal and thematic patterns we can only guess. To Joyce it may have seemed later a 'puerile production',[17] but it would have taken a very extraordinary boy to have written it. The *Portrait* is clearly a work of greater economy and tautness of organization, and far more sophisticated and controlled in its handling, but the contrast is not between chaos and creation, autobiography and art: it is between two novels, one brilliantly promising, the other maturely achieved, which use similar materials, derived from the same experience, and conceived by the same mind, yet expressive of different attitudes and themes. In *Stephen Hero*, Dedalus is a young man 'as much in love with laughter as with combat' (*SH* 78); in the last chapters of the *Portrait*, he is a young artist who rarely laughs and who tries to evade his foes rather than face them. The progress of the artist by his own efforts to the achievement of a lofty destiny was, Joyce came to realize, too simple an account of how things were: isolation and self-mastery, if too complete, were sterile and self-defeating. The paralysing force of the city, diagnosed in *Dubliners*, had to be matched with an uncompromising spirit who would not serve, who would sever his roots rather than submit, because only by such refusal and such severance would it be possible, subsequently, for him to respond fruitfully to contact with a more tolerant and less embittered spirit.

The theories

Although *Stephen Hero* is far from being an unintegrated accumulation of materials, the artistic economy of the *Portrait* is severer, and the subject more precisely defined and coordinated. Reliance on selected and exactly executed and disposed strokes, instead of the filling-in of details, is a sign of growing confidence in the artist, and the theory of aesthetics, with which Joyce had been busied since his university days and at one time hoped to publish,[18] must have pushed his ambition towards the achievement of a form for the novel at least as compactly and elaborately organized as the form he had devised for the stories of *Dubliners*. The long aesthetic discussions which appear in the *Portrait* could hardly have been written with-

[15] Commenting on a reference (in a letter from Stanislaus) to a planned Martello Tower episode in *Stephen Hero*, Richard Ellmann notes that 'Joyce evidently intended to continue his novel through his second departure from Ireland, but he changed this plan' (*Letters* II, 103, n.1).

[16] *Budgen*, 61.   [17] *MBK*, 218.   [18] *Letters* II, 38.

out awareness of their reference to the work of art in which they appear, and cannot be justified except in terms of their role in the novel and their relevance to its aesthetic character. They offer not a logically developed philosophical scheme, but a fictional presentation of an undergraduate engaged in an attempt to reduce to some sort of order his intuitions about art and beauty, and, in particular, to outline for himself the principles which will guide his future career as an artist. The borrowings from logic and philosophy belong to his manner rather than his content; the coherence of the argument matters less than the usefulness of the insights developed from his definition of art as 'the human disposition of sensible or intelligible matter for an esthetic end' (*P* 211).

Stephen relates truth and beauty:

> Truth is beheld by the intellect which is appeased by the most satisfying relations of the intelligible: beauty is beheld by the imagination which is appeased by the most satisfying relations of the sensible. (*P* 212)

Such definitions imply that literary art must involve both truth and beauty, since words are both intelligible and sensible, and possess, in addition to their intrinsic sensible qualities as words, the power of evoking nonverbal sense-memories and associations through their intelligibility. Literature, then, must satisfy the intellect as well as the imagination, truth and beauty alike producing 'a stasis of the mind'. As to the exact relationship between the two, Stephen is uncertain, but quotes Plato as saying 'that beauty is the splendour of truth.'[19] He does not believe that beauty 'has a meaning' but thinks that 'the true and the beautiful are akin.' Certainly both are included in those qualities 'the apprehension of which pleases', and thus the truth is also beautiful. As aesthetics, the passage leaves much to be desired: to distinguish between truth and beauty in terms of a distinction between intellect and imagination is to define the unknown in terms of the unknown. But Stephen (like Joyce in his notebooks) is less occupied with definition of terms than with supplying a formal framework for his own intuitions.

The pretence of logical progression is temporarily dropped when Stephen rejects without argument the materialistic explanation of beauty which would account for the varieties of female beauty in terms of man's perception of 'the manifold functions of women for the propagation of the species': 'it may be so' but he prefers not to accept an explanation which would make the world seem so dreary. Instead he suggests that although different objects may seem beautiful to different people, all people who perceive an object which they call beautiful perceive certain relations in the object experienced 'which satisfy and coincide with the stages themselves of all esthetic apprehension' and which must therefore be 'the necessary qualities of beauty'. There must, then, be a correspondence between 'the necessary phases of artistic apprehension' and beauty: 'Find these and you find the qualities of universal beauty.'

[19] Joyce was fond of this phrase, which he found quoted in a letter by Flaubert (see note 23 in this chapter), and had already used it in his paper on Mangan (*CW* 83) and in *Stephen Hero* (*SH* 85).

At this point he brings in 'another pennyworth of wisdom' from Aquinas: '*ad pulcritudinem tria requiruntur, integritas, consonantia, claritas*', and he translates, '*Three things are needed for beauty, wholeness, harmony and radiance.*' Taking the basket of a butcher's boy for illustration, he demonstrates that these qualities correspond to the phases of apprehension. First the mind separates the image from all which is not it; that is to say, it observes the limits of the image to be apprehended, against the spatial background if the aesthetic image be visual, and against the temporal background if it be aural:

> But, temporal or spatial, the esthetic image is first luminously apprehended as selfbounded and selfcontained upon the immeasurable background of space or time which is not it. You apprehend it as *one* thing. You see it as one whole. You apprehend its wholeness. That is *integritas*.   (*P* 216)

The second stage of apprehension, unlike the first which is a synthesis, is analytic. Led by the formal lines of the object (or image), the mind apprehends the balance of its parts, 'the rhythm of its structure':

> Having first felt that it is *one* thing you feel now that it is a *thing*. You apprehend it as complex, multiple, divisible, separable, made up of its parts, the result of its parts and their sum, harmonious. That is *consonantia*.   (*P* 217)

Claritas gives more difficulty. Stephen rejects the notion that Aquinas had in mind 'symbolism or idealism' (the notion that the object is merely the shadow or symbol of some other reality) although, in fact, he is interested not in what Aquinas meant but in what interpretation, acceptable to himself, he can put upon the word:

> When you have apprehended that basket as one thing and have then analysed it according to its form and apprehended it as a thing you make the only synthesis which is logically and esthetically permissible. You see that it is that thing which it is and no other thing.   (*P* 217)

The 'radiance', then, Stephen identifies with 'the scholastic *quidditas*, the *whatness* of a thing' (although critics have pointed out that the Scotian *haecceitas* would seem a more exact equivalent).[20] Suddenly switching from reception to creation, Stephen affirms that it is this radiance which the artist feels 'when the esthetic image is first conceived in his imagination':

> The instant wherein that supreme quality of beauty, the clear radiance of the esthetic image, is apprehended luminously by the mind which has been arrested by its wholeness and fascinated by its harmony is the luminous silent stasis of esthetic pleasure. . . .   (*P* 217)

Stephen, who has set out to define beauty by reference to the phases of apprehension of a beautiful object in 'all people', seems to have concluded by confining the ultimate and supreme phase to the artist, and this despite the fact that he has said earlier that the terms from Aquinas will serve only for one part of his aesthetic philosophy:

[20] 'What Stephen seems to mean by claritas may have been better expressed by the haecceitas of Duns Scotus than by the quidditas of Aristotle' (*Noon*, 51, and see also 72).

When we come to the phenomena of artistic conception, artistic gestation, and artistic reproduction I require a new terminology and a new personal experience. (*P* 214)

Presumably what he means is that the radiance of the aesthetic image 'apprehended' by everyone who responds to its beauty is the same in kind as the radiance of the aesthetic image 'conceived' by the artist. Thus his theory supposes that, when the aesthetic image apprehended is a work of art, the final phase of apprehension is a kind of re-creation in the imagination of the observer, listener or reader of the radiance of the image as conceived in the artist's imagination, and that the artist's function is, therefore, so to delineate and articulate his vision that its *integritas, consonantia* and, finally, its *claritas* may be apprehended by others. This interpretation is confirmed by *Stephen Hero*, where 'radiance' is equated with the achievement of 'epiphany' (*SH* 218), and the job of the artist is said to be to 'disentangle the subtle soul of the image' in order to 're-embody it in artistic circumstances chosen as the most exact for it in its new office' (*SH* 82).

Despite, then, some gaps in the argument and some undefined terms, Stephen's notions of the nature of beauty and of the role of the artist are tolerably clear. In Van Gogh's room was an old cane chair – not apprehended as an aesthetic image at all by most eyes, but merely part of such generalizations as 'the room', 'the furniture'. Van Gogh, however, apprehended it, first as a distinct aesthetic unity, distinct from the rest of the contents of the room and from all other chairs – apprehended, that is, its wholeness or *integritas*. Next he apprehended the separate parts of the chair (and these 'parts' would include its function, its history, its human connections, its associations as well as its physical parts), the interrelations of the parts with each other and with the whole, and thus 'the rhythm of its structure', its harmony, its *consonantia*. Then, having passed through these two phases of apprehension, his mind apprehended in an instant of artistic insight, an epiphany, the essential, individual nature of the chair, its unique character, its radiance or *claritas*. Through his medium he was then able to recreate, freed from the surrounding confusions, the integrity and consonance of the chair so that through his recreation an observer of the painting could experience, too, the chair's epiphany. The merit of the theory is that it places beauty not merely in the external object or image (which would leave unexplained why different cultures find different things beautiful) nor simply in the eye of the beholder (which would rule out any concept of 'universal beauty'): beauty is manifested in a relationship between observer and observed, governed by the fundamental character of human apprehension. Thus, each observer apprehends beauty differently and in different objects or images, but the basic nature of his apprehension is common to all men. Consequently the artist, recreating such an apprehension, though it be one that he alone has experienced, can, by excluding from his created image all irrelevancies and shaping it according to the threefold nature of human apprehension, enable others to apprehend what he has apprehended. To return to my illustration, although only Van Gogh could see the chair as beautiful (at least, as beautiful in that particular way), he was able through the medium of his art to make his apprehension of its beauty accessible to others: those who would have seen the chair as commonplace or ugly can respond to the beauty of the artist's apprehension. Much of this is dubious as an exercise in abstract aesthetics, but it was of particular relevance to a young artist who planned to create a work which had beauty 'in the sense which the word has in the literary tradition', although it would present what was ugly or vulgar according to the standards of 'the marketplace'. (*P* 218)

A similar concern with his own future development governs Stephen's consideration of the ways in which the aesthetic image is recreated in art. First, he says, it 'must be set between the mind or senses of the artist himself and the mind or senses of others' and this, he continues, necessarily results in three forms: *lyrical*, 'wherein the artist presents his image in immediate relation to himself'; *epical*, 'wherein he presents his image in mediate relation to himself and to others'; and *dramatic*, 'wherein he presents his image in immediate relation to others.' The lyrical form is, says Stephen, 'the simplest verbal vesture of an instant of emotion. . . . He who utters it is more conscious of the instant of emotion than of himself as feeling emotion.' The epical form emerges from this when the artist 'broods upon himself as the centre of an epical event' and develops 'till the centre of emotional gravity is equidistant from the artist himself and from others', the narrative being no longer purely personal; instead the personality of the artist flows round the persons and the action. But it is the dramatic form which is the most advanced:

> The dramatic form is reached when the vitality which has flowed and eddied round each person fills every person with such vital force that he or she assumes a proper and intangible esthetic life. The personality of the artist, at first a cry or a cadence or a mood and then a fluent and lambent narrative, finally refines itself out of existence, impersonalises itself, so to speak. The esthetic image in the dramatic form is life purified in and reprojected from the human imagination. The mystery of esthetic like that of material creation is accomplished. The artist, like the God of the creation, remains within or behind or beyond or above his handiwork, invisible, refined out of existence, indifferent, paring his fingernails. (*P* 219)

Stephen allows that even in literature, 'the highest and most spiritual art', these 'forms' are often confused, and, in fact, the inaptness of their application to other arts is revealed by one of the problems Stephen has set himself ('*Is the bust of Sir Philip Crampton lyrical, epical or dramatic?*'— *P* 218), though the implied answer, that sculpture is an inferior art in which the forms are not clearly distinguished, is a feeble escape: one might say the same of music.[21] The fact is that Stephen's 'forms' are, as their labels suggest, chiefly literary in application, and confusedly combine dif-

---

[21] In *Stephen Hero*, Stephen includes music among the forms inferior in this respect to 'the literary form of art' (*SH* 82).

ferentiations between the degrees of distance which separate the personality of the artist from the image he creates, with the names of traditional literary forms, and with a literary-historical theory about the development of literature from the earliest rhythmical cry to the epic and thence to the drama.

In the paper, 'Drama and Life', which Joyce read in 1900, he had tried to distinguish between 'drama' (the presentation of the 'changeless laws' which govern man's nature and existence) and 'the drama', the 'proper form' and 'fittest vehicle' for such presentation.[22] But, in the *Portrait*, 'the drama', has been replaced by 'the dramatic form', which is clearly not limited to plays. When Joyce compares the artist in the dramatic mode to the God of creation 'within or behind or beyond or above his handiwork', he is echoing Flaubert:

> The artist should be in his work like God in creation, invisible and all-powerful; he should be felt everywhere, but he should not be seen.[23]

Joyce certainly knew this passage and must have seen that Flaubert was discussing not a play but *Madame Bovary*; the allusion confirms that he no longer regarded 'the drama' as the 'proper form' for the impersonal presentation of the drama of life. Stephen is seen, essentially, as an embryo novelist, the younger image of 'the artist' who is now engaged in transforming the comparatively personalized narrative of *Stephen Hero* into the impersonal *Portrait*. It would no doubt have been better from the point of view of aesthetic theory if Joyce had disposed altogether of the confusing terms 'lyrical', 'epical' and 'dramatic'. But they were the terms he, as a young man, had been using to clarify his understanding of art (they first appeared in the Paris notebook on 6 March 1903),[24] and, at least, served to figure the young artist's aspirations, beyond the fervent lyricism of the 'Villanelle of the Temptress' towards an art which should present 'life purified in and reprojected from the human imagination' (*P* 219). It was no part of Joyce's intention to show Stephen as an accomplished aesthetic philosopher; it was an important part of his intention to suggest the intellectual struggle by which Stephen mapped out his artistic future. The aesthetic explorations, however groping and uncertain, promise the eventual production of a work of art which shall be integrated, possessed of structural rhythm and charged with the radiance of the artist's vision, presented in 'dramatic form' with the artist immanent in his creation – a work of art impersonal in that the artist would not obtrude his personality but

[22] *CW*, 40–42. Much of this passage was taken over from an essay, 'Royal Hibernian Academy: "Ecce Homo" ' (*CW*, 32).

[23] Letter to Mlle Leroyer de Chantepie, 11 March 1857. (The translation is given in *Workshop*, 248. Joyce's knowledge of this letter is confirmed by his echoing of Flaubert's assertion that the beauty of the artist's conception 'is the splendour of truth, according to Plato'. See note 19 above.) An earlier letter from Flaubert to Louise Colet, 9 December 1852, makes much the same point: 'The author, in his work, should be like God in the universe, present everywhere and visible nowhere' (*Workshop*, 247).

[24] *Gorman*, 97–8.

would remain invisible, and yet deeply personal in that his personality would be diffused through every aspect of his work.

The highly formalized presentation of the aesthetic ideas is, oddly, as much a method of 'naturalizing' them in the novel as are Lynch's coarse interruptions, since such formulation exemplifies the way in which the Jesuit training has shaped Stephen's mind; after he has rejected the faith, his mode of thought still gives off 'the true scholastic stink'. Despite the declaration '*Non serviam*', he has been trained to depend on external authority; even as a rebel he has to construct his aesthetic rebellion on a foundation of accepted authority. At the same time, he enjoys the irony of calling upon such unchallengeable backers as Aquinas and Aristotle: it was one thing to be of the same party as Ibsen and Hauptmann, but the way to undermine the opposition, who liked to condemn all new ideas as reckless Bohemian threats to accepted truth, was to take one's stand with Aquinas and Aristotle, or, rather, to conscript them to one's cause.[25] As Stephen informs the dean of studies, he uses these two luminaries purely for his own purposes, and will trim them or get rid of them whenever it suits him. Nevertheless he strategically adopts not only their ideas but their manners; while the style of his exposition is consciously scholastic, its circumstances, equally deliberately, are peripatetic. There is always this element of irony in Stephen's employment of authorities and manner: his weapons were to be 'silence, exile, and cunning', and, although the first two apply only figuratively to his situation in the *Portrait*, the cunning is manifest in his conduct at University. The complications arise because, while Stephen is treating his acquaintances with detachment and aloof irony, Joyce is treating Stephen in much the same way. By making the exposition of the theory also function as a revelation of Stephen's personality and pose, of the characteristic operations of his mind in abstract thought, of the conditioning of his mind by his education, of his 'cunning', Joyce is enabled to digest his own early aesthetic insights into a form in which they can operate in his novel.

But the introduction into this severely economical and 'dramatic' novel of an extended theoretical exposition requires that the theory, thus expounded, be a necessary and important constituent in the portrait of the young artist, not only belonging to the *integritas* of the image but also an essential part of its *consonantia*, and one of the means by which a reader is assisted to an apprehension of the *claritas*. Similarly, the *Portrait* itself must measure up to the theoretical analysis, its wholeness clearly delineated, its parts held together in a rhythmic complex of relationships, its essential nature manifested in every detail of handling, and the author's personality not expressed in commentary but pervading the created image. The theory should illuminate the novel which contains it; the novel should exemplify the theory.[26]

[25] This tactic is particularly evident in Stephen's argument with the President in *Stephen Hero* (95–103).

[26] Many critics take the view that to apply the theories to the novel is a gross error. S. L. Goldberg, for instance, says that 'to attempt to assess Joyce's work by the theory as he there presents it, is inevitably to distort his artistic achievement' (*Goldberg*, 43).

Integritas

Although in the *Portrait* the chief concern of the aesthetic discussion is the apprehension of beauty, and Stephen puts off any specific examination of the artist's creative processes, in *Stephen Hero* he does, in general terms, outline the conclusion to which his theorizings obviously point:

> The artist, he imagined, standing in the position of mediator between the world of his experience and the world of his dreams – a mediator, consequently gifted with twin faculties, a selective faculty and a reproductive faculty. To equate these faculties was the secret of artistic success: the artist who could disentangle the subtle soul of the image from its mesh of defining circumstances most exactly and re-embody it in artistic circumstances chosen as the most exact for it in its new office, he was the supreme artist. (*SH* 82)

In the aesthetic image, grasped by the mind gifted with the 'selective faculty', the qualities to be apprehended as *integritas*, *consonantia* and *claritas* are potentially present, though not manifest, prior to the apprehension; but in the aesthetic image created by 'the reproductive faculty' they must be built in, by conscious or unconscious process. The artist must be the God of his creation, must give his image its wholeness, structural rhythm, and, ultimately, through these and round these, its *quidditas*, capable of awaking in those of sufficient penetration 'the luminous silent stasis of esthetic pleasure'.

The change in the title of the planned autobiographical novel is significant of a change in the planned *integritas*. It is as though Joyce, looking back on his childhood and youth, now selected from it the single complex image of himself as an artist in the making – in one light an image of development or process, and in another an image of unchangingness, of 'constant traits'. This was his apprehension of the *integritas* of the image and to reproduce it he had to cut away all incidents, thoughts, emotions, and people which he now saw as inessential to the early development of the artist (however important they may have been to that of the man), as part of the time and space surrounding the image rather than the one thing itself.[27] The Isabel passages of *Stephen Hero*, the fuller treatment of Stephen's family life, the intimacy with Maurice, the bold approach to Emma, whatever their merits as episodes in the growth of the man, were irrelevant to or interfered with the image of the artist gradually achieving his necessary isolation. 'Isolation,' Stephen told his brother, 'is the first principle of artistic economy'

Clive Hart finds 'little ground for thinking that [the theory] has much relevance to his own mature art-works' (*Hart–Ulysses*, 35). Assessment is not really involved, but, without believing that the mature Joyce subscribed entirely to Stephen's theories of art, I would argue that the inclusion of a prolonged discussion of the response to any aesthetic object requires that the discussion have some special relevance to the novel which contains it.

[27] Cf. 'It was no longer an autobiography in the usual sense, but the portrait of an artist' (Stanislaus Joyce, 'James Joyce: A Memoir', *Hudson Review* II (4) (1950), 504).

(*SH* 37).[28] Family life, responsibilities, ties, even friendship and romantic love, together with involvements in religion, nationalism, and society in general had to be cast aside unsparingly, since it was from them that the artist had to free himself, even if, subsequent to the achievement of isolation, he would find a need for human relationships. Regarded as process, the five chapters of the *Portrait* depict the embryo artist's struggle, first to master his environment and then to free himself from it. At the end of each chapter he attains the completion of one stage in his growth; he finds a new world and a point of rest, though in every case a temporary one which collapses under the new strain of some internal pressure.[29]

In the first chapter the chief problem facing the boy is one of social adjustment – the need to be accepted and to achieve a certain competence in dealing with his environment. He is small and weak, no good at games, bullied by bigger boys, unable to understand their jokes and teasing, and desperately homesick. He is bewildered by political and religious dissension in his home, confused by sexual hints and by the behaviour of Eileen, and finally outraged by an unjust punishment. This last confusion provokes the crisis. The other boys tell him to complain of his pandying to the rector, a remote and awful figure; but he realizes this is only schoolboy talk, and concludes that it would be best for him to keep quiet. Nevertheless, he finds himself on the way to the rector's room, propelled, not by a sense of injustice, but by his recall of the affront to his identity in Father Dolan's pretended inability to remember the name Dedalus: 'It was his own name that he should have made fun of if he wanted to make fun. Dolan: it was like the name of a woman that washed clothes' (*P* 56). His satisfactory interview with the rector is Stephen's first social success. He runs to tell his schoolfellows; they fling their caps in the air, cheer and carry him about.

Temporarily Stephen is at peace. By not reporting Wells for shouldering him into a ditch, he has satisfied the code of honour recommended to him by his father – 'whatever he did, never to peach on a fellow' – and he has won the approval of his society. But this is not the whole emphasis of the chapter, nor even of the climactic episode with Father Dolan. Until this point Stephen is submissive. When he is laughed at for admitting to kissing his mother, he denies that he kisses her and is laughed at again. He seems incapable of asserting himself or defending himself. The episode of the beating presents him fairly with a problem. Despite their advice, he knows the other boys would not go to the rector, knows that they would be ready to laugh at him for going, and knows that the most sensible thing to do is to escape trouble by keeping out of the way of it. His visit to the rector is

---

[28] Cf. '. . . the artist, though he may employ the crowd, is very careful to isolate himself. This radical principle of artistic economy applies specially to a time of crisis . . .' ('The Day of the Rabblement', *CW*, 69).

[29] Hugh Kenner, whose essay, 'The *Portrait* in Perspective' (*Givens*, 132–74) outlined the structure of the *Portrait* in a way to which all subsequent accounts (including this one) are indebted, places a slightly different emphasis. He says of the last chapter, 'Each of the preceding chapters, in fact, works toward an equilibrium which is dashed when in the next chapter Stephen's world becomes larger and the frame of reference more complex' (*Kenner*, 122).

his first positive act as an isolated individual, and, significantly, despite his moment of social triumph, he tries to escape from the cheering boys, and having done so feels 'alone' but 'happy and free'. That he has won social acceptance is of less importance than that he has deliberately acted in isolation (and, in consequence, has been liberated) and that he has defended his name, the symbol of his identity. Previously he had submitted to Nasty Roche's ridicule of the name Dedalus, and his assertion of his identity has been private – by writing in his geography book 'himself, his name and where he was' and by thinking, when he read the inscription from the bottom to the top and came at last to his own name, 'That was he.' The name as the symbol of identity recurs several times later in the book, and is crucially alluded to in the very last sentence in the invocation to the fabulous artificer: in defending it against Father Dolan, Stephen begins the assertion of his individuality, and this, leading to his discovery of freedom in isolation, is the chief step in the development of the artist in the first chapter, though there are also certain indications of the kind of artist he will be, such as his fondness for and interest in the sound and meaning of words.

In the second chapter his social adjustment crumples under the pressure of new forces, external and internal. The chapter covers several years during which various stages in the collapse succeed each other. It begins with the close of what is later called 'a two years' spell of revery' (*P* 80). He is engaged in athletic training, learning about 'the real world' through the conversations of his father and uncle, and preparing for 'the great part' he will play in that world, indulging his romantic imagination with imaginary adventures on the pattern of the Count of Monte Cristo's and with mock adventures among a gang of boys. A half-grasped knowledge that his father is in trouble clouds all this, destroys his confidence in the flabby old man who trains him, shocks 'his boyish conception of the world' with changes in what he had thought unchangeable, dissipates visions of the future, and destroys his pleasure in childish games. He feels more strongly than at Clongowes that he is 'different from others' (*P* 66). The melancholy romanticism of his dreams about Monte Cristo's Mercedes are transformed into a feverish unrest: 'He wanted to meet in the real world the unsubstantial image which his soul so constantly beheld.' He feels that he will inevitably encounter this image, 'and in that moment of supreme tenderness he would be transfigured . . . . Weakness and timidity and inexperience would fall from him in that magic moment' (*P* 67). As the family fortunes continue to decline he becomes embittered, sees the world as 'a vision of squalor and insincerity', amongst children at a party begins 'to taste the joy of his loneliness', and refrains from responding to Emma's advances. Instead he writes a poem about her, removing from the scene everything which he thinks is 'common and insignificant', and presenting only the sentimental furniture of 'the night and the balmy breeze and the maiden lustre of the moon', together with 'some undefined sorrow . . . hidden in the hearts of the protagonists.' This stage, in which he begins to perceive the true nature of his family and his environment, and seeks escape in daydreams, is ended by his entrance to Belvedere College, where, superficially, the social position is retrieved: he is described as 'a model youth', and he and Heron are 'the virtual heads of the school'; yet he finds no satisfaction in this eminence:

> While his mind had been pursuing its intangible phantoms and turning in irresolution from such pursuit he had heard about him the constant voices of his father and of his masters, urging him to be a gentleman above all things and urging him to be a good catholic above all things. These voices had now come to be hollow-sounding in his ears. When the gymnasium had been opened he had heard another voice urging him to be strong and manly and healthy and when the movement towards national revival had begun to be felt in the college yet another voice had bidden him be true to his country and help to raise up her fallen language and tradition. In the profane world, as he foresaw, a worldly voice would bid him raise up his father's fallen state by his labours and, meanwhile, the voice of his school comrades urged him to be a decent fellow, to shield others from blame or to beg them off and to do his best to get free days for the school. And it was the din of all these hollowsounding voices that made him halt irresolutely in the pursuit of phantoms. He gave them ear only for a time but he was happy only when he was far from them, beyond their call, alone or in the company of phantasmal comrades.   (*P* 86–7)

The phantoms which draw Stephen away from the aims and services urged upon him by society are sex fantasies, developing from the callow dreams of Mercedes, through the excitement he associates with Emma, to what he at first regards as 'a brutish and individual malady of his own mind'. The word '*Fœtus*' carved on a desk in the anatomy theatre where his father had studied, first shocks him because it is a trace in the outer world of his obsession and then seems to mock him and force him to recognize his weakness and madness, for it alone seems to speak to him: all else in the world seems alien to him, and the sense of loss of identity is so strong that he has to say to himself his name, 'I am Stephen Dedalus', while, remembering himself at Clongowes, he thinks that that boy has passed out of existence, has faded out, been 'lost and forgotten somewhere in the universe.' The presence of his father and his cronies reminiscing produces an even more acute sensation of spiritual death:

> His mind seemed older than theirs: it shone coldly on their strifes and happiness and regrets like a moon upon a younger earth. No life or youth stirred in him as it had stirred in them. He had known neither the pleasure of companionship with others nor the vigour of rude male health nor filial piety. Nothing stirred within his soul but a cold and cruel and loveless lust. His childhood was dead or lost and with it his soul capable of simple joys, and he was drifting amid life like the barren shell of the moon.   (*P* 98)

The money he wins in examinations temporarily revives his ties with his family and he forms resolutions and draws up a household economy: but he is forced to realize that he cannot paint over the squalor of his environment or of his mind, and that he has made no real contact with his family at all. He abandons himself to his secret sexual practices and dreams, accepting the sense of sin. At moments he still has premonitions of the holy encounter with an ideal image, but these are succeeded by desires 'to sin with another of his kind.' Reality unites the two. Wandering in the brothel area, 'he was in another world: he had awakened from a slumber of centuries.' In the arms of a prostitute he finds relief:

> Tears of joy and relief shone in his delighted eyes and his lips parted though they would not speak.
> ... In her ams he felt that he had suddenly become strong and fearless and sure of himself. (*P* 103–4)

That this relief will prove only temporary, this new world very unstable, is so obvious that few authors would have presented the incident, as Joyce does, as one of the triumphs of the boy's life. It is an important step in the development of the artist, for in it he has to assert the claims of his own nature, even when he sees that nature as vile in the eyes of God and man. To choose this defiant course, the boy he was must die: Stephen must enter into 'another world', and then the 'weakness and timidity and inexperience', which he had dreamed would fall away in his holy encounter with his romantic dream-figure, do indeed disappear as he feels 'strong and fearless and sure of himself'. At the end of each chapter there is a similar transfiguration, a similar new world or new life: that none of these is permanently satisfying is of no account: what matters is the courage to be alone, to act according to one's nature, not to be afraid of making mistakes.

The 'dark peace' which has been established between his body and his soul soon proves unstable. He is conscious of mortal sin (the first few pages of the third chapter contain a procession of the deadly sins[30]) and takes pleasure in the rigidity of the Church doctrines which condemn him. The retreat, with the series of addresses on the Four Last Things given by Father Arnall, completely shatters his peace and indifference with terror. The process is again a death of his former self; at first a conviction that he has sunk to the state of a beast; then a growing terror 'as the hoarse voice of the preacher blew death into his soul'; a fear that he had died while 'his brain was simmering and bubbling within the cracking tenement of the skull'; a vision of the 'hell of lecherous goatish fiends' prepared for him; and finally, while hastening to confess, extinction:

> One soul was lost; a tiny soul: his. It flickered once and went out, forgotten, lost. The end: black cold void waste. (*P* 144)

The phrasing recalls his image in the previous chapter of his own vanished childhood 'lost and forgotten somewhere in the universe' (*P* 96): it is his second death. Confession and repentance bring him again into a new life:

> Another life! A life of grace and virtue and happiness! It was true. It was not a dream from which he would wake. The past was past. (*P* 150)

But this new life is unlike the others he has experienced in that it is a communion not an isolation: 'He knelt before the altar with his classmates, holding the altar cloth with them over a living rail of hands.'

[30] See *Kenner*, 126.

The curious thing here is that whereas the boy's turning to the prostitute seems a triumphant rebellion against the frustration, pressures and sanctions of his environment, his reception of an invisible grace seems like a defeat, mainly because it is brought about by the hysterical terror aroused by Father Arnall's vivid depiction of hell. (Of the Four Last Things, heaven is hardly mentioned, death serves merely as an introduction, and even the Last Judgment is not dwelt on with the same relish as the preacher displays in his account of the tortures of the damned.) Stephen's reaction seems feeble-spirited compared to the resilience of Maurice in *Stephen Hero* who, although subjected to a similar retreat, replies when asked about the contents of the sermon on hell, 'Usual kind of thing. Stink in the morning and pain of loss in the evening' (*SH* 62). Stephen has a much livelier sense of guilt than Maurice, as well as a more intense imaginative life to be tormented by the preacher. Yet, although his period of religious exaltation is no more lasting than his other new lives, his achievement of it is not entirely a matter of defeat and intimidation, for, in one sense, this is the refining fire through which his soul must pass in order that its sensual desires should be given a new direction – that the impulse of his lust ('He stretched out his arms in the street to hold fast the frail swooning form that eluded him and incited him'—*P* 102–3) should be transformed into the spiritual impulse of the artist: 'I desire to press in my arms the loveliness which has not yet come into the world' (*P* 255). The artist must be ready to renounce the ordinary world if he is to become 'a priest of eternal imagination, transmuting the daily bread of experience into the radiant body of ever-living life' (*P* 225).[31] He must experience spiritual despair and shame, spiritual ecstasy, and total spiritual commitment, as a kind of apprenticeship to his vocation. At least this particular artist must. The exaltation with which Stephen later recognizes his vocation combines the sense of strength and confidence which came to him in the arms of the prostitute, with the religious ecstasy experienced at the end of this chapter. The occasions which establish these qualities may seem acts of defiance or submission, and their specific effects may be local and transitory; what matters, from the point of view of the artist, is the way in which they have formed his features, or in which the powerful constants in his nature convert such occasions to their own ends.

In the next chapter, for instance, the moment of religious communion is rapidly transformed into a new kind of fanatical religious isolation. In contrast to the parade of deadly sins at the beginning of the third chapter, the fourth presents a life given over entirely and systematically to religious practices. He self-consciously mortifies each of his senses, and feels 'a new

[31] Stanislaus Joyce quotes a conversation with his brother: 'Don't you think, said he reflectively, choosing his words without haste, there is a certain resemblance between the mystery of the Mass and what I am trying to do? I mean that I am trying in my poems to give people some kind of intellectual pleasure or spiritual enjoyment by converting the bread of everyday life into something that has a permanent artistic life of its own . . . for their mental, moral, and spiritual uplift, he concluded glibly' (*MBK*, 116).

thrill of power and satisfaction' in rejecting 'the insistent voices of the flesh', knowing 'he could by a single act of consent, in a moment of thought, undo all that he had done' – thus converting a submission of the self into a new kind of self-assertion, declaring that the eternal welfare of his soul is his to make or mar. The insuperable difficulty is the required surrender of his isolation:

> To merge his life in the common tide of other lives was harder for him than any fasting or prayer, and it was his constant failure to do this to his own satisfaction which caused in his soul at last a sensation of spiritual dryness together with a growth of doubts and scruples. (*P* 155)

When the director, impressed by the boy's piety and good example, invites him to consider whether he has a vocation for the priesthood, these doubts and scruples become dominant and once again his achieved world perishes. Despite his respect for the Jesuits who have educated him, some of their judgements have recently seemed childish to him, 'and had made him feel a regret and pity as though he were slowly passing out of an accustomed world and were hearing its language for the last time.' Though he has long dreamt of becoming a priest, attracted by the possession of secret knowledge and power, now he sees the priest's life in different terms ('It was a grave and ordered and passionless life that awaited him, a life without material cares') and instinctively turns away from it. He imagines himself in a college community, and this flouts one of the principles of his life: 'What had come of the pride of his spirit which had always made him conceive himself as a being apart in every order?' His years of obedience have no hold on him as soon as the surrender of his freedom and more particularly of his isolation is in question; his isolation reaffirms itself: 'His destiny was to be elusive of social or religious orders. . . . He was destined to learn his own wisdom apart from others or to learn the wisdom of others himself wandering among the snares of the world.' Shortly afterwards he has the revelation of his true destiny, first suggested by the boys who call out his name: 'Now, as never before, his strange name seemed to him a prophecy', and, thinking of it, he sees it as

> a prophecy of the end he had been born to serve and had been following through the mists of childhood and boyhood, a symbol of the artist forging anew in his workshop out of the sluggish matter of the earth a new soaring impalpable imperishable being. (*P* 173)

Once more there occurs the imagery of death and rebirth ('His soul had arisen from the grave of boyhood, spurning her graveclothes') and of a new world ('His soul was swooning into some new world, fantastic, dim, uncertain as under sea, traversed by cloudy shapes and beings'), but an even more powerful image presents his vision of this new world:

> A world, a glimmer, or a flower? Glimmering and trembling, trembling and unfolding, a breaking light, an opening flower, it spread in endless succession to itself, breaking in full crimson and unfolding and fading to palest rose, leaf by leaf and wave of light by wave of light, flooding all the heavens with its soft flushes, every flush deeper than other. (*P* 177)

No-one as familiar as Joyce with Dante's work could have written that without recognizing the indebtedness to the image of the Celestial Rose towards the end of the *Paradiso*, though Joyce's flower is properly rose and crimson instead of yellow and white. As the vision of the transcendent beauty of Beatrice leads directly to the Rose vision, so Stephen's ecstasy is introduced by his perception of the 'mortal beauty' of the girl paddling, and, like Dante, he is silenced: 'Her image had passed into his soul for ever and no word had broken the holy silence of his ecstasy.' But Stephen's angel has not been sent from the courts of heaven, and has not come to lead him to the realm of light and love: like Beatrice, she has summoned him with her eyes, but it is 'to live, to err, to fall, to triumph, to recreate life out of life':

> A wild angel had appeared to him, the angel of mortal youth and beauty, an envoy from the fair courts of life, to throw open before him in an instant of ecstasy the gates of all the ways of error and glory. (*P* 176)

The paradisal nature of Stephen's rapture may suggest that the middle three chapters of the book are patterned, like 'Grace', on the *Divine Comedy*, although this time with a different irony. 'The wasting fires of lust' which burn in Stephen as he grows conscious of 'some dark presence moving irresistibly upon him from the darkness', compelling from him a cry 'like a wail of despair from a hell of sufferers', represent his *Inferno*. The flames which seem to consume his flesh and his brain after the hell-fire sermons, the little flakes of fire which fall on the sinful city of his soul, the shame which 'covered him wholly like fine glowing ashes falling continually', are all purgatorial, so that after his confession he can pray from a 'purified heart' and receive God in the communion in a 'purified body'; and it is possible that the 'white pudding and eggs and sausages and cups of tea', which inspire Stephen to think 'How simple and beautiful was life after all!', compose a comical equivalent to the Earthly Paradise at the end of the *Purgatorio*. The significant and ironical contrast is that whereas Beatrice leads her poet to a vision of eternity which transcends mortal life, the Muse-like girl paddling on the shore brings to the embryo artist a vision of the transcendent beauty of mortal life, though, as yet, the raptures of the vision have no real contact with the life he knows.

If the parallel is deliberate (and it seems unlikely that Joyce who had already patterned one story on the *Divine Comedy* could have failed to notice these correspondences), then presumably the first and last chapters must be seen as prologue and epilogue, the first conducting the boy up to the first assertion of his individuality, the beginning of his existence as a separate and responsible being in the transition from innocence to experience, and the last concerned with his first stumbling attempts to translate the rapturous vision into 'some mode of life or art'. Certainly the main action of the book (in the sense of an ordered and developing sequence of psychological events) is presented in the middle three chapters: the first is a series of discontinuous episodes displaying the various pressures exerted on the young boy until the decisive act at the end, and the last, similarly, has no central action, but shows Stephen challenged again by all the old forces, until his final resolve to leave Dublin.

This is not to say that the last chapter, any more than the first, is un-important or incoherent. On the contrary, it is the chapter in which all the features of the artist as a young man, shaped and formed by the interaction of his nature and his environment, are assembled and moulded into a portrait. Joseph Prescott has said that 'what we have of *Stephen Hero* has a better claim to the title *A Portrait of the Artist as a Young Man* than does the so-miscalled work, which treats Stephen's experience from his earliest memories to young manhood.'[32] But a portrait of any man's soul, at any period of his life, must have the temporal dimension; in Stephen's mind in the last chapter of the *Portrait*, his Jesuit teachers, his exposure to Irish nationalism, the collapse of his family's position, his romantic dreams, his sexual experiences, his religious exaltation, his rapture at discovering his vocation are still (as they always will be) potent presences. It is not simply that in the past they fashioned him: they are active in him.[33] Apart from certain constant traits (and these are not really exceptions), Stephen is composed not of a set of characteristics, but of interacting forces.

In the last chapter one can see by comparison with *Stephen Hero* what has been cut away and what boiled down, and perceive how all the earlier themes are recalled and related to Stephen's specifically artistic essence. His problem is to fly past the nets which have been cast to enmesh his soul, without getting caught in others. Throughout this chapter he is presented as steering a way between opposites, from the beginning when he dispels the 'ache of loathing and bitterness' (his initial response to the disorders of his family life and the squalor round his home) by opening his senses to the beauty of the wet morning, to the end where his romantic excitement about the life ahead of him is challenged by realism and a sense of humour:

> O life! Dark stream of swirling bogwater on which appletrees have cast down their delicate flowers. Eyes of girls among the leaves. Girls demure and romping. All fair or auburn: no dark ones. They blush better. Houp-la!
> (*P* 255)

Throughout the chapter he is trying to control the impulses of desire and loathing: the artist's life must be as free of them as his art. Stasis is the appropriate condition for the soul of the artist as artist. Even on the simplest religious questions Stephen is noncommittal: asked whether he believes in the eucharist he says 'I neither believe in it nor disbelieve in it', and pressed further about the possibility of overcoming his doubts he answers 'I do not wish to overcome them' (*P* 243). He turns away from the

---

[32] Joseph Prescott, *James Joyce: The Man and his Works* (Toronto, Forum House 1969), 17. (Originally published as *Exploring James Joyce*, Carbondale, Southern Illinois University Press 1964.)

[33] Cf. 'The features of infancy are not commonly reproduced in the adolescent portrait for, so capricious are we, that we cannot or will not conceive the past in any other than its iron memorial aspect. Yet the past assuredly implies a fluid succession of presents, the development of an entity of which our actual present is a phase only' ('A Portrait of the Artist', *Workshop*, 60).

Catholic Church but not to become a Protestant: he contemptuously rejects Irish nationalism, both Davin's athletic militancy and the cultural chauvinism of the students, yet he will not turn to the internationalism and universal brotherhood proclaimed by MacCann. All his friends are held at a distance: to the idealist, MacCann, he talks materialistically, asking whether he will be paid if he signs the testimonial; with the materialist, Lynch, who thinks only of jobs and women, he discusses his artistic theories and ideals; to Davin, whose courtesy is coupled with 'grossness of intelligence' and 'bluntness of feeling', he repeats poetry, and to the cold, listless, and unsympathetic Cranly he tells 'all the tumults and unrest and longings in his soul.' He rejects both his mother's humble religiosity and his father's noisy conceit. At one moment Dublin is evocative of all the authors he most admires, and, at another, the city is dead, its soul 'shrunk with time to a faint mortal odour rising from the earth.'

Joyce is not presenting Stephen simply as wayward, unstable, inconsistent: it is very much Stephen's deliberate policy to prevent himself from becoming too committed even to an attitude. A clear though minor illustration is when he allows his irritation with the Ulsterman, MacAlister, 'to carry him towards wilful unkindness, bidding his mind think that the student's father would have done better had he sent his son to Belfast to study and have saved something on the train fare by so doing.' But at once he realizes that the thought is not his own; it has been stimulated by the mockery of the 'comic Irishman', Moynihan, and he thinks,

> Can you say with certitude by whom the soul of your race was bartered and its elect betrayed – by the questioner or by the mocker? Patience. (*P* 198)

This is a small matter, but it shows how Stephen is constantly trying to prevent himself from accepting even the most casual and insignificant suggestions of his companions and his environment: he must be free and alone, influenced by no-one and committed to no cause other than his art.

The most important manifestation both of Stephen's elusiveness and of Joyce's shaping of his materials for this chapter is in the treatment of the relationship with the girl, E— C—.[34] In *Stephen Hero*, the girl herself, Stephen's attraction to her, and her rejection of his advances are all much more fully presented. We are shown how the acquaintance between Stephen and Emma Clery was renewed, her nationalist fervour which drew Stephen to Irish language classes, her flirtation with the priest, Father Moran, and Stephen's fluctuations between desire for her body, 'compact of pleasure' and his contempt for 'her distressing pertness and middle-class affectations'. This culminates in the remarkable (and, one might have thought, crucial) incident when Stephen runs after Emma in the street and suggests that, without any bond of love between them, they should spend a night together and then part forever. She thinks him mad, and as she walks away

---

[34] In the *Portrait*, the initials are used only in addressing an early poem 'To E— C—' ((*P* 72). The name, Emma, occurs only in the third chapter, where it appears three times in close succession (*P* 119–20), almost as though Joyce has forgotten to remove it from that small section.

he seems 'to feel her soul and his falling asunder swiftly and for ever after an instant of all but union.' The attraction for him has always been a purely physical one: it seems to him essentially hostile to his art, and, more particularly, to his poetry:

> He knew that it was not for such an image that he had constructed a theory of art and life and a garland of verse and yet if he could have been sure of her he would have held his art and verses lightly enough. (*SH* 163)

In the *Portrait* the real relationship with the girl is faded out. Stephen's attendance at the Irish class is merely mentioned, in passing, as something which has ended. He recalls briefly two occasions when they were together in her parlour and at a ball, but there is no conversation between them during the time covered by the chapter, except for the curious farewell recorded in his journal just before he leaves Ireland. Yet the relationship is now much more central, especially to his development as an artist. The 'Villanelle of the Temptress' which, in *Stephen Hero*, was said to have been prompted by a trivial conversation overheard in the street, is, in the *Portrait*, specifically addressed to the girl, who is so deeply involved in his mind with his spiritual state and poetic inspiration that to break free from the desire for her is one of the last and most difficult of his steps towards isolation. When he first sees her in the chapter he remembers with 'conscious bitterness' her flirting with a priest, but immediately wonders if he has judged her harshly, if she is not simple and gay, 'her heart simple and wilful as a bird's heart'. Immediately afterwards we see him waking to 'a morning inspiration', where she is both identified with his Muse, and imaged in terms of the Virgin Mary:

> O! In the virgin womb of the imagination the word was made flesh. Gabriel the seraph had come to the virgin's chamber. An afterglow deepened within his spirit, whence the white flame had passed, deepening to a rose and ardent light. That rose and ardent light was her strange wilful heart, strange that no man had known or would know, wilful from before the beginning of the world: and lured by that ardent roselike glow the choirs of the seraphim were falling from heaven. (*P* 221–2)

The virgin figure is, to start with, explicitly the visited imagination of the poet, and one would suppose the wilful heart to be that of the Muse, were it not that only three paragraphs earlier we have heard that Emma has just such a heart. The poem which follows certainly seems to refer more intelligibly to a Muse figure, though Emma is identified as 'the temptress of his villanelle'. In the very midst of Stephen's poetic raptures, there is a remarkable collapse:

> Smoke went up from the whole earth, from the vapoury oceans, smoke of her praise. The earth was like a swinging smoking swaying censer, a ball of incense, an ellipsoidal ball. The rhythm died out at once; the cry of his heart was broken. His lips began to murmur the first verses over and over; then went on stumbling through half verses, stammering and baffled; then stopped. The heart's cry was broken. (*P* 222)

This comical interruption of Stephen's poetic frenzy should remove any possible doubts concerning Joyce's irony in the presentation of the artist as a young man. For what completely shatters Stephen's heart's cry is the unfortunate shift from 'a ball of incense' to 'an ellipsoidal ball'. The nature of this object has been defined by Moynihan during the physics lecture:

> Moynihan leaned down towards Stephen's ear and murmured:
> —What price ellipsoidal balls! Chase me, ladies, I'm in the cavalry!
> (*P* 196)

Thus the unfortunate appearance of the word in Stephen's verbal rhapsody comes almost as a jeering comment, besides introducing the sexual note which repeatedly interferes with his spiritual devotion, as it here interferes with his poem. The recollection of her behaviour in the company of others revives the memory of her flirtation with the priest, and anger rudely drives away the remains of his ecstasy, as he sees her reflected in various unattractive women of his recent experience. But then he feels that anger, too, is 'a form of homage', and before long he is recalling the childhood incident on the tram when he had resisted her blandishments. He compares that childish wisdom to his present folly, and imagines her reading out his verses to be mocked at by her family. Once again this provokes a reaction ('He began to feel that he had wronged her') and the thought of her innocence again inflates her image and his language:

> Might it be, in the mysterious ways of spiritual life, that her soul at those same moments had been conscious of his homage? It might be.   (*P* 227)

But in the very next sentence the 'spiritual life' has been replaced by physical desire and an erotic vision of her naked body, waking, 'conscious of his desire' instead of his homage. Now the poem can be finished, the villanelle of the temptress.

Thus, in this chapter, Emma is for Stephen a female body in which his imagination can locate the sexual appeal of the prostitute, the spiritual uplift of the Virgin and the rhapsodic inspiration of the Muse-girl on the shore. But besides serving to provide a bodily form for Stephen's dreams, she is also the chief threat to his assumed detachment. He fluctuates between desire and loathing, until, like the boy in 'Araby', he sees all his highflown dreams of her as vanities. Because so many of his enfeebling dreams have been incarnate for him in the figure of the girl, his perception of the self-deceit which has characterized his feelings towards her serves as a more general self-liberation, and, as this illusion has been represented by the posturing poeticism of the 'Villanelle', so the act of liberation is prompted by a critical recognition, in his next encounter with the girl, of the falseness of this poetic abandonment.

She passes, and the air seems silent after her passage: he thinks of the line, '*Darkness falls from the air*', and, moved by 'a trembling joy', is unsure whether it is her passing or the beauty of the verse which has so moved him. But the verse evokes the Stuart period and with it the sexual squalor beneath the musical and verbal grace of that time – an historical projection of his own physical desire concealed behind poetical and spiritual disguises. He checks himself lest her image be contaminated:

> That was not the way to think of her. It was not even the way in which he thought of her. Could his mind then not trust itself? (*P* 237)

At once he imagines her passing homewards, and senses the smell of her body and her underclothes, 'a wild and languid smell'. The wildness and languor of the 'Villanelle' has been metamorphosed from spirit to matter. A louse crawling on his neck disturbs him; he suddenly remembers that Nash's line was '*Brightness falls from the air*', and all the images prompted by the misquoted line are seen to have been false: 'His mind bred vermin. His thoughts were lice born of the sweat of sloth.' The revulsion, following this new perception of his vanity, is such that he decides to 'let her go and be damned to her. She could love some clean athlete who washed himself every morning to the waist and had black hair on his chest. Let her' (*P* 238).

This curious and involved revolution of attitude is not to be explained in logical terms; but some concatenative mental process is clearly at work. The association of the girl with the misquoted line of verse is part of the habitual poetic aura with which Stephen clothes his feelings towards her, but as a consequence of the sexual images produced by the historical and literary associations of the line (although he denies they have any reference to the girl) 'a conscious unrest seethed in his blood' and an unmistakably physical and sexual desire awakes, focused not on the customary Swinburnian image of nakedness but on the smell of her body 'and the secret soft linen upon which her flesh distilled odour and a dew.' The combination of this poetical perspiration and the appearance of the louse recalls the old superstition that lice were born of human sweat, and induces the image of his own body 'illclad, illfed, louseeaten'; in sudden despair he sees 'the brittle bright bodies of lice falling from the air.' The word 'bright' recalls the true wording of the verse he had misquoted, and makes him see his mind as breeding vermin 'born of the sweat of sloth'. The revulsion is not due to a horrified perception that Emma's body-odours and his lice-breeding sweat are the same, but rather to the realization that the fantasy he has made of the girl is merely a slothful exudation of his mind, disguising physical desire as poetic devotion, very much as the boy in 'Araby' perceived the 'vanity' of his religio-romantic fantasies. The girl in spiritual reality bears no resemblance to his dreams of her; in fact, she belongs to and will be drawn to a world of physical cleanliness and athleticism totally alien to him and his poetry. Once the true nature of his feelings emerges from the 'cloudy circumstance' and rosy afterglow in which his poem was conceived, once the 'wilful heart' and 'look of languor' of the dream image have been transmuted to 'a wild and languid smell', the girl loses her hold on his imagination. Later, talking to Cranly, and perceiving that his friend would shield a woman and bow his mind to her, Stephen knows that his own feelings for the girl have no real place in his life: 'He could not strive against another. He knew his part' (*P* 249). His part, as artist, seems to him, at this stage, to keep out of the struggle, to detach himself, and the obsession with the girl is the last skin but one that he must strip off to be free. Later he writes in his diary he is 'soulfree and fancyfree', and adds, 'And let the dead marry the dead.' The diary reveals a mild concern for her, but he seems untroubled to hear that Cranly is 'the shining light now'. There is almost a tone of contempt (at least of cheerful rejection) in the next entry:

> Certainly she remembers the past. Lynch says all women do. Then she remembers the time of her childhood – and mine if I was ever a child. The past is consumed in the present and the present is living only because it brings forth the future. Statues of women, if Lynch be right, should always be fully draped, one hand of the woman feeling regretfully her own hinder parts.   (*P* 255)

This is the confident assertion of the artist that his past is important only because it serves as the fuel of the present, making him what he is, and being destroyed (in its original form) in the process, while the only importance, for the potential artist, of what he is, is its contribution to what he will become and produce in the future. When he has got thus far in his detachment from the girl and from what she has in the past meant to him, he can chat to her dispassionately in the street, and even, for the first time, like her:[35]

> Then, in that case, all the rest, all that I thought I thought and all that I felt I felt, all the rest before now, in fact. . . O, give it up, old chap! Sleep it off!   (*P* 256)

I have discussed Stephen's relationship with the girl at length, because, although it is treated with so much less detail than in *Stephen Hero*, it has been made the climactic episode in the artist's struggle for isolation: the last chapter is held together by the process of Stephen's decisive break with his environment and his past, and the release from the spiritual, emotional and physical obsessions which have centred in the girl is the crucial and most difficult task, especially since she has become, in his mind, identified with his artistic inspiration. He must liberate himself from her before he can 'discover the mode of life or of art whereby [his] spirit could express itself in unfettered freedom.' The final prospect is again of a rebirth: Stephen must destroy all his old life in order to discover a new one: the severing of roots and ties is not a final step, but a necessary one in the process of rebirth.

Stephen's progress is, in a sense, an achievement of the *integritas* of his own nature as artist with the consequent discarding and rejection of all that is not directly relevant to that nature, and it is a progress reflected in the *integritas* of the created image. Apparently, in *Stephen Hero*, Joyce intended to show how the artist reached maturity through isolation, but the *Portrait*, with its emphatic 'as a young man' is far from suggesting that the romantic figure who leaves Ireland in the closing pages is mature. The earlier conception of the first two books, one of which should show the moribund environment and the other an individual soul's victory over that

---

[35] I agree with S. L. Goldberg who suggests that, in this brief passage, we see 'the first glimmering of Stephen's maturity' (*Goldberg*, 110–11).

environment, has been replaced by a conception in which the second book shows the achievement of freedom, not as a final victory but as the development of a counterforce, extreme and necessarily so. The isolated artist has to pay the cost in humanity of defeating the forces which subdue the gregarious, mutually bound, yet isolated citizens: he does not discover a final solution but creates an opposite and opposing energy. For this reason the *Portrait* demands a sequel, while, as far as one can gather from Joyce's notes and letters, *Stephen Hero* did not – a sequel in which the two opposites, equally sterile by themselves, would fruitfully interact and in which their coming together would be figured.

At the very end of the novel there appears to be one respect in which Stephen has not completely snapped his ties with his past and his environment – the resolve 'to forge in the smithy of my soul the uncreated conscience of my race.'[36] The suggestion here of some sense of responsibility to the Irish race seems inconsistent with his earlier refusal to accept the debts of his ancestors, and, hence, inconsistent with the specific *integritas* of the portrait of the young artist. But there is no real inconsistency. During the last meeting with Cranly, Stephen has wondered how he could hit the conscience of 'the patricians of Ireland',

> how cast his shadow over the imaginations of their daughters, before their squires begat upon them, that they might breed a race less ignoble than their own? And under the deepened dusk he felt the thoughts and desires of the race to which he belonged flitting like bats, across the dark country lanes, under trees by the edges of streams and near the poolmottled bogs. (*P* 242)

This appears an even clearer acceptance of racial responsibility; but the bat image has occurred several times before. The swallows which symbolized his own spirit (as well as being a 'symbol of departure or of loneliness') are bat-like, though their notes were 'long and shrill and whirring, unlike the cry of vermin' (*P* 228). Earlier still he has thought of Emma as 'a figure of the womanhood of her country, a batlike soul waking to the consciousness of itself in darkness and secrecy and loneliness' (*P* 225). The origin of the image is in Davin's story of the countrywoman who invited him to spend the night with her – a story which is linked in Stephen's mind with the childhood memory of the peasant women, standing at their doors as the boys from Clongowes drove past:

> The last words of Davin's story sang in his memory and the figure of the woman in the story stood forth, reflected in other figures of the peasant women whom he had seen standing in the doorways at Clane as the college cars drove by, as a type of her race and his own, a batlike soul waking to the consciousness of itself in darkness and secrecy and loneliness and, through the eyes and voice and gesture of a woman without guile, calling the stranger to her bed. (*P* 186–7)

[36] Joyce puns on 'forging' in *Finnegans Wake*. Although it has become a critical commonplace, I see no reason for supposing that he is doing so here, where the meaning of the word is defined by the related 'smithy', and by its earlier use in the phrase, 'forge out an esthetic philosophy' (*P* 183).

Here Stephen recognizes his own deep involvement in his race, and certainly the idea of the soul becoming conscious of itself 'in darkness and secrecy and loneliness' is more directly applicable to him than to Emma or anyone else in the story. Thus, the resolve to forge the uncreated conscience of his race is not evidence of a remaining fetter: his effort will be to express his own nature, but this will inevitably be an expression of his race. As he told Davin: 'This race and this country and this life produced me ... I shall express myself as I am.' The artist's race, as it were, derives the benefits of his exertions, without any deserving, and without, on his part, a deliberate bending of his nature to serve. The image is exact when he thinks that he will 'cast his shadow over the imaginations of their daughters'. In fact, it is only by leaving 'the old sow that eats her farrow' that the artist, spiritually free, can work out his own salvation, and incidentally create for his race 'in the smithy of [his] soul' the conscience which it lacks: for Stephen to refuse all the claims of his race is paradoxically the only way in which he can serve it.

In the past it was offered as a criticism of Joyce that his hero was too priggish: more recent critics, having recognized the irony in the presentation, have gone to the other extreme of supposing that Joyce was mocking a vain aesthete. Thus Hugh Kenner believes that 'by the time he came to rewrite the *Portrait* Joyce had decided to make its central figure a futile *alter ego* rather than a self-image' and that 'neither Stephen nor any extrapolation of Stephen' could have written *Ulysses*.[37] There can be no doubt that Stephen's development was a transmutation of Joyce's, but it would have been a pointless and ridiculous exercise to make by this transformation a figure of mere absurdity and impotence. All Joyce had available for his portrait of the artist was his own experience, and he used and shaped this to distinguish and present what seemed essential to him in the artistic nature. Naturally there is much that looks absurd in the behaviour of the aspiring artist, as there is always something absurd in the behaviour of a young man who takes himself and his future with profound seriousness. Equally there is something foolish, from the wiser viewpoint of critics, in a young man's attempt to cut free from all ties of family and friends, tear up his roots, and reject his native land. But although the behaviour of a young man, who believes in himself and his purpose, may seem foolish to older, more sceptical men, the energy generated by that foolishness is the means by which some young men pass beyond their immaturity. Stephen's collapsed and deflated condition in the early chapters of *Ulysses* does not prove that his wild ambitions at the end of the *Portrait* were merely futile posings. Joyce, himself, as a young man, was full of similar nonsense, as Richard Ellmann's biography shows and Stanislaus Joyce and others confirm.

Ulysses shows the sterile consequence of Stephen's isolation and dreams: it implies that something more was needed – that, like his creator, he had to become a man as well as an artist. Yet he had first to be free. If he accepted responsibilities, made attachments and ties, rooted all his work in Dublin,

[37] *Kenner*, 137.

he had to do so by choice and not by inheritance or puerile submission. Freedom and choice were not possible without, first, a complete rejection and resurrection: there could be no compromise in acceptance of the artist's vocation, and it is this uncompromising integrity which the *Portrait*, while reflecting the elements of coldness, absurdity and conceit inescapable in such a severance from humanity, sympathetically represents. Stephen's sense of triumph at the end of the *Portrait* is justified: he has triumphed. It may be a partial and temporary triumph, but so are all triumphs in life, and a victory is no less a victory because it does not end the war. In the closing diary, as throughout the book, Joyce uses the style to present, as he sees it, the whole truth about Stephen: his joy in his triumph is boyish and smug, he is insufficiently aware that the struggle is not finished, and his conception of his future is grandiose and unreal; all of these are captured in the style of his self-communings. But the style also hints at the beginnings of a new shrewdness and self-awareness which will eventually moderate his romantic excesses.

As the growth of the artist demanded the cutting-away of all that was inimical or irrelevant to it, so the creation of an integral image of the artist demanded the excision of the elements irrelevant to that aspect of the aspiring soul, even to the extent of making it appear cold, foolish and priggish. While he was writing the book his mind, he said, had been transformed by his wife's love into an opal. That is an image of a mature artist; but we should not be led by our admiration for the opalescent maturity to despise the passionless pearl. No-one knew better than Joyce that he had had to create the pearl before it could be transmuted to an opal, and, although, in presenting the formation of that pearl, truthfulness (as in the episode of the "Villanelle') required the ironic vision of the mature artist, nevertheless it is an understanding, not a hostile, irony. Joyce did not sentimentalize or falsify the artist as a young man, but neither did he spurn him: his endeavour was, instead, to delineate as sharply and precisely as he could those uncompromising qualities which constituted the young artist's *integritas* and enabled him to fly past the nets.

Consonantia

In tracing the 'action' of the novel, I have necessarily emphasized the emerging or developing aspects of the artist; but equally important is the presentation of those aspects which survive rather than develop. Stanislaus Joyce's remark, that his brother conceived the autobiographical novel originally as a representation of how 'a man's character, like his body, develops from an embryo with constant traits', is important and perceptive. The portrait of the artist involves the unchanging as well as the changing. The constancy underlying the development is more apparent when the relationship of parts to each other and to the whole is examined apart from the merely chronological relationship. The *consonantia* of the work, the rhythm of its structure, is articulated by a complex of echoes, cross-references, repeated phrases, memories, parallels, recurring images and symbols, some demanding recognition, others operating at less conscious levels. Their mode of operation is particularly evident in the treatment of one of the artist's dominant 'traits' – his detachment or isolation.

In the second chapter there is a curiously fragmented passage which follows a description of 'a vague dissatisfaction' stirring in the boy. He visits relatives, and does Christmas shopping with his mother, but

> his mood of embittered silence did not leave him. The causes of his embitter-
> ment were many, remote and near. He was angry with himself for being
> young and the prey of restless foolish impulses, angry also with the change of
> fortune which was reshaping the world about him into a vision of squalor
> and insincerity. Yet his anger lent nothing to the vision. He chronicled with
> patience what he saw, detaching himself from it and testing its mortifying
> flavour in secret. (P 69)

His anger is the ordinary human response to the situation: the vision, un-affected by anger, patient, detached, savouring the experience, is the artist's, and the last sentence, in particular, is reminiscent of Joyce's compulsion to record the truth of Dublin without interfering with it and to capture its 'special odour of corruption'.

There follow three, unintroduced, apparently unrelated epiphanies,[38] which mark their formal separateness by each beginning with the same three words. The first begins 'He was sitting on the backless chair in his aunt's kitchen' and describes how two children, a ringletted girl and a boy who enters carrying coal, eagerly look at a picture of a stage beauty. Without transition, the second begins, 'He was sitting in the narrow breakfast room high up in the old darkwindowed house', and tells of the ramblings of an old woman which are interrupted by the appearance of another woman, crazed and senile. Then, again with no transition, there is a fresh start: 'He was sitting in the midst of a children's party', and we are told how he silently watches the other children, especially one girl who eventually sees him to his tram, where he declines the invitation in her manner. Clearly this trilogy of scenes is intended to illustrate the preceding statement, 'He chronicled with patience what he saw'; clearly, too, the repeated 'He was sitting' underlines another part of that sentence – 'detaching himself from it' – as well as presenting him facing passively the dwindling, mortifying environment – an inactive, uninvolved, silent watcher.

The general bearing of these three epiphanies is not obscure, though it is the nature of the epiphany to suggest more than can be stated. The first obviously contrasts the wretched scene with the image of Mabel Hunter, the pantomime queen with 'demurely taunting eyes', but the effect is not merely one of contrast. Even the escapist dream of this family is vulgar, expressed in the image of a pretence, a pantomime queen, gazed at in fascination and hackneyed devotion by the girl ('Isn't she an exquisite creature?') and grabbed at greedily by the boy who brings in the coal.

[38] The last two of these passages are based on recorded epiphanies. See *Workshop*, 13 and 15.

Similarly the second episode contrasts the boy's romantic imaginings as he looks into the fire, 'following the ways of adventure that lay open in the coals, arches and vaults and winding galleries and jagged caverns', with the gloomy room and the senile decay of the old woman. Yet the presentation of the scene in the 'spectral dusk', and the weird and disturbing interruption themselves have a Gothic undertone:

Suddenly he became aware of something in the doorway. A skull appeared suspended in the gloom of the doorway. A feeble creature like a monkey was there, drawn thither by the sound of voices at the fire. (*P* 70)

The method here is not unlike that of 'Araby', placing the adventurous dreams of the boy in a nightmarish reality, and presenting an epiphany of moribund decay. For this artist the 'adventures' of the mind are to be found ultimately in the spectral world around him rather than in fiery daydreams.

Finally, the episode of the party not only contrasts Stephen's 'silent watchful manner' with the noisy merriment of the other children, but more importantly reveals the conflict within him. Although he has begun 'to taste the joy of his loneliness', he is conscious too of 'the feverish agitation of his blood' as he watches the girl dancing, 'flattering, taunting, searching, exciting his heart.' The struggle in him is between the natural human desire and the strange withdrawal of his temperament. When she flirts with him on the steps of the tram, it is Eve tempting Adam:

He heard what her eyes said to him from beneath their cowl and knew that in some dim past, whether in life or in revery, he had heard their tale before. He saw her urge her vanities, her fine dress and sash and long black stockings, and knew that he had yielded to them a thousand times. Yet a voice within him spoke above the noise of his dancing heart, asking him would he take her gift to which he had only to stretch out his hand. (*P* 71)

This reminds him of an incident described in the first chapter when Eileen had put her hand in his pocket, and had then run away laughing. Even in this childish scene the girl had behaved teasingly, erotically, sexually, while the boy had been puzzled rather than excited:

Now, as then, he stood listlessly in his place, seemingly a tranquil watcher of the scene before him. (*P* 71)

He is only 'seemingly' tranquil and sees his resistance as mere 'listlessness' and productive of gloomy regret. Yet already his temperamental isolation compels him instinctively to resist the sexual urge, the lure of feminine vanities, since they threaten his lonely joy and the inherent detachment of the potential artist.

The three brief passages present in the subtle and suggestive mode of the epiphany the boy's vision of himself and his environment, bluntly summed up in the preceding paragraph. They define and realize such abstractions as 'a vision of squalor', 'mortifying flavour' and 'the prey of restless foolish impulses', and establish the separation of the boy as artist, sitting in silence, a patient chronicler, detached from the anger and bitterness of his natural self, a detachment Joyce is not only describing but attempting to practise.

As the reference to the episode with Eileen shows, this detachment was already present in embryonic and unconscious form in the little boy of the first chapter, and it is manifested again and again throughout the book. For instance, in the second chapter, Stephen, remembering the occasion when he had been bullied by Heron, recognizes this strange quality in his temperament:

> All the descriptions of fierce love and hatred which he had met in books had seemed to him therefore unreal. Even that night as he stumbled homewards along Jones's Road he had felt that some power was divesting him of that suddenwoven anger as easily as a fruit is divested of its soft ripe peel. (*P* 84)

An even closer parallel follows when, although furious, hurt, and frustrated at missing Emma after the play, he cannot sustain his passion:

> A film still veiled his eyes but they burned no longer. A power, akin to that which had often made anger or resentment fall from him, brought his steps to rest. (*P* 89)

Consistently, though in different forms, this power quells every passionate outburst. Even the boy's hysterical fear and hate of Father Dolan at once dissolves, so that while the other boys are celebrating the triumph over 'Baldyhead Dolan', Stephen is resolving to be 'very quiet and obedient'. His emotional riot prior to the meeting with the prostitute subsides into 'a cold lucid indifference', 'a dark peace': 'The chaos in which his ardour extinguished itself was a cold indifferent knowledge of himself' (*P* 107).

Both this passage and the passage where his anger about the bullying is suddenly stripped off like peel are verbally echoed when, during his period of devotion, his temperament asserts itself again:

> He had heard the names of the passions of love and hate pronounced solemnly on the stage and in the pulpit, had found them set forth solemnly in books, and had wondered why his soul was unable to harbour them for any time or to force his lips to utter their names with conviction. A brief anger had often invested him but he had never been able to make it an abiding passion and had always felt himself passing out of it as if his very body were being divested with ease of some outer skin or peel. He had felt a subtle, dark and murmurous presence penetrate his being and fire him with a brief iniquitous lust: it too had slipped beyond his grasp leaving his mind lucid and indifferent. This, it seemed, was the only love and that the only hate his soul would harbour. (*P* 152–3)

The repeated phrases and images are important: they reveal the same cast of mind at work in his religious exaltation as in his spiritual hell. Moreover, as this passage echoes the two preceding chapters, so, in similar fashion, it looks forward to the next and final chapter. For it continues by pointing out that despite this temperamental inability to prolong love or hate, his faith will not allow him to 'disbelieve in the reality of love since God Himself had loved his individual soul with divine love from all eternity', and he gradually finds a way out of this difficulty in a new vision:

Gradually, as his soul was enriched with spiritual knowledge, he saw the whole world forming one vast symmetrical expression of God's power and love. Life became a divine gift for every moment and sensation of which, were it even the sight of a single leaf hanging on the twig of a tree, his soul should praise and thank the Giver. The world for all its solid substance and complexity no longer existed for his soul save as a theorem of divine power and love and universality. (*P* 153)

The combination, in this period of devotion, of the detachment from personal love and hate with the revelation of the whole of creation as a 'symmetrical expression' of the divine power and love, manifested in even the smallest experience, is matched by the nature of the aesthetic theory which Stephen expounds in the following chapter. It underlines his rejection, from the work of art, of the kinetic impulses, desire and loathing, in favour of the aesthetic stasis, and it determines his preference for the dramatic form, where the artist's creative vitality, instead of expressing itself in a personal outburst of emotion, or flowing round the characters and action, 'fills every person with such vital force that he or she assumes a proper and intangible esthetic life.' His personality 'finally refines itself out of existence, impersonalises itself', and 'the mystery of esthetic like that of material creation is accomplished'. The artist, like God, creates a work which is a 'symmetrical expression', a 'theorem' of himself:

> The artist, like the God of the creation, remains within or behind or beyond or above his handiwork, invisible, refined out of existence, indifferent, paring his fingernails. (*P* 219)

This much-quoted sentence is not as simple an assertion of the artist's indifference to life as has sometimes been supposed. Certainly in one sense he is detached, but as God may be said to be detached, because all his concern has been projected into the creation, where it fills every person with vital force, as Stephen had seen in his religious period every leaf and twig charged with God's power and love. Like God, the artist is not only behind, beyond and above his handiwork, but also within it. His personality is refined out of existence because it is, like God's, embodied in his creation. Instead of a personal love and hate, there is a universal creative vitality; instead of personal sympathy, there is a more complete and general sympathy flowing into every person. The condition of artistic creation in the dramatic form is a detachment of the spirit from personal concerns in order that there may be a universal penetration into all the concerns of the created world.

The indebtedness of this doctrine (even in its wording) to Flaubert goes far deeper than the mere notion of the artist's divine detachment. Flaubert, too, writes of this detachment as a necessary means of achieving a more universal and penetrating involvement:

> If one gets mixed up with life, one cannot see it clearly; one suffers too much, or enjoys it too much. The artist, in my opinion, is a monstrosity, something outside nature.[39]

[39] This translation of Flaubert's letter of 15 December 1850 is taken from Miriam Allott's *Novelists on the Novel*, (London, Routledge and Kegan Paul 1959), 125–6.

For Flaubert, too, the characters had to be charged with the author's life: 'We must, by an effort of the mind, go over to our characters, as it were, not make them come over to us.'[40] Similarly it is not only in Stephen Dedalus but in the novel as a whole that Joyce's personality finds expression. The character of Stephen is not a reflection of the author's, but draws its energy and life from his. The detachment of the author, both to Joyce and Flaubert, was merely part of his total surrender to his work.

The 'constant trait' of detachment appears in manifold disguises in every chapter, and thereby serves not only as part of the book's and the artist's *integritas*, but also as one of the methods by which a functional interaction between the parts, and between the parts and the whole, is created. This interaction or structural rhythm informs the presentation of all the forces against which the 'constant traits' of the artist are set, and which nevertheless mould, and direct the expression of his art – the pressures of the family and society, of sexual desire, of religion, of politics and nationalism, of the Dublin environment generally. Each is operative in every chapter and becomes dominant in one.[41] The sexual theme, for instance, touched on in the first chapter in Athy's schoolboy suggestiveness, in the row about 'smugging' (associated in Stephen's mind with the urine-stinking yard), and in the episode with Eileen near the hotel-grounds, in the second chapter gradually assumes dominance until sexual fantasies swarm in Stephen's mind and find fulfilment in the prostitute. The priest's sermons produce dreams of lecherous fiends, and Stephen is shamed to think of himself ruled by 'a bestial part of the body'; his confession has mainly to do with sins of impurity (so much so that he wishes he had only murder to confess to), and, in reaction, his own devotions are particularly focused on the Virgin. (Earlier he has been puzzled to find that his lewdness made him wish to be the Virgin's knight.) His revelation of his vocation is associated with the image of a girl paddling with her clothes tucked up, and, finally, sexual attraction, even though dressed up in inspirational raiment, is the most persistent enemy to Stephen's artistic detachment.

The rise and fall of each of the impediments to the artist thus establish another complex of structural relationships – especially as Stephen uses one to liberate him from another – supplemented and enriched by recurring images. His detachment from life is recurrently imaged in terms of the vast cold spaces of the heavens, an image at first humbly suggested by the inscription in his book:

Stephen Dedalus
Class of Elements
Clongowes Wood College
Sallins

[40] Letter to George Sand, 15–16 December 1866. The translation is from *Novelists on the Novel*, 271.

[41] Cf. 'Each chapter in the *Portrait* gathers up the thematic material of the preceding ones and entwines them with a dominant theme of its own' (Hugh Kenner, 'The *Portrait* in Perspective', in *Givens*, 164).

County Kildare
Ireland
Europe
The World
The Universe   (*P* 15–16)

This first relation of himself to the universe provokes thoughts about its extent: 'It was very big to think about everything and everywhere. Only God could do that.' Later, in Cork, he sees himself 'drifting amid life like the barren shell of the moon', and recalls Shelley's lines about the weary moon '*Wandering companionless*', until the poem's 'alternation of sad human ineffectualness with vast inhuman cycles of activity' chills him and subdues his human grieving. The same lines of Shelley are again remembered as a 'distant music' when he is in a state of mortal sin, but now his soul is itself seen in terms of a 'vast cycle of starry life', where his sins are the burning stars, spreading, and fading and going out, leaving a dark chaos, in a reversal of the act of creation. Later, just before his recognition of his vocation, he watches the movement of the clouds across the sky and hears a confused music within him, which recedes leaving one piercing note like a summons. His sudden vision of the 'hawklike man flying sunward above the sea', the 'symbol of the artist', excites him 'as though he were soaring sunward. . . . soaring in an air beyond the world', and he rests, feeling above him 'the vast indifferent dome and the calm processes of the heavenly bodies.' Later, again, the swallows, whose flight symbolizes both his departure and his loneliness, make him feel in his heart 'the soft peace of silent spaces of fading tenuous sky above the waters, of oceanic silence' (*P* 230). Thus the image of vast silent spaces first expresses the boy's sense of his inconspicuousness, then his desolate and barren isolation, then the cold chaos of his sense of sin, and ultimately the detached peace in which his soul can be free, and, like God, create. All the central images of the book have this kind of mutability; they appertain to an uncertainly defined area of experience and of temperament, from which circumstances summon sometimes a misty image and sometimes a fully-formed symbol.

Music plays a similar role of imaging the vague or the inexpressible, beginning with the responsiveness of the boy to sounds (like the 'little song' of the gaslight and the 'quick music' of the railway guards' keys), and becoming the instinctive expression of inarticulate emotions: his feeling for the girl is expressed in 'the tide of flowing music' on which the school theatre floats like an ark; his sense of a cold chaos is introduced by 'distant music'; his sudden antipathy to the idea of becoming a priest is provoked by the 'trivial air' of a concertina which dissolves his fantasies of priestly power and knowledge; his first intuition of his true vocation appears as 'fitful music', 'an elfin prelude'; religion and love make their last appeal in the voice of the girl singing 'Rosie O'Grady' (strangely transformed in Stephen's imagination to a whiterobed woman intoning liturgical music). No single symbolic significance can be fastened on this recurring musical imagery, though it can, at times, harden into something like a symbol: it is clearly related to Stephen's own fondness for music, to his specifically rhythmical and musical response to language, and thus to one aspect of his artistic character; but, as imagery, it usually functions to suggest those aesthetic aspects of his emotional experience of which he fully understands neither the origin nor the nature, as the space imagery expresses intuitions, gloomy or joyous, of his isolation.

There have been many attempts to trace consistent symbolic patterns in Joyce's references to the four elements, especially water,[42] but to impose elaborate interpretations on every reference of this kind is arbitrary and misleading. Because the elements are ubiquitous in our experience, they may operate powerfully as symbols, but equally they may not. If we convert all the elements of life into permanent symbols, we will have nothing left to be symbolic about. Wholesale symbolic interpretation obscures and confuses the reader's response to those passages which have important figurative significance. The elements of water, fire, air and earth have powerful traditional connotations, and, usually, Joyce leaves little doubt which of these is involved: the stream of life, the tides of sin, the fires of lust, the purgatorial flames, the comforting warmth of a fire (Stephen, in fact, points out to the dean of studies that insofar as it satisfies the animal craving for warmth fire is good, but that in hell it is an evil), the 'mortal odour' of 'rainsodden earth', the earth as the mother that bore him and took him to her breast, the thick fog which images the state of mind after the first sermon, the air that was 'soft and grey and mild' in his moment of peace when he had been to see the Rector – none of these give the reader much difficulty; they work on him by suggestion and association, and the puzzles only start if and when the critic tries to fit them all into some prefabricated symbolic system. The recurring elemental imagery is not a set of equations but one of the binding elements which hold together the varied styles and moods of the book. The images of fire and water, though, unsurprisingly, more numerous than those of space and music, are even less fixed, but, like the rest of the imagery, colour and deepen the general *consonantia*, which is fundamentally established by a framework of structural and thematic elements, outlined in the opening paragraphs.

The importance of the 'overture' to the book, the brief impression of the infant mind, is precisely this – that it sketches in, unostentatiously, the main materials and relationships which hold the *Portrait* together in a structural rhythm. The passage represents the dawn of individual consciousness, but this alone would hardly justify its place in a portrait of the artist: it must also show in embryonic form the fundamental traits of the artist and of his environment. Through the child's eyes, Joyce arranges all the chief elements of his composition: the family group, not only individualized, but conceived as a separate entity, distinct from the Vances, and the original model of social approval and disapproval; Irish patriotism represented by the song about '*the wild rose*' and '*the little green place*' and Irish politics symbolized in the coloured brushes; infantile sexual feelings accompanied with a sense

---

[42] See, for instance, *Tindall–RG*, 88–9.

of guilt, figured childishly in the words, 'he was going to marry Eileen. He hid under the table'; moral pressure supported by the threat of super-natural sanctions; the earliest gropings towards artistic expression in the distortion of the little song and the forming of '*Apologise*' and '*Pull out his eyes*' into a verse. Then, as Hugh Kenner has pointed out,[43] Joyce runs over the scale of the awakening senses – sight, hearing, taste, touch and smell – and this, too, introduces one of the dominant traits of the artist. In the early chapters, the small boy's world is overflowing with sensuous experience, so that the simple words of the senses – light, dark, white, pale, black, grey, chilly, cold, warm, hot, quiet, sound, noise, silence, damp, slimy, shivering, tingling, smell, taste, feel – recur with a frequency that would be difficult to parallel elsewhere. A single sentence may embody many sense-impressions:

> As he passed the door he remembered with a vague fear the warm turf-coloured bogwater, the warm moist air, the noise of plunges, the smell of the towels, like medicine. (*P* 23)

This sensuous activity persists into the time when he is a frequenter of the brothel quarter, his appetite now craving coarser sensations – 'thick pep-pered flourfattened sauce', and the 'soft perfumed flesh' of the whores; but 'his senses, stultified only by his desire, would note keenly all that wounded or shamed them' and examples are given of what his eyes and ears found particularly offensive. In this way, gratification of his senses (like the infan-tile bedwetting which was first pleasant and then unpleasant) produces unpleasant consequences, and leads up to the passage where the boy, spiritually reborn, deliberately sets about the motification of his senses. This thoroughgoing campaign against the senses is a reversed echo of the opening: the boy has been reborn, but to a very different kind of life and one which he eventually finds is inimical to his nature and vocation. How-ever, at his first dim apprehension of his destiny, there still remain some traces of this rejection of the senses as he wonders whether 'he drew less pleasure from the reflection of the glowing sensible world through the prism of a language manycoloured and richly storied than from the con-templation of an inner world of individual emotions mirrored perfectly in a lucid supple periodic prose'; but this proves a false opposition as he sees his role as artist will be to forge 'out of the sluggish matter of the earth a new soaring impalpable imperishable being.' His body is 'commingled with the element of the spirit', and his encounter with the girl is not merely a spiritual revelation but a revelation too of 'mortal beauty'. Thus, when he comes to formulate his aesthetic theories, his definition of beauty is in terms of 'the sensible'. Of course, this is a long way from the sense impres-sions of the first few paragraphs, but it illustrates how the main themes of the book grow out of and sometimes refer back to those embryonic mani-festations.

There are other foreshadowings, too, of the nature of this artist. Stephen's

---

[43]*Kenner*, 114. Hugh Kenner was the first to show how the opening paragraphs of the *Portrait* 'enact the entire action in microcosm.'

identification of himself as 'baby tuckoo' and of the road in the story as 'the road where Betty Byrne lived', on the one hand foreshadows Stephen's later assertions of his identity ('I am Stephen Dedalus') and his habit of identifying himself with the heroes of books and plays – the Count of Monte Cristo, Napoleon, Claude Melnotte, Dante and Christ – and, on the other hand, is the beginning of his custom of 'placing' literature in his environment. Clongowes Abbey becomes for him Leicester Abbey, a house near Blackrock, the home of Monte Cristo's Mercedes, and even at university he persists in associating certain Dublin scenes with his literary masters – Hauptmann, Newman, Cavalcanti, Ibsen and Ben Jonson. The modification of the song into '*O, the green wothe botheth*' is Stephen's first imaginative flight, and prefigures the artist's later desire for an unknown beauty. At Clongowes he remembers the song and thinks, 'But you could not have a green rose. But perhaps somewhere in the world you could' (*P* 12); and this desire for the new and undiscovered is similarly present in the artistic ambition towards the end of the book – 'to press in my arms the loveliness which has not yet come into the world' (*P* 255). The beating out of the rhythm in the hornpipe and the rhythmic repetition of '*Apologise*' and '*Pull out his eyes*' foreshadows the sensitivity to sounds which later makes him wonder whether he loved 'the rhythmic rise and fall of words better than their associations of legend and colour' (*P* 171), and sets the rhythmic impulses of his brain operating to compose verse of less meaning than the childish rhyme (*P* 182). The young man's isolation and sense of difference is prefigured when the child hides under the table, and when he considers that the Vances had 'a different father and mother'. This last phrase is picked up later when he feels inferior to the other boys because his father is not a magistrate: 'All the boys seemed to him very strange. They had all fathers and mothers and different clothes and voices' (*P* 13). With the collapse of the family's fortunes, this sense of difference is exacerbated, and listening to children at play makes him feel 'even more keenly than he had felt at Clongowes, that he was different from others' (*P* 66). Thus the most powerful sign of his utter isolation, prior to his abandonment with the prostitute, is the sundering of his family ties: at Cork he is conscious of 'an abyss of fortune or of temperament' between himself and his father, and immediately afterwards, when he has failed to restore order with his prize-money, he seems to himself 'hardly of the one blood' with his mother, brother and sister, related to them only 'in the mystical kinship of fosterage, fosterchild and fosterbrother (*P* 101). When at the end he tries to fix his image of Cranly, he does so by trying to imagine his friend's father and mother.

Besides figuring in this opening section as the unit to which the boy belongs, the family is also particularized: each member of it is caught in a characteristic attitude. His father looks through his eyeglass, and the story he tells, beginning 'Once upon a time and a very good time it was', suggests his habit of reminiscing nostalgically and his son's summary description of him as 'a praiser of his own past'. The mother's nature is reflected in her nice smell (her niceness is again emphasized when the boy is at Clongowes), and in her attempt to shield him from the consequences of his act by persuading him to ask forgiveness: 'O, Stephen will apologise.' Similarly, in the closing pages of the book, although she is shocked and disappointed by her son's loss of faith, Stephen records in his diary,

> Mother indulgent. Said I have a queer mind and have read too much. Not true. Have read little and understood less. Then she said I would come back to faith because I had a restless mind. This means to leave church by back-door of sin and reenter through the skylight of repentance. Cannot repent. (*P* 253)

Still she is hoping that he will escape his punishment by apologizing. All the essentials of Dante's character, too, are sketched in – her fierce devotion to the nationalist cause, her even fiercer devotion to the Roman Catholic Church, her belief in the threat of exemplary punishment from on high for offenders (whether the infant Stephen or Parnell), and her genteel fastidiousness in collecting tissue-paper, presumably for toilet purposes, and in using cachous. Later the boy learns that 'when Dante made that noise after dinner and then put up her hand to her mouth: that was heartburn' (*P* 11).

To underline the multiple suggestions of the overture of infancy in this way may seem to imply something rather mechanically ingenious about the making of the book, but the clumsiness is that of critical explanation not of Joyce. The passage does not function as a contents page, but as a dim childish view of the environment and of the boy's nature, which become clearer and more definite as the book progresses. As in *Dubliners* the initial sounding of the word *paralysis* suggests the thematic metaphor for the city's disease, so here the opening of the *Portrait* attunes the reader's imagination to the apprehension of the *consonantia* of the book, by introducing from the beginning, in muted forms, the themes which through their relationships and interactions create a harmony of structure. This harmony, initiated in the 'overture', is sustained and developed throughout the novel by the 'constant traits' of the potential artist, by the interplay of the forces hostile to his growth, by recurring images and associated imagery, by symbols, echoes, cross-references and memories, until ultimately the changing and the unchanging unite in the one image, since the process of Stephen's development is essentially the process of recognizing his own constant nature.

Claritas

The application of the terminology from Aquinas to works of art, and especially literature, raises questions which Stephen does not pursue. He implies a kinship between the apprehension of a butcher's basket and an artist's conception of an aesthetic image, but does not examine the differences between a basket and, say, a novel, or between a novelist's conception of an image and his reader's apprehension of the completed novel, though these are differences of essence. Looking back on his earlier years to grasp what had shaped him as an artist, Joyce, no doubt, saw irrelevancies fall away and relationships discover themselves, until the essential shone forth in an image of the artist as a young man; but the *claritas* apprehended by a reader of the *Portrait* is fundamentally different, involving a response not only to the represented life-experience of the young Stephen but to the perceiving mind of the mature artist, Joyce, and also to the character and quality of the representing medium, a novel. The author's image was apprehended in 'the world of his experience' (*SH* 82); the reader's apprehension is of 'the human disposition of sensible or intelligible matter for an esthetic end': the nature of life is essential to the first and the nature of literature to the second.

Nevertheless, just as an author may (deliberately or instinctively or, more often, through a mixture of art and intuition) build into his novel features analogous to and expressive of the *integritas* and *consonantia* of the image originally conceived, so he may create an analogous *claritas*, in which represented life, authorial vision, and literary form are fused. Such a fusion, of which *integritas* and *consonantia* are individualizing and formal principles and which makes available to the reader's apprehension the three-fold *quidditas* of the novel, can be achieved only through the choice and ordering of words – through, in the widest sense of the term, 'style'. Certainly Joyce was convinced of this: when Frank Budgen, praising a contemporary writer, began to describe a scene in his work, Joyce said, 'Tell me something of it in his own words', and, when Budgen was unable to do so, remarked,

> When you talk painting to Taylor, Sargent or Suter you don't talk about the object represented but about the painting. It is the material that conveys the image of jug, loaf of bread, or whatever it is, that interests you. And quite rightly, I should say, because that is where the beauty of the artist's thought and handiwork become one.[44]

The title, *A Portrait of the Artist as a Young Man*, suggests some essential aspects of the novel. First, as a portrait (though one with a temporal dimension) it is limited to the immediate experience of the 'young man' and reflects the surrounding world only insofar as it influences, interacts with, or is apprehended by the central figure. Secondly, the author is presenting himself as an artist, not, as another writer might have done, as a storyteller, a biographer or a memoirist, and is declaring an identity of some sort between author and subject. Thirdly, there is a clear distinction between the mature artist painting the portrait and the embryo artist portrayed. Each of these aspects is embodied in the general conduct of the style.

Most novelists, when writing about childhood (even when writing for children), represent, describe and comment upon the child's experience in language and in a manner not themselves childlike. Great things have been achieved with this method (the first three stories of *Dubliners* among them)

[44] *Budgen*, 180.

but something is lost: the created image is more likely to suggest memories of childhood than the direct impact of the experience as known to the child; the mature style anchors the reader too firmly in the adult world. On the other hand, for an author to restrict himself to a child's capacity to penetrate, examine, understand and articulate would be to deprive himself of his mature insights and expressive resources. It can be done – it has been done in *Huckleberry Finn* – but only where the distinction between author and narrator is so emphatic that the author can depend on a sustained and unmistakable irony. Moreover, if, as in the *Portrait*, the title implies that the author is presenting himself as artist, one expects the style to reflect this, and, because of the implied relationship between the author and the 'young man', the novel should itself be related to the aspirations and notions of the embryo artist. The reader might comprehend Stephen's talk about the three things needed for beauty, and about the impersonality of the artist who pervades his work invisibly as God pervades his creation, but he would not apprehend their essential significance unless it was manifest in the writing. Yet, despite the relationship between author and subject, the style should continuously imply the simultaneous and distinct coexistence of the two presences, the 'young man' and the mature artist.

The clumsiest passages of *Stephen Hero* exhibit Joyce's failure in that book to find a style capable of handling consistently this complex relationship between the author and the young man he had been. Though 'the point of view' throughout is Stephen's, there is repeated difficulty in deciding whether the language is meant to represent the hero's or the author's view: the two are sometimes crudely, and sometimes inadequately, differentiated, as in the following laborious paragraph:

> In spite of his surroundings Stephen continued his labours of research and all the more ardently since he imagined they had been put under ban. It was part of that ineradicable egoism which he was afterwards to call redeemer that he conceived converging to him the deeds and thoughts of his microcosm. Is the mind of youth medieval that it is so divining of intrigue? Field-sports (or their equivalent in the world of mentality) are perhaps the most effective cure and Anglo-Saxon educators favour rather a system of hardy brutality. But for this fantastic idealist, eluding the grunting booted apparition with a bound, the mimic warfare was no less ludicrous than unequal in a ground chosen to his disadvantage. Behind the rapidly indurating shield the sensitive answered: Let the pack of enmities come tumbling and sniffing to my high-lands after their game. There was his ground and he flung them disdain from flashing antlers. (*SH* 39)

The uncertainty in creating a lucid relationship between the voices of Stephen and the author is particularly obvious in the last two sentences where, although the romantic metaphor is continued, there is a shift from first to third person. What can be taken as youthful self-dramatizing in the penultimate sentence smacks of authorial melodramatizing in the last one. There are other uncertainties and confusions. Did the notion that his egoism was a 'redeemer' come to Stephen 'afterwards' but when he was still a youth, or is it the author's? Do such words as 'imagined', 'conceived', 'divining' indicate that the young man was deluded or that he was subtly perceptive? 'This fantastic idealist' is blatantly an authorial label, but what then do we make of 'the sensitive', since our response to the word will depend on whether we take it to represent Stephen's egocentric view of his own nature or a congratulatory pat on the head from the author? One can see that Joyce is trying to present a double vision, but there is no fusion of the two: the erratic flickering from one to the other produces vagueness and imprecision, and suggests an author not clearly differentiated from and almost as self-dramatizing as his hero. What was wanted was a style which should be fully appropriate to and expressive of the subject, Stephen; yet, at the same time, one in which the authorial presence of Joyce would be pervasive, instead of having to poke itself clumsily into the narrative; and, also, a style which was manifestly an artifice, the signature of a conscious artist (rather than a storyteller or biographer) as the brushwork is the signature of the painter. In fact, while writing *Stephen Hero*, Joyce had solved the problem: in 'Clay', the style fuses Maria's essential nature, the author's view of her, and the character of the story as a short-story. Most of what we apprehend about Maria we apprehend through the kind of language in which she is presented; the author's complex feelings about his character are experienced through the style, and only through the style; without the special use of language the story would hardly exist – it would be an almost pointless anecdote. In 'Clay' the situation was static, the character paralysed, and her personality humble and commonplace, and all of these are reflected in the style: the *Portrait*, on the other hand, required a style which was 'growing', and which would be expressive of a creature, immature but experiencing intensely, even at times with an exaggerated intensity.[45]

The opening section, in addition to its concentration of thematic seeds, signals the stylistic character of the whole novel. No reader is likely to suppose that Joyce wrote in this way because he knew no better; the style is clearly artifice, created out of babytalk and the manner of infant-readers, and designed to suggest a child's consciousness. Authorial presence is most simply marked by the imitative spelling, '*O, the green wothe botheth*' (not what the child would have thought he was singing but what an adult would have heard him sing), and the author's vision is more complexly implicit in such abrupt juxtapositions as that of the uncomprehended offence, the absurd savagery of the threat, and the conversion of the threat into a jingle. There is plainly an unstated distinction between the child's view of Dante and the author's. Moreover, even in this short space, there is growth from the baby responding to its parents to the child familiar with relatives, neighbours and playfellows, and this growth is matched by the stylistic development from 'a nicens little boy named baby tuckoo' to 'O, Stephen will apologise.' The reader responds to the fused essence of the child's nature and experience, the author's implied commentary, and the function

---

[45] James Naremore's interesting discussion of 'Style as Meaning in *A Portrait of the Artist*' (*JJQ* IV (4) (1967), 331–42) differs from my account mainly in emphasis and some particulars of interpretation.

of the passage in the novel as a whole. Here, at the beginning of the book, it is proper that the general method should be established in an unmistakable, even exaggerated form; as Stephen grows up the differentiation between author and subject is progressively less emphatic. Nevertheless, it is variously and subtly sustained until Stephen's journal at the end.

The stylistic features I have so far discussed are those relating to the most general aspects of the novel's *claritas*; within these bounds, the style responds continually to the local character of particular experiences, incidents and moods. At the simplest level, language converts the sensuous experiences of the boy into sensible aspects of the verbal image:

> He leaned his elbows on the table and shut and opened the flaps of his ears. Then he heard the noise of the refectory every time he opened the flaps of his ears. It made a roar like a train at night. And when he closed the flaps the roar was shut off like a train going into a tunnel. That night at Dalkey the train had roared like that and then, when it went into the tunnel, the roar stopped. He closed his eyes and the train went on, roaring and then stopping; roaring again, stopping. It was nice to hear it roar and stop and then roar out of the tunnel again and then stop. (*P* 13)

The simple alternation of the words creates a verbal equivalent in sound to the boy's sense-impressions; that is all it purports to do. But the alternating sounds are also an aural equivalent for the alternating heat and chill that are symptomatic of his fever, and they become, a little later, an image of the alternation of term and vacation which lies dismally ahead of him. It is possible, too, that the train sounds 'nice' because it reminds him of home (he dreams that night of travelling home by train), and because the rhythmic rise and fall of the noise satisfies that quality of his imagination which leads him, in a much later episode, to fit words to 'the insistent rhythm of the train', and finally to feel a particular delight in 'the rhythmic rise and fall of words'. Moreover, this particular passage with its onomatopoetic effects forms part of an extended rhythmic alternation between such words as *fire, hot, burning, red, warm* and their opposites, *cold, chill, wet, damp, slimy, white*. The pattern involves the juxtaposition of the thought of the 'cold slimy water' of the ditch and that of his mother's 'hot' slippers with their 'warm smell', and the image of the lavatory with the hot and cold taps, the memory of which 'made him feel cold and then hot'; it creates a hectic rhythm of the senses through the whole section:

> He shivered and yawned. It would be lovely in bed after the sheets got a bit hot. First they were so cold to get into. He shivered to think how cold they were first. But then they got hot and then he could sleep. It was lovely to be tired. He yawned again. Night prayers and then bed: he shivered and wanted to yawn. It would be lovely in a few minutes. He felt a warm glow creeping up from the cold shivering sheets, warmer and warmer till he felt warm all over, ever so warm; ever so warm and yet he shivered a little and still wanted to yawn. (*P* 17)

Through this, the reader senses the boy's feverishness long before the illness has been recognized, but the physical waves of hot and cold so variously colour the boy's thoughts that the state of his body seems an image for the state of his spirit: he is desperately homesick, and consequently when Fleming asks if he is 'sick in [his] breadbasket', Stephen thinks that he is not sick there – 'he was sick in his heart if you could be sick in that place.' Here, then, the alternating repetition of words not only figures a much more prolonged and all-embracing experience than the sound-effect of opening and closing the ears, but also contributes to the verbalization of a fever of the mind as well as of the body.

Sense-words and images dominate the first section because for the boy the world of sense and the inner world are not yet separated (if he thinks about the universe, it makes his head feel very big, and his thoughts are repeatedly felt as sensations). In the whole section culminating in the vision when Brother Michael brings news of Parnell's death, Stephen cannot separate his sensations from his thoughts and emotions, and towards the end of the chapter there is a remarkable use of repetition to present an experience which is painful both physically and spiritually. By any ordinary criteria, the account of the pandybatting is overwritten. It is congested with repetitions, assonances, alliterations, laboured onomatopoetic effects, syntactic parallelisms, heaped-up adjectives, and diction which seems excessive for the context, and has a rhetorical flourish which declines into the childish – 'made him feel so sorry for them as if they were not his own but someone else's that he felt sorry for.' Kristian Smidt comments that Joyce's 'violence of expression can only be explained by the sense of having been unjustly punished rankling in his own mind till adult age and magnifying the physical pain beyond all proportions.'[46] Yet, according to the novel, the memory of the incident did not even rankle in Stephen's mind, let alone Joyce's, for, later, thinking of the Jesuits, he recalls that 'during all the years he had lived among them in Clongowes and in Belvedere he had received only two pandies and, though these had been dealt him in the wrong, he knew that he had often escaped punishment' (*P* 159). Even if Joyce had felt bitterness, it is hardly likely that he would have expressed it in this exaggerated and blatantly self-pitying way. What the emotional excess of the style represents is, on the one hand, the hysteria of pain, anger, self-pity and indignation which overwhelms the boy and drives him from his usual posture of submissive obedience, and, on the other, the author's sense that he is presenting a commonplace classroom incident vested in a child's hysteria. If a reader, while sympathizing with the boy, takes his agonies with a grain of salt, it is precisely because the style creates the child's sense of outrage and, at the same time, suggests the author's understanding of the reality of the situation. Similarly, the self-consciousness of the style reminds one that this is not a child's articulation of its experience, but an artist's: it is the phrase, 'unfair and cruel', recurring again and again, which represents the child's limited powers of explaining the emotional catastrophe he has passed through.

[46] Kristian Smidt, *James Joyce and the Cultic Use of Fiction* (Oslo 1955), 4.

The same double nature of the style is evident in the somewhat mawkish ecstasy when Stephen recognizes his vocation:

> Where was his boyhood now? Where was the soul that had hung back from her destiny, to brood alone upon the shame of her wounds and in her house of squalor and subterfuge to queen it in faded cerements and in wreaths that withered at the touch? Or where was he?
>
> He was alone. He was unheeded, happy and near to the wild heart of life. He was alone and young and wilful and wildhearted, alone amid a waste of wild air and brackish waters and the seaharvest of shells and tangle and veiled grey sunlight and gayclad lightclad figures of children and girls and voices childish and girlish in the air. (*P* 175)

This is sentimental stuff:[47] but Joyce could expect that such a passage would be read in the context of the whole novel, where, from the first page, he had developed a stylistic method fusing the attitude of Stephen and his author. As a young man, Joyce had often written in a highfaluting way, but this passage is deliberately excessive: it creates an exact image of the boy's self-admiring fervours, and, at the same time, implies the artist's assessment of the true nature and quality of the experience. This ironic flavour in the style is repeatedly reinforced by abrupt, deflating breaches of the intense, romantic introversion:

> An ecstasy of flight made radiant his eyes and wild his breath and tremulous and wild and radiant his windswept limbs.
> — One! Two! . . . Look out!
> — O, cripes, I'm drownded! (*P* 173)

By neither method is Stephen's mood rendered ridiculous or contemptible; there is nothing dismissive about the irony, any more than there is about the ironic presentation of Maria in 'Clay'. Joyce is trying to apprehend a boy's sense of revelation, to recreate it verbally, and to identify it for what it is – not to mock or scorn it.

The same is true of other passages where the style expresses an elevated mood, suddenly deflated. The agonies of frustration when Stephen misses Emma after the play are swept away by the odour of 'horse piss and rotted straw'; 'ellipsoidal ball' temporarily brings down his poetic flights, partly by the change in diction and partly by the bawdy connotation of the phrase; but a more complete transformation of style expresses the relief he feels at descending from his intellectual heights to squalid reality:

> His thinking was a dusk of doubt and selfmistrust lit up at moments by the lightnings of intuition, but lightnings of so clear a splendour that in those moments the world perished about his feet as if it had been fireconsumed: and thereafter his tongue grew heavy and he met the eyes of others with unanswering eyes for he felt that the spirit of beauty had folded him round like a mantle and that in revery at least he had been acquainted with nobility. But,

---

[47] At least, it seems to me unquestionably so. But Marvin Magalaner refers to it as 'prose of rhythmic and euphonic loveliness, as rare and fragile as the incident it describes' (*Magalaner and Kain*, 120).

when this brief pride of silence upheld him no longer, he was glad to find himself still in the midst of common lives, passing on his way amid the squalor and noise and sloth of the city fearlessly and with a light heart.

Near the hoardings on the canal he met the consumptive man with the doll's face and the brimless hat coming towards him down the slope of the bridge with little steps, tightly buttoned into his chocolate overcoat, and holding his furled umbrella a span or two from him like a diviningrod. (*P* 180)

This is a fine perception of the young man's change of mood, and a fine verbalization of it, with, on the one hand, the descent from the self-inflating reverie to the hard facts of the Dublin scene, and, on the other, a kind of reassurance in the descent so that, despite the squalor, one senses his relief at finding himself alive amid ordinary life again. This suppleness of style articulating paradoxical states and contradictory moods, and combining the scene observed with the mood of the observing consciousness, and with an evaluation of that mood, is everywhere evident in the *Portrait*. The author's personality and commentary are apparently eliminated, but, in fact, pervasive – as Stephen's aesthetic theory requires.

Yet the general stylistic method is at times so violently modified that it may seem to have been abandoned – most remarkably in the long extracts from Father Arnall's sermons at the very heart of the book. Few readers would dispute the energy of the execution, and the general point of giving the sermons for the most part *verbatim* is clear enough: instead of informing us about them and of their effect on Stephen, Joyce makes us experience them – experience both the lip-smacking relish with which the priest, confident of his own salvation, triumphs over the damned, and the shattering impact of such presentations of eternal torment on an imaginative mind already troubled with feelings of guilt. One can appreciate how Joyce has created a powerful pulpit rhetoric in a tradition of addresses designed to terrify the sinner (he seems in particular to have used a work casually referred to in *Ulysses*, Father Pinamonti's *Hell Opened to Christians*[48]), but still object that there is too much of these sermons. Including the brief interludes, they take up nearly two-thirds of the middle chapter of the book, and, what is perhaps more important, for most of the time we do not clearly experience them through the mind of Stephen: we learn at the end of each sermon of its effect on the boy. The one exception to this occurs at the beginning of the first address just after Father Arnall's friendly introductory remarks, which are given in direct speech. But Stephen's mind is befogged, his soul 'fattening and congealing into a gross grease', though a glimmer of fear has begun to penetrate. The preacher gets under way with the sermon on death and judgment, and here at the beginning we are shown only the effect on Stephen's imagination. This shifts to an exact account of the

[48] See James A. Thrane, 'Joyce's Sermon on Hell: its Source and its Background' (*Modern Philology* LVII (1960), 172–198; reprinted in *JJM III*), and Elizabeth F. Boyd, 'James Joyce's Hell-Fire Sermons' (*Modern Language Notes* LXXV (1960), 561–71; reprinted in *Portraits of an Artist: A Casebook on James Joyce's 'A Portrait of the Artist as a Young Man'*, ed. William E. Morris and Clifford A. Nault, Jr. (New York, Odyssey Press, 1962), 253–63).

sermon in indirect speech, until, at the words 'Time is, time was but time shall be no more' (*P* 117), with no sign other than the change from the past tense of reported speech to the present of direct speech, we are given the preacher's actual words, and this continues until the end of the retreat. The development here from the boy's feelings about what he hears, to the account of what he is hearing, and finally to the reproduction of what he is hearing, brings the sermons more vividly before the reader, but raises the question whether the book has not lost its focus. Should it not be creating the image of the boy's experience in the chapel, rather than creating the image of the sermons themselves, and at such length?

What are the effects of Joyce's method? First, the withdrawal from Stephen's mind during the sermons suggests a state of mental paralysis. It is as though the shock and terror are so great that his mind is emptied. It is precisely a death of his self which is described shortly before the shift to the present tense:

> He felt the deathchill touch the extremities and creep onward towards the heart, the film of death veiling the eyes, the bright centres of the brain extinguished one by one like lamps, the last sweat oozing upon the skin, the powerlessness of the dying limbs, the speech thickening and wandering and failing, the heart throbbing faintly and more faintly, all but vanquished, the breath, the poor breath, the poor helpless human spirit, sobbing and sighing, gurgling and rattling in the throat. (*P* 115)

Stephen imagines himself dead, buried, consigned to the worms and rats. What more could be said about what he experiences? 'The bright centres of the brain' have been put out; the words of the preacher have driven all else from his mind; their action is a purging of his whole nature. Similarly the terrible sermon on the physical torments of hell leaves the boy fearing 'that he had already died', and, even when he is on his way to confession, he feels convinced that his is the only lost soul, which 'flickered once and went out' in 'black cold void waste'. The bare presentation of the words of the sermon replaces the representation of his experience because for the length of the sermons they are in effect the whole of his experience: it is as though his life is suspended by them. The feeling that his soul has been extinguished on the way to confession is a similar hiatus in his life: 'Consciousness of place came ebbing back to him slowly over a vast tract of time unlit, unfelt, unlived.' This is exactly the effect of the technique of abandoning the presentation of Stephen's thoughts and feelings during the sermon. It presents the spiritual death which is the necessary preliminary to rebirth. The break with his former self is not like the other new worlds he has found. Although, in one sense, he eventually overcomes his terror, in another it scars him more deeply than anything else that happens. It determines the nature of his artistic development: it is behind his response to the call of art as a vocation to a priesthood; it influences the images of poetic inspiration as the visit of Gabriel, and of his poem as a *'eucharistic hymn'*; and, in his aesthetic theories, it contributes to his notion of the ultimate aesthetic experience, as something akin to the detachment of a mystic, a 'luminous silent stasis'. Similarly it affects his ability to have relationships with others – his family, his friends, women. It makes him, even when an unbeliever, a religious figure in a society of worldlings. After the sermons, Stephen has no time for compromise. In the last conversation with Cranly he speaks of having tried to unite his will with God's, instant by instant: 'In that I did not always fail. I could perhaps do that still.' But the lukewarm and prudent adjustments Cranly urges are impossible for him. As he says in *Ulysses*, 'With me all or not at all' (*U* 549/682); the resoluteness of his decision not to serve is the complement of his attempt to serve utterly, and is expressed by the *Non serviam* of Lucifer quoted by Father Arnall.

To understand the artist we must see him not only in his society and environment: we need to see the cosmos he inhabits. The daily religious life, the religious education are merely parts of the first two: the vision of the universe and eternity which he must defy cannot be expressed in terms of daily life. The sermons present, not in extended but in concentrated form, the universal vision which underlies the superficialities of existence – a vision where the things of the earth are as nothing in an infinity and an eternity. Stephen's crucial denial is not merely a rejection of his world: MacCann, Lynch, Cranly, Temple, all reject it in one way or another. His rebellion is against the universe in which he has grown up, and which has shaped his mind and dominated his imagination. The eagles threatened by Dante, the severity of Father Dolan's punishments and the terrible consciousness of sin, like the joyful discovery of his destiny, the ecstatic sense of inspiration and the spiritualized devotion to Emma, are all related to the universal vision which shapes and inhibits Stephen's development, and to which he finally refuses to pay homage. This vision is given its fullest presentation in the sermons of the retreat: far from being overextended or digressive, they create with extraordinary intensity, coherence and economy an image of something permanent and central in the artist's nature and environment.

The other stylistic variations are easier to accept. The dependence on dramatic dialogue for the justly famous scene at the Christmas dinner table hardly needs justification: Stephen is a bewildered onlooker in a scene of violent political and religious passion and, apart from occasional passages expressing his bewilderment, there would be little point in tracing what is going on in his head. It is the total image of the scene which fills him with terror: he asks himself, 'Who was right then ?', but has no means of knowing. What shocks him is the destruction by violent passions of the adult world, the family circle, and the happy occasion to which he had looked forward. It is an entire experience, a dramatic scene which plunges directly into his imagination without passing through the understanding.

The appropriateness of the peripatetic and scholastic exposition of the aesthetic theories is also obvious enough, as is the appropriateness of the diary form at the end of the novel when Stephen has broken free from his ties. There is now for him no-one worth talking to, save himself, and although he notes a few conversations they serve merely as occasions for self-communing. The disjointedness, incoherence, and occasional obscurity of the entries must also be deliberate, and befit a mind which has renounced the old order without having yet found or created a new one, while the improved consecutiveness of the last few entries suggests the dim emergence of a sense of purpose. But, although the diary with its mixture of symbolic vanities, mysterious dreams, commonplace meetings and ecstatic outbursts seems formally justified, and certainly not, as some have felt, a disastrous anticlimax, I would not rate the execution of the idea very high by Joyce's own standards. There has been no previous mention of a diary,[49] and while one can perceive that Stephen might record a dream or a meeting or an emotion of deep significance, there seems little reason for him, in his isolation, to record the meeting of his father and Davin, or to triumph again over the dean of studies for his ignorance of the word 'tundish'.

The problem Joyce set himself was a difficult one to solve. The emergence of the artist from the shell of his boyhood and adolescence can be marked by the shift from the earlier styles, where the vision and language of the mature artist control our apprehension of Stephen's mind, to Stephen's own style in the self-communings of his journal; but we should feel this as an emergence, not as a sudden change; somehow the manner of the journal has to be convincingly the manner we have earlier associated with Stephen, and yet go beyond it. Stephen's way of writing must mark a step towards maturity, and yet remain convincingly immature; it must express the young man's romantic ambitions while, at the same time, suggesting his self-critical view of his own past-and-present romanticizing. In all these respects, the closing pages of the *Portrait* are fully adequate. Their failing, if there is a failing, is that the illumination is sporadic, that Stephen's *claritas*, at this stage of his life, shines out less vividly and wholly than in the earlier periods. It is in comparison with what has been achieved up to this point that the final image of Stephen seems relatively blurred, and this may be an inevitable consequence of the passing from the mature artist's retrospective vision to the potential artist's groping towards his destiny. However, if it is a flaw in the novel, it is so only by the standards Joyce set himself.

Throughout, the book is heavily charged with imagery, symbol and allusion. The allusions are often literary echoes, though these occur, for obvious reasons, most frequently and strikingly in the last chapter. In the earlier part of the book they tend to be simple and explicit, like the 'sadly proud gesture of refusal' of Monte Cristo refusing the muscatel grapes, or like the fragment of Shelley which expresses the boy's sense of 'sad human ineffectualness'. Later the allusions are more fully integrated in the style. Thus there is no mistaking the Swinburnian flavour of Stephen's mood when writing the villanelle:

A glow of desire kindled again his soul and fired and fulfilled all his body. Conscious of his desire she was waking from odorous sleep, the temptress of

[49] According to Stanislaus Joyce, 'Jim never kept a diary at any time in his life' (*MBK*, 135).

his villanelle. Her eyes, dark and with a look of languor, were opening to his eyes. Her nakedness yielded to him, radiant, warm, odorous and lavish-limbed, enfolded him like a shining cloud, enfolded him like water with a liquid life: and like a cloud of vapour or like waters circumfluent in space the liquid letters of speech, symbols of the element of mystery, flowed forth over his brain. (*P* 227)

After such an addiction to the letter 'l', one expects the poem to begin 'O lips full of lust and of laughter', though, in fact, it seems more indebted to Swinburne's imitators than to the poet himself. Joyce is no more concerned to mock Swinburne than he is, in the 'Nausicaa' episode of *Ulysses*, to mock the style of cheap novelettes. What he is looking for is a verbal image of Stephen's mood: a young poet does not operate in a literary vacuum: his inspirations are deeply affected by the literature he admires, not merely through the desire to imitate but because this literature suggests to him what a poetic mood, for instance, is. A different literary association can set his mind working along an entirely different channel, as when the thought (once again) of Emma's eyes is tied to a misremembered line of Nash's:

Eyes, opening from the darkness of desire, eyes that dimmed the breaking east. What was their languid grace but the softness of chambering? And what was their shimmer but the shimmer of the scum that mantled the cesspool of the court of a slobbering Stuart. And he tasted in the language of memory ambered wines, dying fallings of sweet airs, the proud pavan: and saw with the eyes of memory kind gentlewomen in Covent Garden wooing from their balconies with sucking mouths and the poxfouled wenches of the taverns and young wives that, gaily yielding to their ravishers, clipped and clipped again. (*P* 237)

Stephen is not pleased with this imagery and thinks of it as 'old phrases, sweet only with a disinterred sweetness', but, although there are several expressions that carry the mind fairly directly to specific plays, Joyce is not here using allusion in that way. The romanticized evocation of Jacobean atmosphere and spirit challenges his spiritualized emotions and, in effect, in this particular episode shatters them. Such adopted literary styles, approximating to pastiche, suggest Stephen's current literary allegiances, and his habit of translating his own moods and predicaments into literary terms, and the exaggerations of the adopted manner are evaluative: we know both the character and the worth of Stephen's passion for Emma by the luscious fin-di-siècle style in which it is presented.

The recurrent images and symbols contribute importantly to the *claritas*, but by intensifying and focusing, not by supplying hints of some esoteric significance. What is factual and objective in one place may be figurative in another, and symbolic in a third, though frequently the borders between object, image and symbol are not precisely drawn. For instance, at the beginning of the second chapter, Stephen is revolted by 'the filthy cowyard at Stradbrook with its foul green puddles and clots of liquid dung and steaming brantroughs' (*P* 65). The cows and the filth are real, and the boy's revulsion needs no other explanation than a townchild's natural disgust. Yet what immediately follows shows that for the author, though not consciously for the child, this passing revulsion at the cows which 'had seemed so beautiful in the country on sunny days' is an image of the 'many slight shocks to his boyish conception of the world.' Later, inflamed by the hell-sermon, he has a vision of the hell reserved for him, peopled by goatish creatures moving in a field of excrement with stinking fumes curling up out of canisters, and, although these 'hornybrowed' creatures with 'long swishing tails besmeared with stale shite' are specifically goatish, it is obvious that memories of the cowyard have fused with childish images of hell to produce the vision. The vision itself is symbolic of the boy's guilty sense of the filthiness of his own mind – is, in fact, a self-revelation, an epiphany.[50] But it does not follow that the original passage describing the cowyard was symbolic, or that any general assertion can be made about the symbolic content of cows in the *Portrait*, or that one can then mount symbolic significance on the back of any casual cow or bovine reference that occurs in the novel – the cow in the fairy-story, the milkman's cart, the cowhouse in which the preacher says Jesus was born, Daedalus who made a wooden cow for the convenience of Pasiphae, the cow made by a man '*hacking in fury at a block of wood*' which briefly figures in Stephen's explanations, or the nurse like a heifer whom Stephen and Lynch follow. The whole effectiveness of imagery and symbols is that they can be drawn out of a situation or seen in it by the writer's skill and insight: as soon as a cow ceases to mean a particular animal, it is useless as image or symbol. The cow in the story is an imaginary cow which for that reason does not frighten 'baby tuckoo' when he meets it in the road; the cows in the cow-yard are real stinking cows, acceptable only when seen in a summer field; as the reality of their dung shatters Stephen's pastoral illusions and revolts him, they may be seen functioning as a subdued image of shattered illusions, and colouring the image of vile brutality beneath the goatish exterior of the fiends. But in each case the context creates and controls the function, and it is undiscriminating to suppose that every reference to a cow must be interpreted in the same way.

The most manifest symbol in the whole book is that of Daedalus, but even Stephen's name does not function in a constantly symbolic fashion. At first it is just 'a queer name' like Athy; then a name to be defended against the mockery of Father Dolan; then an assertion of identity ('I am Stephen Dedalus'); then a peg for dreams, 'The Reverend Stephen Dedalus, S.J.', or a nickname 'The Dedalus'; until it becomes 'a prophecy', 'a symbol of the artist' and his flights, and ultimately leads to the uncon-scious irony of Stephen's identification of himself with Icarus in the last sentence of the book, an irony which becomes explicit in *Ulysses*. This is how symbols develop in Joyce's work from materials which have carried no symbolic weight. Birds offer a ready symbol for the flights of the artist, and they acquire special symbolic significances for Stephen as he thinks of the hawklike flight of Daedalus and sees the paddling girl as 'a strange and

[50] The 'epiphany' in its original form is in *Workshop*, 16.

beautiful seabird'; later, while he watches the swallows, to the original symbolic meaning are added those of loneliness and departure. But it is mechanical criticism to link these images with every bird or suggestion of a bird mentioned – the eye-pulling eagles, the football 'like a heavy bird', the birdlike name and face of Heron. The eagles are symbolic agents of divine punishment but in a completely different frame of reference; the 'heavy bird' is a simple visual image; and the bird-face is both a visual and psychological image for Heron's appearance and manner, as the 'hooded reptile' is for Lynch's. Swallows, hawks, seabirds, eagles and herons are all birds, but connotatively and symbolically they have very little in common.[51]

Too much criticism, not only of Joyce, seems to work on the assumption that it does an author credit to show that whenever he uses a given word or image it is always within a consistent symbolic or archetypal scheme, and critics have worked out the most tortuous explanations in order to foist such schemes on various works of art. Fortunately the art of the writer is a much more subtle business, able to use words 'symbolizing' physical objects with or without figurative significance, and able to charge them with a wide range of such significances as and when these are relevant to his purposes. What Joyce is creating is not a symbolic design but a *Portrait* – an 'esthetic image' in a verbal medium – and the *quidditas* of the image is not contained in a symbol or a group of symbols but in the total verbal construct. Yet since words are both sensible and intelligible, the image they form is apprehended by the imagination and comprehended by the intellect, and recognized as a creation of the human imagination and intellect out of 'the daily bread of experience'. Experience has been transmuted into 'the radiant body of everliving life'. The artist-priest has apprehended and understood in life more than the layman and has embodied this in words so that the reader can partially enter this vision of truth and beauty, and experience 'the luminous silent stasis of esthetic pleasure'.

Words, then, in all their uses and all their interrelationships, create the *claritas* of the *Portrait*, the *claritas* of an image of the young Stephen Dedalus as he was and as in the mind of the mature artist he is seen to have been: 'So in the future, the sister of the past, I may see myself as I sit here now but by reflection from that which then I shall be' (*U* 183/249). The mature artist could not exclude (nor had any desire to exclude) his understanding of the young man's occasional foolishness, fanaticism, and mistakes, and his knowledge that it was as Icarus, not Daedalus, that Stephen flew from Dublin, yet, on the other hand, he did not pretend that this young man was an object of scorn, a deluded aesthete. As Stephen says in *Ulysses*, 'A man of genius makes no mistakes. His errors are volitional and are the portals of discovery' (*U* 179/243). Indeed the whole concept of his vocation as it is first revealed to him is of a call, 'To live, to err, to fall, to triumph, to recreate life out of life!' (*P* 176), and in the last conversation with Cranly he again recognizes that the willingness to make a mistake is

---

[51] Joyce's distrust of systematic symbolism is suggested by his attitude towards psychoanalysis: 'Joyce brushed it aside as absurd, saying its symbolism was mechanical, a house being a womb, a fire a phallus' (*Ellman-JJ*, 393).

of the very essence of his destiny: 'I am not afraid to make a mistake, even a great mistake, a lifelong mistake and perhaps as long as eternity too' (*P* 251).

Joyce was not a man to write off his past or even to create from it an image for contemptuous rejection. He believed rather in the interplay of opposites: Stephen was not foolish to have carried so far his own deracination, though that was only a process in the formation of the artist. The deracinated and isolated spirit, nursing his egoism, was a necessary element in the complete artist. Bloom did not replace Stephen but complemented him as the other pole of experience; Shem and Shaun are similarly complementary opposites in *Finnegans Wake*.

The *Portrait of the Artist as a Young Man* is an image of a young man's recognition of his destiny, a destiny determined by those 'constant traits' of the embryo which preserve themselves through all the apparent changes of nature and purpose until they are recognized as the marks of an artist. They demand not merely a renunciation of the environment in which they have survived, for renunciation suggests a sacrifice of what is still valued, but a detachment from it. If to a maturer eye that chosen detachment should seem to be merely a stage in a process, nevertheless it was an essential stage, a 'mistake' which made possible new discovery. Despite the critics who have treated the *Portrait* as a mocking exposure of an aesthete, there is something heroic in Stephen's egoistic struggle to fly past the nets which are cast around him and there is also something comical in his self-dramatizing and posturing. There is irony but it is not destructive irony: it is the irony which belongs to the double view. We see, apparently, only through Stephen's eyes, yet what we see, including Stephen, is part of a mature artist's vision, not concerned with passing simple moral or aesthetic judgment on Stephen but with presenting his experience as he experienced it and at the same time, through control of all the devices of language, placing that experience as belonging to the artist in his formative years. It was failure to respond to the subtleties of style, in the widest sense of the word, which led some early critics to attack Stephen's priggishness, as though the author were unaware of it, and, having taken such pains with the style to make his image clear, Joyce was entitled to feel a little impatient with those who, he told Budgen, 'forget that it is called *A Portrait of the Artist as a Young Man*.'[52]

[52] *Budgen*, 61. S. L. Goldberg's comment on the presentation of Stephen is typically judicious: 'Irony and sympathetic understanding, or even love, are not necessarily incompatible, nor is there any reason why Stephen's potentialities as an artist should be dismissed because he is very immature and clearly portrayed as such' (*Goldberg*, 110).

Chapter 3 *Ulysses:* the form and subordinate structures

What happens

The virulent opposition to *Ulysses*, most memorably represented by the reviewer in *The Sporting Times* who called it 'literature of the latrine' and 'enough to make a Hottentot sick',[1] is now of only historical interest, but radical objections to the book have been made by responsible critics who, refusing to regard it either as a literary freak or as Holy Writ, apply, with appropriate modifications, the same kind of criteria as are appropriate to *Middlemarch, Madame Bovary,* or *War and Peace.* They argue that the book lacks a significant central action; that the patterns and schemes imposed upon it are an arbitrary substitute for organic form; that it exemplifies aesthetic notions which are ninetyish and precious, and lead to obsessive concern with pointless and distracting refinements of technique and style; that the view of life embodied in it – its moral vision – is inadequate or even repulsive, and above all is not 'life-enhancing'.

These are fundamental objections attacking the form of the book, its internal organization, its manner of presentation, and the values implicit in it. They are necessarily interrelated; to complain of a novel's organizing principle or of its techniques is indirectly to complain of its moral position – not necessarily of the moral views of the author, but of the moral vision actually presented by the book. But although form, structure, style and content are not separate constituents of a novel, they are convenient labels for different ways of looking at it, ways which focus attention on certain aspects of the book – what happens in it, its methods of organization, its stylistic features, and the nature and quality of the author's vision of life.

The criticism of the form of *Ulysses* is summed up in Dr Leavis's assertion that it has no 'organic principle'. Such an objection does not ignore the presence of patterns and Odyssean parallels, but finds that these have been imposed mechanically, and indicate the absence of a vital internal pressure to shape sense and give imaginative direction and purpose.[2] The force of the objection is strengthened by the disagreement about the direction in which the book moves and the nature of that movement. Each critic has

---

[1] 'Aramis', 'The Scandal of *Ulysses*', *Sporting Times* XXXIV (1922), 4, reprinted in *CH* I, 192–4.
[2] *The Great Tradition* (London, Chatto and Windus 1948), 25–6.

his own scheme; the book is so intricately made that it is not difficult to distinguish one of the connecting structures and persuade oneself that it carries the central weight. However, one certain and central characteristic of the structure was referred to by Joyce, in a letter written in 1915, when he said that he was 'engaged on a novel which is a continuation of *A Portrait of the Artist* and also of *Dubliners*'.[3] To consider in what ways *Ulysses* continues the earlier works would seem a practical step towards discovering the direction in which it proceeds beyond them.

Dubliners and the *Portrait* are consciously contrasted. One presents the paralysed and paralysing city, the other the movement of the artist away from the city, spiritually and, at last, geographically. Very deliberately, *Ulysses* takes up these two great subjects of the earlier works, the City and the Artist, and places them in thematic and chronological parallel. The book starts twice – once at 8 am in the Martello tower with Stephen, and again, at 8 am, in Leopold Bloom's kitchen. The second chapter shows Stephen at 10 am and the fifth shows Bloom at the same time. In chapter 3 we are with Stephen on the beach just after 11 am and, in chapter 4, at the same time, we accompany Bloom to the cemetery. This curious double opening demands attention as a structural oddity for which there must be a reason, and consideration of its function should have relevance to the book's central action and perhaps to its organic principle.

The first three chapters or episodes take up the themes and recall the chief characters of the *Portrait* – Cranly and Temple are mentioned, and Stephen Dedalus and his mother, father and family are more vividly re-called. The diary entry which closes the *Portrait* is dated 27 April (pre-sumably 1902): *Ulysses* opens, like a sequel, on 16 June 1904. In the interval, Stephen has escaped from Dublin to Paris, having flown above the nets intended to trap him, but, now that he is back in Dublin, the closing triumph of the *Portrait* is seen to have been illusory. At the end of the *Portrait* he had declared that he would no longer serve home, father-land or Church, but the first of these, the home, has, through a telegram, dragged him back to Dublin, and involved him so deeply that he now sees himself as 'a server of a servant', and later as 'the servant of two masters', – 'the imperial British state . . . and the holy Roman catholic and apostolic church.' The church has struck back at him through his mother, for his refusal of her request that he should pray at her bedside has produced in him a recurring torment of conscience – associated in his mind with a vision of his mother in her grave-clothes, with the image of drowning (as his mother had seemed to be drowning in the green bile she had vomited) and, in a characteristically bookish way, with the title of the medieval *Agenbite of Inwit*. The closing conversation of the *Portrait*, in which Cranly reproached Stephen for his refusal to obey his mother's wish that he should make his Easter duty ('Whatever else is unsure in this stinking dunghill of a world a mother's love is not'—*P* 246), seems to lead into the first conversation in *Ulysses* where Buck Mulligan reproaches him in similar terms:

[3] *Letters* I, 83.

—You could have knelt down, damn it, Kinch, when your dying mother
asked you . . . I'm hyperborean as much as you. But to think of your mother
begging you with her last breath to kneel down and pray for her. And you
refused. There is something sinister in you. . .   (*U* 3/4)

Later, Stephen asks himself whether a mother's love was not 'the only
true thing in life' (*U* 196/266). The forces he thought he had escaped have
renewed their attack: his mother's deathbed request had behind it all the
pressures of family, Church, and social approval, and although Stephen
has refused to conform, he is, in consequence of his refusal, guiltridden,
beset by remorse, and spiritually defeated. His confidence in his artistic
vocation has also gone, and when, later, he recalls his flattering dream in
the Daedalus imagery of the *Portrait*, it is in a very different sense:
'Fabulous artificer, the hawklike man. You flew. Whereto? Newhaven–
Dieppe, steerage passenger, Paris and back. Lapwing. Icarus' (*U* 199/270).
He has cut free from all ties, has chosen isolation, yet sees no profit in it.

The first three chapters variously present this isolation – in his alienation
from family and friends, his occupation of a Martello Tower outside the
city limits (symbolizing a makeshift withdrawal to an Ivory Tower), and
the self-identification with Hamlet; it is emphasized by the recurring
adverbs describing his cold, dry, listless manner. Instead of seeing on the
beach the girl who revealed to him his vocation, he recognizes his own
image in the bloated corpse of a drowned dog. To add to his discomfiture,
Buck Mulligan who is prepared to pay lip-service to the idols of the city,
but jibes at them all – parodies the mass, thinks a mother's death merely
'beastly', laughs at Irish nationalism and art –, succeeds where Stephen has
failed. Haines, the Englishman, represents the empire which has usurped
material and political power in Ireland, and the medical student, Mulligan,
the mocker who cares for nothing, has usurped the artist's position in
society. His irresponsible wit and continual blasphemies were meant, Joyce
told Frank Budgen, 'to pall on the reader as the day goes on.'[4] He is the
usurper referred to in the last word of the first chapter, claiming even the
artist's Ivory Tower and accepted by society because he plays the role of
'a jester at the court of his master, indulged and disesteemed, winning a
clement master's praise' (*U* 22/29). (In an article written in 1909, Joyce
had said of Oscar Wilde, 'In the tradition of the Irish writers of comedy
that runs from the days of Sheridan and Goldsmith to Bernard Shaw,
Wilde became, like them, court jester to the English.'[5]) This frivolous
figure has taken the rightful place of the artist who had determined to forge
the conscience of his race, and who now feels not free but disinherited, or,
like Telemachus, in need of a father's help against the usurping powers.
The picture of the romantic artist, rebellious, outcast, haunted, feeding on
resentment, bitterness and remorse, is a familiar one, but the ironies,
implicit in the *Portrait*, are now patent even to Stephen himself. He is a

---

[4] *Budgen*, 118.
[5] 'Oscar Wilde: The Poet of *Salomé*', *Il Piccolo della Sera* (Trieste, 24 March 1909);
translated in *CW*, 202.

romantic poet-hero playing the part with little conviction, having out-grown his belief in it – an artist without purpose, of little achievement, sick of the isolation so painfully won, denied by his contemporaries, and contemptuous of his own dream of being the enigmatic soul addressing itself to posterity.

Now Joyce starts again, with the City, and this time recalling persons and themes from *Dubliners*. The central figure, Leopold Bloom, was origin-ally conceived as the hero of a story to be included in *Dubliners*, and his origin is reflected in the way he links the novel with the short-stories. In the next three chapters, we meet or hear of some twenty characters from the short stories; the city's faded substitutes for art, politics and religion, and its citizens' frustrations, petty preoccupations, social insincerities, oriental fantasies and dreams of escape are all recalled. Even the image of Dublin as a city of the dead is revived as the men attend the event of the day, a funeral: 'The Irishman's house is his coffin' (*U* 102/139).

The two beginnings of the novel, paralleled in time chapter by chapter, set in motion the two opposed forces, and also establish between them a relationship, partly of similarity, partly of contrast. There are temporal and spatial links like the slow cloud covering the sun and saddening alike the thoughts of Stephen and Bloom; there are aesthetic and symbolic links like the contrast between Stephen's disgust at the thought of his devouring 'a urinous offal from all dead' and Bloom's hearty enjoyment of such offal; and there are numerous links between the two men's minds, from the casual coincidences that they both think briefly of Turko the Terrible, foot and mouth disease, Palestrina, and Egypt, to the more significant relationships suggested by their thoughts on death, fathers and sons, navel-cords, ghosts, and life as a bloody struggle for survival. But the general emphasis is on contrast and opposition, even in the locations, the first three chapters being set outside the city limits and the second three inside them, so as to pre-clude contact between the two men. Thus, at the beginning of *Ulysses*, the *Portrait* and *Dubliners* are contained as separate strands, related mainly in contrast.

Yet both synchronized beginnings recall the earlier works with vital differences. The triumphant young artist of the *Portrait* is now defeated and dejected, while the dead city is inhabited by a citizen who, whatever his limitations, seems by no means paralysed, morally or in any other way. Bloom has his frustrations and humiliations but he is temperamentally resilient. He shrugs off dark thoughts and depressing emotions; he is keenly alive to and naively interested in everything about him – the correct pro-nunciation of a phrase in *Don Giovanni*, the functions of a cat's whiskers, communications between graveyard rats, the love-life of a cemetery care-taker – and is constantly developing new schemes – for a prize short story, for irresistible advertisements, for municipal funeral-trams. As Lenehan says, later in the day,

—He's a cultured allroundman, Bloom is . . . . There's a touch of the artist about old Bloom. (*U* 222/301–2)

So the roles of artist and citizen have been almost reversed – the artist paralysed and disheartened, the citizen, in his limited way, lively and creative. The artist is haunted by images of death and drowning: the citizen, despite all his moments of dejection and humiliation, rejoices in life:

> There is another world after death named hell. I do not like that other world she wrote. No more do I. Plenty to see and hear and feel yet. Feel live warm beings near you. Let them sleep in their maggoty beds. They are not going to get me this innings. Warm beds; warm fullblooded life. (*U* 107/146)

The oddity of construction so obvious in the opening six chapters of *Ulysses* points unequivocally to the setting in motion of two opposed themes, or thematic centres, and the principle on which the whole book is organized is the slow moving into relationship of citizen and artist, as the central narrative action is their physical convergence. There are a number of significant near-misses. In the very next chapter ('Aeolus'), Bloom leaves the newspaper office just before Stephen enters and returns just after Stephen's departure. The implication is, perhaps, that the world of journalism and rhetoric is one where artist and citizen might be expected to meet and find common ground – but not the world of Dublin journalism and rhetoric in 1904. Here the editor is interested in the artist only if he can give the public 'something with a bite in it', and for the citizen, Mr Bloom, the journalists and their hangers-on have little time or respect. There is no real possibility of fruitful contact between artist and citizen in the windy confusion of the newspaper office.

The eighth and ninth chapters ('Lestrygonians' and 'Scylla and Charybdis') return to the parallels of the earlier books: they present the city feeding. First it is seen devouring its physical food in a way that quite puts Bloom off the lunch he has been contemplating. He leaves the Burton Restaurant hastily, thinking, 'Every fellow for his own, tooth and nail. Gulp. Grub. Gulp. Gobstuff. . . . Eat or be eaten. Kill! Kill!' The vision of Dublin, red in tooth and claw, depresses him and makes him more sympathetic to vegetarianism than he had been when, seeing A.E. accompanied by a woman with stockings over her ankles, he had attributed their slovenliness and 'etherial' poetry, in part at least, to their diet. If Dublin seeking its physical sustenance expresses its brutal nature in a manner repellent to Bloom, its spiritualized representatives are no more pleasing to him than to Stephen, who meets them in the next episode.

Here, in the library, Dublin takes its mental pabulum, urbanely and genteelly. Dublin's cultural and intellectual life, represented by Dr Best for the scholars, 'John Eglinton' for the critics, 'A.E.' for the poets, and Buck Mulligan for the pseudo-artists or court-jesters, elicits from Stephen a feeling comparable to Bloom's about the eaters. The men of letters pay solemn though rather irritable attention to Stephen's Shakespearean speculations, and, even when he admits that he doesn't believe his theory himself, Best continues to think of how it might be written up for publication. The Young Pretender to the throne of this literary world is Buck Mulligan, whose presence is requested at George Moore's party, while Stephen's is not, and who breaks up the conversation with amusing obscenity. This judgement of Dublin intellectual life as anaemic and trivial is, though based on different standards, not unlike Bloom's. Again, like the newspaper office, the National Library and Museum are, theoretically, establishments where there should be contact between citizen and artist, but Bloom and Stephen pass without speaking. While the artist has been weaving the wind in the library office, Bloom more matter-of-factly has been trying to settle a doubt in his mind concerning the anatomies of the statues of Greek goddesses and to check an advertisement. Stephen peddles pseudo-scholarship, beneath which he hides his own problems, while Bloom gets no nearer to art than a shameful curiosity, and a notion that such things of beauty as Greek statues must, like the Nymph above his bed, be free from such mundane functions as excretion. The world of 'culture' like the world of journalism provides no true ground for a meeting of artist and citizen.

The following chapter is centrally placed (in time it lies at 3 pm, exactly half-way between the setting out of the travellers at 8 am and their meeting in the maternity hospital at 10 pm) and makes a pause in the central movement of the two protagonists. It gives nineteen 'shots' of the Dublin streets and the circulating populace in relation to the passage, through the city, of Church (in the person of the Rev. John Conmee) and state (represented by the viceregal carriage). In the confusion of the city Bloom and Stephen once more just miss each other:[6] both thumb through books, Stephen glancing through a volume of magical charms and incantations, Bloom, in search of something suitable for his wife, finally deciding on a volume entitled *Sweets of Sin*. Business matters took Bloom to the newspaper offices, curiosity to the library and museum, sexual titillation (or pandering to his wife's desire for such titillation) to the bookstall: this is as near as he gets to oratory, the visual arts, or literature, while the artist, approaching the city's intellectual centres from the other side, finds nothing to his purpose. The newspaper editor wants from him journalism, the intellectuals are fascinated by pseudo-learning, while the book of charms reminds him of the time he has wasted on Father Joachim's prophecies.

The next three chapters ('Sirens', 'Cyclops' and 'Nausicaa') are all concerned with Bloom, and in some ways present an approximate afternoon reflection of Stephen's morning. As Stephen had been disturbed in the tower by Mulligan, the usurper of his spiritual kingdom, so in the Ormond bar Bloom is disturbed by the presence of Blazes Boylan, the usurper of his bed; as Stephen had listened to the antisemitic jibes of Mr Deasy and to garbled history, so Bloom is submitted to the Citizen's ignorant chauvinism and antisemitism; as Stephen had contemplated on Sandymount beach his romantic isolation, so Bloom on the same beach contemplates his outcast state, and masturbates, the physical emblem of romantic isolation. The

---

[6] I do not know on what evidence Richard M. Kain says that Bloom buys a book 'at a bookshop which Stephen visits a few moments later' (*Kain*, 27), but certainly both men look at books in Bedford Row (*U* 229/311 and *U* 689/859).

parallels are not exact, but there is enough to suggest how the sense of friendless and fruitless isolation and resignation develops in the two men.

With artist and citizen equally outcast, a relationship between them begins to develop, appropriately enough in the house of birth, the maternity hospital. Bloom conceives a quasi-paternal affection for Stephen, attaches himself to him, and in the succeeding chapters in the brothel, the cabmen's shelter and Bloom's house gradually overcomes Stephen's initial coldness and suspicion. The emotional life of each of them reaches a point of crisis in the brothel, where their inner feelings of guilt and shame are expressed in a drama of the soul. For each the crisis culminates in a symbolic defiance of the ghosts which haunt them and a symbolic reaffirmation of the values they still unhopefully cling to.

Bloom, bent submissively to tie the bawd's bootlace, experiences characteristically a deep sexual guilt, presented dramatically by the apparition of the Nymph (the statue whose photograph, cut from *Photo Bits*, hangs above his marital bed). For him the Nymph stands for chastity, purity, and the feminine ideal, and, while she reproaches him for the scenes she has been forced to observe, he confesses his sins and begs for pardon. But, as he stands up, reality and a sense of reality, as usual, come to Bloom's aid. The Nymph in a nun's white habit, supplied from Bloom's memory of a visit to a Carmelite nunnery, speaks softly:

No more desire. (*She reclines her head, sighing.*) Only the ethereal. Where dreamy creamy gull waves o'er the waters dull.
   (*Bloom half rises. His back trousers' button snaps.*)
                        THE BUTTON
Bip!
   (*Two sluts of the Coombe dance rainily by, shawled, yelling flatly.*)
                        THE SLUTS
         O Leopold lost the pin of his drawers
         He didn't know what to do,
         To keep it up,
         To keep it up.
                        BLOOM
   (*Coldly.*) You have broken the spell. The last straw. If there were only ethereal where would you all be, postulants and novices? Shy but willing, like an ass pissing.   (*U* 523/661)

The Nymph, after an unsuccessful attempt to castrate Bloom, departs – '(*With a cry, [she] flees from him unveiled, her plaster cast cracking, a cloud of stench escaping from the cracks*)' – and Bloom sniffs the air and identifies the smell: 'But. Onions. Stale. Sulphur. Grease.' The commonplace interruption of Bloom's mood of self-reproach, or rather the irruption of the commonplace into the subconscious mood, through the agency of a trouserbutton, rescues Bloom. The vision of woman associated with the Nymph, the statue in the museum, the nun, and the untidy aesthetic woman Bloom had seen with A.E. is destroyed by the other vision of woman, associated with the song of the two sluts he had seen one night in the Coombe, with the odorous appeal of the heroine of *Sweets of Sin*, and hence with Molly and with the young prostitute, Zoe, whose body emits similar smells. The physical world demolishes the ethereal; Bloom reasserts the validity of the life he leads, and, refreshed, can confront the bawd, Bella Cohen, before whom he had previously crouched physically and in spirit, with man-of-the-world confidence. When, a little later, the passage of a hackney-car recalls Boylan, Bloom's sense of guilt is dramatized by scenes where he is pander and voyeur, but now he finds a more philosophic attitude – 'Lapses are condoned' (*U* 537/671).

Stephen's act of defiance, equally characteristically, is romantic, extravagant and violent. After his drunken dance, the reproachful image of his dead mother returns to haunt him, and he is overcome, 'choking with fright, remorse and horror'. She calls again on him to pray for her and to repent, and repeats the old threat – 'Beware! God's hand!' At first he merely reiterates the avowals of the *Portrait* – 'The intellectual imagination! With me all or not at all. *Non serviam!*', but when his mother prays for mercy to save his soul from hell, he cries out,

No! No! No! Break my spirit all of you if you can! I'll bring you all to heel!

and, with Siegfried's cry, '*Nothung!*',

(*He lifts his ashplant high with both hands and smashes the chandelier. Time's livid final flame leaps and, in the following darkness, ruin of all space, shattered glass and toppling masonry.*) (*U* 550/683)

So Bloom, rejected citizen, and Stephen, rejected artist, challenged and condemned in a fantasia built of the frustrations and agonies of their lives, reaffirm in their respective and typical ways the validity of what they live by – Bloom, his tolerant and good-natured worldliness, and Stephen, the artist's egocentric and isolated spirit, as yet with no outlet other than a blind refusal to submit. There is still a gulf between the two, but doubtfully, suspiciously, hesitantly, it is bridged. When the soldier knocks Stephen down, it is Bloom who stands over him protectively, while the supposed friend, Lynch, runs away; and Bloom's movement towards Stephen is accomplished in a sentimental vision of his own dead son, Rudy. The father without a son has found a son without a father.

In the episode centring round the cabman's shelter, Stephen, though still reserved and at times short-tempered, besides being exhausted and half drunk, comes slowly towards an acceptance of Bloom, at least so far as to agree to go home with him; and, finally, in the last chapter involving the two men, when they walk together and drink cocoa together, some kind of communication develops between them. In place of the tense verbal fencing in which Stephen has engaged all day, there is a companionable rambling from point to point, a relaxation which even the catechism technique does not obscure:

Of what did the duumvirate deliberate during their itinerary?
Music, literature, Ireland, Dublin, Paris, friendship, woman, prostitution, diet, the influence of gaslight or the light of arc and glowlamps on the growth of adjoining paraheliotropic trees, exposed corporation emergency dust-

buckets, the Roman catholic church, ecclesiastical celibacy, the Irish nation, jesuit education, careers, the study of medicine, the past day, the maleficent influence of the presabbath, Stephen's collapse.   (*U* 627/776)

With no-one else all day has either man indulged in this kind of conversation, pointless because not seeking to make a point, a kind of communion if only a very limited one. They find they have things in common –

Both indurated by early domestic training and an inherited tenacity of heterodox resistance professed their disbelief in many orthodox religious, national, social and ethical doctrines.   (*U* 627/777)—

and they discover points of disagreement –

Stephen dissented openly from Bloom's views on the importance of dietary and civic self help while Bloom dissented tacitly from Stephen's views on the eternal affirmation of the spirit of man in literature.   (*U* 627/777)

Basically they are different temperaments, one 'the scientific' and the other 'the artistic'; yet the two temperaments do not clash but complement each other. Even Stephen's refusal of Bloom's offer of a night's lodging shows his consciousness of kindness and good nature, and displays his own friendly feelings:

Was the proposal of asylum accepted ?
Promptly, inexplicably, with amicability, gratefully it was declined.
(*U* 656/815)

Expressions of amicability and gratitude indicate how far Stephen has moved from the cold, embittered figure of the early chapters – the figure whom Professor MacHugh had compared to Antisthenes: 'It is said of him that none could tell if he were bitterer against others or against himself' (*U* 138/188). Yet there is nothing really inexplicable about Stephen's refusal: the citizen's notion of an artistic career for his protégé combines writing for the newspapers with a tour of seaside resorts as tenor in a concert party. The artist may be grateful for the offer but cannot serve the citizen's conception of art. Nevertheless, before parting, the two men plan future meetings, see themselves as they stand together, in the relaxed intimacy of making water, *sub specie æternitatis*, and shake hands.

Both artist and citizen have been deprived of their rightful places by usurpers, both have been rejected by society, and both refuse to serve the local idols and tenaciously resist 'many orthodox religious, national, social and ethical doctrines.' This basic kinship is seen as a spiritual father–son relationship. The artist finds his spiritual father not among the witty, the learned, the successful, but in the ordinary man of goodwill, who, like the artist, has to rise up from a never-ending series of humiliations and defeats. In recognizing this bond, the artist qualifies the isolation which was necessary to his growth but which is, in itself, fruitless. Equally, for Bloom, the contact renews his confidence in himself: at last he has been able to take charge of a situation, to achieve a rescue, and hence to feel satisfaction in his role as practical man. He can now regard his humiliators with amusement and even pity, can condone the adultery of his wife with Boylan as merely a consequence of physical attraction, and can retire to bed with 'equanimity' and with such composure that he can, much to his wife's surprise, ask for 'his breakfast in bed with a couple of eggs' (*U* 698/871).

I find it hard to understand those who argue that nothing comes of the meeting. Clearly something important has happened to both men. Of course, nothing dramatic and final has happened – life is rarely like that – but on this day the association of artist and citizen has, if only temporarily, relieved the isolation of the artist and the humiliations of the citizen. Certainly there will be other hostilities to face and other difficulties to overcome: there will be other meetings, on other days, with other men, in other cities. *Ulysses* cannot present a final solution to predicaments which are interesting precisely because they are universal and unchanging aspects of human nature and experience: what it does is to demonstrate a need for relationship and to exemplify one brief satisfaction of that need. It would be unrealistic to expect more.

Molly Bloom's soliloquy is the epilogue to the book of the citizen and the artist. In her uncritical acceptance of life they are united, as artist and citizen are united in her person (for she besides being a housewife is, as singer, something of an artist), and brought together in her thoughts. Hearing that her husband has come home with 'Stephen Dedalus, professor and author' (*U* 696/868), her mind fills with dreams of entertaining the young man – erotically, maternally and musically. Thoughts of him help defeat the image of Blazes Boylan, and fulfil the message of the cards which had told her to expect 'a young stranger'. Thus she anticipatorily accepts the artist into her thoughts and emotions, and, although she frowns on her husband's eccentricities, yet her thoughts finally return to him, to his courtship, and to her reiterated *Yes* to him. Significantly it is the thought of buying flowers to welcome Stephen which initiates the train of thought leading to Bloom's triumph in her mind: in her 'sane' and 'fertilisable' nature[7] the relationship of artist and citizen, symbolically enacted in the kitchen, is psychologically re-enacted in bed by the affirmation of the common flesh.

The convergence and relationship of artist and citizen is not the only thematic and structural principle in the book, but it has claims to being the organic one, because it develops through the central action of the novel, whereas the others are, in varying degrees, static or subordinated. Its centrality is confirmed by the book's structure, in particular the double opening in parallel, as well as by its position relative to Joyce's earlier work: *Dubliners* and the *Portrait* meet in *Ulysses* through their representatives, Bloom and Stephen. Yet it might be said that the predicaments of Stephen and Bloom, their meeting, and their mutual aid in passing constitute an action too slight and insubstantial to carry the weight of a novel of such length and complexity. This is an objection which can be answered only if it can shown that the complexities of the work, so far from being a dis-

[7] *Letters* I, 170.

Title	Scene	Hour	Organ	Art	Colour	Symbol	Technic	Correspondences
I TELEMACHIA								
1 Telemachus	The Tower	8 am		Theology	White, gold	Heir	Narrative (Young)	*Stephen:* Telemachus, Hamlet *Buck Mulligan:* Antinous *Milkwoman:* Mentor
2 Nestor	The School	10 am		History	Brown	Horse	Catechism (Personal)	*Deasy:* Mentor *Sargent:* Pisistratus *Mrs O'Shea:* Helen
3 Proteus	The Strand	11 am		Philology	Green	Tide	Monologue (Male)	*Proteus:* Primal Matter *Kevin Egan:* Menelaus *Cocklepicker:* Megapenthus
II ODYSSEY								
4 Calypso	The House	8 am	Kidney	Economics	Orange	Nymph	Narrative (Mature)	*Calypso:* The Nymph *Dlugacz:* The Recall *Zion:* Ithaca
5 Lotuseaters	The Bath	10 am	Genitals	Botany, Chemistry		Eucharist	Narcissism	*Lotuseaters:* The Cabhorses, Communicants, Soldiers, Eunuchs, Bather, Watchers of Cricket
6 Hades	The Graveyard	11 am	Heart	Religion	White, black	Caretaker	Incubism	*Dodder, Grand, and Royal Canals, Liffey:* The 4 Rivers. *Cunningham:* Sisyphus. *Father Coffey:* Cerberus. *Caretaker:* Hades. *Daniel O'Connell:* Hercules. *Dignam:* Elpenor. *Parnell:* Agamemnon. *Menton:* Ajax
7 Aeolus	The Newspaper	12 noon	Lungs	Rhetoric	Red	Editor	Enthymemic	*Crawford:* Aeolus *Incest:* Journalism *Floating Island:* Press
8 Lestrygonians	The Lunch	1 pm	Esophagus	Architecture		Constables	Peristaltic	*Antiphates:* Hunger *The Decoy:* Food *Lestrygonians:* Teeth

	Scene	Hour	Organ	Art	Colour	Symbol	Technic	Correspondences
9 Scylla and Charybdis	The Library	2 pm	Brain	Literature		Stratford, London	Dialectic	*The Rocks:* Aristotle, Dogma, Stratford *The Whirlpool:* Plato, Mysticism, London *Ulysses:* Socrates, Jesus, Shakespeare.
10 Wandering Rocks	The Streets	3 pm	Blood	Mechanics		Citizens	Labyrinth	*Bosphorus:* Liffey. *European Bank:* Viceroy. *Asiatic Bank:* Conmee *Symplegades:* Groups of Citizens
11 Sirens	The Concert Room	4 pm	Ear	Music		Barmaids	Fuga per Canonem	*Sirens:* Barmaids *Isle:* Bar
12 Cyclops	The Tavern	5 pm	Muscle	Politics		Fenian	Gigantism	*Noman:* I. *Stake:* Cigar *Challenge:* Apotheosis
13 Nausicaa	The Rocks	8 pm	Eye, Nose	Painting	Grey, blue	Virgin	Tumescence, detumescence	*Phaeacia:* Star of the Sea *Gerty:* Nausicaa
14 Oxen of the Sun	The Hospital	10 pm	Womb	Medicine	White	Mothers	Embryonic development	*Hospital:* Trinacria. *Nurses:* Lampetie, Phaethusa. *Horne:* Helios *Oxen:* Fertility. *Crime:* Fraud
15 Circe	The Brothel	12 midnight	Locomotor Apparatus	Magic		Whore	Hallucination	*Circe:* Bella
III NOSTOS								
16 Eumaeus	The Shelter	1 am	Nerves	Navigation		Sailors	Narrative (Old)	*Skin the Goat:* Eumaeus *Sailor:* Ulysses Pseudangelos *Corley:* Melanthius
17 Ithaca	The House	2 am	Skeleton	Science		Comets	Catechism (Impersonal)	*Eurymachus:* Boylan *Suitors:* Scruples *Bow:* Reason
18 Penelope	The Bed		Flesh			Earth	Monologue (Female)	*Penelope:* Earth *Web:* Movement

Joyce's columnar scheme for *Ulysses* (see page 122)

proportionate burden, are made to strengthen and sustain the action, and enrich and extend its significance.

The subordinate patternings and relationships of *Ulysses* have importance largely because they elaborate the central movement and structure and thus develop the applications of what might otherwise have seemed a parable for artists. Stephen and Bloom become (like Shem and Shaun in *Finnegans Wake*) representative of two types of human existence, two kinds of human nature and experience, two forms of human aspiration, endeavour and destiny. The schematic patterns, structures and allusions illustrate the universality of the theme of the interaction of opposed human needs – for isolation and for mutual aid – figured in the chance and apparently inconclusive encounter between two men on an ordinary day. Bloom, Molly and Stephen are related to other trinities – Father, Mother and Son; Ulysses, Penelope and Telemachus; King Hamlet, Gertrude and Hamlet (although Stephen's Hamlet role is clearest in the opening chapters and the library scene, he is also the agent by which the usurper of the marital bed is psychologically eliminated); the World, the Flesh, and the Devil who will not serve; scientific reason, feminine intuition and 'the intellectual imagination'; husband, wife and lover (though Stephen functions in this role only in Molly's mind); the life of common intelligence, the life of the body and the life of the spirit.[8] None of these triads is consistently emphasized; many are repeatedly suggested, while others are comparatively local, but their common function is to extend and enrich the central image of relationship.

Some of the patternings are listed in the author's columnar scheme of the work (first published by Stuart Gilbert and printed in fuller form by Hugh Kenner), where they appear under the headings, 'Title', 'Scene', 'Hour', 'Organ', 'Art', 'Colour', 'Symbol', 'Technic', and 'Correspondences'.[9] Since its appearance, the scheme has been often abused as a piece of laboured and mechanical ingenuity, and used as a stick with which to beat the novel. But it is hard to see how the abuse can be justified: a writer's working notes are his own business, and are usually too brief, too incoherent, and too subject to modification in the course of composition, to provide a basis for criticism of the completed work. In them, the writer may employ a kind of shorthand which only he understands, and may

---

[8] Critics have suggested many other trinities. Harry Levin, for instance, says that Molly 'is the compliant body as Stephen is the uncompromising mind, and as Bloom – torn between them – is the lacerated heart' (*Levin*, 92).

[9] The scheme reproduced on pp. 120–21 is that printed in *Gilbert*, 41, together with the 'Correspondences' column omitted by Gilbert and supplied in *Kenner*, 226–7. The same scheme (apart from incidental details and the naming of the three parts of the novel, *Telemachia*, *Odyssey* and *Nostos*) was supplied to Herbert Gorman and published in *JJM II*. An earlier version, sent to the Italian critic, Carlo Linati, is fuller and differs from the later scheme in many respects, but corresponds less closely to the book as it was finished. This scheme is printed in *Ellmann–Ulysses* and in Claude Jacquet's essay, 'Les Plans de Joyce pour *Ulysse*' (*Bonnerot*, 45–82), which also reprints the Gorman and Gilbert schemes. I shall refer to the Linati scheme only when its special features have some direct relevance to the novel as printed.

resort to various devices which have no more rational bearing on the work-ings of his creative imagination than the private obsessive oddities some writers have of being able to write only at a certain desk, with a certain pen, at a certain time of day or night, on a clean sheet of paper, or with a packet of cigarettes at hand. They may include self-imposed rules which the writer uses, as a poet may use the technical difficulties of a complicated stanza form, because he has found that his imagination, in some mysterious way, responds to certain formal restraints and impediments. Or they may include speculative schemes where a novelist, for instance, having conceived some resource for enriching a particular episode, considers whether this might be extended and varied to contribute to the work as a whole. This is parti-cularly likely to appear in the notes of a writer like Joyce, who was tem-peramentally addicted to the elaboration of exhaustive schemes designed to play a part in the total shape of his works.

Several of these functions seem to have been served by Joyce's notes. Certainly the columns are not similar in kind or importance. Two of them ('Scene' and 'Hour') are merely notes of the place and time of each chapter, with the exception that Molly's closing soliloquy, a kind of epilogue to the day, has no prescribed hour. Of the rest, three ('Colour', 'Symbol' and 'Technics') seem to refer centrally to aspects of the handling of the chapters, while the other four ('Title', 'Organ', 'Art' and 'Correspondences') seem to refer to more specifically structural elements. Joyce originally intended to entitle each section of his novel according to its Odyssean parallel, but finally did not do so, presumably because he felt that it would make over-emphatic what was meant to be contributory. The 'Correspondences' are, for the most part, minor and detailed Odyssean identifications of characters, objects and places in the book, together with notes of a few other allusions such as the echo of Hamlet in the situation and mood of Stephen.

Whilst it would be wrong to regard the columnar scheme as a diagram of *Ulysses* (there are many patterns and relations not included in the scheme, and some of the individual notes are difficult to interpret with reference to the book itself), critical terminology and the whole concept of the book's nature have been shaped by these working notes. Therefore, although the scheme has to be handled with caution, since, as Joyce said, it consists of 'catchwords'[10] rather than precise descriptions, and is, at best, a plan of Joyce's hopes and intentions rather than of what he achieved, it requires and deserves close scrutiny, to see what light it can throw on the *con-sonantia* of *Ulysses*.

The Odyssean scheme

The Odyssean parallels do not, as some have suggested, merely create a framework to which a series of otherwise uncoordinated scenes are pegged in order to belittle contemporary life by comparison with heroic times.

[10] *Letters* I, 146.

They are not a substitute for a linking action, theme, or organic structure. If Joyce had been primarily concerned with writing a burlesque epic, he could easily have kept much closer than he did to the Homeric original. The tripartite division into '*Telemachia*', '*Odyssey*', and '*Nostos*' is retained, but otherwise the order of episodes in the epic voyage is completely disregarded, while the Wandering Rocks, which in Homer's work are merely referred to as dangers on a course which Odysseus does not take, are given a whole chapter. In the National Library, it is Stephen rather than Bloom who plots a course between Scylla and Charybdis, and in the cabman's shelter Bloom has to share the role of Ulysses with W. B. Murphy, ABS. In the *Odyssey*, Telemachus and his father first meet in the swineherd's hut; in *Ulysses*, Stephen and Bloom, apart from passing encounters during the day, come together in the maternity hospital ('Oxen of the Sun'), although their relationship matures later. Plainly, then, Joyce is not using the epic story as a substitute for an action, and, to this extent, T. S. Eliot's remark, in an early article on the novel, that 'instead of narrative method, we may now use the mythical method'[11] is misleading: Joyce's innovation was not to replace narrative, but to supplement it. He establishes the epic as a level of figurative reference (as Pope did in *The Dunciad*), which he can ignore or variously exploit.

The three central areas of relevance are the correspondences between Bloom and Ulysses (from here on it will be convenient to use this name for the hero), between the incidents of Dublin life and the episodes of the *Odyssey*, and between Stephen and Telemachus. For Joyce, as a boy, Ulysses was 'My Favourite Hero', and, in later life, he described him as the only 'complete all-round character' in literature – the only one presented in all the male roles as son, father, husband, lover, companion-in-arms and king.[12] He spoke of Bloom in very similar terms:

> I see him from all sides, and therefore he is all-round in the sense of your sculptor's figure. But he is a complete man as well – a good man. At any rate, that is what I intend that he shall be.[13]

Thus, Joyce did not envisage Bloom as a pitifully diminished and clownish equivalent to the hero: the relation between the two is more nearly that of 'metempsychosis' than of burlesque imitation. If there is something Ulyssean about Bloom, there may also be something Bloom-like about Ulysses. For instance, at first glance, Bloom's encounter with Gerty MacDowell seems a low comedy version of the meeting with Nausicaa – and in some respects it is. But the Homeric episode is itself not without comedy, as when Ulysses, shipwrecked and nearly drowned, and covering his nakedness with a branch, wonders whether to embrace the young princess's knees and pray for assistance, or keep his distance and ask politely, and resolves on the second alternative for fear that the girl might

[11] '*Ulysses*, Order and Myth', *The Dial* LXXV (1923), 480–83; reprinted in *Givens*, 202.

[12] *Budgen*, 15–16.   [13] *Budgen*, 17–18.

be offended if he embraced her knees.[14] Moreover, Bloom's sexual performance inspired by the sight of Gerty's knickers, though ridiculous, is part
of the process by which he overcomes the mood of depression and humiliation produced by his knowledge of what is happening in his bed that
afternoon:

> We'll never meet again. But it was lovely. Goodbye, dear. Thanks. Made me
> feel so young. (*U* 364/498)

The parallels are ironic, but irony is not to be confused with sarcasm. As
Jonathan Swift knew, there is irony on the subject of praise[15] as well as
hostile irony; Joyce's ironic comparisons elevate Bloom as often as they
ridicule him, and often do both at the same time, mocking some aspects of
a situation but discerning in it qualities of courageous and even lofty
motive and behaviour. This is particularly clear in Bloom's defiance of the
violent old man in Barney Kiernan's pub and in his mental triumph over
his enemies and humiliators, where the implicit allusions to the defeat of
the Cyclops and the slaying of the suitors help the reader to recognize,
among the many absurd circumstances, the elements of moral courage and
heroic victory.

The parallel between Bloom and Ulysses extends to the actions and
situations in which they are involved in a manner implicit in the common
figurative use of the term 'odyssey' to mean the journey of a soul through
the perils and temptations of this life – that is to say, by the treatment of
the epic myth as, in part, allegorical. Insofar as the episodes are regarded
as representative of universal human experiences, any specific location will
modify only their accidental particulars, not their essences; and whether in
the Mediterranean region or in Dublin, whether presented in the heroic
or the realistic mode, they will compose a kind of spiritual geography of
the hazards that lie in wait for the 'complete' man in his voyage through
life, menacing or undermining his will to travel on.[16] Seen in this way, the
chief threats to Bloom's preservation of his own moral nature and continued pursuit of his own values are indifference and withdrawal from the
struggle ('Lotuseaters'), nostalgia for the past and preoccupation with death
('Hades'), the animal struggle for survival and sustenance ('Lestrygonians'),
the attractions of tempting women and music and liquor ('Sirens'), the
hostility of ignorant bigotry ('Cyclops'), an escape into sentimental romantic

[14] Joyce laughed when telling Budgen of Ulysses' modest behaviour in approaching
Nausicaa (*Budgen*, 17).
[15] *The Correspondence of Jonathan Swift*, ed. Harold Williams (London, Oxford
University Press 1963), III, 410: 'I pretend to have been an improver of Irony on
the subject of Satyr and praise.'
[16] W. B. Stanford observes that Joyce could have derived this idea, and much else,
from Lamb's *Adventures of Ulysses*: 'The "agents" in his tale, [Lamb] tells his readers,
"besides men and women, are giants, enchanters, sirens: things which denote external
force or internal temptations, the twofold danger which a wise fortitude must expect
to encounter in its course through this world"' ('The Mysticism That Pleased Him:
A Note on the Primary Source of Joyce's *Ulysses*', in *A Bash in the Tunnel: James
Joyce by the Irish*, ed. John Ryan, ... through this world "' ('The Mysticism Brighton,
Clifton Books 1970), 40).

daydream ('Nausicaa'), the sterile cynicism of mockers ('Oxen of the Sun'), and psychological bankruptcy and moral paralysis ('Circe').

Thus, the Lotuseaters of the *Odyssey* are metamorphosed into an aspect of the spiritual climate of Dublin. In his 'Correspondences', Joyce noted, '*Lotuseaters;* the Cabhorses, Communicants, Soldiers, Eunuchs, Bather, Watchers of Cricket', and, in the novel, each of this mixed bunch is variously seen as a manifestation of the city's spiritual lethargy. The cab-horses are gelded ('Might be happy all the same that way'); the communi-cants take the eucharist like an anaesthetic ('Lulls all pain'); the military life mesmerises soldiers ('Half baked they look: hypnotised like'); the eunuchs of the papal choirs suggest the peace possible to those untroubled by sexual desire ('One way out of it'); the bather is Bloom as he foresees himself stretched out in the bath 'in a womb of warmth'; and the cricket-watchers represent the dream of a life of idle leisure ('If life was always like that. Cricket weather. Sit around under sunshades. Over after over. Out.'). All of these image escapes from the struggles and problems of life, but the chapter is filled with similar images and notions which Joyce has not troubled to list. In the first paragraph, Bloom sees a boy smoking a cigarette-butt and thinks of warning him that smoking will stunt his growth, but then recognizes the need for a narcotic: 'O let him! His life isn't such a bed of roses!' Immediately afterwards, the sight of packets of tea in a shopwindow calls up a picture of the far east:

> Those Cinghalese lobbing around in the sun, in *dolce far niente*. Not doing a hand's turn all day. Sleep six months out of twelve. Too hot to quarrel. Influence of the climate. Lethargy. Flowers of idleness.   (*U* 64/87)

Not only the cab-horses but the cabbies have 'no will of their own'. Bloom thinks of the narcotic powers of a cigar to cool down the 'usual love scrim-mage'. The memory of a picture of Martha and Mary of Bethany evokes a peaceful scene where there would be 'no more wandering about. Just loll there:... let everything rip. Forget', while the sound of a train calls to Bloom's mind Dublin's native drug or lotus, as he pictures vast barrels of porter pouring over the country 'a lazy pooling swirl of liquor bearing along wide-leaved flowers of its froth.' The notion of religion as a drug is present not only in the account of the communicants, but in Bloom's thoughts of other religions and races – of the Chinese who would 'prefer an ounce of opium' to the message of Christianity, of Buddha 'taking it easy with hand under his cheek', and of negroes listening entranced to a missionary: 'Lap it up like milk, I suppose.' Even the chemist's shop suggests thoughts of drugs which first excite, and then induce a lethargy, as well as of 'Chloroform. Overdose of laudanum. Sleeping draughts. Lovephiltres.'

Not all sections of *Ulysses* make as much of the Homeric analogue as does 'Lotuseaters', though in all those parts of the voyage which I have men-tioned the nature of the relevance of the Homeric episodes to Bloom's spiritual odyssey is sufficiently clear. The various dangers and temptations that he meets are not each confined to a particular chapter: on the contrary, most of them recur. But, as in the *Portrait*, one inimical force after another becomes dominant or particularly threatening, until their energies coalesce in the final assault on Bloom's nature in the 'hallucinatory' Nighttown chapter.

There are, however, sections of the book where the Homeric parallels have a rather different relevance. Calypso's isle is the place where Ulysses was a solitary captive for seven years, held there by the nymph who loved him: it is a place of exile, rather than of danger. But for Bloom the same house in Eccles Street represents both the isle of Calypso and his Ithaca: what changes is not the place or its occupants but his attitude towards them. Joyce's column of 'Correspondences' identifies Calypso as the nymph whose picture hangs above the Blooms' marital bed, but that nymph is linked in Bloom's mind with Molly: 'Not unlike her with her hair down: slimmer.' And there are other nymphs in the section – Milly, for instance, and the gauze-clad figures who perform the Dance of the Hours in Bloom's projected story. In the *Odyssey*, Ulysses acknowledges the superiority of Calypso to Penelope in beauty, and in the possession of unfading youth and immortality; yet he still longs for the woman, Penelope. Bloom, similarly, has been trapped into an unsatisfying relationship. Sexually he is exiled from his wife: there has been no 'complete carnal intercourse' between them for over ten years, and no 'complete mental intercourse' since Milly reached puberty. He recognizes later that there had been 'a limitation of activity, mental and corporal' and that 'complete corporal liberty of action had been circumscribed' (*U* 697/869. Bloom has become a captive, a submissive slave to the feminine tyranny represented by the nymph in the picture. We see him running about at Molly's beck and call, reading with 'his soft subject gaze', and feeling 'a soft qualm regret' at the prospect of a young man kissing his daughter: 'Useless: can't move.' Even the postcard from Blazes Boylan, promising to call that afternoon to practise *Love's Old Sweet Song* with Molly, seems to upset him more by its impolite disregard of the formalities and of his legal position as husband than by arousing sexual jealousy: 'Mrs Marion Bloom. His quick heart slowed at once. Bold hand. Mrs Marion.' When he tries to invent a sketch, he thinks of the authorship as 'By Mr and Mrs L. M. Bloom'.[17] It seems that Bloom is as much reduced to a husband as Little Chandler who inadvertently accepted the expression 'to put one's head in the sack' as a description of marriage.[18]

Bloom, as Jew, is in exile in another sense: the 'Correspondences' note, '*Dlugacz;* The Recall. *Zion;* Ithaca'. In the shop of Dlugacz, the butcher,

---

[17] Richard Ellmann points out that the authorship should be ascribed to Mr and Mrs L. P. Bloom. Instead Bloom combines his own and his wife's first initials (*Ellmann–Ulysses*, 31).

[18] R. M. Adams has made the interesting suggestion that Bloom garbles '*Vorrei e non vorrei*' as '*Voglio e non vorrei*' (*U* 56/77), because he is combining the Don Giovanni–Zerlina seduction duet with Leporello's '*Non voglio più servir*', as though, in his mind, anticipation of the Boylan/Molly meeting is mixed with resentment of his own servitude (*Adams*, 71). That Bloom is a slave to uxoriousness is also suggested by the Linati scheme, which includes in the '*Persone*' column, 'Calypso (Penelope) *moglie*', identifying Molly, as wife, with Calypso.

Bloom picks up the paper which reminds him of Zion, with promises of model farms by Lake Tiberias, and proposals to establish fruit farms in Palestine. But, unlike the exiles in Babylon, Bloom has no real desire for the Holy Land. He daydreams briefly, but a passing cloud recalls what, to him, is the truth of the matter:

> No, not like that. A barren land, bare waste. . . . A dead sea in a dead land, grey and old. Old now. It bore the oldest, the first race. . . . The oldest people. Wandered far away over all the earth, captivity to captivity, multiplying, dying, being born everywhere. It lay there now. Now it could bear no more. Dead: an old woman's: the grey sunken cunt of the world.   (*U* 54/73)

Natural resilience makes him shake off this vision of desolation, and attribute it to 'morning mouth' or getting out of the wrong side of the bed, but it does not restore any yearning for a national home: 'Well, I am here now.' If there is to be any Ithaca or any promised land for Bloom, it will be found in Molly's bed; and that is where in the penultimate chapter of the book he finds both, and his final satisfaction:[19]

> Satisfaction at the ubiquity in eastern and western terrestrial hemispheres, in all habitable lands and islands explored or unexplored (the land of the midnight sun, the islands of the blessed, the isles of Greece, the land of promise) of adipose posterior female hemispheres.   (*U* 695/867)

As in the cabman's shelter, Bloom, after all the tribulations of the day, finds himself back on his own territory, in charge of a situation which he can manage cheerfully and competently, so in bed he escapes from the role of legal and subservient husband and becomes a man satisfied with the physical presence of a mature woman.

The 'Aeolus' episode in the newspaper office again makes an unusual use of the Homeric analogue. The Ruler of the Winds was not hostile to Ulysses: on the contrary, he shut all the boisterous winds in a sack to facilitate the hero's voyage home, but Ulysses' crew, in sight of Ithaca, opened the bag and the ship was blown back to the Aeolian isle. It was only Ulysses' second application for help that Aeolus refused, on the grounds that a man so unfortunate must be hated by the gods. Joyce retains a faint parallel in that Bloom first gets the promise of help for his proposed negotiation with Keyes, a prospective advertiser, yet receives a rude answer from the editor, Crawford, when he delivers Keyes's request for a 'puff' in the newspaper. But the whole incident is hardly central to the chapter, and Joyce's 'Correspondences' indicate a different emphasis: '*Crawford;* Aeolus. *Incest;* Journalism. *Floating Island;* Press.' Aeolus married his six sons to his six daughters, and Stuart Gilbert suggests that journalism 'involves an illicit union, of aspiration and compromise, of literature and opportunism',[20] but the two pairings, although perhaps illicit, are not between partners sufficiently related to justify the word 'incest'. A more

---

[19] The notesheets are explicit on this point: 'her rump = promised land' (*Notesheets*, Ithaca 11: 29, 463).

[20] *Gilbert*, 185.

likely explanation of the term is the curious atmosphere of inbred kinship among the journalists, together with an obsessional devotion to the tricks of their trade: Crawford describes a smart journalistic stunt as an 'inspiration of genius', Bloom remarks on the inconsistency of journalists ('Go for one another baldheaded in the papers and then all blows over. Hailfellow well met the next moment'), and all the newspaper men exchange names and allusions like family gossip:

> Gregor Grey made the design for it. That gave him the leg up. Then Paddy Hooper worked Tay Pay who took him on to the *Star*. Now he's got in with Blumenfeld. That's press. That's talent. Pyatt! He was all their daddies.
> —The father of scare journalism, Lenehan confirmed, and the brother-in-law of Chris Callinan. (*U* 128/174)

But the real point of the Homeric analogue here seems to be a ridicule of the contemporary press as a noisy, incoherent and sometimes infantile collection of windbags. The rhetoric of the past has been replaced by wordy inanities, and those who regard themselves as belonging to a great profession blunder in a state of hectic confusion, propagating not the word but the wind.

Although the Homeric parallels both honour and mock Bloom, their reference to the city life of Dublin is always belittling. Yet, either way, their relevance is on the plane of moral discrimination: the threats to the moral life of the 'good man' and his ways of avoiding or overcoming them are distinguished and characterized. The relation of Stephen to Telemachus is different in kind. To say, as is often said, that Stephen needs a father as Bloom needs a son is loosely true but confusing, since it joins two quite different metaphors. Bloom needs someone to serve, help, guide and advise, someone in whose fortunes he can take an interest, someone who will provide an object for his paternal feelings and his altruism, and thereby give support to his moral nature and his ego: his is essentially an emotional need. Stephen, on the other hand, needs a relationship which he refers to as 'a mystical estate, an apostolic succession, from only begetter to only begotten' (*U* 195/266), some interaction which will help him pass out of his artistic immaturity: it is essentially a spiritual or imaginative need. (This statement of the contrast is itself oversimplified, in that the imaginative stimulation supplied by the artist is part of Bloom's emotional satisfaction in their relationship, while the maturing of the artist's imagination is partly dependent on the establishment of a sympathetic emotional relationship with another human being.)

For the first chapter of *Ulysses*, the listed 'Correspondences' are '*Stephen:* Telemachus, Hamlet. *Buck Mulligan:* Antinous. *Milkwoman:* Mentor.' The Hamlet reference, clearly established in the text, serves as a link between Stephen and Telemachus, between whose situations and behaviour there is otherwise little obvious connection. However, once the Hamlet connection has been made by repeated and explicit comparison, it can be extended to Telemachus, since both he and Hamlet grieved for a lost father, felt helpless in the evil situation resulting from that loss, and bitterly resented a usurping power. Stephen's grief is for the loss of his mother, his isolation seems to arise from a loss of trust in his supposed friend, and, although his last thought, as the section ends, is 'Usurper', one might think that he is expressing no more than his suspicion that Mulligan wants to get rid of him from the Martello Tower. The relevance of the father–son relationship is hinted at by Mulligan's mocking reference to the *Hamlet* theory ('He proves by algebra that Hamlet's grandson is Shakespeare's grandfather and that he himself is the ghost of his own father'), by the Ballad of Joking Jesus (which refers to Stephen as well as to Jesus), by Haines's memory of a theological interpretation of *Hamlet* ('The Son striving to be atoned with the Father'), and by Stephen's thoughts about the various heretics who had challenged the orthodox notions of the relationship of Father and the Son in the Trinity. But the only indication that Stephen is, in any sense, in need of a father is Mulligan's jibe, 'Japhet in search of a father!', the title of a novel by Captain Marryat about a foundling who tries to find his father. The surface reason for Stephen's decision not to return to the Martello Tower is his disgust with the company there.

The one incident which suggests another, submerged, motive is that involving the old milkwoman. Without Joyce's note it seems unlikely that anyone would have thought of associating this old woman, who ignores Stephen, with the goddess Athene, who, disguised as Mentor, visited Telemachus and encouraged him to seek information about his missing father. Yet on her appearance, Stephen thinks of her as a messenger, an immortal, and a symbol of Ireland. Her identification with Ireland is pursued in Stephen's thoughts as she bows her head to listen to the voice of Mulligan, the medical student: he imagines her subservient before 'her medicineman', her priest, and the Englishman – 'me she slights'; similarly Ireland is submissive to doctor, priest and conqueror, and slights the artist. He has already thought of himself as 'a server of a servant': later, to Haines, he says that he is 'the servant of two masters', the British empire and the Roman Catholic Church. But, at once, the thought enters his mind of 'a crazy queen, old and jealous', and he adds, 'And a third . . . there is who wants me for odd jobs.' The 'crazy queen' is again Ireland which, in the course of the day, wants him for such odd jobs as teaching history, writing for the newspapers, and contributing a pseudo-learned article to some periodical. (The allusion is confirmed by a passage in the early essay on James Clarence Mangan where Ireland is described as 'an abject queen upon whom, because of the bloody crimes that she has done and of those as bloody that were done to her, madness is come and death is coming, but who will not believe that she is near to die.'[21]) In this way, Stephen's feeling that he has been rejected or ignored by his homeland is linked to his suspicion that he is being ousted from the Martello tower, so that when Mulligan is labelled 'Usurper', the word implies a usurpation of the artist's position in Ireland, the country later called a 'paradise of pretenders'. It is a reversal of the position in the *Portrait*: the young man who had proudly

[21] *CW*, 82.

adopted the weapons of 'silence, exile, and cunning', now feels dispossessed, disinherited by the country he had so gladly escaped.

These Odyssean equivalents are certainly much more tenuous than those which refer to Bloom; apart from the sense of usurpation, there is no substantial connection between the motherless Stephen and the fatherless Telemachus. Of course, Bloom and his adventures were invented, and could be shaped and coloured to suggest the epic analogue, whereas, for Stephen, Joyce was drawing on his own experience and seems to have been unwilling to wander too far from the facts as he remembered them. There were other difficulties: for instance, at the beginning of the *Odyssey*, Telemachus is repeatedly helped in his search for information about his father – by Athene, Nestor and his son, Peisistratus, and Menelaus. Where could such sources of help be located in Dublin without undermining the image of the city as a hostile environment through which the young hero was to travel?

The solution to the problem depends on the character of Stephen's 'search'. Its underlying and partly conscious purpose is to enable him, as artist, to move out of his state of barren isolation; any encounter, therefore, which, however accidentally, prepares him for a new relationship with other men, can be seen as a kind of spiritual assistance. Thus, in the first chapter, it is the encounter with the old milkwoman which prompts the thought that his place in Ireland has been usurped, and leads to the decision to abandon the Martello Tower, symbolic of isolation: hence the old woman performs a function analogous to that of Athene disguised as Mentor. In the second chapter, the arithmetic lesson with the 'ugly and futile' schoolboy, Sargent, sets off another train of thought, promising a relaxation of Stephen's secretive silence, and perhaps foreshadowing the composition of the *Portrait*:

> Like him was I, these sloping shoulders, this gracelessness. My childhood bends beside me. Too far for me to lay a hand there once or lightly. Mine is far and his secret as our eyes. Secrets, silent, stony sit in the dark palaces of both our hearts: secrets weary of their tyranny: tyrants willing to be dethroned.
> (*U* 26/34)

Later, the thought of Sargent among the football players suggests another image of involvement in life: 'I am among them, among their battling bodies in a medley, the joust of life.' In this way, Sargent is contributive to Stephen's liberation and is identified by Joyce in the 'Correspondences' as Peisistratus, son of Nestor and companion of Telemachus on the journey to Menelaus.

The 'correspondence' between Mr Deasy and Nestor is less surprising, since both are purveyors of 'old wisdom', though the schoolteacher's pronouncements are, for the most part, materialistic and pompously stupid. Yet he, too, like the milkwoman, unconsciously helps Stephen's mind in the right direction. The thought of the chapter centres round history; it begins with a history lesson and at once considers the nature of the historical past. In his Mangan paper, Joyce had said that history was 'fabled by the daughters of memory',[22] but it was more than that: certain events occur and 'are not to be thought away'; certain possibilities become actualities and 'are lodged in the room of the infinite possibilities they have ousted.' Stephen thinks of the long tradition of Irish comic-writers who had been court-jesters to the English.[23]

> Why had they chosen all that part? Not wholly for the smooth caress. For them too history was a tale like any other too often heard, their land a pawnshop. (*U* 22/29-30)

Like them, Stephen is tired of the recital of Ireland's wrongs, but he cannot regard it as a boring tale; the events happened and their consequences remain. His quandary is like that which concerns his feelings for his mother: perhaps her love was 'the only true thing in life', but 'she was no more', and his bitterness and regret is compared to a fox scraping and listening at his grandmother's grave. Neither the historical wrongs of Ireland nor his mother's death can be brushed aside and forgotten as though they had never happened; but they cannot be allowed to govern his life.[24] The conversation with Mr Deasy does not resolve the dilemma but points to the kind of answer that must be found. The schoolmaster is a patriotic Irishman with a characteristic fondness for living in the past. 'We are all Irish, all kings' sons', he declares proudly: Stephen's reply is short but expressive – 'Alas.' The same sort of historical cliché serves to justify Mr Deasy's antisemitism and explain the sufferings of the Jews:

> —They sinned against the light, Mr Deasy said gravely. And you can see the darkness in their eyes. And that is why they are wanderers on the earth to this day. (*U* 31/41)

Stephen's reaction to this is twofold: in the first place, he thinks of the Jewish race in terms which reflect his own state – 'Their eyes knew the years of wandering and, patient, knew the dishonours of their flesh' – and thus unconsciously prepares for the companionship with Bloom; in the second place, he finds an expression for his attitude towards history:

> —History, Stephen said, is a nightmare from which I am trying to awake. (*U* 31/42)

He cannot, that is, like the jesters, be subservient to the English as though the past had never happened; but he will try to free himself from the incubus of the past. His position is like that adopted by Joyce in a lecture given in 1907, when he summarized Ireland's cultural history and concluded by rejecting the idea of a race attempting to live in the past:

[22] *CW*, 81. The phrase is adapted from Blake, [*A Vision of the Last Judgment.*] *For the Year 1810 (Poetry and Prose of William Blake,* ed. Geoffrey Keynes (London, Nonesuch Press 1943), 637–8).

[23] Cf. *CW*, 202.

[24] Joyce made a similar response to Gogarty's wish for reconciliation: 'O.G.'s request was that I should forget the past: a feat beyond my power. I forgive readily enough' (*Letters* II, 183).

If an appeal to the past in this manner were valid, the fellahin of Cairo would have all the right in the world to disdain to act as porters for English tourists. Ancient Ireland is dead just as ancient Egypt is dead. Its death chant has been sung, and on its gravestone has been placed the seal. . . .

. . . It is well past time for Ireland to have done once and for all with failure. If she is truly capable of reviving, let her awake, or let her cover up her head and lie down decently in her grave forever.[25]

The nightmare from which Stephen is trying to awake is, however, not only the past of Ireland, but also his own past life, in particular the haunting memory of his mother's death. The necessary precondition of his escape is awareness of what he must escape from, and to this extent both Sargent and Mr Deasy, though pitiful shadows of Peisistratus and Nestor, contribute to Stephen's liberation from the position achieved at the end of the *Portrait*, a position which appeared to be a new freedom, but has proved to be a dead end and an obstacle to his development as artist.

For the third chapter, Joyce has taken the struggle with Proteus (undertaken by Menelaus and merely reported to Telemachus) and attributed its modern equivalent to Stephen. Menelaus wrestled with the shape-changing Old Man of the Sea in order to force him to reveal why he, Menelaus, was becalmed and in what direction he should steer for home. Similarly, what Stephen is seeking in this chapter is a course to follow. At the simplest level, it is a question of where he should go, having left both his family home and the Martello Tower. He thinks of going to his Aunt Sara's, but recalls the claustrophobic family life there, representative of Dublin's moribundity: 'Beauty is not there,' he thinks, nor in the esoteric pursuits to which he has abandoned his mind. Yet his first attempt to escape, his flight to Paris, has been a ridiculous failure. Exile is associated in his mind with Kevin Egan, the old militant nationalist he had met in Paris, 'loveless, landless, wifeless'. According to the 'Correspondences', Egan is the Menelaus of this chapter, but the Helen for whom he fought is plainly not the wife who is separated from him, but Ireland. Now a 'spurned lover', he is forgotten by his country, and lives on memories, in exile. This Menelaus has no more useful information to offer than Mr Deasy's Nestor, but remembering him helps Stephen to perceive the futility of his own flight to Paris – the affectations in dress and manner, his self-conceit as a 'missionary to Europe', the 'rich booty' he brought back consisting of a few tattered periodicals. This rejection of alternatives, one after another, is characteristic of the whole chapter, for, as Joyce told Frank Budgen, 'It's the struggle with Proteus. Change is the theme. Everything changes – sea, sky, man, animals. The words change, too.'[26] The universe, as Stephen apprehends it, is an incessant flux like the sea by which he stands, and the movements of his own mind are comparably confused and contradictory. First, he thinks of the universe in Aristotelian terms as composed of the diaphane, the invisible transparent substance of all things, known to man

[25] 'Ireland, Island of Saints and Sages', translated in *CW*, 173–4.
[26] *Budgen*, 49.

only by its limits, the accidents of colour: space and time are the ineluctable
modalities of our seeing and our hearing, but the primal matter (identified
as 'Proteus' in the 'Correspondences', as in Bacon's *Wisdom of the Ancients*
– 'Proteus, or Matter') is 'there all the time without you: and ever shall be,
world without end.' Nevertheless, a little later he is exploring Berkeley's
idealism. God, he thinks, having willed him to be, 'now may not will me
away or ever', yet he is forced to recognize the inevitability of death –
'*Omnis caro ad te veniet.*' The pride of his spirit contrasts with the identification of himself as the bloated corpse of a drowned dog ('poor dogsbody'),
He feels a part of all mankind, linked by the navel cords to their common
origin in Eve, and yet cannot accept involvement: imagining himself faced
with the task of saving a drowning man, he makes excuses, fears being
drawn down himself: 'I want his life still to be his, mine to be mine.' He
sees the scene around him as a Lotusland ('Among gumheavy serpent-
plants, milkoozing fruits, where on the tawny waters leaves lie wide. Pain
is far'), and the next moment in terms of Saint Ambrose's vision of the
whole creation groaning day and night beneath its wrongs. He remembers
lecherous thoughts about naked women and justifies himself – 'What else
were they invented for?' – and later dreams sentimentally of the consoling
touch of a soft hand to heal his loneliness. His poem unites death and love,
and he mouths the phrase 'allwombing tomb'. Theologically, philosophically, morally, linguistically, and, in particular, about his own future, he
vacillates: there seems no way to avoid or reconcile the contraries that
divide him, no way to grasp his situation with sufficient certainty to choose
a course of action. And yet his conclusion is not one of defeat:

> My cockle hat and staff and his my sandal shoon. Where? To evening lands.
> Evening will find itself. . . .
>   . . . Yes, evening will find itself in me, without me.   (*U* 47/63)

The imagery of pilgrimage suggests resolve, even though he does not know
to what goal he must travel. 'Evening lands' has already been established
(in his thoughts about the woman cocklepicker) as an image for death. That
will not be his goal. Death will find him without his seeking it. But before
he leaves the shore, he looks over his shoulder and sees behind him,

> Moving through the air high spars of a threemaster, her sails brailed up on
> the crosstrees, homing, upstream, silently moving, a silent ship.   (*U* 47/64)

In an Odyssean context, a 'homing' ship, especially at the close of the
Telemachus chapters, is a good omen, even though a later use of 'crosstree'
for the cross of Calvary may suggest that the voyage will not be achieved
without suffering. It confirms the hopeful suggestion of the dream Stephen
remembers – the dream of a man who met him in the 'street of harlots',
led him and spoke to him:

> I was not afraid. The melon he had he held against my face. Smiled: cream-
> fruit smell. That was the rule, said. In. Come. Red carpet spread. You will
> see who.   (*U* 43/59)

The struggle with Proteus does not give Stephen a direction – for that the meeting with Bloom is necessary – but it does, as it were, clear the ground for that meeting. This, I take it, was what was in Joyce's mind when he noted the 'Correspondence', *'Cocklepicker:* Megapenthus'. In the *Odyssey*, the part played by Megapenthus is hardly significant. He is the son of Menelaus by a slavewoman, and on Telemachus's arrival is about to be married: when Telemachus leaves, Megapenthus helps to load the departing guest with treasure. The fact that Megapenthus, like the cockle-picker, is of low birth hardly seems to justify the correspondence, but the point may be that the advent of the cocklepicker brings to Stephen's mind words and verses in rogues' cant. Stephen compares this language with that of Aquinas:

> Language no whit worse than his. Monkwords, marybeads jabber on their girdles: roguewords, tough nuggets patter in their pockets. *(U* 44/59)

Stephen's acceptance of 'low' language as a treasure of 'tough nuggets', a kind of treasure from the lowborn, is another preparatory movement in the spirit of the artist, away from his hierophantic narrowness towards a wider acceptance of the whole range of language and life, a movement in the direction which his acceptance of Bloom's companionship will confirm. This seems a slim justification for the inclusion of Megapenthus among the 'Correspondences', but it does conform to the general pattern of Homeric parallels in the first three episodes, where the analogies must be sought in the movements of Stephen's mind rather than in external incidents.

In the other chapter dominated by Stephen, the Shakespeare discussion in the library, the Homeric correspondences are again purely intellectual:

> *The Rock:* Aristotle, Dogma, Stratford. *The Whirlpool:* Plato, Mysticism, London. *Ulysses:* Socrates, Jesus, Shakespeare.

If Bloom is not Ulysses here, neither is Stephen: the hero's correspondents are Socrates, Jesus and Shakespeare, each seen as a man who made his way between opposing extremes. They navigated their lives; Stephen, however, is merely using their example to plot his own future course; the navigation will follow when he is a mature man and artist. In fact, the function of this chapter is very similar to that of the aesthetic discussions in the *Portrait*: there, the literary theorizings focused attention on the book's own nature and served to suggest the future development of the embryo artist; here, the critical speculations indicate by analogy the kind of book *Ulysses* is and show the young artist trying to define by illustration the nature of the creative spirit which will mature in him. The point is most clearly made when Stephen says (with the same Shelleyan allusion that was used in the *Portrait*'s explanation of *claritas*[27]),

> In the intense instant of imagination, when the mind, Shelley says, is a fading coal, that which I was is that which I am and that which in possibility

---

[27] Joyce had already used the image from Shelley's *Defence of Poetry* in his paper on James Clarence Mangan in 1902 *(CW,* 78) and retained it in his Italian lecture on Mangan given in 1907 *(CW,* 182).

I may come to be. So in the future, the sister of the past, I may see myself as I sit here now but by reflection from that which then I shall be.   (*U* 183/249)

The artist, Stephen has said, weaves and unweaves his image, because, as he adds later, 'His own image to a man with that queer thing genius is the standard of all experience, material and moral.' Thus the artist, throughout his life, is creating the image of himself, and at the same time unweaving its threads to discover its nature, and to remake it. Stephen compares the process to that of physical change in the body: all the molecules of the body are re-made time and time again, but 'the mole on my right breast is where it was when I was born.' This, too, corresponds with the fundamental image of the *Portrait* where the 'constant traits' of the artist's nature are shown persisting through the changes and developments in time. What Stephen is primarily concerned with in this chapter is the apprehension of his own nature as artist by an interpretation of Shakespeare's life, or, in other words, with defining his own artistic image and future in terms borrowed from Shakespearian criticism and biography.

Socrates plays a supplementary part. He is there partly because of the Maeterlinck quotation – '*If Socrates leave his house today he will find the sage seated on his doorstep*' – which supports the notion of the man of genius imposing his own image on all that he experiences, and partly because, in Stephen's account of him, he is a type of the artist transforming the daily bread of life into the food of the spirit: from his shrewish wife he learned his dialectic and from his midwife mother 'how to bring thoughts into the world.' This interaction between the material and spiritual worlds is interpreted as a course steered between the materialist definitions of Aristotle ('Horseness is the whatness of allhorse') and 'Plato's world of ideas'. As Ulysses steered deliberately close to Scylla, preferring to sacrifice six of his crew to that monster than to lose everything in the whirlpool of Charybdis, Stephen at this point chooses to keep closer to Aristotle than to Plato, seeing the real threat to his artistic survival in the vague mysticism of George Russell, 'gulfer of souls'. Stephen rejects Russell's view of art – 'Art has to reveal to us ideas, formless spiritual essences' – and decides instead to 'hold to the now, the here, through which all future plunges to the past.'

The relevance of Jesus is equally artistic, as is most clearly seen in the parody of the Creed:

> He Who Himself begot, middler the Holy Ghost, and Himself sent himself, Agenbuyer, between Himself and others, Who, put upon by His fiends, stripped and whipped, was nailed like bat to barndoor, starved on crosstree, Who let Him bury, stood up, harrowed hell, . . . fared into heaven and there these nineteen hundred years sitteth on the right hand of His Own Self but yet shall come in the latter day to doom the quick and dead when all the quick shall be dead already.   (*U* 186/253)

As Jesus, 'being of one substance with the Father, by whom all things were made', was 'begotten not made', through the agency of the Holy Ghost, and came as Redemptor, and mediator between God and man, was tormented and crucified, allowed himself to be buried, but rose again, harrowed hell and sits in judgement – so the artist begets his own consubstantial image (as Joyce begot Stephen), to mediate between himself and others (as, according to the *Portrait*, the artist's image 'must be set between the mind or senses of the artist himself and the mind or senses of others'), suffers at the hands of hostile forces, is banished (or buried, since he becomes 'a ghost by absence'), but, in his image, survives, and passes judgement on men's lives by creating the conscience of his race. Thus God the Father is to Jesus as Shakespeare is to Hamlet ('the son of his soul') and Joyce is to Stephen. The parallels have been suggested earlier, in a passage referring to George Fox, apparently about Shakespeare, figuratively involving Jesus, and implicitly referring to Stephen:

> Christfox in leather trews, hiding, a runaway in blighted treeforks from hue and cry. Knowing no vixen, walking lonely in the chase. Women he won to him, tender people, a whore of Babylon, ladies of justices, bully tapsters' wives. (*U* 182/247)

It is only in the third of these sentences that Stephen would be unable to recognize himself, and that is because for him this lies in the future: the Christ/Shakespeare analogy suggests an association with common but 'tender people', the kind of association he will realize with Bloom.[28] The view of Jesus taken here is of a man, mediating between the spiritual and the worldly, elusive of the dogma by which the Church has tried to define him, but not one of Russell's 'formless spiritual essences', not 'Hiesos Kristos, magician of the beautiful, the Logos who suffers in us at every moment.'

But, in this chapter, both Socrates and Jesus are subordinate and contributory to the central figure of Shakespeare, whose life and works are manipulated (and sometimes falsified) by Stephen, according to the already-enunciated principle that the genius fashions all experience into his own image. According to Stephen, 'the theme of the false or the usurping or the adulterous brother or all three in one' is always with Shakespeare, and all his plays sound 'the note of banishment, banishment from the heart, banishment from home.' The identification of Shakespeare with King Hamlet is partly based on the idea that Shakespeare, in exile from home, was a ghost there 'through absence, through change of manners', and the following sentence reveals Stephen peering through the Shakespearian mask:

> Elizabethan London lay as far from Stratford as corrupt Paris lies from virgin Dublin. (*U* 176/240)

Shakespeare in London carried with him the wounds inflicted in Stratford – the wound to his *amour-propre* through his 'first undoing' by Anne Hathaway, and the wound to his sense of property dealt by his brother's

---

[28] Robert Kellogg has shown that, besides the allusion in 'Christfox', this passage includes many expressions borrowed or adapted from the *Journal* of George Fox (*Hart and Hayman*, 161). The Quaker, too, was not a man to be trapped in dogma or to fear persecution.

usurpation of his bed: all his works are 'the creation he has piled up to hide him from himself, an old dog licking an old sore.' Stephen, in effect, foresees (and Joyce sees with hindsight) that he too will live in exile, forever in his work trying to heal the wounds he received in Ireland, obsessed by the themes of isolation, usurpation and banishment. Stephen describes Shakespeare as a perverted idealist, furious with a world that cannot emulate his ideal:

> Lover of an ideal or a perversion, like José he kills the real Carmen. His unremitting intellect is the hornmad Iago ceaselessly willing that the moor in him shall suffer. (*U* 200–201/272–3)

Again, there is an implicit self-image; Stephen is remaking Shakespeare to portray himself. The 'moor', presumably, is his emotional nature devoted to Dublin and needing the love of others, but infuriated by falseness, insincerity and betrayal, and egged on by the 'unremitting intellect' to destroy what it loves. Whatever play, or episode from a play, Stephen considers, one of the characters begins to dissolve into an image of Shakespeare and thence into a more generalized image of the artist, more particularly the artist that Stephen will become. Thus, the discussion of King Hamlet's ghost concludes:

> But, because loss is his gain, he passes on towards eternity in undiminished personality, untaught by the wisdom he has written or by the laws he has revealed. His beaver is up. He is a ghost, a shadow now, the wind by Elsinore's rocks or what you will, the sea's voice, a voice heard only in the heart of him who is the substance of his shadow, the son consubstantial with the father. (*U* 185/252)

The fusion of the ghost with Shakespeare is there complete, and the two melt into the image of the artist who creates out of his loss and suffering yet is not healed by his creation, whose wisdom is for others not for himself,[29] and whose substance survives in the children of his imagination. When Stephen says, with reference to Shakespeare, 'Where there is a reconciliation, ... there must have been first a sundering' (he repeats the assertion, in almost the same terms, shortly afterwards), he is making a decision about his own future. Isolation is, for Stephen, the necessary prelude to any reunion, and if, in *Ulysses* itself, there is a symbolic reconciliation with the city through Bloom, it can occur only when all other ties have been broken. The isolation sought in the *Portrait* and sought again in *Ulysses* was not a mistake: for the man of genius 'his errors are volitional and are the portals of discovery.' This is said in reply to Eglinton's suggestion that Shakespeare erred in marrying Anne Hathaway, and made the best of a bad job by leaving her and departing to London. To Stephen such a view is superficial: the artist makes a gain out of his loss; it was through the tension of his being divided between London and Stratford that

---

[29] Cf. Joyce's reference to himself, after the publication of *Ulysses*, as 'the foolish author of a wise book' (Stanislaus Joyce, 'James Joyce: A Memoir', *Hudson Review* II (1950), 511).

Shakespeare created his works. Stephen will take the same course: Ireland is his Anne Hathaway as it was Kevin Egan's Helen: it has wounded his soul and all his creation will be a licking of the sore it has left. He has taken flight from Ireland once before, but fell, like Icarus, calling for help – '*Pater ait.*' This time, the Shakespearean analogy implies, he will take Ireland with him as Shakespeare took with him to London 'a memory in his wallet' of Anne Hathaway, and, moreover, this time he will have an image of a father-figure to whom he can turn for encouragement.

Bloom's significance in this chapter is only symbolic. As Stephen and Mulligan leave the library, Stephen becomes aware of the latent hostility between them: 'My will: his will that fronts me. Seas between.' Between these two forces, opposed like Scylla and Charybdis, Mr Bloom quietly passes 'bowing, greeting'. Stephen at once recalls his dream of the previous night of the man who welcomed him in the street of the harlots, this time with the addition that in his dream he flew, 'easily flew'. His attitude towards Mulligan changes: he will 'cease to strive' against the usurper (as in the *Portrait* he had decided not to 'strive against another – P 249), accepting, as it were, the 'peace of the druid priests of Cymbeline', turning the whole earth into an altar for the praise of the gods. But this too will prove a transitory peace, at best a relaxation from the wrong kind of rivalry. The course he has plotted with the help of Shakespeare is one of conflict and tension rather than of peace; it will be a long struggle to escape destruction by the opposed forces within him, and, before facing that struggle, he needs the friendly support of a father figure, like the 'fabulous artificer' to whom he had prayed vainly at the end of the *Portrait*.

In the chapters dominated by Stephen the relationship with the *Odyssey* is less substantial and its relevance more obscure than in the chapters centrally concerned with Bloom. Readers, alerted by the novel's title, might be expected to realize that Bloom was a type of Ulysses and his journey through Dublin an odyssey; once this initial recognition was made, it would be reinforced and developed by the detailed handling of the chapters; and, finally, the parallels would be accepted and responded to as a sustained structural metaphor, enriching the texture with echoes and associations, implying varied moral comment, and focusing attention on the nature and significance of the book's central action – the coming together of artist and citizen. Much the same can be said of the identification of Stephen as a kind of Telemachus, to which recognition of Bloom as a Ulysses-figure would directly lead. But it is very unlikely that an unassisted reader would have associated Athene with the milkwoman, Sargent with Peisistratus, Egan with Menelaus, or the cocklepicker with Megapenthus:[30] even when

---

[30] Most of the other parallels in 'Correspondences' are of very little importance. For instance, in crossing the Dodder, Grand and Royal Canals and the river Liffey, the funeral can be thought of as crossing the four rivers of Hades; Martin Cunningham repeatedly setting up homes for his drunken wife is Sisyphus: Father Coffey, with a belly 'like a poisoned pup', is Cerberus; the caretaker of the cemetery is Hades, ruler of the underworld; the late Paddy Dignam is Elpenor, dead through drink. Daniel O'Connell represents the legendary hero, Hercules; Parnell the betrayed and murdered

these correspondences have been pointed out, they require lengthy justifications which are at best speculative and contribute comparatively little to one's experience of the novel.

Yet it is possible that, although obscure, they represented for Joyce something more than idle or obsessive ingenuity. They may represent a kind of Odyssean shorthand for the presence of certain important factors in the development of Stephen: in a letter to Carlo Linati, the Italian critic, Joyce said with reference to his 'summary-key-skeleton-scheme', 'I have given only catchwords in my scheme but I think you will understand it all the same.'[31] In the *Odyssey* itself, the function of the first four books is not immediately apparent. The presentation of Telemachus' wretchedness stresses the urgent need for the hero's return, and knowledge of the desperate situation awaiting him creates interest, but both of these are largely achieved in the first book. Telemachus' journey neither brings him to his father nor hastens the hero's homecoming: in fact, Ulysses returns to Ithaca before his son. But what the journey brings about is a maturing of Telemachus: partly by his own efforts and partly through the help and encouragement of Mentor (Athene), Nestor, Peisistratus, Menelaus and Megapenthus, the dispirited boy-man who helplessly bewailed his lot has been prepared for the challenge to stand by his father's side and share in the massacre of the suitors. The same is true of Stephen: melancholy and bitterness cannot rescue him from his predicament and Bloom cannot arrive as a miraculous redeemer: first, Stephen has to struggle to free his mind from bondage and begin his own movement towards maturity. Once he has begun, by recognizing his subservient position and determining to leave the Martello Tower, encounters and memories which would otherwise have been of no account play an important part in helping him towards a state of mind in which he can profit from an association with Bloom. The fact that, in his notes, Joyce chose to record these important moments in the process of Stephen's maturation by the names of Homeric figures who assisted Telemachus is of no great concern to the reader. Correspondences which cannot be observed without explanatory notes, and which, even when pointed out, add little to the experience of careful reading are of interest chiefly to the student of the writer's methods of composition, and are different in kind from those Odyssean parallels which

---

king, Agamemnon; and John Henry Menton the resentful and rather stupid Ajax. Corley (in 'Eumaeus') is identified by the scheme with the loafing ne'er-do-well, Melanthius, but Gilbert says that he is Theoclymenos (*Gilbert*, 349). Gilbert is probably right, because the British Museum notesheets show Joyce sketching in a parallel between Theoclymenos, whose genealogy is told at length, who seeks help from Telemachus, and who is sent to Eurymachus, the best of the suitors, and Corley, whose suspect family history is described, who asks Stephen for help, and asks if Bloom could get him a job with Boylan, identified in the scheme as Eurymachus (*Notesheets*, Eumaeus 6: 124 and 129, 404). These and other minor correspondences merely serve to fill in some sort of background to the central and significant Homeric parallels.

[31] *Letters* I, 146.

can be recognized and which contribute to the novel's significance. The reader who is ignorant of the epic reference is not excluded from an understanding and appreciation of *Ulysses*, although, when he is aware of it, his understanding and appreciation is deepened and extended; but such awareness is not dependent on knowledge of all the correspondences listed in Joyce's working notes.

The relevance of the Odyssean parallels depends on Joyce's concept of two men each engaged in a spiritual odyssey, and when there is a temporary hesitation in their progress, it is reflected in the epic analogy. This may be the reason why, for the 'Wandering Rocks' chapter, he chose a parallel which was not one of the adventures of Ulysses or Telemachus. The last we have seen of Bloom and Stephen is their departure from the National Library and Museum, and the concluding note of that chapter has been Stephen's 'Cease to strive'. In this chapter, his relaxed will is subjected to the pressures of commonsense, fear, and guilt: Almidano Artifoni good-naturedly advises him to cultivate his voice as a source of income, instead of sacrificing himself to an idea; a rash challenge to the *dio boia* who rules this world is hastily followed by an apologetic request for a little more time to look around; and a meeting with his sister Dilly associates his remorse for having refused his mother's wish with guilt for doing nothing to help save his sisters. Bloom, meanwhile, has turned from the pursuit of his own affairs to carrying out his wife's instructions to get her another book: the book he chooses, *Sweets of Sin*, reflects his situation as a cuckold and arouses in him sexual desire for Molly's full and odorous body – a desire terminated by the thought that he is no longer young. (I take it that the meaning of his mental exclamations – 'Young! Young!' – is indicated by the next sentence, which begins 'An elderly female, no more young'.) The image is of a city full of people engaged in no odyssey, but pursuing temporary immediate ends, most of them concerned with getting and spending money. The 'Correspondences' are geographical rather than heroic: '*Bosphorus;* Liffey. *European Bank;* Viceroy. *Asiatic Bank;* Conmee. *Symplegades;* Groups of Citizens.'

As the two most prolonged movements in the chapter are the journeys of Conmee and the Viceroy, it may seem curious that these two represent the banks of the stream of city life. But Joyce is concerned with movements of the spirit, not movements in space, and in that respect Conmee and the Viceroy, engaged in their routine duties, are not only stationary, but stand for the unmoving boundaries of Church and state between which the daily activities of the citizens are confined. The structure reinforces this image: the chapter begins with Conmee's journey and ends with the Viceroy's, and every incident between them is, directly or indirectly, located in time by reference to one or both of the containing 'banks'. The citizens are 'wandering rocks' in the sense that their lives have no sense of direction or purpose, other than their immediate occupations, the barren pursuit of petty ends. The only effective action is purely symbolic – the passage down the Liffey of the 'Elijah is coming' leaflet, which Bloom threw away from

O'Connell Bridge, and which is now observed passing down towards Dublin Bay and finally past 'the threemasted schooner *Rosevean* from Bridgwater with bricks.' As, in the 'Proteus' chapter, the arrival of this schooner seemed to symbolize the forthcoming arrival of Bloom, so now the escape from Dublin of the paper 'skiff', launched by Bloom, seems to symbolize Stephen's escape, with impetus derived from Bloom. It is the one promise of new movement in this chapter.

In discussing the Odyssean reference of *Ulysses*, I have (apart from the discussion of the 'Lotuseaters' chapter) paid most attention to those areas where the connection is unusual or puzzling, and this may have had the effect of suggesting that the whole epic level is esoteric or recherché. In fact, the more important allusions are the more apparent and, therefore, less in need of explication. Variety and flexibility are the characteristic qualities of Joyce's use of the *Odyssey*: the parallels vary in centrality, nature and function, according to the local needs in a chapter or the total shaping of the book. An Odyssean character may find a counterpart in a Dubliner, an historical person (Jesus, Socrates, Shakespeare), a philosophical concept ('*Proteus;* Primal Matter'), an appetite ('*Antiphates;* Hunger'), a moral impediment ('*Suitors;* Scruples') or even the earth itself ('*Penelope*'). Conversely, men can correspond to Homeric motives ('*Dlugacz;* The Recall') or features of Homeric geography ('Wandering Rocks') as well as to epic figures. The heroic comparison may elevate or belittle, may refer to a situation, an incident, a state of mind, and usually implies some moral discrimination and judgment. The Odyssean scheme was thus not a Procrustean bed on which Joyce racked his invention and distorted the novel-form: it was a resource which he called on wherever he saw a use for it, and shaped to his purpose, so that, without ever becoming rigid or over-emphatic (indeed many readers of *Ulysses* must still be unaware of it), it could support the central structure and add functional ornament to the texture of his novel.[32] This part of the columnar scheme is merely a formalized record of a device which, in the handling, was the opposite of formulaic.

'Organs'

The column headed 'Organs' refers to a very different element in the novel, since it is concerned primarily with the city background rather than with the action. It is again an adaptation of a traditional literary figure – the analogy between the human body and the body politic.[33] Consequently no 'organs' are listed for the first three chapters, since these concern a solitary

[32] Cf. '. . . only a fraction of the Homeric correspondences collected on the notesheets appear in the text' (*Litz*, 20).

[33] Hugh Kenner has suggested that the organs present a 'vision of Dublin as a mechanization both of the Body Politic and of the Mysterious Body of Christ', without examining either analogy in detail (*Kenner*, 237–8).

young man outside the city limits.[34] In *Dubliners*, Joyce had already
employed the symbol of paralysis to present the city's moral condition: in
Ulysses, the metaphor, though greatly extended, is essentially the same in
kind and function. To assume that the organ of the fourth chapter ('Calypso')
is a kidney because Bloom buys and cooks a kidney for his breakfast, that
the fact that he imagines his genitals floating in the bathwater explains why
the organ of the fifth chapter ('Lotuseaters') is 'genitals', or that the sixth
chapter ('Hades') corresponds to 'heart' because the word 'heart' occurs
frequently in that chapter is to suppose that Joyce was a much more simple-
minded artist than we know him to have been. The general ironic relevance
of the list of organs to the spiritual condition of Dublin is plain enough.
The 'lungs' of Dublin are the newspaper offices, inhaling and exhaling the
fetid air of cheap journalism and stale rhetoric; the voracious struggle for
existence of Dubliners, hastily swallowing belly-fodder, appropriately links
the 'Lestrygonians' chapter with the 'oesophagus'; the 'brain' of the city
is satirically represented by the intellectuals in the library; if, as Hobbes says
in *Leviathan*, 'Money [is] the blood of a Commonwealth',[35] the 'blood' and
business circulating through Dublin in the 'Wandering Rocks' chapter is
sluggish, thin and anaemic; the city's 'ear', in the 'Sirens', responds sentimentally to operatic arias and patriotic ballads, because, as Mr Bloom
observes, the addiction to music is a 'kind of drunkenness' with 'thinking
strictly prohibited'; 'muscle' finds an equivalent in the energy and violence
of the prejudices displayed in the 'Cyclops' chapter; the city's 'womb' is
the maternity hospital where young mockers praise contraception and the
artist hears 'the voice of the god Bringforth'; the 'skeleton' is aptly represented by the hard facts of time, space and the laws of science, on which
the life of the city hangs; and Molly's fleshly soliloquy adequately stands
for the 'flesh' of human physical existence, covering all the rest.

These are the plainest points of the analogy, but they are sufficient to
establish the pattern. Whatever 'organ' one finds in Joyce's Dublin is
likely to be diseased or at least performing its function inadequately. 'Eye
and 'Nose' are the joint organs of the 'Nausicaa' chapter. This is the most
visual of the chapters: Gerty's figure and face are described in detail from
'rosebud mouth' and hands 'of finely veined alabaster' to her eyes 'of the
bluest Irish blue', her 'lustrous lashes and dark expressive brows', and the
'luxuriant clusters' of her hair. Even her clothes are itemized and described
in the gushing manner of a fashion correspondent. Something is evidently
amiss with Dublin's eyes, since everything is seen through a haze of sentimental fantasy, which conceals a much coarser exercise of the visual sense
– for Gerty is aware of Mr Bloom's regard, and finally leans back to give

---

[34] In the Linati scheme the *Telemachia* chapters have, in the 'Organs' column,
'(*Telemaco non soffre ancora il corpo*)'. Translating this as 'Telemachus does not yet
bear a body', Richard Ellmann suggests that, as yet, Stephen 'remains abstract' and
is only incipiently 'corporeal' (*Ellmann–Ulysses*, 31). Insofar as the sentence applies
to the book as published, I take it to mean that, outside the city, and before engaging
with the citizen, Stephen is, as it were, an unattached spirit without a local habitation.
[35] *Leviathan* II, 24.

him a view of her underclothes. The vision of Dublin is thus represented, on the one hand by self-willed delusion, and on the other by Peeping Tom voyeurism. Its sense of smell is characterized similarly. Gerty's romantic fantasy is expressed, in terms of smell, by the perfume-soaked cottonwool she waves, in the hope of leaving with Bloom a fragrant memory: he thinks the scent is of roses, but considers it 'sweet and cheap: soon sour', before going on to think of the more intimate smells distilled by the female body and their function in attracting the opposite sex. Further thoughts on 'man-smell' lead him to attempt to smell his own body, not entirely successfully because of the lemon soap in his pocket. The chapter, then, images Dublin's spiritual eyes and nose as organs of sense in which a coarse and unpleasant reality is veiled beneath a genteel or romantic cloud.

The reason why 'locomotor apparatus' is given as the organ for the Nighttown chapter is more fiercely satirical. The movement in question is moral or spiritual locomotion and, for Joyce, Dublin suffered from moral paralysis. In *Ulysses* two forms are referred to – general paralysis of the insane, and locomotor ataxy – both much more specific than the paralysis of Father Flynn in 'The Sisters' and both among the consequences of syphilis: the connection between syphilis and locomotor ataxy is made by the whores. For Joyce a convenient etymology for syphilis was 'συφιλις = swinelove?';[36] Circe turned men into swine, as Madam Bella Cohen's establishment made them behave like animals. Joyce told Frank Budgen that the chapter was 'an animal episode, full of animal allusions, animal mannerisms', and that 'the rhythm is the rhythm of locomotor ataxia';[37] and he speculated in letters as to what the 'moly' might be that saved Bloom – 'chance, also laughter, the enchantment killer' or 'the invisible influence (prayer, chance, agility, presence of mind, power of recuperation) which saves in case of accident' or 'indifference due to masturbation, pessimism congenital, a sense of the ridiculous, sudden fastidiousness in some detail, experience', or 'absinthe the cerebral impotentising (!!) drink of chastity'.[38] As Budgen rightly observes, 'Joyce regarded the Circean metamorphosis in this double sense of a corruption of the mind . . . and the downfall of the body' and adds that 'the real saviour of Bloom was a spiritual "Moly", a state of mind.'[39] Symbolically the whorehouse represents the moral corruption of the city and, just as syphilis produces general paralysis of the insane, the moral corruption produces a paralysis of the locomotor apparatus of the soul.

The 'nerves' of the city, represented by its communications, appear in the 'Eumaeus' chapter to be severely run down. It is not surprising, seeing that it is one in the morning, that Bloom cannot find a cab, and that in the Great Northern railway station 'all traffic was suspended', but the deficiencies of the communications system mount up; the dredger is 'quite possibly out of repair'; 'the falling off in Irish shipping, coastwise and

---

[36] *Letters* I, 147.   [37] *Budgen*, 234.

[38] *Letters* I, 144, 147–9. Many other possible equivalents for the 'moly' were jotted down in the notesheets (see *Litz*, 25–6).

[39] *Budgen*, 236.

foreign as well' is loudly lamented – 'Right enough the harbours were there only no ships ever called'; and the facilities for travel available to the citizen are quite inadequate. 'Uptodate tourist travelling,' it is concluded, 'was as yet merely in its infancy.' The conversation is full of accidents, disasters and shipwrecks. All these are only the physical images of the collapse of communications in Dublin. The newspaper report of the funeral has gross errors, the conversation rambles on incoherently with confusions and tall stories, and, as often as not, Bloom and Stephen are at cross purposes. The citizens encountered or referred to are, in one way or another, in a state of debility – Corley chronically broke, Gumley come down in the world, the prostitute an idiot, O'Callaghan an example of 'cultured fellows that promised so brilliantly, nipped in the bud of premature decay', and the keeper of the cabmen's shelter supposedly 'the once famous Skin-the-Goat, Fitzharris, the invincible.' It is this 'decidedly miscellaneous collection of waifs and strays and other nondescript specimens of the genus *homo*' who are the manifestations of the exhausted nerves of the city.

The only organs I have not so far discussed are the kidney, the genitals and the heart, respectively corresponding to the first three chapters of Bloom's day. On the basis of the pattern of the other organs, I take it that these, too, are ironic in their reference. If the function of the kidney is to remove waste products from the blood, and control the body's water and salt contents, Dublin's metaphorical kidney seems not to be in good working order. Because of drought there is a shortage of 'pure fresh water' and eggs; 'flabby' whiffs exude from Larry O'Rourke's bar and cellar; the houses Bloom passes are 'blotchy brown'; the soil in his backyard is 'scabby'; and there is thunder and heaviness in the air. Even Molly's bedroom has a stale smell from yesterday's incense, 'like foul flowerwater'. There are waste products in Bloom's spiritual system, too, souring the day for him. He is weighed down with husbandly cares, especially when he sees Boylan's letter; the pleasure he derives from his daughter's postcard is spoiled by fears; the dream of the Promised Land is blotted out by thoughts that Palestine is now a barren and poisonous desert; and he feels 'age crusting him with a salt cloak'. However, at the end of the chapter, Bloom's excretory organs function, and he emerges from the jakes 'lightened and cooled in limb'. The pattern is repeated throughout the book: Bloom's physical and mental systems operate, even though the metaphorical organs of the city are not functioning very effectively.[40]

The organ of the 'Lotuseaters' chapter is 'genitals' because, amongst other things, the chapter presents an image of the sexual life of the city, ranging from the brutal and commercial transactions of the soldiers 'rotten with venereal disease' and the sluts of the Coombe, to the feeble sentimentality of the 'language of flowers'. But this language is a thin disguise for the sly titillation of Bloom's secret correspondence. Apart from the coarseness of the soldiers and Boylan, the sex life of Dublin is a timid and

[40] Cf. *Budgen*, 81: 'Bloom's moral staying power is, rooted in his body's regularity.'

shameful business in this chapter. Bloom becomes excited when there seems to be a chance of seeing a well-dressed woman step up into her carriage, and indulges in fantasies alien to his usually gentle and submissive nature: 'Possess her once take the starch out of her.' This pusillanimous Peeping Tom-ism – it hardly qualifies for the label 'voyeurism' – appears elsewhere, in various forms, as when Bloom imagines married women confessing to their priest, or thinks of 'glimpses of the moon' seen through an unhooked placket. It is not sexuality which governs the chapter, but tawdry substitutes for sexuality, best represented by the correspondence with Martha, in which Mr Bloom indulges in lukewarm suggestiveness; he does not intend that this shall lead to a meeting, in case the 'usual love scrimmage' should follow. The enervated state of the sexual life of the city is pictorially symbolized by Bloom's vision of 'the limp father of thousands, a languid floating flower.' In the circumstances, it is not surprising that he almost envies the gelded cab-horses.

After 'The Dead', with its image of a city obsessed with the past and inhabited by shades, the placing of the 'heart' of Dublin in Glasnevin cemetery is a natural development. The citizens of *Ulysses* are only too ready to grieve with empty nostalgia for departed leaders or friends or loved ones: 'How many broken hearts are buried here, Simon!' The curious relish for death and the pretences of mourning make Bloom's matter-of-factness (as when he thinks of hearts as 'old rusty pumps: damn the thing else') seem positively healthy. The self-dramatizing emotion of Simon Dedalus, weeping to himself, – 'I'll soon be stretched beside her. Let Him take me whenever He likes' – is contrasted with Bloom's declaration for 'warm fullblooded life'. Whatever the defects of Bloom's moral kidneys and genitals, his heart, unlike that of his fellow-citizens, is in the right place.

As with the Odyssean parallels, some parts of the scheme of the city's 'organs' are more apparent and more meaningful than others, but it is doubtful how much of this would have been perceived by a reader who had not been briefed by Joyce's notes, and how much, even when the physical references have been pointed out, they can profitably affect the reader's response to the novel. Yet Joyce has plainly made some attempt to set his reader's mind working, perhaps unconsciously, with the metaphor of the human body. That, I take it, is why in the first three chapters which relate to organs, the author has introduced explicit images of real kidneys, genitals and hearts: these images are not themselves the points of correspondence,[41] but are deliberately planted clues to Joyce's extended metaphor, just as in *Dubliners*, although he did not mention moral paralysis, he hinted at the correspondence of spiritual and physical incapacity by using the word 'paralysis' in his first paragraph. Does an author need to go further

[41] But commentators continue to suppose that they are. For instance, Claude Jacquet (in 'Les Plans de Joyce pour *Ulysse*') writes, 'Si dans *Calypso* l'organe est le rein, c'est que Bloom mange un rognon à son petit déjeuner' (*Bonnerot*, 63). On this reasoning, one would expect the liver to be the organ of 'Sirens', because Bloom dines on liver and bacon at the Ormond Restaurant.

than this in establishing a submerged metaphor? Joyce would presumably have said 'No!', since it was apropos of this very set of correspondences that he told Budgen, 'I want the reader to understand always through suggestion rather than direct statement.'[42] He seems to have thought that a reader whose imagination had been prompted unobtrusively might respond to the image of the corrupted body politic as to a poetic symbol operating below the conscious level. Yet, as he showed by the assistance he gave to Stuart Gilbert and Carlo Linati (and later to the authors of *Our Exagmination*), Joyce was not averse to supplying critical pointers to ensure that readers did not miss what he had so carefully embedded in his work.[43] My own feeling is that the pattern of 'organs' (like that of the Odyssean parallels, though less importantly) does contribute to the total image of a city whose moral and intellectual life is diseased – with the reservation that, while some parts of the scheme operate powerfully and meaningfully, others (the 'kidney', for instance) are more ingenious than functional.

'Arts'

The significance of the 'Arts', allocated to each chapter except the last, seems to me to have been both exaggerated and complicated. There are, in some places, indications of a correspondence between the 'art' and the mode of presentation of a chapter. For instance, the art, 'Rhetoric', of the newspaper chapter seems to be manifested in the rhetorical modes employed; similarly 'Music', in the Ormond bar, is exemplified in verbal imitations of musical devices; and 'Science', the art of the penultimate chapter, finds a parallel in appropriately scientific language. Such coincidences have suggested a relationship between 'Art' and style or mode of presentation, with the result that vain searches are made for something 'architectural' in the style of the 'Lestrygonians' chapter, something 'mechanical' in the manner of 'Wandering Rocks', or something characteristically 'political' in the form of the 'Cyclops' chapter. Yet however painstakingly such explorations are made, they are bound to find it impossible to discover anything 'historical' in the way we are told of Stephen's school-teaching, anything 'economical' in the presentation of Bloom's breakfast-hour, anything 'navigational' in the style of the chapter set in the cabmen's shelter.

I can perceive no way of interpreting this section of Joyce's notes plausibly and consistently, except to take it literally as referring to arts and sciences spoken of or exemplified in the respective chapters. There is, again, a precedent in *Dubliners*: as the Odyssean scheme is a development of the three-part Dantean pattern of 'Grace', and the 'organs' are an

---

[42] *Budgen*, 21.
[43] Yet, curiously, Joyce objected strongly to the publication of the scheme in Gorman's possession. See H. K. Croessman, 'Joyce, Gorman, and the Schema of *Ulysses*' in *JJM II*, 9–14.

elaboration of the metaphor of paralysis in 'The Sisters', so the 'arts' column relates to the kind of categorization of Dublin's politics, art and religion employed in the three stories of public life. The purpose is similar – to show how, in Dublin, every art and science has become decadent or trivial.[44] As in the other structural schemes, the degree of emphasis varies: some of the 'arts' are treated extensively in the chapters in which they occur – for instance, rhetoric, literature, music, politics – while others, like architecture, mechanics and painting, are almost incidental, according to Joyce's view of their importance in the life of the city.

In the Martello Tower, Irish 'theology' is represented on the one hand by the jibing materialism of Mulligan and, on the other, by the old woman who, as symbol of Ireland, bows her head to the medicineman, the priest and the Englishman. As for Stephen, though 'a horrible example of free thought', he responds to 'the proud potent titles' of the Church and imagines her 'embattled angels' overthrowing the heretics who question 'the consubstantiality of the Son with the Father'. The unbeliever has 'the cursed jesuit strain . . . , only it's injected the wrong way': the supposed believers and the conformists are attached to the material world. In the second chapter, 'history', as known to Dublin, is a matter of meaningless names and dates learnt by schoolboys, or 'a tale like any other too often heard', or the garbled and confused stuff that Mr Deasy uses to justify his prejudices and glorify the Irish of the past. As for 'philology', Stephen is its representative (apart from Kevin Egan's fascination with the word 'postprandial') and he, for all his use of foreign and cant terms and expressions, has a useless expertise: he is embedded in words as in sand:

> A bloated carcass of a dog lay lolled on bladderwrack. Before him the gunwale of a boat, sunk in sand. *Un coche ensablé*, Louis Veuillot called Gautier's prose. These heavy sands are language tide and wind have silted here. (*U* 41/55)

Stephen's philology is at a dead end.

In 'After the Race', the Dubliners form a 'channel of poverty and inaction', and this view of the city's 'economics' is implied in the first chapter of Bloom's day. His financial interests are on a very small scale; he admires Major Tweedy's shrewdness in making a corner in stamps, considers the adequacy of his daughter's weekly wage of twelve and six, wonders whether he might save the half-a-crown return fare to visit her by getting a press pass, and envies Mr Beaufoy for having won three pounds thirteen and six for his prize story. The most sustained economic considerations to enter his head concern the ways by which young men from the country come to Dublin as barmen and finish as grocers. Even his dreams of an investment in a fruit plantation in Palestine, though very limited, are beyond his means. Thus, in Bloom's thoughts, we have an impoverished Dublin parody of the art of 'economics'. The 'botany' and 'chemistry' of Dublin appear together in the 'Lotuseaters' chapter; the first is humbly represented

----

[44] Without explaining the point in detail, Hugh Kenner says that, in Dublin, 'The arts are perverted' (*Kenner*, 239).

by Bloom's dream of happy lethargy among the 'flowers of idleness' in Ceylon, by the language of flowers, by the flowers of froth on the porter which Bloom imagines flooding the country, and by the 'languid floating flower' of his penis; the second is manifested in the drugs and cosmetics of the chemist shop and in such chemical notions as 'Test: turns blue litmus paper red.' The 'religion' of Dublin is appropriately illustrated by a burial service conducted in 'a fluent croak' by the 'muscular christian', Father Coffey. The Dubliners wear their hearts on their sleeves, enjoying the public display of mourning, and indulging in pretentious platitudes about the dead. The word for this kind of religion is suggested by Bloom's thoughts of those who scrape up the earth 'to get at fresh buried females': it is necrophily.

The decline of Dublin 'rhetoric' from the great past of Burke, Grattan and Flood, and the more recent eloquence of John F. Taylor and Seymour Bushe, to the windy verbiage of Dan Dawson and the sensationalism of newspaper headlines is plain enough, and part of the central content of 'Aeolus'; but 'architecture' is less important in Dublin life and is mainly confined to a single paragraph of 'Lestrygonians', where Bloom thinks of Dublin as, apart from a few relics of the distant past, an architectural mess:

> Round towers. Rest rubble, sprawling suburbs, jerrybuilt, Kerwan's mushroom houses, built of breeze. Shelter for the night. (*U* 153/208)

(Modern critics' delight in the Georgian architecture of Dublin is due less to any improvement in the city itself than to a change in taste: a pre-1914 *Pictorial and Descriptive Guide to Dublin and its Environs* is apologetic in tone –

> The street architecture of Dublin is not beautiful, the houses generally being of the uninteresting Georgian period.[45]

Even the modern visitor has little to say in favour of the suburbs.)

According to most judgements, the year 1904 occurred in the middle of a remarkable revival of Irish literature, but the picture of the 'literature' of Dublin in the 'Scylla and Charybdis' chapter is far from flattering. To Stephen all the writers he meets – the poet, the critic, the scholar and the mocking parodist – and with whom he discusses Shakespeare are fit inhabitants of the 'paradise of pretenders' and the level of their achievement is illustrated by lines quoted from the verse of A.E., Louis H. Victory, Padraic Colum and Mulligan (Gogarty) as well as by their critical inanities. On the other hand, there are only two significant references to 'mechanics' in the 'Wandering Rocks'; the machine to indicate the programme-number of the act being performed in a music-hall is a symbol of the quality of Dublin's inventive genius, and the sounds from the powerhouse suggest

---

[45] *A Pictorial and Descriptive Guide to Dublin and its Environs* (London, Ward Lock, n.d.), 9. C. P. Curran confirms the prevalence of this attitude in the Dublin of 1904: 'This was in 1904, years before the Georgian Society began its study of Dublin architecture and before our eighteenth century became a fashion' (*James Joyce Remembered* (London, Oxford University Press 1968), 40).

to Stephen the 'beingless beings' which drive on the physical universe. Dublin is not so much the mechanic as the machine.

It is not surprising that 'music' is more fully treated than any of the other arts, since it was the aspect of Dublin life to which Joyce himself was most responsive. Songs, from operatic arias to patriotic ballads, dominate 'Sirens', but there are also references to instrumental and orchestral music and to a representative selection of the city's musical occasions. It might seem that Joyce's personal relish has interfered with the ironic scheme, if it were not that he is suspicious of the nature of Dublin's musicality and sees it as in decline.[46] Simon Dedalus and Ben Dollard are both past their prime: their singing is a shadow of the past surviving into a world better represented by the two barmaids trilling a song from *Floradora* and Blazes Boylan (who 'can't sing for tall hats') and his ditty about *Those lovely seaside girls*. The older men exhibit the same nostalgia for the songs and singing of days gone by as was manifested in 'The Dead', and to Bloom it seems that their absorption in music has become a 'kind of drunkenness', a way of evading thought and responsibility. In a letter to Harriet Weaver, Joyce spoke of 'the seductions of music beyond which Ulysses travels':[47] of all the seductions of Dublin these were the ones he found most alluring.

For Dublin 'politics', however, he had little but contempt, and they are exposed in Barney Kiernan's pub as a combination of cheap cynicism, blind prejudice, ignorant chauvinism and loud-mouthed violence. This ridicule is fierce and bitter, while the ridicule of 'painting' (extended to include such allied arts as photography and embroidery) is more humorous, being directed against folly rather than vice. At the simplest level, 'painting' begins with Gerty MacDowell's use of cosmetics, in particular the 'eye-browleine' to give 'that haunting expression to the eyes'; and this instance of superficial decoration, inspired by novelettes and responded to with false emotion, is symbolic of the city's 'painting'. In her dream-home Gerty MacDowell would have a photograph of the savage dog which had growled at Bloom in the previous chapter, but it would be sentimentalized into 'grandpapa Giltrap's lovely dog Garryowen that almost talked, it was so human', and the nature of the pictures and engravings which would adorn her 'beautifully appointed drawingroom' is indicated by her appreciation of the picture, torn from a grocer's almanac, which she has tacked up in the outside lavatory,

> the picture of halcyon days where a young gentleman in the costume they used to wear then with a threecornered hat was offering a bunch of flowers to his ladylove with oldtime chivalry through her lattice window. You could see there was a story behind it. The colours were done something lovely. She was in a soft clinging white in a studied attitude and the gentleman was in chocolate and he looked a thorough aristocrat. She often looked at them dreamily when there for a certain purpose ... (*U* 338–9/462)

[46] Stanislaus Joyce was equally suspicious: 'They all used to sing. The singing of sentimental ballads was a backwash of that ebbing wave of romanticism, in which poetry and all it is wont to express had degenerated, Tommy Moore assisting, to a drawing-room accomplishment' (*MBK*, 38).

[47] *Letters* I, 129.

For the rest, she enjoys the landscapes in coloured chalks of the pavement artist, and the linoleum with 'artistic standard designs, fit for a palace, gives tiptop wear and always bright and cheery in the home', and dreams of presenting to her favourite priest 'a ruched teacosy with embroidered floral design' or 'an album of illuminated views of Dublin or some place'. She even aspires briefly to paint a picture herself:

> And she could see far away the lights of the lighthouses so picturesque she would have loved to do with a box of paints because it was easier than to make a man . . . (*U* 346–7/473)

There is, of course, quite another aspect of Dublin's taste in the visual arts. Gerty has heard of a gentleman 'that had pictures cut out of papers of those skirt-dancers and highkickers' and Bloom recalls the 'Mutoscope pictures in Capel street: for men only. Peeping Tom.' But for him, too, painting promises a nostalgic sentimentality as he wishes he had 'a full length oil-painting' of Molly as she was the night he kissed her shoulder.

If painting in Dublin is trivial, so too is 'magic', at least as it is represented in Nighttown by Bloom's 'Potato Preservative against Plague and Pestilence', Zoe's dabbling in palmistry and wrinkle-reading, or the 'parlour magic' by which, to the drunken Stephen, a cigarette suddenly appears out of nowhere. The real 'magic' however, is something much more sinister – it is the power to paralyse men's wills and turn them into beasts.[48]

The *Nostos* section of *Ulysses* has only two arts, since Molly's earthy monologue is, appropriately, excluded from the scheme. In the 'Eumaeus' chapter, the declining 'navigation' of Ireland is a recurring theme, and, finally, in Bloom's home, the 'science' of the city is presented, chiefly through Bloom himself, the man of scientific temperament. But however scientific his temperament, Bloom as a scientist is a comical figure. His knowledge is adequately represented by the contents of his bookshelf which include *The Useful Ready Reckoner*, *A Handbook of Astronomy*, *Physical Strength and How to Obtain It* and *Short but yet Plain Elements of Geometry*: Bloom has more knowledge of the sky than of anything else, yet even here astrology intrudes into astronomy, and the guiding light of the moon is converted into a vision of female buttocks. His scientific preoccupations in the past consisted of attempts at squaring the circle (for which he apparently thinks there is a one-million-pound prize) and the imaginary inventions

[48] Phillip F. Herring shows that the 'Circe' notesheets in the British Museum include 'jottings on such diverse subjects as palmistry, fortune-telling by cards, astrology, the language of gesture (fan, parasol, umbrella, handkerchief), botany, pharmacology (and home remedies), common superstititions, Egyptology, the symbolism of jewelry, the Black Mass, demonology, bestialogy, sinistrism (my word), fetishism, and psychophysics' (*Notesheets*, 39). Many of these notes were not used in the chapter, and, of those that were, more occur in the 'hallucinatory' sections to represent figuratively the magic transformation of men into beasts. See also Norman Silverstein's 'Magic on the Notesheets of the Circe Episode' (*JJQ* I (4) (1964), 19–26) and 'Some Corrections and Additions to Norman Silverstein's "Magic on the Notesheets of the Circe Episode" ', by Phillip F. Herring and Norman Silverstein (*JJQ* II (3) (1965), 217–26).

which he adduces 'to prove that his tendency was towards applied, rather than towards pure, science':

> Were these inventions principally intended for an improved scheme of kindergarten?
> Yes, rendering obsolete popguns, elastic airbladders, games of hazard, catapults. They comprised astronomical kaleidoscopes exhibiting the twelve constellations of the zodiac from Aries to Pisces, miniature mechanical orreries, arithmetical gelatine lozenges, geometrical to correspond with zoological biscuits, globemap playing balls, historically costumed dolls. (*U* 643–4/799)

His scientific apparatus is similarly on a small scale: besides 'Sandow-Whiteley's pulley exerciser', he has the prospectus of 'the Wonderworker, the world's greatest remedy for rectal complaints'. Among the means to future wealth that fill his head are 'a prepared scheme based on a study of the laws of probability to break the bank at Monte Carlo', and plans, worthy of the Academy of Lagado, for the utilization of waste paper, ratskins and human excrement. The science of the Dubliner is as unreal, ineffectual, minuscule and inflated as his art.

This account of the 'arts' column in Joyce's notes may seem rather matter-of-fact and literal, but, as far as I can see, it is the only one which consistently tallies with what Joyce wrote, although in a few places the scheme is a little finely drawn. Certain major aspects of Dublin life – religion, rhetoric, literature, music, and politics – would have been impossible to omit in any extensive portrayal of the city; many other 'arts' no doubt came to mind quite naturally once the general pattern had been conceived; but, here and there, the art (architecture, for instance) seems to have been allocated to a vacant rather than to an especially appropriate chapter, and elsewhere Joyce may have been hard put to it to find an art (mechanics?) for the chapter.

The column of 'arts' differs in kind from both the Odyssean parallels and the organs. While the epic reference forms a commentary on the central themes, situations and action of the novel, and the 'organs' compose a metaphor for the corporate life of the city, the 'arts' column is essentially a checklist for the benefit of the author – its effect on the reader is achieved, not by recognition of the scheme, but by his total impression that the condition of all the fields of intellectual endeavour in Dublin has come under scrutiny. In other words, it belongs to that part of Joyce's design which was expressed in his statement to Frank Budgen: 'I want . . . to give a picture of Dublin so complete that if the city one day suddenly disappeared from the earth it could be reconstructed out of my book.'[49] The objection that this is a design for a social historian rather than a novelist has no force when applied to a novel in which the city is presented as a powerful, even a dominant, force in the working out of the action – as the hostile being against which the two protagonists contend.

[49] *Budgen*, 69.

'Colours'

The other columns in Joyce's work-notes seem, in the broadest sense of the word, stylistic, in that they refer to aspects of presentation rather than to contents or structures, and, therefore, discussion of them might be properly postponed to the next chapter. But there is some advantage in considering Joyce's schematic framework as a whole, and, in some respects, the modes of presentation also have structural relevance.

The most curious of these sets of notes are those headed 'Colours', for there are only eight of the eighteen chapters to which colours are attributed, and the connections between the chapters and their respective colours are not immediately clear. As a result, critics have either condemned these notes as arbitrary, or offered explanations so ingenious that, in effect, they repeat the charge of arbitrariness. For instance, of the 'colours' of the three chapters of the *Telemachia*, one critic has this to say:

> The association of the colours – first, white and gold; second, brown; and third, green – appears to be arbitrary, for, as a matter of fact, gold appears only once in the breakfast scene, and then in describing the fillings of Mulligan's teeth! Scarcely an important symbol, especially as green occurs eight times in the same chapter. On the other hand, gold appears no less than nineteen times in the 'Sirens' episode and fifteen in 'Circe', for neither of which a colour symbol is given.[50]

At the other extreme, Hugh Kenner, developing a suggestion initiated by Valery Larbaud,[51] relates the colours to the colours of ecclesiastical vestments. In his discussion of the first chapter, he argues that the relevant colours, white and gold, are displayed in the first six lines of the book (in Mulligan's shaving lather and yellow dressing-gown), and continues,

> When the colours of the sacred vestments are explicitly mentioned some twenty-five lines later, it is in an image of shark-like rapacity forecasting the priest-king-cannibal motifs of the Lestrygonians episode: '. . . his even white teeth glistening here and there with gold points.'

One might wonder what could be less 'shark-like' than even and gold-stopped teeth, or what they have to do with sacred vestments, but a footnote explains:

> Gold (on a white ground) is the generic colour of sacerdotal vestments. With certain exceptions, it may be worn at all masses, except during Advent and Lent and at masses for the dead. The 16th of June, 1904 (St John Francis Regis in the liturgical calendar) is no exception. White is prescribed, with gold optional, because of the feastday of a Confessor.[52]

If such a trivial and imprecise reference was all that Joyce had in mind, why would he have entered it in the columnar scheme of the whole book? And if 'white and gold' are needed because Mulligan parodies the Mass, why are no colours at all given for the brothel chapter in which a black mass

---

[50] *Kain*, 40.   [51] 'The *Ulysses* of James Joyce', *Criterion* I (1) (1962), 101.
[52] *Kenner*, 228.

is celebrated? But the attempt to explain all the colours in terms of liturgical vestments, however industriously pursued, soon breaks down. It gets round the 'grey' in the 'grey, blue' of the 'Nausicaa' chapter by suggesting that it is the colour of twilight subduing 'blue', 'the colour of the Virgin Mary', and struggles past the 'green' of the 'Proteus' chapter, but founders on 'brown' ('Nestor') and 'orange' ('Calypso'), which, it has to confess, are 'nonliturgical'.[53] The notion of simplicity in the explanation of 'orange' is comical:

> As for Orange, suffusing 'Calypso', where the charms of sun-warmed orange-groves of Jaffa impel Mr Bloom's *Drang nach Osten*, the clue is simple. It was the colour of Greek harlots' dresses.[54]

Fortunately, it is not necessary to go to these lengths to explain Joyce's list of colours. Among his literary heroes was Flaubert, every line of whose writings he claimed to have read and pages of whose work he could recite by heart;[55] he could not have been ignorant of Flaubert's remark, recorded by the Goncourts, about his methods of composition:

> When I write a novel, I have in mind rendering a colour, a shade. For example, in my Carthaginian novel I want to do something purple. In *Madame Bovary* all I was after was to render a special tone, that colour of the mouldiness of a wood louse's existence.[56]

No-one is led by this to count the occurrences of the word 'purple' in *Salammbô* or the references to the shade of woodlice in *Madame Bovary*. The notion of a relationship between colours and sounds, or colours and styles, was a commonplace in late nineteenth-century literature, and Joyce was familiar with it. Stephen had read 'Rimbaud on the values of letters' (*SH* 37), and other writers Joyce refers to, like Gautier, employed this particular kind of synaesthesia. Joyce's own early writings not infrequently refer to the colour of words and styles: the word 'wine' made Stephen think of 'dark purple' (*P* 48); a poem recalled outside the library has 'soft long vowels ... shaking the white bells of their waves' (*P* 230); a misquoted line of Nash's poem has 'black vowels' (*P* 237); Newman's prose is 'silverveined' (*P* 179)[57] In *Ulysses* itself Stephen thinks of a song by Yeats as 'Wavewhite wedded words shimmering on the dim tide' (*U* 7/9), and

---

[53] In the Linati scheme, colours are ascribed to every chapter except 'Scylla and Charybdis' and 'Eumaeus'. The colours for some chapters differ from those given in the Gilbert scheme: 'Nestor' is 'chestnut' instead of 'brown', 'Proteus' 'blue' instead of 'green', 'Nausicaa' 'grey' instead of 'grey, blue'. Liturgical colours are totally out of the question here, but I suspect that the Linati scheme represents what Joyce thought he might do rather than what he in fact did.

[54] *Kenner*, 241.   [55] *Budgen*, 181.

[56] *The Goncourts' Journals, 1851–1870*, ed. and tr. Lewis Galantière (London, Cassell 1937), 98.

[57] Cf. 'Words. Was it their colours? He allowed them to glow and fade, hue after hue: sunrise gold, the russet and green of apple orchards, azure of waves, the greyfringed fleece of clouds' (*P* 171). Is it accidental that the listed colour for the sunny scene on the Martello Tower includes 'gold', and that, in 'Nausicaa', the seascape with nightclouds moving up is, according to the scheme, 'Grey, blue'?

images Dante's rhymes as trios of entwining girls, in green, rose, russet, mauve, purple and 'in gold of oriflamme' (*U* 129/175).

One may, like Dr Johnson, who scorned the idea that there was any relationship between scarlet and the sound of a trumpet,[58] deny that any correspondence between colours and sounds or styles exists, but even if the idea is illusory it is widespread and long-established, and in Joyce's formative years was particularly prevalent.[59] It seems probable that, like Flaubert, Joyce was using colour-words as a shorthand to plot out overall effects he wanted to achieve in the styles of the various episodes. There would seem to be nothing very arbitrary in aiming at a general stylistic colour of 'white and gold' for the sunny morning on the Martello Tower, and, provided that one doesn't spend one's time counting the words, the colours Joyce named can seem a rough visual equivalent for the cool, bright atmosphere of the episode. Similarly one can see what an author had in mind who thought a 'brown' style suitable for the classroom, the smoky leather-upholstered study, Stephen's thoughts about the darkness of the soul, and the drab Nestorian wisdom of Mr Deasy; a 'green' style for Stephen's morning walk by the sea; 'black and white' for a funeral; 'red' for the brash and sensational newspaper office; 'grey and blue' for late afternoon and early evening on the beach; and 'white' for an episode set in a hospital. The only difficulty is presented by the colour 'orange' for the first Bloom episode; of course, it is related to Bloom's daydream about the orange-groves of Agendath Netaim, but perhaps the 'orange' was meant rather to characterize the more homely warmth and light of Bloom's morning as compared to the purer, chiller, 'white and gold' of Stephen's.

Joyce's 'Colours' seem primarily interesting for what they reveal of the writer's mode of composition, and its place in the history of synaesthesia. Joyce may have remarked to Larbaud that his chapters (or some of them) had a characteristic colour like the colours prescribed in the Catholic liturgy. It is even likely that, in considering the appropriate colour for each chapter, the author's choice was influenced by the traditional associations of a given colour: as the regal associations of 'purple' must have played a part in Flaubert's choice of that colour to represent the general stylistic qualities of *Salammbô*, so the association of 'blue' with the Virgin may have affected Joyce's notion of the colour appropriate for 'Nausicaa', with the oncoming evening and Bloom's deflation of the romantic tone providing the 'grey'. But as the colours do not all relate to the liturgy or to any other scheme, and as word-counts and other examinations show that there is no way in which a reader could have identified the colours for himself, it seems

[58] *The Rambler* 94.
[59] C. P. Curran confirms Joyce's interest in this fashionable kind of correspondence: 'Huysmans's symbolism of colours fitted in, too, with the Rimbaud sonnet, *Voyelles*, which Joyce would repeat to me. Imitating Rimbaud and *A Rebours*, we would push these fin-de-siècle fancies, as I imagine students were doing in every university town, to the correspondence of colours with the sounds of musical instruments and with the sense of taste, compiling, for example, monochrome meals, tables d'hôte in black puddings and caviare, black sole with Guinness and black coffee' (*James Joyce Remembered* (London, Oxford University Press 1968), 29).

reasonable to suppose that Joyce was merely using a well-established device of stylistic colour symbolism to provide a shorthand for certain unanalysable qualities which he hoped would 'colour' the atmosphere of certain chapters.

'Symbols'

The column of 'Symbols', too, may have been intended as a guide in the process of composition rather than as a list of symbols which a careful reader could identify. Certainly it is surprising that, despite the numerous and exhaustive explanations of the symbolism of the novel, there has been very little detailed examination of the eighteen symbols, one for each chapter, listed by Joyce. The fact is that it is often not easy to determine what Joyce had in mind. Some of the words listed refer to the central figure of a chapter, some to figures or things relatively inconspicuous, and some to notions not explicitly mentioned at all. It is always difficult to analyse or interpret a symbol, but here the first difficulty is to determine what Joyce meant by the heading 'Symbol'.

Reference to the uses of the word and cognate terms in *Ulysses* indicates the nature of the problem. Joyce talks of algebraic symbols, phonic symbols, large letters and figures in advertisements, religious emblems, hermetic symbols like the red triangle on a bottle of Bass and traditional symbols like the anchor tattooed on the sailor's chest. None of these have any apparent relevance to Joyce's column, nor does Bloom's contemptuous dismissal of the literary symbolism represented for him by A.E. and his disciple, Lizzie Twigg. Only three passages look helpful: Stephen's remark that the cracked looking-glass of a servant is a symbol of Irish art; his thought in Mr Deasy's study that coins are symbols of beauty and power; and Seymour Bushe's quoted allusion to the Moses of Michelangelo as 'that eternal symbol of wisdom and prophecy'. All of these suggest that a symbol is a real object which, by its complex nature, function and associations, can represent a complex relationship, concept or intuition. However, none of these is the symbol attributed by Joyce to the chapter in which it occurs. Instead of 'looking-glass', the symbol for 'Telemachus' is 'Heir' – a word which does not occur in the chapter. Mr Deasy's coins are symbols of beauty and power partly because they are gold and silver and include three 'sovereigns' and two 'crowns', but, because they are money, they are also for Stephen 'symbols soiled by greed and misery': in them, many of the themes of the 'Nestor' chapter seem to focus. But the listed symbol is 'Horse'. It is less surprising to find that in the 'Aeolus' chapter the listed symbol is not 'Moses' but 'Editor'.

Yet, in the last two chapters of *Ulysses* (the only two for which there is reliable evidence as to what Joyce intended) the meaning of 'symbol' implied in the three passages fits well enough. Joyce told Frank Budgen in a letter that, in 'Ithaca', Bloom and Stephen 'become heavenly bodies, wanderers like the stars at which they gaze',[60] and this clearly relates to

---

[60] *Letters* I, 160.

the symbol for the chapter – 'Comets'. Comets are referred to only twice, once literally when Bloom and Stephen look up at the night sky and consider, amongst other things, 'the almost infinite compressibility of hirsute comets and their vast elliptical egressive and reentrant orbits from perihelion to aphelion', and once figuratively when the unlikely possibility of Bloom's abandoning his home is considered:

> Would the departed never nowhere nohow reappear?
> Ever he would wander, selfcompelled, to the extreme limit of his cometary orbit, beyond the fixed stars and variable suns and telescopic planets, astronomical waifs and strays, to the extreme boundary of space, passing from land to land, among peoples, amid events. Somewhere imperceptibly he would hear and somehow reluctantly, suncompelled, obey the summons of recall. (*U* 688/858)

The words 'egressive' and 'reentrant' link the first passage to Stephen and Bloom; Bloom opens the garden-door to permit Stephen 'free egress' before 'reentering the passage'. Stephen is 'centrifugal' and Bloom 'centripetal'. As the throwaway, outward bound, passed the homing threemaster, so the artist is setting out on his venture from the known to the unknown and the citizen returning from the unknown to the known. Like two comets, the two men have passed, but their courses do not coincide. Thus the symbol of 'Ithaca' has a real existence in the physical world, and reflects directly the situation and behaviour of Bloom and Stephen.

Another letter to Budgen indicates why the symbol for 'Penelope' is 'Earth'. The chapter, Joyce said, 'turns like the huge earthball slowly surely and evenly round and round spinning',[61] and, although there is no explicit reference to the globe's rotation, the symbol is suggested by the comparison, at the end of the previous chapter, of Molly's position to that of Gea-Tellus, and supported by the continuous circling repetitiveness of her monologue, its 'earthiness', and her repeated praises of the beauty of the natural world. (In his notes for *Exiles*, Joyce similarly identified the wife, Bertha, with 'the earth, dark, formless, mother, made beautiful by the moonlit night, darkly conscious of her instincts.'[62] There is an implied contrast between the symbolic characters of the two last chapters. While the two men in their pursuit of ideals are as erratic, airy and insubstantial as comets (hence the reference to 'the almost infinite compressibility of hirsute comets'), Molly brings the book down to earth with her steadily revolving, self-centred, solid and physical monologue.

This link of contrast between the two symbols suggests the possibility of a similar link with the preceding chapter, since, in Joyce's scheme, the three chapters of the *Nostos* frequently form a triad. The symbol for 'Eumaeus' is 'Sailors', which presumably refers not only to W. B. Murphy, ABS, but also to the 'superannuated old salt' Bloom used to see at Dollymount, to the men lost in the various shipwrecks mentioned, to fictitious

---

[61] *Letters* I, 170.
[62] *Exiles: A Play in Three Acts*, with the author's own notes and an introduction by Padraic Colum (London, Cape 1952), 167.

travellers like Ben Bolt, Enoch Arden and Sinbad, and to a variety of people who are only metaphorically sailors – like Corley who is 'on the rocks', the diseased prostitute referred to as 'the gunboat', and the driver of the roadsweeper, 'the ship of the street'. The emphasis is on the perils of the deep as the men discuss 'accidents at sea, ships lost in a fog, collisions with icebergs, all that sort of thing', but Bloom is more particularly concerned with the plight of husbands who, returning after a long absence, find their wives have taken another man. At one point in the chapter, this concern leads into a recollection of the Tichborne case and, thus, by allusions to a lost heir and a false claimant, involves – for the reader rather than Bloom – Stephen's predicament. Finally, as the two men set out for Eccles Street, Stephen begins to sing the ballad about the cunning of the Sirens, and they walk on talking 'about sirens, enemies of man's reason, mingled with a number of other topics of the same category, usurpers, historical cases of the kind.' The voyages of both men have been threatened by temptations, and their homecomings troubled by usurpers, while Stephen was wrecked in Bella's brothel and rescued by his companion. Now the immediate dangers are past; they are tired and by no means sure of a welcome, but they are together and temporarily at rest. Their situation is thus variously reflected in the real, remembered and metaphorical sailors of the chapter. The shift to the comet symbol in the next chapter, as they briefly move in 'parallel courses', implies that the homecoming is short-lived – that Stephen will now embark on his egressive orbit of exile, while Bloom, although for the moment his course is re-entrant, will pass away from home again on his daily odyssey, subject always to 'the summons of recall'.

If these interpretations of the three last symbols are correct (and for two of them the letters offer confirmation), it seems that for Joyce the listed symbols indicated in some sense the ruling spirit or motif of the chapters, whether they referred to objects or figures important in the story (like the sailors), or comparatively inconspicuous (like the comets), or merely implicit (like the earth). They seem, that is, points of focus lying near the centre of the chapter's content, or towards its circumference, or outside it.

The symbols of the *Telemachia* reveal a similar but reversed order since neither the word 'Heir' nor the idea of inheritance is explicit in the first chapter, 'Horse' appears relatively unimportant in the second, and 'Tide' is an important element in the third. (As most of the symbols in the centre of the novel relate to central figures in the story, it may be that Joyce intended a gradual initial increase in the centrality and weight of the symbols, matched by a corresponding diminution at the end.) Yet, although no reader unassisted by the scheme could have identified 'Heir' as the 'symbol' of 'Telemachus', it is intelligible as a catchword for that aspect of Stephen's symbolic role which is presented in the Odyssean parallel, the Hamlet references, the encounter with the milkwoman and the Father–Son theme. It would be too much to say that the notion that Stephen is deprived of his inheritance is emphasized in any of these, yet it is their accumulated weight which gives full meaning to the closing word 'Usurper' and to later expressions – like 'a dispossessed' and 'the dispossessed son'.

The symbol 'Horse' for the second chapter is more puzzling. The only horses to which attention is drawn are the racehorses of the past whose pictures decorate Mr Deasy's study, and these seem to have no obvious relevance to Stephen or his situation. This is perhaps because we too readily think of racehorses as images of grace, beauty and power: in Stephen's response to the pictures the emphasis is different. He observes the way the horses stand 'in homage, their meek heads poised in air', ridden by 'elfin riders', belonging to various English noblemen or wearing 'king's colours'. Thus, if they are images of grace and power, they are images of these qualities tamed and docile, controlled by figures neither graceful nor powerful, and the servants of their English owners. They may thus represent genius submissive and used for alien purposes: this image is explicit when, in Nighttown, Stephen tells Lynch that 'even the allwisest stagyrite was bitted, bridled and mounted by a light of love.' On the other hand, genius refusing to submit is given an equally equine image in the 'Proteus' chapter when Swift is imagined fleeing from the service of the rabble 'to the wood of madness, his mane foaming in the moon, his eyeballs stars.' In 'Nestor', the pressures are on Stephen to submit to Mr Deasy's worldly wisdom; to apply his talents to the instruction and amusement of schoolboys in order to clear his debts and share the Englishman's proud boast that he always paid his way; to follow Iago's advice, 'Put but money in thy purse', for in this world, as Mr Deasy observes, 'money is power'; to accept the current historical fantasies of Ireland's past and of the decay of England in the hands of Jews; and to act as Mr Deasy's agent in his campaign for inoculation of Irish cattle against foot-and-mouth disease. In the last respect, at least, Stephen is compliant, and, generally, in the chapter, his behaviour is more subdued and respectful than elsewhere. Economic pressure and the circumstances of school could reduce him to the level of a docile horse, submitting quietly to Mr Deasy's control.[63] It is perhaps accidental that Mr Deasy is riding his own hobby-horses, but certainly when he reappears in the 'Circe' chapter he is still on horseback:

> (*A dark horse, riderless, bolts like a phantom past the winningpost, his mane moonfoaming, his eyeballs stars. The field follows, a bunch of bucking mounts. Skeleton horses: Sceptre, Maximum the Second, Zinfandel, the Duke of Westminster's Shotover, Repulse, the Duke of Beaufort's Ceylon, prix de Paris. Dwarfs ride them, rusty armoured, leaping, leaping in their saddles. Last in a drizzle of rain, on a broken-winded isabelle nag, Cock of the North, the favourite, honey cap, green jacket, orange sleeves, Garrett Deasy up, gripping the reins, a hockey stick at the ready. His nag, stumbling on whitegaitered feet, jogs along the rocky road.*) (U 541/675)*

'A dark horse' suggests Mr Bloom,[64] but in this race, where the runners

---

[63] Cf. *Gilbert*, 114: 'The symbol of this episode is the *horse*, noble houyhnhnm, compelled to serve base Yahoos. Stephen, too, is restless beneath the pedagogic yoke.'

[64] Bloom, who is regarded as 'a dark horse' by his fellow citizens (in 'Cyclops' he is so described three times on one page – U 319/435), may be felt to be somehow sharing in Stephen's victory.

include the horses from Mr Deasy's study as well as those involved in that day's Ascot Gold Cup, the riderless steed which wins is Stephen, refusing to be 'bitted, bridled and mounted'. (The winner of the Ascot Gold Cup was Throwaway, and this horse has already been associated with the artist through the throwaway, the leaflet, which has floated out to sea from Dublin.) The symbol 'Horse' colours other thoughts and expressions in the 'Nestor' chapter. It was to the racecourse that Cranly had led Stephen 'to ger rich quick', and, appropriately, the racecourse itself with its bookies, smells, slush, gamblers and cheats, its 'vying caps and jackets' becomes an image of the competitive struggle of the world to put money in its purse. The same conflict is also described as 'the race of the world' in which, Stephen thinks, Sargent would have been trampled underfoot, had it not been for his mother's protection. More importantly, it is from the 'nightmare' of history that Stephen is trying to escape, and the dead metaphor is revived by the form of Stephen's afterthought: 'What if that nightmare gave you a back kick?' Probably, the notion of this symbol was suggested to Joyce by the Homeric 'Nestor, tamer of horses', for Mr Deasy's role in the chapter is to bring Stephen's wild spirit under control and make it a competitor in 'the race of the world'. Again, despite the demonstrable relevance of the symbol to Stephen's situation in Mr Deasy's school, no reader would have identified it without Joyce's assistance, and one can only suppose that it represented for the author a way of operating on the reader, below the conscious level, through a collocation of related images, to focus his apprehension on the second stage in Stephen's liberation.

The 'Tide' of the 'Proteus' chapter is easier to recognize, although perhaps more complex in its relevance. It symbolizes the continual flux and reflux in a universe of continuous change; the sea of life in which Stephen fears to drown; the inevitable approach of death, the westering tide in the blood; the wearying vicissitudes of all worldly things, 'To no end gathered: vainly then released, forth flowing, wending back: loom of the moon.' Traditionally it symbolizes the moment of decision or opportunity, 'a tide in the affairs of men', and on it symbolically arrives the threemaster.

All of the later symbols are similarly complex, although it is not always clear why they have been singled out as the ruling symbols of their chapters. But the symbol 'Nymph' for Bloom's breakfast-hour is obviously appropriate. It refers to the picture which Bloom has cut out, framed, and hung above his marital bed, and which symbolizes the idealization of womanhood by which he is enthralled: in the 'Circe' chapter he tells the Nymph, 'I was glad to look on you, to praise you, a thing of beauty, almost to pray.' It is because the picture is the symbol of Bloom's abasement before the female idea that when the Nymph appears in the brothel he crawls humbly before her and abjectly confesses his offences against the purity which she represents. Significantly, when reality intrudes and he rejects the Nymph and her wishes, he calls after her,

> Eh! I have sixteen years of black slave labour behind me. And would a jury give me five shillings alimony tomorrow, eh? Fool someone else, not me. (*U* 524/662)

The sixteen years of slavery are the sixteen years of Bloom's marriage; he has been enslaved not by Molly, the woman, but by the idealized notion of feminity to which he has submitted voluntarily.

The 'Eucharist', the symbol of the next chapter, is different in the direction of its reference. The symbolic centre has now shifted from Bloom himself to the city through which he moves. Bloom sees the 'eucharist' as the main Dublin drug – taken childishly ('Shut your eyes and open your mouth'), stupefying the communicants with its Latin, and turning them into, 'blind masks'. It has other effects too: on the religious level it gives a 'kind of kingdom of God is within you feel'; on the social level, it makes the communicants feel 'all like one family party' and 'not so lonely'; on the personal level, it sends them out of church feeling 'a bit spreeish' and ready to 'let off steam'. Wine adds an aristocratic touch to the proceedings for those accustomed to Guinness or mineral waters, and, above all, there are narcotic, anaesthetic, soporific effects:

> Blind faith. Safe in the arms of kingdom come. Lulls all pain. Wake this time next year. (*U* 73/99)

It is the symbol which Stephen feared in the *Portrait*:

> I fear . . . the chemical action which would be set up in my soul by a false homage to a symbol behind which are massed twenty centuries of authority and veneration. (*P* 247)

Bloom, unlike the other Dubliners, is not enslaved by the magic of the eucharist: but his involvement in the lotus-eating mood is his own partaking of the city's communion, and his surrender to the sensual attractions of the anticipated bath is presented as a narcissistic eucharist: 'This is my body.'

In 'Hades', for the first time Joyce makes one of his characters the symbol of the chapter. In the 'Correspondences', John O'Connell, the caretaker of the Glasnevin cemetery, is said to be Hades, the god of the underworld, and as 'Caretaker' he is the chapter's symbolic figure. He, not Father Coffey, the croaking clergyman who, as Cerberus, guards the entrance to the grave, is the lord and master of the realms of the dead. He runs it almost like a hotel, saying to Simon Dedalus, 'My dear Simon, . . . I don't want your custom at all', putting his guests at their ease with a funny story, bearing his keys, supervising the proceedings when the latest arrival is shown to the room allocated, and collecting the dockets from the undertaker. The Dubliners with their fondness for mourning[65] – later, Stephen observes that 'sorrow for the dead is the only husband from whom they refuse to be divorced' (*U* 201/273) – treat him with proper respect, since, as Bloom thinks, 'all want to be on good terms with him', while he seems to have 'a sense of power seeing all the others go under first'. Bloom regards

---

[65] In his lecture on Mangan (1907), Joyce referred to the Irish 'love of grief' (*CW*, 186), and, in 'Fenianism: The Last Fenian' (1907), he said that 'the Irish, even though they break the hearts of those who sacrifice their lives for their native land, never fail to show great respect for the dead' (*CW*, 192).

with some admiration and wonder this portly, prosperous man, father of eight children, who presides over the necrophiliac sentimentality of the Dubliners with such good-natured efficiency.

In the remaining chapters of the *Odyssey* proper, the symbols – 'Editor', 'Constables', 'Stratford-London', 'Citizens', 'Barmaids', 'Fenian', 'Virgin', 'Mothers' and 'Whore' – are, with one exception, individuals or groups who are fairly plainly representative of the character of the chapters. The exception is the 'Scylla and Charybdis' chapter, where everything demands a pair of contrasting symbols to represent the two extremes between which Stephen must plot his course. The theme is the duality of the artist's nature, and as the theme is explored in terms of Shakespeare's life and the tension between the home, which wounded him and from which he was exiled, and London where he licked his wounds and produced his creation, the central polarity is well enough symbolized by 'Stratford-London'. The confusion, distraction, inconsistency, incoherence and noisy intemperance of the newspaper office are focused in the person of the 'Editor', and the 'Constables' are thoroughly representative of the coarse physical tone of the 'Lestrygonians' chapter. Bloom's thoughts about the squads of policemen draw together the characteristic themes of the chapter: as one squad leaves the station 'after their feed with a good load of fat soup under their belts', and another returns to it, 'bound for their troughs', they embody the Dubliners' greedy stuffing away of belly-fodder; the brutality of the struggle for survival is represented by police brutality ('Nasty customers to tackle'); and the crude materialism of the city is centred in its police:

> For example one of those policemen sweating Irish stew into their shirts; you couldn't squeeze a line of poetry out of him. Don't know what poetry is even. (*U* 154/210)

There is no group which symbolizes the 'Wandering Rocks' as the constables do the 'Lestrygonians': all the citizens as presented in that chapter are equally barren and devoid of any but the most trivial sense of purpose as they wander about the city's streets on their petty business, and consequently the 'Citizens' as a whole symbolize the spirit of the chapter. The Sirens are well represented by the silly, vulgar and flirtatious 'Barmaids' who draw the men of Dublin to the Ormond Bar, and all the ignorance, falseness, hatred and deceit of the city is focused in the person of the 'Fenian' in Barney Kiernan's pub.

The three symbols, 'Virgin', 'Mothers', and 'Whore', look like another triad, and their appearance in the last stages of Bloom's voyage suggests that they may be related to the weakness of his attitude to women, earlier symbolized by the figure of the Nymph. The link between these three symbols is strengthened by the fact that, in one place at least, each is related to the figure of the Virgin Mary: in 'Nausicaa', the voices from the nearby church praise her as virgin ('the Virgin most powerful, Virgin most merciful'); in the 'Oxen of the Sun' chapter, Stephen speaks of her as mother ('our mighty mother and mother most venerable'); and in 'Circe', she is paralleled to the diseased whore, Mary Shortall, and described by

Virag as the whore of Panther, the Roman centurion. Similar feminine trinities are mentioned in the maternity hospital when Costello declares his readiness to 'dishonest a woman whoso she were or wife or maid or leman', and in 'Circe', when among the inhuman faces crowding round the humiliated Bloom are those of 'the girl, the woman, the whore'. Perhaps the simplest way of relating the three symbols (although each has quite distinct subsidiary aspects) is to say that each is expressive of some element in the composition of Bloom's attitude towards women. He has a sentimental feeling for feminine innocence and purity (as represented, for instance, by his daughter Milly and the Nymph), yet is attracted sexually by young girls: 'I begin to like them at that age. Green apples. Grab at all that offer.' Gerty, like the Virgin Mary 'a beacon ever to the storm-tossed heart of man', satisfies his craving for a young girl and makes him feel young. Similarly Bloom has a particular concern for women as mothers, though oppressed by the thought that he is sonless. In the maternity hospital, he is aware of the conflict – a champion of fertility who has at home 'a seedfield that lies fallow for the want of a ploughshare' – but he is lifted out of his depression partly by the vision of an apotheosized Milly, and partly by his increasingly paternal feeling towards Stephen. Finally, the lecherous side of his attitude towards women is exposed in the 'Circe' episode and related to his masochism: only his commonsense rescues him from a crushing sense of guilt. After these three symbolic experiences, Bloom is ready to return to his Ithaca. Of course, there are other aspects of these symbols. The 'Virgin' is not only Gerty but the Virgin Mary, because Joyce seems to see something characteristically enfeebled and enfeebling in the Roman Catholic devotion to the Madonna, perhaps something spiritually correspondent to masturbation: at least, he told Budgen that 'mariolatry' was one of the ingredients of the style in which Gerty is presented[66] (a similarly sentimental style had been used to describe Stephen's devotion to Mary in the *Portrait*), and, in the Shakespeare discussion, Stephen had declared that the Church was founded on the mystical estate of fatherhood, and 'not on the madonna which the cunning Italian intellect flung to the mob of Europe'. The worship of the Virgin which is proceeding in the nearby church is parodied by Bloom's masturbation, and Gerty's own self-induced orgasm builds up to the chanting of the Litany of Our Lady of Loreto. The subsequent symbols relate equally, though differently, to Stephen's predicament as well as Bloom's, and thus imitate, in the symbolic pattern, the coming together of the two men.

But, that the significance of such an apparently deliberate and structural triad of symbols should be a matter of speculation is itself a comment on this part of Joyce's columnar scheme. All the listed symbols can be justified in one way or another, but the justifications are often laborious and rarely more than plausible. Few are easily recognizable; in many chapters there are other persons or objects which carry as much, if not more symbolic weight; and it is hard to demonstrate that any advantage accrues to the

[66] *Letters* I, 135.

reader when he has been enlightened as to the author's intentions. But it does not follow that the column is merely a record of futile ingenuity. The 'catchwords' seem to stand for certain subtle emphases, images or figures which Joyce hoped to establish and meant to operate subliminally, and possibly a number of them do affect one's subconscious response – for instance, 'horse', 'tide', 'nymph', 'eucharist', 'comets', 'earth'. Yet they are rarely symbols in the ordinary literary sense of the term, but rather cryptic notes for the author's benefit. Like the 'Colours', they contribute more to an understanding of Joyce's processes of composition than to the interpretation of his novel.

'Technics'

The adoption of a different technique of presentation for every chapter in *Ulysses* is, essentially, a development of the stylistic variation in *Dubliners* and the *Portrait*, where the style of each story or episode is controlled by two interacting factors, sometimes one dominant, sometimes the other – its place in the book as a whole and the nature of the incident, situation, character and mood to be represented. In the short stories, the local demands predominate, but both factors are operative: for instance, the first-person narrative of 'Araby' is determined by its place among the stories of childhood and the romantic rhythms and images reflect the boy's emotional condition, while, in 'Ivy Day in the Committee Room', the detached, dramatic manner marks the shift to 'public life' as well as suggesting the superficiality of Dublin politics. In the *Portrait*, the interaction is more sustained, balanced and complex, because all the special stylistic effects (of, for instance, the pandybatting or the vision on the beach) have to be consistent with the general scheme of a style gradually 'growing up'. There is a similar dual control in *Ulysses*: the techniques respond to the particular characteristics of each episode, but there is a general design of increasing stylistic complexity, culminating in 'Circe', and thereafter diminishing. In the next chapter I shall be looking more closely at the local relevance and significance of the 'technics': here I am concerned only with their part in the total shaping of the novel, especially where such shaping is particularly evident, in the parallelled 'technics' of the *Telemachia* ('Narrative-young', 'Catechism-personal', 'Monologue-male') and the *Nostos* ('Narrative-old', 'Catechism-impersonal', 'Monologue-female').

It seems to have been Joyce's intention to make the techniques of his novel progressively more complex, and, then, in the *Nostos*, progressively simpler. Some such intention is suggested in two letters to Harriet Weaver: in the first, dated 6 August 1919, he comments on her dismay at the increasing complexity of his novel, and says that she may 'prefer the initial style much as the wanderer did who longed for the rock of Ithaca', and in the second, dated 12 July 1920, he informs her that 'a great part of the Nostos or close was written several years ago and the style is quite plain.'[67] 'Quite

[67] *Ibid.*, 129 and 143.

plain' is hardly a phrase that many would apply to the styles of the *Nostos* chapters, and yet one can see that they are relatively straightforward when compared to the styles of 'Sirens', 'Cyclops', 'Nausicaa', 'Oxen of the Sun' or 'Circe'. In the reference to the wanderer who longed for Ithaca there may be an implication that Joyce wanted his readers to apprehend their own experience of his novel as a kind of Odyssey – that after struggling through the increasing difficulties of his method, up to the climactic complexity and turmoil of 'Circe', they should feel, on coming to the comparative simplicity and calm of 'Eumaeus', that they had at last reached shore.

But the formal parallelism of the 'technics' of the *Telemachia* and the *Nostos* is the most emphatic indication of Joyce's intention to lead the reader into and out of the complexities of the novel. In the *Portrait* Joyce had already introduced narratives expressive of different ages: one could, for instance, label the technique of the first chapter of that novel 'narrative-boyish', and the technique of the fourth 'narrative-adolescent'; and one might reasonably expect some similar explanation of the 'narrative-young', 'narrative-mature' and 'narrative-old' labels, applied respectively to the 'Telemachus', 'Calypso', and 'Eumaeus' chapters of *Ulysses*. The manner of presentation of the scene in the cabmen's shelter can easily be recognized as 'old': it is garrulous, long-winded, incoherently rambling from one point to another; it is full of clichés, hackneyed turns of phrase, proverbial sayings and wise saws, and has a Polonius-like assumption of the tolerant prudence that comes with age. Equally, the manner of 'Telemachus' is plainly 'young' in the sense that the manner of the closing sections of the *Portrait* is young; it is often very reminiscent of the earlier novel. The somewhat lush, romantic, emotive, introverted style of Stephen's dream of his mother – 'Silently, in a dream she had come to him after her death, her wasted body within its loose brown graveclothes giving off an odour of wax and rosewood, her breath, that had bent upon him, mute, reproachful, a faint odour of wetted ashes' – is akin, for all the difference of content, to his image of the body of his beloved – 'Yes, it was her body he smelt: a wild and languid smell: the tepid limbs over which his music had flowed desirously and the secret soft linen upon which her flesh distilled odour and a dew' (*P* 238). 'Wavewhite wedded words shimmering on the dim tide' in *Ulysses* echo the moment in the *Portrait*, when Stephen imagines words 'lapping and flowing back and ever shaking the white bells of their waves in mute chime and mute peal and soft low swooning cry' (*P* 230). The self-dramatizing self-pitying manner which is used to present Stephen's mood when, in the *Portrait*, he thinks,

> To him she would unveil her soul's shy nakedness, to one who was but schooled in the discharging of a formal rite rather than to him, a priest of eternal imagination, transmuting the daily bread of experience into the radiant body of everliving life (*P* 225),

is used again, in *Ulysses*, when he feels ignored by the old milkwoman:

She bows her old head to a voice that speaks to her loudly, her bonesetter, her medicineman; me she slights. To the voice that will shrive and oil for the grave all there is of her but her woman's unclean loins, of man's flesh made not in God's likeness, the serpent's prey.   (*U* 12/16)

The passages from *Ulysses* are handled more subtly, but the similarities are enough to suggest that, in this first chapter, Joyce was aiming at a technique, not far removed from that of the closing chapter of the *Portrait*, and devised to represent the consciousness of the young artist, compounded of touchiness, resentment, disappointment, frustration, remorse, bitterness, self-pity, and uncertainty as to whether his own feelings and attitudes are genuine or part of a pose. But one cannot sum up a consciousness with a string of abstract nouns, however extended: they are still too few, too discrete and too imprecise. What Joyce had done in *Dubliners* and the *Portrait* was to try to capture the impalpable essence of experience, temperament or mood through style: what he does in *Ulysses* is to use similar stylistic devices more confidently, so that the *quidditas* of Stephen is presented, in the few pages of 'Telemachus', more exactly, more variously and more numinously than in the much longer closing chapter of the *Portrait*.

The same is true of Bloom's first chapter, the technique of which is 'narrative-mature'. One can extract from it a list of nameable aspects of maturity (allowing for Joyce's ironic use of the term): the relish of minor sensual pleasures like eating or excreting; the uneasy awareness of approaching age; the husbandly submissiveness and paternal sentimentality; the abandonment of ambitions and the nursing of little daydreams; the mood of resignation which converts the sound of the bells to 'Heigho! Heigho!'; the prudence and tolerance. But what creates the image of Bloom's mature consciousness is the way in which it is presented, where all these and many other elements are combined by words and rhythms in an organic whole. The two chapters which set in motion Stephen and Bloom also introduce us to two contrasted style-complexes, each of which will undergo transformations during the course of the day, will reach a pitch of extravagance and near-hysteria in the brothel, and will, thereafter, progressively lose their complexity and nervous tension. What happens to them is, in effect, what happens to the two protagonists: the styles are structural.

The 'personal' and 'impersonal' catechisms of 'Nestor' and 'Ithaca' are apparently at odds with the relationships presented in these chapters. Nothing seems less 'personal' than Stephen's questioning of his pupils or his dialogue with Mr Deasy, and nothing that happens to him during the day is more 'personal' than his conversation with Bloom. But the techniques are purposefully and rightly in contrast with the contents. Stephen's manner with the schoolboys and the schoolmaster is detached, but covers an intense self-questioning prompted by the answers of the boys or the shallow wisdom of the old man. He questions himself about the nature of the past and of history, about the tradition of Irish comic-writers, about the soul, about mother love, about his role in the school and in the joust of life, about God – and every question leads to a painful examination of himself, of his role, and of his destiny. The technique reflects the quasi-spiritual catechism beneath the surface. In 'Ithaca', on the other hand, while he chats to Bloom, the 'impersonal' technique reflects the comparative calm of spirit as the two men agree or disagree, question each other, and declare their allegiances. They are able to have a personal relationship because neither is obtruding his personality on the other and because for both the inner, personal turmoil is temporarily quiet. Here, too, the parallelism of techniques is structurally significant.

The monologues of Stephen in 'Proteus' and Molly in 'Penelope' seem more arbitrarily associated by their labels in the column of 'Technics'. There are very marked differences between the techniques of the two chapters, but these are hardly described or accounted for by labelling one 'male' and the other 'female'. Moreover, the parallel arrangement of techniques in the opening and closing triads raises the question why the *Telemachia* should end in a male monologue and the *Nostos* (and the whole novel) in a female monologue. To answer such questions it is necessary, I think, to forget about the physical sexual differentiation between Stephen and Molly, and to see them rather as representatives of two forces in human life – forces which Joyce seems to have thought of as masculine and feminine principles.[68] The first is expressed in the compulsion to seek truth, in the questing, self-doubting spirit, challenging its human limitations, active, combatant, aspiring, and, in consequence, troubled, disillusioned, disappointed, frustrated, and, at times, despairing: Stanislaus Joyce's Yeatsian pun the 'world-troubling semen',[69] sums it up. The feminine principle, on the other hand, accepts life as it is, makes the best of things, is not profoundly disturbed by hope or disappointment, and, though involved in contradictions, is either unaware of them or brushes them aside as of no moment. (It is Stephen, not Bloom, who best exemplifies the male principle, because mixed with Bloom's masculine moral striving is a resilient feminine element: as Dr Dixon is supposed to say in the 'Circe' chapter, 'Professor Bloom is a finished example of the new womanly man.') The technique of the monologue in 'Proteus' is expressive of the struggling, divided and weary spirit, grasping at insoluble philosophical or theological problems, divided to the point where the monologue repeatedly becomes a dialogue between a scornful accusing voice and a voice offering hesitant and feeble excuses, expressing weary disgust with the world in languid rhythms and repeated phrases of boredom, exhaustion and death. But in Molly's soliloquy, the voice presses unhesitatingly on, one thing leading to another, ignoring incompatibles, untroubled by abstractions, syntax or punctuation, and content to go on living despite passing griefs and resentments.

The paralleled sequences of 'technics' in the *Telemachia* and the *Nostos* thus seem designed not to mark similarity or recurrence, but to emphasize contrast and countermovement. In the first three chapters the focus of attention on Stephen narrows from the suspicious relationship with his so-called 'friends', to the detached contacts and self-questionings at the

[68] See passage from *Stephen Hero* quoted on page 338.   [69] *Letters* III, 104.

school, and finally to his isolation on the beach. Stephen's bitterness and frustration are only superficially associated with his companions or job: their causes are deep in his own mind and temperament, and it is there that he must trace and subdue them. The narrowing focus is represented and intensified by the gradual increase in the proportion of interior monologue. Conversely, in the last three chapters, Stephen moves out of focus, first, blurred by the pompous jargon of 'Eumaeus', then observed from a scientific distance, and finally reduced to a figment in Molly's erotic fantasies. Similarly, the tensions and strains which have been the motive-power of the whole novel are relaxed in the verbose and smug manner of 'Eumaeus', stripped of passion and energy in the factual question-and-answer of 'Ithaca', and eventually submerged in the undifferentiated, undiscriminating flow of existence of Molly's nocturnal reverie. While Stephen's soliloquy on the beach had drawn everything to focus in his self-tormenting isolation, Molly's soliloquy reduces everything and everybody to the basic common factors of human nature and experience.

*

The apparent distinction observed at the beginning of this chapter between those columns which seemed to relate primarily to total structure and those which seemed to relate primarily to methods of presentation has proved to be misleading. In a novel, ordered sequence is generally a feature of all central structures. But the Homeric order governs only the first four and the last three of the Odyssean parallels; in the 'Organs' column only the final shift to the general physical structures of nerves, skeleton and flesh suggests a significant order; there is no sequential pattern in the 'Arts' or the 'Symbols'; and the only column which relates to some ordered process in the novel is 'Technics' – and even there the broad, general design is dominated, except for the beginning and the end, by stylistic adaptation to the specific character of each chapter. There is thus no possibility that Joyce began with such a scheme and, as it were, pinned a story to it, shaping the story according to the demands of the scheme. On the contrary, it is obvious that, like any other novelist, he began by conceiving the organic principle, action and basic structure of his book, and that these controlled and determined the columnar scheme. Basically the columns represent various areas of reference, imagery, content and manner, materials from which were to be worked into the fabric of each chapter (where possible and appropriate) to enrich its significance. If, as seems likely, Joyce had this scheme, or some version of it, before him as he wrote, then he was usually more interested in the horizontal relationships than in the vertical sequences. It is of no special consequence that, under 'Title', 'Cyclops' follows 'Sirens' and precedes 'Nausicaa', or that, under 'Organ', 'Muscle' comes between 'Ear' and 'Eye, Nose': what is important is that the encounter in Barney Kiernan's pub should be enriched by the complex of meaning, manner and association represented by the horizontal rank, 'Cyclops – The Tavern – 5 pm – Muscle – Politics – Fenian – Gigantism – Noman; I. Stake; Cigar. Challenge; Apotheosis.' Thus the columnar notes often contribute more importantly to the *consonantia* of the individual chapters than to that of the novel as a whole – except where the patterns reinforce and elaborate the basic structural features in the double beginning, the central pause in the action, the developing relationship in the cabman's shelter and the kitchen, and the final dissolve as the protagonists and their problems and concerns are subsumed in the consciousness of Molly Bloom. But the two kinds of *consonantia* are not entirely separate: the fact that each chapter includes in its organization elements of common patterns ensures a degree of consistency and coherence underlying the apparently extreme variety of the manners of presentation.

The columnar notes do not in themselves cover the structure and patternings of the novel, or of the chapters. They include no mention of many important structural features. They do not mark the persistence of certain thoughts, memories and images – of the dead mother or the self-poisoned father. They ignore recurring motifs – for instance, the motif of the Mass, introduced by Buck Mulligan's performance on the Martello Tower, considered critically by Bloom in church, parodied in the physical eucharist offered by Bloom's body in its bath, dominating Stephen's image of the role of the artist's miracle of transubstantiation, blasphemed against in the Black Mass of the brothel chapter, and, perhaps, finally figured in the two men's partaking of cocoa, the 'massproduct'.[70] They do not mention the literal, symbolic and thematic keys, which Bloom forgets and Stephen surrenders, which appear in the symbol of the Isle of Man used for an advertisement of the House of Keyes, and which are related to the central action when the incompetent keyless artist is rescued by the 'competent keyless citizen'. More surprisingly, they make no reference to such quasi-religious identifications as Bloom-Elijah, Bloom-Christ, Lynch-Judas, and Stephen-Lucifer, or to the consubstantiality of Father and Son. Above all, they do not indicate the central structural principle – the convergence of citizen and artist, the near-encounters in the newspaper office, the library and the bookstalls, and the relationship which begins in the maternity hospital and develops in the brothel, the shelter and the kitchen.

It appears, then, that Joyce's notes are less a diagram of the novel than a set of partially cryptic memoranda referring to certain submerged patterns to be kept in mind by the author but not necessarily traced consciously by his readers. Nevertheless Joyce certainly hoped that his readers would, at various levels of awareness, respond to these submerged patterns: his willingness to show his notes to chosen commentators implies that he was anxious to encourage such a response. The consequences of the publication of the notes have been very mixed: the relationship of some notes to the work itself is so obscure as to have been a source of mystification rather than elucidation, while others, in particular the Odyssean parallels and the

[70] W. Y. Tindall's interesting interpretation of this word is that ' "Massproduct," the key word, means three things: the cocoa is mass-produced for the trade; as the product of a symbolic Mass, it is the sacrament; and it suggests the masses for whom it is produced' (*James Joyce: His Way of Interpreting the Modern World* (New York, Scribner 1950), 29.

'technics', have provided essential elements of the critical terminology in which the book is discussed. If it is impossible to regard the scheme as the complete framework on which *Ulysses* was constructed, it is equally impossible to regard it merely as evidence of Joyce's obsessional and trivial ingenuity.

Its true role may be suggested by comparison with the *Portrait*. In that novel there are two contrasted principles in the composition of the *consonantia* – the process of development in the growth of the potential artist, and the static complex of permanent traits, which react to changes in situation while remaining themselves essentially unchanged. Somewhat similarly, in *Ulysses*, there are some aspects of the structure (especially the converging central action) which emphasize the changes produced in Stephen and Bloom by the events of this particular day, and other aspects (such as the patterns recorded in the notes) which are static in that their function is to relate the characters, incidents, situations and environment to various categorical and analytical schemes of what is permanent in human experience, society and arts. But in *Ulysses* the relation between the two aspects is much more involved than in the *Portrait*. On the one hand, the principle of development and change is less emphatic and less climactic: the changes produced in the two men are symbolic and representative of the fruitful interaction of opposites rather than indicative of a final transformation of their lives and natures, and, being representative, are thus seen in part as expressive of something constant in human relationships. On the other hand, the schematic patterns include, especially in the Odyssean parallels, patterns of recurring process. Thus, the two aspects of the structure are more closely interwoven than in the *Portrait*, and, although the dominant and organic principle is still that of process and development to which the static patterns are subordinate and supplementary, the distinction between the two is less heavily marked.

There is nothing unusual in the occurrence of dual or multiple principles in a novel's structure: what is characteristic of Joyce is the degree of elaboration in the subordinate patterns – an elaboration beginning in the symmetrical groupings of the *Dubliners* stories and culminating in *Finnegans Wake*, where the two principles become one, and what is constant is cyclic development. Joyce's fondness for such structures is related to his apprehension of experience as the product of interacting polar opposites. His disposition, as artist, inclined him to approach the problems of combining complexity and order, whether in form or content, by establishing opposed forces or currents. In *Ulysses* the static patterns, such as 'Organs' and 'Arts', relate to the paralysed city; the developing patterns, such as the Odyssean parallels and 'technics', relate to the principles of real or potential growth. Whereas in the earlier books the movement of the artist is directly contrasted with the city's stagnation, in *Ulysses* Bloom, structurally as well as thematically, is a bridge between the two: he belongs to the city but not to its paralysis, his cometary orbit is within the city's system but is a constant cyclic moral activity. The novel's structure, like its content, grows out of the earlier opposition of city and artist, but reflects a much more complex relationship between them.

Chapter 4 *Ulysses:* techniques and styles

Whatever may be said of Joyce's skill in the manipulation of language, no great claims can be made for *Ulysses* as a novel unless the stylistic and technical innovations can be shown to be functional, and necessary to the articulation of some new and important vision of life. The more attention a book requires, the more it has to justify. The initial difficulties of reading the interior monologues are beside the point: any plausible and detailed image of mental processes must involve allusions, transitions and associations at first sight obscure, and in *Ulysses* such obscurities can usually be dispelled by a second or third reading or by the use of works of reference. In fact, what is remarkable about the early interior monologues is their clarity and comprehensibility. Joyce succeeds in representing the apparently random and unpredictable movements of the mind, shifted from one course to another by casual links, by the mood of the moment, or by passing sense impressions, and yet, at the same time, in creating sharp and coherent images of the complex natures of Stephen and Bloom. So convincing are the images that many readers are persuaded to recognize in what they are reading the processes of their own minds, and to regard the interior monologue as a kind of mental taperecording. It then becomes easy to see the novel as consisting of some sections which realistically record what Stephen and Bloom and their acquaintance did, said, thought and felt, and of other, later, sections in which quite unrealistic styles are arbitrarily adopted. This is a fundamental misconception of the process of a book which creates its own stylistic conventions from beginning to end, and in which the developing and declining complexity of these conventions is deliberate and significant.

The artificiality of the interior monologues is evident. Consider three passages where Stephen, Bloom and Molly think about death, among other things. Stephen is watching the cocklepickers on the beach:

> Across the sands of all the world, followed by the sun's flaming sword, to the west, trekking to evening lands. She trudges, schlepps, trains, drags, trascines her load. A tide westering, moondrawn, in her wake. Tides, myriadislanded, within her, blood not mine, *oinopa ponton*, a winedark sea. Behold the handmaid of the moon. In sleep the wet sign calls her hour, bids her rise. Bridebed, childbed, bed of death, ghostcandled. *Omnis caro ad te veniet.* He comes, pale vampire, through storm his eyes, his bat sails bloodying the sea, mouth to her mouth's kiss. (*U* 44/59–60)

Bloom's thoughts are prompted by Mr Kernan's praise of the language of the Anglican burial service:

> Mr Kernan said with solemnity:
> —*I am the resurrection and the life*. That touches a man's inmost heart.
> —It does, Mr Bloom said.
> Your heart perhaps but what price the fellow in the six feet by two with his toes to the daisies? No touching that. Seat of the affections. Broken heart. A pump after all, pumping thousands of gallons of blood every day. One fine day it gets bunged up and there you are. Lots of them lying around here: lungs, hearts, livers. Old rusty pumps: damn the thing else. The resurrection and the life. Once you are dead you are dead. That last day idea. Knocking them all up out of their graves. Come forth, Lazarus! And he came fifth and lost the job. Get up! Last day! Then every fellow mousing around for his liver and his lights and the rest of his traps. Find damn all of himself that morning. Pennyweight of powder in a skull. Twelve grammes one pennyweight. Troy measure.   (*U* 97–8/133)

Death crosses Molly's mind from time to time, but she rapidly dismisses such morbid thoughts:

> ... well its a poor case that those that have a fine son like that theyre not satisfied and I none was he not able to make one it wasnt my fault we came together when I was watching the two dogs up in her behind in the middle of the naked street that disheartened me altogether I suppose I oughtnt to have buried him in that little woolly jacket I knitted crying as I was but give it to some poor child but I knew well Id never have another our 1st death too it was we were never the same since O Im not going to think myself into the glooms about that any more ...   (*U* 737–8/926–7)

Naturally the content of the three consciousnesses differ: Stephen's response to death is poetic and morbid, Bloom's materialistic and down-to-earth,[1] and Molly's sentimental yet dismissive of depressing thoughts. But the monologues are not recordings of consciousness; they are verbal representations of it, and consciousness consists of much more than words. When William James spoke of 'a stream of consciousness' he was referring to a psychological process with certain verbal aspects: the interior monologue, as used by Joyce, is a literary convention which may be variously modified to represent the processes of different minds or different states of consciousness. Moreover, the conventions in *Ulysses*, besides being verbal, often exist only on the page, or for the reader's inner ear. If one listens to Miss Siobhan McKenna's excellent reading of Molly's closing monologue,[2] what one hears is not a woman thinking but a woman talking to herself, because, in order to read aloud what Joyce has put on the page, Miss McKenna has to introduce what Joyce deliberately excluded – the pauses and intonations conventionally indicated by punctuation – while it is quite

---

[1] Erwin R. Steinberg has shown in detail how the sentence patterns of Bloom's and Stephen's monologues reflect the characterising features of their minds ('Characteristic Sentence Patterns in "Proteus" and "Lestrygonians" ' in *New Light*, 79–98).

[2] *James Joyce's 'Ulysses': Soliloquies of Molly and Leopold Bloom*, read by Siobhan McKenna and E. G. Marshall (Caedmon Literary Series, TC 1063).

impossible to read words like 'dont', 'itd' and 'wouldnt' in a way that responds to the missing apostrophes. Both the absence of punctuation and the long succession of loose sentences are conventions to suggest to the eye and inner ear of the reader some aspects of Molly's mental rhythm – a slow continuous flow in which one thought or feeling or sensation leads on to another, each as it were replacing what has gone before, so that Molly is unaware of inconsistencies or contradictions; thus, the final turning of her thoughts to her husband is a symbolic obliteration of the other men who have passed through her mind.[3]

Punctuation and syntax are only the most obvious stylistic features of the monologues. The passage from Stephen's monologue is poetic, full of literary imagery and allusion, but it does not tell us that Stephen thought in poetry: it tells us that his experience is of a kind best suggested by a somewhat highly-coloured poetic style. The poetry which his conscious mind is capable of producing and which emerges from his mood is illustrated by the self-conscious closing words – 'mouth to her mouth's kiss' – which is different from and inferior to the rest of the passage and closer in its immature poeticizing to the 'Villanelle of the Temptress'. As yet his mind is that of a potential artist, at the moment oppressed by thoughts of death and failure and in a highly emotional state. The words of the monologue are not his words, but the words chosen by Joyce to express the character's experience and condition – just as they were in the third-person narrative of the *Portrait*. Of course, words and literature are particularly operative in Stephen's consciousness:[4] the allusion to the expulsion from Eden, the Homeric phrase and the Latin tag presumably pass through his conscious mind, but it is not always easy to distinguish between what words are present in his consciousness, and what represent it: does, for instance, the succession of verbs – 'schlepps, trains, drags, trascines' record his search through several languages for *le mot juste*, or does it represent his sense of the universal movement towards death 'across the sands of all the world'? The distinction is not hard and fast, because the mind represented is itself often consciously engaged in finding verbal equivalents for its experience, while Joyce's handling of the interior monologue creates an image of the mind, through language, imagery and rhythms appropriate to it, and thus articulates what is itself not fully articulate. Out of Joyce's mind comes this paragraph providing an image of an episode in Stephen's consciousness: out of Stephen's mind the episode produces a line of self-conscious verse.[5] Once the representational character of these early monologues is recognized,

[3] The convention seems to have been suggested by Nora Joyce's letters. Remarking on them in a letter to Stanislaus, Joyce asked, 'Do you notice how women when they write disregard stops and capital letters?' (*Letters* II, 173).

[4] Joyce told Larbaud that the reader 'will know early in the book that S.D.'s mind is full like everyone else's of borrowed words' (*Letters* I, 263).

[5] Moreover, as Joseph Prescott has shown, the verse is largely indebted to Douglas Hyde's 'My Grief on the Sea' in *Love Songs of Connacht* (1895) ('Notes on Joyce's *Ulysses*', *Modern Language Quarterly* XIII (1952), 149–62).

it is easier to follow the novel's progress to other and more unusual forms of representation.[6]

In Bloom's thoughts on death, the abrupt, comic, downright, colloquial style is quite unlike his ordinary way of speaking – that is why it differs fundamentally from the speech of Mr Jingle in *Pickwick Papers*, to which it has often been compared. It is not an automatic product of Bloom's mind, but a compact and subtle style, devised by Joyce, to represent the current state of Bloom's consciousness, involving an unexpressed mockery of Mr Kernan's solemnity, a genially materialistic view of death, a suspicious rejection of religious comforts, some irrelevant scraps of information, some familiar clichés, and some old saws and jokes. Unless this is recognized, difficulties are likely to arise when the reader reaches the 'Sirens' chapter and is faced with distortions and confusions of words and sense which cannot be supposed to have emanated directly from Bloom's mind:

> Up the quay went Lionelleopold, naughty Henry with letter for Mady, with sweets of sin with frillies for Raoul with met him pike hoses went Poldy on. (*U* 274/372)

Here there is no mistaking that some kind of stylistic convention is at work, but it is an intensification of the mode of the earlier monologues rather than something entirely new. The elements in it are intelligible enough. The lolloping rhythm suggests Bloom's characteristic walk, earlier mocked by the newsboys; the compound 'Lionelleopold', indicates his self-identification with the hero of the opera *Martha*, whose aria, sung by Simon Dedalus, has reminded Bloom of his first meeting with Molly ('*When first I saw that form endearing*') and troubled him with the fear that he has lost her ('*Come, thou lost one!*') – besides recalling his clandestine correspondent, Martha Clifford; in another role, he is Henry, the name under which he conducts his epistolary flirtation with Martha, who, in her last letter, has called him 'naughty', and to whom he has just written a letter beginning, familiarly, 'Dear Mady'; together with his letter for Mady, he carries with him the book, *Sweets of Sin*, which he has bought for his wife. There is further confusion in his emotional state, since he has made a mental identification of Raoul, the triumphant lover of *Sweets of Sin*, with Blazes Boylan, and has pictured Molly, like the heroine of the novel, awaiting her lover in her

---

[6] According to Stuart Gilbert, Joyce said that, from his point of view, 'it hardly matters whether the technique in question is "veracious" or not' – once it had served his purpose (*Gilbert*, p 28). Erwin Steinberg, in a minutely detailed examination of Joyce's 'stream-of-consciousness technique' (he is referring, in particular, to 'Proteus' and 'Lestrygonians') says that it 'certainly does not provide an "exact reproduction" of thought or "the total contents of thought" as some critics have claimed; it *simulates* the psychological stream of consciousness' (*Steinberg*, 255). For the purposes of his analysis, Steinberg differentiates between various kinds of mental process, such as stream of consciousness, stream of thought, internal monologue, soliloquy etc. (*Steinberg*, 255): I recognize the need for such differentiation for his purposes, but for mine a simpler discrimination is sufficient, and I therefore use 'interior monologue' for any of Joyce's conventional literary representations of the processes of the mind, and 'stream of consciousness' only for the psychological process.

'frillies'; but, having himself been sexually excited by reading of the meeting between Raoul and his mistress, Bloom is also vicariously Raoul. Finally a more realistic memory of his relationship with his wife is recalled by her mispronunciation of 'metempsychosis' (and this sentence illustrates the application of the term to Bloom's own experience) and by the half-affectionate, half-patronizing pet-name she has for him, Poldy. Thus this one sentence weaves into the rhythm of Bloom's walking-pace the emotional confusion of his mood, and the conflicting images of himself as sad romantic lover, shy writer of titillating letters, masterful enjoyer of voluptuous women, cuckold and subservient husband. The complexity of the human mind is such that many conflicting images can coexist in it, but plainly the sentence itself was never in Bloom's consciousness: probably he would not even have been able to understand it. It is a conventional representation of the involved emotions stirred up in him by his experience in the Ormond Restaurant.

'Telemachus'

Even in the early chapters, the handling of the interior monologue varies subtly in response to mood and to the specific function of the chapter in the novel as a whole. The proportion of monologue increases in the three chapters of the *Telemachia*, as the focus of attention narrows to Stephen's introspection, and its character develops. The interior monologue is introduced almost tentatively as though the reader is to be gradually accustomed to its conventions. In the opening lines of the novel Stephen is not present, and when he arrives at the top of the Martello Tower his state of mind is particularized only by implication:

> Stephen Dedalus, displeased and sleepy, leaned his arms on the top of the staircase and looked coldly at the shaking gurgling face that blessed him, equine in its length, and at the light untonsured hair, grained and hued like pale oak. (*U* 1/1)

Formally the sentence appears to offer the author's description of Mulligan; it is only because the description follows immediately the statement about Stephen's displeasure that we infer that the image of Mulligan as a kind of dissolute monk is in Stephen's mind. Similarly, when the account of Mulligan's echoing whistle is interrupted by the single word 'Chrysostomos', we suppose that the word must be in Stephen's mind because there is no other way of accounting for its abrupt interpolation. But the word is an unspoken comment rather than monologue: it is a kind of associative reaction, in part suggested by the sound of the word 'Christine', in part a dry application of the Greek 'golden-mouthed' to the gold stoppings in Mulligan's teeth, and in part a reference to St John Chrysostom, one of the founders of the Catholic doctrine of transubstantiation which Mulligan is parodying. The glimpse into Stephen's mind is momentary, and yet illustrative of his responsiveness to words, his interest in languages, and his

176 Ulysses: *techniques and styles*

readiness to relate his experience to figures from history, literature or theology. When, a little later, we are for the first time unmistakably taken into his consciousness, the entry is made in the traditional mode of a descriptive statement using the third person and the past tense: 'Pain, that was not yet the pain of love, fretted his heart.' The word 'yet' implies the presence of an author who knows more than his character. The form is traditional, but the language and rhythms suggest violent emotional strain: 'A bowl of white china had stood beside her deathbed holding the green sluggish bile which she had torn up from her rotting liver by fits of loud groaning vomiting.' Not until Stephen looks into the cracked mirror held out to him by Mulligan does interior monologue briefly appear: 'As he and others see me. Who chose this face for me? This dogsbody to rid of vermin. It asks me too.' Two short unspoken comments ('Parried again. He fears the lancet of my art as I fear that of his. The cold steelpen', and 'Cranly's arm. His arm')[7] suggest the latent suspicion and hostility behind the conversation with Mulligan, and lead to the first passage of any length directly representing Stephen's thoughts: Mulligan's offer to give Haines a ragging calls up the memory of an earlier ragging, whose crude horseplay is ironically juxtaposed in Stephen's mind with Mulligan's lofty talk of hellenizing Ireland. Yet this is still a very uncomplicated presentation of the psyche, no more, in fact, than a remembered scene vividly recalled, and Stephen's feelings are still described in the traditional way, though in painfully extravagant language, when he is said to be 'shielding the gaping wounds which the words had left in his heart'.

It is not until Stephen is left alone on the top of the tower that a prolonged interior monologue begins. Mulligan has gone down the stairs singing, 'Who will go drive with Fergus now', and the words of the song colour Stephen's impressions as he looks across the sea, phrase-making. 'The shadows of the wood' become the 'woodshadows' floating past him; 'white breast of the dim sea' is remembered entirely from Yeats; and the structure of the song itself provides an image of the wind-ripples on the water 'merging their twining chords'. But the song has deeper significance for Stephen: he had sung it to his dying mother, and recalls how she had wept at the words, 'love's bitter mystery'. Consequently his vision of Dublin Bay changes: it has earlier reminded him of the bowl into which his mother had vomited, and now that image returns tinged with the language of the song – 'a bowl of bitter waters'. The memory of the dying woman leads to other images associated with her – her pathetic souvenirs and reminiscences, the trivial objects which symbolize for him her daily life, the dream he had had of her wrapped in graveclothes, the scene when he had refused to kneel at her deathbed. The order is not that of the events and situations in time, but of the succession of his thoughts, growing in intensity until his mother seems present and still willing him to submit, and he interrupts the chain of emotion with denunciation of a cruel God ('Ghoul! Chewer of

---

[7] Steinberg notes the odd introduction of 'Chrysostomos', says that 'As he and others see me, etc.' is Stephen talking to himself, and describes 'Cranly's arm. His arm' as the first brief attempt to simulate the stream of consciousness (*Steinberg*, 29–30).

corpses!') and a renewed refusal to surrender – 'No, mother. Let me be and let me live.' Throughout this passage, Joyce shifts to and fro between third and first person, between description of Stephen's thoughts and direct representation of them, as though from the recalled memories ('In a dream, silently, she had come to him') there are sudden explosions of immediate emotion ('Her eyes on me to strike me down'). The reader is familiarized with the monologue convention by encountering it blended with a traditional convention; he observes the workings of Stephen's mind and is intermittently involved in them.

By this point, Joyce has established the chief characteristics of Stephen's interior monologue, and can repeat and vary them. The echoing of Fergus's song is paralleled when Stephen, hearing Mulligan sing *Coronation Day* ('O won't we have a merry time'), sees 'warm sunshine merrying over the sea'. There are more brief unspoken comments on Mulligan and Haines, and such literary allusions as 'Agenbite of Inwit' and 'Yet here's a spot'. But there are only two more passages of interior monologue of any length – the first when Stephen sees the old milkwoman as a symbol of Ireland and of Ireland's disregard of the artist, and the second when, having spoken of 'the holy Roman catholic and apostolic church', he responds to 'the proud potent titles' by forming a rhetorical image of the history and power of the Church militant overthrowing the heretics – a train of thought finally rejected, like his thoughts about Mulligan's ragging and his dead mother, with a dismissive verbal gesture: 'Hear, hear. Prolonged applause. *Zut! Nom de Dieu!*' The interior monologue of the chapter ends, as it began, with a single word, 'Usurper', as though to summarize the conclusion to which Stephen's thoughts about Mulligan during the chapter have led him.

Even in this short chapter, where the technique is essentially 'narrative', Joyce makes the brief and interrupted passages of monologue carry much of the weight. In terms of the novel's central action, they present Stephen's motives for deciding to leave the Martello Tower and his friends; thematically they show the effects on him of four main relationships – with Mulligan, his dead mother, Ireland, and the Church; and they also establish a number of motifs and symbols which, later in the book, can stand for whole areas of his experience, obsessive emotions, and recurring ideas – the dream of the mother, the self-contempt in the word 'dogsbody', Fergus's song, the Latin prayer for the dying, the notion of the *dio boia* or 'chewer of corpses', the awareness of change and permanence in the self ('I am another now and yet the same'), the old woman symbolizing Ireland, 'Agenbite of inwit', the key, the doctrine of the consubstantiality of Father and Son, the fear of drowning, and the image of himself as one dispossessed by a usurper.

Yet although interior monologue is so important in this first chapter, it is far from being the only or even the dominant stylistic feature. The dialogues, for instance, are brilliantly managed, and perhaps leave the deepest impression on the reader's mind. The latent hostility lying beneath the surface friendship is finely suggested, and the representation of the spoken word, with short sense units often linked by association rather than logic or grammar, is itself a preparation for the manner of the interior monologue in later chapters:

> —God, he said quietly. Isn't the sea what Algy calls it: a grey sweet mother? The snotgreen sea. The scrotumtightening sea. *Epi oinopa ponton.* Ah, Dedalus, the Greeks. I must teach you. You must read them in the original. (*U* 3/3)

Critics have often remarked on the adverbs used to qualify Stephen's speech or behaviour (in this chapter, 'coldly', 'wearily', 'quietly', 'gloomily', 'very coldly', 'gravely', 'listlessly' and 'drily') and have sometimes supposed them indicative of Joyce's sharing in the priggishness of his hero. Certainly their consistency of tone is remarkable, especially when compared to the inconsistency of the adverbs, five times as many, applied to Buck Mulligan: Mulligan is described as speaking or behaving 'coarsely' and 'quietly', 'solemnly' and 'lightly', 'gravely' and gaily', 'sternly' and 'pleasantly', 'frankly' and 'warily', 'thickly' and 'blandly', 'abruptly' and 'evenly', 'seriously' and 'casually', 'contentedly' and 'impatiently', 'nervously' and 'vigorously', 'earnestly' and 'casually', 'tragically' and 'happily', besides 'smoothly', 'briskly', 'hastily', 'neatly', 'suddenly', 'kindly', 'quickly', 'nimbly', 'piously' and 'tritely'. The effect of this plethora of adverbs of manner is to set Stephen's fixed and bitter detachment against Mulligan's superficial and chameleon-like play-acting, and thus point the contrast implicit in the dialogue.[8]

The language of the narrative is also noticeably deliberate in matching sound to sense – sometimes laboured as in Stephen's phrasemaking ('Wavewhite wedded words shimmering on the dim tide'), sometimes richly sonorous ('The proud potent titles clanged over Stephen's memory the triumph of their brazen bells'). Everywhere the style is exactly evocative of Stephen's observations and experience, whether in monologue or narrative. For instance, the description in the monologue of 'a sail veering about the blank bay waiting for a swollen bundle to bob up, roll over to the sun a puffy face, salt white' is vivid and precise, but not more so than the narrative's image of the bathing-place: 'A young man clinging to a spur of rock near him moved slowly frogwise his green legs in the deep jelly of the water.' In the first explicitly, in the second implicitly, we are seeing through Stephen's eyes, and sharing the intensity of his impressions. Because the passages describing Stephen's thoughts use the same highly-coloured language as the passages representing them, there is no sense of sudden shifting between an objective and a subjective viewpoint.[9] The interior monologue is thus introduced into the novel as little more than an

---

[8] Harry Levin's account is typical of the usual simplification: 'There are still certain adverbial distinctions between Stephen's innate refinement and the vulgarity of the rest of the world: his speeches are spoken "coldly", Mulligan's "coarsely" ' (*Levin*, 62).

[9] Steinberg makes the interesting suggestion that 'in effacing himself, in attempting to become "invisible", Joyce tried to make his omniscient author's sentences less obtrusive by flavouring them with the characteristics of the stream of consciousness of the character with whom he was dealing at the time' (*Steinberg*, 121).

intensification of the traditional conventions, already stretched to their limit in the *Portrait*, but through its use Joyce is able to present Stephen, not as a static character, but as a consciousness, sensitive and alert, swept by emotions of distrust, remorse, and frustration – a consciousness entered into, not merely described.

'Nestor'

The other two chapters of the *Telemachia* are, for the most part, based on developments and refinements of the monologue techniques introduced in the first chapter. In 'Nestor', for instance, although Stephen's mind is still revolving his own problems, these occur in passages of comparatively detached speculation about historical or philosophical matters, more intellectually complex than anything in 'Telemachus' but less emotionally charged:

> Thought is the thought of thought. Tranquil brightness. The soul is in a manner all that is: the soul is the form of forms. Tranquillity sudden, vast, candescent: form of forms. (*U* 23/30–31)

These speculations themselves seem to have a calming effect: even when the pathetic schoolboy, Sargent, reminds Stephen of a child's dependence on maternal protection, and momentarily recalls the dream-vision of Mrs Dedalus ('an odour of rosewood and wetted ashes' – the phrase is now enough), the resultant emotion is controlled, finally, to a degree of abstraction: '*Amor matris;* subjective and objective genitive.' Partly this is because the dialogues with the schoolboys and with Mr Deasy merely set Stephen's thoughts in motion; unlike the dialogues of the first chapter, they do not themselves pierce or bruise him. He can afford to be ironic or amused by his own self-dramatization:

> I am among them, among their battling bodies in a medley, the joust of life. You mean that knockkneed mother's darling who seems to be slightly crawsick? (*U* 30/40)

The adverbs of manner which before, by their consistency, had helped to suggest Stephen's terse and bitter isolation no longer occur: he is more isolated, still feels threatened, but is now less despairing: 'Three nooses round me here. Well. I can break them in this instant if I will.' The monologue reveals a more attractive and promising aspect of Stephen's consciousness – a capacity for seeing his own problems in a wider context, glimmers of resolution, sympathy for others (whether for the boy, Sargent, or for the Jewish race), a sense of humour which in his dealings with Mr Deasy is not sour, and a readiness to mock himself as the fox scraping at a grave or as 'the bullockbefriending bard.'

'Proteus'

All these developments are taken further in 'Proteus', where the interior monologue is dominant to the extent that even the occasional passages in narrative become merely a conventional indication of a change in the focus of Stephen's attention. In general, the past-tense, third-person form is used to represent only Stephen's simpler observations of his surroundings: paragraphs, and even sentences, which begin in this way, frequently shift into the present-tense, first-person monologue:

> Turning, he scanned the shore south, his feet sinking again slowly in new sockets. The cold domed room of the tower waits. Through the barbicans the shafts of light are moving ever, slowly ever as my feet are sinking, creeping duskward over the dial floor. (*U* 41/55)

In some sentences, narrative and monologue are interwoven: 'His gaze brooded on his broadtoed boots, a buck's castoffs *nebeneinander*.' If the opening clause suggests to the reader that he is watching Stephen brood, the closing words (especially the German word which has figured in Stephen's speculations at the beginning of the chapter) make it clear that the sentence is representing Stephen's consciousness of himself and his own behaviour. This repeated shift, without obvious transitions, from narrative to monologue is partly what gives the chapter its Protean character; there is a fusion of experience of the outer and inner worlds. Often what seems to be an authorial description of a scene reveals, by the sudden intrusion of an expression from Stephen's mind, that it is a representation of his response to the scene. For instance, an echo of the song about 'old Mary Ann', which Mulligan had sung in the Martello Tower, springs up in the middle of a poetic description of seaweed:

> Under the upswelling tide he saw the writhing weeds lift languidly and sway reluctant arms, hising up their petticoats, in whispering water swaying and upturning coy silver fronds. (*U* 46/62)

Apart from the intruded phrase, there is nothing to suggest that the actual words of the sentence are in Stephen's mind: the deliberate rhythms and alliteration and assonance are not his devices, but an expression of the deliberate intensity with which he is experiencing. Similarly when Stephen recalls Kevin Egan in Paris, his mental picture of the man lighting a cigarette is fused with his knowledge of Egan's past as a dynamitard, and that fusion of visual and non-visual memory is expressed in the style:

> The blue fuse burns deadly between hands and burns clear. Loose tobacco shreds catch fire: a flame and acrid smoke light our corner. (*U* 40/54)

Even the series of animal metaphors in the description of the dog and the sea – 'hare', 'buck, trippant', 'forehoofs', 'seamorse', 'serpented', 'bearish fawning', 'wolf's tongue', 'calf's gallop', 'dogsbody', 'pard', 'panther', 'vulturing' – are not necessarily words from Stephen's mind. Some probably are: 'buck, trippant' is presumably a memory of 'Tripping and sunny like the buck himself', 'dogsbody' is the label which Stephen has already applied to himself, and 'panther' may, perhaps, be related to Haines, the 'panthersahib'; but the device as a whole is not some kind of word-game played by Stephen, but Joyce's way of suggesting Stephen's apprehension of the dog and the waves as representative and symbolic of the protean flux in the physical universe. Alliteration, assonance and onomatopoeia are often so dense and elaborate that their literal presence in the casual process of a young man's mind is implausible; on the other hand, they would seem laboured and self-conscious in ordinary authorial description or narrative. But if recognized as part of a literary convention designed to suggest the nature of this young man's experience – the experience of a mind full of literature, sensitive to words and rhythms, and deliberately cultivating intensity of impression – then these stylistic devices seem finely appropriate, the virtuosity as functional as the simple, repetitious style used to present Maria in 'Clay'.

The conscious verbal play of Stephen's mind is often ingenious, but much less complex than this. He notes the 'catalectic tetrameter of iambs' in a childish verse, or the imagined bobbing of a drowned body shoreward – 'a pace a pace a porpoise'; he tries to verbalize various sounds; he imagines a clumsy speech for the giant builders of the past, and mouths the sounds of the verse he has composed: 'Oomb, allwombing tomb'. Occasionally there is some play on words, as when the memory of Patrice Egan lapping milk is linked through the French *lapin* to the image of his 'bunny's face', or when the 'gentleman poet' is called 'Lawn Tennyson'. Besides numerous literary allusions, there are a few references twisted humorously – 'isle of dreadful thirst', '*Lui, c'est moi*', and 'the simple pleasures of the poor' – and there are many words from other languages – Greek, Latin, Sanskrit, Hebrew, German, Italian, French, Celtic, Swedish and thieves' cant – and such inventions as 'lourdily' and 'contransmagnificandjewbangtantiality'. All of these variously illustrate Stephen's love of words ('philology' is the 'art' of this chapter), but they are quite different in quality from the stylistic brilliance of the chapter as a whole.

In this, the first chapter dominated by monologue, Joyce converts the somewhat narrow, alienated and unsympathetic young man of the Martello Tower into a figure of human complexity, interest and sympathy, capable of sharing with Leopold Bloom the central place in the novel, and this is achieved by a bold and inventive handling of the convention. What goes on in a mind is rapid and multifarious beyond observation, and far beyond verbal representation. Interior monologue, of the kind Joyce attempts, must suggest this rapidity and variety, yet create a coherent and consistent image of a human being; must appear to be unselective when governed by the strictest relevance; must seem to follow random impressions and associations while being, in fact, highly organized, condensed and purposeful. To this end Joyce developed his abbreviated notation of thoughts and feelings, his elided or implied transitions, his use of repeated words or phrases as leitmotifs for important memories and experiences, and, above all, the stylistic variety to provide verbal equivalents for mental processes ranging from a general mood to a trivial observation. The clarity of the image of a consciousness is remarkable in itself – but additionally remarkable in that it is offered as an image of a young man of genius. The difficulty of creating such a fictional figure is a commonplace; there are plenty of novel-heroes who are supposed to be writers, painters, sculptors, musicians, but few of whose genius the reader is convinced. It is even more difficult to present the inner workings of potential genius, especially when they are mingled with naivety, conceit, sentimentality, self-pity, self-dramatization and immaturity. This is what is attempted and, I think, achieved in 'Proteus': the monologue is a plausible representation of the way everyone's mind works, yet expresses, too, the intensity, sensitivity and fertility of a mind of great promise – an artist's mind, though one as yet immature and incompletely articulate. The embryonic qualities are manifested less in the thoughts and feelings attributed to Stephen (which, summarized, would suggest little more than a clever and complicated young man, conscious of rejection and disturbed by the collapse of youthful dreams and hopes) than in the intensity, sensitivity and fertility of the style which Joyce has devised as a verbal equivalent for Stephen's consciousness. The style is not merely appropriate; it is an essential part of the content, since, unless Stephen is established as an artist of unrealized potential, the central action and themes of the book are crippled from the start.[10]

'Calypso'

The changes in the use of interior monologue in the first three chapters of *Ulysses* are progressive: monologue occupies more and more space, is increasingly central in function, and becomes more complex in character and manner. The inner portrait of Stephen is gradually deepened and extended, and, in the process, the reader is familiarized with the techniques and devices Joyce needs for the full practice of his form of the monologue convention.[11] But, with the shift to Leopold Bloom, the novel begins again, and this is reflected in a qualitative change of style. Bloom's first chapter is related to 'Telemachus' by the time of day and the narrative method, and to 'Proteus' by the use of a fully developed interior monologue, but the difference in the nature of the mind represented demands a sudden change of manner.

The dissimilarity of the two minds and of the modes of representation is shown by a comparison of the passages dealing with animals. On a factual level, Stephen is afraid of the dog and Bloom fond of the cat; but the significant differences between the two men are manifested in the contrasting styles of their monologues. Stephen's is poetic, seeing the dog in metaphorical terms and relating it to his own concerns and obsessions: he identifies it with the hostility he feels around him ('Dog of my enemy'),

[10] Goldberg has a similar view of the importance of the 'Proteus' chapter (*Goldberg*, 158).

[11] The gradual introduction of interior monologue is analysed in detail in *Steinberg;* the conclusions are summarized on pp. 60–61. See also Steinberg's article, 'Introducing the Stream of Consciousness Technique in *Ulysses*' (*Style* II (Winter 1968), 49–58), and the essay by William M. Schutte and Erwin R. Steinberg, 'The Fictional Technique of *Ulysses*' (*Approaches*, 163–4).

with the people he despises but wants to give him 'the bark of their applause', with Mulligan, with death and his own spiritual death ('dogsbody'), with his guilt and remorse about his dead mother, and with his general sense of the protean physical universe. Bloom's monologue, on the other hand, is, for the most part, affectionate, literal, and scientific. He wonders how tall he seems to the cat, why mice do not squeal when caught, what the functions of a cat's whiskers may be, and why cat's tongues are rough. As Joyce says, he views the cat 'curiously, kindly'. While for Stephen the dog is a multifaceted symbol, for Bloom the cat is an attractive and interesting creature, on which he can pour some of his affection.

Thus the structural re-start of the novel is matched by a change in the stylistic characteristics of the interior monologue. In the *Telemachia*, the handling of the monologue developed progressively because the overriding aim was to reveal more and more of the comparatively fixed character of Stephen; in the chapters immediately following 'Calypso', the style of the monologue varies in response to changes in the mood or situation of the flexible and resilient Bloom. Because interior monologue is a highly selective convention, it can be shaped to represent a general disposition in the consciousness, so that whatever is experienced – an impression, an emotion, a thought – tends to lead in some common direction. Such unspecific states of mind as general euphoria or general depression can be represented by showing the stream of consciousness moving characteristically towards happy or unhappy conclusions. Such terms as 'euphoria' and 'depression' are no more than abstract labels for mental predispositions: one's response to a given impression depends on the mood of the moment, or, to put it another way, a mood is recognized by the prevailing tendency of thoughts to move in a roughly common emotional direction.

In 'Calypso', no dominant mood is as yet established in Bloom's mind: he fluctuates between feeling young and feeling old, between satisfaction and regret, between the bitter vision of a barren Palestine and the idyllic dream of Agendath Netaim. The sketch, based on *The Dance of the Hours*, which he thinks of writing, is expressive of such fluctuation: 'Still true to life also. Day, then the night.' A sudden change in weather conditions can sweep him from one mood to another. After a cloud passing over the sun has provoked the image of the desolation in the Holy Land, and oppressed Bloom with a sense of 'age crusting him with a salt cloak', the sun breaks through:

> Quick warm sunlight came running from Berkeley Road, swiftly, in slim sandals, along the brightening footpath. Runs, she runs to meet me, a girl with gold hair on the wind. (*U* 54/74)

The factual content of these two sentences is simply that the cloud has passed away from the sun. Whatever else is conveyed is conveyed by the style, which is lively, gay, and, for Bloom, poetical. It is all these things, because Bloom is nearing his home and the sudden moving sunlight is associated with the image of his daughter, Milly, running to greet him. Bloom's love for and delight in his daughter are among the most powerful of his emotions; he is worried about what may happen to her away from home, and when he recalls 'her slim legs running up the staircase' smiles 'with troubled affection', but, in general, the memory of her lightens his heart. This little episode foreshadows the more extended passage in the maternity hospital chapter, when Bloom, again oppressed by a vision of infertility and universal desolation, is restored by the image of 'Millicent, the young, the dear, the radiant . . . shod in sandals of bright gold.' Yet to suppose that the two sentences presenting Bloom's response to the sudden sunlight indicate that he thought of the metaphor of the running girl, or remembered how Milly used to run to meet him, is mistaken; the language is plainly not the language of Bloom. The style evokes his response, and that response is vaguely associated in his mind with the pleasure he used to get when Milly welcomed him home. One can hardly say that the style echoes the sense – the style largely is the sense.

There is a range of such stylistic devices to represent aspects of Bloom's consciousness of which he is not fully aware – sometimes aspects of which he does not wish to be fully aware. For instance, when he arrives home he finds a letter from Boylan to Molly: 'Mrs Marion Bloom. His quick heart slowed at once. Bold hand. Mrs Marion.' His mind does not comment on Boylan's breach of epistolary etiquette, nor dwell on its implications, yet his heart at once reacts. His mind notes the trivial solecism, twice: he does not allow himself to consider what his heart knows is implied in the form of address. But the style records the shock, the sense of threat to his status as husband, and, subsequently, twice more in this chapter and thereafter recurrently through the book, the simple words 'Mrs Marion' or 'Marion' are enough to represent the painful flash into his mind of a situation which he does not wish to contemplate. Again, style and content are inseparable.

'Lotuseaters'

It is the inner monologue's capacity for suggesting a pervasive mood that presumably explains the otherwise obscure 'technics' listed by Joyce for the next two chapters – 'Narcissism' and 'Incubism'. Both words seem to refer to the contents of a mind rather than to techniques of representation, but because they are general characteristics they can be expressed in the handling of the monologue. The dictionary defines Narcissism as 'a morbid self-love or self-admiration'; in Bloom, it is not a permanent condition, but a mood of self-satisfaction induced mainly by the receipt of a letter from Martha Clifford and partly by the warmth of the day. At the beginning of the chapter it is betrayed by a gesture – 'While his eyes still read blandly he took off his hat quietly inhaling his hairoil and sent his right hand with slow grace over his brow and hair' – and by the manner in which he crosses the road, 'sauntering' with a self-consciously 'careless air'. At the end of the chapter, he walks 'cheerfully' towards the baths as he contemplates his oiled and scented body floating 'in a womb of warmth'. He has no need, at this point of the day, for the company of others: as M'Coy approaches him, he thinks 'Get rid of him quickly. Take me out of my way. Hate company when you', and, later, accosted by Bantam Lyons, he decides 'Better leave him the paper and get shut of him.' He is uncharacteristically smug about himself and contemptuous of others. He is 'fine', he tells M'Coy, and Molly is 'tiptop', and, when he has got rid of M'Coy, he smiles to himself at the superiority of himself and his wife to the M'Coys. Even less characteristic are the dreams of bullying dominance over women: the sight of a well-dressed woman makes him want to 'Possess her once take the starch out of her', and he plans to be more 'brutal' in the language of his next letter to Martha. All the lotuseating fantasies are equally evidence of that same desire to retire from life and human involvement, which culminates in his vision of himself in the warm seclusion of the bath.

Bloom's state of mind is responsible for another stylistic device introduced in this chapter – one which becomes increasingly important in the three chapters which follow it. Bloom's pen-name is Henry Flower; he receives a letter with a flower pinned to it; he buys lemon soap and a lotion containing sweet almond oil and orangeflower water; imagining himself in the bath, he thinks of his navel as a 'bud of flesh' and of his penis as 'a languid floating flower'; and these are only a few of the fifty or so words or phrases referring to flowers or vegetation. Sometimes they occur because Bloom thinks of a tropical Eastern scene, or of 'the language of flowers' or of the herbs and simples used by chemists. But they influence the language in less direct ways: seeing a poor boy, Bloom thinks 'His life isn't such a bed of roses'; Martha Clifford's bad headache is explained by the vulgarism 'Has her roses probably'; the vast production of Guinness suggests a land flooded with liquor 'bearing along wideleaved flowers of its froth'; he supposes that familiarity with eating corpses is why cannibals 'cotton' to the idea of the eucharist; and, later, he notices 'a widow in her weeds'. None of these phrases would, by itself, catch the reader's attention; as A. Walton Litz observes,

> As readers we do not catalogue the references to flowers . . . but we do feel the accumulative force of their repetition.[12]

What is this accumulative effect on the reader? If the device merely indicates that the Odyssean parallel is 'Lotuseaters' and the technique 'narcissism', then it is no more than a rather laborious cryptogram. But if, as I believe it does, the vegetal colouring of the language ('vegetal' is more precise than 'flowery', because trees, shrubs, fruits, leaves and other plants are included) helps to induce in the reader a sense of a relaxed, passive, sensuous quality in Bloom's consciousness at this period of the day, then it is inconspicuous but functional.

'Hades'

The change of mood and technique from the 'Lotuseaters' chapter to

---

[12] *Litz*, 52. Litz points out that many of the 'vegetal' words were late additions to the chapter (46–9).

'Hades' is most clearly marked in the passages where Bloom remembers his dead father. In 'Lotuseaters', he recalls the old man's quoting from a play in which a son is reproached for having 'left the house of his father and left the God of his father.' Later, in the brothel, Bloom recognizes the application of his father's self-reproach to his own behaviour,[13] but, here, he seems pettily self-centred and anxious to forget about his father's death:

> Poor papa! Poor man! I'm glad I didn't go into the room to look at his face. That day! O dear! O dear! Ffoo! Well, perhaps it was the best for him.
> Mr Bloom went round the corner and passed the drooping nags of the hazard. No use thinking of it any more. Nosebag time. Wish I hadn't met that M'Coy fellow.   (*U* 69/93)

In 'Hades', his companions' contempt for suicides reminds Bloom of the tradition of driving a stake through the heart of a suicide ('As if it wasn't broken already'), and sets in train a much more vivid memory of the inquest on his father and the circumstances of his death:

> That afternoon of the inquest. The redlabelled bottle on the table. The room in the hotel with hunting pictures. Stuffy it was. Sunlight through the slats of the Venetian blinds. The coroner's ears, big and hairy. Boots giving evidence. Thought he was asleep first. Then saw like yellow streaks on his face. Had slipped down to the foot of the bed. Verdict: overdose. Death by misadventure. The letter. For my son Leopold.
> No more pain. Wake no more. Nobody owns.
> The carriage rattled swiftly along Blessington Street. Over the stones. (*U* 89/121)

The last words of the last two paragraphs are suggested by the song, *The Pauper's Drive*, which echoes in Bloom's mind throughout the journey to the cemetery, but the song is only one of the ways in which Joyce shows a mind turning persistently to thoughts of death.

Bloom and his fellow-mourners are not a particularly solemn lot, and, at times, forget decorum, but death is like a heavy presence, an incubus, in their minds. It is not surprising that Bloom, attending a funeral, should be reminded of death by the sight of a child's coffin, the bereaved family or the funeral service, but Joyce's handling of the interior monologue shows a constant drift of thought in that direction. A woman's face at a window calls up the image of the laying-out of the corpse; Simon Dedalus's anger about Stephen's friends makes Bloom remember painfully the loss of his own son; the sight of Boylan leads to a visualization of the increasing flabbiness of Molly's body ('I suppose the skin can't contract quickly enough when the flesh falls off'). O'Callaghan is said to be 'on his last

---

[13] Bloom's father had turned from the Jewish faith to Protestantism, Bloom from Protestantism to Catholicism. The fact that Rudolf retained certain Jewish 'beliefs and practices' (*U* 685/853) suggests that his conversion was skin-deep; Bloom became a Catholic 'with a view to his matrimony' (*U* 677/843). Although Bloom now has no religious faith, he sometimes, like his father, feels himself to be an apostate from his race.

legs',[14] a tramp emptying stones from his boot is doing so 'after life's journey', and the appearance of Reuben J. Dodd stimulates Bloom to begin the story of the attempted suicide of Dodd's son. Animals have similarly mortal associations: seeing a drove of cattle and sheep, Bloom thinks, 'Tomorrow is killing day' in what he calls the 'dead meat trade'; a braying ass recalls the superstition that asses hide when dying, and then the memory of Bloom's father going away to kill himself; a bird on a tree in the cemetery seems stuffed, reminding Bloom of Milly's burial of a dead bird; and a rat suggests the decaying flesh in the graves – 'Saltwhite crumbling mush of corpse: smell, taste like raw white turnips.' If Bloom picks up the newspaper, his eyes immediately rest on the obituary notices; when he hears a street organ, 'Has anybody here seen Kelly?' suddenly becomes the 'dead march from *Saul*', and the sight of a bunch of flowers on Smith O'Brien's statue suggests it must be 'his deathday. For many happy returns.' Buildings, too, lead into similar trains of thought: the gas-works reminds him of children convulsed with whooping cough, the dogs' home of the pathetic death of his father's dog, the hospital of the 'dead-house handy underneath', and the house in which Childs was murdered of the public appetite for gruesome details. Even Bloom's usual inventiveness of mind is now directed towards municipal funeral trams, canal-borne hearses, the advantages of upright burial, re-usable coffins, the possible provision of electric clocks, telephones or canvas airholes in graves in case of premature burial, more interesting gravestone inscriptions, and the preservation of the voices of the dead on gramophone records.

To supplement the 'incubism' of the presentation, Joyce colours the language of the chapter with phrases and clichés suggestive of mortality. Molly is remembered expressing her sexual appetite in the words, 'God, I'm dying for it'; the cabhorses have 'too much bone in their skulls'; the bootlace seller has been 'kicked about like snuff at a wake'; Mrs Cunningham has been leading her husband 'the life of the damned' and 'would wear the heart out of a stone'; the Childs house has 'gone to hell'; there is a 'funereal silence' outside the cemetery; Martin Cunningham describes his embarrassment by saying 'I was in mortal agony'; the bald Dick Tivy is said to have 'nothing between himself and heaven'; the priest has 'a belly on him like a poisoned pup'; and even Ivy Day is 'dying out'. In addition, there are such expressions as 'more dead than alive', 'dead side of the street', 'dead weight', 'a few bob a skull', 'death's number', 'dead letter office' and the description of cheese as 'corpse of milk'. Bloom's mental habit of adapting or misquoting familiar quotations is modified to produce '*Habeat corpus*', 'Silver threads among the grey', 'In the midst of death we are in life', '*De mortuis nil nisi prius*', 'The Irishman's house is his coffin', and 'Eulogy in a country churchyard', while Simon Dedalus neatly applies an obituary phrase to Tom Kernan's failure to pay his debts to Fogarty:

---

[14] Victory Pomeranz has shown that O'Callaghan is not the name of the bootlace-seller, but an allusion to a play by William Bayle Bernard, *His Last Legs*. performed at the Queen's Theatre, Dublin in 1866. O'Callaghan was the name of the chief character (*JJQ* IX (1) (1971), 136–8).

'– Though lost to sight, Mr Dedalus said, to memory dear.' When Bloom's point of view is briefly abandoned, it is only so that Martin Cunningham can whisper to Mr Power about the suicide of Bloom's father.

Bloom resists and finally escapes from the prevalent mood, and that too is reflected in the handling of his monologue, but this chapter is particularly interesting stylistically for the way in which it articulates the moribund mental atmosphere of Dublin, already presented in 'The Dead', by selection and control of the mental processes represented, and by the use of words and expressions, mostly commonplace, but, in accumulation, suggestive of mortality.

The recurrence of the word 'heart' (or 'hearts) in the chapter (on a rough count twenty-two times, seventeen of them in the second half, after the arrival at the cemetery) is a device, related to the accumulation of mortal phrases, but different in effect. Whereas the phrases suggest the underlying mood of the chapter, the recurrence of 'heart' is nearer to an irony – the heart of the Dubliners is in the grave, in a buried past. The first contributes to the 'incubism' of the 'technic', the second underlines the metaphor of the column headed 'Organ'.

'Aeolus'

The use of words and phrases, sometimes literal, sometimes figurative, concealed in the narrative or the interior monologue but by their recurrence operating subliminally on the reader, is a development of the 'hot-cold' alternation to express the child's feverishness in the *Portrait* and culminates in the hundreds of river-names woven into the texture of the 'Anna Livia Plurabelle' chapter of *Finnegans Wake*. It is a technique of which Joyce seems to have been particularly fond – perhaps because of its indirectness and its capacity to give a subtle colouring to an episode – and one which he handles with extraordinary skill and variety. It occurs again in the 'Aeolus' chapter where, as has been often observed, there are about forty expressions related in some way to wind: besides such obvious forms as 'what's in the wind' and 'raise the wind', Joyce ranges from 'breath' to 'puff', 'draught', 'zephyrs', 'breeze', 'squalls', 'gale', 'whirlwind', 'hurricane' and 'cyclone', introduces allusive references in nouns like 'flatulence', 'bladderbags' and 'afflatus', and even makes such etymological puns as 'vent' and 'window'. Here, the handling of the technique is more overt than in 'Hades', but it serves a more complex role: it contributes to the windy atmosphere in the newspaper office, points to the Odyssean parallel (one headline, 'O, HARP EOLIAN', is a patent clue) and, more importantly, register's Joyce's comment on the 'art' of the chapter, 'Rhetoric', as practised in Dublin.

Unlike the three preceding chapters of Bloom's day, 'Aeolus' is not dominated by Bloom's interior monologue or point of view. We see through his eyes and perceive his unspoken thoughts when he is talking to the advertisement clerk, when he is in the printing works, and when he arrives in the *Evening Telegraph* Office, but this merely prefaces the main business of the chapter; when Bloom goes into the editor's room to make his telephone call, we do not follow him, but stay to listen to the conversation of the editor and his cronies, and, when he returns, it is merely as a minor figure quickly given his dismissal by the editor. As he leaves the building, he is watched from the window and we get our first indication of his physical appearance seen from outside, as Lenehan ridicules the flat-footed walk mocked by the newsboys. The succeeding conversation is presented dramatically, with no point of view, as in 'Ivy Day in the Committee Room', until the arrival of Stephen, when, at once, we begin to get snatches of his interior monologue. But they are only snatches: the emphasis is still on dialogue, until, having left the office, Stephen begins to tell MacHugh his parable. Halfway through the parable, Bloom accosts Myles Crawford and a brief paragraph of interior monologue expresses his observation of the editor, Stephen and their companions; then Bloom is left behind and the parable is concluded with no further glimpse into Stephen's mind except the association provoked by MacHugh's reference to Penelope: 'Poor Penelope. Penelope Rich.'

Thus, in this chapter, the monologues are subordinate to the dialogue, and there is no occasion to modulate their style in order to present some characterizing and pervasive mood. Instead, Joyce labelled the 'technic' of the chapter 'enthymemic', which (like the 'art', 'Rhetoric') principally refers to the dialogue. According to Aristotle, the enthymeme is a rhetorical syllogism based on probable rather than necessary premises: it starts from a generally accepted or granted principle and infers a probable application to the matter in hand. Aristotle claims that all rhetoric (in which he includes not only the public forms of deliberative, forensic and epideictic oratory[15] but all forms of persuasion when men 'endeavour to criticize or uphold an argument, to defend themselves or to accuse'[16]) depends on the use of enthymemes and examples, corresponding to the use of the syllogism and induction in dialectic.[17] Presumably, then, what Joyce meant by 'enthymemic' (the usual form of the adjective is 'enthymematic') relates to his presentation of the various kinds of persuasion exhibited in the chapter.

The three specimens of oratory quoted in the newspaper office – those of Dan Dawson, Seymour Bushe, and John F. Taylor – are obviously epideictic, forensic and deliberative respectively, but the rhetorical nature of the chapter has, I think, been somewhat obscured by Stuart Gilbert's well-known list of rhetorical devices exemplified in 'Aeolus' – a list so full, he believes, that the chapter might be 'adopted as a text-book for students of the art of rhetoric'.[18] The list of nearly a hundred devices looks impressive. But on closer examination it is less so. It includes, for instance, chiasmus, metaphor, anacoluthon, apostrophe, irony, parenthesis, tautology, professional jargon, Hibernicism, epigram, sarcasm, oratio recta-obliqua, anticlimax, hyperbole, and neologism – all of which could be illustrated equally

---

[15] The *'Art'* of Rhetoric, translated by John Henry Freese (Loeb Classical Library (London, Heinemann 1926) I, iii, 3, p. 33.
[16] *Ibid.* I, i, 1, p. 3.   [17] *Ibid.* I, ii, 8, pp. 19–21.   [18] *Gilbert*, 187.

well from any chapter in the book: the same could be said of most of the other devices. Certainly, other chapters could be used to illustrate an equally formidable list of figures of speech.[19] Moreover, when Gilbert wants to exemplify 'enthymeme' (which Joyce's label would suggest is the key rhetorical feature of the chapter) he offers Bloom's remark to Hynes: 'If you want to draw the cashier is just going to lunch'.[20] This is not an enthymeme at all – not even according to the non-Aristotelian use of the term (a 'syllogism with one premise suppressed') which Gilbert attributes to Aristotle:[21] formally Bloom's remark is a conditional sentence with the apodosis or conclusion partly suppressed (and immediately added by Bloom): 'If you want to draw [you'd better look sharp because] the cashier is just going to lunch.' This list of rhetorical devices has rarely been questioned because Stuart Gilbert specifically claims for it Joyce's authority:

> Thus the long list of examples of rhetorical forms which concludes my commentary on the 'Aeolus' episode was compiled at his suggestion, and we spent several industrious afternoons collaborating on it.[22]

Yet this account of the composition of the list hardly agrees with Gilbert's description of the nature of the chapter as a 'gathering together ... of nearly all the important, misleading enthymemes elenchated by Quintilian and his successors' to form 'a lively organic part of a very living organism.'[23] If Joyce had consciously made of his chapter 'a veritable thesaurus of rhetorical devices', one wonders why it took him and Gilbert 'several industrious afternoons' of collaboration to compile the list. Why could Joyce not have pointed out the devices he had introduced into the chapter? Why, in fact, should he have asked for the list to be compiled? The likely answer is that, in writing the chapter, Joyce had had the general idea of

[19] Arnold Goldman (*The Joyce Paradox: Form and Freedom in his Fiction* (London, Routledge and Kegan Paul 1966), 90) suggests that the figures of rhetoric found in 'Aeolus' 'could probably be found in any other chapter as well', and Robert Humphrey, pointing to twenty rhetorical figures and devices in a short passage from 'Proteus', says 'I suspect that Joyce seldom did so well in the "Aeolus" episode' (*Stream of Consciousness in the Modern Novel* (Berkeley, California University Press 1954), 74–6).
[20] *Gilbert*, 192.
[21] *Gilbert*, 186. The *Shorter Oxford English Dictionary* gives for 'enthymeme': '1. *Rhet.* An argument based on probable premisses, as dist. from a demonstration – 1841. 2. *Logic* A syllogism with one premiss unexpressed; as *Cogito, ergo sum*. (A misapprehension of "imperfect syllogism" applied to 1.) – 1588.' The Glossary of the Loeb edition of Aristotle's *Rhetoric* makes the same point: 'an enthymeme (lit. thought, argument) in the *Rhetoric* is a rhetorical syllogism, that is, it is drawn from probable premises and is therefore not a strictly demonstrative proof. The use of the term for a syllogism in which one of the premises is suppressed is due to a misunderstanding....' 475–6). Phillip Tompkins notes the incorrectness of Gilbert's definition and points out that his illustration of an enthymeme is both dubious and unimportant ('James Joyce and the Enthymeme: The Seventh Episode of *Ulysses*', *JJQ* V (3) (1968), 199–205). However, he regards John F. Taylor's speech as an enthymeme, whereas I regard it as an 'example'.
[22] *Gilbert*, 12. M. J. C. Hodgart observes that Gilbert's list 'is not exhaustive and not completely accurate', and notes that his supposed 'enthymeme' is 'just an elliptical sentence' (*Hart and Hayman*, 122 and 124).
[23] *Gilbert*, 187.

giving his treatment a rhetorical flavour, and, subsequently, was interested and amused to discover how much of the loose talk of his journalists could be formally catalogued. He must have been amused, for instance, to find that the simple protestation of the newsboy – 'It wasn't me, sir. It was the big fellow shoved me, sir' – could be solemnly identified as an example of 'Epanaphora (combined use of Anaphora and Epiphora)'.[24] A similar investigation of 'Eumaeus' would have produced an equivalent range of devices.

However, Gilbert's reference to 'all the important, misleading enthymemes' rightly notes that most of the rhetoric displayed in the chapter is false. Aristotle lists nearly thirty different types of enthymeme but there are few, if any, valid examples in 'Aeolus': it is much easier to illustrate his list of ten apparent or seeming enthymemes,[25] corresponding in rhetoric to the fallacious syllogism in logic. For instance, Bloom's successful attempt to persuade Nannetti to insert the Keyes advertisement illustrates Aristotle's second kind of apparent enthymeme:

> The second kind of fallacy of diction is homonymy. For instance, if one were to say that the mouse is an important animal, since from it is derived the most honoured of all religious festivals, namely, the mysteries.[26]

This argument, based on the mere similarity of sound in the Greek words for 'mouse' and 'mysteries', is paralleled in Bloom's persuasion of the home-ruler Nannetti that the heading, 'the house of keys' will, by an implied reference to the Manx parliament, offer an 'innuendo of home rule': the homonymic point is emphasized by the headline, 'HOUSE OF KEY(E)s'. On a more serious plane, the argument attributed to Mr Justice Fitzgibbon – 'We were weak, therefore worthless' – belongs to the first category of apparent enthymemes, which consists 'in ending with a conclusion syllogistically expressed, although there has been no syllogistic process.'[27] Professor MacHugh's eloquence is full of fallacious arguments. In his assertion of the superiority of the Greek civilization to the Roman or British, although he has warned Molloy not to be misled 'by sounds of words', he uses a more learned form of the homonymic fallacy employed by Bloom: the Latin 'dominus' suggests 'material domination', the English 'Lord' does not distinguish between 'Lord Jesus' and 'Lord Salisbury' ('Where is the spirituality?'), but 'Kyrios' is a 'Shining word! The vowels the Semite and the Saxon knew not. Kyrie! The radiance of the intellect'; and by this play on words MacHugh concludes that Greek is 'the language of the mind' and the Athenian empire 'the empire of the spirit'. When he praises by implication the loyalty of the Irish to lost causes, he associates them with Pyrrhus who was also 'loyal to a lost cause'; but since, when Pyrrhus 'made a last attempt to retrieve the fortunes of Greece', the cause was in his opinion not yet lost, the argument belongs to the ninth category of apparent enthymemes, dependent on 'the omission of when and how'.[28] Even more blatantly, he dismisses the Roman Empire as 'vast, . . . but vile'

---

[24] Ibid., 193.   [25] Rhetoric II, xxiv, 2, pp. 325–35.   [26] Ibid. II, xxiv, 2, pp. 325–7.
[27] Ibid. II, xxiv, 2, p. 325.   [28] Ibid. II, xxiv, 9, p. 333.

on the grounds that wherever the Romans went they built sewers: here an accidental circumstance is treated as essential, the fallacy of the sixth kind of apparent enthymeme – 'derived from accident'.[29] In this instance, J. J. O'Molloy detects and exposes the fallacy by observing that 'we have also Roman law.'

There are many other fallacious rhetorical syllogisms scattered through the chapter, though few are in clear syllogistic form and many are concealed by the incoherencies of conversation. Whatever purports to be a process of syllogistic argument aiming at persuasion proves to be fallacious, not always in conclusion but in method. The three exceptions to the general debasement of rhetoric in this chapter are John F. Taylor's speech, Seymour Bushe's period on the Moses of Michelangelo, and Stephen's parable. On the first of these, Stuart Gilbert provides a perceptive comment:

> This speech is an apt example of the manner in which eloquence aided by the rhetorical device of a far-fetched, not to say false, analogy, can produce conviction in the listener's mind. The resemblance between the movement for a revival of the Irish tongue and the situation of the Chosen People in the land of Egypt was really of the slightest; the question at issue for the latter was not the revival of a dead or moribund tongue, nor is there any reason to believe that the Egyptians sought to impose their culture on the Jews. The speaker uses the *argumentum ad hominem* by comparing his hearer's race with the Chosen People, an *argumentum ad fidem* in exploiting for the purposes of his similitude their belief in the miraculous origin of the tables of the law, and an *argumentum ad passiones* in his description of the browbeating of a small, inspired race by the arrogant spokesman of a mighty empire. Yet it is impossible to read, *a fortiori* to hear, this speech without being in some measure convinced by the speaker's eloquence.[30]

Each of the three forms of argument listed by Gilbert is referred to by Aristotle as legitimate rhetorical practice but, formally, Taylor's speech is not enthymematic at all; it is a fine use of the rhetorical 'example' – the form of argument which, according to Aristotle, is 'most suitable for deliberative speakers, for it is by examination of the past that we divine and judge the future.'[31] Gilbert's objection that there is only a partial resemblance between the situation of the Irish and that of the Israelites does not invalidate the rhetorical process, for an example 'is neither the relation of part to whole, nor of whole to part, nor of one whole to another whole, but of part to part, of like to like, when both come under the same genus, but one of them is better known than the other.'[32] Aristotle distinguishes between two kinds of 'examples',

> namely, one which consists in relating things that have happened before, and another in inventing them oneself. The latter are subdivided into comparisons or fables, such as those of Aesop and the Libyan.[33]

Obviously Taylor's example belongs to the first category, Bushe's to the

---

[29] *Ibid.* II, xxiv, 6, p. 331.   [30] *Gilbert*, 186 n. 1.   [31] *Rhetoric* I, ix, 40, p. 105.
[32] *Ibid.* I, ii, 19, p. 29.   [33] *Ibid.* II, xx, 2–3, p. 273.

subdivision of comparison, and Stephen's to that of fable.[34] It seems odd that, in a chapter supposedly 'enthymemic', the three valid passages of rhetorical persuasion should all be based on the 'example', but these three passages are related by their common reference to Moses and distinguished from the rest of the chapter by their quality as well as by their form. They provide the standard by which the impoverished rhetorical argument in the newspaper office is to be judged; when Joyce labelled the 'technic' of the chapter 'enthymemic', he was using the term ironically.

It is impossible to be certain that, in writing 'Aeolus', Joyce had Aristotle's *Rhetoric* consciously in mind (although it seems in keeping with his general readiness to refer to Aristotle[35]), but the book does in many respects provide a useful commentary on the chapter. For instance, the splendid closing sentence of Taylor's speech exhibits all the features recommended by Aristotle for a periodic sentence – antithesis, parisosis (balanced clauses), and paromoiosis (similarity of syllables at the beginnings or ends of clauses):

> He would *never have* spoken with the Eternal amid *light*nings on *Sinai's mountaintop*
> *nor ever have* come down with the *light* of inspiration *shining in his countenance* and bearing in his arms the tables of the *law*,
> graven in the language of the *outlaw*. [My italics and line divisions]. (*U* 133/181)

Aristotle says, 'All these figures may be found in the same sentence at once – antithesis, equality of clauses, and similarity of endings',[36] and Joyce's sentence seems to have been composed to this very prescription.[37] At the other extreme of eloquence, all four abuses which, according to Aristotle, produce 'frigidity of style' – the inappropriate use of compound words, of strange or unnatural words, of epithets which are 'long or unseasonable or too crowded', and of metaphors which are ridiculous, inflated or far-fetched[38] – are exemplified in combination in Dan Dawson's speech. Moreover, Bloom's unspoken defence of Dawson's fustian ('All very fine to jeer at it now in cold print but it goes down like hot cake that stuff') has an Aristotelian precedent:

> [The speeches] of rhetoricians, however well delivered, are amateurish when read. The reason is that they are only suitable to public debates; hence

---

[34] W. Rhys Roberts clarifies the distinction between the two subdivisions of invented examples by translating the terms as 'illustrative parallel' and 'fable'. (*Aristotle: 'Rhetoric' and 'Poetics'* (New York, Random House 1954), 133).

[35] Joyce had at least some knowledge of the *Rhetoric* as a schoolboy. In an essay, 'The Study of Languages', he wrote that 'The notion of Aristotle and his school, that in a bad cause there can be true oratory, is utterly false' (*CW*, 28).

[36] *Rhetoric* III, ix, 9, p. 395.

[37] A pamphlet quoting Taylor's speech confirms that Joyce carefully patterned the peroration, although the pattern was partially present in Taylor's play on 'law' and 'outlaw': 'Would he ever have come down from the Mount with the light of God shining on his face and carrying in his hands the Tables of the Law written in the language of the outlaw?' (See *Workshop*, 157).

[38] *Rhetoric* III, iii, 1–4, pp. 361–7.

speeches suited for delivery, when delivery is absent, do not fulfil their proper function and appear silly.[39]

Even Lenehan is catered for by Aristotle, who lists such devices as 'clever riddles', paradoxes, 'slight changes in words', 'jokes that turn on a change of letter' and puns;[40] though Lenehan's constant attempts to ingratiate himself belong to the behaviour of a buffoon:

> Irony is more gentlemanly than buffoonery; for the first is employed on one's own account, the second on that of another.[41]

The direct or indirect influence of Aristotle on the chapter is an issue of minor importance: the principal function of Joyce's handling is to contrast the true rhetorical tradition of Ireland, represented by men of an earlier generation like Taylor and Bushe, with the debased forms displayed by the editor and his cronies. It is probably of this corruption that Stephen is thinking when, in the middle of Taylor's speech, he recalls the words of St Augustine:

> It was revealed to me that those things are good which yet are corrupted which neither if they were supremely good nor unless they were good could be corrupted.   (*U* 132/180)[42]

The implied defence of the art of rhetoric again approximates to Aristotle's:

> If it is argued that one who makes an unfair use of such faculty of speech may do a great deal of harm, this objection applies equally to all good things except virtue, and above all to those things which are most useful, such as strength, health, wealth, generalship; for as these, rightly used, may be of the greatest benefit, so, wrongly used, they may do an equal amount of harm.[43]

Immediately before recalling Augustine's words, Stephen, listening to Taylor's exordium, has thought, 'Noble words coming. Look out. Could you try your hand at it yourself?', and his recognition that rhetoric, however it may be corrupted, is in itself good leads him, in fact, to try his hand – 'I have a vision too' – with a '*Pisgah Sight of Palestine*', which responds in opposition to Taylor's eloquent example. The scheme of the whole chapter and its relation to the central action of the novel depends on the distinction between true rhetoric and its corruption. Rhetoric is one of the fields of activity where citizen and artist should theoretically meet: but, in 'Aeolus', Bloom hears only the turgid nonsense of Dan Dawson (which he regards as 'high falutin stuff', but popular stuff), while Stephen hears and is moved by the remembered speeches of Bushe and Taylor. Bloom, as canvasser, depends on the fickle and turbulent wind-god, Crawford, while Stephen ignores Crawford's attempt to recuit him into 'the pressgang', and offers instead an ironic variation on Taylor's vision of the Promised Land.

---

[39] *Ibid*. III, xii, 2, p. 419.   [40] *Ibid*. III, xi, 6–7, pp. 409–11.

[41] *Ibid*. III, xviii, 7, p. 467.

[42] The quotation was used in the original short form of *A Portrait of the Artist*, though there it was applied to 'the beauty of mortal conditions' (*Workshop*, 65).

[43] *Rhetoric* I, i, 13, p. 13.

The degeneration of rhetoric is part symptom and part cause of the separation of citizen and artist.

The most corrupt form of rhetoric, current in Dublin, was in the newspapers themselves. The contemptuous ridicule of Dawson's speech, and the admiration of Bushe's and Taylor's might suggest that the pressmen in the office were defenders of true rhetoric against debasement; what prevents this view are the headlines,[44] which show journalism to be the ultimate corruption of rhetoric; and I believe that it was to perform this function that they were added after the first publication of the chapter in the *Little Review*. Stuart Gilbert's observation about their character is again perceptive:

> It will be noticed that the style of the captions is gradually modified in the course of the episode; the first are comparatively dignified, or classically allusive, in the Victorian tradition; later captions reproduce, in all its vulgarity, the slickness of the modern press. This historico-literary technique, here inaugurated, is a preparation for the employment of the same method, but on the grand scale, a stylistic *tour de force*, in a later episode, the *Oxen of the Sun*.[45]

But despite their comparative dignity, the early headlines are as false as the later ones: the inflation is only of a different kind. 'IN THE HEART OF THE HIBERNIAN METROPOLIS' is a highfaluting heading for the description of a tram-terminus; 'THE WEARER OF THE CROWN' turns out to be a mailvan; and the 'GENTLEMEN OF THE PRESS' consist of an advertisement canvasser, an advertisement clerk and a newsboy. There is not much to choose in point of vulgarity between the faked-up emotion of 'WITH UNFEIGNED REGRET IT IS WE ANNOUNCE THE DISSOLUTION OF A MOST RESPECTED DUBLIN BURGESS', and the attempt to inject a false excitement into Antisthenes' preference for Penelope above Helen: 'SOPHIST WALLOPS HAUGHTY HELEN SQUARE ON PROBOSCIS. SPARTANS GNASH MOLARS. ITHACANS VOW PEN IS CHAMP.' And, finally, there is an equal irrelevance, in early and late captions to the 'news' which they introduce: the last form of speech which Dawson can be accused of using is 'HIS NATIVE DORIC'; it is hard to conceive a more inappropriate heading for MacHugh's attack on the 'cloacal obsession' of the Romans than 'THE GRANDEUR THAT WAS ROME'; and the old woman's response to Nelson's pillar is entirely falsified by 'SOME COLUMN! – THAT'S WHAT WADDLER ONE SAID.' Thus, despite the variety of manner, which not only traces a 'historico-literary' development but also reflects the changing moods of the chapter from Bloom's respectful admiration to Stephen's ironic contempt, the headlines consistently exhibit the inflation, insincerity, vulgarity and ignorant lying of the journalistic corruption of rhetoric. They are not an idle, if amusing, trick, but an important element in the presentation of Dublin rhetoric, and, consequently, of the barriers between citizen

[44] M. J. C. Hodgart argues persuasively that what are usually referred to as the 'headlines' of the chapter are more like 'captions under imaginary illustrations' (*Hart and Hayman*, 129). Yet, in 'Aeolus', they look like and act like headlines and subheadings.
[45] *Gilbert*, 178 n. 1.

and artist in those very areas of public life where, traditionally, there was a relationship.

But the shaping technique of the 'Aeolus' chapter is the movement to a climactic focus in Stephen's parable. Besides its function as a dry antidote to the somewhat syrupy flavours of Dublin rhetoric, it rounds off the chapter by echoing the scene presented in the opening paragraph. At the end of the parable the trams are suddenly paralysed, 'becalmed in short circuit', and Nelson's Pillar is the scene of Stephen's story. The Moses-theme, introduced in Bloom's memory of the Passover ritual, suggested in Dawson's distant prospect of *'Our Lovely Land'* seen from 'the serried mountain peaks' and in MacHugh's image of the Jews in the wilderness building an altar to Jehovah on the mountaintop, and developed in the speeches of Bushe and Taylor, culminates in the anticlimax of *'A Pisgah Sight of Palestine'*. Stephen's vision focuses rhetoric, setting, symbol and theme, and is given added emphasis by its placing and by the sudden change in Stephen's manner. That taciturn and reserved young man, whose thoughts when he entered the newspaper office were of his verse about the 'pale vampire' Death, now, uninvited, unburdens himself of his vision, and declares secretly, 'Let there be life' (*U* 135/183).

The emphasis on his story and its description as a parable invite critical interpretation, though there is very little agreement as to what Stephen meant and even less as to what Joyce meant. Some of the difficulties are illustrated by Hugh Kenner's comment that 'the vision [Stephen] enunciates is a parable of infertility: plumstones dropping over Dublin from a phallic monument.'[46] No doubt the sexual innuendoes playing round the story justify the phallic significance of the pillar, but this makes nothing of the Mosaic reference, and, as plumstones are the seeds of the plum, they seem an inept symbol of infertility. Before speculating about the meaning of the parable, it would be sensible to consider its nature and function in the total fabric of the novel. It is not a self-contained authorial interpolation, but an effusion of Stephen's mind at a certain point in the action, and the climax to the chapter. With the exception of the imitative verse which accompanies his entry into the chapter, the parable is the first manifestation, in the novel, of the young artist's talent. In it, many disparate thoughts and experiences are fused: the two old women seen on the beach; the lane where he had embraced a prostitute; Mr Deasy's money-box; the girl selling plums at the foot of Nelson's pillar (whose cry Bloom had heard on his way to Glasnevin); old Mary Ann, of Mulligan's song, 'hising up her petticoats'; the speeches of Bushe and Taylor; and Crawford's advice to write 'something with a bite in it' about him and his fellow Dubliners. Some links have already been established in Stephen's mind: on the beach he had imagined the two old women to be hiding a baby in the bulrushes, and, listening to Taylor's Moses analogy, he had linked this image with that of Michelangelo's Moses, described in the speech of Seymour Bushe. But other less explicit trains of thought are involved.

[46]*Kenner*, 251.

When Stephen calls Nelson 'the onehandled adulterer', MacHugh cries out, 'I like that. I see the idea. I see what you mean.' There seems to be no great wit in the epithet 'onehandled',[47] but, in Stephen's phrase, the adjective distinguishes Nelson from the other famous Dublin adulterer, the man at whose memory Dante, in the *Portrait*, had screamed out 'Adulterer!' and whom Bloom remembered 'clothed in the mantle of adultery' – Charles Stewart Parnell. Parnell had been the Moses of the Irish people: Richard Ellman records that 'Mosaic imagery was commonly applied to Parnell'[48] and Joyce himself, in 1912, described Parnell as the leader who, 'like another Moses, led a turbulent and unstable people from the house of shame to the verge of the Promised Land'.[49] It is Parnell who is suggested by the figure of Moses in Taylor's speech, and his premature death which seems to be regretted in J. J. O'Molloy's comment, 'And yet he died without having entered the land of promise'. Stephen's '*Pisgah Sight of Palestine*' sets the reality against Taylor's 'prophetic vision'. Despite MacHugh's talk of the Irish people as 'liege subjects of the catholic chivalry of Europe that foundered at Trafalgar', and despite the eloquence of the Moses analogy, it was the adulterous victor in that battle whose statue dominated the main thoroughfare of Dublin, while at the far end of the same street the foundation stone for a statue of Parnell, rejected and dishonoured for his adultery, remained unoccupied. (The foundation stone was laid in 1899 – Bloom noticed it on his way to the cemetery – but no statue was erected until 1911.[50]). MacHugh might well, at the end of the chapter, look up at Nelson, and repeat Stephen's phrase yet again, but this time 'grimly'. Nelson was the symbol of English domination, of 'the seas' ruler' before whose representative the old milkwoman had bowed her head. She, too, already identified as a symbol of Ireland, contributes to the two old women who take their view of Dublin from the commanding height of Nelson's Pillar, and show no interest in what they see except the position of the different churches. The parable relates to Stephen's earlier statement about the servitude of Ireland beneath 'the imperial British state . . . and the holy Roman catholic and apostolic church.' In an essay, published in 1907,

[47] Both J. Mitchell Morse (*The Sympathetic Alien: James Joyce and Catholicism* (New York University Press 1959), 38) and Arnold Goldman (*The Joyce Paradox: Form and Freedom in his Fiction* (London, Routledge and Kegan Paul 1966), 174, n. 19) suppose that Nelson is being compared to a chamberpot, on the grounds that in *Gas from a Burner* such a receptacle is called a 'onehandled urn'. If this were all, Stephen's point would be feeble as well as obscure, and would hardly deserve MacHugh's comment. Robert M. Adams remarks on the Nelson–Parnell contrast but without relating it to 'the onehandled adulterer' phrase: 'Prudent, chaste and beefy, Dublin nonetheless admires romantic adultery, condoning in Nelson what it condemned in Parnell' (*James Joyce: Common Sense and Beyond* (New York, Random House 1966), 143).

[48] *Ellmann–JJ*, 32n.   [49] *CW*, 225.

[50] Presumably Joyce had this in mind when he said, in 1907, that in Ireland 'even when the monuments are for the most popular men, whose character is most amenable to the will of the people, they rarely get beyond the laying of the foundation stone' (*CW*, 176). Weldon Thornton notes that the foundation stone of a monument to Wolfe Tone, laid in 1898, also remained without its statue (*Allusions*, 227).

Joyce had commented on Ireland's 'long parade of churches, cathedrals, convents, monasteries, and seminaries':

> Ireland, weighed down by multiple duties, has fulfilled what has hitherto been considered an impossible task – serving both God and Mammon, letting herself be milked by England and yet increasing Peter's pence . . . .[51]

In contrast to his earlier poeticizing, Stephen's parable is his first, characteristic creative act – moved by a dominant and oppressive idea, gathering to itself thoughts, associations and experiences, and finally provoked into expression by MacHugh's praise of Taylor's 'prophetic vision'. Stephen's counter-vision sets against the dream of the Promised Land the reality, and, against Taylor's poetic eloquence, a style of matter-of-fact bluntness:

> —Two Dublin vestals, Stephen said, elderly and pious, have lived fifty and fiftythree years in Fumbally's lane.   (*U* 135/183)

The mind of the artist, dejected and despairing at the beginning of the day' is now beginning to assert itself and to behave, as Stephen said in the *Portrait*, 'like the God of the creation', saying 'Let there be life' (*U* 135/183). It is still immature, as is suggested by the 'sudden young laugh' with which Stephen closes his story, and by the adolescent bitterness MacHugh perceives in him: although there is a closer relationship to life than could have been found in the 'deeply deep' epiphanies or the romantic verse, the relationship is as yet detached, cold and mocking. But the parable marks a stage in the young man's movement away from sterility, and although it does not, as Crawford might have hoped, 'paralyse Europe', yet its end coincides with a paralysis of the Dublin tramways system, a chance illustration of Stephen's vision of the state of Ireland. It is the promise of future achievement that Bloom acknowledges when the parable is repeated to him in his kitchen, although for Bloom achievement is measured in terms of 'financial, social, personal and sexual success' (*U* 646/802).

This examination of the nature and function of the parable incidentally goes some way towards interpreting it. Why it is called '*A Pisgah Sight of Palestine*' is clear enough; but it is not so clear why it is subtitled '*The Parable of the Plums*'. To look for a symbolic interpretation is dangerous in such a deliberately matter-of-fact story – if the plums are symbols, why not the brawn or the striped petticoats? The story is a parable, not an allegory or a symbolic image; its central meaning lies in what happens, not in what can be read into the details. The old women and Nelson's Pillar may be called 'symbols', but only in the sense that they are representative of the Irish people and English domination. Oversubtlety in the interpretation of plums and plumstones obscures the point of a story which MacHugh and, later, Bloom, easily understand. Two old women who want to survey their city, save their money, buy provisions, make their journey, and are then too exhausted, too frightened, too dizzied to continue looking at the prospect: 'too tired to look up or down or to speak', they sit and eat

[51] *CW*, 190.

their plums and carelessly spit the stones down on the city they had climbed to view. The Moses analogy becomes a parody. On Sinai, Moses had looked upon the back parts of God, had touched neither bread nor water for forty days and nights, and had brought down the stone tablets of the law; the two old women look up at 'the onehandled adulterer', settle down to eat their plums, and, as the headlines put it, 'DONATE DUBLIN'S CITS SPEEDPILLS VELOCITOUS AEROLITHS.' Stephen's vision of Ireland in the parable is like the vision which informs *Dubliners*: it presents the same hemiplegia of the will, the same bovine dullness, the same servility of spirit, and it does so in that tone of ironic detachment which characterizes the short stories. The sense of isolation and deprivation which underlies Stephen's bitterness is recognized by him when, in the hospital, he recalls his parable:

> Remember, Erin, thy generations and thy days of old, how thou settedst little by me and by my word and broughtest in a stranger to my gates to commit fornication in my sight and to wax fat and kick like Jeshurum. Therefore hast thou sinned against the light and hast made me, thy lord, to be the slave of servants. . . . Look forth now, my people, upon the land of behest, even from Horeb and from Nebo and from Pisgah and from the Horns of Hatten unto a land flowing with milk and money. But thou hast suckled me with a bitter milk: my moon and my sun thou hast quenched for ever. And thou hast left me alone for ever in the dark ways of my bitterness: and with a kiss of ashes hast thou kissed my mouth. (*U* 376/514)

The turning of Stephen's talent away from morbid versifyings about the kiss of death and towards a vision of the life of Dublin does not end his isolation or diminish his bitterness, but it affects his subsequent thoughts and behaviour; it influences the account he gives, in the Shakespeare discussion, of the productive enmity between the artist and his home, and sets him on a mental course that will make a relationship with Bloom possible and fruitful.

'Lestrygonians'

The 'technic' of 'Lestrygonians' was labelled by Joyce 'peristaltic', and this has inspired a number of critical attempts to find parallels between the narrative movement of the chapter and the involuntary muscular movement that propels food through the body. Stuart Gilbert, for instance, has suggested that

> this process is symbolized by Mr Bloom's pauses before various places of refreshment, the incomplete movements he makes towards satisfaction of the pangs of hunger which spasmodically urge him onward, and their ultimate appeasement.[52]

There are a few passages which might suggest peristalsis, but too few to justify the label for the 'technic' of the whole chapter, and I doubt whether there is anything peristaltic about Bloom's movements through the city.

[52] *Gilbert*, 204–5.

What is certain is that throughout the chapter, Bloom feels hungry: 'I'm hungry too', he thinks, and, later, 'Must eat', and then 'Ah, I'm hungry.' Just as the labels 'narcissism' and 'incubism' referred to a technique for representing, in interior monologue, a pervasive mood which repeatedly turns Bloom's thoughts in a certain direction and colours the language in which they are expressed, so 'peristaltic', too, seems to refer to a handling of the monologue to represent a feeling of hunger, at first unconscious but gradually becoming more assertive and urgent. When Bloom thinks of 'the gnaw of hunger' or hopes that there will be liver and bacon for lunch because 'Nature abhors a vacuum', he is referring to those feelings of abdominal discomfort, produced by peristaltic contractions, which we call hunger.[53] It is these feelings which shape his mental processes throughout the chapter: his belly is signalling to his mind, and in this sense the conduct of the chapter is 'peristaltic'.

As in 'Lotuseaters' and 'Hades', Bloom's general condition colours the style throughout. Many foods are named, and the common expressions which occur frequently to Bloom's mind have reference to food also: 'living on the fat of the land', 'have a finger in the pie', 'a feast for the gods', 'I was souped', 'drop him like a hot potato', 'the next thing on the menu', 'gammon and spinach', 'go to pot', 'country bred chawbacon', 'all the beef to the heels', 'couldn't swallow it all', and 'eat, drink and be merry'. Bloom's humour is given an alimentary flavour: he parodies Moore in 'the harp that once did starve us all'; he imagines a man talking with his mouth full – 'Table talk. I munched hum un thu Unchster Bunk un Munchday'; the sight of a sandwich suggests 'Ham and his descendants mustered and bred there'; the coffined Dignam becomes 'Dignam's potted meat'; the limerick Bloom recalls is about a cannibal who ate a clergyman's private parts; and thoughts of a city banquet produce such witticisms as 'too many drugs spoil the broth', and 'Do ptake some ptarmigan.' The physical world about him also becomes transformed: above 'the treacly swells' of the Liffey swerve 'hungry famished' gulls; the jerrybuilt suburbs consist of 'mushroom houses' and the architecture of the National Museum has 'cream curves'; poplin in one shop window looks like 'lustrous blood', and closestools in another turn his thoughts to the idea of tracing the passage of a foreign body through the entrails; even the clock in Davy Byrne's looks 'bilious'. Food dominates the descriptions of the Dubliners whom Bloom meets or remembers: Dilly Dedalus seems underfed on a diet of 'potatoes and marge', while Ben Dollard 'has legs like barrels', an 'appetite like an albatross', and would 'get outside of a baron of beef'; John Henry Menton has 'oyster eyes', Pat Kinsella 'parboiled eyes', a man in the Burton Restaurant 'sad booser's eyes' and John Howard Parnell 'poached eyes on ghost'; Mr Purefoy has 'muttonchop whiskers', Bob Doran 'bottle shoulders', and Tom Wall's baby son a 'head like a prize pumpkin'; Mrs Breen was once 'a tasty dresser', Molly 'looks out of plumb' and has

[53] Cf. 'Peristaltic movements taking place in an empty stomach give rise to the sensation of hunger' (W. Gordon Sears and R. S. Winwood, 5th edn, *Anatomy and Physiology for Nurses and Students of Human Biology* (London, Arnold 1974), 217).

'gumjelly lips', old Mrs Riordan was the possessor of a 'rumbling' stomach, and Queen Victoria is described as 'a good layer'; Professor Goodwin's tall hat had provided a 'flies' picnic', while on Nosey Flynn a flea is 'having a good square meal'; the blind boy's coat is slobbered with food, and Sir Frederick Falkiner seems replete with a good lunch and vintage wine; most significantly for Bloom, he remembers seeing Boylan at the door of the Red Bank restaurant that morning, and wonders whether he has been eating oysters to prepare himself sexually for the meeting with Molly. Even the civic, cultural, spiritual and business life of the city is presented in terms of food. Bloom's attitude to the police is sufficiently indicated by the description of them marching in 'goose step' at 'pudding time', some 'let out to graze' and others 'bound for their troughs'; but he is equally critical of the so-called republicans, 'halffed enthusiasts', who can be won over by stuffing them with meat and drink and who are always ready for a 'penny roll and a walk with the band'. The ethereal poetry of George Russell is blamed on his vegetarian diet, while Dan Dawson's eloquence is 'flap-doodle to feed fools on'. The Irish clergy have well-stocked 'butteries and larders', the nuns of Mount Carmel ('Sweet name too: caramel') fry everything 'in the best butter', the method of the Methodist Mr Purefoy is characterized as 'eating with a stopwatch, thirtytwo chews to the minute, a teetotaller is a 'dog in the manger' and the evangelist Dr Dowie preaches that 'God wants blood victim'. In the streets, the sandwichboardmen walk the gutters for 'bread and skilly', the cities are built by slaves feeding on 'bread and onions', while the upperclasses are '*Crème de la crème*', and hunters who, although pursuing the 'uneatable fox' are 'pothunters too' – pothunters being those who hunt for food.

These are only a selection from a chapter congested with references to food and eating which suggest the progressive permeation of Bloom's mind by his hunger. But Joyce is not merely concerned with creating an image of a hungry man's consciousness: Bloom's hunger is a threat to his moral nature, a threat he must either overcome or elude. In Odyssean terms, Bloom/Ulysses is in the land of the Lestrygonians, who devoured the crews of all the Greek ships, except Ulysses', who were saved by the prudence of their master. In Joyce's list of 'Correspondences', Antiphates is equated with 'Hunger', his daughter (who decoyed the Greeks) with 'Food', and the Lestrygonians with 'Teeth'. Although this is a set of correspondences which no reader would have discovered unaided, it does metaphorically represent a feature of the chapter which is both important and clear – that Bloom's hunger could deflect him from his lonely course, and absorb him like all the other citizens of Dublin, into a way of life of which the motto is 'Eat or be eaten. Kill! Kill!'

The risk is that much greater because, at this hour of the day, Bloom is at the lowest ebb of his moral resources:

This is the very worst hour of the day. Vitality. Dull, gloomy: hate this hour. Feel as if I had been eaten and spewed. (*U* 153/208)

It is less that he is depressed because he is hungry than that he is hungry because he is depressed, though both factors influence him. A few passages suggest ways in which the body affects the mind: Bloom thinks that a vegetarian diet 'produces the like waves of the brain the poetical', that 'hungry man is an angry man', and that 'peace and war depend on some fellow's digestion.' But, on the other hand, there is a strong implication that his physical hunger is related to his hunger for Molly's love, and that he hopes, by eating, to dispel the unhappiness that shakes him whenever he thinks of her forthcoming session with Boylan. For instance, recalling an evening walk with Boylan and Molly, he suspects that it was then, by touches of the elbows, arms and fingers, that Boylan made his approach and Molly silently consented, and, as usual, Bloom tries to dismiss these painful thoughts: 'Stop. Stop. If it was it was. Must.' The half-expressed decision to do something to escape from these thoughts is completed in the passage closely following, when silks in a shopwindow afflict Bloom with a longing for his wife's embraces:

> A warm human plumpness settled down on his brain. His brain yielded. Perfume of embraces all him assailed. With hungered flesh obscurely, he mutely craved to adore.
>
> Duke Street. Here we are. Must eat. The Burton. Feel better then. (*U* 157/214)

Evidently Bloom hopes, in eating, to subdue his craving for his wife's body. His memory of the afternoon on Howth when Molly gave herself to him is thick with oral imagery, associating sexual and physical hunger:

> Ravished over her I lay, full lips full open, kissed her mouth. Yum. Softly she gave me in my mouth the seedcake warm and chewed. Mawkish pulp her mouth had mumbled sweet and sour with spittle. Joy: I ate it: joy. Young life, her lips that gave me pouting. Soft, warm, sticky gumjelly lips. . . . Wildly I lay on her, kissed her; eyes, her lips, her stretched neck, beating, woman's breasts full in her blouse of nun's veiling, fat nipples upright. Hot I tongued her. She kissed me. I was kissed. All yielding she tossed my hair. Kissed, she kissed me.
>
> Me. And me now. (*U* 165/224)

Bloom's ecstasy, shaping the rhythms of the monologue (they are frequently metrical), is suddenly dispelled by the recollection of his present situation, and the sad irony of his memory is pointed by the fact that the whole passage is framed between his observations of two flies stuck together, buzzing. He is tormented by thoughts of Boylan; a momentary panic seizes him when the possibility that Boylan has venereal disease enters his mind; he briefly wonders whether the sandwich-board men are Boylan's employees; he looks round the Burton restaurant to ensure that Boylan is not there; and his composure is shaken when Nosey Flynn, enquiring about Molly's tour, asks innocently, 'Who's getting it up?' The same question had been asked by M'Coy earlier in the day, but now the sexual innuendo temporarily silences Bloom, and, when Flynn mentions Boylan's name, he looks at the clock: 'Not yet.' Again his physical hunger and his hunger for love interweave:

His midriff yearned then upward, sank within him, yearned more longly, longingly.

Wine. (*U* 161/220)

After this, it is not surprising that Bloom's heart and breath react violently when, on his way to the library, he almost bumps into Boylan.

In his troubled state of mind and body, Bloom's visions are gloomy. He imagines a desolate universe without sense or purpose, one 'cityful' of men following another in meaningless succession, and life itself a monotonous series of births and deaths:

> Things go on same day; day after day: squads of police marching out, back: trams in, out. . . . One born every second somewhere. Other dying every second. (*U* 153/208)

Even the struggle for existence is a mechanical cycle of 'stuffing food in one hole and out behind: food, chyle, blood, dung, earth, food: have to feed it like stoking an engine.' It is a grim vision of a world governed by soulless material forces in which such things as love and sympathy are absurdities. The proper inhabitants of such a world are those who follow the rules for survival: 'Every fellow for his own, tooth and nail', 'Eat or be eaten', 'All for number one', 'Hate people all round you.' The proper God for such a world is one who requires blood victims, and finds his sustenance in 'birth, hymen, martyr, war, foundation of a building, sacrifice, kidney burnt-offering, druid's altars.'

Although, in his lowered condition, Bloom sees himself in a world like this, he doesn't succumb to it. However hungry he may be, he will not eat in the restaurant where men feed like animals, and contents himself with a cheese sandwich and a glass of wine. He may be low-spirited but he will not deny his own moral nature by joining in the selfish struggle: he knows the gulls are moved by 'greed and cunning' but he feeds them; he feels pity for Dilly Dedalus, for Mrs Breen, for Mrs Purefoy, for all who suffer, and shows tact and sympathy when he helps the blind boy across the road. In *Stephen Hero*, Stephen had expressed his contempt for the religion of blood and had associated it with the eating habits of western man:

> Renan's Jesus is a trifle Buddhistic but the fierce eaters and drinkers of the western world would never worship such a figure. Blood will have blood. There are some people in this island who sing a hymn called 'Washed in the blood of the Lamb' by way of easing the religious impulse. Perhaps it's a question of diet but I would prefer to wash in rice-water. (*SH* 194)

Bloom, reading the 'Blood of the Lamb' throwaway handed to him outside Graham Lemon's, has a similar revulsion. The gods (or rather, goddesses) he admires are those of Ancient Greece, who feed on nectar and ambrosia, and are so far removed from mortal animals that they need no excretory orifices. It is to check this theory that he visits the Museum, escaping with relief from the turbulent emotions aroused by the sight of Boylan to 'cold statues: quiet there. Safe in a minute.' It is only a temporary safety, but it does constitute an escape from the savage Lestrygonian world through which he has passed.

Thus the prevalence in the chapter of the language of food and eating is not merely a verbal representation of Bloom's physical hunger: it expresses, too, the general desolation of his mood, his yearning for Molly, and his vision of the savagery of life. This is a black hour in his day: he is torn by emotions of longing and revulsion so powerful that to represent them Joyce had to concentrate and exaggerate the language of the interior monologue. The scene in the Burton restaurant is not an uncommon one, but the sound of the words is itself so thickly repellent ('swilling, wolfing gobfuls of sloppy food, their eyes bulging') that we share Bloom's revulsion and his feeling that the scene is symbolic of human selfishness and savagery. We can understand Bloom's veering towards vegetarianism merely through our own response to the sickening language used to present his image of a butcher's shop: 'Flayed glasseyed sheep hung from their haunches, sheepsnouts bloodypapered snivelling nosejam on sawdust.' The passage where he recalls the embrace on Howth enacts in its rhythms and words the overwhelming excitement and emotion still aroused in him by Molly, as the broken and incoherent stammerings of the monologue when he fears Boylan may have a venereal disease enact the shattering distress and confusion produced by the thought:

> If he . . .
> O!
> Eh?
> No . . No.
> No, no. I don't believe it. He wouldn't surely?
> No, no. (*U* 142/193–4)

Everywhere in the chapter, Joyce intensifies the language and finds new resources for the interior monologue, shaping both styles and techniques to present the consciousness of a man almost overwhelmed by a complex of physical, emotional and spiritual distresses, yet surviving with the help of his own prudence and good nature.

'Scylla and Charybdis'

The stylistic character of the 'Scylla and Charybdis' chapter is obviously dominated by the exposition and discussion of Stephen's Shakespeare theory: the term 'Dialectic' in the column headed 'Technic' presumably refers both to 'the art of critical examination into the truth of an opinion' (*SOED*) and to Stephen's search for a resolution of contending opposites. The men involved in this discussion are representative of Dublin's intellectual life, the topic of discussion is literary, and consequently the dialogue is far more allusive, mannered and artificial than in any earlier chapter. It is less like normal conversation than like the formal presentation and examination of a thesis. Mr Lyster, the librarian, the essence of formality, sets the tone from the start:

> Urbane, to comfort them, the Quaker librarian purred:

—And we have, have we not, those priceless pages of *Wilhelm Meister*? A great
poet on a great brother poet. A hesitating soul taking arms against a sea of
troubles, torn by conflicting doubts, as one sees in real life. (*U* 172/235)
The old-fashioned manner as much as the platitudes and clichés are
characteristic of Mr Lyster – everyone in the chapter has a characteristic
way of speaking – but a similar bookish artificiality is present in the speech
of Eglinton, Russell, Best and Stephen himself. Not only is Stephen's
language mannered, the conduct of his argument is according to Jesuitical
precept, beginning with 'Composition of place', as advised by St Ignatius
Loyola and defined and practised by Father Arnall in the *Portrait*:

> —The play begins. A player comes on under the shadow, made up in the
> castoff mail of a court buck, a wellset man with a bass voice. It is the ghost,
> the king, a king and no king, and the player is Shakespeare who has studied
> *Hamlet* all the years of his life which were not vanity in order to play the part
> of the spectre. (*U* 177/241)

From the beginning of his exposition Stephen (clad in Buck Mulligan's
castoff shoes) is present behind the Shakespeare mask, not merely the
mask of the dramatist but also that of the actor. The whole of his speech
in the library is a performance, as the style itself suggests:

> If others have their will Ann hath a way. By cock, she was to blame. She put
> the comether on him, sweet and twentysix. The greyeyed goddess who bends
> over the boy Adonis, stooping to conquer, as prologue to the swelling act, is a
> boldfaced Stratford wench who tumbles in a cornfield a lover younger than
> herself. (*U* 179/244)

These few sentences run together allusions to the *Sonnets*, *Hamlet*, *Twelfth
Night*, *Venus and Adonis*, *Macbeth* and *As You Like It*, together with an
old joke about Hathaway, a bawdy innuendo, and a phrase from Goldsmith.
It is a mock literary argument, an attempt to overwhelm the audience with
a show of learning (though few of the references have any relevance to the
point at issue) in accordance with Stephen's original plan: 'Work in all
you know. Make them accomplices.' As snatches of his interior monologue
indicate, Stephen is putting on a show:

> Smile. Smile Cranly's smile. (*U* 173/235)

> Now your best French polish. (*U* 181/246)

> They list. And in the porches of their ears I pour. (*U* 185/252)

> I think you're getting on very nicely. Just mix up a mixture of theolologico-
> philolological. *Mingo, minxi, mictum, mingere.* (*U* 193/263)

> Flatter. Rarely. But flatter. (*U* 196/267)

> Don't tell them he was nine years old when it was quenched. (*U* 198/269)

Stephen is playing a role, beating these literary men, for whom he has little
respect, at their own game. But the deceit is not just a trivial trick; as in
'Aeolus' he borrowed the Mosaic imagery to articulate his vision of the
Irish people, so now he uses the life of Shakespeare as a way of discovering

and understanding his own nature – 'W.H.: who am I?' For him, the men in the library form an audience on which to sharpen his wits and his self-understanding:

> Where is your brother? Apothecaries' hall. My whetstone. Him, then Cranly, Mulligan: now these. Speech, speech. But act. Act speech. They mock to try you. Act. Be acted upon. (*U* 199/271)

This is a modification of the policy of silence, exile and cunning, decided on in the *Portrait*. He will break silence, make the required speech, but it will be acted speech. They mock him to test his intellectual claims; he meets the test but in a spirit of mockery. He will act, and thus take part in their mummery, and, in doing so, will be exposed to it, will be acted on. The importance of these words, 'Act. Be acted on', is, almost at once, made clear when Stephen accepts Eglinton's assertion that Shakespeare is 'all in all' in Hamlet:

> —He is, Stephen said. The boy of act one is the mature man of act five. All in all. In *Cymbeline*, in *Othello* he is bawd and cuckold. He acts and is acted on. Lover of an ideal or a perversion, like José he kills the real Carmen. His unremitting intellect is the hornmad Iago ceaselessly willing that the moor in him shall suffer. (*U* 200–201/272–3)

For the boy to become the mature man, for the artist to become 'all in all', he must both act and suffer; he must sacrifice his real self to the claims of his ideal artistic self. He plays 'bawd' to his audience, at the cost of becoming himself the 'cuckold'. Yet it is only by acting this role, by exposing himself to the 'real' world, that he can discover and understand himself:

> Every life is many days, day after day. We walk through ourselves, meeting robbers, ghosts, giants, old men, young men, wives, widows, brothers-in-love. But always meeting ourselves. (*U* 201/273)

The style of the dialogue of this chapter is, then, deliberately artificial and yet, like the Shakespeare theory itself, expressive of a development in Stephen towards a recognition of the necessary interaction between the artist's true self and the world around him, not adapting to it or corrupted by it, but acting on it and being acted on. To his audience, it is a remarkable performance, though, since they themselves are mummers unconscious of their mummery, they are puzzled by Stephen's prompt declaration that he does not believe his own theory. For Stephen, it has all been play-acting, but, nevertheless, acting in earnest. As he leaves the room he asks himself, 'What have I learned? Of them? Of me?'

The theatrical character of the dialogue is supported by a few devices of lay-out: the advertisement for

HAMLET
ou
LE DISTRAIT
Pièce de Shakespeare

is set out on the page like a playbill, and Mulligan later introduces the title-page and *dramatis personae* of his 'national immorality in three orgasms'. The prosaic discussion of Shakespeare's will is printed as blank verse (though it is flat, unmetrical and incompetent); thanks to John Eglinton's ironic remark, 'The plot thickens', the beginning of the talk about Shakespeare's brother is set out in dramatic form, and accompanied by musical instructions like the libretto of an opera; and the chapter ends with some lines from Cymbeline's concluding speech. None of these devices is important in itself (though some of them become important in later chapters) but each helps to strengthen the image of play-acting.

The interior monologue is affected by the same image. Because Stephen is playing a role, his monologue frequently falls into stagy parodies – of Yankee or Cockney slang, of theosophical or advertising jargon, of medieval, Elizabethan, Irish and Quaker styles, and of the Lord's Prayer, accompanied by a *Gloria in Excelsis Deo* in neume notation. Mulligan's arrival signals for Stephen an '*entr'acte*' in the discussion, and at times the monologue splits into a dramatic dispute between Stephen's divided selves:

How now, sirrah, that pound he lent you when you were hungry?
Marry, I wanted it.
Take thou this noble.
Go to! You spent most of it in Georgina Johnson's bed, clergyman's daughter. Agenbite of inwit.
Do you intend to pay it back?
O, yes.
When? Now?
Well . . . no.
When, then?
I paid my way. I paid my way. (*U* 178/242)

But most remarkably the authorial narrative itself is infected with theatricality. Mr Lyster's movements are presented as a series of Elizabethan dance-steps, and the sentences themselves are sometimes set to a dance rhythm: 'Swiftly rectly creaking rectly rectly he was rectly gone.' Buck Mulligan, too, enters, with 'a ribald face', 'blithe in motley' and carrying his hat like a 'bauble', exits like 'a lubber jester', goes downstairs 'iambing, trolling' ('Puck Mulligan footed featly, trilling') and, finally, whispers to Stephen 'with clown's awe'. The other characters at different times assume different roles: Russell, seen first 'bearded amid darkgreener shadow, an ollav, holyeyed', emerges from the shadow as 'a tall figure in bearded homespun' examining his 'cooperative watch'; Eglinton can seem like the villain of a melodrama, exerting 'the bane of miscreant eyes, glinting stern under wrinkled brows', yet, later, when flattered, appear 'gladly glancing, a merry puritan, through the twisted eglantine'; and Best makes his appearance like a juvenile lead, in neat and dapper sentences rounded with a rhyme:

Mr Best entered, tall, young, mild, light. He bore in his hand with grace a notebook, new, large, clean, bright. (*U* 174/237)

The language of the narrative frequently echoes that of the dialogue: when Stephen says that the errors of a man of genius are 'the portals of discovery', immediately the librarian enters, not through a door, but through 'portals of discovery', and when Best quotes Hamlet's speech, 'Those who are married, . . . all save one, shall live. The rest shall keep as they are', he laughs 'unmarried, at Eglinton Johannes, of arts a bachelor.' Even more frequently, the way in which things are said reflects, in a very selfconscious manner, what is said, as though the speakers were actors, underlining their words with exaggerated gesture and intonation: the following are just a few examples of this device.

—A shrew, John Eglinton said shrewdly . . . (*U* 179/243)

—Yes, Mr Best said youngly, I feel Hamlet quite young. (*U* 183/249)

—The most brilliant of all is that story of Wilde's, Mr Best said, lifting his brilliant notebook. (*U* 187/254)

—History shows that to be true, *inquit Eglintonus Chronolologos*. (*U* 195/265)

In earlier chapters, where the interior monologue influenced or was echoed in the language of the narrative, it was reasonable to assume that the outside world was being viewed through the eyes of the monologist, but the sustained theatricality of 'Scylla and Charybdis' cannot plausibly be attributed to Stephen. One is conscious, rather, of an authorial vision shaping and colouring everything in the chapter, and presenting Joyce's perception and assessment of the behaviour of the characters through style and technique. It is not only Stephen who is acting: the others, too, are involved in a pretentious mummery: 'Mummed in names: A.E., eon: Magee, John Eglinton.' Stephen is out-mumming the mummers ('O, you peerless mummer!'), but purposively and seriously. His audience, who fail to recognize the mockery, fail, too, to recognize the purpose. The Quaker librarian observes, concerning Wilde's Shakespeare theory, that 'the mocker is never taken seriously when he is most serious' and the group talks 'seriously of mocker's seriousness', but they cannot perceive the relevance of this to Stephen. In this chapter, even God becomes 'the playwright who wrote the folio of this world and wrote it badly'; he is 'the lord of things as they are' against whom the artist, 'lover of an ideal', must struggle.

'Scylla and Charybdis' is the conclusion of the first half of the novel.[54] Stephen is, as it were, ready for the fertilizing contact with Bloom: he has entered, however ironically, into the life of the city, has examined his own nature as artist, and, through his Shakespeare theory, has begun to apprehend his future course. In the previous chapter, Bloom has thought '*Hamlet, I am thy father's spirit*', and, in his exposition, Stephen has repeatedly presented Shakespeare in Bloomian terms – as a betrayed husband, 'bawd and cuckold', as inheritor of the 'mystical estate' of fatherhood, and, in answer to Eglinton's challenge, as a Jew. Eglinton accuses Stephen of having reduced Shakespeare's plays to projections of 'a French

[54] *Letters* I, 145.

triangle', as Joyce might be said to have reduced the *Odyssey* to the French triangle, Bloom–Molly–Boylan. And, finally, leaving the library, Stephen, conscious of the 'seas between' himself and Mulligan, sees Bloom pass quietly through, and recalls his dream of the street of harlots and his easy flight. This first notice of Bloom by Stephen properly concludes the first half of the novel.

The chapter marks a turning point in the handling of style and technique. The three elements characteristic of most novels – the representation of what is done, the presentation of what is said, the description of what is thought – have each been developed and complicated, and their inter-relationships multiplied, until in this chapter they become similarly and equally expressive of the author's vision. In the styles and techniques of the first nine chapters there is no comparatively consistent mode of pre-sentation, suddenly discarded in the latter half of the book, but a constant and gradual development to the complexity of 'Scylla and Charybdis'. The subsequent chapters continue this development, they do not suddenly break with it. The musical colouring of 'Sirens' is foreshadowed in the theatrical colouring of 'Scylla and Charybdis'; the inflated passages of 'Cyclops' are foreshadowed in Dan Dawson's windy rhetoric and the headlines of 'Aeolus'; the qualifying of the interior monologue by the physical processes of tumescence and detumescence in 'Nausicaa' is an extension of what happens to Bloom's monologue in 'Lestrygonians', under the influence of physical hunger and its satisfaction. The later developments are bolder, but are based on the same general principle of making the style progressively carry more and more of the burden of significance, until it becomes the means by which Joyce simultaneously creates, interprets and assesses.

'Wandering Rocks'

The 'Wandering Rocks' chapter continues the methods already developed to present narration, dialogue and thoughts, but requires of the reader a new distancing. With few and minor exceptions – the opening paragraphs of the novel, a whispered conversation in the cemetery, the brief gap between Bloom's departure and Stephen's arrival in 'Aeolus', and Bloom's visit to the lavatory in 'Lestrygonians' – the reader has been present only when Bloom or Stephen was present: now he moves freely about Dublin. Up to this point in the novel the only interior monologues have been those of Bloom and Stephen; now there are interior monologues of the Very Reverend John Conmee, Miss Dunne the typist, Mr Kernan and young Patrick Dignam, briefly of Dilly Dedalus and M'Coy, and even of Blazes Boylan, though Boylan's is limited to a single characteristic thought – 'A young pullet' – as he looks into the neckline of the girl in the fruitshop. Through *oratio recta obliqua* we also get glimpses into the mind of the shop girl, looking at Boylan 'got up regardless, with his tie a bit crooked', of the reverend Hugh C. Love 'mindful of lords deputies whose hands benignant had held of yore rich advowsons', and of Gerty MacDowell who, looking at the viceregal cortege, 'knew by the style it was the lord and lady lieutenant but she couldn't see what Her Excellency had on because the tram and Spring's big yellow furniture van had to stop in front of her on account of its being the lord lieutenant.' The reader, accustomed to the integrating viewpoints of Bloom and Stephen, is, in this chapter, sent wandering like them among the citizens of Dublin. But although this chapter does not concentrate on the experience of Stephen and Bloom, their monologues are stylistically so much more intense and troubled than anything else in the chapter that they continue to be the focus of interest.

Stephen's conversation with Artifoni seems friendly and relaxed. When the older man says that Stephen is sacrificing himself to an idea, Stephen remarks smilingly that it is a bloodless sacrifice. But he is deceiving himself. The language of his later monologue is congested with revulsion, fear and misery. A jeweller's window calls up a Swiftian vision of men struggling for precious stones – 'Muddy swinesnouts, hands, root and root, gripe and wrest them' –, and the Yahoo reference is sustained in the image of the old jeweller, like 'grandfather ape gloating on a stolen hoard.' The sounds of the powerhouse produce a desperate feeling that he is caught between 'two roaring worlds', the physical body he occupies and the world about him:[55] a momentary challenge to the God of this universe, 'bawd and butcher', to shatter him is quickly withdrawn. The most painful moment is when he sees his sister Dilly, whose eyes are like his, whose mind is a shadow of his mind, reduced to buying a secondhand French primer to feed her mind. He knows the poverty of his home, with the children dependent for food on charity and on what can be cadged from their irresponsible father, and he feels the pressure to help. The girl's plight reminds him of his dead mother and of his thoughts, earlier that morning, of his inability to rescue a drowning man. Stephen, who has been paid that morning, who has bought drinks for the newspapermen and will later buy drinks for his companions in the hospital, and who will readily give the contemptible Corley half-a-crown, offers nothing to Dilly, who has just with great difficulty extracted one-and-twopence from her father. His behaviour seems both sentimental and cold; he can agonize for his sister, without doing anything to help. But it is the essence of his position to refuse to submit to family ties and responsibilities: he suffers because he refused his dying mother's wish, and he suffers because he refuses to rescue his sisters. Yet, as the drowning image shows, he fears that once he commits himself to the service of his family he will destroy the ideal he pursues. As he had said of Shakespeare, he sacrifices his humanity to the ideal.

[55] Richard Ellmann and Ellsworth Mason have drawn attention to the apparent reflection in this incident of a passage from James Lane Allen's novel, *The Mettle of the Pasture*, quoted by Joyce in his review of that novel in 1903: '. . . but without us and within us moves one universe that saves us or ruins us only for its own purposes' (*CW*, 118).

Bloom's short monologue is equally intense; in search of a book for
Molly, he opens and reads some sentences from *Sweets of Sin* which
excite him sexually and, at the same time, force into his mind an image
of the animality of the sexual act which will take place that afternoon in his
bed – an image which, until now, he has studiously avoided:

> Warmth showered gently over him, cowing his flesh. Flesh yielded amid
> rumpled clothes. Whites of eyes swooning up. His nostrils arched themselves
> for prey. Melting breast ointments (*for him! For Raoul!*). Armpits' oniony
> sweat. Fishgluey slime (*her heaving embonpoint!*). Feel! Press! Crushed!
> Sulphur dung of lions! (*U* 223/303)

Nothing else in the chapter has the stylistic intensity of the presentation
of these experiences. On the contrary, Joyce demonstrates that interior
monologue can be a distancing as well as an involving device. This is
especially true of the first section where the monologue is one of the many
methods by which Joyce exposes Conmee, the representative of the Church,
to irony. Conmee is setting out on a charitable errand, to obtain a place for
young Dignam at the Artane orphans' school, but the first snatch of monologue reveals the depth of his concern:

> Just nice time to walk to Artane. What was that boy's name again? Dignam,
> yes. *Vere dignum et justum est.* Brother Swan was the person to see. Mr
> Cunningham's letter. Yes. Oblige him, if possible. Good practical catholic:
> useful at mission time. (*U* 206/280)

His mind is so little occupied with the fatherless boy that he has forgotten
his name, and, when he does recall it, uses it for a little clerical jest. One
can understand Conmee's giving the onelegged sailor a blessing instead of
money because he has only one silver crown in his purse, but his subsequent thoughts, prompted by the sailor's condition, are harder to condone:

> He thought, but not for long, of soldiers and sailors, whose legs had been shot
> off by cannonballs, ending their days in some pauper ward, and of cardinal
> Wolsey's words: *If I had served my God as I had served my king He would not
> have abandoned me in my old days.* (*U* 207/80)

The parenthesis 'but not for long' is suggestive of Joyce's judgement of
this kind of priest, whose response to the sight of a cripple is a smug
satisfaction, and who interprets Wolsey's words to mean that those who
serve God (such as priests) will be looked after in economic terms and not
allowed to die in a 'pauper ward'. Conmee's respect for worldly power,
wealth and position becomes increasingly evident. He cannot refer even in
his thoughts to Mrs Sheehy's husband without giving him his full title,
'Mr David Sheehy M.P.'; his uneasiness about the preaching of Father
Bernard Vaughan is relieved by the thought that Vaughan is probably 'of
good family'; Mrs M'Guinness, the pawnbroker, seems to him to have 'a
queenly mien'; and he dreams of the old days when he might have been
'don John Conmee', honoured among the nobility. The closing sentence of
the section is read by Conmee in his breviary:

Sin: *Principes persecuti sunt me gratis: et a verbis tuis formidavit cor meum.*
(*U* 212/88)

Stuart Gilbert's comment on this sentence is very curious. He says that the words 'are here symbolical of the rôle of Father Conmee in this chapter; as will be shown later, he is pitted against the counter-subject of the episode, the Viceroy, as the Irish Catholic Church against British rule, Christ against Caesar.'[56] Father Conmee, so far from being opposed to the Viceroy, remembers with nostalgia 'oldworldish days, loyal times in joyous townlands'. In fact, the quotation from *Psalm CXIX* is the crowning irony of the section. There is no fear of princes persecuting Conmee, the Jesuit, the representative of that order whose influence on its students is presented in *Stephen Hero*:

> They respected spiritual and temporal authorities, the spiritual authorities of Catholicism and of patriotism, and the temporal authorities of the hierarchy and the government.   (*SH* 177/8)

Father Conmee is a mild and well-meaning man, but it can hardly be said of him, as Gilbert says, that he stands for 'the spiritual antithesis of material glory.'[57] He has failed to read nones before lunch for what seems to him the sufficient reason that 'lady Maxwell had come': this is less suggestive of spirituality than of an analogy between Conmee and the person whose passage is briefly interpolated in this first section:

> Mr Dennis J. Maginni, professor of dancing, &c., in silk hat, slate frockcoat with silk facings, white kerchief tie, tight lavender trousers, canary gloves and pointed patent boots, walking with grave deportment most respectfully took the curbstone as he passed lady Maxwell at the corner of Dignam's court. (*U* 208/82)

Father Conmee 'liked cheerful decorum' and is a little too ready to dismiss problems with the thought that the ways of God are not the ways of men. Everywhere in his section, in interior monologue, narrative, dialogue, *oratio recta obliqua*, imagery, language, there is a sustained and detached humorous irony more reminiscent of the manner of 'Grace' than of anything in the earlier chapters of *Ulysses*.

The styles of the other monologues are similarly distancing in effect. Mr Kernan's presents him as a figure of comic self-satisfaction, admiring his own skill in handling a customer, priding himself on his 'dressy appearance', seeing in the mirror a 'returned Indian officer': in his own mind, he is not a commercial traveller but a 'knight of the road', able to forget, in his contempt for the graft that prevails in America, his own deserved reputation as an evader of debts. In contrast to Kernan's inflation, Master Patrick Aloysius Dignam's monologue is deflatory: there has been plenty of gloom and solemnity occasioned by his father's death, but Patrick's thoughts are presented in a cheerfully colloquial style. He is relieved to have escaped from the parlour, where his mother and her neighbours sit

[56] *Gilbert*, 227, n. 1.   [57] *Ibid*, 234.

sniffing and drinking sherry, 'and they eating crumbs of the cottage fruit cake jawing the whole blooming time and sighing.'

There is little stylistically or technically difficult in the narrative or dialogue sections; they throw light (usually sardonic) on some aspects of Dublin life. For instance, Bloom's earlier suspicion that Corny Kelleher is a police informer suggests some dramatic undercover work, but when, in the second section, this suspicion is confirmed, the tone is of squalid and absurd gossip rather than conspiracy. The refrain *'For England, home and beauty'* is angrily growled by a one-legged beggar, listened to by two barefoot urchins beslobbered with liquorice juice. Ned Lambert declaims, in the manner of a guide, 'We are standing in the historic council chamber of saint Mary's abbey where silken Thomas proclaimed himself a rebel in 1534. This is the most historic spot in all Dublin'; yet this most historic spot is now a dark and dirty warehouse filled with sacks. Bloom's response to the rich animality of the heroine of *Sweets of Sin*, *'the beautiful woman'* of *'opulent curves'*, *'queenly shoulders and heaving embonpoint'* and *'perfect lips'* is discoloured by the presence of the decrepit bookseller, unshaven, unkempt, stinking of onions, shaken by phlegmy coughs and peering through eyes 'bleared with old rheum', who recommends the book as 'a good one'. Over much of the chapter, there is an atmosphere of cheap squalor, physical and moral.

The most striking feature of the chapter is its division into sections, each presenting an episode in a different part of the Dublin streets, linked to each other by brief snatches of conversation or incident taken from earlier or later sections. The effect is to place each episode in time relative to other episodes. This is the technique which Joyce labelled 'Labyrinth': it is reminiscent of the way in which a person wandering in a maze glimpses, from time to time, other wanderers simultaneously following other routes. The interpolated links are not only temporal; they are often associated in some other way. The curve of the spit sent 'arching' by Corny Kelleher is linked to the trajectory of the coin flung by Molly from her window; the sound of the lacquey's bell coincides with the last-lap bell in a cycle race; Miss Dunne's typewriter is connected with Tom Rochford's machine. But the juxtapositions are often more significant than this. The deferential deportment of Mr Maginni, the dancing master, seems to comment on the Reverend Conmee, in whose section it occurs; the begging sailor is juxtaposed to J. J. O'Molloy calling on Ned Lambert to borrow money; while Boylan is buying fruits for Molly, we suddenly glimpse Bloom searching for a book for her; when Lambert is examining points of vantage for a camera in St Mary's Abbey, the picture of John Howard Parnell concentrating on the chessboard suddenly intrudes; Martin Cunningham prepares to accost Jimmy Henry, and, in another part of Dublin, Boylan waylays Bob Doran; and when Bloom, reading *Sweets of Sin*, exclaims to himself 'Young! Young!', we immediately switch to the elderly female, 'no more young', who has been at the law courts. It is characteristic of Joyce to use this linking device, which apparently serves only to relate the episodes in time, as a source of imagery, comment or comparison.[58]

All the business of the citizens of Dublin is confined between the opening and closing sections which present respectively the journeys of Conmee and the Viceroy, Church and state, each engaged on an ostensibly charitable mission, each accompanied by a series of salutes, though most of the salutes given to the viceregal cortege belie the bland officialese of the statement that 'the viceroy was most cordially greeted on his way through the metropolis.' The movements of the citizens to and fro are represented in essence by the shuttling of the sandwichboardmen or the madman, Cashel Boyle O'Connor Fitzmaurice Tisdall Farrell: the one object seen symbolically escaping from the confines of the city labyrinth is the Elijah throwaway, launched by Bloom, whose course along the Liffey towards the open sea is traced to the moment when it passes the homecoming Rosevean, the schooner noticed by Stephen at the end of the 'Proteus' chapter.[59]

The chapter serves to supply information lacking from the earlier chapters – for instance, besides confirming Bloom's guess about Corny Kelleher's police contacts, it shows the wretchedness of the Dedalus home, and gives the first close view of Blazes Boylan –, and to introduce characters who will appear in subsequent chapters – Ben Dollard, Father Cowley and the barmaids of the Ormond hotel reappear in 'Sirens', Bob Doran and Nolan in 'Cyclops', and Gerty MacDowell in 'Nausicaa'. Technically and stylistically it suggests the purposeless activity of the Dublin streets and dissipates the concentration on Bloom and Stephen. The reader is prepared to see them from a greater distance, as participants in, rather than observers of, the life of the city, and is, thus, also prepared for the more impersonal authorial techniques of the succeeding chapters.

'Sirens'

There is little in the technique of 'Sirens' which is intrinsically new in *Ulysses*. Earlier chapters have shown a mood or situation pervasively colouring the style; in 'Wandering Rocks', scenes geographically separated in Dublin have been juxtaposed; and there have been many mimetic

[58] Clive Hart has demonstrated that 'Wandering Rocks' is 'in terms of timing, realistically exact (or at any rate very nearly so)', and has explained most of the thirty-one interpolations (*Hart and Hayman*, 200 and 203–14).

[59] According to Richard Ellmann, Joyce told Paul Suter that 'he had found an analogy for the Homeric pigeon which flies safely between Scylla and Charybdis: it was the throwaway which is cast by Bloom into the Liffey to float successfully between the North and South Walls' (*Ellmann-JJ*, 452). But there is no Homeric pigeon; the passage of a dove between the Wandering Rocks occurs in the *Argonautica* of Apollonius of Rhodes. Homer makes no mention of it, but says that the Argo was the only ship ever to pass between the rocks. Stuart Gilbert calls the throwaway 'a miniature Argo', and three times in the 'Wandering Rocks' chapter the throwaway is referred to as a skiff. Paul Suter's memory must have been at fault in confusing the Argo with the Argonauts' bird, or in thinking that the bird was Homeric, and certainly in replacing the Wandering Rocks with Scylla and Charybdis.

modifications of the ordinary sounds and rhythms of language. Sounds like
those of waves, cats, machines, have been verbalized; overheard songs have
affected the phrasing of interior monologues; sentence rhythms have
responded to described movements, like those of the Quaker librarian; and
there have been varied distortions or manipulations of sound and syntax to
express some passing sensation or emotion. Consequently, there is no
reason for surprise that, in a chapter centring round an impromptu concert,
a teatray should be 'transposed' rather than shifted, that such expressions
as 'paying the piper' should occur with some frequency, and that musical
performances should influence the words and rhythms of the narrative and
the monologues. The general musical reference of the style is plain enough;
the usual objection to it is that Joyce engaged in a vain and pointless
attempt to impose musical forms on prose.

To identify the musical devices supposedly imitated by Joyce (Stuart
Gilbert illustrates *trillando, staccato, appoggiatura, martellato, sordamente,
portamento* or *glissando, rondo, fermata, affrettando, stretto,* suspension and
resolution, hollow fifth, polyphony, augmentation and final cadence [60] – other
commentators have added to the list) is of some academic interest, but the
real question concerns the effects in prose of the various devices adapted –
for the effect of a device in music may bear no resemblance to the effect of
the linguistic device suggested by it, if only because what is natural and
familiar in music may seem laboured and artificial in language. Take for
instance the sentences describing Miss Kennedy's departure from the
window where Miss Douce is enjoying the backward gaze of the Honourable Gerald Ward in the viceregal cortege:

> Miss Kennedy sauntered sadly from bright light, twining a loose hair
> behind an ear. Sauntering sadly, gold no more, she twisted turned a hair.
> Sadly she twined in sauntering gold hair behind a curving ear. (*U* 244/331)

One important effect produced by Joyce's 'musical' elaboration has nothing
to do with the musical origin of the style; the laboured verbal grace suggests
Mina Kennedy's self-conscious endeavour to display a romantic yet ladylike melancholy. The deliberate artificiality of the style reflects the affectation of the barmaid's manner – an affectation betrayed by her natural
vulgarity as soon as she speaks: 'It's them has the fine times, sadly then
she said.' The two sirens of the chapter are both silly creatures, who see
themselves as romantically attractive and, despite lapses, try to preserve a
flirtatious gentility. Joyce's devices frequently reflect the barmaids' manner
by setting what is vulgar or commonplace to tripping or languishing
rhythms, so that reality is mingled uneasily with their silly fantasies and
affectations. Miss Douce looks in the mirror to ballad metre, but despite
the poetical presentation the reader soon learns that the gilded lettering is
an advertisement for mineral water and the shell a souvenir of a seaside
holiday:

[60] *Gilbert,* 249–51.

> Miss Douce halfstood to see her skin/
> askance in the barmirror gilded-lettered/
> where hock and claret glasses shimmered/
> and in their midst a shell. (*U* 245/332)

To mark the line-endings, as I have done, draws attention to the metre, but to relate either of these passages to some specific musical device adds nothing to their effect; what matters in reading is to perceive and respond to the implications and suggestions of the sentence rhythms.

Both of these passages are exaggerated forms of what is commonly referred to as 'musical' prose, but it is not in this sense that the word 'musical' can be applied to the chapter as a whole: on the contrary, much of it is deliberately flat, discordant, clumsy, or disjointed. In 'Sirens', the surface action mainly consists of musical performance and discussion, Bloom's thoughts are dominated by music, the barmaids are representative sirens, and the language is full of musical references, but Joyce goes beyond mere verbal music; he derives from a range of musical forms and devices an analogous range of stylistic devices, responsive to every shift in the action or mood of the chapter. The problem for a reader is not to identify what lies beneath a layer of musical decoration, but to respond to a concentrated variety of functional devices, the effects of which are often cumulative and often complexly interwoven.

They serve primarily to delineate and evaluate character and behaviour: the sentences about the barmaids are comparatively simple and self-contained examples. Miss Douce and Miss Kennedy, as the sirens who lure men to the 'reef' of the Ormond Bar, have also a more remote and seductive aspect. The opening sentence of the chapter proper refers back to their appearance, in 'Wandering Rocks', watching the viceregal procession from their window, and prepares for the early sounding of the siren theme in its most rhythmic form:

> Yes, bronze from anear, by gold from afar, heard steel from anear, hoofs ring from afar, and heard steelhoofs ringhoof ringsteel. (*U* 245/332)

Apart from its mimetic sound, the sentence establishes the paired phrasings 'bronze ... gold', 'anear ... afar', which become the recurrent identifying patterns of this blest pair of sirens. Part of their charm lies in the 'exquisite contrast' in their colouring, and between the languid gentility of Miss Kennedy and the flirtatious vivacity of Miss Douce; and Joyce repeatedly makes variations on this contrasted pairing. Thus, when the barmaids burst into laughter, after they have been exchanging rude remarks about 'that old fogey in Boyd's', there is a romanticized parody of their laughter, heard as a chime of bells:

> Shrill, with deep laughter, after bronze in gold, they urged each each to peal after peal, ringing in changes, bronzegold goldbronze, shrilldeep, to laughter after laughter. (*U* 246/334-5)

Again the artificiality of the repetitions, assonances and rhythms suggests the element of affection in this girlish laughter, with each encouraging the other to laugh more: the sentence presents their dream of themselves, and the image they present to the customers, but there is a deflating sequel when the two girls return to their natural selves:

> —O saints above! Miss Douce said, sighed above her jumping rose. I wished I hadn't laughed so much. I feel all wet.
> —O, Miss Douce! Miss Kennedy protested. You horrid thing! (*U* 246/335)

The sexual undertones of the conversation about the old fogey are developed in the exchanges with Lenehan and Boylan. Neither barmaid has much time for the persistent but poor Lenehan, but Miss Douce's vulgarity responds to Boylan's ('Sparkling bronze azure eyed Blazure's skyblue bow and eyes'), and at his request she performs her little exhibitionist trick:

> Smack. She let free sudden in rebound her nipped elastic garter smackwarm against her smackable woman's warmhosed thigh. (*U* 252/343)

Here the style enacts the sound and action, and suggests as well the sexuality which underlies Miss Douce's manner and is the bait which draws the men to the bar. She tells Boylan, 'You're the essence of vulgarity', but this is part of his attraction for her, and she watches his departure pensively and wonders why he left so quickly after she had plucked her garter for him. In Boylan's absence, she consoles herself with the tamer attentions of George Lidwell, though Bloom, watching her listening to the song, *The Croppy Boy*, is sure that she is aware of his gaze, and deceives himself into thinking that her pose is for his benefit:

> At each slow satiny heaving bosom's wave (her heaving embon) red rose rose slowly, sank red rose. Heartbeats her breath: breath that is life. And all the tiny tiny fernfoils trembled of maidenhair. (*U* 271/369)

Miss Douce's undulations are supposed to be a natural reaction of sympathy and pity for the unfortunate hero of the song, but the slow sensual music of the style (supported by the fragment from *Sweets of Sin*) suggests a performance designed to titillate – as Bloom perceives, though he does not at first see that the show is aimed at Lidwell, not at him. In case there should be any doubt about the motivation behind the rise and fall of Miss Douce's breasts, she at once begins a performance, equally unconscious and innocent in appearance, but more frankly sexual:

> On the smooth jutting beerpull laid Lydia hand lightly, plumply, leave it to my hands. All lost in pity for croppy. Fro, to: to, fro: over the polished knob (she knows his eyes, my eyes, her eyes) her thumb and finger passed in pity: passed, repassed and, gently touching, then slid so smoothly, slowly down, a cool firm white enamel baton protruding through their sliding ring. (*U* 272/369)

The paragraph illustrates the economy of Joyce's style. In a few sentences, by manipulation of rhythm, repetition and alliteration, he vividly presents the scene, enacts the regular sensual movements of the hand, suggests the focusing of the men's attention on the hand and their sexual response to it, and observes Miss Douce's air of abstracted pity, her awareness of being watched (as well as Bloom's awareness of her awareness), and her siren-like instinct for the combination of gentle touching and firm movement which will most excite the watchers. What draws men to the bar is Miss Douce's manner of pert girlish innocence – an innocence which covers a latent sexuality and is designed to produce in the customers fantasies of being the first to arouse her. Bloom has just such a fantasy:

> Thrilled, she listened, bending in sympathy to hear.
> Blank face. Virgin should say: or fingered only. Write something on it: page. If not what becomes of them? Decline, despair. Keeps them young. Even admire themselves. See. Play on her. Lip blow. Body of white woman, a flute alive. Blow gentle. Loud. Three holes all woman.   (*U* 271/368)

Thus the theme of the sirens is developed through the chapter as the nature of the barmaids' allure is progressively revealed.

Boylan's passage through the chapter is even more emphatically developed to a reverberating climax. First, comes the isolated and unexplained word 'Jingle', reminiscent of Molly's jingling bed and of the jingling harness which seemed to pursue Bloom in 'Lestrygonians' (*U* 156–7/213–14). When it occurs again, 'Jingle jaunty jingle', a suggestion of Boylan 'jauntily' walking at the end of 'Wandering Rocks' is added. Soon the subject of the phrase is identified as we see Lenehan waiting for 'jingle jaunty blazes boy'. Bloom catches sight of Boylan and the source of 'jaunty' and 'jingle' is now clear, for Boylan is riding on a jauntingcar: 'Jingling on supple rubbers it jaunted from the bridge to Ormond quay.' Here the characteristically bounding, bold rhythms used to image Boylan's progress begin, but are soon halted by his arrival at the bar: 'Jingle jaunted by the curb and stopped.' His stay in the bar is brief, but long enough for Miss Douce's performance with her garter, and for the style to suggest his sensuality and appetite, tempted by the call of the sirens:

> Boylan, eyed, eyed. Tossed to fat lips his chalice, drank off his tiny chalice, sucking the last fat violet syrupy drops. His spellbound eyes went after her gliding head as it went down the bar by mirrors, gilded arch for ginger ale, hock and claret glasses shimmering, a spiky shell, where it concerted, mirrored, bronze with sunnier bronze.   (*U* 253/343)

Unfortunately for the barmaid, her attempt to excite Boylan is only too successful; his desire reminds him of the more accessible charms of Molly, and 'I'm off, said Boylan with impatience.' His urgency leads Lenehan to ask, 'Got the horn or what?', and this, too, becomes part of the Boylan music. It is traditionally considered a gross error of prose style to fall into regular metrical rhythms, but for Joyce everything is to be judged by its appropriateness and expressiveness in a particular context, and, here, the bouncing rhythms create an image of Boylan's coarse sexual self-confidence. They become even more stressed as he travels towards Molly ('Jingle jaunted down the quays. Blazes sprawled on bounding tyres') and the sexual reference becomes more blatant and heated:

By Bachelor's walk jogjaunty jingled Blazes Boylan, bachelor, in sun, in heat, mare's glossy rump atrot, with flick of whip, on bounding tyres: sprawled, warmseated, Boylan impatience, ardentbold. Horn. Have you the? Horn. Have you the? Haw haw horn. (*U* 255–6/347)

The thumping and trumpeting music accompanies Boylan across Dublin, at times breaking into song rhythms and rhyme:

Slower the mare went up the hill by the Rotunda, Rutland Square. Too slow for Boylan, blazes Boylan, impatience Boylan, joggled the mare. (*U* 262/356)

As Boylan reaches his destination, the rhythms become the beat and roll of a drum, heralding his arrival, expressive of his sexual eagerness and arrogance, and appropriate to his coarse, insensitive nature:

One rapped on a door, one tapped with a knock, did he knock Paul de Kock, with a loud proud knocker, with a cock carracarracarra cock. Cockcock. (*U* 268/364)

Before dismissing Joyce's rhythmic manipulations as idle ingenuities or mere decorations, one should consider how much of the total image and assessment of Blazes Boylan derives from them. Boylan's stay in the Ormond bar is brief and, while there, he neither says nor does much. If the reader experiences him as one of the dominant, driving forces of the chapter, and understands his nature and his animal energy, it is largely through the musical devices by which Joyce traces his self-confident and expectant journey, 'jiggedy jingle jaunty jaunty', to the rendezvous with Molly Bloom.

Another character whose passage through Dublin is followed with increasing attention, though with very different rhythms, is the blind piano-tuner. First, there are a number of unexplained, isolated and quite widely separated taps, each 'Tap' with a line to itself; then, at intervals, come 'Tap. Tap' (twice), 'Tap. Tap. Tap' (twice), 'Tap. Tap. Tap. Tap' (twice), until, eventually, as Bloom walks along the quay, the source of the sound is revealed: 'Tap blind walked tapping by the tap the curbstone tapping, tap by tap.' The tapping increases as the blind boy draws nearer to the bar – four taps, five, eight – until he reaches the shop where, earlier, Bloom had stopped to buy notepaper and had seen the advertisement for Mermaids, 'coolest whiff of all'. Here the blind boy theme is again given a brief development:

Tap. Tap. A stripling, blind, with a tapping cane, came taptaptapping by Daly's window where a mermaid, hair all streaming (but he couldn't see), blew whiffs of a mermaid (blind couldn't), mermaid coolest whiff of all. (*U* 275/374)

The parentheses refer back to 'Lestrygonians', where Bloom helped the blind boy across the road, and thought of his inability to see women or enjoy tobacco. Finally, he enters the bar as a Croppy Boy ('Tap. A youth entered a lonely Ormond hall'):

> Tip. An unseeing stripling stood in the door. He saw not bronze. He saw not gold. Nor Ben nor Bob nor Tom nor Si nor George nor tanks nor Richie nor Pat. Hee hee hee hee. He did not see.   (*U* 276/375)

The blind pianotuner's hesitant entry and journey is plainly contrasted with Boylan's assured jog-trot, with which it overlaps: as Boylan's journey leads up to the emotional climax of the chapter, the blind boy's brings the music of the chapter to a retarded close. The musical performances in the saloon were introduced by the sounding of the tuning-fork, and are completed (save for Bloom's flatulent *coda*) by the pianotuner's arrival to collect the tuning-fork which he had left behind. In his blindness, the Mermaid's advertisement, the visual symbol of the sirens, and the assembled company in the bar are obliterated.

Other musical devices represent more localized characters or behaviour:

> Miss Douce reached high to take a flagon, stretching her satin arm, her bust, that all but burst, so high.
> —O! O! jerked Lenehan, gasping at each stretch. O!
> But easily she seized her prey and led it low in triumph.   (*U* 251/341)

Here, Joyce depends on straining and relaxing rhythms, and rising and declining intonations, without going far beyond what is fairly common in carefully written prose. But for the boots, who rudely and discordantly interrupts the barmaids' fantasies, a curious and original device is used in both the arrival and departure of the boy:

> The boots to them, them in the bar, them barmaids came. For them unheeding him he banged on the counter his tray of chattering china.
>
> .   .   .   .   .
>
> —Imperthnthn thnthnthn, bootsnout sniffed rudely, as he retreated as she threatened as he had come.   (*U* 244/331–2)

The boy's jeering mockery of Miss Douce's complaint about his 'impertinent insolence' is straightforward, but his entry and departure are marked by triplets of brief expressions, linked in the first case by 'them' and in the second by 'as'. This seems intended to make the reader feel the discordant intrusion of the boots by jarring grammatical constructions: in the first passage, 'them' appears, in close succession, as dative pronoun, as colloquial demonstrative pronoun, and as demonstrative adjective; in the second, 'as' is successively a conjunction of time, of reason and of manner. Such an intrusion of grammatical and syntactic clumsiness dislocates the siren music, and jerks Miss Douce back to her native coarseness:

> —Most aggravating that young brat is. If he doesn't conduct himself I'll wring his ear for him a yard long.   (*U* 244/332)

The other male employee at the Ormond is Pat the waiter, bald, bothered and hard of hearing. He is the link between the three rooms of the hotel, the dining-room, the bar, and the saloon. His abrupt staccato rhythms, expressive of his hurried movements to and fro, and, perhaps, also suggesting the short words and expressions with which he is addressed because of his deafness, are modified by circumstances. They are established on his first appearance: 'To the door of the diningroom came bald Pat, came bothered Pat, came Pat, waiter of Ormond.' Bloom's sudden decision to write to Martha and consequent request for writing-materials produces an exaggerated abruptness: 'Bald Pat at a sign drew nigh. A pen and ink. He went. A pad. He went. A pad to blot. He heard, deaf Pat.' When Pat brings the materials, Bloom has been thinking of girls practising 'scales up and down', and the delivery is made in three evenly-accented octaves of mono-syllables: 'Bald deaf Pat brought quite flat pad ink. Pat set with ink pen quite flat pad. Pat took plate dish knife fork. Pat went.' But the fullest development of the Pat theme is more complicated. Between the songs of Simon Dedalus and Ben Dollard, Cowley is improvising at the piano, while Bloom, unhappily aware that by now Boylan is nearing Molly, tries in vain to catch the attention of the deaf waiter:

> Car near there now. Talk. Talk. Pat! Doesn't. Settling those napkins. Lot of ground he must cover in the day. Paint face behind on him then he'd be two. Wish they'd sing more. Keep my mind off.
> Bald Pat who is bothered / mitred the napkins. / Pat is a waiter / hard of his hearing. / Pat is a waiter / who waits while you wait. / Hee hee hee hee. / He waits while you wait. / Hee hee. / A waiter is he. / Hee hee hee hee. / He waits while you wait. / While you wait / if you wait / he will wait / while you wait. / Hee hee hee hee. / Hoh. / Wait while you wait. /   (*U* 266/362)

Marking the metrical divisions emphasizes how the passage, which Frank Budgen describes as a burlesque of 'the more banal tiddleypom aspects of music',[61] suggests the rhythms of the '*Largo al factotum*' from *The Barber of Seville*. Bloom's letter to Martha has already been coloured by his emotional response to Cowley's improvization of an intermezzo, and later his thoughts are influenced by the performance of the minuet from *Don Giovanni*: it seems likely that, at this point, Cowley has shifted to the Rossini aria, which has for Bloom, watching the way in which Pat is hurrying to and fro at everyone's beck and call, a special aptness.

Like the boots, bald Pat does not fit easily into the florid music of the sirens; when Miss Douce sees him conversing with Miss Kennedy, the pair are in 'inexquisite contrast'. This kind of contrast is essential to a chapter in which moments of nostalgia and pathos are set in a context of comic incongruity. Bloom is deeply moved by Simon Dedalus's singing of '*M'Appari*', and, when the song is finished and the other listeners relax, 'Bloom sang dumb.' The voice seems to him a lamentation and the song of the lost one a universal theme. The tension inside him is expressed in the stretching of the elastic band, wrapped round his fingers, until it snaps. At this point, suddenly, there is an intrusion of the meaningless chitchat of the bar, expressed in a style of inane repetitiveness, in which even indivi-duality is dissolved:

> George Lidwell told her really and truly: but she did not believe.
> First gentleman told Mina that was so. She asked him was that so. And second tankard told her so. That that was so.

[61] *Budgen*, 141.

> Miss Douce, Miss Lydia, did not believe: Miss Kennedy, Mina, did not
> believe: George Lidwell, no: Miss Dou did not: the first, the first: gent with
> the tank: believe, no, no: did not, Miss Kenn: Lidlydiawell: the tank.
> (*U* 263/358)

Again, after Dollard's performance of *The Croppy Boy*, the superficiality of
response to what has disturbed Bloom profoundly is betrayed by empty
chatter between a barmaid and a customer identified by his tankard:

> Miss Mina Kennedy brought near her lips to ear of tankard one.
> —Mr Dollard, they murmured low.
> —Dollard, murmured tankard.
> Tank one believed: Miss Kenn when she: that doll he was: she doll: the
> tank.
> He murmured that he knew the name. The name was familiar to him, that
> is to say. That was to say he had heard the name of Dollard, was it? Dollard,
> yes. (*U* 273/371)

All this humdrum stuff is as important to the music of the chapter as the
elaborate passages representing the piano or the voices of the singers,
because it suggests the dull and petty reality hidden behind the pretended
emotions. The irony of the chapter is partly in the contrast between
Bloom's intense spasms of feeling and the escapist playing with emotions
indulged in by the rest of the company, and partly in the absurd coexistence
in Bloom's mind of deep and disturbing feelings with nonsense and triviality. Consequently even the most melodious and passionate parts of the
interior monologue stagger and fumble, are confused with bathos, vagueness, crudities of expression and bombast, as though the experiencing mind,
however profoundly moved, cannot entirely free itself from its inarticulacy,
incoherence and ordinary dullness. This seems shrewdly observed: we talk
of our musical or other aesthetic responses as though they transport us
above our commonplace selves, but in fact the mind is so fickle and inconsistent that even the most intense experiences are rarely free from
unwanted, irrelevant and silly thoughts or shifts of attention. The presentation of Simon Dedalus's performance of '*M'Appari*' exhibits this
unreliability of the mind very effectively. Dedalus begins softly:

> Through the hush of air a voice sang to them, low, not rain, not leaves in
> murmur, like no voice of strings of reeds or whatdoyoucallthem dulcimers,
> touching their still ears with words, still hearts of their each his remembered
> lives. Good, good to hear: sorrow from them each seemed to from both
> depart when first they heard. When first they saw, lost Richie, Poldy, mercy
> of beauty, heard from a person wouldn't expect it in the least, her first
> merciful lovesoft oftloved word. (*U* 260/353)

There is real pathos and sentiment in the response of the two men to the
song, but it is a response interrupted and conditioned by their unheroic
natures. Bloom's indecision about the word 'dulcimer', observed earlier in
the day, intrudes irrelevantly, as does his sense of getting more than his
deserts in having been chosen by Molly. He thinks, 'Love that is singing'
and supposes that this is the reason 'Tenors get women by the score.'

Consequently, when the singer's voice swells out, it takes on for him a sexual connotation:

> Tenderness it welled: slow, swelling. Full it throbbed. That's the chat. Ha, give! Take! Throb, a throb, a pulsing proud erect. (*U* 260/354)

With his mind full of what will soon be taking place between his wife and another singer, Boylan, Bloom's imagination converts the emotion of the song into an orgasm. And, finally, to express the ecstatic last sustained high note, the language sets off poetically and slides into bathetic echoes of Dan Dawson's speech:

> —*Come!*
> It soared, a bird, it held its flight, a swift pure cry, soar silver orb it leaped serene, speeding, sustained, to come, don't spin it out too long long breath he breath long life, soaring high, high resplendent, aflame, crowned, high in the effulgence symbolistic, high, of the ethereal bosom, high, of the high vast irradiation everywhere all soaring all around about the all, the endlessness-nessness . . .
> —*To me!* (*U* 261–2/355–6)

Stuart Gilbert's comment – 'There is a *fermata* effect (a note held beyond its normal duration), the aftermath of an *affrettando* passage . . ., in the "held" word *endlessnessnessness* . . .'[62] – is not quite satisfactory, because the whole paragraph represents a note sustained beyond its normal duration: 'endlessnessnessness' seems rather to suggest, by its sense, the effect of indefinite prolongation that one sometimes feels when listening to gramophone records of the period where final high notes are spectacularly sustained, and, by its sound, the increasing *vibrato* of the voice holding such a note. But these are only the imitative aspects of the paragraph: its essential function is to represent Bloom's reaction – his mounting emotion, his growing identification with the singer so that he himself seems to draw a deep breath as he wills Dedalus not to spin the note out too long, his vague association of long breath with long life, and finally the sense of being borne upwards above mundane concerns – an escape linked in his mind with the highflying bombast of Dan Dawson and the ethereal symbolism of A.E.'s poetry. At the end of the song, the next word is 'Siopold!'; in the intensity of the emotion Leopold has fused with the singer, Simon, and the romantic hero, Lionel.

The handling of Simon Dedalus's performance is, in itself, sufficient to show how far Joyce's mind was from any naive intention to do in prose what can be done only in music. The use of sound as an echo to the sense or a contributing to it is as old as literature: Joyce's devices are adventurous extensions of traditional methods. As Bloom's mind is swamped with emotions provoked by the romantic aria, so rational syntax dissolves and sentences melt into each other; as his transports are pulled back to earth by his more pedestrian qualities, so the poetic language and rhythms tumble into the prosaic. The one truly musical effect is produced by the

[62] *Gilbert*, 250.

flow of quotations and references which keep the tune of the famous aria running at the back of the reader's mind.

In fact, the persistent background of music, sung, hummed, whistled and played, is both essential to the action of the chapter and dominant among the techniques of presentation, to the extent that a reader unfamiliar with the music cannot experience the chapter as Joyce meant it to be experienced.[63] The songs, representative of the Dubliners' fondness for strongly-flavoured, vicarious emotionalizing, are 'the seductions of music' beyond which Bloom must travel: without knowledge of them, some of the interior monologue and even some passages of dialogue cannot be understood, much less apprehended, and, besides moulding and colouring Bloom's mood, they constitute, in their succession, a condensed programme of the chapter's developing theme. The airy, waltzing song from *Floradora*, sung by Miss Douce, is the quintessence of escapist fantasy, and no doubt Joyce wanted his readers to remember the tune and the references to a romantic dream-world, set not only in 'Eastern seas' but also in 'sweet Arcadia', 'this valley of Eden', and 'Elysian vales'. The fervent pastoral song of the lover unwilling to leave his beloved, *Goodbye, Sweetheart, Goodbye*, is ironically interwoven with Boylan's coarse and impatient departure from bar and barmaid. The duet, *Love and War*, sums up the double sentimentalizing of Simon Dedalus and his cronies: just as, in the song, the initial opposition of amorous tenor and martial bass is resolved in liquor –

> Since Mars lov'd Venus, Venus Mars,
> Let's blend love's wounds with battle's scars,
> And call in Bacchus all divine,
> To cure both pains with rosy wine.
> And thus, beneath his social sway,
> We'll sing and laugh the hours away[64]—

so, after the aching love-aria, 'When first I saw', has been succeeded by the patriotic sentiment of *The Croppy Boy*, we have a final view of the men in the bar reconciling Venus and Mars with drink and Bacchic song:

> —True men like you men.
> —Ay, ay, Ben.
> —Will lift your glass with us.
> They lifted.
> Tschink. Tschunk. (*U* 276/375)

But, by this time, Bloom has freed himself from the siren charms to which

---

[63] According to Zack Bowen, the chapter contains '158 references to forty-seven different works of music' ('The Bronzegold Sirensong: A Musical Analysis of the Sirens Episode in Joyce's *Ulysses*', in *Literary Monographs* I, ed. Eric Rothstein and Thomas K. Dunseath (Madison, Wisconsin University Press 1967), 251).

[64] Since Weldon Thornton (*Allusions*, 240) says that after much search he has been unable to locate the song or information about it, it may be useful to mention that it is in the once-popular collection, *British Minstrelsie* (5 vols., London, Caxton Publishing Co., n.d., and 6 vols, Edinburgh, Jack, n.d.).

the others have succumbed, and has, for the time being, erased the mournful passions which have troubled him – by associating the words of Dedalus's song with the frowzy whore of the lane ('When first he saw that form endearing') and by allowing his flatulence to fire a dismissive salute to the martyred hero, Robert Emmet.

As for the more extreme devices, they are rarely musical in effect; they are adaptations of musical 'shapes' to prose purposes to which the musical origins have little relevance. Nothing is added to the reader's understanding of 'Yrfmstbyes. Blmstup' by the information that the words are 'examples of the "hollow fifth" ';[65] in prose, the omission of the vowels merely suggests the suddenness with which Bloom, after some indecision, rises and says goodbye to Goulding. The passage in Bloom's monologue, 'Will? You? I. Want. You. To', which, according to Gilbert, is a *staccato* effect,[66] has, in context, nothing to do with *staccato* in music: Bloom, who has been eyeing Miss Douce lecherously, thinks (as many men have thought) of the possibility of directing her mind by a kind of unspoken ventriloquism ('Ventriloquise. My lips closed. Think in my stom. What?') and the series of isolated words represents the concentration of his attention on each individually in order to project his desire into the barmaid's mind.

Of all the devices in 'Sirens', none has provoked so much critical debate as the so-called 'overture', though no commentator has added much to Stuart Gilbert's account of its function:

> The episode of the *Sirens* opens with two pages of brief extracts from the narrative which follows. These fragmentary phrases appear almost meaningless to the reader till he has perused the chapter to its end; nevertheless, they should not be skipped. They are like the overtures of some operas and operettes, in which fragments of the leading themes and refrains are introduced to prepare the hearer's mood and also to give him, when these truncated themes are completed and developed in their proper place, that sense of familiarity which, strangely enough, enhances for most hearers their enjoyment of a new tune.[67]

Functionally the passage resembles the opening of the *Portrait* which sounds the embryonic themes to recur and be developed throughout the novel, but whereas in the *Portrait* the passage is plausibly related to the rest of the novel as fragmentary infantile impressions, now Joyce makes no attempt to disguise the separate and introductory character of his opening, and ends it with the word 'Begin!' before starting the chapter proper. Yet this opening is not a series of themes, even truncated themes. Many of the fragments are very different in form from anything to be found in the chapter: 'Where bronze from anear? Where gold from afar? Where hoofs?' refers, the sequence suggests, to the arrival of the unseeing pianotuner, but there are no such questions in the chapter. Words which occur casually in the chapter ('avowal', for example) are reiterated and emphasized in the phrases. The sequence of phrases roughly corresponds to the order in which their materials occur in the chapter, but it is only a rough corres-

[65] *Gilbert*, 250. [66] *Ibid.*, 249. [67] *Ibid.*, 239.

pondence, and many phrases are considerably displaced. Gilbert says that the phrases 'appear almost meaningless' until the reader has read the chapter, but the situation is more extreme than this, in that frequently they suggest a wrong meaning. A reader coming to 'Boomed crashing chords. When love absorbs. War! War! The tympanum' reasonably assumes that the reference is to a dramatic call to arms, summoning the lover to war with a drum-beat. But the passage referred to is very different in character. Almost as soon as he enters, Ben Dollard plumps himself down at the piano and thumps out *Love and War*, a duet for tenor and bass, which begins with the amorous voice of a lover, who is answered by the thundering voice of a soldier. When Ben absentmindedly booms out the lover's part in a very martial style, Cowley quickly corrects him ('War! War! cried Father Cowley. You're the warrior') and Simon Dedalus comments 'Sure, you'd burst the tympanum of her ear, man, ... with an organ like yours.' But there is nothing in the phrases of the 'overture' to indicate that the cry 'War! War!' is a correction rather than a summons, or that the tympanum is an eardrum rather than a military drum. Confusion is increased by the way in which some phrases, belonging to quite unrelated incidents or characters, are misleadingly linked:

> A husky fifenote blew.
> Blew. Blue bloom is on the
> Gold pinnacled hair.   (*U* 242/329)

Despite the repetition of 'Blew' and the absence of punctuation after 'the', Simon Dedalus's attempt to clear out his pipe has nothing to do with Bloom or with the song *When the Bloom is on the Rye* (*My Pretty Jane*), and there is no bloom on Miss Kennedy's golden hair. Similarly the juxtaposition of the phrases –

> Peep! Who's in the . . . peepofgold?
> Tink cried to bronze in pity.
> And a call, pure, long and throbbing. Longindying call.   (*U* 242/329)—

suggests that the question is cried pityingly by 'Tink' to 'bronze', and that it is followed by a sustained throbbing call; in fact, Lenehan's teasing of Miss Kennedy ('Peep! Who's in the corner?') is quite unconnected with the tinkle of the diner's bell which interrupts Miss Douce's expression of pity for the blind pianotuner, and neither is related to the call of the tuning-fork sounded by Simon Dedalus.

These characteristics complicate the question about the nature and function of the opening of 'Sirens': it is plainly not a catalogue of themes, and although the links are evidence of a planned sequence, this is not the sequence of the chapter itself. Stuart Gilbert is certainly right in supposing that the opening fragments prepare the reader, and give him a 'sense of familiarity' when they recur in the narrative, but this does not explain why they have been changed, why their meanings have been disguised, or why false relationships have been established between them. It may be that the terms 'overture' and 'themes' are themselves misleading. One would expect

a '*fuga per canonem*' to be introduced by a 'prelude' rather than an 'overture':
in fact, the latter word occurs in *Ulysses* only in the expression 'to make
overtures to someone', whereas 'prelude' occurs only in the musical sense.
In 'Circe', the pianola plays the prelude of *My Girl's a Yorkshire Girl*: in
'Sirens', before the beginning of Dedalus's aria, 'the harping chords of
prelude closed.' This last sentence suggests that if the opening section is
thought of as a prelude, then the separate fragments may correspond to
chords. The chapter has many references to chords, 'all twinkling, linked,
all harpsichording', or quavering and faltering, or bombarding, or harping
or deepening and rising, or black and deepsounding, or consenting, or in
'curlycues', or plumped out, and Bloom, listening to Cowley improvising,
thinks that chords are 'vibrations':

> Might be what you like till you hear the words. Want to listen sharp. Hard.
> Begin all right: then hear chords a bit off: feel lost a bit. In and out of sacks
> over barrels, through wirefences, obstacle race. Time makes the tune.
> Question of mood you're in. (*U* 264/359)

If, then, one takes the opening as a prelude, intended to 'form a suitable
preparation of the listener's ear and mind for what is to follow',[68] it is
possible to suppose that Joyce deliberately disguised or distorted the fragments from the chapter in order to remove their specific meanings. As
Bloom recognizes, musical chords are given specific significance only by
the words of the songs to which they are set: yet they can, as the chords
described in the chapter show, seem to have various general emotional
connotations ('Trails off there sad in minor. Why minor sad?'). If Joyce
wanted to produce some verbal equivalent to a chord, he had to find a way
of muffling the specific denotations and reference of the words in order
that the emotional 'vibrations' could reverberate without limitation by
specific context or reference. Thus the fragment already examined, 'Boomed
crashing chords. When love absorbs. War! War! The tympanum', has
been deprived of intelligible reference to the events of the chapter or to
any coherent sequence, in order that it may exist merely as a general martial
summons suggested by the sounds as well as the meanings of the words.
The next fragment, 'A sail! A veil awave upon the waves', cannot be
understood, since its reference to the picture, '*A Last Farewell*',[69] has been

[68] Percy A. Scholes, *The Oxford Companion to Music* (5th edn, London, Oxford
University Press 1944), 745. L. L. Levin also describes the opening of the chapter as a
'prelude' which 'contains all eight voices developed, both thematically and poly-
phonically, in a shorthand utilizing leitmotifs combined in a quintessential and abstract
form of narrative' ('The Sirens Episode as Music: Joyce's Experiment in Prose
Polyphony', *JJQ* III (1) (1965), 14). However, Zack Bowen insists that it is an 'overture' 'piecing together the main leitmotifs' and linking them with 'bits of third person
narrative description gleaned from the body of the episode.' His case is fully argued in
'The Bronzegold Sirensong' (see n. 63 above), and its conclusions repeated in 'Libretto
for Bloomusalem in Song: The Music of Joyce's *Ulysses*' in *New Light*, 156–158.

[69] Zack Bowen ('The Bronzegold Sirensong', 261) takes '*A Last Farewell*' as a
reference to a song, but it is clearly a romantic seascape, and the details given suggest
that it is a picture on the wall of the bar or restaurant. The song supposedly referred
to has no relevance to the scene described.

removed, but it still retains, through its sounds and through the general connotations arising from the combination 'sail-veil-waves', a vague plaintive emotion. The same is true of the other fragments: they associate certain words and phrases from the chapter in such a way and with such effects of sound and rhythm as to communicate various emotional colours – as though, together, they make up the palette of emotions to be used in the chapter, though often in quite unpredictable or unexpected ways. Some chords are comparatively simple: 'Lost. Throstle fluted. All is lost now' is without rational meaning, but there is no mistaking its tone of subdued and melancholy surrender. On the other hand, many are puzzling and discordant: 'Amen! He gnashed in fury' vaguely suggests religious fanaticism and persecution: the romantic isolation suggested by the sound of a seashell is rudely interrupted by a sexual enquiry in 'The spiked and winding cold seahorn. Have you the? Each and for other plash and silent roar'; and other contrasted moods are associated, as in the alternation of the words of *Goodbye, Sweetheart, Goodbye* and the performance of the garter-trick:

> Avowal. *Sonnez*. I could. Rebound of garter. Not leave thee. Smack. *La cloche!* Thigh smack. Avowal. Warm. Sweetheart, goodbye!   (*U* 242/329)

Here, two attitudes to woman, romantic and sensual, are interwoven – so effectively that 'Warm' might refer equally to the avowal or the thigh. The reordering of the fragments seems to suggest that Joyce was aiming at some kind of musical patterning: after a brief percussive opening, he modulates on 'Blew' into a more lyrical vein, shifts into jaunty rhythms, fades into a tone of amorous regret and loneliness, moves through an uncertain and questioning transition into a passage of solemn passion, and closes with a little wind music. Whereas the chapter's other adaptations of musical devices produce effects which belong characteristically to language, the 'prelude' aims at giving an experience comparable to the experience of music – an ordered series of emotional and sensuous responses evoked without explicit reference to any framework of discursive or narrative sense. It is not simply a passage to be understood only after the chapter has been read, but a predisposing of the reader's mind to put him in key with and condition his responsiveness to what follows, as though the mental and physical events of the chapter are concretizations of the generalized emotional suggestions of the prelude. It is one of the boldest experiments in the whole novel, and, by its nature, very difficult to analyse or assess: my own view is that this curious opening does condition importantly the reader's response to the 'Sirens' chapter.

Apart from its musical function, the prelude has a distancing effect in that it suggests that 'Sirens', like the preceding chapter, will not be confined to a single point of view. The reader sees and hears the barmaids in the Ormond bar while Bloom is still drifting along the streets; the journeys of Boylan and the blind boy are indicated; and, at the end, although Bloom's thoughts in the street are represented, there are glimpses of the bar after he has left. The passages describing Boylan's journey towards Molly do not represent Bloom's heated imaginings of what his rival is doing: Bloom does think of Boylan's triumphant ride, but his thoughts are quite distinct from the jaunty paragraphs naming the landmarks of Boylan's journey, and his picturing of the moment of arrival – 'Jing. Stop. Knock. Last look at mirror always before she answers the door' – occurs before Boylan is halfway to Eccles Street: it is a faint anticipation of the bold statement of Boylan's arrival. The controlling point of view in the chapter is one which can range across Dublin, and which knows of earlier events, witnessed by the reader but unknown to any of the people present in the Ormond bar. For instance, when Lydia Douce expresses pity for the blind boy, the following sentence is 'God's curse on bitch's bastard'; when in Dollard's song, the Croppy Boy confesses that he has cursed three times since Easter, there is the incomplete phrase, 'You bitch's bast'; and when, in the same song, the yeomen captain curses the boy, he does so 'swelling in apoplectic bitch's bastard'. The reader recalls the origin of the phrase – it comes from 'Wandering Rocks' where the blind boy, bumped into by the crazy pedestrian, Farrell, snarls after him 'God's curse on you, . . . whoever you are! You're blinder nor I am, you bitch's bastard!' – but the curse has not been heard by Miss Douce or, for that matter, by anyone else. Its presence in 'Sirens' can be explained only as the work of the author, using motifs he has established earlier in the book, first to mock Miss Douce's sentimentality and then to introduce the parallel, later developed, between the blind pianotuner and the Croppy Boy.

There are several similar interpolations of motifs from earlier chapters introduced without explanation. For instance, in the account of Boylan's journey to Molly, the epithet 'onehandled', applied to Nelson, is borrowed from Stephen (in 'Aeolus'), and, while Bloom is trying to deceive Goulding in the dining-room, 'down the edge of his *Freeman* baton ranged Bloom's your other eye', although Bloom was not in the hotel when the barmaids screamed with laughter at the phrase, 'your other eye'. Most surprisingly, when Bloom casually thinks of Shakespeare as a supplier of 'quotations every day in the year', the next paragraph echoes a passage of Stephen's monologue in the library chapter: 'In Gerard's rosery of Fetter lane he walks greyedauburn. One life is all. One body. Do. But do.' Robert M. Adams, discussing this passage, says that it 'interrupts strikingly the prevailing tenor of the novel', and wonders whether it occurs 'by accident or design'; but his difficulty is caused chiefly by the assumption that Bloom is 'thinking Stephen's thoughts'.[70] In fact, the passage is merely the largest of several extracts from earlier chapters introduced into 'Sirens' by the author, with no implication that they are present in the minds of the people in the Ormond hotel.

These unexplained intrusions add to the impression given by the prelude and by the musical manipulations of style that the reader is being deliberately distanced from what is going on in the hotel. At times he occupies Bloom's mind to see with Bloom's eyes as in earlier chapters, but he is not allowed to stay there. He is forced to recognize an authorial presence, and

[70] *Adams*, 98–9.

to realize that he is not witnessing a scene or sharing a character's point of view but reading a verbal representation of what takes place in the hotel and its neighbourhood, as well as of the course of Boylan's drive. The author's intention is made even plainer by the use (unprecedented in Joyce's writings) of the clumsy formula 'as said before', which on four occasions marks brief recapitulations of material about to be given further development. The reader's attention is now focused on the manner of presentation rather than on an observing intelligence; although Bloom's interior monologue is dominant, it is no more the organizing principle of the chapter than it was in 'Wandering Rocks'. His comparative sub-ordination is humorously indicated from the beginning. Miss Kennedy's sad thought that men have 'the fine times' is followed by the phrase, 'A man', and then we observe Bloom, as a man of uncertain identity, passing along the street:

> Bloowho went by by Moulang's pipes, bearing in his breast the sweets of sin, by Wine's antiques in memory bearing sweet sinful words, by Carroll's dusky battered plate, for Raoul. (*U* 244/331)

After Miss Douce's encounter with the boots, the isolated word 'Bloom' occurs, but it turns out to be a false entry, leading not to the man but to the flower on Miss Douce's bosom. After further conversations between the barmaids, a sudden question asks 'But Bloom?' as though enquiring what has become of him, but there is no answer. It is not until Miss Douce's exclamation, '– And your other eye!', that we shift to 'Bloowhose dark eye' and to a fragment of his interior monologue, and his next appearance is heralded by a similarly false connection, when the barmaid's laughter at the thought of being married to the 'old fogey' with his greasy nose is misleadingly applied to Bloom: 'Married to Bloom, to greaseaseabloom.' In this confusing and uncertain way Bloom is allowed to enter the chapter.

There has been a gradual change in the author's relationship to the two central figures of his novel: in the first six chapters he took us more and more deeply into their consciousness; in the next three, the increasingly obtrusive techniques of presentation added an implied authorial commentary; and in 'Wandering Rocks' the viewpoint was that of an omniscient author, able to switch from one part of the city to another, and to enter such minds as suited his local purposes. The question, then, is not why Joyce should have abandoned, in 'Sirens', an established and consistent mode, but why he gradually distanced his central figures, reduced their roles as the observing intelligences whose moods shape the stylistic character of the early chapters, and made his manipulations of style and technique increasingly obtrusive.

There are some fairly clear general objectives attained by this gradual modification of the mode of the narrative. There have been brief glimpses of Bloom, seen from outside by such observers as Nosey Flynn, Mulligan, Lenehan and Martin Cunningham, but more prolonged external observations – cynical and contemptuous, romantic and sentimental, and in the light of varied authorial attitudes – are needed: no man, certainly not Bloom, is fully conscious of himself; he misunderstands himself as much as others misunderstand him. He is not a single self, capable of revealing himself through interior monologue, but a multiplicity of selves, often conflicting, and any comprehensive image of this 'allroundman' must present him from a succession of different angles. Moreover, the problems and distresses of Bloom and Stephen as revealed in their interior monologues are the tips of icebergs: the conscious mind is aware of and responds to only the local and temporary manifestations of what is deeply submerged. Guilts and anxieties of which neither man is fully aware are the sources of their troubles, and the critical relationship which develops between them assists them without their understanding why – it solves none of their immediate problems but strengthens them spiritually or subconsciously. To illuminate these concealed essences of the two men and their predicaments, Joyce must devise methods which permit a penetration deeper than the conscious levels represented in interior monologue.

He has achieved very nearly as much as can be achieved in the mode of interior monologue. He has manipulated the style, within this mode, to suggest fluctuations of mood, involuntary responses to the environment and to bodily needs, and a variety of rational and irrational mental processes. But interior monologue, however modified, restricts the author to the insights and judgements of his characters: it hardly allows for the full presentation of his own vision of the nature and quality of the life in which they are involved. In most novels, the author's criticism of life can be expressed in direct authorial commentary or through a character whom the novelist uses as a mouthpiece, but neither of these methods is suitable for *Ulysses*. The whole character of the book is shaped by Joyce's determination to represent as much and state as little as possible, and both Bloom and Stephen are, by design, characters whose perceptiveness is, in different ways, limited. Consequently, the process in *Ulysses* is away from the more representational conventions of interior monologue, where the style is tied to the thoughts and feelings of the central characters, towards styles and techniques which present in more and more complexity the author's judgement of and insights into the essence of his characters, their situations and their relationships, and his vision of the life of the city in which they move. The distancing in the style permits a fuller range of irony, and also moves towards the impersonality which will be necessary for the later chapters when two men as fundamentally dissimilar as Bloom and Stephen have to be presented in relationship.

As for the 'technic' of 'Sirens', according to Joyce a *'fuga per canonem'*, attempts to make a detailed musical analysis of the chapter have not proved very profitable or convincing. Stuart Gilbert says,

> The various themes are introduced in the fugal manner: the first, the *Subject*, is obviously the Sirens' song: the *Answer*, Mr Bloom's entry and monologue; Boylan is the *Counter-Subject*. The *Episodes* or *Divertimenti* are the songs by Mr Dedalus and Ben Dollard. [71]

[71] *Gilbert*, 248.

This sounds straightforward but it hardly justifies the label '*fuga per canonem*'. If Bloom supplies the *Answer*, why is his entry in no respects a fugal imitation of the *Subject*? In a fugue, the *Counter-Subject* is sung or played by the first voice while the second voice is occupied with the *Answer*, but between Bloom and Boylan there appear on the scene Lenehan, Dedalus and Pat the waiter. In a letter to Harrier Weaver, Joyce referred to 'the eight regular parts of a *fuga per canonem*',[72] and, taking 'parts' to mean 'voices' as is usual in discussions of fugal music, the eight voices, characterized by distinguishing phrases or rhythms, may be, in order of appearance, as follows: 1, the barmaids; 2, Bloom; 3, Dedalus (joined later by Dollard, Cowley, Lidwell, Kernan and the two gentlemen); 4, Pat the waiter; 5, Lenehan; 6, Boylan; 7, Goulding; 8, The blind boy. (The chorus of drinkers, linked with Dedalus, are similarly associated several times towards the end of the chapter.) This list suggests some patterning, the first, third, fifth and seventh voices representing those who are caught and held by the deceptive siren music – including the sirens themselves, and the alternate voices those who escape its fascination – Bloom through prudence, Boylan because he is too impatient for idle flirtation, and the other two through deafness and blindness. Some other analyses of the musical form of the chapter are equally plausible,[73] because only certain aspects of the fugal form can be imitated verbally. A number of voices, each with characteristic phrases or rhythms, are introduced one after the other; each voice can appear in different keys, so that, for instance, the gold-bronze of the barmaids can occur in a laughing or melancholy passage; two, three or four voices may occur, at any time, in close association; and the tone of any one voice may be modified by the presence of others: these seem to be the chief formal characteristics borrowed from the fugue. Their main function is obvious enough; they enable Joyce to show Bloom, at the first major crisis of his day, the hour fixed for Boylan's rendezvous with Molly, pursued by a series of voices painfully forcing into his mind what he has been trying to forget. The behaviour of the barmaids frequently brings Molly into his thoughts and he perceives, through their response to Boylan, what it is that has attracted Molly:

> They want it: not too much polite. That's why he gets them. Gold in your pocket, brass in your face.   (*U* 271/368)

Listening to Dedalus's voice, he feels the sexual excitement of the throbbing notes, and thinks that that is why tenors (like Boylan) get women by the score; Dollard reminds him of the night Molly laughed to see the old man, no eunuch, 'with all his belongings on show', and is an image of lonely old age; Cowley's piano-playing makes him conclude his letter, 'I feel so sad today'; Kernan speaks of a wronged husband who, unlike Bloom, seized an adulterous tenor by the throat and spoiled his voice. Pat, the waiter,

---

[72] *Letters* I, 129.
[73] For instance, L. L. Levin also distinguished the eight voices, but differs from me in regarding Dollard as a separate voice and seeing Goulding as merely part of the free counterpoint ('The Sirens Episode as Music', *JJQ* III (1) (1965), 14).

may be deaf and bothered, but, while he waits, 'perhaps he has wife and family waiting, waiting Patty come home', whereas Bloom's wife, who sang *Waiting* when he first met her, is now waiting not for her husband but for her lover. Lenehan's chief contribution to Bloom's distress is his departing question to Boylan: 'Got the horn or what?' The jaunty jingling of Boylan is constantly in Bloom's thoughts, as he fluctuates between vain impulses to intervene in some way and resignation. Goulding, who seemed an innocuous companion, turns out to be equally a source of pain: his harping on his daughter reminds Bloom of Dedalus's contemptuous comment – 'Wise child that knows her father, Dedalus said. Me?' –, the final word suggesting a doubt that the fair-haired Milly is his child, and Goulding's whistling of *Tutto è sciolto* ('All is lost now') supplies words for Bloom's gloom and hopelessness. The blind boy comes into Bloom's consciousness only through his identification with the Croppy Boy of the song, of which the words 'Last of my name and race' and 'I bear no hate against living thing' touch Bloom in his most vulnerable spot:

> I too, last my race. Milly young student. Well, my fault perhaps. No son. Rudy. Too late now. Or if not. If not? If still?
> He bore no hate.
> Hate. Love. Those are names. Rudy. Soon I am old. (*U* 270/367–8)

These are only a few illustrations of the ways in which Bloom is moved by the interweaving themes and motifs. At the beginning of this chapter, I have shown how they are used to represent the emotional turmoil within Bloom as he walks away from the Ormond Hotel; and this is the real justification for the adaptation of musical forms in the style and organization of 'Sirens'. Joyce establishes, through his fugal method, a range of themes and motifs, easily recognizable and therefore capable of modulation and variation, whose interlacings and juxtapositions can create the over-charged and sentimental atmosphere of the Ormond Hotel and suggest the disturbing emotional pressures experienced there by Bloom.

Critical opinion about the chapter is very divided: one critic says, 'The attempt at a *fuga per canonem* form . . . is not only unsuccessful in practice; more fundamentally, it is meaningless in conception';[74] another calls it 'Dublin's great fugue of passion'.[75] I suspect that a careful and responsive reader, quite uninformed about the fugal 'technic' or the adaptations of musical forms, would, apart from a few local difficulties, feel the emotional tensions beneath the sentimentality, would recognize Bloom's distressed awareness of Boylan's journey to Molly, and would apprehend the way in which the overheard song and talk trouble and almost overwhelm him. These are the central matters of the chapter, and there can, I think, be little doubt that the stylistic and technical virtuosity are in their service. One may argue about the effectiveness of this or that device, but I do not see how one can deny the functional nature of the general conduct of the chapter.

[74] *Goldberg*, 281. [75]*Kenner*, 254.

'Cyclops'

In 'Cyclops', the unnamed narrator's account of what happened in Barney Kiernan's pub provides the sequential framework on which the inflated interpolations are hung, and is so lively and straightforward in manner that its oddity is easily overlooked. In the two preceding chapters, the novel has shifted from its confinement to the viewpoints of Bloom and Stephen, but now the main speaking voice is that of someone who has not previously appeared and whose name remains unknown: all that we learn of him is that he is a man who has, in his own opinion, come down in the world ('How are the mighty fallen!'), and is at present a debt-collector and an ever-ready consumer of free beer, gathering and distributing Dublin gossip in a malicious and foul-mouthed way.

Even the nature of his narrative is not immediately obvious. At first sight, it appears to be his story of the events in Barney Kiernan's, related, at a subsequent time, to some cronies. Yet a few passages contradict this reading:

> So I just went round to the back of the yard to pumpship and begob (hundred shillings to five) while I was letting off my (*Throwaway* twenty to) letting off my load gob says I to myself I knew he was uneasy in his (two pints off of Joe and one in Slattery's off) in his mind to get off the mark to (hundred shillings is five quid) and when they were in the (dark horse) Pisser Burke was telling me card party and letting on the child was sick (gob, must have done about a gallon) flabbyarse of a wife speaking down the tube *she's better* or *she's* (ow!) all a plan so he could vamoose with the pool if he won or (Jesus, full up I was) trading without a licence (ow!) Ireland my nation says he (hoik! phthook!) never be up to those bloody (there's the last of it) Jerusalem (ah!) cuckoos.   (*U* 319/435–6)

The parentheses alone show that we are not overhearing a reported tale, but observing the state of mind of the narrator while he is making water and brooding on Bloom's alleged win on the Gold Cup.[76] The colloquial narrative is interior monologue, now plainly not a recording of the narrator's thoughts, but a manner devised by Joyce to represent the consciousness of this garrulous, contemptuous, gossiping, Dublin scrounger. (In fact, his contributions to the conversation in the bar are usually much more cautious, ingratiating and moderate than the representation of his thoughts would suggest, perhaps because he is unwilling to risk offending possible

[76] In order to explain the apparent time-confusion in the quoted passage, David Hayman argues that the narrator 'has probably told the tale at least once before and he is retelling it now in the hope of shaming another dupe into buying drinks.' As for what Hayman calls 'the famous gonorrheal micturition', he supposes that, while urinating in some other pub, the narrator is telling a companion about what he was thinking while urinating in Barney Kiernan's (*Hart and Hayman*, 264–5). The explanation is ingenious, although it is hard to regard the latter part of the passage as spoken rather than thought, and the need for ingenuity disappears if one regards the gossiping voice as a technique for presenting the narrator's stream of consciousness, as proper to him as Gerty Macdowell's convention is to her.

suppliers of free drinks.) Although the manner of this part of the chapter makes it (apart from a few Irishisms and slang expressions) the easiest reading in the novel, it is the most radical development so far in the handling of interior monologue. Apart from the few passages to which I have already referred, Joyce adopts a style which suggests a man telling a story rather than thinking. The nuances of experience in this narrator are of little interest: Joyce creates for him a style which in its coarse, humorous, exaggerated way represents his essential nature; in this respect it is closer to the styles of 'A Little Cloud' or 'Clay' than to those of the earlier interior monologues. The medium through which the narrator's experience is presented indicates how much we can believe his account and interpretation of what he witnesses, and at once characterizes and judges him, just as the manner of the authorial voice in 'Sirens' characterized and judged such figures as the barmaids and Boylan.

'Gigantism' is the label Joyce gave to the 'technic' of this chapter. It is usually taken as referring to the interpolated passages, but it is equally applicable to the narrator's way of thinking and talking, and to the conversation in the bar. For example, the first interpolation is an agreement, swollen with legal terminology, concerning the sale of tea and sugar to the total value of 'one pound five shillings and sixpence sterling'. The legal pomp and ceremony is an absurd inflation of the transaction, but it is no more inflated than the language of the narrator, who refers to 'any God's quantity of tea and sugar' and describes the plumber who has failed to pay the weekly amount of three shillings as 'the most notorious bloody robber you'd meet in a day's walk and the face on him all pockmarks would hold a shower of rain.' The legal agreement imitates the habitual exaggeration of the narrator and his companions, and a similar relationship exists between all the interpolations and the conversation of the men in the bar. It is the Irish tendency to wild exaggeration which makes the city a dangerous place for a moderate man like Bloom.

The Cyclopean giant who threatens the Dublin Ulysses is not something real in the situation of the country or its inhabitants: the danger comes from the swollen dreams and illusions which are the compensation for pointless and trivial lives, and from the giant hatreds and prejudices which originate in such dreams and give rise to blind nationalism, religious intolerance, antisemitism and all the other symptoms of spiritual poverty and frustration. The bar-flies utter with seriousness and fervour exaggerated opinions on matters about which they are both ignorant and indifferent: the interpolated passages extend these absurdities into historical, mythological, spiritual, political, sporting, social, legal, archaeological, journalistic and other contexts. In particular they reflect, in more literary manners, the way in which the foolish topers in the bar, with no genuine convictions at all, inflate their egos with puffed-up visions of The Golden Age of Erin, and of themselves as sons of kings, loyal and devout Catholics, and guardians of Gaelic traditions and culture. Although the unnamed narrator is himself an habitual exaggerator his cynicism helps him to see that the citizen's rhetoric is 'all wind and piss like a tanyard cat', and reveals that all the pretended devotion and nationalistic passion is a thick froth concealing a total absence of religious and political principle. His gossip confirms what the interpolated inflations suggest. For all the old citizen's boasted devotion to the cause of Ireland, we learn that he dare not show his face in one district because he would be murdered 'for grabbing the holding of an evicted tenant', and the depth of his religious zeal is sufficiently exposed when, angered by Bloom's assertion that Christ was a Jew, he screams out, 'By Jesus, . . . I'll brain that bloody jewman for using the holy name. By Jesus, I'll crucify him so I will.'

The interpolated passages do not merely translate the exaggerations of the bar into a series of pompous prose styles; if that were their sole function, the device would be laborious, repetitive and uneconomical. In the first place, their relationship to what happens in the bar varies: sometimes they take over the narrative role and record the entry of various characters or relate such incidents as the buying of a round of drinks; sometimes they give a rhetorical equivalent of what the narrator tells in a more disparaging way, as when Bergan darts in and Mr and Mrs Breen pass the door; sometimes they describe events in and around the bar which are quite imaginary, such as the procession of saints to Barney Kiernan's door; sometimes they are ornamental fantasies springing from some phrase in the conversation; and sometimes they are gratuitous rhapsodies like the description of the abundance in 'the land of holy Michan'. More importantly, the interpolations variously ridicule different aspects of the national paranoia, and parody the current literary modes and tastes of the Irish.[77]

The initial target is the romantic medievalism of the Celtic Renaissance. The narrator sets the exaggerated tone, when he asks of Hynes, who has been at a cattle traders' meeting, 'Anything strange or wonderful, Joe?' What Joe cannot supply, the interpolated passage does, in a description of abundance which hides beneath its eloquence the Dublin food markets. The dream of abundance is indebted to James Clarence Mangan's poem, 'Prince Alfrid's Itinerary through Ireland', from which several phrases are taken ('unfettered Munster', 'Connacht the just', 'Cruachan's land', and 'Armagh the splendid'),[78] but the general effect parodies the congestion of foodstuffs in many late nineteenth-century translations of Celtic elegiac and descriptive poetry.

The next interpolation draws on the epic tradition, represented by such works as *The Stealing of the Dun Cow*. The style is prompted by the citizen's preposterous revolutionary pose:

—Stand and deliver, says he.
—That's all right, citizen, says Joe. Friends here.
—Pass, friends, says he. (*U* 280/381)

This time the citizen himself is transmuted into 'a broadshouldered deep-

[77] As Hugh Kenner says, the parodies in 'Cyclops' are 'a critique of the en tire neo-Celtic movement' (*Kenner*, 255).
[78] The relevant passages of the poem are quoted in *Allusions*, 256–7. Joyce himself quotes the poem in his lecture, 'Ireland, Island of Saints and Sages' (*CW*, 159).

chested stronglimbed frankeyed redhaired freely freckled shaggybearded widemouthed largenosed longheaded deepvoiced barekneed brawny-handed hairylegged ruddyfaced sinewyarmed hero.' Again the style strains so hard to impress that it collapses into a clumsy absurdity which mockingly parodies the translations of Irish epics (such as those of Standish O'Grady) or the pseudo-medievalism of Ossian and his imitators.

The critical fashion for enthusing over the harsh verses of the Celtic bards of the eighteenth century is ridiculed in a passage about the dog, Garryowen. The citizen has been fooling about with it and talking to it in Irish, with the dog 'letting on to answer', though the narrator, in his usual hyperbolic way, expresses his loathing of the animal, 'growling and grousing and his eye all bloodshot from the drouth is in it and the hydrophobia dropping out of his jaws.' The subsequent interpolation about this gifted dog's power of reciting its own verses, translated 'by an eminent scholar', amusingly parodies the critical manner of the time, and culminates in eight lines of verse, said to recall metrically 'the intricate alliterative and iso-syllabic rules of the Welsh englyn', but consisting of a prolonged curse on Barney Kiernan for not supplying a drink of water. The verses, to be 'spoken somewhat slowly and indistinctly in a tone suggestive of suppressed ran-cour', are very reminiscent of some of the cursing poems, translated or imitated 'from the Irish', the implication being, of course, that these 'satirical effusions' on which so much learning was expended and so much critical praise lavished were hardly to be distinguished from the growlings of a thirsty dog.

The revival of interest in Celtic art, especially in illustrated manuscripts, is parodied in a passage about the citizen's handkerchief, described as 'the muchtreasured and intricately embroidered ancient Irish facecloth.' Joyce captures the pompous and plummy tone of guidebooks and patriotic travel-lers ('No need to dwell on the legendary beauty of the cornerpieces, the acme of art'), imitates the incidental displays of anti-British sentiment (as in the reference to the North American puma – 'a far nobler king of beasts than the British article, be it said in passing'), and develops an hysterical catalogue of Irish beauty-spots, ranging from Glendalough and the lakes of Killarney to 'the brewery of Messrs Arthur Guinness, Son and Company (Limited)' and 'Rathdown Union Workhouse at Loughlinstown.' These parodies are closer to journalese than to the mock-medievalism of the earlier passages, though they are equally marked by a fumbling and bathetic pretentiousness. Other kinds of Irish journalism are ridiculed, all exhibiting a similar verbosity, a similar fondness for superlatives, and a similar chauvinism, turning a boxing-match into an Irish victory over the British by repeated stressing of the nationality of the two fighters, 'Dublin's pet lamb, . . . the Irish gladiator, . . . the fistic Eblanite' knocking out 'the welterweight sergeantmajor, . . . the redcoat, . . . the Englishman, . . . the Portobello bruiser'. A parody of the Creed, adapted to the British ('They believe in rod, the scourger almighty, creator of hell upon earth . . .') exemplifies the more extreme and bitter forms of political hatred.

To the discussion of Irish games, Joyce appends a passage ridiculing another aspect of the people whom, in the *Portrait*, Mr Dedalus had called 'a priestridden Godforsaken race'; the report, after referring to the large audience 'amongst which were to be noticed many prominent members of the clergy as well as representatives of the press and the bar and the other learned professions', gives a list of those present, a list consisting of the titles, names and orders of twenty-four clerics, with the feeble addition that 'the laity included P. Fay, T. Quirke, etc., etc.' The pseudo-religiosity of the bar-flies, on whose lips 'God' is a commonplace, is laughed at in a more extended passage when Martin Cunningham says 'God bless all here is my prayer', and the citizen, who has been savagely sneering at Bloom, answers 'Amen'. There follows a long procession of church-attendants, minor clerics, monks, nuns and friars of all kinds, leading the saints, martyrs, virgins and confessors, all proceeding to Barney Kiernan's to pronounce a blessing on the house, though the effect is diminished by the presence among the saints of all the men in the bar, spontaneously canonized, together with 'S. Owen Caniculus', 'S. Marion Calpensis', and such mysterious figures as 'S. Anonymous and S. Eponymous and S. Pseudonymous and S. Homonymous and S. Paronymous and S. Synonymous.' What, no doubt, seemed to Joyce the more ridiculous aspects of the Catholic worship of the saints appear in the robes worn by them,

> whereon were woven the blessed symbols of their efficacies, inkhorns, arrows, loaves, cruses, fetters, axes, trees, bridges, babes in a bathtub, shells, wallets, shears, keys, dragons, lilies, buckshot, beards, hogs, lamps, bellows, beehives, soupladles, stars, snakes, anvils, boxes of vaseline, bells, crutches, forceps, stags' horns, watertight boots, hawks, millstones, eyes on a dish, wax candles, aspergills, unicorns. (*U* 323-4/441)

Nevertheless, *en route* to Barney Kiernan's, this remarkable procession performs 'divers wonders such as casting out devils, raising the dead to life, multiplying fishes, healing the halt and the blind, discovering various articles which had been mislaid, interpreting and fulfilling the scriptures, blessing and prophesying.' Although this passage shares with earlier passages the exaggerated manner, the extensive and absurd catalogues and the collapses into bathos, the nature and point of the satire are now quite different. Here Joyce is laughing at the curious literal-mindedness of much Irish Catholicism, with its almost casual appeals to the saints, its blindness to the ludicrous side of its beliefs, and its simple superstitious confidence in the efficacy of the repertoire of saints about whom the ignorant worshipper knows nothing but the symbols. It is a simplicity of mind as apparent among the blasphemous scroungers of Barney Kiernan's as among the superficially more sophisticated people who swallow the spiritualist and theosophical jargon used to describe the return of Paddy Dignam's spirit.

The account of the execution of an Irish hero, the longest interpolation in the chapter, is more bitterly satirical, presenting the Irish as a nation greedy for cheap excitement, always ready to shed an easy tear, fickle and for sale. It begins by mocking the swollen rhetoric of Irish grief:

The last farewell was affecting in the extreme. From the belfries far and near the funereal deathbell tolled unceasingly while all around the gloomy precincts rolled the ominous warning of a hundred muffled drums punctuated by the hollow booming of pieces of ordnance. (U 291/396)

To this, thunder, lightning and torrential rain are added, while the crowd of five hundred thousand are entertained by a band and streetsingers, and a special word of praise is given to the Little Sisters of the Poor, who have brought children from the foundling hospitals, 'for their excellent idea of affording the poor fatherless and motherless children a genuinely instructive treat.' Among those present are members of a foreign delegation 'known as the Friends of the Emerald Isle', who, after denouncing 'the nameless barbarity which they had been called upon to witness', fall into an argument about the correct birthday of St Patrick, which develops into a violent combat involving 'cannonballs, scimitars, boomerangs, blunderbusses, stinkpots, meatchoppers, umbrellas, catapults, knuckledusters, sandbags, lumps of pig iron.' To this point, the satire seems largely directed against a vulgar seeking for sensation of any kind, a total absence of sympathy or patriotic feeling, and the attitudes of the foreign powers who, though fond of expressing sympathy for Ireland, were far more concerned with petty quarrels of their own. But the tone becomes more savage when the headsman arrives and is 'greeted by a roar of acclamation', while admirers of the executioner provide him with a flock of sheep on which to test the sharpness of his blade. The combination of a penny-pinching materialistic economy, bloody violence, and sentimental religious gestures is symbolized by the provision of a saucepan to receive the hero's innards after he has been disembowelled, and two milk jugs 'destined to receive the most precious blood of the most precious victim', all these utensils to be carried, when filled, to 'the amalgamated cats' and dogs' home'. Emotions run high when 'the blushing bride elect', a figure representing Ireland, embraces the hero who is about to die for her sake and promises to cherish his memory. She leads the audience, first, to hearty laughter by reminiscences of childhood on the banks of the Liffey, and, then, to torrents of tears and 'heartrending sobs', and immediately accepts an offer of marriage from 'a handsome young Oxford graduate', who wins her by showing her 'his visiting card, bankbook, and genealogical tree'. This episode reflects the same view of Ireland's treatment of her patriots as Stephen had put to Davin in the Portrait:

—No honourable and sincere man, said Stephen, has given up to you his life and his youth and his affections from the days of Tone to those of Parnell, but you sold him to the enemy or failed him in need or reviled him and left him for another. (P 207)

The insincerity of Ireland's mourning for her hero is the concluding theme of Joyce's article about the Fenian, John O'Leary:

Now that he is dead, his countrymen will escort him to his tomb with great pomp. Because the Irish, even though they break the hearts of those who sacrifice their lives for their native land, never fail to show great respect for the dead. [79]

The method here is essentially allegorical fable, and the exposure of the treacherous emotionalism of the Irish is contemptuous and bitter.

At the other extreme are passages ridiculing Bloom's pedantic remarks about scientific phenomena (to explain posthumous erections in hanged men) or Doran's drunken request to Bloom to tell Mrs Dignam 'that he said and everyone who knew him said that there was never a truer, a finer than poor little Willy that's dead.' These and similar passages are less serious in purpose: they laugh at the earnestness and self-importance with which the idiocies in Barney Kiernan's are exchanged. In the same vein is the report of the marriage of the chevalier Jean Wyse de Neaulan to Miss Fir Conifer, which springs from a conversation in which Nolan complains of the deforestation of Ireland, the citizen makes an impassioned plea to save 'the giant ash of Galway and the chieftain elm of Kildare with a fortyfoot bole and an acre of foliage', and Lenehan comes in with, 'Europe has its eyes on you.' The silly notion that Europe was deeply interested in the preservation of the stock of noble Irish trees no doubt suggested the grandiose style of a society columnist, in whose eyes a few ladies anxious to get their names into society journals can be seen as 'the fashionable international world': the whole passage smacks of the petty and provincial trying to pass itself off as high society, although, of course, Joyce is not mocking society columnists, but merely using their style to ridicule Irish provincialism and pretentiousness in general.

Sometimes the interpolated passage runs counter to the implications of the bar-room talk. A conversation about a Jew who has that day appeared before the Dublin Recorder, Sir Frederick Falkiner, on a charge of swindling, and has been remanded, develops into an idealized eulogy of Sir Frederick's soft-heartedness and sympathy towards the poor. The succeeding interpolation takes up the image of justice in the loftiest way, even the date being defined in classical, ecclesiastical and lunar terms. The court is a similar conglomerate of traditions. The recorder is medievally transfigured into Sir Frederick the Falconer, who comes to administer 'the law of the brehons' (the ancient Irish law), together with 'the high sinhedrim' (the Jewish court of justice) consisting of representatives of the twelve tribes of Iar (combining the twelve tribes of Israel with Irish legend and history) who form the 'twelve good men and true' of an English jury. This jury is conjured that it should 'well and truly try and true delivrance make', and give a true verdict, and the members swear in God's name 'that they would do His rightwiseness'. After all this solemn preparation for justice, a man is led forth from the dungeons, having been apprehended 'in consequence of information received', and the paraphernalia of justice at once collapses:

And they shackled him hand and foot and would take of him ne bail ne mainprise but preferred a charge against him for he was a malefactor. (*U* 308/419)

[79] *CW*, 192.

The last word arbitrarily and without evidence brings in the verdict which all the judicial forms and procedures were supposed to reach 'according to the evidence'; it is a verdict comparable to that of the Citizen, who follows it immediately with a display of antisemitism:

—Those are nice things, says the citizen, coming over here to Ireland filling the country with bugs. (*U* 308/419)

Bloom pretends not to have heard this, but it is ominous. So too is the interpolation, for it is in just this arbitrary way, on the totally unreliable information of Lenehan, that Bloom is found guilty of being a secretly successful punter, too mean to buy a drink. While he is spending his time trying to help Mrs Dignam and her children, he is accused of 'defrauding widows and orphans', and is convicted without trial. Here the interpolation not only ridicules the fine talk in the bar, but anticipatorily indicates the real prejudices and cruelty hidden behind the talk.

Towards the end of the chapter, the interpolations begin to serve an additional purpose. It is obvious to everyone that trouble is about to start, and Bloom's friends endeavour to hurry him away: the inflated styles are now at least related to a situation of some tenseness. The epic description of the jaunting car, in terms proper to the chariot of Poseidon, and the journalistic description of a ceremony of farewell appropriate to the departure of a distinguished foreign guest, seem to prepare for a climactic action, and, curiously, seem both to laugh at Bloom's predicament and to draw attention to the heroic elements in his behaviour. For once, the man whom Joe Hynes calls 'the prudent member' and who entered the chapter as 'he of the prudent soul', abandons prudence and responds boldly if confusedly to the snarling citizen. Similarly, although the account of the impact of the biscuit-tin as a natural catastrophe devastating a large area of Dublin is very funny, and develops from the narrator's exaggerated assertion that the citizen threw it so vigorously 'he near sent it into the county Longford', it is not merely another example of the trivial grossly magnified: it also suggests the real destructiveness and violence of the old man's anger. At one level, his threat to 'crucify' Bloom is just another example of the 'gigantism' of language from which he, the narrator and most of their companions suffer, but at another it expresses accurately enough the depth of malice working in him. Consequently Bloom's departure, though a farcical parody of Elijah's chariot of fire and the light which surrounded Christ at the Transfiguration, relates to his conduct as a prophet of love among savages and pagans, and as the only man in Barney Kiernan's pub with the moral courage to stand up to the citizen:

And they beheld Him even Him, ben Bloom Elijah, amid clouds of angels ascend to the glory of the brightness at an angle of fortyfive degrees over Donohoe's in Little Green Street like a shot off a shovel. (*U* 329/449)

This last sentence draws together the inflations of the interpolations and the colloquial exaggeration of the dialogue; both are laughable, and yet the swollen illusions which they represent constitute the real threat to Bloom.

While his final departure, like his behaviour throughout, has its ludicrous aspect, the style humorously suggests that, in his resistance to the patriotic cant and affected fanaticism of his fellow citizens, he has acted with heroic independence and moral courage.

The interpolations are associated with the conversation in a variety of ways and with varying effect, but, in general, they mock the inveterate Irish (and human) tendency to exaggerate in order to dress up the commonplace in a vesture of passion or importance, and form an ironic commentary on the talk and behaviour of the bar-flies. They might be seen as a *reductio ad absurdum*, if it were not that the exchanges in the bar are absurd beyond the possibility of reduction. Indeed, reduction to absurdity, itself a mode of exaggeration, is one of the ways in which the interpolations handle whatever does not accord with the simple prejudices of the men in the bar. Bloom's concern for the suffering of animals is first sneered at by the cynical narrator ('Gob, he'd have a soft hand under a hen'), and then mocked in an absurdly childish interpolation:

> Ga Ga Gara. Klook Klook Klook. Black Liz is our hen. She lays eggs for us. When she lays her egg she is so glad. Gara. Klook Klook Klook. Then comes good uncle Leo. He puts his hand under black Liz and takes her fresh egg. Ga ga ga ga Gara. Klook Klook Klook. (*U* 300/408)

Similarly, when Bloom speaks out against 'Force, hatred, history, all that', and urges that what is proper to mankind is 'Love', both the old citizen ('He's a nice pattern of a Romeo and Juliet') and the interpolation misconstrue his use of the term in order to ridicule him:

> Love loves to love love. Nurse loves the new chemist. Constable 14A loves Mary Kelly. Gerty MacDowell loves the boy that has the bicycle. M.B. loves a fair gentleman. . . . You love a certain person. And this person loves that other person because everybody loves somebody but God loves everybody. (*U* 317/433)

The highfaluting and sentimental response of the interpolated passages to fake nationalism, superstition and prejudice is matched by their supercilious and sneering ridicule of whatever is, however lamely expressed, humane and genuine.

The whole chapter is the most consistently satirical in *Ulysses*. It is often suggested that, in his writings, Joyce was apolitical and amoral, but this chapter alone proves the contrary. He does not advocate any political creed or any moral code, but, partly through the events in Barney Kiernan's pub and partly through the styles in which they are presented, he exposes and ridicules antisemitism, chauvinistic nationalism, and several forms of religious cant and hypocrisy.[80] The satire is always implicit in the styles –

---

[80] Cf. 'Patriotism was for my brother as for Johnson 'the last refuge of a scoundrel'' ' (*MBK*, 201). Phillip F. Herring, both in *Notesheets* (13–15) and in an article, 'Joyce's Politics' (*New Light*, 3–14), argues that Joyce 'was incapable of any sort of altruistic political commitment' and merely 'endorsed the politics of self-interest' (*Notesheets*, 15). Self-interest plays its part in the most committed political attitudes – for that matter, in the most altruistic behaviour. We should not judge Joyce by totally unreal standards.

whether of the narrator's monologue or of the rhetorical interpolations –
and penetrates more deeply than most political or social satire, because it
goes beneath the superficial displays of ignorance and folly, traces such
attitudes as antisemitism to their roots in the frustrations and disappointments of trivial lives, and relates them to the various forms of vain self-
glorification or morbid 'gigantism' which afflict men and nations.

'Nausicaa'

The unnamed narrator's interior monologue resembles a protracted bar-
room anecdote because such a manner best reflects the nature of his self-
awareness: he feels himself and others to be permanently involved in an
endless gossipy tale. Gerty MacDowell's consciousness, on the other hand,
is like a flattering mirror before which she performs, just as she performs
before a real mirror: 'she knew how to cry nicely before the mirror. You
are lovely, Gerty, it said.' Although the style borrows freely from novelettes
of the time, it is not critical parody – Joyce is not out to ridicule the
patently ridiculous – nor even pastiche. It is rather a purée of clichés,
extracted and condensed not only from the stories in girls' papers, but from
their beauty pages, cookery tips, fashion notes, advice to the lovelorn,
correspondence columns and advertisements, to which are added clichés,
equally sickly, from religious tracts, temperance propaganda, popular
superstitions and all the current affectations of popular culture and respectability. Through this oversweetened mess, the dry facts of Gerty's real
situation occasionally emerge, and the vulgarities of her undoctored self
erupt. Her monologue is not a repetitious or laborious exercise. There are
continuous fluctuations of style from high-flown romanticism to coarse
spitefulness, from pious pretence to naive exhibitionism, from airy vagueness to drab particulars. Joyce himself found it impossible to describe the
style fully:

> Nausikaa is written in a namby-pamby jammy marmalady drawersy (alto là!)
> style with effects of incense, mariolatry, masturbation, stewed cockles,
> painter's palette, chit chat, circumlocution, etc., etc. [81]

There is a constant tendency to sink from the fantasy levels of consciousness towards the mundane and vulgar, so that Gerty repeatedly has to
snatch up her thoughts again, and this erratic movement is reflected in a

---

That he was an egoist he was the first to admit; it does not follow that he was incapable
of sympathy with the oppressed and hatred for the tyrannous. He was primarily an
artist; it does not follow that political sympathies could not enter his work. No doubt,
like most of us, he was more certain of what was politically bad than of what was
politically desirable.

[81] *Letters* I, 135. I find incomprehensible Father W. T. Noon's opinion that 'there is
nothing satirical about the opening paragraph of this chapter. Here is the sort of praise
of Our Lady that might be found in St. Bernard' (*Noon*, 100). On the contrary, here are
'effects of incense, mariolatry'.

style far removed from the comparative inflexibility of parody. Illusion is repeatedly interrupted by the commonplace facts of Gerty's life and resentments. The dream of being 'pronounced beautiful by all' stumbles a little on the memory of real comments about her resemblance to one or other side of her family; the image of a graceful figure breaks up into the less elevated particulars of iron jelloids, pills, discharges and the advertisers' catchphrase, 'that tired feeling'. The stock phrases of loveliness from advertisements for creams, powders and lipsticks raise the tone again until it is lowered by the names of specific preparations, and shattered by Gerty's anger at Bertha Supple's 'deliberate lie'. The attempt to modulate into the 'little tiffs' of 'girl chums' doesn't succeed, but Gerty dismisses this unfortunate, catty episode by creating the dream of her own 'innate refinement', leading upwards to the view of herself as a natural aristocrat, presented in such appropriate terms as '*hauteur*' and 'devoirs'. Deprived by fate of her true position in society, she quickly transmutes the loss into a love-deprivation and so brings in the note of melancholy passion. Through mention of Gerty's 'eyes of witchery', the train of association leads to eyebrows, and thence to the synthetic world of 'eyebrowleine' and remedies for blushing, shortness and small noses. Gerty cannot resist a sly dig at Mrs Dignam's button nose, before returning to her dream of her own beauty, of her crowning glory, and a momentary slip into superstitions about haircutting and nailparing is quickly recovered by consciousness of her own shy and rosy flush at Edy's remark about Gerty's being Tommy Caffrey's sweetheart.

The style is as various as Gerty's moods, and the manner in which her experience of what lies around her is presented changes abruptly and radically. The Caffrey twins, first seen as 'darling little fellows with bright merry faces and endearing ways about them', later become 'exasperating little brats', and their sister, Cissy, undergoes more complex transformations. At first she is seen as a girl of merry sweetness:

> A truerhearted lass never drew the breath of life, always with a laugh in her gipsylike eyes and a frolicsome word on her cherryripe red lips, a girl lovable in the extreme. (*U* 330/450)

When Cissy makes an unladylike remark about smacking Tommy 'on the beetoteetom', Gerty is able to reconcile herself to this by the image of 'Madcap Ciss with her golliwog curls'. However, when Cissy's tomboy behaviour threatens Gerty's dream about the gentleman on the beach, resentment presents Cissy in quite a different light, mounting through sarcastic comments on Cissy's skimpy hair, 'long gandery strides' and tomboy behaviour to scorn for this 'forward piece' who is trying to show off by exposing 'her skinny shanks up as far as possible'. The coarsening of the language and the reference to the vulgar joke about 'up as far as possible' indicates how far Gerty's anger is carrying her. At this point the reader does not know that the bitterness towards Cissy's running and tight skirt and 'her high crooked French heels' is because Gerty is lame and cannot compete in that sort of display. She can pull herself out of a mood of cattiness only by assuming feelings of haughty superiority – represented in the monologue by such terms as '*Tableau!*' and 'exposé' – and then by associating herself with the overheard prayer to the Virgin. The ease with which her religious sentimentality can coexist with her erotic dreams is comically expressed by her foot-swinging, moving to the rhythm of the hymn, but designed to reveal titillating glimpses of her legs in their transparent stockings. The religiosity provides a disguise for her desire to compete with the brazen revelations of Cissy. Even the interweavings of the elements in the style of the monologue expose aspects of Gerty's mind of which she herself is not fully aware.

The function of the style is not to ridicule the silly daydreams of a young girl; Gerty is ridiculous but she is also pitiable, and the image of her circumstances and nature is too complex to permit of a simple response. The style, like that of the earlier monologues, serves to represent the essence of her consciousness and the fluctuations of her moods; what we are told about Gerty is, for the most part, exaggerated, misleading, garbled or quite untrue, yet, through the style, we experience the quality of her experience. Gerty's escapism represents a temptation to which Bloom is vulnerable, as Nausicaa was a temptation to Ulysses to abandon the long struggle homeward. Her daydreams are a flight from her homelife with a drunken and violent father and from her lameness; Bloom too has family and personal disabilities. The 'tumescence' of the 'technic', culminating in her self-induced orgasm and his masturbation, is figured equally in the action and the style of her monologue.

For Gerty, the self-deception and the auto-eroticism are enough; tomorrow or another day she will attach similar fantasies to Reggy Wylie or Father Conroy or some other stranger. The danger is that it will also be enough for Bloom. For a moment, he is caught up in the false romanticism of the style:

> He was leaning back against the rock behind. Leopold Bloom (for it is he) stands silent, with bowed head before those young guileless eyes. What a brute he had been! At it again? A fair unsullied soul had called to him and, wretch that he was, how had he answered? An utter cad he had been. He of all men! But there was an infinite store of mercy in those eyes, for him too a word of pardon even though he had erred and sinned and wandered. (*U* 350/478)

Perception of Gerty's lameness jerks him back to reality, and the return to the characteristic style of his earlier monologues signifies that a 'detumescence' of his imagination is accompanying his physical detumescence.

The sudden shift back to the earlier kind of monologue is the most important feature of the style of the latter part of the chapter, representing as it does a release from the strains and pressures that have been building up in Bloom:

> Did me good all the same. Off colour after Kiernan's, Dignam's. For this relief much thanks. (*U* 355/485)

The silent relationship with Gerty has the double effect of tiring him physically ('Exhausted that female has me. Not so young now') and restoring him psychologically ('Goodbye, dear. Thanks. Made me feel so young.') He can now face up to what has happened between Boylan and Molly and see it as something over and done with: 'O, he did. Into her. She did. Done': though it may happen again on the Belfast tour, he can't be bothered about it. Molly is again a source of pride to him rather than humiliation and distress: she can 'knock spots off' other men's wives, and now, if he wonders why she chose him, he recalls her answer, 'Because you were so foreign from the others.' Gerty has strengthened him, not only by providing the stimulus for his masturbation, but by choosing him now as Molly chose him in the past. He cannot be as contemptible as some of his recent encounters have suggested: 'Saw something in me. Wonder what.' One cannot distinguish the style of the monologue from its content. Both are relaxing, quiescing: the paragraphs draw out longer and more leisurely than before, because Bloom is less troubled by turbulent emotions. The scene, too, grows sleepy as the light fails and Bloom prepares to have a short snooze:

> Twittering the bat flew here, flew there. Far out over the sands the coming surf crept, grey. Howth settled for slumber tired of long days, of yumyum rhododendrons (he was old) and felt gladly the night breeze lift, ruffle his fell of ferns. He lay but opened a red eye unsleeping, deep and slowly breathing, slumberous but awake.   (*U* 362/494-5)

Howth has become a projected image of Bloom's own sleepiness. The 'yumyum rhododendrons', a mocking reference to the courtship of Molly, the memory of which had so excited Bloom in Davy Byrne's, no longer disturb him. Like Howth, Bloom intents to rest – not sleeping, but 'slumberous'. After the tensions of his day and the unexpected relief supplied by Gerty, Bloom dozes off, and the style represents the dissipation of his consciousness, with words and phrases echoed from earlier phases of his interior monologue:

> O sweety all your little girlwhite up I saw dirty bracegirdle made me do love sticky we two naughty Grace darling she him half past the bed met him pike hoses frillies for Raoul to perfume your wife black hair heave under embon *señorita* young eyes Mulvey plump years dreams return tail end Agendath swoony lovey showed me her next year in drawers return next in her next her next.   (*U* 365/498)

The fusion of Bloom's memory of Gerty's display with his awareness of what has happened in his bed that afternoon is clear and effective enough but Joyce tracks the movements of Bloom's dozing mind more closely to suggest the resumption of its odyssey after this temporary distraction. At first, feelings of gratitude ('O sweet little, you don't know how nice you looked'), the memory of his excitement ('Darling, I saw your. I saw all'), the vision of Gerty's white underclothes are all confused with his notion that women's lingerie is designed to tempt men ('I'm all clean come and dirty me') and that Gerty's performance was somewhat stagy, like the fascination exerted by such actresses as Mrs Bracegirdle. This leads, via

the image of their mutual excitation and subsequent stickiness to the phrase
from Martha's letter (which he had remembered just before), 'naughty
darling', the name 'Grace' being intruded as a result of his passing thought
of the Victorian heroine, Grace Darling. Martha's letter had borne the
address 'P. O. Dolphin's Barn', and this had led his mind to his early
courtship of Molly; thus 'naughty darling', though borrowed from Martha,
leads at once to 'she him', Molly and Boylan, to their meeting that afternoon at half-past four (the time at which his watch had stopped), and to
the bed in which the adultery took place. In that bed, that morning, Molly
had asked him to explain 'met him pike hoses' (the word, 'metempsychosis',
has occurred to him, in another connection, just before): 'met him' is a
euphemism for what has taken place between Molly and Boylan, while
'hoses' leads, through the memory of the Mutoscope pictures of 'A dream
of wellfilled hose', to the 'frillies' worn by the heroine of *Sweets of Sin* for
her lover, 'for Raoul'. In 'Sirens' Bloom had imagined Molly awaiting
Boylan, 'perfumed for him', and that now blends with Gerty's farewell
wave of a piece of perfumed wadding to leave behind a scented memory,
and with Martha's enquiry about his wife's perfume. He remembers
Molly's first meeting with Boylan, when she was 'wearing her black and
it had the perfume of the time before', and his earlier thoughts of the
sources of female odour, in particular the hair, 'strong in rut'. All of these
thoughts of Molly and Boylan, of Raoul and the heroine of *Sweets of Sin*,
and of perfume shift easily to the picture of a woman's 'heaving embonpoint' (Molly's, the novel heroine's, and Miss Douce's – already shortened
to 'her heaving embon') lying under a lover, and thence to Molly as she must
have been at the time of her first affair with Mulvey, a young 'señorita'
with her fine 'Spanishy eyes' and her breasts already 'developed' – the
word 'plump' seems to link this with an earlier image of Molly when she
was just beginning to plump out her elephantgrey dress. He has remembered, too, his own first wooing of his wife, in an earlier June, and the
passage of time has brought to his mind the succession of years, 'The year
returns.' Mixed with this motion of the returning year is a later thought
that a dream 'never comes the same', and the succession of 'years dreams
return' is also associated with the charades at Dolphin's Barn, when he was
courting Molly, and he played the part of Rip Van Winkle. 'Return' is an
aspect of his earlier thoughts of sailors, 'smelling the tail end of ports',
while 'tail end' is linked to another kind of return, the smutty picture of a
husband returning to find his wife with her lover – on which Joe Hynes
had commented, 'Get a queer old tailend of corned beef off of that one,
what?' But the word 'end' suggests by its sound 'Agendath', the name of
the plantation company, a symbol of the return of the Jews to Palestine.
These various returns now become confused as Bloom's consciousness
fades: the sexual image recalls the image of orgasm suggested to his mind
when he first read *Sweets of Sin* ('Whites of eyes swooning up'), and his
own sensation while watching Gerty 'on show'; but the Agendath memory
brings in a phrase from the Passover ritual, 'Next year in Jerusalem', the
dream of return. (He has just recalled, or misrecalled, the *Exodus* praise of

God who 'brought us out of the land of Egypt and into the house of bondage.') Does 'drawers' refer to Gerty's underclothes or to Molly's: 'Drawers: little kick, taking them off. By by till next time'? The combination of 'drawers' and 'next' may suggest that it is the reference to Molly's underclothes which is in his mind, but Bloom is now close to sleep; Molly and Gerty are blending in his dim consciousness as are the notions of returning home, of the possibility of returning to see Gerty again, and of the Jewish return to Palestine. Similarly there is no knowing whether 'next' refers to next year in Jerusalem, the next time he sees Gerty or the next of Molly's infidelities. Everything is fusing as Bloom dozes off. The paragraph thus presents a kaleidoscopic image of a mind slowly fading into sleep, joining together remembered words and phrases (as in the closing paragraph of 'The Dead') moving along a train of associations, sometimes verbal, sometimes phonetic, sometimes emotional, sometimes of linked thoughts and experiences. It shows how, in Bloom's mind, despite the certainty of Molly's adultery and despite his own sexual satisfaction through masturbation, the image of his wife slowly absorbs the images of Gerty and of Martha; the dominant thought in his darkening consciousness is that of return – a return essentially to Molly, for she is his Ithaca and the Promised Land to which he hears the summons of recall.

As the cuckoo-clock in the priest's house sounds nine o'clock, everything inconclusively fades away. Bloom, openmouthed, leaning sideways, thinks 'just for a few'; the priests are at their supper 'and talking about'; Gerty notices that the gentleman 'that was sitting on the rocks looking was'. The nine times repeated cry of 'Cuckoo' seems to publish Bloom's situation: earlier, in the library, Mulligan had quoted 'Cuckoo! Cuckoo! O word of fear!': and later, in the brothel, the clock again signals Bloom's place in the register of Dublin cuckolds. But if the cuckooing was simply to announce Bloom's cuckoldry, one would have to say that the clock was four and a half hours slow, and that the stale joke was a feeble conclusion to the chapter. In fact, it offers a brief image of the attitudes of the two central figures of the chapter. Gerty's persistent romanticism transforms the cuckoo into 'a little canarybird bird', while Bloom, now able to accept the situation which has troubled him all day, shows his resigned unconcern ('Let him') by falling asleep while his cuckoldry is being proclaimed.

But Gerty is more than an agent by whom Bloom is enabled to achieve physical and emotional 'detumescence'; for that purpose, the whole chapter could have been restricted to Bloom's point of view. She also incarnates a temptation to which Bloom is vulnerable. The vague doctrine of 'love', with which he countered the old Citizen's racial and religious prejudices, could, in its own sentimental and religiose way, be just as blinding and paralysing as bloodyminded chauvinism. In 'Cyclops', Gerty has been used as an image of this tendency in Bloom; the paragraph, ridiculing Bloom's affirmation of love, includes the sentence, 'Gerty MacDowell loves the boy on the bicycle.' To realize, focus and pass judgement on this kind of escapism, it has to be shown at work in the consciousness of one of its victims; but to use a convention of interior monologue, akin to that used for Bloom and Stephen, would be uneconomical and inappropriate. Gerty is a subordinate figure: to capture her essence, a convention is needed which, without ignoring the girl's specific qualities or the fluctuations of her mood, will characterize and assess the retreat from reality which she represents. The conglomerate of clichés establishes and implicitly comments on the escapist fantasy; the variations among the phrases belonging to schoolgirl slang, bitchy gossip, and romantic, patriotic, moral and religiose sentimentality create Gerty's individuality within the general image. It is an image not simply of a silly girl who has read too many novelettes but of an impoverished, handicapped, disappointed and frustrated existence, consoling itself with the illusions offered by the Dublin environment and the prevailing attitudes to love, friendship, family, country and religion.

'Oxen of the Sun'

For this chapter Joyce provided, in a letter to Frank Budgen, what appears to be a detailed scheme:

Am working hard at *Oxen of the Sun*, the idea being the crime committed against fecundity by sterilizing the act of coition. Scene, lying-in hospital. Technique: a nineparted episode without divisions introduced by a Sallust-ian-Tacitean prelude (the unfertilized ovum), then by way of earliest English alliterative and monosyllabic and Anglo-Saxon ('Before born the babe had bliss. Within the womb he won worship.' 'Bloom dull dreamy heard: in held hat stony staring.') then by way of Mandeville ('there came forth a scholar of medicine that men clepen, &c') then Malory's *Morte D'Arthur* ('but that franklin Lenehan was prompt ever to pour them so that at the least way mirth should not lack') then the Elizabethan 'chronicle style' ('about that present time young Stephen filled all cups'), then a passage solemn, as of Milton, Taylor and Hooker, followed by a choppy Latin-gossipy bit, style of Burton-Browne, then a passage Bunyanesque ('the reason was that in the way he fell in with a certain whore whose name she said is Bird-in-the-hand'). After a diarystyle bit Pepys-Evelyn ('Bloom sitting snug with a party of wags, among them Dixon jun, Ja. Lynch, Doc. Madden and Stephen D. for a languor he had before and was now better he having dreamed tonight a strange fancy and Mistress Purefoy there to be delivered, poor body, two days past her time and the midwives hard put to it, God send her quick issue') and so on through Defoe-Swift and Steele-Addison-Sterne and Landor-Pater-Newman until it ends in a frightful jumble of Pidgin English, Nigger English, Cockney, Irish, Bowery slang and broken doggerel. This procession is also linked back at each part subtly with some foregoing episode of the day and, besides this, with the natural stages of development in the embryo and the periods of faunal evolution in general. The double-thudding Anglo-Saxon motive recurs from time to time ('Loth to move from Horne's house') to give the sense of the hoofs of oxen. Bloom is the spermatozoon, the hospital the womb, the nurse the ovum, Stephen the embryo.

How's that for high?[82]

[82] The letter is included in *Letters* I, 138–9, but the version is defective, omitting altogether 'the Elizabethan "chronicle style"'. The version in the text is, therefore, taken from *Ellmann–JJ*, 489–90.

In a letter to Harriet Weaver the structure is again described, though without the trimmings, as consisting of 'nine circles of development (enclosed between the headpiece and tailpiece of opposite chaos).'[83]

The Budgen letter seems helpful. All the reader has to do to see to the bottom of Joyce's intent is to distinguish the nine parts, identify the links to earlier episodes, embryonic development and faunal evolution, perceive how the meeting of Bloom and the nurse results in the symbolic gestation of Stephen, and consider why 'the crime committed against fecundity' should be represented by a technique which follows the process from conception to birth. The general implication of the scheme – that here the entry of Bloom initiates the growth of the embryo artist – is plain enough and the proposed technique plausible: it remains only to observe and respond to the details of handling.

Unfortunately, the details are very difficult to identify, let alone respond to. Although the British Museum has Joyce's notesheets which contain, besides many notes on the embryo, a large onion-shaped diagram recording the details of its shape, size and length, month by month,[84] the scheme of embryonic development in the chapter remains surprisingly obscure, apart from a few obvious hints: at one point there is mention of the infusion of a human soul 'at the end of the second month', a little later Costello begins to sing '*The first three months she was not well*', and the moment of birth is signalled when Stephen and his companions burst out of the hospital. The two commentators whose personal access to Joyce gave them special advantages are of little help. Frank Budgen merely repeats the terms of Joyce's letter to him, and Stuart Gilbert, after listing a few dubious 'allusions', derived mainly from the notesheets, is content to assert that anyone who has (as he has not) 'more than a superficial acquaintance with the facts of pre-natal development' will detect 'many more such correspondences'.[85] That is to say, he does not know where they are, but believes, on the evidence of the Budgen letter and the notesheets, that they are somewhere there.[86] A much more determined examination by A. M. Klein[87] lists what purport to be other allusions, but most of these are farfetched and many quite implausible. I find no discernible, coherent, complete scheme of embryological reference: the acceptable allusions –

---

[83] *Letters* III, 16.

[84] The diagram is reproduced in *Notesheets*, facing p. 162. Details of a similar chart in the Cornell Joyce Collection are given by J. B. Lyons, *James Joyce and Medicine* (Dublin, Dolmen Press 1973), 75.

[85] *Gilbert*, 302.

[86] It may be significant that although J. B. Lyons, who has the specialist knowledge Gilbert lacked, says that 'it is certainly possible to uncover laboriously within the literary gestation many references to fertilization and foetal growth' (*James Joyce and Medicine*, 75), the illustrations he gives are the same as those given by Gilbert, apart from two which are given in A. M. Klein's article (see next note). J. S. Atherton has found a few more embryological hints – for instance, he sees 'naked pockets' as 'a rendering of "scrotum empty"' ' (*Hart and Hayman*, 325).

[87] A. M. Klein, 'The Oxen of the Sun', *Here and Now* I (1949), 29–31.

acceptable by the most unexacting standards of evidence – are few in number and of little significance.

The parallels to faunal evolution are even fewer and less significant.[88] Presumably Joyce had in mind the theory of 'recapitulation', which explains the embryo's development of such features as rudimentary gills and tail by supposing that, during gestation, it briefly passes through the stages of evolution of the species. The theory is alluded to in the passage where the occurrence of 'harelip', 'breastmole', and 'swineheaded ... or doghaired infants' is attributed to 'an arrest of embryonic development at some stage antecedent to the human.' The animalism, as of incompletely evolved human beings, of the students who rush out of the pub is suggested in the rhetoric of a revivalist American preacher: 'Come on, you dog-gone, bull-necked, beetlebrowed, hogjowled, peanutbrained, weaseleyed fourflushers.' But for any ordered evolutionary parallel to be apprehended, however subliminally, it must be first continuous and chronological, and second not buried in a mass of irrelevant and disordered faunal material; in fact, such allusions as may be found (or imagined) are without continuity and are swamped with uncoordinated animal images and references.

After prolonged search, and despite the efforts of the commentators, I cannot find more than a few scattered allusions to embryonic development and faunal evolution,[89] and the most plausible of these are in the early part of the chapter. They are too rare, fragmentary and insignificant to contribute anything to the reader's response, even when he has been forewarned of their presence. As Stuart Gilbert remarked, the letter to Budgen was written 'while Joyce was working on the episode', and comparison of it with the published chapter 'shows that he made some changes in his programme.'[90] I think it likely that Joyce abandoned both schemes during composition or, at least, did not bother to complete their working-out. The notesheets confirm this supposition for, although there are thirty or more jottings referring to embryonic development month by month (and sometimes week by week), comparatively few of them have been crossed through to indicate that they have been incorporated in the chapter. What purpose could such schemes have served? Presumably Joyce's plan was that they should constitute a developing embryological and evolutionary metaphor for what happens to the artist, Stephen; but such a metaphor is already much more effectively established by the procession of styles and the constant talk among the young men concerning the processes of gestation.

The subtle links to foregoing episodes are just as difficult to identify –

[88] Unfortunately in the transcript of the Budgen letter supplied to A. M. Klein, 'faunal evolution' was miscopied as 'formal evolution', and consequently he related each of the nine parts to geological periods. That his case for these imaginary parallels is almost as well supported as the other parts of his argument says more for his ingenuity than for the reliability of his exegetical method.

[89] J. S. Atherton says that the faunal evolution and the embryology in the chapter are 'equally sketchy' (*Hart and Hayman*, 317–18).

[90] *Gilbert*, 292 n. 1.

this time because there are too many allusions.[91] Joyce could not have written the chapter without constant links to earlier events of the day, and, although some of these may be regarded as 'subtle' (for instance, the headless fish may be intended to recall the sardine in Davy Byrne's bar), no system of association, one for 'each part', can be recognized in the maze of references to and reminiscences of preceding episodes. It is hard to see what Joyce hoped to achieve. Possibly he meant to suggest a parallel between Bloom's odyssey (which has, to this point, occupied nine chapters) and the development of the embryo artist, struggling, as Bloom had done, past inimical forces. But there is little in the chapter to support such a conjecture.

Even the account, given in the letter, of the procession of styles has its difficulties. Many of the parodies in the chapter, including some of the most striking, are not mentioned,[92] and, despite the reference to nine parts, Joyce appears to list eleven varieties of style besides the prelude and the chaotic conclusion. No two critics entirely agree in relating the months of gestation to the styles, but the few reliable clues to the embryological parallel suggest that the scheme envisaged in the letter was as follows:

Gestation	Main content	Style
Unfertilized ovum (and womb)	Hospital and midwives	Latinate
Sperm and conception	Bloom's arrival and entry	'Anglo-Saxon' etc.
First month	The drinking party	Mandeville etc.
Second month	Discussion – mothers and babies	Malory etc.
Third month	Discussion – Virgin and Logos	Elizabethan chronicles etc.
Fourth month	Stephen reproaches Ireland	Milton–Taylor–Hooker–Burton–Browne etc.
Fifth month	The God Bringforth and Stephen the Prodigal	Bunyan etc.

[91] The notesheets contain lists of references to 'Nestor', 'Proteus', and 'Calypso', many of which were incorporated in the 'Oxen of the Sun' chapter (*Notesheets*, 34–5).

[92] Adrienne Monnier gave a different list, 'according to Joyce's own hints', in '*L'Ulysse* de Joyce et le public français' (*La Gazette des Amis des Livres* III (10), (1940), 50–64; translated by Sylvia Beach in *Kenyon Review* VIII (1946), 430–44; reprinted in *CH* II, 463): 'Mandeville, Malory, Bunyan, Defoe, Swift, Sterne, Addison, Goldsmith, Junius, Gibbon, Walpole, Lamb, De Quincey, Landor, Macaulay, scientific reviews of the first half of the 19th century, Dickens, Thackeray, Carlyle.' The best account of the parodies is given by J. S. Atherton in *Hart and Hayman*, 313–39.

Sixth month	Rainstorm	Pepys–Evelyn etc.
Seventh month	Foot-and-mouth disease and the fable of the Bull	Defoe–Swift etc.
Eighth month	Talk of copulation, fertility and contraception	Steele–Addison–Sterne etc.
Ninth month	Discussion – births, abortions and monsters	Landor–Pater–Newman etc.
Post-natal infant	Drinking in Burke's	Slangs and jargons

It is necessary to add 'etc.' to the authors named by Joyce, because they are not, and were probably never meant to be, the only ones parodied. They are representative of various stages in the development of English prose; this is why many paragraphs blend together materials from several different sources, why such additions as the parodies of Goldsmith, Lamb, De Quincey and Dickens do not dislocate the general scheme, and why Carlyle could be introduced to present the moment of birth, as mock Anglo-Saxon presented the moment of conception. Joyce is less concerned with individual writers or even with correct chronological sequence than with what he thought were the main stylistic developments in our prose. His general view was probably influenced by Saintsbury's *History of English Prose Rhythm*, which he is known to have been reading at the time,[93] and the recurrence of 'the double-thudding Anglo-Saxon motive' throughout the chapter may have been suggested by Saintsbury's assertion that the 'general trochaic rhythm' of Anglo-Saxon 'has beyond all doubt persisted in English prose more fully than it has in English poetry.'[94] The metaphor, implicit in the procession of styles and pointed to unmistakably by the scene and the talk of conception, gestation and birth, is of the embryonic development of English literary prose from a fusion of Latin and Anglo-Saxon, through stages ('without divisions') of progressive complexity to the present. The obvious application of the metaphor is to Stephen, the embryo artist: it suggests that, as the human embryo, developing in its environment, passes through phases corresponding to earlier evolutionary adaptations before being born into a world where it must make its own adaptations,

[93] See *Notesheets*, 32–3. In writing his parodies Joyce used, besides passages quoted by Saintsbury, an anthology edited by W. Peacock, *English Prose from Mandeville to Ruskin* (World's Classics. London, Oxford University Press 1903). See James S. Atherton's 'The Peacock in the Oxen' and 'Still more Peacock in the Oxen' (*A Wake Newslitter*, n.s. VII (5) (1970), 77–8 and n.s. VII (4) (1971, 53), and Phillip F. Herring's, 'More Peacock in the Oxen' (*A Wake Newslitter*, n.s. VIII (4) (1971), 51–3). *Notesheets* supplies many other deatils of the plundering of Saintsbury's and Peacock's volumes.

[94] *A History of English Prose Rhythm* (2nd edn, London, Macmillan 1922), 21.

so the embryonic literary artist, developing according to the constant traits of his nature, is in part shaped by the literature of the past – the earlier adaptations of language to experience – and emerges into the chaos of modern 'marketplace' speech, where his task is to create a new adaptation of language to experience.

The underlying metaphor, in both its embryological and evolutionary aspects, is firmly established by recurring images as well as by the conversations of the young men; this may be why the schemes envisaged in the Budgen letter, proving unnecessary elaborations, were not persisted with. The assumption that the letter gives a detailed account of the basic techniques of the chapter has led many critics to praise or condemn 'Oxen of the Sun' for the use of devices which are not effectively operative in it; the letter's usefulness is that it indicates clearly what Joyce had in mind, although he eventually depended on other methods to accomplish it. There is, for instance, a repeated metaphorical association of literary and physical generation. It is made explicit by Stephen:

> Mark me now. In woman's womb word is made flesh but in the spirit of the maker all flesh that passes becomes the word that shall not pass away. (*U* 374/511)

In the thunder, he is said to hear the reproachful voice of the god Bringforth, and later his literary infertility is mocked by Lynch, who says that Stephen should not crown his head with vineleaves until 'something more, and greatly more, than a capful of light odes can call your genius father.' 'All desire,' he adds, 'to see you bring forth the work you meditate.' In these passages, Stephen, it will be noticed, figures not as the embryo to be brought forth, but as the progenitor failing in his duty to bring forth: perhaps he may be thought of as a case of what in the obstetric discussion is called 'acardiac *foetus in foetu*'.

From the beginning, the chapter implicitly relates physical and literary gestation. The ritual invocation, 'Send us, bright one, light one, Horhorn, quickening and wombfruit', is addressed both to the master of Horne's National Maternity Hospital and to the sun-god Apollo, owner of the Oxen of the Sun, bringer of fertility and god of poetry. The Latinate passage which follows this invocation has a similarly ambiguous reference: literally it asserts that a nation's prosperity is to be judged by its care for the 'proliferent continuance' maintained by motherhood and that every just citizen should encourage his fellows to be fruitful; but figuratively the assertions apply equally well to the need to foster and encourage artists, 'lest what had in the past been by the nation excellently commenced might be in the future not with similar excellence accomplished.' It is this notion of the literary artist as the renewer and developer of the inherited traditions which is exemplified in the procession of parodies; the essence of Stephen's complaint against Ireland is that she has failed to be solicitous for his welfare, and has welcomed his usurper:

> Remember, Erin, thy generations and thy days of old, how thou settedst little by me and by my word and broughtest in a stranger to my gates to commit

fornication in my sight and to wax fat and kick like Jeshurum. Therefore hast thou sinned against the light and hast made me, thy lord, to be the slave of servants. (*U* 376/514)

Bloom, whatever his personal failings as a procreator, does at least carry out the citizen's duty of displaying and encouraging a concern for women in labour, and similarly is disturbed to see a young man 'of real parts' wasting his talents, 'for that he lived riotously with those wastrels and murdered his goods with whores.' The repeated positive of this chapter is 'Bring forth' – 'that evangel simultaneously command and promise' – a difficult and painful task for Mrs Purefoy and Stephen alike, and one which exposes them to indifference and mockery, while Bloom's concern and goodwill extend to each of them.

Yet why should the handling of the chapter figure a process of conception, gestation and birth, when its idea was 'the crime committed against fecundity by sterilizing the act of coition'? In an important sense, the form of the chapter is directly opposed, in implication, to its apparent content, which presents the sterilizing and abortifacient influence of Stephen's companions. Can the discrepancy be connected with Stephen's dual role as embryo-artist and artist-progenitor? His failure in the latter role has been a source of self-contempt since the first chapter, and here it is associated with the spiritual self-abuse he and his companions are engaged in, which earns them the wrath of the god Bringforth, who 'would presently lift his arm and spill their souls for their abuses and their spillings done by them contrariwise to his word which forth to bring brenningly biddeth.' Stephen spills his wit and talent as wastefully as he pours out the beer which he calls his 'soul's bodiment', and 'the Word' to which he finally gives utterance and which is introduced by references to the birth of Christ and to a portentous cloudburst, is no creative Logos but merely the name of the pub to which he leads the company: as a progenitor he produces no more than an abortion.

On the physical level, it is Bloom who is the masturbator in the company, 'his own and his only enjoyer' the neglecter of his own marital 'seedfield', his vital juice now 'stagnant, acid and inoperative'. Yet according to Joyce's letter Bloom represents the spermatozoon, and certainly in the chapter he is the defender and advocate of fertility. But in what way does his arrival and behaviour in the hospital initiate the emergence of the embryo-artist? Among Bloom's reasons for staying with the party are his feeling of 'fast friendship' towards Stephen, and later his concern at seeing a promising young man wasting his talents, but there is no indication until the very end of the chapter that Stephen recognizes Bloom's quasi-paternal attitude towards him, much less that he consciously responds to it in any way. But this is not to say that Bloom's behaviour is without effect. Stephen's infertility derives directly from his bitterness:

But thou hast suckled me with a bitter milk: my moon and my sun thou hast quenched for ever. And thou hast left me alone for ever in the dark ways of my bitterness: and with a kiss of ashes hast thou kissed my mouth. (*U* 376/514)

His bitterness is linked to his 'agenbite of inwit' about his mother's death: the kiss of ashes recalls her dreamed-of breath, 'mute, reproachful, a faint odour of wetted ashes', and the vampire kiss of death, 'mouth to her mouth's kiss'; thinking of her, he had seen Dublin Bay as 'a bowl of bitter waters', and he had remembered her weeping over the words, 'love's bitter mystery'. It is this bitterness which pervades his spirit: his fear at the thunder is not allayed by Bloom's calming words because 'he had in his bosom a spike named Bitterness which could not by words be done away.' The whole passage describing his response to Bloom's reassurance that the thunder was 'all of the order of a natural phenomenon' is interesting and important:

> Heard he then in that clap the voice of the god Bringforth or, what Calmer said, a hubbub of Phenomenon? Heard? Why, he could not but hear unless he had plugged up the tube Understanding (which he had not done). For through that tube he saw that he was in the land of Phenomenon where he must for a certain one day die as he was like the rest too a passing show. And would he not accept to die like the rest and pass away? By no means would he and make more shows according as men do with wives which Phenomenon has commanded them to do by the book Law. Then wotted he nought of that other land which is called Believe-on-Me, that is the land of promise which behoves to the king Delightful and shall be for ever where there is no death and no birth neither wiving nor mothering at which all shall come as many as believe on it? Yes, Pious had told him of that land and Chaste had pointed him to the way but the reason was that in the way he fell in with a certain whore of an eyepleasing exterior whose name, she said, is Bird-in-the-Hand and she beguiled him wrongways from the true path by her flatteries that she said to him as, Ho, you pretty man, turn aside hither and I will show you a brave place, and she lay at him so flatteringly that she had him in her grot which is named Two-in-the-Bush or, by some learned, Carnal Concupiscence. (*U* 377–8/516–17)

The opening question appears to ask whether Stephen heard in the thunder the voice of the god or a mere phenomenon, but the answer indicates that that is not really the question. The question is whether he heard at all; the voice of the god and the hubbub of Phenomenon are the same – God is 'a shout in the street'. It is the understanding that he is living in a world of physical phenomena, that he is one of them and must one day die, which commands him to bring forth. Yet he is not content with the ordinary procreation of children, which would merely be to bring forth new passing phenomena. Despite the religious terminology, the land of the King Delightful is, with reference to Stephen, the land of literature where 'all flesh that passes becomes the word that shall not pass away', and it is from the path to this land that he has turned aside to dally with Bird-in-the-Hand in her grot, Carnal Concupiscence. This is the pilgrimage from which the embryo artist has strayed, hence the Bunyanesque manner. Bloom's commonsense words of comfort do not help, because Stephen is only too well aware that he is in the land of Phenomenon, and because he is unable through bitterness to bring forth 'the word that shall not pass away'. His bitterness is directed against an omnivorous god impartially devouring 'cancrenous females emaciated by parturition' or newborn babies; against a Church which commands that in difficult births the child shall be saved even at the cost of the mother's life; against a nation which has suckled him with 'a bitter milk'; in all, the bitterness is shaped by a mother-image. It disguises itself in sarcasm against everything maternal; although he had been wounded by Mulligan's reference to Mrs Dedalus as 'beastly dead', he echoes the expression when ironically defending the Church's position that 'that earthly mother which was but a dam to bring forth beastly should die by canon.' Yet this cynical, antimaternal pose covers a persisting sensitivity; when Lenehan (presumably referring to Stephen's earlier comparison of the artist, whose spirit created the immortal out of the transient, to the Virgin Mary, who was *vergine madre figlia di tuo figlio*) says mockingly that Stephen will one day write his book because 'He could not leave his mother an orphan', Stephen is so painfully affected that he 'would have withdrawn from the feast had not the noise of voices allayed the smart.'

It is in the light of the bitterness associated with his mother's death, and of the consequent pose of cynicism towards the maternal, that the nature and importance of the final exchange in this chapter has to be interpreted: Stephen

> is reported by eyewitnesses as having stated that once a woman has let the cat into the bag (an esthetic allusion, presumably, to one of the most complicated and marvellous of all nature's processes, the act of sexual congress) she must let it out again or give it life, as he phrased it, to save her own. At the risk of her own was the telling rejoinder of his interlocutor none the less effective for the moderate and measured tone in which it was delivered. (U 401-2/550)

The narrative shifts for a paragraph to a sentimental Dickensian picture of the parental bliss of Mr and Mrs Purefoy, but returns to illustrate the effect of Bloom's rejoinder on Stephen:

> There are sins or (let us call them as the world calls them) evil memories which are hidden away by man in the darkest places of the heart but they abide there and wait. (U 403/552)

'A chance word' will suddenly call up these memories (in this instance, Stephen's memory of having refused his dying mother's wish) and they will appear as a vision or a dream to confront him even 'at the feast at midnight when he is now filled with wine':

> Not to insult over him will the vision come as over one that lies under her wrath, not for vengeance to cut him off from the living but shrouded in the piteous vesture of the past, silent, remote, reproachful. (U 403/552)

Stephen's assumed cynicism about motherhood is pierced by Bloom's reminder that the mother risks her life in giving birth to her child. He could pretend that his anger at Mulligan's dismissive phrase, 'beastly dead', was occasioned by the offence to him, not to his mother, and he could try to ignore Lenehan's insensitiveness; but Bloom's sympathy for mothers stirs in Stephen the emotion which he is hiding from himself and from others:

The stranger still regarded on the face before him a slow recession of that false calm there, imposed, as it seemed, by habit or some studied trick, upon words so embittered as to accuse in their speaker an unhealthiness, a *flair*, for the cruder things of life.   (*U* 403/552)

Looking at Stephen, Bloom remembers having seen him as a boy, standing on an urn above a pool, held there by a group of young women, Molly and her friends:

He frowns a little just as this young man does now with a perhaps too conscious enjoyment of danger but must needs glance at whiles towards where his mother watches from the *piazzetta* giving upon the flower-close with a faint shadow of remoteness or of reproach (*alles Vergängliche*) in her glad look.   (*U* 403–4/553)

Stephen's reaction to the few moderate words appended to his cynical disparagement of motherhood is remarkable, and particularly so because of the change in his sense of the mother vision. On the Martello Tower, its reproach had seemed hostile, the eyes seemed fixed on him to strike him down, and his mind had cried, 'No, mother, let me be and let me live'; now the reproach seems a gentle maternal anxiety, with no anger in it and no suggestion that it has come 'to cut him off from the living'. Equally remarkable is Bloom's imaginative apprehension of what lies behind Stephen's change of expression; a seventeen-year-old memory enables him to interpret Stephen's frown as that of a child, consciously enjoying danger but looking round for reassurance in its mother's 'glad look', tinged with fleeting reproach. The styles used are appropriately sentimental: '*amor matris* (subjective and objective genitive)' is at once one of the most powerful of human emotions and one of the most overflowing sources of human sentimentality; we revel in it, and the strength of the feeling bears little or no relationship to the real worth of its object. Stephen has been caught in a coarse and affected denial of *amor matris*, and it at once dissolves his pretence of calm and bitter cynicism. The importance of the change in him is signalled by the first words of the next paragraph: 'Mark this farther and remember. The end comes suddenly.' The paragraph represents the moment before birth, when, after all the 'vacant hilarity', the temporary quietness among the company is like 'the vigilant watch of shepherds and of angels about a crib in Bethlehem of Juda long ago':

But as before the lightning the serried stormclouds, heavy with preponderant excess of moisture, in swollen masses turgidly distended, compass earth and sky in one vast slumber, impending above parched field and drowsy oxen and blighted growth of shrub and verdure till in an instant a flash rives their centres and with the reverberation of the thunder the cloudburst pours its torrent, so and not otherwise was the transformation, violent and instantaneous, upon the utterance of the Word.
Burke's! Outflings my lord Stephen, giving the cry.... (*U* 404/553–4)

In terms of Stephen's own artistic creativity, the word may be an anticlimactic abortion, but, in context, it has a different significance; it suggests that the few words of Bloom, which have so plainly shattered Stephen's cynical pose that even the noisy company is momentarily silenced, have driven Stephen to escape from his own discomfiture and nervous tension by rushing off to the public house. The image of the electric atmosphere before the sudden storm and cloudburst is certainly a reference to the release of the waters of the womb before childbirth, but it also clearly enough presents a fertilizing flood pouring down on the barren situation. Stephen has been obliged to leave what has earlier been called his 'refuge' and he goes out into the 'scintillant circumambient cessile air' to the triumphant strains of Carlyle, celebrating a milk which is not bitter:

> *Deine Kuh Trübsal melkest Du. Nun trinkst Du die süsse Milch des Euters.* See! It displodes for thee in abundance. Drink, man, an udderful! Mother's milk, Purefoy, the milk of human kin, milk too of those burgeoning stars overhead, rutilant in thin rainvapour, punch milk, such as those rioters will quaff in their guzzlingden, milk of madness, the honeymilk of Canaan's land. Thy cow's dug was tough, what? Ay, but her milk is hot and sweet and fattening. No dollop this but thick rich bonnyclaber. To her, old patriarch! Pap! *Per deam Partulam et Pertundam nunc est bibendum!* (U 405/555)

The triumph is the progenitive triumph of Mr Purefoy, but the language refers back to Stephen's reproach to the Irish nation – that though it looked upon a promised land 'flowing with milk and money' it had suckled him with a bitter milk and abandoned him to the dark ways of his bitterness. Purefoy has drawn sweet milk from the cow Adversity, despite the toughness of her udders – mother's milk, the milk that unites man and flows through the universe, the intoxicating milk of fertility. Stephen, on the other hand, has drawn only a sterile bitterness from adversity, until Bloom's words have penetrated his self-pitying egotism. The birth imagery also goes back to the complaint against Ireland, where Stephen had spoken of his bitterness as a 'tenebrosity of the interior' appropriate only to 'the nights of prenativity and postmortemity'; now he emerges from that dark womb into the air, 'life essence celestial, glistering on Dublin stone there under starshiny *coelum.*' By forcing Stephen out of the stagnant bitterness which has been his defence against the remorse associated with his mother's death, Bloom makes possible the artist's emergence into life. This, I take it, is what Joyce meant by calling him the 'spermatozoon', and presumably Nurse Callan is referred to as the 'ovum' for similar reasons – at least, I can see no other justification for the term. From the beginning of the chapter, Bloom and Nurse Callan have been the representatives of the ordinary and often sentimental concern for others, in particular for women in labour, which eventually liberates Stephen. Both have been mocked, but together they have offered 'the milk of human kin' or human kindness, lacking in the rest of the company. This is the serious aspect of their joint role: as always, Joyce mixes absurdity and comic irony in his presentation of altruism. The man who praises fertility and procreation has just arrived from masturbating on the beach: the virginal nurse, described as 'a woman endued with every quality of modesty and not less severe than beautiful', turns out to be pregnant. (Punch Costello is almost thrown out of the company for asserting that she is 'in the family way', but Bloom notices her condition more discreetly when, as he leaves, he whispers, 'Madam, when comes the storkbird for thee?') Their personal imperfections or failings are beside the point; Stephen is shifted out of the closed circle of his bitterness and sterility, not by a pair of personified virtues or pene-trating moral intelligences, but by two very limited people moved by ordinary compassion. Their commonplaces of speech and behaviour, though hackneyed and sentimental, are closer to a real appreciation of human nature, more genuinely felt, and more creative psychologically and practically than the ingenious witticisms and intellectual chitchat of Stephen and his companions; they eventually compel Stephen to recognize in himself, beneath the cynical and embittered pose of the disillusioned artist, the common humanity, and on that recognition depends his emerg-ence as artist from the embryo stage.

Some of the formal devices and imagery seem quasi-allegorical, because they have to suggest the implications and the unrealized importance for Stephen of this casual encounter. He is not, however, suddenly transformed; he does not emerge from the hospital an artist; he is not freed from his tormenting remorse. Yet something has happened to him if it is no more than an undermining of his bitter egotism.[95] Even in the confusion at the end of the chapter, there is a discernible change in his manner. His reaction to the news that he has been abandoned by Mulligan and Haines ('Aweel, ye maun e'en gang yer gates') is without the customary resentment of betrayal, and his invitation to Lynch to accompany him to the brothel has even a drunken gusto – '*Laetabuntur in cubilibus suis*', or, as the Authorized Version has it, 'Let them sing aloud upon their beds.' Still more interesting is his answer to Lynch's question about Bloom:

> Whisper, who the sooty hell's the johnny in the black duds? Hush! Sinned against the light and even now that day is at hand when he shall come to judge the world by fire. Pflaap! *Ut implerentur scripturae*. (*U* 409/561)

'Sinned against the light', by echoing Mr Deasy's words in his study, identifies Bloom as a Jew, but recalls, too, Stephen's inner commentary on Deasy's notion that 'you can see the darkness in their eyes': 'Their eyes knew the years of wandering and, patient, knew the dishonours of their flesh' (*U* 31–42). It is presumably because he has felt Bloom's behaviour and words in the hospital to be an implicit judging of his own attitude that he now applies to Bloom the words from the Absolution after a Mass for the Dead, asking for deliverance on the Day of Judgement 'when thou shalt

---

[95] In *Notesheets* Phillip F. Herring, arguing that the letter to Budgen has led critics on false scents, writes, 'Do we see any dynamic artistic growth in Stephen in "Oxen"? And in nine successive stages? Is he any maturer when he leaves the hospital? He is a good deal drunker, but hardly changed in any other measurable way' (35–6). I agree that too much reliance has been put on the letter (and on nine-partedness); but Stephen's mood is clearly becoming more distressed, and not merely through drunkenness. The contrast between the attitudes towards mothers, shown, on the one hand, by Bloom (and Nurse Callan), and, on the other hand, by his drinking companions, externalizes and exacerbates his inner conflicts.

come to judge the world by fire.' 'That the scriptures [of the prophets] might be fulfilled' (*Matthew* xxxvi, 56), spoken by Jesus in the Garden of Gethsemane, is usually taken as a reference to the prophecy of the coming of a Messiah, who should be 'despised and rejected of men; a man of sorrows and acquainted with grief' – a scapegoat who should suffer for 'the iniquity of us all' (*Isaiah* liii, 3 ff.). Usually, Stephen sees himself as the Messianic artist sent to the Irish and rejected by them. Yet the passage implies some intuition on his part that it is through Bloom that the scriptures shall be fulfilled, the artist's destiny accomplished. Of course, Stephen is in a drunken and extravagant mood, but these mocking allusions suggest that he senses more importance in Bloom's arrival than can be explained by the surface action, and seems to have a vague notion that the meeting with Bloom is of special consequence to him.

The closing jibes about the 'Elijah is coming' poster on the Merrion Hall may have a different kind of relevance. The preceding biblical allusions are expressions of Stephen's uneasy reaction to Bloom's presence, and it is possible that he may be associating Bloom with Alexander J. Christ Dowie, 'that's yanked to glory most half this planet'. But Stephen knows nothing of the 'Elijah is Coming' leaflet, handed to Bloom that morning, launched by him on the Liffey, and by now making its way beyond the restricting banks of the port of Dublin out to the open sea. If, as I have suggested earlier, the launched throwaway symbolizes Stephen, as the homing schooner symbolizes Bloom, the reminiscence of it at the end of this chapter is an indirect and sardonic tribute to the part Bloom has played – to push the artist out of the stagnant waters of his own bitterness and his companions' barren jocularity into a renewal of the voyage prematurely embarked on at the end of the *Portrait*.

Joyce's label for the technique of the chapter, 'embryonic development', is appropriate, despite the apparent abandonment of some of the refinements mentioned in the letter to Budgen, because the long discussions of gestation and birth provide a metaphor to illuminate and unite the procession of styles, the attitudes of Stephen's companions and Stephen's response to Bloom's presence. The most remarkable feature of the chapter, the succession of parodies, is not only functional but also perhaps serves a more important function than any of the preceding techniques, since here it has to sustain the implication of a growth and development in Stephen of which he himself is hardly aware, in face of the repeated implications of sterility and fruitlessness in the surface action. Through its agency, two directly opposed movements coexist in the chapter. The whole conception is brilliantly ingenious – Joyce could well exclaim, 'How's that for high ?' – and the management of the parodies is equally brilliant. The skill and humour with which Joyce bends the styles of the past to suit his shifting purposes make the chapter a *tour de force* whose sheer ingenuity and energy are difficult to resist. I have referred to the styles as parodies (rather than, as some would prefer, pastiches) because they exaggerate, rather than merely imitate, the manners of other writers. But they seem to me in no sense critical parodies. They celebrate earlier successful adaptations of language to literary purposes as stages in the evolutionary process which has helped form the modern literary artist. He is born into a world where language has been reduced to 'a frightful jumble' of slang, jargon and cliché, the 'language of the market place' of which Stephen complained in the *Portrait*, and has to create from it a medium which continues the earlier developing tradition while responding to the language he hears spoken about him. The meeting of the literary and the colloquial is a stylistic analogy to the meeting of artist and citizen, and, equally, should lead to a fruitful interaction from which a new literary manner may be born. The exaggerations of past styles are always good-humoured; even the imitations of Dickens's sentimentality or Carlyle's heartiness are more suggestive of an enjoyment of the creative eccentricities of these great writers than of any mocking criticism, and other passages, such as the Swiftian fable of the Irish bull, are manifestly acts of homage. There is no chapter in the book where Joyce's delight in the exercise of his talents is more evident.

It is not an irresponsible exercise. One of Joyce's declared aims was to see and present the characters and situations of *Ulysses* from many 'points of view'.[96] Ways of looking at life change with time, but the outmoded are not invalid. Twentieth-century points of view have the characteristics of their time; they have no monopoly of the truth; they apprehend differently, but not wholly. The nearest we can get to the truth is to look at it from many different angles and in many different lights. One purpose of the Odyssean parallels is to supplement the unheroic view of life with intimations of the heroic view, and to these 'Oxen of the Sun' adds a series of ways of looking embodied in a series of literary manners. It is not absurd or ridiculous to see Bloom as a pious wanderer grieving for the lost and the imperilled, as a gentle knight in the company of scorners, as a kind of Worldly Wiseman, as an eighteenth-century moralist, as a hypocritical denouncer of others' failings, as a Romantic visionary, as a Victorian rationalist or as an apostle of the life-force: they are all literary simplifications and interpretations, each forming a coherent image around one particular aspect of his nature or behaviour. Similarly, Stephen can be legitimately seen as a sly medieval scholar, a Prodigal Son, a deliverer of comminatory homilies, a pilgrim, a Swiftian satirist, an atheistic sceptic, a decadent malcontent and a Bohemian student. The only way to compensate for the partiality of every individual vision is to combine a representative selection of contrasting 'points of view'. This, at least, was the principle governing the total organization of *Ulysses*, and fundamentally the same principle lies behind the parodic sequence of 'Oxen of the Sun'. The method is a special development (extended into the literary past) of the method of the book as a whole.

Yet this is also the one chapter where I find it difficult to resist the objection that the techniques are insufficiently subordinated to their thematic purpose. The conspicuous comic brilliance of the parodies draws attention away from the process in Stephen which they should suggest; in

96 *Letters* I, 167.

discussions of *Ulysses*, the 'Oxen of the Sun' is more often referred to as the chapter of parodies than as the chapter where Stephen's sterile bitterness is undermined. Moreover, the scheme has a built-in principle of order – approximate chronological sequence – which makes it less flexible than any of the other techniques: if there is to be a responsiveness of style to subject, the events of the chapter must be ordered to match the procession through the history of English prose. There is such matching: the sober discussion of Bloom and Nurse Callan about Mrs Purefoy's labour and Dr O'Hare's death is appropriately represented in the solemn imitation of Anglo-Saxon and Early Middle English; Mandeville's style is right for the traveller finding himself in strange and unexpected company, and Malory's for a gentle 'knight', on an errand of kindness, surrounded by callous roisterers. The effect of the thunder on Stephen is suitably depicted as the guiltiness of a young man who has strayed from the straight and narrow path of his pilgrim's progress; the Swiftian manner reflects the spirit of the satire against the Irish Church as a gelded bull; Dickens's style is proper for postnatal sentimentalities and Carlyle's for postnatal celebration; and, throughout, the style matches the particular incidents or discussions. But because the stylistic order is predetermined, the incidents seem to respond to the style rather than vice versa – that is to say, the sequence of events, external or psychological, seems dominated by the historical sequence of the styles. The technique is too powerful; it overwhelms what it should serve. Consequently, while the chapter in itself is an extraordinary achievement and one to which readers of *Ulysses* frequently return for its exuberant comedy, it does not to my mind fit comfortably into the total *consonantia* of the novel.

'Circe'

The technique of the 'Circe' chapter is 'Hallucination', but this does not refer to hallucinations experienced by the characters. The technique is operative in the descriptions of the Mabbot street entrance of Nighttown before Stephen and Bloom arrive there and in the interval between Stephen's departure to the brothel and Bloom's entry. 'Hallucination' is the mode of the chapter, and some aspects of it are established from the start in passages uncomplicated by the presence of the central figures.

First, it describes, accurately if somewhat colourfully, scenes, people and incidents – '*rows of flimsy houses with gaping doors*', '*a form sprawled against a dustbin and muffled by its arm and hat*', '*two night watch in shoulder capes, their hands upon their staffholsters*', and the drunken entry of Private Carr and Private Compton. Secondly, it gives a bizarre and grotesque distortion to elements of the scene, so that whistled calls and answers figure as characters in a drama, icecream under the harsh light appears as '*lumps of coal and copper snow*', and a totter among the rubbish becomes '*a gnome*'. Thirdly, it evokes things which did not happen, and are not heightened presentations of the scene, but fantastic symbolic images of the pervasive chaos and nightmarish atmosphere:

> *Tommy Caffrey scrambles to a gaslamp and, clasping, climbs in spasms. From the top spur he slides down. Jacky Caffrey clasps to climb. The navvy lurches against the lamp. The twins scuttle off in the dark. The navvy, swaying, presses a forefinger against a wing of his nose and ejects from the farther nostril a long liquid jet of snot. Shouldering the lamp he staggers away through the crowd with his flaring cresset.* (U 414/565)

The climbing boys belong to the first category, the stream of snot to the second, and the carrying off of the gaslamp to the third, and the hallucinatory quality of the passage derives in part from the shifting between reality, heightened reality, and unreality.

These three aspects of the technique in the presentation of the scene roughly correspond to three aspects of its use in the main business of the chapter. It presents what is said and done, what is thought or consciously apprehended, and what is plainly not said or done nor, in the ordinary sense of the word, thought. Although these three aspects blend together in the dramatic form, it is usually easy to distinguish between them:

> (*Jacky Caffrey, hunted by Tommy Caffrey, runs full tilt against Bloom.*)
>
> BLOOM
>
> O!
>
> (*Shocked, on weak hams, he halts. Tommy and Jacky vanish there, there. Bloom pats with parcelled hands watch, fobpocket, bookpocket, pursepocket, sweets of sin, potato soap.*)
>
> BLOOM
>
> Beware of pickpockets. Old thieves' dodge. Collide. Then snatch your purse.
> (*The retriever approaches sniffling, nose to the ground. A sprawled form sneezes. A stooped bearded figure appears garbed in the long caftan of an elder in Zion and a smoking cap with magenta tassels. Horned spectacles hang down at the wings of the nose. Yellow poison streaks are on the drawn face.*)
>
> RUDOLPH
>
> Second halfcrown waste money today. I told you not go with drunken goy ever. So. You catch no money.
>
> BLOOM
>
> (*Hides the crubeen and trotter behind his back and, crestfallen, feels warm and cold feetmeat.*) *Ja, ich weiss, papachi.* (U 417-18/568-9)

A boy certainly collides with Bloom and makes him cry out and check his pockets – though whether Jacky and Tommy are the same two boys as appeared in 'Nausicaa' is doubtful. Bloom's concern about pickpockets is clearly something that passes through his mind, and is in the manner of his interior monologue in earlier chapters. But his dead father is no more in the interior monologue than he is in Nighttown, and Bloom does not respond shamefacedly to his reproaches either in speech or thought. The father's appearance has been provoked by the collision and by Bloom's fear of having been robbed. If such manifestations happened occasionally during the chapter, one might suppose them to be vivid images passing through Bloom's mind: here, his doubts about the way he has been spending money and wasting time and energy pursuing a gentile might have recalled paternal reproaches for being a spendthrift and drifting away from Jewish tradition in the company of gentile wastrels. But such apparitions are not occasional; they form a major part of the chapter. They are presented in the manner of hallucinations, although Bloom is clearly not in an hallucinated state. Moreover, while he recalls in later chapters what he said, did and thought during his adventure in Nighttown, he does not remember any of the 'hallucinatory' material, even as something which passed through his mind.

What goes on in Bloom's conscious mind proceeds as though the 'hallucinatory' episodes have never occurred. For instance, after extraordinary encounters with his father, his mother, Molly, Sweny the druggist, Bridie Kelly, Gerty MacDowell, Mrs Breen and Richie Goulding, interspersed with various transformations in his dress, and passing appearances of a minstrel band and various Dublin figures, Bloom's interior monologue shows no awareness of this hectic experience:

BLOOM

Wildgoose chase this. Disorderly houses. Lord knows where they are gone. Drunks cover distance double quick. Nice mixup. Scene at Westland row. Then jump in first class with third ticket. Then too far. Train with engine behind. Might have taken me to Malahide or a siding for the night or collision. Second drink does it. Once is a dose. What am I following him for? Still, he's the best of that lot. If I hadn't heard about Mrs Beaufoy Purefoy I wouldn't have gone and wouldn't have met. Kismet. He'll lose that cash. Relieving office here. Good biz for cheapjacks, organs. What do ye lack? Soon got, soon gone. Might have lost my life too with that mangongwheeltrack-trolleyglarejuggernaut only for presence of mind. (*U* 431/579–80)

This is unmistakably the representation of Bloom's mental processes with which Joyce has familiarized us. Bloom takes note of his surroundings, recalls how he came to lose Stephen and Lynch at the station, makes his usual confusion between the names Beaufoy and Purefoy, and remembers the incident, just before the passage about his father, when he was nearly run over by a street sandstrewer. But there is no hint of the fantastic encounters which have occurred since. The only inference is that his conscious mind is totally unaware of them. Yet they are clearly related to his mood.

As the 'unreal' elements in the description of the scene are symbolic images of the general atmosphere of fantastic disorder, so the unreal encounters of this chapter are best understood as dramatic representations of the unconscious, affecting and affected by the conscious mind, but never entering it even as images. It is as though, in order to represent the unconscious activity of the psyche, Joyce has used a dramatic method suggestive of dreams, and, like dreams, only symbolically representative of the climate of the unconscious. Unconsciously, something deeply buried in Bloom responds to his fear of having been robbed and is symbolized by Joyce in the family and racial terms associated with Bloom's father; unconsciously, Bloom is afraid of being seen in Nighttown and this fear is symbolically represented by the imaginary encounter with Mrs Breen, while a certain furtive sexuality aroused by the place is figured in the flirtatious exchanges; unconsciously, the conversation with the Jewish whore Zoe stimulates Bloom's desire for appreciation, admiration and love, and for recognition of his philanthropic nature, and, to present this unconscious surge in Bloom, we have the founding of the new Bloomusalem; unconsciously, the entry of the dominant and overbearing bawd, Bella Cohen, causes a flood of timid self-abasement and cringing submissiveness to sweep over Bloom, and his reaction is dramatized by his conversion into a bisexual slavegirl and Bella's into a moustachioed slave-auctioneer, Bello. These and similar episodes cannot be said to pass through Bloom's mind. For the representation of the workings of the conscious mind, Joyce had a model – his own consciousness – but the nature of unconscious experience is by definition inaccessible, except through the symbolic hints which we may remember having dreamed, and which some psychologists claim to interpret. Bloom is not dreaming, but Joyce uses (it is hard to see what else he could use) a dreamlike method to symbolize what is going on beneath the level of Bloom's consciousness.

The special propriety of this technique for the brothel scene is that it is here the subconscious pressures on Stephen and Bloom become almost overwhelming; its special usefulness is that it enables Joyce to integrate, in a single dramatic method, three distinct levels of the psyche, the continuity of the method expressing the continuous interaction of the levels – subconscious forces, thought, and conscious behaviour – which proceeds despite apparent discrepancies and incongruities between them. As a rule it is not difficult to recognize and distinguish the three levels represented, yet the distinction is often confused. For example, the apparition of Rudy is sometimes described as an hallucinatory vision or as an image passing through Bloom's memory or imagination, and frequently blamed for its sentimentality. There is no question that it is sentimental in tone, and, equally certainly, the sentimentality is intentional. Some seem to think that Joyce is trying to have it both ways – to achieve a sentimental climax to his chapter while, by his tone, mocking the sentimentality. Others suppose that it is Bloom who has suddenly become feebly sentimental.[97] But once we recognize and respond to the nature of the convention, neither of these accounts is necessary or relevant. That dreams symbolically present exaggerated emotions is obvious: our critical faculties are in abeyance and the mind abandons itself freely to excesses of sentiment, emotion, melodrama or horror. Or, to put it another way, it is in such excessive terms that the unconscious dramatizes its impulses in dreams. It hardly makes sense to speak of the sentimentality of the unconscious, because the term can only be understood of conscious thought or behaviour. What the conclusion of the chapter shows is not that Bloom, looking at Stephen, was reminded of Rudy or remembered his sonlessness, but that, in his conscious

[97] John Gross, for instance, finds 'the grotesquely namby-pamby vision of the dead Rudy at the end of "Circe" unnecessarily demeaning, too inconsistent with what we already know and feel about Bloom' (*James Joyce* (London, Collins 1971), 63).

defence and protection of the young man, he experienced a sudden and unexplained access of paternal emotions, sentimental inasmuch as they were without adequate object or motivation in his conscious mind, but springing from the depths of his unconscious, and giving release to frustrated and stifled impulses. The technique presents not only an image of the impulses, but also the physical and conscious circumstances which led to their release.

Most of the extended hallucinatory episodes of the chapter are similarly representative of unconscious workings and similarly induced by passing situations or remarks. A prolonged psychic disturbance is provoked by the arrival of the raincaped watch just as Bloom is surreptitiously giving his crubeen and his trotter to a dog. The guilty fears in Bloom's unconscious are dramatized in a series of mounting accusations – first, of committing a nuisance, of cruelty to animals, of offering false names and addresses, of 'unlawfully watching and besetting'. As so often in dreams, minor offences develop into graver ones: he is charged with being an enemy of the state, a seducer, a political turncoat, a plagiarist and pretender, 'the arch conspirator of the age', an interferer with a servant-girl, a defecator in a bucket of ale, a bankrupt, a writer of indecent letters to society ladies, Jack the Ripper, 'dynamitard, forger, bigamist, bawd and cuckold and a public nuisance', a white-slaver, and Judas Iscariot – and he is on the point of being hanged when the corpse of Paddy Dignam arrives with the alibi that Bloom had that morning attended his funeral. The dream-logic is convincing: Bloom's sense of guilt dramatizes itself with reference to his fear of being arrested, his memory of shameful episodes (like his advances to the servant-girl) or secret impulses (like the sending of indecent letters), and his notions of the most disgraceful crimes of which a man might be accused. There is no more reason for supposing that Bloom actually posted rude letters to the improbable society ladies than for supposing that he was Jack the Ripper, but Joyce's method brilliantly suggests the characteristic nature of the unconscious movements below the surface of Bloom's mind.

Similarly, it takes only a casual remark from the whore Zoe to stir up Bloom's longing to serve mankind and win public love and admiration. As a spokesman for the working class, he becomes an alderman, progresses triumphantly through the streets, is acclaimed as 'the world's greatest reformer', is declared 'emperor president and king chairman', marries the moon-goddess, founds the new Bloomusalem, distributes universal charity, and, Solomon-like, acts as a fountain of wisdom and justice. But his fears break into his smug dreams: like all Irish leaders, he is denounced ('He's as bad as Parnell was'), and to escape the accusations has various witnesses give evidence that he suffers from hereditary diseases, that he is an example of 'the new womanly man', and that he is about to have a baby, whereupon (in expression of the Jewish desire to found a successful family) he gives birth to eight handsome, brilliant, successful sons, born rich. The interplay of grandiose illusion and fear finally translates him into the Messiah, who after performing various absurd miracles, becomes the scapegoat for the sins of the people, is accused of being a false Messiah, and is martyred.

But, after this martyrdom, he appears again like the phoenix, wearing 'a seamless garment *marked I.H.S.*' and is celebrated in the Litany of the Daughters of Erin. As Zoe's voice continues, 'Talk away till you're black in the face', Bloom abandons his mood with a feeling of self-pity: 'No more. I have lived. Fare. Farewell.' Other episodes follow a similar pattern: a lecherous but half-hearted desire for Zoe is developed in the bizarre sexuality of Lipoti Virag (Bloom's grandfather but also an animalized version of Bloom himself); the appearance of Bella Cohen induces a submissive, self-abasing masochistic drama; the sight of the whores secretly giggling because Zoe has read 'henpecked husband' in Bloom's hand gives him a sense of his having acted shamefully in the adultery of Boylan and Molly; trying to escape the observation of Corny Kelleher and his friends, Bloom becomes like a hunted fox; and, finally, his paternal feelings towards Stephen are imaged in the apparition of Rudy.

As these representations of unconscious hopes, fears and desires are the central uses of the 'hallucination' technique, it is important to recognize their special character. Although they include fragmentary and distorted references to Bloom's past life and even echo some of his characteristic mistakes and slips of the tongue, they are no more filmed records of his unconscious than the interior monologues are taped records of his consciousness. Most commentators agree that the hallucinatory episodes refer to the unconscious, but frequently discuss them as though they present what we should see if we could penetrate into the unconscious minds of Bloom and Stephen. This leads to serious difficulties, because the episodes use materials which could not have reached the two men's unconscious minds, unless through some form of telepathy or collective unconscious. There are many examples: the day-dream figures of Molly and Bloom refer to the formula '*Nebrakada Femininum*', which occurred in a book read by Stephen; in the passage where Bloom is accused of many crimes, Myles Crawford repeats the expression, 'Paralyse Europe', which he spoke after Bloom had left the newspaper office; in the subsequent courtroom scene there are several allusions to the discussion of the Mosaic Code and the speeches of John F. Taylor and Seymour Bushe, which took place in Bloom's absence; there are references to Canon O'Hanlon's cuckoo-clock (known to Gerty MacDowell but not to Bloom), to the silent thoughts of the nameless narrator of the 'Cyclops' chapter, to the imaginary buttermilk drunk by Paddy Dignam's ghost in one of the inflated interpolations in 'Cyclops', to Rochford's machine and his rescue of a man from a sewer (known to Lenehan, not Bloom) and to Mother Grogan, a fictitious figure in Mulligan's joke and his 'national immorality'. One or two of these could be explained away or attributed to authorial carelessness, but their number makes such explanations impossible, and in most places the confusion is plainly deliberate.[98] To suppose that the minds of Bloom and Stephen are

---

[98] There are many other deliberate deformations of place and time. For instance, although commentators have discovered some accidental anachronisms in Joyce's account of 16 June 1904, such gross errors as allowing the apparition of Rumbold to

linked telepathically would explain nothing: such detailed interaction goes far beyond anything claimed for telepathy, and, in any case, the minds of other characters (Lenehan and Gerty MacDowell, for instance) are involved. It would also be impossible to explain how Bloom's mind can employ technical medical terms (such as 'hypospadia' and 'teratological'), nonce worlds like 'angriling' and 'basilicogrammate', and a wide range of obsolete and exotic language, not attributable to any character in the novel. As for collective unconscious, no such psychological theory has suggested the spontaneous transmission between minds of the peculiarities of personal experience and vocabulary.

The only mind in which all these experiences and words can so fantastically fuse is the mind of the author, using all the materials at his disposal to create a symbolic drama of the unconscious. In dreams, the unconscious symbolically communicates with the dreaming mind. If I dream that I am walking to work and suddenly discover that I have forgotten to put on my trousers, no interpreter will deduce that I am obsessed with the fear of such an unlikely eventuality: they will agree that the dream is merely a projection from the unconscious, a translation into a symbolic situation or action of some quite different aspect of my unconscious. In 'Circe', the communication is between the author and the reader's mind: he creates a series of symbolic actions, using all the earlier incidents, observations and images of his novel and all his resources of language to express his intuitions of the deeper mental levels of his characters, regardless of whether the materials used belong to the particular character's conscious mind. This is how he had used such previous techniques as *'fuga per canonem'*, 'gigantism' and 'embryonic development', and, even in the representation of Gerty MacDowell's consciousness, he had not limited himself to words and constructions which Gerty herself would have been capable of using. These techniques are methods of controlling and integrating the handling of a chapter; one of their purposes is to illuminate the inner experience of certain characters, but this is not their only purpose, nor are they tied to or limited by the characters' own vocabularies or experiences.

In 'Circe' the 'hallucination' technique is employed for all the purposes which any novelist might have in a given chapter – to present the scene, to suggest developing relationships between characters, to shape the action significantly, to relate the business of the chapter to the total business of the novel, and even to imply authorial commentary. This last is, I take it, the function of the curious passage where Bloom and Stephen, looking into a mirror, are reflected as Shakespeare:

LYNCH
(*Points.*) The mirror up to nature. (*He laughs.*) Hu hu hu hu hu hu.
(*Stephen and Bloom gaze in the mirror. The face of William Shakespeare, beardless, appears there, rigid in facial paralysis, crowned by the reflection of the reindeer antlered hatrack in the hall.*) (U 536/671)

---

speak of such famous murder cases as Voisin (1917) and Seddon (1912) cannot have been mere slips. They are part of a technique which makes no pretence of being confined to the minds, the space or the time of the characters.

Lynch's remark and gesture suggests that the whispering and giggling of
the whores which has so embarrassed Bloom is due to the fact that, in the
mirror, Bloom's head seems to be crowned by the antlers of the hatrack in
the hall. Lynch's *Hamlet* tag makes a link with the Shakespeare mirror-
image, but who, even unconsciously, combines the joint reflections of
Bloom and Stephen into a beardless Shakespeare? Shakespeare's beardless
image speaks:

SHAKESPEARE

(*In dignified ventriloquy.*) 'Tis the loud laugh bespeaks the vacant mind. (*To
Bloom.*) Thou thoughtest as how thou wastest invisible. Gaze. (*He crows with
a black capon's laugh.*) Iagogo! How my Oldfellow chokit his Thursdaymomun. Iagogogo! (*U* 536/671)

The first sentence is addressed to Lynch, the second to Bloom, whose
vague notion of Elizabethan English is reflected and who thought his
cuckoldry was not known to others, and the third to Stephen who has
suggested in the library discussion that Iago's tormenting of Othello
expressed the conflict of artist and man in Shakespeare. The distorted
forms of the *Othello* reference can be only speculatively interpreted: that
morning Stephen had pointed out to Mr Deasy that the advice 'Put but
money in thy purse' is from Iago's speech to Roderigo, which concludes
with a series of urgings ('go, make money – go, provide thy money. . . . Go
to; farewell') – hence the urgent corruption of the name to 'Iagogo . . .
Iagogogo'; 'Othello' has presumably become 'Oldfellow' under the influence
of Mulligan's remarks in the library linking Bloom and Simon Dedalus –
'He knows your old fellow'; I assume that 'Thursdaymomun' has been
influenced by the just-concluded exchange between Stephen and Zoe where
he is identified as 'Thursday's child' – as he is his mother's child, the
possessive case may have linked mother, mom, mum, with Thursday. Thus
one possible explanation of Shakespeare's cryptic remark, related to the
passage in the library discussion and to Stephen, would be that 'his unremitting intellect . . . the hornmad Iago' has caused 'the moor in him'
(the natural man) to suffer, by making him suppress his innate love for his
mother. This is a somewhat finedrawn interpretation of a difficult passage:
yet one thing is clear – that the reflection speaks in three different ways to
three different men, 'in dignified ventriloquy' adapting its voice to each of
them. The immediate developments in the passage are equally confused:
the image of Mrs Dignam takes all its characteristics from Bloom's experience, except for the comparison to 'a pen chivvying her brood of cygnets'
which derives from Stephen's description of Shakespeare's walk along the
riverbank; similarly, the refeaturing of beardless Shakespeare into the
bearded Martin Cunningham refers to Bloom's thought in the funeral-
carriage that Cunningham's face is like Shakespeare's, but the speech of
the refeatured paralytic face, 'Weda seca whokilla farst' ('None weds the
second but who killed the first' – *Hamlet* III, ii), echoes Stephen's allusion
in the library to Shakespeare's granddaughter who, 'to use granddaddy's
words, wed her second, having killed her first.' It may just be possible to

suppose that the image of the beardless Shakespeare relates to Stephen' unconscious, and those of Mrs Dignam and Martin Cunningham to Bloom's (borrowing some expressions from Stephen's experience), but the passage is then very empty and obscure. What seems to be suggested by the combined reflection of Bloom and Stephen as Shakespeare is that the artist, even if he is suffering from facial paralysis, develops from the fusion of the two men. It was foreshadowed in the library, by Stephen's presentation of Shakespeare as a divided soul, on the one hand prudent businessman ('He drew Shylock out of his own long pocket'), lover, deceived husband, father, and on the other the artist, 'the unremitting intellect' tormenting the natural man. As Stephen foresaw that it would be necessary for his own development to be a man as well as intellectual imagination, to act and to be acted on, so Shakespeare was, as Stephen said in the library, boy and mature man (hence 'beardless' and 'bearded'), bawd and cuckold, acting and acted on. In the mirror-image, the reader recognizes (though Stephen has not yet done so) that Bloom is the man involved in the suffering and actions of life who is the necessary counterpart of the isolated creative impulse – necessary that is, for the growth of the artist. The passage presents, in hallucinatory technique, an insight into the interrelationship of Bloom and Stephen which neither man has apprehended: it is the means by which the author suggests to his reader through a symbolic action an aspect of his theme rather than of the world he is representing.

The fusing of the images of the two men in the beardless and bearded face of Shakespeare is expressive of one of the central structural ideas of the novel, one which powerfully influences, in this chapter, both content and technique – the meeting of opposites. The idea is hesitantly and uncertainly introduced by Stephen when Bloom first enters the brothel. Stephen is playing 'empty fifths' on the piano and talking in rambling fashion of the prevalence of that musical interval in rituals ranging from the Hymn to Demeter to a Psalm of David, in widely differing musical modes and in settings of widely divergent texts.[99] He is apparently making some point about the coincidence of contraries, because Lynch mockingly reminds him of other oppositions he has asserted: 'Jewgreek is greekjew. Extremes meet. Death is the highest form of life.' Stephen observes that Lynch memorizes all his 'errors, boasts, mistakes', and adds another dogma of opposition to explain the prevalence of the interval of a fifth: 'The reason is because the fundamental and the dominant are separated by the greatest possible interval which .... Interval which. Is the greatest possible ellipse. Consistent with. The ultimate return. The octave. Which.' Stephen is half-drunk, confused and fumbling for expression, but seems to be developing

[99] E. L. Epstein points out that the 'empty fifths', played by Stephen, are part of Marcello's setting of Psalm XVIII, *Coeli enarrant gloriam Domini*, and that Marcello had used 'what he thought was an ancient Greek melody originally employed as the melody of a "Homeric" hymn to Demeter' ('King David and Benedetto Marcello in the works of James Joyce', *JJQ* VI (1) (1968), 83).

his earlier cryptic assertion, 'The rite is the poet's rest'.[100] If this means
that in rites the insights of the poet are ordered and fixed, that ritual,
whether pagan, Jewish or Christian, is the *stasis*, the stable art-form,
founded on, created by and expressive of the activity of the poetic mind,
then presumably he is now trying to formulate the nature of the poetic
insight responsible for the prevalence of the fifth in such rites. His formulation is in terms of the relationship between extremes – that the
dominant is as far removed in pitch from the fundamental as is consistent
with the return in the completed octave. He relates this to the curve of an
ellipse because the point in the curve which is farthest from one of its two
foci is the very point at which it curves back towards that focus and thus
to the completion of the ellipse. This image, in turn, leads to an image of
existence as an elliptical orbit:

STEPHEN

(*Abruptly.*) What went forth to the ends of the world to traverse not itself.
God, the sun, Shakespeare, a commercial traveller, having itself traversed in
reality itself, becomes that self. Wait a moment. Wait a second. Damn that
fellow's noise in the street. Self which it itself was ineluctably preconditioned
to become. *Ecco!*   (*U* 479/623)

The obscurity of Stephen's gropings is lightened by reference to the earlier
Shakespeare discussion. The self sets out to traverse the universe of 'not-
self'. But, as Stephen observed in the library, 'we walk through ourselves,
meeting robbers, ghosts, giants, old men, young men, wives, widows,
brothers-in-love. But always meeting ourselves.' Every person and experience we encounter, we apprehend only through ourselves, only in terms
of ourselves, only by recognizing in them some part of ourselves: Socrates
finds Socrates, Judas finds Judas: Shakespeare's Iago is as much Shakespeare as is his Othello. But the self, thus traversing and finding itself
variously reflected, is extended and developed, becoming that self which
it has traversed. One cannot say that the self has changed, because it has
experienced only what was from the beginning potential within it. In the
library, Stephen said of Shakespeare, 'He found in the world without as
actual what was in his world within as possible.' Thus, through experience,
the self becomes that 'self which it itself was ineluctably preconditioned to
become.' Just as a planet cannot complete its elliptical orbit without passing
through the aphelion, the farthest point consistent with the completion of
the orbit, so the self cannot complete its self-discovery without finding
those aspects of itself at the farthest remove from the centre of its nature.
In terms of the novel, Stephen must encounter Bloom's nature to realize
his own potential self. The idea plainly derives from an application of
Bruno's theory of the coincidence of contraries, is related to that current of
ideas which found similar expression in Yeats's theory of Self and Anti-Self,
and perhaps explains the defiant cry '*Nothung!*' (needful) – a declaration

[100] This sentence occurs in the Trieste notebook among materials for use in the
Portrait (*Workshop*, 97).

that man's self-discovery in life is governed by a Shelleyan Necessity.[101] (I will consider later the application of the idea to the nature of God.)

In this passage, coincident with the arrival of Bloom, Stephen is not alluding to Bloom, whose entry he has not yet noticed, but the author's allusion is unmistakable. The hallucination technique is now being used to expound some of the theoretical ideas of the novel (suitably befogged by circumstances and Stephen's condition). For each of the two men, the brothel chapter represents the dominant of their fundamentals, the aphelion of their orbits. Stephen is at the farthest point consistent with 'the ultimate return' from his true centre as the isolated creative imagination of the artist. Bloom, the ordinary decent citizen, is at the farthest remove from his true Ithaca, his home and his role as husband and father. Both men are at the end of their tethers in that sense, and each is at the end of his tether in a psychological sense. In their extremities, when their paths meet, they may through their encounter complete the realization of their potential selves. In this chapter, although Bloom and Stephen are in the same room, their encounter is only at an unconscious and symbolic level; when the relationship becomes conscious, in the next chapter, they are on their paths of return, mutually aided.

The hallucination technique marks diversely for the two men their turning-points. For Bloom, it is the moment of abject submissiveness while he bends, 'stifflegged, ageing', to tie Bella Cohen's bootlace: he feels unconsciously that he has lost everything – his home, his wife, his daughter and his manhood – and is condemned by his own sentimentalized standards represented by the Nymph. But, as he straightens up, 'his back trousers' button snaps', and the intrusion of the real world to which his nature belongs (the world of practicality where, 'if there were only ethereal', human life would come to an end) restores him. For Stephen, on the other hand, the threat and the rescue are on a very different level. During the chapter, as he grows progressively drunker, the boundary between his consciousness and his unconscious becomes confused and uncertain, until, in the giddiness following his whirling and frenzied dance, his conscious mind loses control. His dialogue with his mother's corpse differs from the other 'hallucinatory' episodes because Stephen does not know where he is or what he is doing: this is real hallucination. Dream and reality are so fused that, as in many nightmares, the unconscious terrors produce externalized phenomena. When, choking with rage, he cries out 'Shite!', the cry is heard, though not understood, by Bloom, and the final act of defiance, the blow of the sword *Nothung*, is projected into the outer world in the blow of the ashplant which smashes the brothel's chandelier.[102] Stephen's

---

[101] Cf. 'If you ask me what occasions drama or what is the necessity for it at all, I answer Necessity. It is mere animal instinct applied to the mind. Apart from his world-old desire to get beyond the flaming ramparts, man has a further longing to become a maker and a moulder. That is the necessity of all art' ('Drama and Life', *CW*, 42–3).

[102] The accounts of the damage done by Stephen's blow again illustrate the three aspects of the 'hallucination' technique, distinguished at the beginning of this section.

struggle has to take place on the unconscious level, because it is at that level that the powers of mother-love, family duty, and religion remain undefeated. As Joyce well knew from personal experience, a spirit like Stephen's, which has been moulded by a loving if disordered family, and in a Church and faith which has shaped its whole nature, cannot escape such influences by a conscious rejection or gesture of denial. Stephen may have abandoned the Church and refused to pray at his mother's deathbed, but such conscious and willed acts are comparatively simple: they cannot remove what has been bred in him, and consequently they generate fear at his obduracy in face of death, grief at his denial of comfort to the mother whom he had loved and who had loved him, and remorse for the egoism which forbade him to sacrifice his will in return for the many sufferings his mother had endured for him. Similarly, he may have rejected faith and refused to serve God, but he cannot eradicate from his mind what a lifetime's conditioning has implanted – fear of the wrath of an offended God, belief in the possibility of repentance even at the last minute, and hope in the intervening mercy of Jesus. This last is the most insidious enemy to his professed 'all or not at all', but all three are painful threats; the hand of God clutches the centre of his being – '*A green crab with malignant red eyes sticks deep its grinning claws in Stephen's heart.*' In the *Portrait*, it was the external pressures of his environment against which his need for spiritual independence had to struggle; now the necessary conflict is with the elements in his own nature formed in loving submission to mother, family, Church and country. By means of the hallucination technique, Joyce presents this conflict at the deepest levels, shows how, in Stephen's drunkenness, it erupts into his consciousness and behaviour, and images the consequent darkness of the spirit ('*Time's livid final flame leaps and, in the following darkness, ruin of all space, shattered glass and toppling masonry*'), symbolizing the obliteration of the whole universe, as Stephen has been brought up to apprehend it, by his '*Non Serviam!*' No spoken defiance can free Stephen's spirit; as he later says to Private Carr, tapping his brow, 'But in here it is I must kill the priest and the king.'[103] In his hallucination

---

In reality, as Bloom points out, the paper shade of a lamp is crushed; in exaggerated terms, the chandelier is smashed; and, in nightmare symbolism, 'Time's livid final flame leaps.'

[103] In his letter to Ibsen (March 1901), Joyce said how he had been inspired by the dramatist's battles – 'not the obvious material battles but those that were fought and won behind your forehead' (*Letters* I, 52). The image of his enemies as the combined forces of 'the priest and the king' was taken from Blake. According to Stanislaus Joyce, his brother used to quote (and mean), 'prophetic couplets of Blake's, which declare that

> The harvest shall flourish in wintry weather,
> When two virginities meet together.
> The king and the priest must be tied in a tether,
> Before two virgins can meet together.' (*MBK*, 161)

The verses, 'Merlin's Prophecy', were obviously familiar ground to both brothers. In a letter of 31 July 1905, Stanislaus wrote to Joyce, 'few sons are born as free as yours because the priest and the king are so seldom tied in a tether' (*Letters* II, 102).

he is engaged in such an internal struggle, and its successful outcome is apparent in his behaviour when threatened by the soldiers; despite intoxication and danger, he is absurdly calm and composed, and, abandoning his old obsession with death ('Death is the highest form of life'), now declares, as Bloom himself might have done, 'Damn death. Long live life!' When struck down by the soldier, he turns on to his side and curls his body in the foetus position as though waiting to be reborn.

This suggests one last important resource Joyce found in the hallucination technique. In the series of Christ-parallels that run through the chapters involving Stephen, this chapter presents his Passion and Crucifixion. The Mass consists of 'the Rites, Ceremonies and Prayers prescribed for the celebration of the Eucharistic Sacrifice of the Body and Blood of Christ, offered, under the forms of Bread and Wine, in remembrance of his Passion and Death', and this chapter is, in part, a Mass. When Stephen first enters Nighttown he is chanting *'the* introit *for paschal time'* (in fact, the Antiphon used with the Asperges) and soon he is devising, for Lynch's benefit, a movement which 'illustrates the loaf and jug of bread and wine in Omar.' Thereafter the Mass becomes corrupted: in honour of the whore, Georgina Johnson, *'Ad Deum qui laetificat juventutem meam* is changed to *'ad deam'*, and the 'Agnus Dei' is applied to the commercial traveller, Mr Lambe from London, who, because he has married Georgina Johnson, becomes 'Lamb of London, who takest away the sins of our world'; the Gospel is represented by a story about Mary Shortall who caught the pox from Jimmy Pidgeon and also had a child by him; Stephen sees himself as the Prodigal Son, and Lynch sees the whores as 'Three wise virgins'; there is a mock Blessing from 'His Eminence, Simon Stephen Cardinal Dedalus', a mock litany in honour of Bloom, and a mock confession by the three whores; the Beatitudes are reduced to a confused version of the eight British Beatitudes ('Beer beef battledog buybull businum barnum buggerum bishop'), the Blessed Trinity is Ireland, the British Empire and the Church, and Lucifer becomes a fallen box of matches. The street-quarrel swells into a vision of Armageddon, and culminates in the celebration of a Black Mass on the belly of Mrs Purefoy, goddess of unreason; and Stephen's destruction of the chandelier is the act of uncreation, restoring original chaos and night. These are only a few of the very numerous allusions to the rites of the Church, but they are enough to suggest how Joyce used the hallucination technique to establish a parallel with the Mass, though the rites celebrated in this chapter are those of Circe, as Stephen's slip of the tongue indicates when he speaks of 'priests haihooping round David's that is Circe's or what am I saying Ceres' altar'.

When I discussed earlier this passage about rites, and Stephen's explanation of the prevalence of the interval of a fifth in ritual music, and its relation to the theory of the self discovering itself in experience of its opposite, I referred only to the applications of that theory to the human self and human life. But the passage itself is more encompassing: 'What went forth to the ends of the world to traverse not itself. God, the sun, Shakespeare, a commercial traveller, having itself traversed in reality itself, becomes that self.' There is a hierarchy of beings: the commercial traveller, in his humbler way, discovers his self through the variety of his wandering experiences (there is, of course, an unconscious allusion to Bloom) just as the artist or Shakespeare (or Stephen) does through the range of his imaginative experience. The extreme points of the sun's nature are summer and winter, life and death, fertility and decay – the seasonal cycle formalized and celebrated in the Hymn to Demeter and the rites of Ceres. The traversing of God may be a reference to the Gradual for the Mass on the Saturday in the Ember-Week of Advent: 'From the end of heaven is His going out; and His circuit even to the end thereof', but, in theological terms, God's traversing of the opposite pole to his nature was in the Incarnation, and, more particularly, in his experience of human suffering in Christ's Passion and Death. According to Stephen's formulation, it was through becoming suffering man that God's self was completed and became what it was 'ineluctably preconditioned to become'. Through this experience, as Stephen said in the library, God became 'all in all in all of us'. Stephen has argued that rites are the formal representation of the poet's insight into the coincidence of contraries; the Mass is specifically that rite which formally represents the nature of a God who is both he whose glory the heavens show forth (the passage from Psalm XVIII occurs frequently in Masses, for instance in the Introit for the Fourth Sunday of Advent) and he who was despised and rejected of men. Thus the ritual character of the chapter and the numerous references to the Mass are a reflection not only of Stephen's isolation and suffering, but also of the whole theme of the meeting of extremes, where artist and commercial traveller, both 'separated by the greatest possible interval' from their starting-points, make contact. The chapter is itself a ritual.

I have by no means exhausted the variety of uses Joyce makes of the hallucination technique. It is the most extended and bizarre of all the techniques of the novel and, like the others, was not devised for some single purpose but as a means of fulfilling simultaneously a number of very different purposes. It gives a nightmarish vision of an area of Dublin life where all is chaos and disorder; it suggests a parallel with Circe's ingle where men were transformed into beasts; it is a means of presenting the continuous interaction of unconscious, consciousness and behaviour; it represents the culmination and combined results of the psychological stresses which have troubled Bloom and Stephen all day; it provides a symbolic commentary focusing on some of the central developing themes and patterns of the novel; it enacts a ritual of the meeting of extremes; and it is technically a frenzied climax to the '*Odyssey*' preparing for the shift to the quieter tones of the '*Nostos*'. Certainly, in devising this technique, Joyce must have been influenced by Goethe's '*Walpurgisnacht*', Flaubert's *La Tentation de St Antoine*, and Strindberg's *Dream Play*, but the developments and applications are entirely his own and, so far from being idle ingenuities and oddities, are inseparable from the conception and nature of the chapter and from its complex function in the novel as a whole.

'Eumaeus'

The techniques of the *'Nostos'* are, in accordance with the overall rhythm of the novel, less complicated, bizarre and strenuous than those of the second half of the *'Odyssey'*. The psychological explosions in the brothel have relieved both men of their swollen emotional pressures, and the technique of 'Eumaeus' ('Narrative-old' in contrast with the youthful intensity of 'Telemachus') is consequently bathetic, anticlimactic. (In the Linati scheme, it is labelled *'Prosa rilassata'*, loose or relaxed prose.)

The usual explanation is that both men are tired out, their exhaustion being mirrored in exhausted language, a limp string of hackneyed phrases and worn-out clichés. Stuart Gilbert reports that Joyce told him that the episode represents 'the intercourse and mental state of two fagged-out men',[104] and the style indeed suggests a relaxation of the sinews, with sentences that collapse or fade out, stale and confused metaphors and allusions, and a general flabbiness of syntax. The danger of this stylistic decorum is that the representation of an exhausted condition may be in itself tedious, and Hugh Kenner has accurately summed up one kind of critical response to it: 'Like "The Oxen of the Sun", the episode has incurred the displeasure of those who don't read closely, and imagine that Joyce is conveying the sense of exhaustion by exhausting the reader for fifty pages.'[105]

It is true that we are told at the beginning of 'Eumaeus' that both men were 'e.d. ed', but the nature of their tiredness is not the same. Stephen is 'not yet perfectly sober' and is 'fagged out', but Bloom, although no doubt weary, is more active, physically and mentally, than at any other time during the day. In one sense, the style is exhausted, but in another it is very busy. Consider these passages from the first few paragraphs of the chapter:

> Preparatory to anything else Mr Bloom brushed off the greater bulk of the shavings and handed Stephen the hat and ashplant and bucked him up generally in orthodox Samaritan fashion, which he very badly needed. . . . For the nonce he was rather nonplussed but inasmuch as the duty plainly devolved upon him to take some measures on the subject he pondered suitable ways and means during which Stephen repeatedly yawned. . . .
>
> This was a quandary but, bringing commonsense to bear on it, evidently there was nothing for it but put a good face on the matter and foot it which they accordingly did. So, bevelling around by Mullet's and the Signal House, which they shortly reached, they proceeded perforce in the direction of Amiens street railway terminus, Mr Bloom being handicapped by the circumstance that one of the back buttons of his trousers had, to vary the time-honoured adage, gone the way of all buttons, though, entering thoroughly into the spirit of the thing, he heroically made light of the mischance. . . .
>
> *En route*, to his taciturn, and, not to put too fine a point on it, not yet perfectly sober companion, Mr Bloom, who at all events, was in complete possession of his faculties, never more so, in fact disgustingly sober, spoke a word of caution *re* the dangers of nighttown, women of illfame and swell

---

[104] In a letter to Richard Ellmann (*Ellmann–JJ*, 372 n.). [105] *Kenner*, 260.

mobsmen, which, barely permissible once in a while, though not as a habitual
practice, was of the nature of a regular death-trap for young fellows of his
age particularly if they had acquired drinking habits under the influence of
liquor unless you knew a little juijitsu for every contingency as even a fellow
on the broad of his back could administer a nasty kick if you didn't look out.
... (*U* 575–6/704–6)

One might describe such language as exhausted, but the adjectives appropriate to the style and manner are very different – smug, conceited, self-
congratulatory, patronizing, attitudinizing, knowing, officious, opinionated,
pedantic, moralizing, bumptious, pompous, pretentious, affected, perky,
jocular and garrulous. It is a style which variously reflects Bloom's mood,
as the content variously presents his character. In the first few paragraphs
he is shown as encouraging, helpful, astute, ready, responsible, practical,
prudent, level-headed, undismayed, wholehearted, courageous, alert, admoni-
tory, worldly-wise, watchfully critical of the social roles of the police and the
army; thrifty of time, money, health and character; tolerant; discriminating
as a connoisseur of wine; well-informed on the nutritional and medical
qualities of drink; abstemious; and, unlike Stephen's other companions, a
loyal friend in need. The passage verbalizes the admiring self-portrait
Bloom is creating in his own mind. Even when he speaks, his mind translates his actual words into the same stilted and verbose style:

—I met your respected father on a recent occasion, Mr Bloom diplomati-
cally returned. Today, in fact, or, to be strictly accurate, on yesterday. Where
does he live at present? I gathered in the course of conversation that he had
moved. (*U* 581/713)

None of the other characters in the chapter is credited with this kind of
language; it expresses how Bloom feels when, after all the rejections and
distresses of the day, he at last finds himself in charge of a situation where
the resources of his practical nature are called upon. There is, in the worn-
out language, an undercurrent of tiredness, but above it Bloom is enthusiastic
and active, absurd but effective, displaying all his attributes to impress
Stephen and restore his own *amour-propre*.

Apart from implicit approval of Bloom's good sense and helpful behaviour, there are repeated idealized statements about him. When he moves
away from Stephen and Corley, he is 'actuated by motives of inherent
delicacy, inasmuch as he always believed in minding his own business'
and, in later passages, he is presented as 'a levelheaded individual who
could give points to not a few in point of shrewd observation', as 'at heart a
born adventurer', as 'a student of the human soul', as a 'much-injured but
on the whole eventempered person', as 'a bit of an artist in his spare time'
and as a man 'often considerably misunderstood and the least pugnacious
of mortals'. These assertions are not literally Bloom's thoughts, and the
style is not his style; they are verbal images of his self-awareness. By the
comparatively simple technique of the chapter, Joyce combined Bloom's
euphoric and eager officiousness, his underlying weariness, and an ironic
exposure of the conceit with which his charitable behaviour fills him – and

yet at the same time one has to recognize that Bloom is, in fact, being a Good Samaritan.

Although the technique of 'Eumaeus' reflects the emotional relaxation after the storms of 'Circe', as well as Bloom's officious pleasure in his adopted role of guide, counsellor and friend, the chapter's place in the total action of the novel requires that, through the artificialities of the style, the first stirrings and tentative developments of the relationship between the two men should begin to appear. Initially the technique only emphasizes their incompatibility. The fussy activity of Bloom is set against Stephen's passivity; in the dialogue, Bloom's garrulous enthusiasm contrasts with Stephen's terse ironic detachment; even the workings of their imaginations in response to their surroundings are fundamentally different – while Stephen associates Ibsen with Baird's, the stone cutter's, Bloom, responding with satisfaction to the smell of bread, recalls an advertising jingle, 'O tell me where is fancy bread? At Rourke's the baker's, it is said.' Bloom's attempts to engage Stephen in conversation fail because the two men find themselves radically opposed or at cross-purposes. Bloom declares that he is a patriotic Irishman because, for him, one's fatherland is 'where you can live well . . . if you work' and Stephen, having hardly listened to what was being said, remarks, 'Count me out.' Bloom pursues the matter: the literary artist, like Stephen, works for and belongs to Ireland as much as does the peasant:

—You suspect, Stephen retorted with a sort of a half laugh, that I may be important because I belong to the *faubourg Saint-Patrice* called Ireland for short.
—I would go a step farther, Mr Bloom insinuated.
—But I suspect, Stephen interrupted, that Ireland must be important because it belongs to me. (*U* 606/748)

This exchange is typical of Bloom's difficulties. How can a man anxious for 'friendlier intercourse between man and man' make contact with the arrogant egoism of the artist? The more the style of the chapter represents Bloom's ingratiating attempts to interest Stephen, the more it reveals the discrepancy between the two minds and natures. After a vain effort to discuss the soul and 'the existence of a supernatural God', the opposition of the two minds is described as polar and total:

On this knotty point, however, the views of the pair, poles apart as they were, both in schooling and everything else, with the marked difference in their respective ages, clashed. (*U* 596/733)

The different manners in which Bloom's speech and Stephen's speech are presented express the apparent impossibility of any real communication between them. For most of the chapter, even where there are points of similarity or contact, they seem minimized by the technique. Though the two agree about the absurdity of political violence, the difference in tone makes Stephen's assent seem impatient and sardonic:

I resent violence or intolerance in any shape or form. It never reaches any-thing or stops anything. A revolution must come on the due instalments plan. It's a patent absurdity on the face of it to hate people because they live round the corner and speak another vernacular, so to speak.

—Memorable bloody bridge battle and seven minutes' war, Stephen assented, between Skinner's alley and Ormond market.

Yes, Mr Bloom thoroughly agreed, entirely endorsing the remark, that was overwhelmingly right and the whole world was overwhelmingly full of that sort of thing.   (*U* 605/745–6)

The coincidence of opinions is less emphatic than the contrast between Bloom's pompous, cliché-ridden, repetitious, tautological manner (or, rather, the manner attributed to him) and Stephen's deflating specifics.

The benefits the two men can draw from their meeting depend on their differences, rather than on what they have in common. Bloom is the first to begin to grasp the nature of a possible relationship: 'Though they didn't see eye to eye in everything, a certain analogy there somehow was, as if both their minds were travelling, so to speak, in the one train of thought.' Their physical link, imaging their spiritual link, is itself associated by Stephen with a sense of their difference:

—It will (the air) do you good, Bloom said, meaning also the walk, in a moment. The only thing is to walk then you'll feel a different man. It's not far. Lean on me.

Accordingly he passed his left arm in Stephen's right and led him on accordingly.

—Yes, Stephen said uncertainly, because he thought he felt a strange kind of flesh of a different man approach him, sinewless and wobbly and all that. (*U* 621–2/769)

The linking of arms, symbolic of friendship and interdependence, is thus, through a confused misapplication of Bloom's cliché, used to enforce Stephen's awareness of his difference from his companion, a difference in kind.

This is typical of the way in which the technique of the chapter expresses the nature of the meeting between the two men, the hesitant and circum-locutory approaches, the uncertain and suspicious responses, the tentative acceptance of a relationship based on dissimilarity and muddled with mis-understanding. Immediately before the agreement that Stephen should lean on Bloom, a trivial exchange represents the kind of help Stephen can derive from the association; for once initiating talk, he says that he has never understood why at night chairs in cafes are placed upside down on tables, and 'the never failing Bloom' at once replies, 'To sweep the floor in the morning.' Question and answer are equally at the lowest level of communication, but their significance is representative and symbolic – the unworldly artist, puzzled by the most ordinary things in daily life, finds a ready answer to his problem from the practical commonsense of the citizen just as, conversely, the latter confusedly hopes to profit from an acquaint-ance with 'someone of no uncommon calibre who could provide food for reflection': 'Intellectual stimulation as such was, he felt, from time to time a firstrate tonic for the mind.' (Of course, the overturning of the day's order in the cafe in readiness for a clean sweep in the morning in itself contributes to the mood of the chapter, as the two men prepare for a fresh start.)

The concluding conversation about music is the resolution of the chapter. Now, consciously and literally depending on Bloom, Stephen, instead of needing to be prodded into reluctant speech, converses freely, sings and translates a song for Bloom's benefit, and, as they move away, is 'singing more boldly'. This despite the fact that their tastes in and attitudes towards music are diametrically and explicitly opposed. Bloom talks eagerly about 'a form of art for which [he], as a pure amateur, possessed the greatest love.' He considers Wagner too heavy and Mendelssohn to be of 'the severe classical school'; he attributes *Les Huguenots* to Mercadante, *The Seven Last Words* to Meyerbeer, the spurious *Twelfth Mass* to Mozart, and thinks that Herrick's *Bid me to live and I will live thy protestant to be* is a Protestant hymn; in general, he shares the Dublin musical tastes exhibited in the 'Sirens' chapter. Stephen, on the other hand, limits his praise to Elizabethan and Jacobean composers, to Sweelinck, and Johannes Jeep. While Stephen sings the song about the Sirens (who for him represent any force which would draw him from his literary vocation), Bloom perceives the possibilities of financial and social benefits to be derived from his companion's fine tenor voice (with Bloom supplying 'some impetus of the goahead sort'), and considers that Stephen could 'practise literature in his spare moments.' The two men are, as it were, singing different tunes, yet there is an easy relationship between them, as between the *dux* and *comes* (subject and answer) in the musical conceits referred to by Stephen. Stephen's dawning realization of the significance for him of the day and the meeting, marking the end of the artist as a young man, is clearly suggested by the musical work he describes for Bloom's benefit – Sweelinck's variations on the air '*Youth here has End*' ('*Mein junges Leben hat ein End*').

It is again in musical terms, though humbler ones, that the final image of the developing friendship is presented. In the closing paragraph, the driver of a streetsweeper, seated 'on his lowbacked car', looks after the retreating backs of the two men and, into the account of what he sees, two quotations from Samuel Lover's song, *The Low Back'd Car*, intrude: '*to be married by Father Maher*' and '*and looked after their lowbacked car*'. Most commentators agree about the general relevance of these quotations from the song about 'sweet Peggy' – Bloom and Stephen, linked arm in arm, are off to celebrate their new relationship – a marriage of opposites. But there is, just before the quotations, another allusion to the song, which seems to been ignored – though it is the allusion which may have prompted the later ones. While his horse dungs, the driver sits 'patient in his scythed car', but, on his next appearance, is described as sitting 'on his lowbacked car'. 'Scythed' is usually explained as a reference to the brushes attached to the wheels of the cart, and, because Bloom has jocularly spoken of the cart as a 'peril' to the lives of himself and his companion, to the scythes attached to the wheels of war chariots. Both of these explanations are certainly correct, but the transformation of the 'scythed car' into the 'lowbacked car' is probably in response to the second verse of Lover's song:

In battle's wild commotion
The proud and mighty Mars,
With hostile scythes, demands the tithes
Of death in warlike cars;
While Peggy, peaceful goddess,
Has darts in her bright eye,
That knock men down in the market town,
As right and left they fly;
While she sits in the low back'd car,
Than battle more dang'rous far,
For the doctor's art
Cannot cure the heart
That is hit on the low back'd car.

The shift from the image of the streetsweeper as 'scythed' to the image of it as 'lowbacked' seems to be a shift from regarding it as an emblem of hostility and war to regarding it as an emblem of love and peace. (I take it that the devastations of Peggy's eye are not relevant here.) After the strife and perils of the day, both men have reached the peaceful state where they can walk along 'chatting about music', and their linked arms, as they continue their '*tête-à-tête*', suggest the physical link between Peggy and the singer of the song, who would prefer to marry Peggy than any lady in the land,

For the lady would sit fornenst me,
On a cushion made with taste;
While Peggy would sit beside me,
With my arm around her waist.
While we drove in the low back'd car,
To be married by Father Maher.

The two men appeared at the beginning of the chapter, walking separately with Bloom pouring out unwanted advice and Stephen silent, morose and, half-drunk: they depart from the chapter arm in arm, walking and stopping and walking again, without interrupting their conversation about 'sirens, enemies of man's reason, mingled with a number of other topics of the same category, usurpers, historical cases of the kind.' They have different sirens and different usurpers in mind, but they are associated like *dux* and *comes* because, as Bloom has perceived, 'their minds were travelling . . . in the one train of thought', or, as the first sentence of the next chapter indicates, because they are following 'parallel courses'.

This transformation of their relationship has been presented throughout in a manner of deliberate banality, partly because such a manner represents and evaluates Bloom's mood, and partly because it is only at a banal level that the two men can meet. They are separated by age, race, disposition, temperament, family background, ambition and, as the chapter say, 'everything else'. They can make contact only when, in a state of lassitude, the passions which have ruled them all day are comparatively subdued, and they are reduced to a man and 'a different man,' each needing the other because he is different. The relationship between them is commonplace: they do not find themselves to be soul-mates; they cannot understand each other very well; there is little they can do for each other on any level but that of the banal. One man needs someone to help him along, the other needs someone he can help along: on that basis they give mutual aid. It seems essential to the whole scheme of *Ulysses* that the meeting to which the novel leads, the resolution of its tensions, should be no emotional climax, but a mere (though none the less important) encounter of two men in need of temporary companionship and setting off together to find food, drink and shelter. Stephen's acceptance that, for him, youth has come to an end, that the artist, no longer a young man, must acknowledge and exist arm in arm with the commonplace life represented by the citizen, that the artist's human ties are in Eccles Street not in the Martello Tower, is marked by the shift from the strained tension of the 'narrative-young' of 'Telemachus' to the relaxation of the 'narrative-old' of 'Eumaeus'.

'Ithaca'

After the relaxing of pressures in the cabman's shelter, the emotional state of the two men becomes calmer still. The '*prosa rilassata*' of 'Eumaeus' sinks, according to the Linati scheme, to the '*stile pacato*' (the pacified or calm style) of 'Ithaca'. In the Gilbert scheme, however, the technique of the new chapter is called 'Catechism-impersonal', referring back to the 'Catechism-personal' of the second chapter of the novel, and emphasizing the method rather than the style. Certainly it is the catechistic method which is the dominant feature of 'Ithaca'. Unlike all the other techniques of *Ulysses*, question-and-answer (especially question-and-answer of this formality) is not naturally a narrative method; it implies a static situation which is being examined and analysed rather than the unrolling of a concatenated series of events or developments. There are events and developments in the chapter – some of them important ones – but the method blurs their place in a sequence and deadens their impact; instead it puts all the emphasis on a detached and apparently ill-ordered enquiry into the state of the two men and the nature of their relationship.

The enquiry, though detached from Bloom and Stephen, reflects the comparative detachment they have attained. Bloom can view coolly the adultery of Molly with Boylan, and Stephen can refer to the haunting memory of his mother, first experienced on the Martello Tower, as 'a matutinal cloud . . . at first no bigger than a woman's hand.' Both are now more concerned with understanding their situations than with elaborating plans for the future; although Bloom does try to arrange future meetings, he knows from experience that such arrangements are rarely fulfilled. The movement of the novel is retarded until it reaches the same point of rest as Bloom, falling asleep.

Joyce's letter to Frank Budgen seems to indicate his intentions quite clearly:

> I am writing *Ithaca* in the form of a mathematical catechism. All events are resolved into their cosmic, physical, psychical etc. equivalents, e.g. Bloom jumping down the area, drawing water from the tap, the micturating in the garden, the cone of incense, lighted candle and statue so that the reader will know everything and know it in the baldest and coldest way, but Bloom and Stephen thereby become heavenly bodies, wanderers like the stars at which they gaze.[106]

The intention seems clear, but the described scheme suggests a more consistent handling of the material than is, in fact, found. As in earlier chapters, Joyce's technique is only a general frame within which there is a remarkable variety of styles and effects. At times, instead of questions, there are blunt instructions, reminiscent of an examination paper: 'Recite the first (major) part of this chanted legend', 'Catalogue these books', 'Compile the budget for 16 June 1904.' The answers differ widely in form: some are monosyllabic, some prolix; some are in song, rhyme, anagram, acrostic or processional form; some are determinedly literal, some riddling, some allusive; they include advertising slogans, an unsolicited testimonial, a balancesheet, a booklist and fragments of Latin, Irish and Hebrew. Their content is also diverse: many are simple statements of observed or remembered facts, sometimes relating to important matters and sometimes to trivialities or irrelevancies; others give events a specific and often laborious placing in time or space, or relate them to the physical universe or to universals of a moral or a spiritual order; there are long passages enumerating or speculating on what might have happened but didn't, or what might have been said but wasn't; there are meticulous references to past parallels, to memories, to biographical information; there are accounts of the two men's ideas of reflections, sometimes treated impressionistically, sometimes encyclopaedically, sometimes confused, and sometimes logically categorized: there are facts and figures, and there are poetic, even onomatopoetic, images. 'A mathematical catechism', however well it may have suited Joyce as a 'catchword' for what he had in mind, is a very inadequate description of the varied forms and styles of the chapter, and, although some events are 'resolved into their cosmic, physical, psychical etc. equivalents', many are not.

Yet, for all these differences, the chapter feels homogeneous: the difficulty is in defining the quality of attitude or purpose which unites the variations of tone as the catechistic method unites the variations in form. First, there is a recurring lack of discrimination in many answers. The answer about the topics of conversation as the two men walk towards Eccles Street solemnly lists besides such matters as music, literature, Ireland, woman and the Roman Catholic Church, 'the influence of gaslight or the light of arc and glowlamps on the growth of adjoining paraheliotropic trees' (though a subsequent answer informs us that on this matter 'their views

---

[106] *Letters* I, 159–60.

were equal and negative') and 'exposed corporation emergency dust buckets'. Bloom's recall of his father's suicide includes the fact that that afternoon the old man had bought 'a new boater straw hat, extra smart', together with the name and address of the shop and the precise time of purchase. Bloom's final position in bed is not only precisely described but compared to 'the attitude depicted on a snapshot photograph made by Percy Apjohn'. The implication of these and similar passages seems to be that we are no longer confined to what seems important to Bloom or Stephen, or even to any normal human system of values – that any available piece of information is as interesting or uninteresting as any other.[107] Yet the total effect is more complicated than this. The undiscriminating list of topics of conversation suggests the ordinary irrelevancies and wanderings of a friendly exchange, unlike any other conversation in which either man has been involved that day; the reference to the straw hat represents the way in which, when not simplified by powerful emotion, memories retain significant and insignificant details alike; the comparison to the snapshot taken by Percy Apjohn, the friend of Bloom's youth, relates Bloom's middle age to his childhood and leads to the image of him as 'the childman weary, the manchild in the womb'. In one sense, then, such details are of no account; in another, they suggest aspects of the relationship between the two men, qualities of Bloom's current mood, and the consistency of personality underlying the changes brought about by time. There is a surface of indifference, yet this surface is itself a means of presenting new insights.

Another recurring feature of many answers is a flat encyclopaedism, though, here again, the flatness is largely of the surface. The question, 'What in water did Bloom, waterlover, drawer of water, watercarrier returning to the range, admire?', elicits an answer of over 450 words, praising water for its universality, democratic equality, vastness, profundity, restlessness; the independence of its units; its variability, quiescence, turgidity, subsidence, sterility; its climatic and social significance, preponderance, hegemony in the southern hemisphere; the stability of the ocean bed; the capacity to dissolve and hold in solution; its erosion, weight, volume and density; its imperturbability, gradation of colours, ramifications, violence, circumterrestrial curve, secrecy, latent humidity; the simplicity of its composition; its healing virtues, buoyancy, and penetrativeness; its cleansing, quenching, and nourishing qualities; 'its infallibility as paradigm and paragon'; its metamorphoses, strength, variety of forms, solidity, docility, utility, potentiality, submarine fauna and flora, ubiquity, and 'the noxiousness of its effluvia' in marshes and stagnant pools. This detailing of water's attributes is unconnected with the action of the chapter, is certainly not an account of what is passing through Bloom's mind as he carries the kettle from the sink to the range, and is hardly more convincing as a description of Bloom's reasons for admiring water. The encyclopaedic method seems to exist for its own sake. Yet its very completeness is expressive of water's

[107] Clive Hart says that the answers in 'Ithaca' 'seem to be the answers of a computer which has not been programmed to distinguish between what is important and what is not' (*Hart–Ulysses*, 74).

'infallibility as paradigm and paragon'; because of water's universality, flexibility and multiple aspects it can serve as an illustrative example and model for the life of common humanity – a symbol of that human universality, flexibility and multiplicity of which Bloom is the representative. His response to it is less one of conscious admiration than of instinctive fellow-feeling. The function of the passage as an image of Bloom's acceptance of his role as one of the independent units in the ocean of life is immediately reinforced by the counter-image of Stephen's hydrophobia, 'distrusting aquacities of thought and language', and Bloom's recognition of 'The incompatibility of aquacity with the erratic originality of genius'. The long and apparently irrelevant catalogue becomes a paradigm of Bloom's ready acceptance of human life and human nature, and of the fundamental difference between the attitudes of the two men, the one glad to share in and feel identity with common mankind, the other asserting his separateness and committed to 'erratic originality'.

Other catalogues are different in kind and effect, yet combine similarly a matter-of-fact surface with subtle implications. Most remarkable is the passage which begins with the question, 'In what ultimate ambition had all concurrent and consecutive ambitions now coalesced?', and then presents, over several pages, Bloom's dream-house – 'a thatched bungalowshaped 2 storey dwellinghouse of southerly aspect' – from its stucco front and its toilet furnishing down to 'a fingertame parrot (expurgated language)'. The style is borrowed from houseagents' advertisements and home-and-garden magazines; the details seem absurdly trivial; the intention is apparently to mock Bloom's suburban ambition. Yet the resultant image of an aspect of Bloom's nature is particularly exact. A man's house and furnishings are a projection of him; when Balzac describes the house of M. Grandet he depicts and evaluates the man, and the descriptions of Bloom's kitchen-dresser, sitting-room, bookshelves, and of the contents of the two drawers he·opens present exactly aspects of his life, his personality and his family situation. The extended account of his 'ultimate ambition' is a development of this familiar novelist's technique. Bloom has never particularized the contents of his dream-house in this way; the passage translates into specific terms his vague, commonplace and sentimental ambition, and by employing a vocabulary of objects belonging to domestic architecture, furnishings and horticulture, and combining them in a style of bourgeois aspiration, articulates a precise vision of Bloom's imprecise dream. It foreshadows the passage in *Finnegans Wake* when Shem the Penman is seen 'writing the mystery of himsel in furniture' (*FW* 184), and, like that passage, uses a catalogue of material objects (each with its own associations) to represent one of the most immaterial and indefinable areas of a man's personality.

There are, however, other answers which do not relate to Bloom or Stephen at all, such as the account of the source of the water which flowed through Bloom's tap and the scientific description of the boiling of the kettle. Such passages are more striking than frequent, but set the characteristic tone of much of the chapter. They seem pedantically and pointlessly elaborate ways of saying that a tap flowed and a kettle boiled. But there is rather more to them than that. They pay proper attention to remarkable phenomena which are so commonplace that we take them for granted. They comically present Bloom as the master of the extraordinary features of ordinary life. As a practical man, by merely turning a tap, he can call upon the resources of the city's water-supply, a supply paid for and primarily intended for men like him, 'selfsupporting taxpayers, solvent, sound', unlike the wretched paupers who have wasted the water; as a scientific man he can, by lighting a match and placing a filled kettle on the range, draw upon the heat stored up in bituminous coal, 'containing in compressed mineral form the foliated fossilised decidua of primeval forests which had in turn derived their vegetative existence from the sun, primal source of heat (radiant), transmitted through omnipresent luminiferous diathermanous ether.' He can do these things because he is a competent citizen and a householder. Stephen speculates philosophically about the nature of space and time; Bloom, without thinking, conquers space and time. At the turn of a tap, he fetches water from a reservoir over twenty-two miles from the city; with 'one ignited lucifer match', he releases energies transmitted from the sun and stored for his use since times primeval. The style's fussy exactness may also mirror the self-conscious efficiency which Bloom adopts to 'prepare a collation for a gentile', the same mood which induces him later to offer proofs 'that his tendency was towards applied, rather than towards pure, science.' Again it is the manner which is the real content of the passage; the particular information given is there only because it is part of the manner.

However, the pseudoscientific manner does not always present Bloom as the practical man manipulating the forces of the universe. If a materialist vision makes man's scientific control of nature possible, it also reveals a bleak and terrifying universe in which man seems minute, insignificant and at the mercy of powers beyond his imagination. Philosophically abstract terms reduce Bloom's life to a meaningless progression:

> From inexistence to existence he came to many and was as one received: existence with existence he was with any as any with any: from existence to nonexistence gone he would be by all as none perceived. (U 628/778–9)

Calculations as to the proportional relations between his age and Stephen's are pointless:

> What events might nullify these calculations?
> The cessation of existence of both or either, the inauguration of a new era or calendar, the annihilation of the world and consequent extermination of the human species, inevitable but impredictable. (U 640/794)

These are only hints at the cold images of man in the universe which follow. When the question asks whether Bloom thought human life 'infinitely perfectible', the answer mockingly excepts 'the generic conditions' imposed by nature – killing for food, birth, death, menstruation, accidents, sicknesses, madness, epidemics, cataclysms 'which make terror the basis of human mentality', earthquakes, and growth from childhood to decay. In comparison with the infinite eons of the stars, 'the years, threescore and ten, of allotted human life formed a parenthesis of infinitesimal brevity.' Even if there were to exist on the planets or their satellites another quasi-human race, such 'an apogean humanity . . . would probably there as here remain inalterably and inalienably attached to vanities, to vanities of vanities and all that is vanity.' Left alone in the garden, Bloom feels 'the cold of interstellar space'.

Yet, like most things in this chapter, the vision *sub specie aeternitatis* which chills Bloom with its reduction of man's life and values, also contributes to the state of mind, the equanimity, with which he conquers the forces which have threatened him all day. In such a vision, all his wife's suitors (that is to say, all whom he believes to have desired her[108]) are, abstractly viewed, deluded:

> . . . each one who enters imagines himself to be the first to enter whereas he is always the last term of a preceding series even if the first term of a succeeding one, each imagining himself to be first, last, only and alone, whereas he is neither first nor last nor only nor alone in a series originating in and repeated to infinity.   (*U* 692/863)

The adultery, which has distressed him all day, seems, in the wider view, no more than natural, less calamitous than the annihilation of a planet, less reprehensible than a variety of crimes ranging from theft to murder, no

---

[108] I agree with those critics (e.g. *Ellmann–JJ*, 388, *Adams*, 35–43, *Sultan*, 431–3, and David Hayman, 'The Empirical Molly' in *Approaches*, 113–14) who discount the list of Molly's supposed lovers – though not with some of the conclusions they reach. For Bloom, the lovers are all those men whom he has, at one time or another, thought to have desired Molly or to have been desired by her. If he had known of so many other love-affairs, he would hardly have been so distressed by his knowledge of the appointment with Boylan. As Sultan points out, Molly indicates clearly enough that it is her first actual adultery – '. . . anyhow its done now once and for all with all the talk of the world about it people make its only the first time after that its just the ordinary do it and think no more about it . . .' (*U* 700–01/875) – and thinks that the thunder comes to punish her sin. I do not see the force of the arguments that abstinence does not accord with what we know of Molly's sexual appetite (*Adams*, 38), or that her remark 'I never in all my life felt anyone had one the size of that' (*U* 702/877) necessarily implies 'a good deal of experience' (Darcy O'Brien, 'Some Determinants of Molly Bloom', *Approaches*, 144). Adultery for a married woman was not as simple a matter in 1904 as it is now: Molly may have strong sexual appetites, but she does not want to lose her marital status or social respectability, and with a husband 'plottering about the house', and, until recently, a servant and a daughter as well, an adulterous appointment would not have been easy to arrange: 'youve no chances at all in this place' (*U* 718/899). Had opportunities been as numerous and as easy to seize as the list of 'lovers' suggests, she would presumably not have been as sex-starved as she is, '. . . O thanks be to the great God I got somebody to give me what I badly wanted . . .' (*U* 718/899). As for her experience, we are told that she has caressed Mulvey's genitals, that soldiers are always trying to exhibit themselves to her, that she has watched naked young men bathing, that she has been kissed by Bartell D'Arcy and has touched Gardner with her hand 'to keep him from doing worse': she has had all the experience she needed to pass comment on Boylan's equipment without having previously committed adultery in the legal sense of the word. It is the men who have entered Molly's mind (or whom he believes to have entered her mind) that Bloom must drive out – not those who have physically entered her bed.

more abnormal than other forms of adaptation to changed circumstances, and 'more than inevitable, irreparable'. Among other reasons justifying his calm acceptance of his wife's adultery are 'the futility of triumph or protest or vindication: the inanity of extolled virtue: the lethargy of nescient matter: the apathy of the stars.'

For Bloom, in this chapter, any mode of thought or vision leads towards a point of rest and satisfaction. He does not understand Stephen's affirmation of his significance as a rational being proceeding from the known to the unknown, but comfortably borrows its terminology to justify his own role of competent citizen proceeding 'energetically from the unknown to the known through the incertitude of the void.' His hidden fears of a decline from poverty to mendicancy to destitution to the 'nadir of misery: the aged impotent disfranchised ratesupported moribund lunatic pauper' lead him to contemplate escape by leaving home and family and becoming a wanderer, 'Everyman or Noman', to be rewarded with tributes – 'Honour and gifts of strangers, the friends of Everyman. A nymph immortal, beauty, the bride of Noman.' Although for the course of this day Bloom has been both Everyman and the disguised Ulysses, a number of forces render further travelling undesirable, induce inertia:

> The lateness of the hour, rendering procrastinatory: the obscurity of the night, rendering invisible: the uncertainty of thoroughfares, rendering perilous: the necessity for repose, obviating movement: the proximity of an occupied bed, obviating research: the anticipation of warmth (human) tempered with coolness (linen), obviating desire and rendering desirable: the statue of Narcissus, sound without echo, desired desire. (*U* 689/859)

Like Ulysses, Bloom is no wanderer by choice; his movement is always spiritually homeward, and it will take more than unlikely fears or dreams of escape to draw him away. The statue, which with its 'candour, nudity, pose, tranquillity, youth, grace, sex, counsel' has already consoled him after the departure of Stephen, is his household god. Rather than pursue 'a nymph immortal', he will rest satisfied with what he is and what he has and what he dreams, self-contained and self-contented. As Narcissus had no need for the nymph Echo or desire for anyone beyond himself, Bloom's spirit has no need in this mood for an echo outside itself or a desire beyond itself. The time of Bloom's painful voyage through the perils of the day is over; he looks back on it, in his present calm state, as 'a perfect day' with a few minor imperfections – his failures to arrange for the renewal of Keyes's advertisement, to obtain tea from Mr Kernan, to check whether the statues of Greek goddesses had a 'posterior rectal orifice', and to obtain a ticket for Mrs Bandman Palmer's performance of *Leah*. All the other hazards and humiliations are forgotten or seen as of no consequence, and all his conflicting thoughts and feelings converge in a 'final satisfaction':

> Satisfaction at the ubiquity in eastern and western terrestrial hemispheres, in all habitable lands and islands explored or unexplored (the land of the midnight sun, the islands of the blessed, the isles of Greece, the land of promise) of adipose posterior female hemispheres, redolent of milk and honey and of

excretory sanguine and seminal warmth, reminiscent of secular families of curves of amplitude, insusceptible of moods of impression or of contrarieties of expression, expressive of mute immutable mature animality.   (*U* 695/867)

In 'mute immutable mature animality', Bloom finds rest and satisfaction after the struggles of the day – just as the novel itself finds its close in Molly's soliloquy. Even Bloom's dreams before going to bed are not really signs of dissatisfaction with his life, but preparatives for the ultimate satisfaction:

> For what reason did he meditate on schemes so difficult of realization?
> It was one of his axioms that similar meditations or the automatic relation to himself of a narrative concerning himself or tranquil recollection of the past when practised habitually before retiring for the night alleviated fatigue and produced as a result sound repose and renovated vitality.
>
> His justifications?
> As a physicist he had learned that of the 70 years of complete human life at least 2/7ths, viz., 20 years passed in sleep. As a philosopher he knew that at the termination of any allotted life only an infinitesimal part of any person's desires has been realised. As a physiologist he believed in the artificial placation of malignant agencies chiefly operative during somnolence.   (*U* 680–81/848)

Thus, as far as Bloom is concerned, the unifying principle behind the varieties of style and manner is a slow movement towards the point of rest at the end of the chapter. The passages which indiscriminately associate the important and the trivial suggest the gradual subsiding of the purposes and values of the day; the encyclopaedism emphasizes the absorption of individuality into universal human nature and commonplace bourgeois dreams; the scientific particularization of ordinary acts and phenomena presents Bloom's role as the practical citizen and householder; the materialist vision with its inhuman scales of time and space leads him to an acceptance of what is, after all, natural and inevitable, and to satisfaction with the pleasures of simple animality. The lonely, striving, Odyssean figure of the voyager reaches home when it returns to its starting-point, the elementary human attributes which all inherit and which all have in common.

The progress of the relationship between the two men is affected by the same influences but moves to a different conclusion; there is a developing calm and detachment producing, not a stasis, but an inevitable parting. They were brought together by mutual needs which their differences from each other enabled them to satisfy, and, once the needs are satisfied, the differences conduct them on diverging courses. Initially Bloom is concerned to cement the friendship; as he looks for 'common factors of similarity', and while Stephen dissents openly from Bloom, Bloom's dissent is tacit. He recalls similar conversations with friends in the past, and regretfully notes the decline in his relations with others. He is eager to please but, at the same time, aware of 'four separating forces', 'Name, age, race, creed', and subsequent questions and answers concern each of these.

Not only are the 'educational careers' of the two men dissimilar, but their natures are such that had Stephen had Bloom's education he would have become not Bloom but Stoom, while Bloom, with Stephen's education, would have become Blephen. They are of opposed temperaments, 'The scientific. The artistic.' In arts, as well as in sciences, Bloom's flair is for the 'applied', the practical. His rhymed acrostic on his name shows him to be a 'kinetic poet', and the little invented scene, which he describes to Stephen, was designed to sell stationery. Characteristically, Stephen transforms the scene into an epiphany of boredom and apathy, set in the Queen's Hotel, and, equally characteristically, the incurably kinetic Bloom sees in the transformation 'certain possibilities of financial, social, personal and sexual success'.

Up to this point, the differences between the two men are mainly matters of temperament, age and background, brought to Bloom's attention because, besides giving Stephen the food and shelter needed, he wishes to extend and deepen their relationship. The unfortunate reference to the Queen's Hotel, the name of the hotel in which Bloom's father committed suicide, is dismissed by Bloom as 'coincidence', but it is a coincidence which symbolizes the distance between the two, a distance which grows because each man is in movement. A further attempt to discover similarities between Irish and Hebrew, and between the Irish and Jewish peoples leads first to a deeper awareness of difference, and then to further misunderstanding. Bloom chants a Zionist hymn, now the national anthem of Israel, to foreshadow 'the restoration in Chanan David of Zion and the possibility of Irish political autonomy or devolution': Stephen hears 'in a profound ancient male unfamiliar melody the accumulation of the past', while Bloom sees 'in a quick young male familiar form the predestination of a future'. The ancient melody with its promise of a national liberation is associated for Stephen with that nightmare of history from which he has determined to escape, while Bloom perceives that Stephen's future is already pre-determined, not to be shaped by Bloom's quasi-paternal assistance. The following question-and-answer form one of the more obscure parts of the chapter:

> What were Stephen's and Bloom's quasisimultaneous volitional quasi-sensations of concealed identities?
> Visually, Stephen's: The traditional figure of hypostasis, depicted by Johannes Damascenus, Lentulus Romanus and Epiphanius Monachus as leucodermic, sesquipedalian with winedark hair.
> Auditively, Bloom's: The traditional accent of the ecstasy of catastrophe.
> (*U* 650/808)

These 'quasisensations' are complementary to the 'sensations'. While listening to the ancient melody, Stephen associates Bloom with the figure of Christ incarnate, as traditionally described – perhaps because the Hebrew chant reminds him of Bloom's assertion that Christ was a Jew, and his own reply that in the flesh Christ belonged to the Jewish race: *'Christus* or Bloom his name is, or, after all, any other *secundum carnem'*. Bloom, watching a young male form, seems to hear the traditional note of the abandon which precedes disaster. Stephen sees in Bloom a representative of *hypostasis*, the union of God and man, the spirit incarnate; Bloom hears in Stephen a representation of ecstasy or *ekstasis* – the state of being alienated, outside oneself, in particular 'the erratic originality of genius' out of touch with the needs of its bodily substance. Only in the flat terminology of the catechism can these intuited 'quasisensations' be translated into abstract statements of contraries, just as it is only in the quieter mood, after they are at rest and have drunk their cocoa, that the two sense the full extent of the differences between them, differences which can now be apprehended without fear or hostility.

This emotional quiescence is tested further when Bloom, still thinking of the analogies between Jews and Irish, encourages Stephen to sing 'a strange legend on an allied theme'. But the legend is the ballad of *Little Harry Hughes*, which unites the two races only insofar as it tells the story of a Christian boy who twice played his ball into a Jew's garden and was then enticed within and murdered by the Jew's daughter. The responses of the two men to the story are, not unnaturally, very different, though both identify themselves with the 'victim predestined'. Stephen's commentary ignores the racial and religious features of the legend; for him, it symbolizes acceptance of his vocation as artist:

> One of all, the least of all, is the victim predestined. Once by inadvertence, twice by design he challenges his destiny. It comes when he is abandoned and challenges him reluctant and, as an apparition of hope and youth holds him unresisting. It leads him to a strange habitation, to a secret infidel apartment, and there, implacable, immolates him, consenting.   (*U* 653/810)

Twice he has solemnly but vainly declared his intention to devote his life to art – once, as a schoolboy, in response to a chance inspiration on the beach, and once when he left Ireland deliberately to pursue his vocation. Now, in Bloom's kitchen, he feels that his destiny has challenged him; his earlier fervours and defiances have been like a boy breaking windows; now he consents to the total submission of his life to his vocation – '*And now he'll play his ball no more.*'[109] The commentary is itself illustrative of this submission; Stephen knows that Bloom is a Jew, but, in his artistic egoism, never thinks of the possible effect on Bloom of the ballad of little Harry Hughes. For Bloom, concerned as citizen not with what the ballad might symbolize about the artist's destiny, but with 'the accumulation of history' exemplified in it, is reminded of charges of ritual murder, and the superstition, fear, envy, atavism and fanaticism which has made the Jew the

---

[109] William Empson believes improbably that the paragraph means 'that Stephen will consent to the Bloom offer, though he is automatically nasty about it', the offer being of a relationship with Molly ('The Theme of *Ulysses*', *JJM3*, p. 135). Zack Bowen suggests that 'The victim of Stephen's song is both himself, as he exposes himself to Bloom through inadvertence at Bella Cohen's, and through design at the cabman's shelter by consenting to return home with Bloom, and Leopold, who is misled by Stephen, his 'apparition of hope and youth'' ('Libretto for Bloomusalem in Song: The Music of Joyce's *Ulysses*', *New Light*, 163). I find it difficult to see why Stephen's 'destiny' should be equated with Bloom.

'victim predestined' for centuries. Both men see themselves as victims but not as fellow-victims. They will both suffer, but in different ways, for different reasons and at the hands of different forces; Stephen is singled out for suffering, Bloom shares his with his race; Stephen consents to his destiny, Bloom is resigned to his.

What now separates the two men is more fundamental than differences of opinion, of 'name, age, race, creed', of education, or of temperament; they are separated by their essential natures and destinies. Yet this divergence has nothing to do with a loss of mutual sympathy; on the contrary, the friendliness of their relationship increases, and culminates in Bloom's offer of accommodation and Stephen's amicable and grateful refusal. When Stephen leaves the citizen's house to pursue his destiny, he does so to the silent accompaniment of the 113th psalm, '*In exitu Israël de Egypto: domus Jacob de populo barbaro*', led by Moses/Bloom, who will not himself see the Promised Land Stephen seeks. As they stand together in the garden, their reciprocal fellowship and their dissimilarities are fused; they stand 'silent, each contemplating the other in both mirrors of the reciprocal flesh of theirhisnothis fellowfaces'. As, in fellowship, they urinate together, each man's thoughts 'concerning the invisible audible collateral organ of the other' are representative of their fundamental differences: Bloom is occupied with the physical properties of Stephen's organ, and Stephen concerned with speculations as to whether Christ's prepuce deserves 'simple hyperduly' (the highest form of worship which may be paid to what is human, such as the Blessed Virgin) or 'the fourth degree of latria' (the form of worship paid only to God). One, that is, is concentrated on the flesh, and the other on the pervasion of the flesh by the spirit.

It is at this point that both observe a 'celestial sign':

> A star precipitated with great apparent velocity across the firmament from Vega in the Lyre above the zenith beyond the stargroup of the Tress of Berenice towards the zodiacal sign of Leo. (*U* 664/826)

That the Lyre relates to Stephen and Leo to Bloom is obvious, but commentators differ on other points of interpretation – for instance, whether Vega is mentioned because it means 'falling', and whether the Tress of Berenice refers to Stephen's mother, Bloom's wife or both. It is characteristic of Joyce's handling of such symbolic passages that he allows some inexplicit but suggestive hints to fly off from the central image. Here the emphasis seems to be on the relative position of the two constellations Lyra 'above the zenith', seemingly at the greatest distance from the earth, and Leo on the horizon, seemingly closest to the earth, so that the shooting star apparently links two constellations separated as far as possible from each other in the sky – a bright but momentary linking like a spark. Since it starts from the Lyre, the star may suggest the flash of imaginative understanding proceeding from the artist, the brightest star in its constellation, towards the citizen. As for the Coma Berenicis, it seems unnecessary to drag in Berenice's husband or her death at the hands of her son.[110] Tradi-

110 *Sultan*, 398–9.

tionally the constellation's name is an image of the immortalizing of mortal beauty, as at the end of *The Rape of the Lock*. Such giving of immortality to the mortal is precisely Stephen's (and Joyce's) conception of the act of the artist: 'in the spirit of the maker all flesh that passes becomes the word that shall not pass away.' Without wishing to diminish the suggestiveness of the symbolic sign in the heavens, I would argue that what it figures chiefly is the distance between the spirit of the artist and the life of common man, the spark that leaps across that gulf 'towards' the mortal, and the mediating image of the work of art in which the mortal is given immortality. This is the kind of interaction towards which the events of the day have led, and which is now figured in the heavens.

The whole course of the relationship – the increasing friendliness and the diminution of any likelihood of prolonged intercourse – is traced in the catechism. The state of comparative calm which has been attained by the two men's association, yet which makes the necessity of their divergence plain, is reflected in the prevalent unemotional flatness. But, within that prevalent tone, many different stylistic forms – biographical summaries, generalized assertions, advertisements, stage directions, songs and responses to songs, symbols, heavenly signs – all contribute to show the gradual separation of mind even before the physical parting takes place. When Joyce said that the two men become as 'heavenly bodies, wanderers like the stars at which they gaze', he was not thinking of physical wandering (Bloom, at least, has reached home); what the technique conveys is that they become to each other wandering spirits, as far removed from each other as stars or constellations in distant parts of the sky, and each committed to a different course, Bloom's orbital, Stephen's parabolic.

The few places in the chapter where the style becomes poetic or elevated are not really exceptions to the matter-of-fact calm, because they are either comically misplaced or quickly deflated. The most striking example is on the first emergence from the house into the garden:

> What spectacle confronted them when they, first the host, then the guest, emerged silently, doubly dark, from obscurity by a passage from the rere of the house into the penumbra of the garden?
> The heaventree of stars hung with humid nightblue fruit. (*U* 659/819)

The answer is consciously poetic. Reading it, one is lifted out of the drab realities of Bloom's kitchen, as both men, despite their calm, are momentarily lifted up by the beauty of the nightsky. But Bloom's rationality asserts itself as he proceeds to point out the constellations and mention some scraps of scientific information about them, and soon reaches the 'logical conclusion' that 'it was not a heaventree, not a heavengrot, not a heaven-beast, not a heavenman': it was a Utopia, an infinity, 'a mobility of illusory forms', 'a past which possibly had ceased to exist as a present before its future spectators had entered actual present existence.' He is convinced of 'the esthetic value of the spectacle' not by his own experience on entering the garden but because of the many examples of poets fervently addressing the constellations or the moon. Similarly, when he considers the possibility of staying in the garden to watch the dawn break, he recalls, with some poetic feeling showing through the catalogue, the signs of dawn as he had once before witnessed them:

> More active air, a matutinal distant cock, ecclesiastical clocks at various points, avine music, the isolated tread of an early wayfarer, the visible diffusion of the light of an invisible luminous body, the first golden limb of the resurgent sun perceptible low on the horizon. (*U* 666/828)

At once, he takes a deep breath, as though to clear away such poetic mists, and goes indoors. In this chapter, poetry and rhetoric occur only to be dissipated by the matter-of-fact and the rational, save for the melancholy tolling that marks the parting of the two men: 'The sound of the peal of the hour of the night by the chime of the bells in the church of Saint George.'

At last, as Bloom sinks to sleep, even the rational voice of question-and-answer becomes uncertain and befogged. Bloom's posture in bed is described as that of 'the childman weary, the manchild in the womb'; a somnolent echo questions and a tired voice answers:

> Womb? Weary?
> He rests. He has travelled. (*U* 697/870)

The figure falling asleep is both Bloom, the middle-aged husband, weary after the day's business, returned to the marital bed from which he rose that morning, and Bloom, the human essence extended in time from childhood to manhood, weary of the voyage of life, returned as though to the womb of his origin. The questions can now hardly frame a question: 'With?' The answerer rambles:

> Sinbad the Sailor and Tinbad the Tailor and Jinbad the Jailer and Whinbad the Whaler and Ninbad the Nailer and Finbad the Failer and Binbad the Bailer and Pinbad the Pailer and Minbad the Mailer and Hinbad the Hailer and Rinbad the Railer and Dinbad the Kailer and Vinbad the Quailer and Linbad the Yailer and Xinbad the Phthailer. (*U* 697/871)

One commentator, taking the hint that in the 'Eumaeus' chapter the supposed sailor, Murphy, is referred to as 'friend Sinbad', attempts to refer the variations to other men Bloom has met or thought of – George Mesias the Tailor, Alf Bergan the Jailer, Corny Kelleher the Nailer, Simon Dedalus the Failer, Martin Cunningham the Bailer, Lenehan the Hailer, the old Citizen the Railer and one of the friends of Bloom who died of phthisis the Phthailer[111] – but even such ingenuity is stumped by the Whaler, the Kailer, the Quailer and the Yailer. Another commentator says that the whole litany is 'a piece of inspired stupidity' and suggests that 'the more we project conscious intellectual meaning into the process, the less it serves its overt purpose.'[112] Yet if the nonsense is 'inspired', it is presumably pertinent nonsense – otherwise any other string of words would do as well.

[111] *Sultan* 413. [112] *Adams*, 82.

In the first place, it is pertinent because the rational answerer sets off on his usual flat cataloguing and continues until the catalogue becomes more and more meaningless and even the alliteration breaks down. Secondly, as Robert M. Adams discovered, Tinbad and Whinbad were characters in the pantomime *Sinbad the Sailor* about which Bloom has thought earlier in the day;[113] the cropping up of their names, in vague association with Sinbad's, sets the litany in motion. Thirdly, in the weariness of the childman, the list of those who have travelled with Bloom adopts the form of the childish litanies, supposedly exhaustive of human occupations, like 'Tinker, Tailor, Soldier Sailor, Rich man, Poor man, Beggarman, Thief', and echoes such childish cries as 'Jollypoldy, the rixdix doldy'. Sleepiness, fading rational consciousness, a return to childishness, and a cloudy vision of all men of all pursuits involved with Bloom in a voyage through life and now at rest with him – all these cooperate in an answer which, though nonsense, is relevant nonsense. The next question 'When?' is itself hardly intelligible (does it mean when did he rest or when did he travel?), and provokes not an answer but an incoherent response:

> Going to a dark bed there was a square round Sinbad the Sailor roc's auk's egg in the night of the bed of all the auks of the rocs of Darkinbad the Brightdayler. (*U* 698/871)

Again the problem is not what kind of sense does the sentence make, but what kind of nonsense. Sinbad is an Eastern analogue of Ulysses, repeatedly drawn to perilous voyages, usually spending most of his time trying to reach home safely, and engaged in a number of adventures closely resembling those of the Greek – notably the adventure in his third voyage when he and his companions fall into the hands of a maneating giant from whom they escape by blinding him in his sleep. Here, Sinbad seems to be the type of the traveller; he is not simply Bloom, for Bloom is in bed, not going to it, and his bed is not dark but lit by a lamp. Moreover, the occurrence of the phrase 'auk's egg', taken from the library chapter where Stephen thinks of Lyster's bald head as an 'auk's egg, prize of their fray' suggests that the confusions of this sentence are taking place, not in Bloom's mind, but in the mind of the catechizing voice. There are other dubious matters. Several commentators have pointed out that 'a square round' seems to allude to Bloom's fantasy of winning a million pound prize for squaring the circle, but there may also be an allusion to Sinbad's third voyage when in order to defeat a huge serpent, which every night swallows one of his companions whole, Sinbad fastens a wooden rectangular frame round his body and is thus preserved. As for the roc's egg, the Arabian tale refers to two. In the fifth voyage, Sinbad's fellow-travellers find and destroy a roc's egg and eat the young bird inside, with the result that their ship is destroyed by the parent rocs and only Sinbad survives: but this seems analogous to Ulysses' encounter with the Oxen of the Sun and has no apparent relevance to sleep and rest. In the second voyage, however,

[113] *Adams*, 80.

Sinbad, stranded and despairing on an uninhabited island, finds a huge
white object; he is exploring it, when the sun disappears and day turns to
night as a huge roc arrives to settle on its egg; by attaching himself to one
of the bird's toes as it sleeps, Sinbad is flown, the next morning, out of the
island to the Valley of Diamonds. If the sentence seems to begin by referring to Sinbad's going to bed, it shifts in the confused syntax to the roc
going to sleep on its egg 'in the night of the bed of all the auks of the rocs
of Darkinbad the Brightdayler.' The day itself seems to be going to bed,
or, since 'Darkinbad the Brightdayler' follows the same name-plus-
occupation pattern of 'Sinbad the Sailor' and the variations, what is now
darkened in sleep is that whose occupation is the bright-day – the working
consciousness. Thus in the sentence there is a misty blending of several
suggestions – the descent of darkness in the minds of all travellers, the
achieving of some prize or reward after the struggles of the day as though
sleep itself was the reward towards which all men strive, and a final dimming of the cold rational light which has illuminated the chapter. There
are other associated possibilities: perhaps 'egg' occurs because, as we learn
at the beginning of the next chapter, Bloom has just asked his wife to give
him eggs for breakfast in bed; perhaps the egg can be imagined as containing the embryo of the next day's voyage as the parent roc now settles on it
to sleep; perhaps the roc is the bird of night which will carry away the
travellers into the world of dreams, where their fantasies can be realized.
But the passage intentionally prevents any coherent or precise interpretation. The pedantically exact mind which has conducted the catechism now
slips out of focus and into the darkness of sleep; the grammatical relationships, still methodical in appearance, become mere suggestions and hints of
a fading awareness, finally obliterated in the black spot which is the only
response to the last question, 'Where?' The technique, the novel itself,
has fallen to sleep with Bloom.[114]

According to Frank Budgen, 'Ithaca' was Joyce's favourite chapter,[115]
perhaps because of the extraordinary range and variety of effects he had
been able to achieve within the limits of a matter-of-fact, detached manner,
and the realized subsidence of all the tensions and struggles of the novel.[116]
In many ways this was the most difficult chapter to write. The relationship
between Bloom and Stephen has to wax and wane simultaneously; their
friendly interaction becomes reciprocal and fruitful in the very process
which brings it to an inevitable end. Stephen must respond to Bloom's
hospitality and yet, through it, recognize and accept isolation as his destiny.
Bloom's dreams of mutually profitable and prolonged intercourse with
Stephen must develop while he is gradually being forced to perceive their

[114] Joyce told Harriet Weaver that 'Ithaca . . . is in reality the end' (*Letters* I, 172),
and wrote to Robert McAlmon that he found the chapter to be 'of a tranquilising
spectrality' (*Letters* I, 176).
[115] *Budgen*, 264.
[116] Cf. the letter to Claud Sykes, where Joyce refers to his 'struggling with the
acidities of Ithaca – a mathematico-astronomico-physico-mechanico-geometrico-
chemico sublimation of Bloom and Stephen' (*Letters*, I, p. 164).

impossibility, and, in the overwhelming sense of his own insignificance before the vastness of the universe, he must discover that equanimity which destroys in his mind his obsession with Boylan and the other suitors. The chapter must demonstrate that there can be no final solution to problems rooted in the natures of the two men, and, yet, at the same time show them strengthened by their encounter to face these problems and to feel that, having successfully ridden out the storms of this day, they can survive others. The story and structure and techniques of the novel must climax in an anticlimax.

All of these contrasted purposes are fulfilled in a technique which by its coolness suggests the pacification of the emotions. Our attention remains focused on the two men, but they are emotionally distanced. The movements of their lives no longer seem arbitrary, fortuitous or spontaneous; they follow the courses which they are destined to pursue by their natures, and become like 'heavenly bodies' whose wanderings are reduced to the stability and stillness of a pattern.

'Penelope'

The mounting technical complexity, which rises to a crest in 'Circe' and subsides in 'Eumaeus' and 'Ithaca', finally disappears in the long smooth flow of 'Penelope' where not even such familiar devices of written language as punctuation break the surface. The technique now is an apparent abnegation of technique. Although it is the only chapter in which nothing is spoken (even 'Proteus' has the cocklepicker's cry to his dog), the manner is closest of all to ordinary, rambling speech, and hence closer than any other of the interior monologues to the traditional form of soliloquy – all the more so because the circumstances ensure the least possible interruption of the train of thought by external experience. It is still a verbal representation of consciousness rather than a tape recording of an inner voice – this is evident even in such details as the verbalizing of a train's whistle, 'frseeeeeeeefronnnng' or of a dog's bark, 'rrrsssst awokwokawok' – but the distinction is blurred: we have hardly heard Molly speaking, so cannot distinguish her interior monologue from her speech, as we can with Bloom and Stephen; there are no linguistic forms which might not have been plausibly used by Molly speaking aloud to herself; and, besides her Irishisms and the Spanish words picked up in Gibraltar, her monologue is full of turns of speech, idiosyncratic phrases, vulgarisms, malapropisms, sentimental, humorous and abusive expressions, and characteristic rhythms proper to Molly's nature. The chapter is restricted not only to the contents of Molly's mind but also to her resources of expression.

This is the most adventurous of all the novel's techniques – to put the responsibility for bringing the complex work to a satisfying close on a character of whom the reader has had only two brief glimpses and whose intelligence and command of language are seemingly so limited. She has, of course, been a dominant presence in the mind of Bloom all day, her influence all the more impressive because of her physical absence from the action. Joyce, having in this way built up a formidable image of Molly's force and fascination, now takes the risky step of putting her before the reader in undress, mental and linguistic as well as physical. She has now to display the charms which have captivated Bloom to a reader who, inasmuch as he has learnt to appreciate the husband, is likely to be unsympathetic towards the woman who has enslaved and cuckolded him, and the successful conclusion of the novel will depend largely on her power to project herself as a person of sufficient energy and richness of personality, and liveliness of mind and speech, to play the role of the Penelope who is the goal of Bloom's odyssey.

Joyce was well aware of the importance of this last chapter:

> Penelope is the clou of the book. The first sentence contains 2500 words. There are eight sentences in the episode. It begins and ends with the female word Yes. It turns like the huge earthball slowly surely and evenly round and round spinning. Its four cardinal points being the female breasts, arse, womb and cunt expressed by the words because, bottom (in all senses, bottom button, bottom of the glass, bottom of the sea, bottom of his heart) woman, yes. Though probably more obscene than any preceding episode it seems to me to be perfectly sane full amoral fertilisable untrustworthy engaging shrewd limited prudent indifferent Weib. Ich bin das Fleisch das stets bejaht.[117]

While Bloom and Stephen have been traversing Dublin, Molly has spent most of the day in bed; if they have followed their courses like 'heavenly bodies', she, like the earth, has revolved on her axis, and clearly Joyce hoped to suggest this self-centred movement in the manner of the chapter. But the details, like those in the letter about 'Oxen of the Sun', are puzzling. It is true that the chapter begins and ends with 'Yes' and that there are eight 'sentences', and the four listed words do occur very frequently – on a rough count, because 44 times, bottom 20 times, woman 72 times and yes 88 times. But although the letter seems to hint at some designed recurrence of these words, I am unable to see any such pattern, apart from a much greater frequency of appearance in the first and last sentences, which, between them, account for half of the occurrences.

One critic has asserted that Joyce's reference to four cardinal points is one of those authorial statements which 'deserve to be disregarded as at best unimportant': 'There is no rendering of form and theme through four "cardinal points", each "expressed" by its own word.'[118] Yet another critic, after a close study of the notesheets, declares, 'There is no more apt description of the technique of Penelope than the adjective coined by Joyce on one of the notesheets: "gynomorphic". The form of the episode is shaped by the physical characteristics of the female sex.'[119] The matter is further confused by Stuart Gilbert who discovered or was given a different

---

[117] Letters, I, p. 170.
[118] Sultan, 416.
[119] Walton A. Litz, 'Joyce's Notes for the Last Episodes of Ulysses', Modern Fiction Studies IV (1968), 16.

set of words – 'woman', 'bottom', 'he' and 'man'[120] – which he calls the 'wobbling-points' on which the chapter turns. He says that 'after each of these there is a divagation in [Molly's] thoughts, which, as a general rule, revolve about herself.' He then suggests a detailed analogy between the conduct of the chapter and the ten distinct movements of the earth – revolution, lunar precession, solar precession, solar nutation, lunar nutation, planetary precession, secular motions, annual motions, diurnal motions and variation of latitude. Unfortunately he does not demonstrate the interpretation of these motions in the monologues, beyond a few references to lunar influence tilting Molly's thoughts towards a woman ('symbol of lunar precession'), or to the word 'bottom' marking a deviation towards 'the ruling planet of the moment, her lover Boylan'.[121]

What can one make of Gilbert's account? His list of words omits not only *because*, but *yes*, the most frequently recurring word of Budgen's list and one of the characteristic words of the chapter, and is not associated, as Budgen's is, with the four main female physical characteristics. It is possible that the list given in the letter was merely part of Joyce's original scheme and was revised, but Gilbert's list has the appearance of the first list partially remembered. Did Joyce make a mistake in recalling for Gilbert his four key-words, or did Gilbert make a mistake in recalling what Joyce had told him? As for the ten distinct earth-movements, the analysis seems an attempt by the critic to refine on the image of the spinning earth-ball, and, as far as I can see, bears no relationship to the conduct of the monologue.

We are left with the obscurities of Joyce's letter. How can the word 'because', however frequently it occurs, express breasts? Why should nearly half its appearances occur in the first sentence, while in the remaining sentences its frequency is quite unremarkable, except for two where it does not occur at all?[122] The 20 appearances of 'bottom', too, are not very striking in the course of reading the long chapter, although statistically the frequency is extraordinary since the word occurs only 6 times in the whole of the rest of the book. The evidence of the initial and closing 'yes', of the frequency of the listed words (especially in the first and last sentences as though Joyce were trying to establish them in the reader's unconscious) and of the division into eight sentences confirms that Joyce was not fooling in his letter to Budgen, but it is difficult to perceive what he had in mind and how he expected his scheme to function.

---

[120] Further confusion is added by Herbert Gorman, also the recipient of inside information, who says 'there are four key words that serve, so to speak, as foci about which circle the thoughts of the reclining woman, "he", "bottom", "women" and, the last (an affirmation of life), "yes"' (*Gorman*, p. 278). A Walton Litz (*James Joyce*, Twayne Publishers, N.Y.: 1966: p. 84), without explanation, gives yet another list of words which 'provide the pivots for the episode: these are "he", "bottom", "because" and "Yes".' Thus, in the four lists, the only word included in all is the one which occurs least often in the chapter – "bottom". As the Budgen list is in Joyce's own letter, it seems the safest choice.

[121] *Gilbert*, 387–8.

[122] A note in the notesheets, 'Incipit – Because', suggests that Joyce may have originally intended to start the chapter with this word (*Notesheets*, Penelope 4:5, p. 502).

My guess is (and it is no more than a guess) that the four key-words were not intended as equivalents for the distinguishing physical characteristics of women, but were related to what Joyce took to be the four dominant characteristics of the female mind, analogous to the four anatomical differentiations. Thus, if the female mind characteristically depends not on reason but on intuition, located figuratively in the breast rather than the head, then this feminine intuition may be regarded as the mental equivalent of the physical breasts and may be linguistically represented by the use of the word 'because' to introduce a non-logical hunch rather than a rational cause.[123] The first page of Molly's soliloquy has three such uses:

> Yes because he never did a thing like that before as ask to get his breakfast in bed with a couple of eggs . . .
> . . . I suppose she was pious because no man would look at her twice . . .
> . . . shes as much a nun as Im not yes because theyre so weak and puling when theyre sick . . . (U 698/871–2)

There is no logic about any of these observations; Molly depends on intuition instead of reasoning, and perhaps it was this feminine characteristic which Joyce hoped to suggest by the repeated irrational use of 'because'. The female quality symbolized or expressed by 'bottom' has been sufficiently identified in 'Ithaca' in the passage describing Bloom's satisfaction at the proximity of Molly's 'adipose posterior female hemispheres, redolent of milk and honey and of excretory sanguine and seminal warmth, reminiscent of secular families of curves of amplitude, insusceptible of moods of impression or of contrarieties of expression, expressive of mute immutable mature animality' (U 695/867). That this passage was related to 'Penelope' in Joyce's mind is confirmed by Molly's reference to 'a womans bottom . . . where we havent 1 atom of any kind of expression in us all of us the same', and by Joyce's letter to Sykes where he speaks of preparing for 'the final amplitudinously curvilinear episode Penelope'.[124] Presumably 'woman' (related to the physical womb) expressed for Joyce, amongst other things, the maternal instinct, the *Amor matris* which distresses Stephen, the motherliness celebrated in 'Oxen of the Sun', and, as Molly says, unknown to men: 'they dont know what it is to be a woman and a mother.' The significance of 'the female word *Yes*' is pointed to by the German sentence '*Ich bin das Fleisch das stets bejaht*' – there are no English verbs which retain the forms of 'Yes' and 'No' as do the German *bejaht* and *verneint*. Joyce seems to identify the feminine nature with acceptance, submissiveness, even passivity: on the sexual level (hence the equivalence to 'cunt') a, constant, but not acute concupiscence resident in a bodily and mental female organism, passive but not obtuse' (U 693/864); on the spiritual level the instinct about which the priest had reassured Gerty MacDowell, 'because that was only the voice of nature and we were all subject to nature's laws, he said, in this life and that that was no sin because that

---

[123] There may be some slight support for this guess in the note, 'L.B. She clasped him to her bosoms (intellects)' (*Notesheets*, Cyclops 5:7, p. 100).
[124] *Letters* I, 164.

came from the nature of woman instituted by God, he said, and that Our Blessed Lady herself said to the archangel Gabriel be it done unto me according to Thy Word' (*U* 342/466–7).

So far I have merely been speculating as to what Joyce might have had in mind when writing the letter to Budgen – a female mental anatomy where feminine intuition, 'mature animality', maternal feelings and readiness to accept whatever or whoever comes along correspond to the four distinguishing features of the female physical anatomy. The question remains whether such a scheme is traceable in the finished chapter, and more particularly whether the key-words are, in any way, operative. Although it is not demonstrable, I find it easy to believe that the recurring 'yeses' help to induce an apprehension of some general accepting, assenting quality in Molly's nature, especially manifested in her sexual responses. Similarly, though even less certainly, the repeated non-logical use of 'because' may help to suggest Molly's dependence on intuition rather than reason, especially when the word draws attention to itself by its frequency:

> ... her face a mass of wrinkles with all her religion domineering because she never could get over the Atlantic fleet coming in half the ships of the world and the Union Jack flying with all her carabineros because 4 drunken English sailors took all the rock from them and because I didnt run into mass often enough in Santa Maria to please her. . . .   (*U* 718–19/900)

I have already indicated some of the animality associated with 'bottom' by Molly's unconscious echo of the passage in 'Ithaca', and there are other animal associations, though it is an aspect of her nature (and of her body) of which Molly tends not to approve: she may have animal instincts but she is, and likes to picture herself as, a romantic. She disapproves of her husband's kissing her bottom, and resents Boylan's having slapped her there:

> ... I didnt like his slapping me behind going away so familiarly in the hall though I laughed Im not a horse or an ass am I. . . .   (*U* 701/876)

> no thats no way for him has he no manners nor no refinement nor no nothing in his nature slapping us behind like that on my bottom because I didn't call him Hugh the ignoramus that doesnt know poetry from a cabbage thats what you get for not keeping them in their proper place . . . of course hes right enough in his way to pass the time as a joke sure you might as well be in bed with what with a lion God Im sure hed have something better to say for himself an old Lion would O well I suppose its because they were so plump and tempting in my short petticoat he couldnt resist. . . .   (*U* 735–6/923–4)

Both passages suggest something animal about attention to the bottom, and it seems possible that, in writing the chapter, Joyce allowed 'behind' sometimes to substitute for 'bottom'. The double key-word would then occur about as frequently as 'because', and provide further links to animality:

> ... better for him put it into me from behind the way Mrs Mastiansky told me her husband made her like the dogs do it. . . .   (*U* 709/887)

... we came together when I was watching the two dogs up in her behind in the middle of the naked street. .... (*U* 737/926)

The ideas associated with the word 'woman' are more complex. The maternal instinct, for Joyce, is something deeper and more far-reaching than motherliness; it involves the whole conception of the woman as a gentle, suffering, healing creature, the source of creativity and beauty, yet not sufficiently appreciated by ungrateful and destructive man. Even the function of motherhood, though a source of pride, can also be resented as an imposition:

... nice invention they made for women for him to get all the pleasure but if someone gave them a touch of it themselves theyd know what I went through with Milly nobody would believe cutting her teeth too ... (*U* 702/877)

Menstruation is another aspect of woman's maternal role that Molly resents as unfair:

... whoever suggested that business for women what between clothes and cooking and children. .... (*U* 729/914)

All the other maternal qualities are similarly reason for as much resentment as pride:

... they want a woman to get well if his nose bleeds youd think it was O tragic ... but if it was a thing I was sick then wed see what attention only of course the woman hides it not to give all the trouble they do. .... (*U* 698–9/ 872)

In their love-making men often seem like greedy babies,

... an hour he was at them Im sure by the clock like some kind of a big infant I had at me they want everything in their mouth all the pleasure those men get out of a woman. .... (*U* 714/893);

and, as rulers of the earth, they are like wild and irresponsible children:

... I dont care what anybody says itd be much better for the world to be governed by the women in it you wouldnt see women going and killing one another and slaughtering when do you ever see women rolling around drunk like they do or gambling every penny they have and losing it on horses yes because a woman whatever she does she knows where to stop. .... (*U* 737/ 926)

As with the other central mother-figure in the book, Mrs Dedalus, Molly's maternal feelings contain as much reproach as affection. Women, she thinks, besides being more sensible and prudent than men, are also more sensitive ('a woman is so sensitive about every thing') and more beautiful ('the woman is beauty of course thats admitted'), but they are the oppressed and underprivileged sex, burdened by nature and deprived in their social and personal relationships. Molly is no more consistent about this than about any other subject – in one place she will ridicule men's physical appearance and in another enthuse about the bodies of the young bathers 'standing up in the sun naked like a God or something' – but, in general, she asserts the physical and moral superiority of women, and, even in her most outspoken attack on the behaviour of her own sex, explains it as due to all that women have to put up with:

> ... I hate that in women no wonder they treat us the way they do we are a dreadful lot of bitches I suppose its all the troubles we have makes us so snappy Im not like that. . . .   (*U* 738/927)

These maternal qualities, always associated with the word 'woman' and corresponding to the physical womb, are not those of benign and uncomplaining motherliness, but rather a confused medley of feelings and attitudes stemming from the woman's childbearing role – womanliness.

This explanation of the scheme obscurely referred to in the letter to Budgen is tentative, and does little to justify the claim that the form of the chapter is 'gynomorphic', but, on the other hand, it may suggest that Joyce's hints cannot be dismissed 'as at best unimportant'. The four mental characteristics I have described were regarded by Joyce as specifically feminine, and demonstrably exert powerful influences on the slow rotation of Molly's mind. Moreover, my impression is that the repeated key-words do, in various degrees, affect the reader's unconscious apprehension of Molly's nature, and I doubt whether Joyce would have expected more from their use. Explicit statements about techniques inevitably make them seem more rigid and mechanical than they are in practice. Some scheme of the 'cardinal points' of the female consciousness would have helped Joyce to control the interior monologue without too severely restricting its tendency to digress, and the repeated key-words would have served as a verbal representation of the persistence of these dominant and shaping characteristics as Molly's soliloquy proceeded on its apparently fortuitous course.

There are, of course, other shaping devices in the monologue – notably, what Joyce calls its 'eight sentences'. These are so elaborated with digressions and so linked by cross-reference, that their separate characteristics are not at once obvious. Yet each has its own tenuous but more or less coherent and developing area of concern, perhaps most easily illustrated from the *first sentence*, where Molly's surprise at Bloom's request for breakfast in bed gives rise to guessing about the causes of his behaviour, and then to a reassuring conviction that she is still in control:

> Yes because he never did a thing like that before as ask to get his breakfast in bed with a couple of eggs . . . yes he came somewhere Im sure by his appetite anyway love its not or hed be off his feed thinking of her so either it was one of those night women . . . or else if its not that its some little bitch or other he got in with somewhere or picked up on the sly . . . because all men get a bit like that at his age . . . not that I care two straws who he does it with or knew before that way though Id like to find out . . . 1 woman is not enough for them . . . yes because he couldnt possibly do without it that long so he must do it somewhere . . . theyre lost for a woman of course . . . I suppose it was meeting Josie Powell and the funeral and thinking about me and Boylan set him off . . . I know they were spooning a bit when I came on the scene . . . I could quite easily get him to make it up any time I know how Id even

supposing he got in with her again . . . I know plenty of ways . . . 1 kiss then would send them all spinning . . . Id rather die 20 times over than marry another of their sex of course hed never find another woman like me to put up with him the way I do know me come sleep with me yes and he knows that too at the bottom of his heart. . . . (U698–704/871–80)

The isolation of this strand in the first long sentence emphasizes the complexity of Molly's feelings: she has plainly been discomfited by her husband's unexpected request, and, despite the declaration that she doesn't care what he is up to, her anger against Mary the maid and other possible rivals, and her need to reassure herself that she can always get Bloom back, show that she is more concerned than she is prepared to admit, even to herself.

In the *second sentence*, concern about her husband is replaced by concern about the impression she has made on Boylan, a development of the earlier passing thought, 'I wonder was he satisfied with me.' She needs to please, and she desires to please Boylan not from love but, primarily, in the hope that he will reward her with the gifts her husband fails to supply:

. . . well he could buy me a nice present up in Belfast after what I gave . . . he has plenty of money and hes not a marrying man so somebody better get it out of him if I could find out whether he likes me. . . . (U 709/886–7)

Molly's nature is liberal and extravagant; she is irritated by her husband's carefulness with money, which, she feels, lowers her in the eyes of others. The nature of Boylan's appeal is clear ('hes certainly welloff'), as is the essence of Bloom's inadequacy as a provider:

. . . he ought to chuck that Freeman with the paltry few shillings he knocks out of it and go into an office or something where hed get regular pay . . . of course he prefers plottering about the house so you cant stir with him any side . . . or pretending to be mooching about for advertisements when he could have been in Mr Cuffes still only for what he did then sending me to try and patch it up I could have got him promoted there to be the manager . . . (U 712/890–91)

Her conviction that Bloom could have been manager derives from her having noticed Mr Cuffe looking very hard at her chest: her sexual charms are Molly's only way of getting more money than Bloom provides. Again the shaping of the sentence is a means by which Joyce reveals something about Molly's motivation underlying the elaborations and particularities of her monologue.

The memory of Mr Cuffe's stare draws her attention to her breasts, and the motif of the *third sentence* is the thought of Boylan's prolonged and passionate attentions to them, culminating in her repeated orgasms. Yet, even here, her feelings about the man who has just been her lover are complicated: admiring her breasts, she thinks that 'theyre supposed to represent beauty':

. . . are they so beautiful of course compared with what a man looks like with his two bags full and his other thing hanging down out of him or sticking up at you like a hatrack no wonder they hide it with a cabbageleaf . . . (U 713/892)

Despite her own sexual excitement, she seems more impressed by 'all the pleasure those men get out of a woman', and her desire is certainly not directed specifically to Boylan: 'I wished he was here or somebody to let myself go with.' His coarseness seems at once to stimulate and repel her – 'you want to feel your way with a man theyre not all like him thank God some of them want you to be so nice about it I noticed the contrast he does it and doesnt talk'. She can't wait until Monday when Boylan will return, yet thinks of him as 'the savage brute'.

Up to this point, we have been shown little of what lies behind Molly's acceptance of Boylan, apart from his wealth and her impersonal lust. The *fourth sentence* goes deeper into her nature, suggesting her boredom with the monotony of her life, her fear of growing old, her need for a lover to occupy her mind. The heat becomes an image of a stifling existence, whether in Gibraltar or Dublin. She recalls how 'stifling it was today' and Bloom's litter 'making the place hotter than it is', and she remembers the greater heat in Gibraltar. The memory of her Gibraltar friends reminds her of the passage of time:

> ... what became of them ever I suppose theyre dead long ago the 2 of them its like all through a mist makes you feel so old. . . . (*U* 715/895)

In Gibraltar, too, after the Stanhopes had left, she had been bored to desperation, and her situation now is much the same, 'with the hands hanging off me looking out of the window.' The young men whose interest she would have welcomed were too stupid to notice, and her days are dreary:

> ... the coalmans bell that noisy bugger trying to swindle me with the wrong bill he took out of his hat what a pair of paws and pots and pans and kettles to mend any broken bottles for a poor man today and no visitors or post ever except his cheques or some advertisement. . . . (*U* 717/898)

She hopes for a longer letter from Boylan, 'if its a thing he really likes me', and congratulates herself that he offers some excitement in the monotony:

> ... O thanks be to the great God I got somebody to give me what I badly wanted to put some heart up into me youve no chances at all in this place like you used long ago. . . . (*U* 718/899)

She needs to be told that she is loved (and Boylan's letter was a disappointment in this respect), even if it is not true:

> ... silly women believe love is sighing I am dying still if he wrote it I suppose thered be some truth in it true or no it fills up your whole day and life always something to think about every moment and see it all around you like a new world ... my goodness theres nothing else its all very fine for them but as for being a woman as soon as youre old they might as well throw you out in the bottom of the ashpit. (*U* 718/899–900)

This sentence puts Molly in a more sympathetic light. She is a vital and lively woman, who is, not unnaturally, bored, and like Emma Bovary, her need is for some romantic relationship to fill her mind and her days. Plainly her husband is not suitable for the purpose, and it is her misfortune to have found a lover who is coarse rather than romantic and cannot even write a decent love-letter.

This brings to mind her first love-letter, from Mulvey; and the brief encounter which followed provides most of the subject-matter of the *fifth sentence*. This was Molly's first affair – for her it is romance – and she looks back to it with tenderness, recalling her girlish excitement and impatience. Everything was romantic – a first kiss, spring, a meeting in 'a wild place', the sea, the sky, his blushes: 'but it was too short'; he promised to return, she thought of him 'for weeks and weeks', and even now it seems like yesterday; she sings to herself the opening words of *Love's Old Sweet Song*: 'once in the dear deaead days beyond recall.' But this is only half the remembered story: Molly doesn't merely sentimentalize over girlhood; there was innocence, and romance, and naivety, and love of fun, but they coexisted with instinctive, developing and experimental sexuality, and the blend of simplicity and knowingness is exactly rendered. It is surprising and pathetic to recognize that this romance, so vivid in Molly's mind that it seems 'just like yesterday', has left her without certain memory of her lover's Christian name, his naval rank or even his appearance. But the emotions were real enough at the time and remain real to Molly:[125] the mixture of sentiment and sexuality survived even the parting, when Molly, 'for weeks and weeks', kept beneath her pillow the handkerchief in which she had caught her lover's semen 'for the smell of him'. There is certainly not in Molly's mind (nor, I think, in Joyce's) any intention to mock the romance of the girl's affair by recognizing her budding sexuality; but it is equally certain that the latter part of this fifth sentence dwells on the incongruity between Molly's image of herself as a great lover and her commonplace nature. The memory of Mulvey is sentimentally symbolized by *Love's Old Sweet Song*, at first with sadness, then with scorn for other female singers whom Molly regards as her rivals but who, she feels, lack the experience to sing that song as it should be sung:

> ... theyd die down dead off their feet if ever they got a chance of walking down the Alameda on an officers arm like me on the bandnight my eyes flash my bust that they havent passion God help their poor head I knew more about men and life when I was 15 than theyll all know at 50 they dont know how to sing a song like that ... let them get a husband first thats fit to be looked at and a daughter like mine or see if they can excite a swell with money that can pick and choose whoever he wants like Boylan to do it 4 or 5 times locked in each others arms or the voice either I could have been a prima donna only I married him comes looooves old deep down chin back not too much make it double ... (*U* 722/905)

In her eagerness to emphasize her superior qualifications to sing *Love's Old Sweet Song*, Molly speaks well of her husband's appearance, while Boylan

---

[125] It was presumably with reference to Molly's affair with Mulvey that Joyce wrote in his notesheets, '1st passion loves lover after loves love' (*Notesheets*, Penelope, 1:30, p. 491).

is distinguished only by being a swell and having money; but the range of feminine experience is complete – virgin, wife, mother and whore. Now her romantic superiority has to be sustained by display ('Ill change that lace on my black dress to show off my bubs and Ill yes by God Ill get that big fan mended make them burst with envy'), while her inner rendering of *Love's Old Sweet Song*, like her husband's patriotic recall of the last words of Robert Emmet, is concluded with a release of wind:

> ... I feel some wind in me better go easy not wake him ... I wish hed sleep in some bed by himself with his cold feet on me give us room even to let a fart God or do the least thing better yes hold them like that a bit on my side piano quietly sweeeee theres that train far away pianissimo eeeeeeee one more song. (*U* 722–3/906)

Molly has returned from her dream of romance to the reality of her body and a shared bed.

Despite the relief of having given vent to her wind and her romantic memories, Molly suddenly becomes uneasy as, in the *sixth sentence*, her mind returns to more immediate things. Was there anything wrong with the pork-chop she has eaten? Is the night-lamp smoking? She has always been nervous about the gas being left on all night: 'why am I so damned nervous about that though I like it in the winter its more company.' Whatever the reason, she thinks 'Goodbye to my sleep for this night anyhow.' Her unsettled state derives chiefly from her husband's late arrival home (which she exaggerates) and his asking for breakfast in bed (which she also exaggerates):

> ... I hope hes not going to get in with those medicals leading him astray to imagine hes young again coming in at 4 in the morning it must be if not more ... then he starts giving us his orders for eggs and tea Findon haddy and hot buttered toast I suppose well have him sitting up like the king of the country ...   (*U* 723/906–7)

Until now, Molly's objections to Bloom's lateness and his 'orders' have seemed to be resentment of the implied challenge to her domination. But she also enjoys his familiar presence ('I love to hear him falling up the stairs of a morning with the cups rattling on the tray'), and feels insecure by herself:

> ... besides I dont like being alone in this big barracks of a place at night I suppose Ill have to put up with it ...   (*U* 725/908)

She will have to put up with it because she knows that she can hardly continue her affair with Boylan and at the same time insist on Bloom being at home with her, and the main content of this sentence is the series of dilemmas in which she is involved by her affair. She remembers Bloom's promises before marriage and complains of their non-fulfilment:

> ... whatever I liked he was going to do immediately if not sooner will you be my man will you carry my can he ought to get a leather medal with a putty rim for all the plans he invents then leaving us here all day you never know what old beggar at the door for a crust with his long story might be a tramp

and put his foot in the way to prevent me shutting it like that picture of that hardened criminal he was called in Lloyds Weekly News. . . . (*U* 725/909)

It does not seem to occur to Molly that if Bloom had not left her all day the session with Boylan would not have been possible, but her fear of being alone is real enough:

> . . . I couldnt rest easy till I bolted all the doors and windows to make sure but its worse again being locked up like in a prison or a madhouse. . . . (*U* 725/909)

That figuratively expresses her dilemma – she wants the security of her home and husband but hates the consequent restriction of her freedom. Milly is a similar problem: she may not have been much help in the house, was beginning to flirt with the boys, critical of her mother, and sometimes impudent, but she was company, and Molly is in two minds about her absence from home. Again, the basic problem is Boylan. Molly recognizes how difficult it would have been to carry on her affair with Milly about the place, yet without her feels unsafe. She would like to blame Bloom – 'its his fault of course having the two of us slaving here instead of getting in a woman long ago am I ever going to have a proper servant again' – but perceives that a servant would create new problems – 'of course then shed see him coming Id have to let her know or shed revenge it arent they a nuisance.' This sentence is more than usually full of Molly's self-contradictions, and this time they are not casual inconsistencies but express real dilemmas:

> . . . every day I get up theres some new thing on sweet God sweet God well when Im stretched out dead in my grave I suppose Ill have some peace . . . (*U* 728/913)

When Molly is in this mood of weary self-pity, her menstruation begins, the last straw:

> . . . wait O Jesus wait yes that thing has come on me yes now wouldnt that afflict you. . . . (*U* 728/913)

There is no doubt in Molly's mind that Boylan's 'poking and rooting and ploughing' are responsible for the early onset of the period, and it is Boylan's Monday visit which is threatened. Although it seems to her almost evidence against Boylan's virility ('anyhow he didnt make me pregnant as big as he is'), Molly goes on to think about his love-making, but the general cast of the sentence has been about the problems and difficulties of being a woman, and the complications added by the affair with Boylan. The memory of Mulvey has already slightly diminished the glamour of her new and coarser lover, and now she has begun to perceive that her involvement, though it may bring some needed excitement into her life, will have to be paid for in stress, in loneliness, and in some loss of her marital authority. She is not yet ready to turn away from Boylan, but, from the middle-point of her nocturnal soliloquy, the curve of his attraction for her is beginning to bend downwards.

Correspondingly, though not obviously, Molly's attitude towards her husband begins to change character in the *seventh sentence*. The early onset of menstruation makes her wonder whether there may be something wrong with her 'insides', and this recalls an occasion, before her marriage, when she had had to visit a doctor because of a vaginal discharge – caused, she believes, by the frequent masturbation induced by Bloom's 'mad crazy letters', extolling her 'glorious Body' and all its products: 'he had me always at myself 4 or 5 times a day sometimes.' This is in complete contrast to Boylan's disappointing letter and the first clear reference to the sexual attraction that Bloom once had for Molly, love at first sight:

> ... it was he excited me I dont know how the first night ever we met when I was living in Rehoboth terrace we stood staring at one another for about 10 minutes as if we met somewhere. ... (*U* 730/916)

She remembers, too, being amused by his remarks and impressed by his political talk. She laughed then and continues to laugh at his peculiarities, in particular his sleeping upside-down in bed with his feet near her face, but, looking at his calm sleep, sees it as further evidence that he has been sexually satisfied:

> ... hes sleeping hard had a good time somewhere still she must have given him great value for his money of course he has to pay for it from her. ... (*U* 731/917)

In this thought there are three suggestions which will be developed later: first, a dislike of the idea of Bloom spending his money on other women; second, the unconscious implication that, if Bloom's deep sleep is a sign of satisfaction, her own sleeplessness may indicate something not wholly satisfying in her sexual encounter with Boylan; and, third, a curious jealousy of her husband, which develops to the point where her own adultery is brushed aside as unimportant, while he seems to be the one who has been having 'a good time' and who needs to be watched and made to toe the line. She is still bothered by their lack of social and financial stability ('God here we are as bad as ever after 16 years'), their constant shifting from house to house, and Bloom's inability to keep a job, but she is more immediately troubled by the lateness of his arrival home and, for the first time, decides, as any injured wife might, to take corrective action: 'Ill knock him off that little habit tomorrow.' Forgetting or dismissing her own unfaithfulness, she plans to seek evidence of his:

> ... first Ill look at his shirt to see or Ill see if he has that French letter still in his pocketbook I suppose he thinks I dont know deceitful men all their 20 pockets arent enough for their lies then why should we tell them even if its the truth they dont believe you. ... (*U* 732/918)

Even in her first sentence Molly has betrayed more concern about her husband's activities than she can admit to; but now the concern is evident. The more she thinks of him as the deceiver and herself as the deceived, the more important and even desirable he becomes in her mind. His request for breakfast in bed only adds to the picture of the wronged wife and the tyrannical husband: 'then tea and toast for him buttered on both sides and newlaid eggs I suppose I'm nothing any more.' She recalls an occasion when she had at first resisted and then submitted to her husband's sexual desires, but even this memory increases her image of herself as a victim ('he does it all wrong too thinking only of his own pleasure') and leads her back to speculations about Bloom's new woman: 'yes its some little bitch hes got in with ... and thats the way his money goes.' Suddenly she thinks of Bloom's Dublin companions and, in doing so, recognizes his comparative merits as a husband and a father:

> ... theyre a nice lot all of them well theyre not going to get my husband again into their clutches if I can help it making fun of him then behind his back I know well when he goes on with his idiotics because he has sense enough not to squander every penny piece he earns down their gullets and looks after his wife and family goodfornothings.... (*U* 733/920)

Here the change of attitude is marked: Bloom becomes 'my husband', superior to other Dublin husbands, and Molly is now occupied with thoughts, not of how to maintain her affair with Boylan, but of how to keep her husband out of bad company. What next occurs to her results in a further supplanting of Boylan in her mind. Thoughts of Bloom's drinking companions lead naturally to Simon Dedalus ('always turning up half screwed singing the second verse first') and then to Stephen whom her husband has brought home with him and to whom he has shown her picture. Molly may well wonder what her husband is 'driving at': besides showing Stephen her photograph, Bloom has praised her talents as a singer and her 'opulent curves', while, in telling his wife of his day's adventures, 'the salient point of his narration' has been 'Stephen Dedalus, professor and author'. In fact, Bloom has conceived the extraordinary idea of using Stephen as a means of dispelling Boylan's influence; the two advantages for Molly which he had hoped might result from Stephen's residence in the house were 'disintegration of obsession, acquisition of correct Italian pronunciation' (*U* 656/815). As Molly was right about her husband when she had earlier thought of 'the way he plots and plans everything out', so Bloom is proved right in foreseeing how Stephen's youth, intelligence and poetry would appeal to Molly. She soon persuades herself that it was Stephen, not Boylan, whose coming the cards had foretold, and a few calculations re-assure her about the difference in age ('Im not too old for him if hes 23 or 24'). But because Molly is a romantic rather than a sensualist, she is most fascinated by the idea of being the muse and mistress of a poet. 'Besides hes young': whereas thoughts of Boylan had earlier led to a ridiculing description of man's naked body, thoughts of Stephen's youth recall the memory of the fine bodies of the young men she had seen bathing: 'why arent all men like that thered be some consolation for a woman.' Before, she had thought 'the woman is beauty of course'; now, she thinks of the statue of the naked Narcissus – 'theres real beauty and poetry for you.' The sentence concludes with her vision of a distinguished future:

... Ill read and study all I can find or learn a bit off by heart if I knew who he likes so he wont think me stupid if he thinks all women are the same and I can teach him the other part Ill make him feel all over him till he half faints under me then hell write about me lover and mistress publicly too with our 2 photographs in all the papers when he becomes famous O but then what am I going to do about him though ... (*U* 735/923)

The beginning of the next sentence makes it clear that the fly in the ointment is not Bloom, but Boylan. Bloom's scheme has worked just as he had hoped. His late arrival home and his evident self-satisfaction have troubled Molly to the point where, as a husband at least, he seems worth striving to keep, and in Stephen he has found a figure to attract Molly's dreams and desires away from Boylan. (His ultimate scheme is for a union between Stephen and Milly – 'Because the way to daughter led through mother, the way to mother through daughter' (*U* 656/815) – but this is merely an eventual possibility.)

By the beginning of the *eighth sentence*, Boylan's image has been comprehensively defeated: compared with her idealization of Stephen, Boylan has 'no manners nor no refinement nor no nothing in his nature', 'doesnt know poetry from a cabbage', and has no more conversation than 'an old Lion'; he is dismissed from any important position in her mind. It is the way Joyce presents the expulsion of the usurper. There is no sudden and implausible shift from obsession with a lover to a renewed passion for the husband: the struggle is not immediately for Molly's love, but for occupation of her mind. In her last 'sentence', Bloom comes to dominate her memories of the past and her plans for the future, but not by any process of wifely forgiveness or idealization. On the contrary, all his deficiencies, referred to in earlier sentences, are remembered, but, instead of being reasons for turning away from him, they now motivate Molly's decision to reclaim her erring husband: his faults, real or supposed, are as important in restoring his hold on Molly's mind as his virtues. The concern implicit in the first sentence has developed to the point where Molly sees herself as the injured party and her own adultery as of little consequence. There is a clear suggestion that, if only Bloom offered more embracings and demonstrations of love, she would feel no compulsion to seek satisfaction elsewhere:

... what else were we given all those desires for Id like to know I cant help it if Im young still can I its a wonder Im not an old shrivelled hag before my time living with him so cold never embracing me except sometimes when hes asleep the wrong end of me not knowing I suppose who he has ... what a madman nobody understands his cracked ideas but me still of course a woman wants to be embraced 20 times a day almost to make her look young no matter by who so long as to be in love or loved by somebody if the fellow you want isnt there. .... (*U* 736/925)

Men's dependence on women and, in particular, on their mothers brings Stephen again to mind (it is because he has no mother that he is 'running wild'), but her thoughts of him are now more maternal than amorous and link him (as he has been linked in her husband's mind) with her dead son, Rudy:

> . . . well its a poor case that those that have a fine son like that theyre not satisfied and I none was he not able to make one it wasnt my fault. . . . (*U* 737/926)

It was the death of Rudy which 'disheartened' her ('I knew well Id never have another'), and damaged her relationship with her husband ('we were never the same since'), and, although she puts it out of her mind ('O Im not going to think myself into the glooms about that any more'), the memory plainly modifies her attitude towards Stephen. She sees herself less as a poet's mistress than as a substitute mother:

> . . . I wonder why he wouldnt stay the night . . . instead of roving around the city meeting God knows who nightwalkers and pickpockets his poor mother wouldnt like that if she was alive ruining himself for life perhaps. . . . (*U* 738/927)

Significantly, whereas earlier she had tended to exaggerate Stephen's age in order to convince herself that he was old enough to be her lover, she now underestimates it in order to feel motherly towards him:

> . . . he could easy have slept in there on the sofa in the other room I suppose he was as shy as a boy he being so young hardly 20 of me in the next room. . . . (*U* 738/927)

Her concern and sympathy for Stephen (reminiscent of her husband's) leads to a revision of her earlier determination not to get breakfast:

> . . . what a pity he didnt stay Im sure the poor fellow was dead tired and wanted a good sleep badly I could have brought him in his breakfast in bed with a bit of toast. . . . (*U* 738/928)

It would be 'great fun', she thinks, if Stephen stayed with them – it could all be easily arranged – and she anticipates with pleasure 'a long talk with an intelligent welleducated person'. But these plans obviously involve some improvement in her relations with her husband – he must be allowed to redeem himself: 'Ill just give him one more chance.' This is Molly's way of putting it, but, in fact, she is prepared to go to some lengths to recapture him. In the first place, she resolves to get up early and get him his breakfast; she will even let him have her 'nice cream'. In the second place, she will deliberately arouse his sexual interest in her:

> . . . I know what Ill do Ill go about rather gay not too much singing a bit now and then mi fa pietà Masetto then Ill start dressing myself to go out presto non son più forte Ill put on my best shift and drawers let him have a good eyeful out of that to make his micky stand for him. . . . (*U* 739/929)

Don Giovanni Boylan is being replaced by Masetto Bloom, and she even contemplates letting him know of her adultery – after all, it is of no account and Bloom's own fault:

... its all his own fault if I am an adultress as the thing in the gallery said O
much about it if thats all the harm ever we did in this vale of tears God knows
its not much doesnt everybody only they hide it I suppose thats what a
woman is supposed to be there for or He wouldnt have made us the way He
did so attractive to men. . . . . (U 739/929)

Molly's attitude towards adultery is now approaching her husband's
equanimity: he had regarded it as of little importance in the scales of
human wrongdoing or universal disaster; for her it is merely part of the
order of nature ordained by God. Then, if Bloom wants to indulge his odd
sexual tastes, she will let him, and use the occasion to get money from him.
Previously it had been Boylan from whom she expected to get gifts and
money; her demands from her husband will be more modest:

... then Ill tell him I want £1 or perhaps 30/ Ill tell him I want to buy underclothes then if he gives me that well he wont be too bad I dont want to soak
it all out of him like other women do. . . . (U740/929-30)

That will deal with her fear of his wasting his money on other women, and,
by similar methods, she can appease her curiosity about his activities and
her worry that he is losing interest in her:

... Ill do the indifferent 1 or 2 questions Ill know by the answers when hes
like that he cant keep a thing back I know every turn in him . . . Ill be quite
gay and friendly over it . . . then Ill go out Ill have him eyeing up at the
ceiling where is she gone now make him want me thats the only way. . . .
(U 740/930)

With all her problems theoretically solved, Molly tries to settle herself to
sleep so that she can rise early. The thought of the next day and of Stephen's
possible return turns her mind to preparations – dusting, cleaning the
piano, buying some cakes and flowers – and flowers introduce the rhapsody
about the beauty of nature: 'God of heaven theres nothing like nature.'
This is Molly's affirmation of the goodness of the world and of life as God
created it; she has no time for atheists, among whom she would number
Bloom, but what redeems her husband is that he understands the poetry of
her womanhood:

... they might as well try to stop the sun from rising tomorrow the sun
shines for you he said the day we were lying among the rhododendrons on
Howth head in the grey tweed suit and his straw hat the day I got him to
propose to me yes . . . after that long kiss I near lost my breath yes he said I
was a flower of the mountain yes so we are flowers all a womans body yes
that was one true thing he said in his life and the sun shines for you today yes
that was why I liked him because I saw he understood or felt what a woman is
and I knew I could always get round him and I gave him all the pleasure I
could leading him on till he asked me to say yes. . . . (U 741/931-2)

She had delayed answering while memories of Mulvey and Gibraltar ran
through her head:

... Gibraltar as a girl where I was a Flower of the mountain yes when I put
the rose in my hair like the Andalusian girls used or shall I wear a red yes and

how he kissed me under the Moorish wall and I thought well as well him as
another and then I asked him with my eyes to ask again yes and then he asked
me would I yes to say yes my mountain flower and first I put my arms around
him yes and drew him down to me so he could feel my breasts all perfume yes
and his heart was going like mad and yes I said yes I will Yes.   (*U* 742/932-3)

Bloom has already driven out the image of Boylan: here he absorbs both
Stephen and Mulvey. He may not be a poet but his amorous words were
exactly of the kind to which the poetic strain in Molly could respond, while
the memory of the first kiss becomes part of the kiss with which Molly
accepted him. The indifference of 'as well him as another' is belied by the
breathless excitement of the language; for Molly, as for Bloom, the episode
on Howth was the most intense experience of poetry, of romance, of sexual
excitement, of mutual understanding – in short, of love. All the emotions
she has hoped to find elsewhere were united in her on that afternoon and
are now relived in her mind. There is no reason to suppose that this marks
the end of Molly's and Bloom's marital difficulties. What is suggested is
that, just as in 'Ithaca' Bloom was imaged as a heavenly body inevitably
drawn back to its orbital starting-point, Molly's thoughts are cyclical, and,
for all their turnings and aberrations, will repeatedly come back to the
husband who excites her indignation, curiosity, and jealous affection.

Unless the characteristic gist of each of the eight sentences is recognized,
this intricately organized novel appears to finish in a formless drift instead
of a movement 'slowly surely and evenly round and round spinning'. Joyce
seems to have designed the soliloquy on a roughly circular scheme, with the
eight sentences corresponding to the eight chief compass-bearings, and
Bloom, Boylan, Mulvey and Stephen standing at North, East, South and
West.

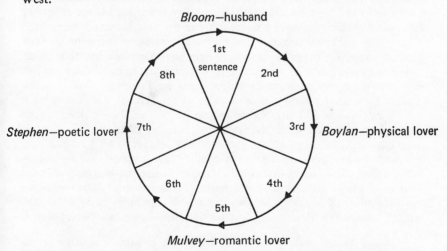

The diagram is simplifying – for instance, Mulvey is most prominent at the
beginning of the fifth sentence, and Stephen at the end of the seventh
sentence – but the details do not matter. The design of the chapter is a

cyclic movement from Bloom and to Bloom, with the difference that, in the return, he combines the qualities of physical, romantic and poetic lovers within the familiar shape of husband.

Certain recurring features of content and manner help the reader to track the course of Molly's slowly changing attitudes. On the one hand, there are such topics as Bloom's request for breakfast, which sets the soliloquy in motion, recurs many times, and marks the concluding phase when Molly, after varying reactions of surprise, indignation and contempt, reconciles herself to satisfying her husband.[126] On the other hand, there are the frequent references to the songs which symbolize and articulate Molly's moods and desires. When she expresses her anticipation of some escape from monotony in the words of the song, *Waiting* ('Waiting always waiting to guiiiide him toooo me'), the reader is reminded that this was the song she was singing when Bloom first met her: *Love's Old Sweet Song*, which she has been singing with Boylan that afternoon, is nevertheless associated not with him but with Mulvey, her romantic lover 'in the dear dead days beyond recall'; *In Old Madrid*, linked to thoughts of Boylan and Stephen, and *Shall I Wear a White Rose?*, expressive of her preparations to receive Mulvey and Stephen, are both echoed and absorbed into the closing re-enactment of her acceptance of Bloom. Other recurrences, especially the frequent inconsistencies and contradictions, help trace the fluctuations of Molly's moods.

The problems Joyce faced in the composition of his last chapter were many and crucial. The central action of the novel was completed with Bloom's falling asleep, yet it left much unanswered. Bloom may have mastered his own troublesome emotions, but what of his relationship with Molly? There have been only two glimpses of her, and, although her presence in the background has been massive, such knowledge of her as has been supplied is certainly unreliable and possibly distorted. For all the reader knows, Bloom's jealousy may have converted an innocent singing-practice (whatever other hopes Boylan may have had) or a harmless flirtation into an adulterous appointment. In any case, the successful completion of Bloom's odyssey depends on his regaining his Penelope. The Homeric analogue required a symbolic destruction of the suitors. Violence is alien to Bloom's nature and principles, and, as Joyce told Frank Budgen, the final slaughter had once seemed to him 'un-Ulyssean'.[127] Bloom's essential concern is not with the presence of a usurper in his house or bed, but with the usurper's occupation of Molly's mind; his aim is 'disintegration of obsession'. Only in her mind could Boylan be defeated and the husband's image reinstated. The catastrophe has to be enacted in some representation of Molly's thoughts. Stephen's comradeship is a psychological weapon: it is not Stephen himself nor Stephen's poetry which

---

[126] Stanley Sultan carefully traces the fluctuations in Molly's response to the request for breakfast in bed, and says that it is 'both the principal manifestation of Bloom's attempt to win Molly back and the principal issue in the resolution of her attitude toward him and his attempt' (*Sultan*, 421).

[127] *Letters* I, 160.

exposes to Molly her lover's coarseness – the thought of Stephen's youth and poetry is what matters. Similarly, Bloom's triumph is achieved not in a sudden wifely affection for the real person of her husband lying beside her but in the gradual domination of her thoughts and plans by his image, past, present and future.

It was necessary, then, to introduce and enter the mind of what was in effect a new character; but to do so would have important thematic consequences. The theme of the coming together of artist and citizen ended, apparently, in 'Ithaca', and was rounded off by Bloom's retirement to bed. To bring in, at this point, a different kind of figure, could confuse and obscure the argument of the novel. The solution Joyce found to this problem was to make the final chapter expressive of a third dimension of human nature, involved in and underlying the spiritual and moral struggles of Stephen and Bloom, but requiring at the end its own voice, the voice of the feminine life-principle speaking in the person of 'sane full amoral fertilisable untrustworthy engaging shrewd limited prudent indifferent *Weib*'. The soliloquy represents both the particular and unique woman in whose mind Bloom's triumph is achieved and a universal principle expressed with sufficient force and coherence to prevent its being crushed by the combined weight of the two great opposites whose interplay governs the course of the book.

Consequently, this closing chapter had to be substantial in length, character and impact, and this, in turn, presented formal difficulties. In 'Ithaca', the shape of the novel, as well as its action and theme, seems to have been completed: the double stories of the opening chapters have converged and blended, and their protagonists have again gone their separate ways; the movements of Bloom and Stephen have been symbolically reduced to the orbits of two heavenly bodies; the technique has presented a vision of final flatness and distance, leading to a fading-out of consciousness; the stylistic complexities which have mounted to 'Circe' have subsided to a matter-of-fact *stile pacato*. To conceive of a chapter even flatter, more distancing and more abstract than 'Ithaca' would be difficult, and, in any case, such a chapter could hardly serve as the necessary catastrophe for the action or establish a new figure and principle capable of holding its own against Bloom and Stephen. The chapter as written overcomes all these formal difficulties. In part it is an epilogue, throwing a new light on the characters and actions of the novel, and, in part, a culmination, uniting the opposites more profoundly by emphasizing their common origin and roots in the assenting flesh. The formal reduction of human endeavours to celestial orbits is balanced by a formal reduction to a slow rotation, through its eight phases, of the earth-ball. The technique is not flatter than the scientific catechism of 'Ithaca', but more even and steady in movement, and more distanced from the activity of life, since there are very few external distractions: moreover, for the first time in the novel, there is a sustained and penetrating presentation of Bloom as seen through the eyes of one who knows him only too well. Finally, the character of the style, though as lively as that of any chapter in the novel, takes simplicity beyond the limits of established literary forms, beyond even the elementary conventions of written language.

To represent the mental processes of an ordinary woman like Molly the style needs to be fairly straightforward; yet, after the book's abundance of stylistic intricacy and innovation, anything short of a *tour de force* would seem an anticlimax. Joyce supplied a *tour de force* of the ordinary, a demonstration of the range and eloquence of the linguistic resources of an uneducated mind. Molly's vocabulary is limited and she does not seek refinement of expression, but she is in full command (in her mind at least) of all the resources of colloquial speech, and creates expressive words and images when she needs them – as, for instance, when she thinks of Boylan 'scrooching down' on her with his big hipbones, or describes Bartell d'Arcy's voice as 'tinny', or Simon Dedalus's as with 'no art in it all over you like a warm showerbath'. She has no talent for precise or ordered thinking and is consequently untroubled by inconsistencies, ambiguities or *non sequiturs*, but she has a complex emotional life and, for the articulation of this, her inner language is unfailingly adequate. The style of her soliloquy is often humorous, witty, ironic, sarcastic, pathetic, opinionated, romantic, passionate, dreamy, brutal, particularizing, generalizing (and usually several of these are blended), and when the occasion demands she can be rhetorical or poetic, as in her praise of nature and her reminiscent image of Gibraltar. Of course, the mastery of the resources of colloquial language, is, strictly speaking, Joyce's, not Molly's: she could no more have dictated the chapter than she could have written it. But to insist on the distinction between the verbal representation of mental processes and the literal recording of them would here be pedantic. In a way which is true of no other interior monologue in the novel, the reader believes himself to be listening to the very words Molly's mind addresses to itself as it slowly revolves, completing the action of the book, adding a new dimension to the theme, fulfilling the form, and bringing the whole stylistic odyssey to a commonplace but brilliant conclusion.

*

The styles and techniques of *Ulysses*, like the other elements of the columnar scheme, are primarily responsive to and expressive of the local characteristics of the chapters. Joyce told Carlo Linati that each chapter 'should not only condition but even create its own technique.'[128] On the other hand, the succession of techniques is not random or pointless; there is design in the increasingly complex handling of interior monologue in the early chapters, in the mounting technical excitement culminating in 'Circe', and in the stylistic subsidence indicated in the Linati scheme by the phrases, '*prosa rilassata*', '*stile pacato*' and '*stile rassegnato*'. Joyce thought of the composition of the book as an odyssean journey – towards the end he wrote of looking forward to rounding 'the last (and stormiest) cape'[129] –

[128] *Letters I*, 147.   [129] *Ibid.*, 163.

and he planned a similar voyage for his readers, who would be exposed to greater and greater strains on their patience, understanding and imagination until, after the emotional and stylistic tempest of 'Circe', they found themselves in the calmer waters of the *Nostos*. He told Harriet Weaver that he understood why she should be dismayed by the more difficult styles and prefer the simpler styles of the opening, 'much as the wanderer did who longed for the rock of Ithaca'.[130]

Yet these increasing difficulties are why many readers, starting hopefully, have been exhausted and irritated by the latter half of the book. They may recognize that a new vision requires new literary conventions, and may be ready to welcome a method which, like the earlier interior monologues, gives the very feel of life; they may be undisturbed by such modifications as the headlines of 'Aeolus', the word-play of 'Hades' or 'Lestrygonians', or the special effects of 'Scylla and Charybdis', since all of these can be accepted as minor refinements of a convention designed to represent the inner experience of Stephen and Bloom. They might have adapted even to such an extreme convention as the drama of 'Circe', if it had been used throughout. What they find tiresome is that, after learning to respond to such a demanding, concentrated and flexible convention as Joyce's version of the interior monologue, they find it replaced by a series of unexpected, obscure and bookish techniques, and they conclude that Joyce has become more interested in displaying his own cleverness than in exploring the predicaments and inner lives of his characters. Though all the techniques may be shown to serve relevant purposes, the question remains, 'But what overall function is served by this kaleidoscopic switching from one technique to another?'

The answer is related to the nature of Joyce's mature vision. Most authors who create a distinctive personal manner or convention, whether intuitively or deliberately, do so in response to the demands of their peculiar vision, whether that be fundamental to their whole sense of life or (as in a novelist like Peacock) a view adopted to bring into special focus some aspect of human activity. The established conventions may be inadequate or inimical, because literary conventions have their own implications. In general, radical innovations are made by authors who feel that current conventions would stifle, falsify or impair the representations of their personal sense of what life is like or of what is important in our experience, and consequently such innovations, designed to express a total and consistent vision, tend to be characteristic of an entire work or series of works. But if an essential principle in an author's way of looking at life is that no one way of looking at it is adequate or dependable, that life itself is a complex of many kinds of existence, and that our individual experience of life is a mixture of quite different and often contrasted modes of experience, then he finds that no one convention of representation is proper to his purpose. Joyce told Carlo Linati, referring to *Ulysses*, that 'each adventure is so to say one person',[131] and, in a letter to Harriet Weaver, said that he had set

[130] *Ibid.*, 129.   [131] *Ibid.*, 147.

himself the task of 'writing a book from eighteen different points of view and in as many styles'.[132] He was not using 'points of view' in the Jamesian sense to refer to the experiences of different observers: the chapters of *Ulysses* do not have eighteen different observers, and, if they had, this would not in itself have necessitated changes of style and technique. Joyce meant different modes of experience: it is not simply that various people have differing opinions and impressions of Bloom, but that he plays different roles in different kinds of consciousness. The strong romantic gentleman seen by Gerty MacDowell and the absurd pliant husband known to Molly belong to the mental worlds which have invented them and in which they move. Gerty, Molly, Stephen, the Unnamed One and the other Dubliners who believe they know Bloom have each a different vision of life and inhabit mental worlds differing in kind from each other: the figures called Bloom in these worlds are fictions rather than approximate reflections of some absolute and essential individual. In fact, the way Bloom is presented in the novel suggests that no such absolute essence can be said to exist. Even to his own mind, Bloom presents no consistent self-image; his sense of his own nature and identity varies according to his mood and inner situation. The figure of Leopold Bloom, citizen of Dublin, is a composite of all the ways in which he is apprehended by himself, by others, and by the unidentified 'points of view' which penetrate his unconscious in 'Circe' and view him scientifically in 'Ithaca'. This, I take it, is what Joyce meant when he spoke of seeing Bloom 'from all sides'.[133]

Stephen, too, is presented as a multiple existence; to Mulligan he is 'the loveliest mummer of them all', to Mr Deasy a young man in need of good advice, to Myles Crawford a potential journalist, to the men in the Library an extravagant *littérateur*, to Bloom a gifted youth fallen into bad company and a substitute son, to Molly a poetic lover or a motherless boy roaming the streets, while his self-image ranges from a proud and defiant spirit to a miserable and remorseful failure. Even the events of the day derive such meaning and consequence as they have from the part they play in various modes of experience. Molly's act of adultery is not presented directly and immediately: its importance lies in its different roles in Bloom's mental drama; it matters far less in Molly's vision of life, and less still in the context of the universal catalogue of crimes and catastrophes. The crucial event of the novel, the meeting of Bloom and Stephen, is an event of utter insignificance except for the way in which it is interpreted and shaped in the mental worlds of the two men and Molly. Like the word 'metempsychosis' (which Molly was unable to understand), the word 'parallax' (which Bloom failed to understand) recurs as a pointer to the nature of the book's vision and method; figuratively it means the apparent change in the nature, position or size of an object as a consequence of change in the nature, position and concerns of the observer or point of observation.

The sense of the relativity of experience dominates Joyce's vision in *Ulysses*, and its representation made necessary the sudden and emphatic

[132] *Ibid.*, 167.   [133] *Budgen*, 17.

changes of manner and convention. Of course, the relativity is not an abandonment of discrimination. Joyce is not implying that any vision is as good as any other: Bloom's self-images may be partial and inconsistent but they encompass more, explore more of the object's complexity and depth than do the more or less casual impressions of his fellow-Dubliners; the figure of Bloom which appears in Molly's soliloquy is distorted and inadequate but it is far more solid and extensive than the romantic stereotype of Gerty's fantasy-world. What is implied by the 'eighteen different points of view' is that our experience, even of ourselves, is made up of numerous, dissimilar and often irreconcilable ways of looking at life, so different in kind that each demands a different kind of literary representation.

Chapter 5   *Ulysses:* the moral vision

Moral vision has nothing to do with visions, religious, mystical, prophetic or otherwise transcendental; it refers to an artist's characteristic ways of seeing and presenting life, as distinguished from any moral ideas, attitudes, beliefs or faiths to which he may adhere and which he may seek to express in his work. Such ideas and attitudes – religious or humanist, spiritual or materialist, social or personal, optimistic or pessimistic, life-celebrating or life-decrying – may be, in part, a product of his moral vision, may provide a vocabulary for expressing it, and cannot be ignored in critical discussion of his work: but they do not constitute the work's moral value, and frequently mark the limits of the author's vision. With ideas and attitudes we can agree or disagree: to a way of seeing, agreement or disagreement is irrelevant. Even the greatest artists can illuminate only a small area of human experience, and artists whom we regard as sick, mad or advocates of evil can nevertheless light up something in us which more congenial artists fail to do. There is nothing inconsistent about preferring the moral attitudes of Joyce Cary to those of Wyndham Lewis, while regarding Lewis's moral vision as far keener; or in rejecting the moral doctrines of *The Pilgrim's Progress*, while responding to Bunyan's moral vision. As far as art is concerned, what matters is the quality of the vision, not the acceptability of the ideas and attitudes associated with it, often quite arbitrarily.[1]

Differentiation between and evaluation of the moral visions implicit in literature depend on the degree of penetration into human experience, on the range of experience into which the author has insight, and on the coherence of the vision within its own range. The penetration is not necessarily a matter of probing psychological depths; it can be equally evident in the grasp of superficial social behaviour. Range may refer to the different kinds of experience explored and presented, but refers more importantly to the centrality of the experience; Jane Austen is a case in point. Coherence is not merely consistency; it is more apparent in a work which struggles with the contradictions and incompatibilities of experience

[1] Anthony Cronin makes a similar distinction: 'To speak of the quality of a man's vision is not to speak of the worth of his mere, paraphrasable opinions abou thistory or religion or our place in the cosmos: an ideology which could be discovered and exclaimed over like that of any other fashionable sage' (*A Question of Modernity* (London, Secker and Warburg 1966), 69–70).

than in one which achieves consistency by ignoring them. All three are plainly both moral and aesthetic qualities; they do not exist in literature unless an appropriate means for their articulation has been created.

It seems necessary to begin the discussion of the moral vision of *Ulysses* with these elementary generalizations, because so much of the controversy about the book has, from the beginning, been about Joyce's supposed moral attitudes, or, more absurdly, about whether he is a 'moral' or an 'aesthetic' novelist. Like any other man, Joyce had moral attitudes which have left their mark on his work and cannot be disregarded, but the moral quality of the work does not depend on them. Whether one describes Molly Bloom's soliloquy as 'affirming' or 'cynical', the quality of the insight into human nature is not affected by the label affixed to it. Indeed, the labels are often more indicative of the reader's attitudes than of the author's, and admiration and disapproval accompany directly opposed formulations of the novel's moral implications. Of those critics who regard *Ulysses* as a comic affirmation of life, some find it sentimentally benevolent; of those who describe it as bitterly negative, some feel that this is the proper response to the degenerate confusion of contemporary life; of those who consider it morally uncommitted, some believe it is right for the artist to abstain from judgement. This variety of opinion, not only in the evaluation of the book's moral vision, but also in the characterization of it, at least suggests that it is a vision of some complexity, and that critical judgements of works of art should not be founded on what the critic takes to be the moral attitudes of the author.

Much of the criticism of the moral vision of the book has been directed at the unacceptability of Bloom and Stephen as figures for whom our sympathy and approval is sought. The interior monologues, it is said, purport to reveal the workings of the mind, but reveal instead the author's lack of moral penetration, sensibility and discrimination; Joyce's view of the experience of the ordinary man never gets below a superficial layer, fails to discern what is admirable and vital in human nature, and presents life as a deterministic flux in which men vainly and sordidly float, and his conception of the nature of the artist is vapid, pretentious and false, a hangover from the decadent aestheticism of the nineties. There is sometimes implied or explicit comparison with D. H. Lawrence: Lawrence leads away from what is vitiated and dead in life and morality, enlarges one's sense of human nature and potential, exposes destructive and inhibiting forces and ideas, demonstrates a finer, fuller and more discriminating awareness; in figures like Birkin and Ursula, without evading the difficulties, he suggests the direction of a struggling, uncertain and erratic movement towards an enrichment of life and a clearer, more exploratory moral vision; his creative impulse and his best works spring from a vital moral energy and a firm grasp of the totality of human nature. Looking back to the twenties and thirties, Dr Leavis sees the Joyce–Lawrence opposition as representative of the fundamental conflict in criticism:

> Those two, it seems to me, were pre-eminently the testing, the crucial
> authors: if you took Joyce for a major creative writer, then, like Mr Eliot, you
> had no use for Lawrence, and if you judged Lawrence a great writer, then
> you could hardly take a sustained interest in Joyce.[2]

Whatever may have been the case in the twenties or thirties, it is not now
true that admiration of the one writer necessarily precludes admiration of
the other; nevertheless, there are still critics who, in effect, complain that
Joyce does not do what Lawrence does or *vice versa*, instead of rejoicing
in the diversity of the two novelists' visions, gifts and artistic temperaments.
Certainly in many respects their penetrations into human nature and
behaviour are contrasted in methods and effects.

When Joyce said that Bloom was 'a good man',[3] he could hardly have
meant that he was a man like Birkin, struggling towards a new awareness,
breaking free from a false established view of life. Joyce seems to have used
'good' in a vague and unparticularized sense. In this he resembles his hero,
for whenever Bloom ties to formulate his ideas of what seems to him good
he flounders ineptly – as, for instance, when he tries to define his position
to the men in Barney Kiernan's:

> And then he collapses all of a sudden, twisting around all the opposite, as
> limp as a wet rag.
> —But it's no use, says he. Force, hatred, history, all that. That's not life
> for men and women, insult and hatred. And everybody knows that it's the
> very opposite of that that is really life.
> —What? says Alf.
> —Love, says Bloom. I mean the opposite of hatred.   (*U* 317/432)

One could hardly have a purer expression of woolly benevolence. Bloom is
no thinker about fundamental moral issues, nor a cogent articulator of such
ideas as he does have. But it is perfectly possible to present a penetrating
and coherent vision through the medium of a muddled and inarticulate
character: more important than what Bloom says is why and how and in
what circumstances he says it, and what he is and does is more important
than anything he says, and may provide the particularizing definition of the
vision which he vainly attempts to express verbally.

The confusion of Bloom's notion of 'love' as the key to life is ridiculed
by the interpolation, beginning 'Love loves to love love', and its social
implications are ludicrously developed in 'Circe', when Bloom, as the new
ruler of Ireland, founds the new Bloomusalem – '*a colossal edifice, with
crystal roof, built in the shape of a huge pork kidney*'. (Bloom's breakfast, his
memory of the glass-roofed Dublin Food Market and his thoughts about
communal feeding are combined to shape the architecture of the new
Bloomusalem.) His administration is represented as a universal distribution
of charity:

[2] *D. H. Lawrence: Novelist* (London, Chatto and Windus 1955), 10.
[3] *Budgen*, 18.

Bloom's bodyguard distribute Maundy money, commemoration medals, loaves and fishes, temperance badges, expensive Henry Clay cigars, free cowbones for soup, rubber preservatives, in sealed envelopes tied with gold thread, butter scotch, pineapple rock, billets doux in the form of cocked hats, readymade suits, porringers of toad in the hole, bottles of Jeyes' Fluid, purchase stamps, 40 days' indulgences, spurious coins, dairyfed pork sausages, theatre passes, season tickets available for all tram lines, coupons of the royal and privileged Hungarian lottery, penny dinner counters, cheap reprints of the World's Twelve Worst Books. (U 461–2/607)

This social projection of Bloom's doctrine of love goes beyond the earlier definition of love as 'the opposite of hatred': it is an expression of his goodwill towards humanity, though the subsequent action, when he is kissed and acclaimed, a throng of women call him 'Little father!' and even the Old Citizen brushes away a tear and prays 'May the good God bless him!', suggest his benevolence and generosity are at least partly motivated by the desire to win the love and approval of others.

Both incidents have a vaguely Christian reference, as is recognized in Barney Kiernan's:

—A new apostle to the gentiles, says the citizen. Universal love.
—Well, says John Wyse, isn't that what we're told? Love your neighbours.
(U 317/432)

Yet the Christian reference is ironic, because it is by declared Christians and in the name of Christ that Bloom is threatened. There is nothing consciously Christian in his views: his insistence that he is saying what 'everybody knows' indicates that for him it is all a matter of ordinary experience and commonsense.[4] There is nothing new about Bloom's moral attitudes; they seem to him and are, commonplace. His implied criticism of his society is not that it is attached to dead or false moral principles but that it pays lip service to principles which it makes no attempt to observe. In *Ulysses*, as in *Dubliners*, Joyce's enquiry is not into the validity of accepted moral propositions but into the behaviour which purports to acknowledge and rest on these propositions. He penetrates into what, in the conditions of ordinary life, constitutes moral behaviour. Bloom's woolly notions are not principles which direct his life; they are inadequate attempts to verbalize his way of seeing. It is no part of Joyce's business to frame accurate statements about Bloom or to show Bloom framing such statements about himself. The penetration will reveal itself in the discriminating and exact presentation of Bloom's nature as it is continuously expressed in his thoughts, feelings and behaviour, and in the general insight into human nature implied by that presentation. In the Bloomusalem episode, for instance, the image is not of Bloom's daydreams (even Bloom's daydreams do not show such total lack of awareness of absurdity and incongruity), nor of his benevolence, nor of his conceit and absurd egoism:

[4] Yet in his confused and unpretentious way, Bloom is plainly supplying the answer to the question which Stephen asks in both 'Proteus' and 'Circe': 'What is that word known to all men?' The answer is 'love'.

it is an image, and a very specific image, of a quite unparticularized, unspecific aspect of Bloom's character and disposition – at once egoistic and altruistic, clouded with absurd dreams yet affecting his behaviour in practice, loving and desiring to be loved. Bloom would be totally unable to articulate such an image of himself or even to recognize it; it is the novelist who apprehends this aspect of Bloom in all its complexity and contradictions and creates an exact and significant image of it. Similarly in the 'Eumaeus' episode, Bloom's smug officiousness, his sense of acting 'in orthodox Samaritan fashion', does not reduce or damage his true Samaritanism. Joyce is not sneering at self-conceit disguised as kindness, or cynically ridiculing Bloom's assumption of a virtuous role; he perceives that in life there is no such thing as unadulterated altruism. Virtuous conduct does not exist in human experience without some impurity of motive, some thought of self-interest, self-approval, self-importance, self-dramatization. But it is none the worse for this: this is what 'virtue' means as a term applicable to human beings. We abstract moral terms from our experience and, having abstracted them, proceed to use them as though they refer to qualities or conduct which exist in pure or absolute forms. The cynic uses the abstractions as a stick to beat human behaviour, without recognizing that it is from human behaviour that his terms have been abstracted.[5] Joyce's discrimination and penetration are shown not by the creation of ideal images of 'good' behaviour but by presenting such behaviour in the only forms in which we ever experience it, in the only terms, that is, in which the word 'good' is humanly significant. If we refuse to call an act generous because the man felt pleased with himself or was anxious to win approval, if we belittle an act of courageous defiance because the man spoke foolishly or acted absurdly, we shall soon have to remove all terms of moral commendation from our vocabulary. In *Ulysses* Joyce is concerned not with defining these terms, nor with creating fictional images expressive of their abstract meanings, but with delineating the kinds of behaviour that gave rise to them, in the confusion of circumstances in which they really occur. The moral vision of an artist goes beyond abstractions; it is specific where they are general; it cannot be reduced to discursive statement, not because it is too vague, impressionistic and confused but because it is too exact, detailed and coherent.

There is nothing essentially new in what Joyce is trying to do, although he gives us extremities of absurd behaviour beyond what novelists usually ask us to stomach in their heroes. Onto Bloom are heaped all the attributes and conditions which our society most despises. He is a cuckold and a resigned one at that; he is in will, if not in deed, unfaithful, but resorts to masturbation rather than adultery; he has masochistic tendencies and other unacceptable sexual inclinations; he is often, even generally, lacking in spirit, and physically timid; he writes suggestive letters under a pseudonym; he is feebly ingratiating both to his dominant wife and to his contemptuous

---

[5] Cf. Joyce's remark to Budgen concerning *Ulysses*: 'It is the work of a sceptic, but I don't want it to appear the work of a cynic' (*Budgen*, 156).

fellow citizens; his head is filled with ridiculous fancies, notions and hopes; socially, financially, maritally he is considered a failure; his bearing is such that newsboys mock it; racially he is an outcast, a renegade from his fore-fathers' race and religion, an unwelcome and unbelieving recruit to the race and religion of those who despise and humiliate him. He is am an for whom, it would seem, one could feel at most sympathy and pity. Instead Joyce presents him not as a figure claiming our pity and sympathy but as a general dispenser of these emotions, and it is this which preserves his moral stature and raises him above his fellow citizens. By Simon Dedalus he is regarded as an inferior, but he demonstrates his superiority in his pity for Dedalus's daughter whom her father has treated with scorn, and in his undertaking of quasi-paternal responsibility for Stephen; despite his own marital problems, he feels sorry for Martin Cunningham, burdened with a drunken wife, and, despite his own financial problems, feels concerned for the fallen state of J. J. O'Molloy; he gives more than he can afford to Paddy Dignam's widow and sympathizes with Mrs Breen whose half-crazy husband is merely a source of amusement to the other Dubliners; he understands the emotions of the lame girl, Gerty, and takes Stephen home with him as he had once carried home a lame dog; he feeds the animals – the cat in the morning, the gulls at mid-day, the dogs in Nighttown; he pities all women, from the fertile Mrs Purefoy to the haggard prostitute ('If you don't answer when they solicit must be horrible for them till they harden'); and at the end of the day his sympathetic understanding extends even to the adulterer, Blazes Boylan, whose behaviour he attributes to 'comparative youth subject to impulses of ambition and magnanimity, colleagual altruism and amorous egoism.'

Inperfectly, erratically, comically, ludicrously and often smugly, Bloom's attitudes and behaviour express the moral sense which he tried vainly to proclaim in Barney Kiernan's. He is, generally, a man of goodwill, and it is not accidental that the few occasions when he overcomes his natural timidity and submissiveness and speaks or acts boldly are when he is defending others. In the pub he speaks up incoherently and ungrammatic-ally for the Jewish race:

—And I belong to a race too, says Bloom, that is hated and persecuted. Also now. This very moment. This very instant.

Gob, he near burnt his fingers with the butt of his old cigar.

—Robbed, says he. Plundered. Insulted. Persecuted. Taking what belongs to us by right. At this very moment, says he, putting up his fist, sold by auction off in Morocco like slaves or cattles.

—Are you talking about the new Jerusalem? says the citizen.

—I'm talking about injustice, says Bloom. (*U* 317/431–2)

Again, at the end of the 'Cyclops' chapter, when the Citizen calls out insultingly, 'Three cheers for Israel', Bloom, despite the intervention of those who foresee violence, turns back to defend his race, once more with a confused mind but with undeniable spirit and resolution:

—Mendelssohn was a jew and Karl Marx and Mercadante and Spinoza.
And the Saviour was a jew and his father was a jew. Your God.
—He had no father, says Martin. That'll do now. Drive ahead.
—Whose God? says the citizen.
—Well, his uncle was a jew, says he. Your God was a jew. Christ was a jew
like me.   (*U* 326/444–5)

In response to the sneer at the Jewish people, Bloom temporarily lays aside
his customary prudence, as he recognizes when he later recalls the incident:
'People could put up with being bitten by a wolf but what properly riled
them was a bite from a sheep' (*U* 619/766).

On a few other occasions, Bloom's courage is aroused by injustice or
threats to others. It sweeps aside his psychological discomfiture in the
brothel, when, in defence of Stephen, who has drunkenly damaged the
gaslamp, he outfaces and even alarms the aggressive bawd whose mere
presence had at first intimidated him.

BELLA

(*Her eyes hard with anger and cupidity, points.*) Who's to pay for that? Ten
shillings. You're a witness.

BLOOM

(*Snatches up Stephen's ashplant.*) Me? Ten shillings? Haven't you lifted
enough off him? Didn't he . . .!

BELLA

(*Loudly.*) Here, none of your tall talk. This isn't a brothel. A ten shilling
house.

BLOOM

(*His hand under the lamp, pulls the chain. Pulling, the gasjet lights up a crushed
mauve purple shade. He raises the ashplant.*) Only the chimney's broken. Here
is all he . . .

BELLA

(*Shrinks back and screams.*) Jesus! Don't!

BLOOM

(*Warding off a blow.*) To show you how he hit the paper. There's not a six-
penceworth of damage done. Ten shillings!   (*U* 551–2/683–4)

Again, Bloom's outrage at the overcharging and his attempt to illustrate his
argument by repeating the blow against the lampshade are farcical – he is
not a man to behave with cool dignity when roused – but the farce does
not conceal the fact that he is acting boldly, and without his usual caution,
in defence of Stephen's interests. The same concern nerves him to elbow
his way through the noisy mob, to intervene between Stephen and the
angry soldier, to push back the crowd gathering round the unconscious
young man, and finally to fend off the police.

Bloom does not consciously endeavour to pursue virtue: he is as incapable of adhering to a moral code as he is of formulating one. His concern
for Mrs Purefoy is not simply a consequence of views about motherhood
or women in labour – it is curiously related to his love for Molly; his
feelings for Stephen are not just an expression of some general interest in
young men or artists – they are an extension of his love for his dead son,

Rudy; his defence of the Jewish race is not motivated by a belief in racial solidarity but by an instinctive revulsion against the injustice from which he too suffers; even his dreams of a better society for all are rooted in his personal dream of retired comfort in 'a thatched bungalowshaped 2 storey dwellinghouse of southerly aspect'. To speak of him as a benevolent man is misleading, because benevolence suggests a detached, almost theoretical goodwill, whereas Bloom's goodwill is part of his nature, and just as likely to manifest itself in trivial or ludicrous thoughts as in the performance of deeds of kindness. This is why the novelist, who can show us what Bloom thinks, feels, says and does and can represent subconscious levels, all in the context of ordinary muddled human experience, can articulate a vision of 'goodness' far more exact than the seeming exactness of statement. Joyce's statement that Bloom is a 'good man' does little or nothing to define Bloom's nature, but the image of Bloom created in *Ulysses* defines with some precision what the word 'good' meant for Joyce. His moral insight in the portrait of Bloom is most evident in his perception and presentation of the qualities, which 'everybody knows' to be good but often fails to recognize or acknowledge because they are lost among the confusions and obfuscations of commonplace human circumstance and mixed with vanity, foolishness and squalor.

It might still be argued that, however deep the insight into Bloom, to present as a good man one who is so psychologically crippled is to carry tolerance to a point where moral discrimination disappears. One might admit Bloom's good nature, resilience and enjoyment of life, and yet feel that his masochism, transvestism, submissive cuckoldry, sexual inadequacy, sly satisfactions and general oddity make him a fitter subject for a psychiatrist's casebook than for the hero of a great novel. It might be that, in trying to find 'goodness' in a man rejected by his society, Joyce created an image of abnormality rather than of the central human experience. If the experience and behaviour of Bloom together represent a special case, then one might find the moral vision of the novel penetrating but lacking general human relevance, limited in range.

I doubt whether Bloom's sexual idiosyncrasies can be legitimately called abnormal.[6] The people whom we call perverts do not experience impulses

---

[6] The point is fiercely disputed among the critics, whose views often depend on the sense in which they use such words as 'abnormal' and 'perverse'. Darcy O'Brien, for instance, says, 'The fact that Bloom turned out to be an entirely plausible character shows how typical Joyce's sexual nature actually is, at least in the Western world, and how logical a step it was for Joyce to name his next and last major male character HCE or Here Comes Everybody. Sex for HCE is again tormented and perverse, and in *Finnegans Wake* there is again a notable scarcity of that union of tenderness and affection we call love' ('Some Psychological Determinants of Joyce's View of Love and Sex, *New Light*, 24). To label a sexual nature both 'typical' and 'perverse' suggests that one's quarrel is with 'the Western world' rather than with Bloom, Joyce or HCE, and if we were so typically perverse it would throw some doubt on our definition of love as a 'union of tenderness and affection'. I cannot improve on Clive Hart's level-headed summary. After pointing out that 'assumptions about sexual normality have . . . bedevilled much recent Joyce criticism', he says that Bloom's sexual characteristics and philanderings 'do not really matter': 'Joyce's view of Bloom's sexual problem is

unknown to their fellow human beings; they are people afflicted with exaggerated and often uncontrollable forms of tendencies which are present in everyone, though usually repressed or censored. There is nothing perverted about Bloom's behaviour. Much of the supposed abnormality is suggested in the psychological drama of the brothel chapter, and belongs not to Bloom's consciousness but to the representation of his unconscious climate. If we apply the standards of ordinary behaviour to the unconscious, no-one will escape the charge of abnormality. Bloom's correspondence with Martha and his masturbation on the beach are unusual and secretive, but they are not perversions; they are fantasy-substitutes for the sexual satisfactions which have been missing from his married life since the death of his son – that is to say, they are products of the circumstances of his life, not of some abnormality in his nature. The peculiarities of his marital relationship are partly due to his submissiveness before the ideal of femininity, but have become chronic because, after the death of Rudy, he and his wife seem to have lost heart. The loss of Rudy and fears of losing Molly affect Bloom's thoughts and behaviour all day, and the transference of his frustrated paternal feelings to Stephen, represented by the image of Rudy's apparition appearing above Stephen's prostrate figure at the end of the brothel chapter, produces a significant change: from this point on, to the moment when he goes to bed, weary but relaxed in mind, Bloom behaves like a man who has found a sense of purpose.

Bloom's consciousness is pervaded by all the silly, conceited, incoherent, platitudinous and distasteful notions, images and dreams that flicker through everyone's mind every day, though, as a rule, we quickly obliterate awareness and memory of them.[7] If Bloom's mind is abnormally silly or dirty, then so too was Joyce's, since it is only by introspection that one can observe the inner workings of consciousness, and so too is that of any reader who recognizes the truthfulness of Joyce's image of the workings of the mind. In presenting Bloom, Joyce presents what is clearly an ordinary human consciousness, though one, like every other consciousness, with its own characterizing limitations and peculiarities. Yet Bloom is not typical in the sense of being the highest common factor of mankind. If he were, he would not be so out of step with his fellow citizens. We are not all subject to the special difficulties facing a Jew in Dublin in 1904; we are not all cuckolds, sons of suicides, social failures and objects of contempt. Bloom is not an average man, but rather a compendium of the burdens which ordinary men bear and of the psychological and social handicaps

---

not so much that he should try to solve it as that he should learn to live with it. Bloom's salvation, in so far as he needs any, is to be sought not in purgation but in acceptance of and equanimity before his nature, whether or not we choose to call that nature fallen' ('The Sexual Perversions of Leopold Bloom', *Bonnerot*, 131).

[7] Joyce said to Arthur Power that 'most lives are made up like the modern painters' themes of pigs, pots, and plates, backstreets and blowsy living-rooms inhabited by blowsy women, bars and binges, the thousand sordid daily incidents which seep into our minds no matter how we strive to keep them out' ('Conversations with James Joyce', *JJQ* III (1) (1965), 47).

they have to live with. His centrality as a representative of humanity depends partly on his encompassing more than the average, both in his burdens and in the resilience and goodwill with which he bears them.

The comparison between the moral visions of Joyce and Lawrence is, I have suggested, a comparison between the insights of two great writers whose aims, methods, gifts and personal and literary characters were, much to our advantage, essentially different; but, if a comparison is made, then against Lawrence's passionate and adventurous moral energy as he seeks to 'inform and lead into new places the flow of our sympathetic consciousness', and to 'lead our sympathy away in recoil from things gone dead',[8] must be set Joyce's greater readiness to trace what is humbly good, in the meanest circumstances and forms of experience, confused, as it always is, with the infirmities and incongruities of our complex nature. Both men, in Lawrence's phrase, 'reveal the most secret places of life', though they are not the same places nor seen in the same light, and, if Joyce is right in supposing that, in the ordinary commerce of life, men like Bloom are ridiculed, despised and rejected, then he too, in effect, creates a moral revaluation, and brings about a redirection of 'our sympathetic consciousness'.

The account of the moral vision of *Ulysses* given so far is one-sided; it has concentrated on the nature and experience of Bloom, and is coloured by moral attitudes very like Bloom's own. It reflects a sense of the co-existence of contrary impulses and motives similar in kind to Bloom's acceptance of the mixture of ambition and magnanimity, altruism and egoism in Boylan. But there is a very different vision in the novel and a very different attitude to life – those of Stephen. Bloom's pity and sympathy are antithetical to Stephen's response to those he meets, towards whom he characteristically feels resentment or contempt. When he is almost moved to pity for the wretched schoolboy, Sargent, or for his own sisters, he steels himself against the impulse. Bloom's altruistic concern for others is contrasted with the egoism of the artist, Bloom's genial appreciation of 'warm fullblooded life' with Stephen's death-obsession. At the end of the book the two visions come close and interact but they cannot be blended or fused.[9] Stephen cannot share Bloom's, nor Bloom his. Their fundamental opposition is made explicit in 'Ithaca':

> Stephen dissented openly from Bloom's views on the importance of dietary and civic selfhelp while Bloom dissented tacitly from Stephen's views on the eternal affirmation of the spirit of man in literature. (*U* 627/777)

And this opposition is still further developed, when we learn that Bloom would be depressed by 'a recurrent frustration':

> Because at the critical turningpoint of human existence he desired to amend many social conditions, the product of inequality and avarice and

---

[8] *Lady Chatterley's Lover*, ch. IX.
[9] In the Linati scheme, Joyce headed the *Nostos* '*Fusione di Bloom e Stephen*'. Their ways meet, their natures interact, but they can hardly be said to fuse. Perhaps Joyce meant that, in terms of the novel itself, the two opposed forces are fused in the *Nostos* – that is to say, the two visions meet in the mind of the reader.

332 Ulysses: *the moral vision*

international animosity.

He believed then that human life was infinitely perfectible, eliminating these conditions?

There remained the generic conditions imposed by natural, as distinct from human law, as integral parts of the human whole: the necessity of destruction to procure alimentary sustenance: the painful character of the ultimate functions of separate existence, the agonies of birth and death: the monotonous menstruation of simian and (particularly) human females extending from the age of puberty to the menopause: inevitable accidents at sea, in mines and factories: certain very painful maladies and their resultant surgical operations, innate lunacy and congenital criminality, decimating epidemics: catastrophic cataclysms which make terror the basis of human mentality: seismic upheavals the epicentres of which are located in densely populated regions: the fact of vital growth, through convulsions of metamorphosis, from infancy through maturity to decay.

Why did he desist from speculation?

Because it was a task for a superior intelligence to substitute other more acceptable phenomena in place of the less acceptable phenomena to be removed.

Did Stephen participate in his dejection?

He affirmed his significance as a conscious rational animal proceeding syllogistically from the known to the unknown and a conscious rational reagent between a micro- and a macrocosm ineluctably constructed upon the incertitude of the void.

Was this affirmation apprehended by Bloom?

Not verbally. Substantially.

What comforted his misapprehension?

That as a competent keyless citizen he had proceeded energetically from the unknown to the known through the incertitude of the void. (*U* 658/817–18)

This difficult but important part of the catechism concludes the discussion in the kitchen, and brings into final focus the essential difference between the two men. But surprisingly they seem almost to have changed roles. Bloom's hopeful altruism, dreaming of a continuous process towards the perfecting of human life (apart from 'the generic conditions'), leads inevitably to recurrent frustration and dejection, and to a view of life as conditioned by inescapable pain and disaster – a view in which 'vital growth' is itself seen as a progress towards decay: his optimism can be sustained only by his ceasing to occupy himself with the problems it creates, by leaving them to some 'superior intelligence'. On the other hand, Stephen's unhopeful egoism now becomes an affirmation of his own significance, of his rationality and its power to proceed from what it does know to what it does not know.[10] His consciousness is the sensitive and

---

[10] The complementary functions of altruism and egoism are linked in Joyce's notes: 'Altruism makes survive race, egoism individ. $\frac{1}{2}$ and $\frac{1}{2}$' (*Notesheets*, Cyclops, 1:34–5, p. 82). There is a slight variation later: 'Altruism saves race, anarchy individual, half & half' (Eumaeus, 5:61, p. 395).

aware point of contact and interaction between the microcosm of individual existence and the macrocosm of the external universe, both of them ineluctably shaped and created upon the unknowable void by his consciousness, his Self being the creation of his own consciousness just as the world of space ('the ineluctable modality of the visible') and time ('the ineluctable modality of the audible') is created by the nature of the seeing and hearing aspects of consciousness. His consciousness, a spark of awareness in the void, creates an inner self and an external universe, as God created a universe out of chaos. In the formulation of this egocentric affirmation, several of Stephen's earlier assertions, thoughts and images intersect – the comparison, in the *Portrait*, of the artist to 'the God of the creation', the affirmation of the spirit of man in literature, the philosophical speculations on the beach, and the declaration that the Church was founded on the mystical estate of fatherhood 'and founded irremovably because founded, like the world, macro- and microcosm, upon the void. Upon incertitude, upon unlikelihood' (*U* 195–6/266). Pushed to extremes, Bloom's optimism turns to despair, and Stephen's negativism to proud affirmation, as though in accordance with the doctrine of the coincidence of contraries, derived from Bruno Giordano, which plays so important a part in *Finnegans Wake*.

Bloom's response to Stephen's affirmation is characteristic: he does not understand it, yet recognizes that it is alien to and dismissive of his own view of life, and so comfortingly reasserts his own values by recalling that it was his practical good sense that had brought both of them safely home. Bloom is right in his apprehension of the substance of the affirmation: Stephen's claim is for himself, not for all mankind. His phrase, 'a conscious rational animal', reminds the reader of Swift's dismissal of man's claim to be called 'animal rationale';[11] Stephen is placing himself, as he had earlier placed Swift, among the rational animals, the Houyhnhnms, living in a world of Yahoos, 'the hundredheaded rabble'. But for all Stephen's rationality and syllogistic process, he has floundered ineptly and feebly when faced with the practical problems of living, while Bloom, though equally 'keyless', has proceeded with competence and energy, has found a way both psychologically and geographically 'from the unknown to the known', and has successfully escorted his companion 'through the incertitude of the void'.

In this concluding exchange, before their departure from the kitchen, both men reaffirm the values they live by, Stephen explicitly, Bloom by implication. It would be ridiculous to ask who is right. Their two visions are opposite but touching at their extremes, polarized but complementary. *Ulysses*, as a whole, is committed to neither; they are the two poles upon which the moral vision of the novel turns. The vision of man as a social animal, erratic, confused and inconsistent but capable of concern for others, moved by 'love' and a vague desire to improve the human lot, and struggling

[11] *The Correspondence of Jonathan Swift*, ed. Harold Williams (London, Oxford University Press 1963) III, 103.

to deal practically and competently with the problems of living, is involved with the vision of man as an isolated individual, self-contemplative, seeking the truth of his own nature and its fulfilment, regarding the universe in which he lives as his own creation and significant only through him. Joyce, in this novel, does not choose between these visions; there is no choice to be made, because each is valid, within its limits, and both coexist in the mind of every man, though in different forms and with different emphases. In *Ulysses*, one extreme is embodied in Stephen and the other in Bloom, and there is no way in which either man can adopt the other's vision. Their meeting is not a fusion, but a spark of sympathetic understanding leaping across the poles. Stephen's bitterness and isolation is, temporarily at least, alleviated by Bloom's practical good nature, so that he declines the offer of a night's lodging with amicability and gratitude, agrees to further meetings, and shakes hands in a friendly parting. Bloom's frustrations and humiliations are relieved by the opportunity to exercise his paternal feelings and display his competence, so that he can escape the immediate pressure of his social and domestic problems and see them in a more detached and philosophic light. When, on going to bed, he detects signs of the prior presence of Boylan, his sentiments move through envy, jealousy and abnegation to equanimity, and the reason for his final equanimity is that he can view the adultery, which has troubled his mind all day, as part of the natural order of things and as of little moment in a wider, even cosmic, perspective:

> As natural as any and every natural act of a nature expressed or understood executed in natured nature by natural creatures in accordance with his, her and their natured natures, of dissimilar similarity. As not as calamitous as a cataclysmic annihilation of the planet in consequence of collision with a dark sun. As less reprehensible than theft, highway robbery, cruelty to children and animals, obtaining money under false pretences, forgery, embezzlement, misappropriation of public money, betrayal of public trust, malingering, mayhem, corruption of minors, criminal libel, blackmail, contempt of court, arson, treason, felony, mutiny on the high seas, trespass, burglary, jail-breaking, practice of unnatural vice, desertion from armed forces in the field, perjury, poaching, usury, intelligence with the king's enemies, impersonation, criminal assault, manslaughter, wilful and premeditated murder. As not more abnormal than all other altered processes of adaptation to altered conditions of existence, resulting in a reciprocal equilibrium between the bodily organism and its attendant circumstances, foods, beverages, acquired habits, indulged inclinations, significant disease. As more than inevitable, irreparable. (*U* 693–4/865)

The ability to adjust to what cannot be helped is characteristic of Bloom, but the manner suggests that Bloom is under the influence of Stephen's air of philosophic detachment, a suggestion supported by the form of a subsequent question – 'By what reflections did he, a conscious reactor against the void incertitude, justify to himself his sentiments?' The answer to this question, culminating in references to 'the futility of triumph or protest or vindication: the inanity of extolled virtue: the lethargy of nescient matter: the apathy of the stars', shows again Bloom somewhat comically adopting to his own purposes the intellectual manner that he admires in Stephen. If the artist has been helped through practical difficulties by the competence and energy of the citizen, so, too, has the citizen been enabled, by the lofty unconcern of the artist for the common business of life, to rise above the troublesome emotions of envy and jealousy.

The parting handshake, indicative of the friendly contact made between the two men, is accompanied by a sound ('the sound of the peal of the hour of the night by the chime of the bells in the church of Saint George'):

> What echoes of that sound were by both and each heard?
> By Stephen:
> > *Liliata rutilantium. Turma circumdet.*
> > *Iubilantium te virginum. Chorus excipiat.*
>
> By Bloom:
> > *Heigho, heigho,*
> > *Heigho, heigho.* (U 665/826–7)

This recall, at the very hour of parting, of the words from the *Ordo Commendationis Animae* associated by Stephen in his first chapter with his dead mother, and of the sigh which in Bloom's first chapter reflected his sadness at Dignam's death, has been taken to mean that the two men are back where they started as far as any relationship between them is concerned.[12] But to place such weight on this local device, ignoring the very different and unmistakable implications of all that has preceded it and of Bloom's subsequent meditations and attitudes, is as unjustifiable as to treat Molly's closing 'Yes' as proof of the book's ultimate affirmation. Of course the meeting and communion of the two men cannot wipe from their memories their personal griefs and distresses; they have given each other temporary relief. What other relief from the problems of living is conceivable? It is natural that Stephen, hearing the bell, should remember his dead mother and that Bloom should remember the last time he heard it, when he was preparing to go to the funeral. However, there are subtle changes in the echoes: Stephen omits 'te confessorum', and, as the punctuation suggests, hears the words of the prayer robbed of meaning and swaying to the peal of the bells; Bloom's earlier sighs had been marked by capitals and exclamation marks ('Heigho! Heigho!') but the new punctuation is quieter, as though a faint echo of his earlier gloom. To imply that through their meeting the two men had escaped from their predicaments would be foolish: their problems are still with them, but, as the modified echoes suggest, they are subdued and manageable. This is what has come from the meeting of the opposites.

The two visions of life represented by Bloom and Stephen must remain opposites if there is to be any profitable interaction between them. The

---

[12] *Sultan*, 386–7. Sultan thinks that the outcome of the meeting is entirely on a spiritual plane, 'that by Bloom's agency Stephen shall achieve atonement with God and be free of the oppressions that constitute his story in *Ulysses*' (387).

resemblance between their fruitful interaction and Blake's declaration in *The Marriage of Heaven and Hell* is not, I think, coincidental:

> Without Contraries is no progression. Attraction and Repulsion, Reason and Energy, Love and Hate, are necessary to Human existence.

When, in Italy, Joyce was asked to lecture on English literature, he chose as his title *Verismo ed idealismo nella litteratura inglese (Daniele De Foe: William Blake)*. As this title suggests, he saw in realism and idealism the two poles on which literature turned, and in Defoe and Blake their two great English exemplars. (Defoe was one of the four authors of whom he claimed to have read everything, while Blake, besides being a potent influence in Stephen's mind, is centrally important in *Finnegans Wake*, the cycles of which turn on interacting opposites.) The opposition is a literary parallel to the opposition of Bloom and Stephen. But as with the characters, so with the nature of the novel: Joyce does not confine himself to either pole, which is no doubt why some critics have called the novel 'realist' and some 'symbolist'. Similarly, the fact that the vision of *Ulysses* embraces the opposed visions of Bloom and Stephen is perhaps the reason why some call the novel an affirmation of life and some a negation. It is more complex than either of these labels would make it out to be, but it is not incoherent, since its two poles are not unrelated but complementary. Joyce sees in human nature coexisting opposites: since he is a man, his own moral vision must share in this duality; consequently he shapes his novel to articulate in its narrative, characters, themes, structure and manner his twofold vision. He is far from being the first writer to see life in this double aspect or to use a dual vision as a central principle of his work, though in most novels, the novelist, for temperamental reasons or in response or reaction to the social *mores* of his time, gives more emphasis to one side or the other. We like to think of ourselves as consistent, though everything tells us we are not. However intellectual or spiritual we may be or aspire to be we have to come to terms with the physical practicalities of living and staying alive, and for this we have to depend on some more down-to-earth notions of what we are and what life is; however practical, realistic and earthy we may be, our existence is from time to time troubled by ideas of purpose, fears of death, hopes of some kind of immortality, notions of truth, or right and wrong, or beauty (in senses other than purely practical ones), and, however limited our responses may be, by the impulses loosely associated with art, religion or dreams of human progress. What Joyce has done is to give the moral vision of his novel the same coherence of coexisting polar opposites that characterizes all human moral vision in life.

But there remains Molly Bloom. How does she relate to the moral vision of the work as a whole? Clearly she cannot be said to share in the natures and attitudes of Stephen or of her husband, and her way of looking at life is quite distinct from theirs. One critic, S. L. Goldberg, has suggested that her soliloquy 'confuses all the subtle moral distinctions to which the whole book has been devoted', because 'her artistic function . . . is to affirm the possibility of *everything*.'[13] Joyce himself described Molly as 'amoral', but it is possible for a character to contribute to the moral vision of a novel without being a moral figure or agent. She represents the basic material of human nature and experience, not concerned with aspirations to penetrate and understand life or with hopes of improving and enriching it; she is not seriously disturbed by thoughts of the past nor concerned with plans for the future beyond those arising immediately from her present mood and situation. She doesn't confuse 'subtle moral distinctions' because as a person she doesn't bother her head with them, and as an element in the novel she is not involved with them. She is capable of discrimination; in some respects she prefers Boylan to her husband; in some respects she prefers her dream of an affair with a poet, Stephen, to either; and finally she turns affectionately, in her mind, to her husband and his courtship. But there is no consistency: her attitudes and opinions fluctuate, vary, contradict each other, and it is as easy to extract passages from the soliloquy to present her as a benign, maternal, natural figure embracing all life as to extract passages which show her to be squalid, selfish and fundamentally depraved. Bloom and Stephen are by no means always consistent, but they are guided by visions of their roles in life: they are the active voyagers in the odyssey, while Molly sits at home and waits, prepared to receive whoever may come along, Boylan, Stephen or her husband. If she represents '*das Fleisch das stets bejaht*', as opposed to the Mephistophelean Stephen who is '*der Geist, der stets verneint*',[14] it has to be remembered that just as the denying spirit affirms itself ('the eternal affirmation of the spirit of man') so too does the affirming flesh make a cavalier rejection of the claims of the spirit, of moral or spiritual purpose. Joyce is not making through Molly a sentimental world-embracing life-affirming declaration: he is merely acknowledging a truth about human nature which moralists tend to forget – that for most people (and for all people for the greater part of the time) the moral and spiritual purposes which trouble and motivate Stephen and Bloom are comparatively inactive. People, like Molly, have their lives to lead, and for the most part lead them without more than occasional thoughts of what is 'good' or 'true', and yet, despite annoyance and frustration and sadness, find life on the whole worth living – at least to the extent of not wanting it to stop. And even the lives of those who are most passionately engaged in pursuit of truth or what is good in the individual or in society, are for much of the time caught up in the daily undiscriminating demands of the flesh. The affirmation of the flesh is instinctive and amoral, but it is part of the human context in which all affirmers of the spirit of man and all who aspire to improve man's behaviour have to live and operate. It may seem a confusion and a cause of despair to visionaries and reformers, but it is the bedrock of human nature, which rests on no moral or rational convictions but simply is, and which makes for survival. Any insights or moral discriminations, however subtle, which ignore the foundation on which all human discrimination ultimately rests, may achieve clarity but

[13] *Joyce*, (London, Oliver and Boyd 1962), 99–100. [14] Goethe, *Faust* I, l.1338.

at the expense of oversimplifying. When Stephen has gone, and Bloom is asleep, this is what is left.

Arnold Kettle perceives this aspect of Molly's soliloquy, without I think, fully stating its relationship to the strenuous moral activity which precedes it:

> The only affirmation that Molly Bloom is permitted is in fact the sort of affirmation associated with a principle rather than a person. Her yes, like Anna Livia's, is the yes of the Eternal Feminine, no more an act of volition than the journey of the river to the sea, without which life would stop altogether, a possibility which even Joyce does not seem seriously to contemplate.[15]

This account of Molly's role associates it with Stephen's notion, in *Stephen Hero*, when 'puzzled and often maddened' by 'the general attitude of women towards religion', 'he toyed ... with a theory of dualism which would symbolise the twin eternities of spirit and nature in the twin eternities of male and female'; but even as early as this Joyce recognized the oversimplification of Stephen's views: 'It did not strike him that the attitude of women towards holy things really implied a more genuine emancipation than his own' (*SH* 215). Moreover, Stephen, despite his immaturity, does not identify spirit and nature with male and female; he toys with the idea of using the male-female polarity to symbolize the spirit-nature polarity. If Molly represents the basic life-urge 'without which life would stop altogether', it is not simply because she is a woman; the same urge exists in all humans irrespective of sex. All that Stephen postulated, and all that Joyce made use of in *Ulysses*, is a symbolic analogy between the natural force and the feminine nature. As a type of the fruitful female, Molly, with one living and one dead child and with no full marital intercourse for ten and a half years, cannot compete with the fecund Mrs Purefoy; if she represents the Eternal Feminine principle, she does so not because that principle is absent from the male characters, but because in her it is not obscured by moral and spiritual aspirations and endeavours.

It is true that Molly does not affirm as 'a person': Stephen can declare for 'the intellectual imagination' and Bloom for 'love', because they are motivated by aspirations; but Molly is not, and any personal affirmation from her, other than the cliché that 'nature is wonderful', would be totally out of character and, even if made, casual and not expressive of any pervading or persisting attitude to life. Her affirmation, such as it is, is implicit in her nature – implicit in the nature of everyone, but most evident in Molly because not confused with other, more personal, affirmations. It does not follow that, because her affirmation is expressive of a fundamental principle of life, she lacks personal identity, though this seems implied in Kettle's account of her, and is explicit in Goldberg's conclusion:

[15] Arnold Kettle, 'The Consistency of Joyce' in *The Pelican Guide to English Literature 7, The Modern Age*, ed. Boris Ford (Harmondsworth, Penguin Books 1961), 309.

Joyce had to be more concerned with the general idea Molly represents than with the specific quality of life embodied in his rendering of her. 'The now, the here' had finally to be sacrificed to its formless essence.[16]

I doubt whether anyone but a critic who had thought long and hard about the thematic significance of *Ulysses* could have come to this conclusion. In my experience, the ordinary reader, whatever he may think of the rest of the novel, at once apprehends the immediacy and reality of Molly's character and presence without troubling his head about 'the general idea' she may be supposed to represent. The critic, properly concerned with her place in the total vision of the book, tends to abstract the 'formless essence' and to label it in order that he may talk about it, but the abstraction is his work, not Joyce's. Molly's moral neutrality is not some abstract condition, it is the condition in which most of us lead most of our lives. It does not confuse the moral distinctions of the earlier parts of the novel: it underlies them and becomes apparent when they are quiescent. Nor does her neutrality sum up or represent the moral vision of the novel; it is a single but basic element in that vision as it is a single and basic element in life. So far from requiring a sacrifice of 'the specific quality of life', Molly's soliloquy is evidence of Joyce's refusal to sacrifice the sense of the particularized and transient flow of life as we daily experience it, in order to simplify the presentation of moral issues. One of the essential qualities and virtues of *Ulysses* is the scrupulous refusal to lift questions of moral discrimination out of the bewildering context of ordinary life: if we come to recognize and admire Bloom's goodness it is as a quality inseparable from his silliness, pettiness and smugness; if we learn to respect Stephen's intellect and singleness of purpose it is not by ignoring his vanity, arrogance and naive posings.

The moral vision of *Ulysses* is penetrating, extensive and coherent. Its complexity may be difficult to grasp on a first reading, but, because it is a complexity founded on every reader's own experience, it is ultimately not merely comprehensible but clarifying and illuminating. It shapes everything in the novel – narrative, structure and local methods of presentation. The polar opposites, Bloom and Stephen, are established and moved towards each other to the point where a spark of sympathy and understanding passes between them, and then they separate as they must. The dry and cynical narrative of the Unnamed One is interwoven with the inflated fantasies which are its complementary opposite. The presentation of Bloom's Samaritanism needs the contrary implications of the smug and officious style. The meeting in Bloom's kitchen, where the opposites approach each other most closely, requires a detached style uncommitted to the characteristic assumptions and attitudes of either man. The interior monologues are essential because the contrasting visions of life must be shown, not described, felt rather than understood. The more we know what it feels like to be Stephen, Bloom or Molly, the more we learn to recognize

[16] Goldberg, *Joyce*, 100.

our own experience in theirs, and thus to share the complexity of Joyce's vision instead of leaping to hasty and oversimplified moral judgements.

From early in his career (what follows was written soon after his twenty-first birthday), Joyce held that 'tragedy is the imperfect manner and comedy the perfect manner in art':

> An improper art aims at exciting in the way of comedy the feeling of desire but the feeling which is proper to comic art is the feeling of joy. Desire, as I have said, is the feeling which urges us to go to something but joy is the feeling which the possession of some good excites in us. . . . All art which excites in us the feeling of joy is so far comic and according as this feeling of joy is excited by whatever is substantial or accidental in human fortunes the art is to be judged more or less excellent. . . .[17]

A writer cannot be held to the formulations of his youth, but it seems typical of Joyce that he should have aimed, in *Ulysses*, at the highest excellence in what he took to be 'the perfect manner in art', for there is nothing more substantial in human fortunes than our daily experience itself nor any good of which we are more surely possessed. *Ulysses* is a comedy not in the sense of being a work designed to make the reader laugh (though it continually does that) or looking steadily away from whatever is harsh, painful or pathetic. It is comedy in that it includes so much – death and birth, remorse and self-congratulation, ambition and stagnation, pride and shame, isolation and companionship, love and hate, a variety of moods and relationships, the human qualities which most excite condemnation or disgust, the ordinary occupations which seem commonplace, trivial or unpleasant – and yet finds in it all cause for what Joyce calls 'joy'. Before his eighteenth birthday, he had foreseen the possibility of such a vision and such a work:

> Still I think out of the dreary sameness of existence, a measure of dramatic life may be drawn. Even the most commonplace, the deadest among the living, may play a part in a great drama. . . . Life we must accept as we see it before our eyes, men and women as we meet them in the real world, not as we apprehend them in the world of faery. The great human comedy in which each has share, gives limitless scope to the true artist, today as yesterday and as in years gone.[18]

[17] *Gorman*, 97. [18] *CW*, 45.

Chapter 6 'The traits featuring the *chiaroscuro* coalesce'

There can be no compromise between the artist and his society when the artist chooses isolation, is committed to a vocation which requires and justifies the refusal of other responsibilities and ties, and defines his own values largely in terms of opposition to those of society. This may be an extreme and romantic notion of the artist's nature, but it is one which Joyce as a young man certainly adopted, and there is nothing to suggest that, in later years, he abandoned it. What he did was to recognize in his own nature and present in his writings another and opposed position, equally necessary and valid. *Ulysses* implies that opposition, not integration, is the natural and healthy state, both in the individual and in society; the citizen and the artist are of value to each other precisely because they strive in different directions. There is 'a touch of the artist' about Bloom, and more than a touch of the citizen about Stephen (hence his remorse and bitterness), but their relationship does not depend on these. They meet on the basic ground of their common humanity: the need for some kind of genial human inter-course predates and underlies all arts and societies. *Ulysses* combines the recognition of that common elementary need with the acceptance of division; the reconciliation it images is a reconciliation to the necessity, if there is to be any vital living, of conflicting forces operating in every man and every society. The society and the individual become morally paralysed if one opposite is subdued in the interests of the other or for the sake of comfort and consistency – if the egoistic, aspiring spirit is subjugated to the service of family, nation, current *mores*, ideology or Church, or the altruistic goodwill of the citizen replaced by egoism masquerading as responsible citizenship, patriotism, morality or religion. Artist and citizen are, as it were, forces on opposite points of a wheel, pushing in opposite directions, but it is their energies, not 'the still centre', which make the wheel turn.

The wheel image and the polar interaction of artist and citizen, implicit in *Ulysses*, are elaborated in *Finnegans Wake* into an intricate and involved apparatus of general ideas, theories, schemes and patterns, embodied in an unprecedented density of form and language. No commentator has, as yet, provided a comprehensive, coherent and widely accepted account of the book's total ordering and significance. In so complex a work it is difficult even to distinguish what is central from what is subordinate or incidental,

or what is certainly (though subtly) present from what is the product of
overingenious reading. In such a situation, all interpretations are tentative.
But as the themes and organic structure of *Ulysses* are illuminated by
recognizing in them the convergence of *Dubliners* and the *Portrait*, so the
central concerns and governing ideas and patterns of *Finnegans Wake* are
clarified by seeing the book in relation to the earlier works. In Joyce's first
notebook for *Finnegans Wake*, the so-called *Scribbledehobble* book, the early
materials were sorted in categories headed by the titles of the fifteen stories
of *Dubliners*, the five sections of the *Portrait*, and the Odyssean titles of the
eighteen chapters of *Ulysses*, together with a few other headings. Some of
these preliminary notes refer to 'S.D.' and 'L.B.',[1] and, as is well-known,
the finished work, besides rehearsing in one paragraph all the *Dubliners*
titles in modified form, refers to all the other published writings – to
'shamebred music', 'gash from a burner', 'a poor trait of the artless' and
'his usylessly unreadable Blue Book of Eccles'. I do not propose offering
here more than some indications of the ways in which the developing art
and vision of the earlier books were continued in *Finnegans Wake*, but, at
least, it can be said that such an approach is in keeping with the nature of
Joyce's career as an artist and not mere airy speculation.

All children learn early that the life which goes on inside their heads is very
different from and has to be concealed in the social life which involves
them at school or at home, and in Joyce the awareness of division must have
been exacerbated by the assertiveness of the demands made on him. He
was clever, and therefore was expected to serve; in a declining home he was
to restore the family's status, in a subjugated country he was to engage in
the struggle for national independence, in a world of sin he was to fight the
good fight as an officer of the Church militant. In various ways, as a child,
he responded dutifully to these calls – won scholarships, hero-worshipped
Parnell, behaved with piety – and, in a less exacting situation, might have
found a way of reconciling the claims of family, country and Church with
his own dreams and aspirations. But too much was required of him, and
too little understanding of his difficult nature offered. Other Irish artists
were able to compromise, and satisfy the claims of society with a veneer of
conformity or an acceptable nonconformity, but Joyce seems to have been
forced, by the extremity of his gifts and the extremity of the demands
pressed on him, to make a choice between submission and recalcitrance.
He took refuge in 'silence, exile and cunning', adopted as his motto the
Luciferian 'I will not serve', and left Ireland.

In leaving Ireland, he figuratively turned his back on his family, his
nation, and his faith, but, as every reader perceives, they had shaped and
marked his nature permanently. He was recurrently troubled by feelings of

[1] *James Joyce's Scribbledehobble: The Ur-Workbook for 'Finnegans Wake'*, ed. Thomas
E. Connolly (Northwestern University Press and London, Oxford University Press
1961). Phillip F. Herring has observed that some of the *Scribbledehobble* materials were
transferred from the British Museum notesheets for *Ulysses* (*Notesheets*, 525).

responsibility towards the family he had left in Ireland (though rarely able to translate these feelings into any sustained course of action); Dublin and Ireland remained major interests and sources of inspiration; and his methods, functions and nature as an artist all reveal the effects of his training in the Roman Catholic Church. Stephen's fears, remorse, and bitterness, in the early chapters of *Ulysses*, reflect the pain and conflict of renunciation, and for many years Joyce seems to have dreamt of a recon-ciliation – though a reconciliation on his own terms, when his countrymen would recognize his genius and admit that they had been wrong. It was a dream which his own writings showed was wildly improbable and which they themselves made impossible. It is as though the Bloom in him longed for approval, while the Stephen in him put such approval quite out of reach. He might have gained, in time, a modest recognition by continuing in the vein of *Chamber Music*, but most Dublin readers were irritated by the exposure of the life of the city in the short-stories, angered by the arrogance of the young artist who implied that the free spirit could not survive in Ireland, revolted by the content and language of *Ulysses*, and persuaded by *Finnegans Wake* that the man who had cut himself off from the traditions and hopes of his people had finally, and deservedly, wandered into a state of mental alienation.

Yet while his books widened the split between him and his origins, absence made Joyce more tolerant, or, perhaps, freed from the imminent pressures, his defensive reaction was less violent. (The violence was quickly restored by return; in 1909, when he was visiting Ireland, he wrote to Nora, 'Dublin is a detestable city and the people are most repulsive to me.'[2]) But from Europe things looked not quite so bad. The change in attitude is already apparent in the letter, written to his brother in September 1906, where he speaks of the attraction of Dublin, and wonders whether, in *Dubliners*, he has been 'unnecessarily harsh' to Ireland.[3] The increasing understanding of the city he had abandoned was associated with an increas-ing acceptance of what was ordinary and vulgar in his own nature. In *Dubliners*, the wretched predicaments of Mr Duffy and Gabriel Conroy are, at least in part, images of what he felt might have happened to him if he had stayed in Dublin – a barren isolation or a ludicrous conformity – yet there is already a difference in tone between the sardonic presentation of Mr Duffy's Pharisaism and the sympathetic treatment of Gabriel Conroy's awareness of failure. From this point onwards, Joyce's work begin to recognize that the commonplace man in him could no more be obliterated by the egoistic artist, who admitted no responsibilities save to his own vocation, than the artistic self could be submitted to the dominion of the citizen. In his life, too, the flamboyant, reckless, defiant, irresponsible bohemian was gradually replaced by the bourgeois family man. Freed from the compulsion to offer an heroic posture to the outside world, the artist could concentrate

[2] *Letters* II, 243. Cf. *Letters* II, 239: 'How sick, sick, sick I am of Dublin! It is the city of failure, of rancour and of unhappiness. I long to be out of it.'
[3] *Letters* II, 166.

on a more appropriate heroism – the accomplishment of Herculean literary tasks.

Yet Joyce's career is not an illustration of art as therapy or of art made possible by the healing of psychological wounds. What Joyce himself felt to be the crucial action in his development, both as man and as artist, was his union with Nora Barnacle, though that, as the history of the early years of their relationship shows, did not produce any dramatic transformation or integration of his personality. What it perhaps did was to increase the strained opposition between his two selves, to force him at length to submit to claims which clashed with his earlier fantasies of absolute artistic freedom, and to induce in him a greater respect for people not fired by 'the intellectual imagination'. He quickly perceived in Nora a disposition 'much nobler than my own'.[4] From the time of his elopement, one can trace in the letters a growth, weak and uncertain at first, frequently interrupted, but persisting, towards an involvement in and dependence on others, a renewal of the ties of family which he had earlier so painfully rejected as inimical to his spirit.[5] It is not a shift from being an artist to being a citizen, but a change in the relationship between the two aspects of Joyce's nature, a change manifested in his writings as well as in his life.[6]

In *Dubliners* (apart from 'The Dead') little is conceded openly to the *mores* of the city. The figure of the artist does not appear except in trivial or corrupted forms, although his presence is felt in the disciplined and refined conduct of the stories, and implicit in the criteria by which the city is judged. The dominant attitude is that of the artist identifying and exposing the city's endemic spiritual disease, although already that attitude is coloured with the estranged citizen's sense of loss and his reluctant enjoyment of the remembered variety and comic peculiarity of his fellow citizens.

The appearance of the artist as the central figure in the *Portrait*, instead of the off-stage observer of *Dubliners*, may seem a further step in the rejection of the city. Certainly the growth of the artist replaces the stagnation of the city as the focus and unifying principle. Yet, in fact, the inter-relationship of the two attitudes is much more firmly and pervasively realized. In *Dubliners*, the artist's view of the city, being implicit in the content and manner of the stories, is, within the book itself, unchallengeable, but in the *Portrait* he becomes part of the comedy, exposed to the same ironic light as the world about him, and thus his serious pursuit of his destiny and his progressive withdrawal from his environment can seem, at one and the same time, both admirable and priggish. In other ways, too, the very nature of the *Portrait* necessitates a more sympathetic attitude

---

⁴ *Letters* II, 80.

⁵ Stuart Gilbert thought that he had 'never met anyone else with such a strong sense of the family tie and its obligations' ('Introduction', *Letters* I, 32).

⁶ Joyce called the *Portrait* 'the book of my youth' and *Ulysses* 'the book of my maturity': 'Youth is a time of torment in which we can see nothing clearly, but in *Ulysses* I have seen life clearly, I think, and as a whole. It has taken me half a lifetime to reach the necessary equilibrium to express it, for my youth was exceptionally painful and violent' (Arthur Power, 'Conversations with Joyce', *JJQ* III (1) (Fall 1965), 45).

towards Dublin life and a fuller recognition of its appeal to Joyce himself. The closing departure to Europe has to seem, to Stephen at least, not a defeated flight, but a hard-won detachment, and this entails some indication of the attractions of what is abandoned. There is, consequently, a swaying balance between sympathy and rejection. When the family moves to Dublin, Stephen finds the city 'a new and complex sensation', and, despite resentment and depression, everything and everyone he encounters affects him intimately, 'whether alluring or disheartening'. Ultimately, it is the squalor of his home and 'the dull phenomenon of Dublin' which is destined 'to win the day in his soul' over the life of quiet and order offered by the Church. His soul does not surrender to disorder, but his image of the artist becomes that of one who creates 'out of the sluggish matter of the earth a new soaring impalpable imperishable being'. The presence in the city of a sensitive, responsive, articulate and developing imagination means that the environment is more intimately and positively sensed than in *Dubliners*; the reader is as aware of its contribution to the growth of the artist as of the impediments it puts in his way. The rejection of the city is more explicitly motivated and decisive than in the short-stories, but the association of the city with sensuous delight, intellectual interest, imaginative experience and feelings of nostalgia is made more forcefully and continually. The *Portrait* presents a counter-force to the influence of Dublin and Ireland, and the focus of attention shifts from the stunted life of the community as a whole to the intense inner life of the embryo artist; but at the same time the interaction of artist and city is more richly and complexly apprehended. This is why most readers have recognized (and some exaggerated) the irony implicit in Stephen's triumphant and self-dramatizing farewell to Ireland. It is the culmination of a self-liberating process which is the main forward movement of the novel, but everything in the handling of the process – the structure, the various styles, Stephen's fluctuating responses to the world around him, even the nature of his early attempts to understand and practise his vocation – indicates that this liberation is not the final step into maturity and artistic achievement; all Stephen has achieved is a clearing of the ground, a necessary preparation for a deeper insight into his own inner conflict and for a more balanced acceptance of it.

Before any resolution could be achieved, it was necessary to develop the concepts of artist and citizen and transform their mode of presentation. *Ulysses* imposes this transformation abruptly and forcefully. The artist's painfully chosen isolation has proved sterile; detachment, however necessary, has proved as unfruitful as submission; it is now equally necessary for him to renew sympathies. He has had to reach the position where he seemed to need no one before he could recognize his true needs. The citizen, too, is transformed. Bloom has the weaknesses and frustrations of the citizens of *Dubliners*: like Eveline he dreams impotently of escape, like Jimmy Doyle he feels excluded from the life of the wealthy, he has vicarious sexual experiences like Lenehan, and is dominated like Bob Doran by women; in his sentimental fantasies and subordination at home he is like little Chandler, like Farrington he is bullied at work, in the ordinary life of the city he is as much an outsider as Maria, and he shares Mr Duffy's prudence and fears of emotional involvement; like Mrs Kearney, he sees art primarily as a means to status and money, he is as capable of absurd self-deception and ignorance as Tom Kernan and his friends, he settles like the men in the Committee Room for reminiscences of past political activity, and like Gabriel Conroy he wavers between self-congratulation and a sense of his own ludicrous inadequacy. He even resembles the boy of the first three stories in his inability to find intellectual nourishment in the city, his romanticizing of his sexual desires, and his timid longings for adventure. But he is not defeated, nor morally paralysed, and he is motivated by a general good nature which, though entangled with self-interest, is not distorted or disabled by it. He is as much in need of someone on whom to exercise his altruism as Stephen is in need of someone whose simple good-will may help him to break out of his isolation. The mutual needs of citizen and artist are the forces which make for and bring about a temporary resolution of their inner conflicts.

They are also the bases of the main secondary patterns of the novel – the Odyssean scheme and the search of Son for Father, Father for Son – which express in terms of a fundamental human relationship the spiritual need of the artist, and give mythological and theological parallels to the humble need of the citizen, thus helping to preserve the sense of its genuineness, dignity and importance through all the follies and confusions of Bloom's day. The other patterns, the organs and the arts, create a static image of the diseased and corrupted city: Joyce is neither withdrawing the damning account of Dublin presented in the short-stories nor saying that Stephen was wrong to turn his back on such a city. The resolution is arrived at not by a softening or compromising of the opposed attitudes, but through an unexpected movement of sympathy between the man who is rejected by the city and the artist who rejected it – a sympathy which helps both to sustain their contrasted roles.

Yet this resolution might have been little more than a formulaic gesture of reconciliation if it were not accompanied by a fundamental change in the author's handling of his subject. In *Dubliners* the city is experienced entirely through the medium of the artist whose values are implicit in the authorial voice; when we enter a character's mind, we are always being told about it, or else its operations are being represented in language and imagery manifestly devised by the author, however responsive to the particular character or situation. Even the first-person narrator of the first three stories is plainly not the boy himself but the mature artist looking back to his childhood. The modulations of style in the *Portrait* are more intricate and bolder, but are still the methods of the mature artist designed to represent the experiences of the boy and the young man. The striking difference in *Ulysses* is that for the first time (apart from Stephen's journal at the end of the *Portrait*) both artist and citizen are apparently speaking for themselves and in their own terms, through the convention of the interior monologue. Of course, the convention is itself a medium created by the mature artist, but it is a medium which gives equal rights to the opposed varieties of life, and demands from the author himself a total cooperation between the two aspects of his nature. To write the interior monologues of Bloom and Molly, Joyce had to focus on that part of himself which was most commonplace and least artistic, and yet call upon the most powerful resources of his intellectual imagination to express and order what he saw. This kind of interplay is more fundamental to the nature of *Ulysses* than even the action and the patterns; the artist is now engaged in that transmutation of common life which he believed was his destiny. The interior monologues are themselves only the most direct expression of the governing principle of the whole novel. No other novel had concerned itself at such length and in such detail with daily life, the casual humdrum of the citizen, and yet no other novel had been so consciously and even ostentatiously 'artistic'. Some said that Joyce had abandoned the essential selectiveness of art in his obsessive recital of the squalid and trivial minutiae of existence, while others objected that the sense of real life was lost in a pointless display of artistic virtuosity. Similar criticisms of the novel continue to be made, and they are not wholly without foundation: *Ulysses* is the most realistic and the most artificial of novels. But neither the realism nor the artificiality is arbitrary; they coexist in the novel because they are formal polarities which characterize Joyce's mature vision of man's nature. Their interaction determines not only the contrasted interior monologues of Stephen and Bloom but also the more elaborate techniques of the latter half of the novel, where an extraordinarily articulate artist deliberately confines himself to the limited expressive ranges of girls' papers, officialese, matter-of-fact statement, or the inconsequential mind of an uneducated and unintelligent woman – and out of these makes refined instruments of expression. The citizen and the artist come gradually together in the styles and techniques of the novel as well as in its action.

The thoroughness with which the artist-citizen theme is embodied in *Ulysses* seems to leave little room for new developments in its handling. Yet that thoroughness was possible only within severe spatial and temporal restrictions. The novel raises questions about space and time, from the point where Stephen, on the beach, defines them respectively as the 'ineluctable modality of the visible' and the 'ineluctable modality of the audible' to his self-affirmation, in Bloom's kitchen, as 'a conscious rational reagent between a micro- and a macrocosm ineluctably constructed upon the incertitude of the void'. But these concepts of the dimensions of space and time as projected by and focussing in the individual consciousness exist mainly as ideas: they are not importantly realized in the handling of the book. It contains a few divergencies from the usual space-time system of the novel form: in 'Wandering Rocks', time is retarded while we view incidents taking place in close temporal proximity all over Dublin, and, in "Circe', there are, as it were, stops in the time of the novel and holes in its space, which are occupied by the representations of the characters' subconscious climate. But, in general, both space and time in *Ulysses* are exceptionally limited to a city and its suburbs during a period of eighteen hours. These limitations are formally apt and functional, suggesting the claustrophobic parochialism of Irish life and the oppressive weight of Irish history as clogs and burdens experienced through every hour of every day. Yet the influence of Ireland as a spatial and temporal environment is only an immediate and localized aspect of a much greater influence – that of the world in which we live and the history of man back to his first emergence and development. Many of the qualities for which Stephen condemns or rejects his native city are plainly no more than Dublin manifestations of universal conditions; the nightmare of history from which he is trying to awake began with Adam.[7] But although it is easy enough to accept the abstract idea that our experience is conditioned by the space-time continuum in which we find ourselves, it is very difficult to apprehend the immanence of such influence in the particulars of our daily life, and even more difficult to conceive of literary conventions capable of representing it. To focus a four-dimensional universe in the conscious and unconscious experience of a single man would require a new kind of writing, which could represent simultaneously our experience as we are aware of it, and as it is related to our specific location in time and space, and as it is involved in the whole of human experience, regardless of location in time and space. Moreover, the connection between the particular and the universal would have to be two-way: no doubt the space-time continuum exerts an influence on the experience of the individual, but, equally, since space and time themselves are merely the modalities of seeing and hearing, the nature of the seeing and hearing individual is projected into and expressed by the universe he apprehends.

What kind of individual, or, more properly, what kind of image of an individual could operate as the microscopic centre of this macrocosm? In one sense he would have to be an Everyman, representative of all the varieties of men and of all human experience; yet, in another sense, he would have to be an individual man in order to suggest how all history and space are factors in and modalities of the experience of every single human being. He would have to be seen as the point in which all the forces in man's history and environment – rises and falls, loves and hates, hopes and fears, the natural world and the manmade world – intersect; and, on the other hand, as the point from which all the temporal and spatial universe is projected. All men and women, whether real or fictional, all historical movements and conflicts, all societies, all institutions, all environments would have to meet in this one man as influences, and yet be seen as externalizations of his complex nature.

Not surprisingly, in *Finnegans Wake*, Joyce has made his figure an Irishman, though one of uncertain origins, and has placed the story in Dublin and its suburbs; if all space and time are to be focused in a microcosm, the microcosmic point of view must be the one familiar to the author. The people, forces, conflicts, environments and institutions most palpably

[7] Cf. ' "For myself," Joyce answered, "I always write about Dublin, because if I can get to the heart of Dublin I can get to the heart of all the cities in the world. In the particular is contained the universal" ' (Arthur Power, *From the Old Waterford House* (London, Mellifont Press 1944, 65)).

operating on him and reflecting his nature are Irish, although they are seen as local manifestations of universal factors. He stands, as it were, immediately surrounded by the situation of his life: beyond it stretches, on the one hand, his personal history, the history of his family, of his fellow citizens, of his race, of all mankind, and, on the other hand, the physical and social environment of the place where he lives, of his country, his continent, his world, his universe. Each of these is a force helping to shape him; and something which he helps to shape; and, also, something which translates his inner nature into terms of space and time. For instance, as a citizen, he is influenced by the physical and social characteristics of his city, and, through that, by the characteristics of all cities and human communities; yet those characteristics are determined, both physically and socially, by his nature and the nature of all who have dwelt in that city or in any city or community; and, finally, the essence of the place as he experiences it is inseparable from his own essence – the very idea of a city or of city life is a creation of the common human mind and has no other existence. Man piles 'buildung supra buildung' – erects buildings, deposits his waste, forms cultures and civilizations (German: *Bildung*) – and, in doing so, makes an environment in his own image (German: *Bild*). The citizen projects from his mind the physical world he inhabits: from his experience of that physical world, the artist creates a new world of the imagination, which then modifies the citizen's mind and, with it, the world it projects. This is to reduce to formula what in *Finnegans Wake* is an organic cycle.

Such a figure makes it possible to take the fictional representation of the artist-citizen polarity a stage further. In *Ulysses*, as in the traditional forms of the novel and the drama, the polarities of human nature are figured in terms of the relationships and conduct of individuals. Thus, although in the Shakespeare discussion Stephen may use the labels of Iago and Othello to refer to conflicting forces within Shakespeare, in the play itself the emphasis naturally falls on two contrasted men, not on quasi-allegorical figures. This traditional literary externalization of inner polarities reflects a similar process of externalization in our daily lives: our behaviour is a simplified expression of the balance and intensity of inner forces; we categorize and judge others according to what we take to be the dominant forces inside them; we interpret their behaviour in the light of the polarities, conscious or unconscious, within ourselves. If all human experience was to be focused in the new fictional figure, it would have to include this kind of externalized opposition, but without allowing it undue emphasis at the expense of the fluctuating and role-changing polarities basic to all human nature. Consequently the 'persons' of *Finnegans Wake* are both individuals and representatives of aspects of our nature; they are presented both as people surrounding in life the central figure, and as parts of his own psychological make-up. Wherever he looks, he discovers himself.

Because all the opposed forces working in human nature are interacting and related, their plainest external manifestation and their clearest image is the family. The central figure is himself a family of interacting opposites ('a family all to himself' – *FW* 392) whose immediate externalization is in the people who share his home. All the main polarities in our nature – male and female principles, altruist and egoist, saint and sinner, innocence and experience, parent and child, virgin and whore, master and servant, artist and citizen, or whatever other labels can be attached to these forces – are projected in familial terms; the family is the innermost parts of the radiating lines of force connecting the individual centre with the whole of universal experience. Stephen's notion, in *Stephen Hero*, of a 'dualism which would symbolise the twin eternities of spirit and nature in the twin eternities of male and female' (*SH* 215), is figured in the husband-wife relationship, from courtship through all the ups and downs of married life and parenthood to viduity. The more obviously warring opposites, such as artist and citizen, saint and sinner, altruist and egoist, are mirrored in the contentions of twin brothers (each, as it were, an aspect of the father), combining only to overthrow and supplant the father. As open conflict of this kind seems characteristic of the male principle, so the more continuous and insidious natural process by which one state or one generation is replaced by its successor can be represented by a daughter who gradually and inevitably takes her mother's place as the symbol of femininity; within both mother and daughter are opposed aspects (simplified in such opposites as temptress and loyal wife, whore and virgin), but to Joyce these seem merely two ways of looking at the same qualities, a woman and her mirror-image. A manservant and a maidservant, representing subordinated and practical aspects of male and female, complete a 'howthold of nummer seven' (*FW* 242). Through these seven intermediary figures, human nature in all its basic roles and aspects is projected through all space and time, including mythical, legendary and fictional space and time.

Yet if these figures were given too great a consistency, they would be merely allegorical representations suggesting a much too rigid categorization of the kaleidoscope of experience. The same impulse or quality takes on very different appearances in different contexts; the same man behaves very differently in different situations: the historical analogues to our varying moods and predicaments will be found in very different, even opposed, figures. For instance, in his courtship of his bride, the father plays a Tristan-role, but, when he is forestalled by his sons in his pursuit of young women, they are Tristan (their symbolic images, Tree and Stone, coalescing in the name of the young lover) and he King Mark. As the old order being supplanted by the new, he plays Isaac Butt to his sons' Parnell, but as a public man brought low by a woman he himself plays Parnell. He can figure as God observing the conflict between Nick (Lucifer, old Nick) and Mick (St Michael) – his contending sons and the opposed forces in his own nature –, and, at other times, is himself a fallen angel or an archangel. His wife is both the cause of his fall and the agent of his resurgence, a mourning Isis or a Merry Widow, while his daughter's role ranges continuously between childlike innocence and accomplished seductiveness: she is the Virgin Mary and Mary Magdalene, Stella and Vanessa, Marie-Louise and Josephine, Hetty Jane the 'child of Mary' dressed in white and gold and Essie Shanahan who 'has let down her skirts' and is exposing her person on the stage. Even the warring sons frequently exchange parts, frequently coalesce into a single figure, and frequently become a trinity, the third person of which is an amalgamation of the opposites. The black sheep is false Jacob deceiving his simple brother, Esau, but, as the outcast who sold his birthright, he is Esau. When the father plays Julius Caesar, he is overthrown by the rising forces of Brutus and Cassius, but replaced by their combined form, Mark Antony. All the projections into time and space are of aspects and processes of human nature and experience rather than of consistent human selves, and therefore they find their parallels in similar aspects and processes, not in prototypical figures of the past. In one aspect of experience or one member of the family several historical figures may, at a given time, coalesce, and, similarly, one historical figure, because of the variousness of his nature and life-story, may at different times be associated with different members of the family. Thus, although there is a family of types of experience, they are not permanently linked to specific human selves, 'since in this scherzarade of one's thousand one nightinesses that sword of certainty which would identifide the body never falls' (FW 51). Like the inhabitants of a dream, all the figures of the comedy are the manifold and protean night-forms adopted (or, figuratively, the various nightdresses put on) by the mind of the one dreamer, and between them there can be no sharp divisions. The very notions of a distinct self and of a mankind composed of innumerable selves, each unique, consistent, and as identifiable as a fingerprint are questioned, and it is impossible 'to identifine the individuone' (FW 51).

To abandon these notions is to abandon the fundamental assumptions on which literature has been based. Our images of ourselves and of the people we know become hardly distinguishable from the characters who inhabit literature; all are abstractions from the welter of experience, attempts to invent an order out of a confusion. Ordered representations of experience are equally fictional whether they are composed of declared fictions (Hector and Achilles, Othello and Iago, Stephen and Bloom), of abstractions (Right and Wrong, Good and Evil, Altruism and Egoism), of categorical types (Artist and Citizen, Parent and Child, Man and Woman), of inner subdivisions (Reason and Imagination, Ego and Libido, Me and Not-me), or of supposedly real existences (I, You, He, She). If all these kinds of abstracted fictions coexist equally in a single work, then the elements are bound to shift about, not only between fictions of the same kind, but also from one kind to another, and be at various times related to figures from the past or literature, to abstract qualities, to human types, to mental faculties and to 'real' individuals: the work is indeed 'a collideorscape'.

Even in this respect, *Finnegans Wake* is the extreme and unexpected culmination of a development traceable in Joyce's earlier writings. The people of *Dubliners* are subtly perceived and understood, but the nature of their delineation implies a world of unique selves. They are representative of the range of Dublin life and have in common the one moral sickness, but their distinctness from each other has to be emphasized in order to illustrate the prevalence of the sickness in widely varying individuals and situations: they are a set of differentiated specimens, shrewdly identified, and defined in terms of traditional literary characterization. In the *Portrait*, however, although Joyce has deliberately limited his image to those elements which were formative in the growth of the artist, the presentation of Stephen is far more impressionistic, fluctuating, undetermined, and complex, with the consequence that readers whose lives and dispositions bear no resemblance to Stephen's and who know nothing at first-hand of Jesuit education or Irish society, recognize, in this highly specific image of an exceptional childhood, a reflection of their own childhoods. It is not simply a matter of 'identification' with the hero or heroine of a book; because of a narrative method which suggests the forms, processes and developments of Stephen's mind as well as its contents, we do not think, 'My childhood was something like that', but 'Being a child was something like that.' Thus, although the portrait is of a very unusual child and youth who became increasingly aware of the gulf between his own nature and the natures of those who surrounded him, we respond to and recognize an image, implicit in Joyce's method, of the common basis of human experience. The concept of the self and of self-awareness is far more complex than in the *Dubliners* stories. In *Ulysses*, the direct representation of self-awareness and the interplay of incongruous elements within the individual self is taken much farther, as is the coexistence within the one book of two apparently incompatible emphases – on the distinctness of identities and on the community of experience. Stephen and Bloom are not merely separate individuals but polar opposites, yet the movement of the book is towards their meeting, and, more importantly, its very method depends on the reader's ability to recognize the existence of both poles within his own experience. The interior monologues are intelligible to him only because he can perceive in them images of some aspects of his own mind; just as they all sprang from the multifaceted mind of a single author, so they are responded to by the multifaceted mind of each reader. The polar opposites are sometimes combined, and sometimes inverted. There seems to be adumbrated a double apprehension of the nature of the self: when Joyce looks at society, he sees its movements dependent on the interaction of contrasted individuals; when he looks at the individual self he sees its movements dependent on the interaction of contrasted forces analogous to warring selves. The self can appear single or multiple according to the observer's point of view.

Yet this notion is something implicit in the conception of the book rather than fully articulated in its execution. In *Finnegans Wake* it is not only fundamental, but explicit, as in Anna's 'mamafesta memorialising the Mosthighest':

> Closer inspection of the *bordereau* would reveal a multiplicity of personalities inflicted on the documents or document and some prevision of virtual crime or crimes might be made by anyone unwary enough before any suitable occasion for it or them had so far managed to happen along. In fact, under

the closed eyes of the inspectors the traits featuring the *chiaroscuro* coalesce, their contrarieties eliminated, in one stable somebody similarly as by the providential warring of heartshaker with housebreaker and of dramdrinker against freethinker our social something bowls along bumpily, experiencing a jolting series of prearranged disappointments, down the long lane of (it's as semper as oxhousehumper!) generations, more generations and still more generations. (*FW* 107)

The passage recognizes the same principle of multiplicity in singularity in both the 'stable somebody' and the 'social something', and suggests the only action in which such a 'somebody' can be involved – an action implicit in his very nature. As the progress of society derives from 'the providential warring' of the opposed elements within it and consists of a bumpy rising and falling, 'prearranged' because a necessary consequence of its constitution, so the progress through life of the 'stable somebody' is brought about by the interacting forces of his multiple contrarieties, as a wheel moves by the complex movements, in different directions and varying speeds, of the opposed points of its circumference. The wheel image recurs frequently in *Finnegans Wake*, is fundamental to the organization of the book, and was in Joyce's mind from the beginning. In 1927 he told Harriet Weaver,

All the engines I know are wrong. Simplicity. I am making an engine with only one wheel. No spokes of course. The wheel is a perfect square. You see what I am driving at, don't you? I am awfully solemn about it, mind you, so you must not think it is a silly story about the mouse and the grapes. No, it's a wheel, I tell the world. *And* it's all *square*.[8]

The importance of the wheel image was that it not only represented the union of contrarieties in a single whole but suggested the way in which these opposed forces inevitably and predictably created movement. Such a movement, implicit in the very nature of what moves, is the only conceivable type of action for a universal being. Yet because a smooth and unhesitant progress from one state to another hardly figures the nature of our experience, the wheel has to be a square one jolting along bumpily like 'our social something'.

Joyce was never very interested in inventing complicated actions for his fictions.[9] In *Dubliners*, there was so little action of the kind critics expected that many called the book a collection of sketches rather than stories; the *Portrait* has no 'plot' nor even a sustained and concatenated series of events – Stephen's course is essentially determined by the permanent constituent forces of his nature, despite the various pressures to which he is subjected; and certainly what happens in *Ulysses* bears little resemblance to what is usually thought of as the action of a novel. The events of all three books are deliberately ordinary. The theory of the epiphany is the work of an artist who sees his function as the perception and presentation of the *claritas* of the commonplace not the devising of stories to convey or illustrate an idea.

[8] *Letters* I, 251.
[9] According to Stanislaus Joyce, his brother 'came to consider a well-ordered plot in a novel or story as a meretricious literary interest, like the story in a *tableau de genre*' (*MBK*, 106).

There was also, from the beginning, a suggestion of cyclic movement. In *Dubliners*, the wheels of the characters' lives are turning on the spot, giving only an illusion of movement; their pointless turning is figured in the story, told in 'The Dead', of Patrick Morkan's horse which became so accustomed to walking round and round in a circle to drive the mill, that, when taken out for a drive, it continuously circled round the statue of William III. The movement through the five chapters of the *Portrait* can also be seen as cyclic, the upward movement of the spirit at the end of each chapter flattening out and then beginning to descend, until at the bottom of the cycle there is some new rising impetus. But here the turning wheel is not stationary – it moves into a new situation. The same is true of *Ulysses*, where the encounter of the two orbits of Bloom and Stephen gives each the energy to move out of what might have become a vicious circle. The home which Bloom leaves as Calypso's island, he returns to as his Ithaca; the wheel of his life has turned and, in turning, has altered to some extent both the position in which he finds himself and his capacity for handling the new situation.

The action of *Ulysses* is certainly both ordinary and representative of a relationship basic to human life, but nothing as specific as that can encompass all possible actions as the central figure of *Finnegans Wake* is intended to encompass all possible experience. What is wanted is an action implicit in and consequent upon the constitution of any unity composed of conflicting opposites, and also, since it has to be the essence of all actions, something implicit in the very concept of an action. The only action that satisfies these requirements is the movement from birth through maturity to death, with the renewal of movement resulting from the seed planted in each completed cycle. The terms, 'birth', 'maturity', 'death' and 'seed' are metaphors; the same cycle is followed by inorganic as by organic existence; it applies equally to the atom and the physical universe, to all objects, plants and animals, and to man, his groupings, his institutions, and to all he creates or experiences. (Or it may be that just as space and time are the modalities of our seeing and hearing, cyclic movements are projected on to our experience by the modality of our consciousness.) It depends on the interplay of opposites and illustrates their underlying identity, since the first moment of birth is the first moment of dying[10] and the same cyclic movement produces simultaneously ascent and descent.

It is with the moral or spiritual cycles experienced directly by man that Joyce is centrally concerned. He is not a philosopher, an historian or a psychologist presenting theories or constructing hypothetical models but a novelist creating an image of his own sense of what being a man is like and what living is like. The conceptual schemes that he borrowed from various theoreticians served as metaphorical representations of the intricate two-way network of forces which he felt operating within him and binding his own experience to the universe of space and time in which he existed.

[10] In the *Portrait*, Temple is credited with this commonplace: '– The most profound sentence ever written, Temple said with enthusiasm, is the sentence at the end of the zoology. Reproduction is the beginning of death' (*P* 235).

One of them, Giambattista Vico's cyclic theory of history, like the *Odyssey* in *Ulysses*, contributed a structural metaphor. Vico's hypothesis was that the history of human society could be reduced to a four-part cycle, moving from anarchy, to theocratic monarchy, aristocracy, democracy and thence back to anarchy. According to Vico, God's first thunderclap initiated the cycle by terrifying primitive and homeless nomads into taking refuge in caves, whence developed family life and tribal groups ruled by priest-kings, skilled in the propitiation of the heavens. Later arrivals in these societies became a slave-class, while, in the struggles between the tribes, there emerged a feudal aristocracy of leaders and heroes. The resistance of the serfs to the privileges and authority of the aristocracy led to the gradual appearance of democracy which, through the destruction of hierarchical order, eventually collapsed into anarchy and chaos, out of which came a new authoritarian monarchy. It seems likely that more people know about Vico's theory through commentaries on *Finnegans Wake* than through direct acquaintance with the philosopher's work; Joyce himself was less interested in the historical validity of the scheme than in its convenience. It offered a four-part cycle for the movement of societies, analogous to the basic action of birth–maturity–death–generation. It presented, as Samuel Beckett has observed,

> the spectacle of a human progression that depends for its movement on individuals, and which at the same time is independent of individuals in virtue of what appears to be a preordained cyclicism. . . . Individuality is the concretion of universality, and every individual action is at the same time superindividual. The individual and the universal cannot be considered as distinct from each other.[11]

The theoretical concepts and structures which Joyce employed in *Finnegans Wake* are there not because they commanded his full intellectual assent, but because they were formulations which projected into the outer world of time and space what he intuitively apprehended in his own experience, and helped him to represent his sense of the interplay between the individual and the universe: as he told Harriet Weaver, in recommending to her the works of Vico and Giordano Bruno, 'I would not pay overmuch attention to these theories, beyond using them for all they are worth, but they have gradually forced themselves on me through circumstances of my own life.'[12]

Even more than its predecessors, *Finnegans Wake* approximates to autobiography. Like Shem the Penman, the artist-self, Joyce had 'scrabbled and scratched and scriobbled and skrevened nameless shamelessness about everybody ever he met' (*FW* 182), and now, with an indelible ink made of his own excrement,

> the first till last alshemist wrote over every square inch of the only foolscap available, his own body, till by its corrosive sublimation one continuous

---

[11] 'Dante . . . Bruno. Vico . . . Joyce', in *Our Exagmination round his Factification for Incamination of Work in Progress* (London, Faber and Faber 1936), 6–7.

[12] *Letters* I, 241. Cf. ' "Of course," Joyce told me, "I don't take Vico's speculations literally: I use his cycles as a trellis" ' (Mary and Padraic Colum, *Our Friend James Joyce* (London, Gollancz 1959), 123).

present tense integument slowly unfolded all marryvoising moodmoulded cyclewheeling history (thereby, he said, reflecting from his own individual person life unlivable, transaccidentated through the slow fires of consciousness into a dividual chaos, perilous, potent, common to allflesh, human only, mortal). (FW 185–6)

Finnegans Wake is here summed up in terms of its manner, its shaping and its movement. 'Marryvoising' alludes to Marivaux whose stylistic refinement is described as 'la finesse de l'analyse psychologique et la délicatesse d'un style qui se modèle sur les nuances mêmes du sentiment';[13] the noun, 'Marivaudage', is defined, less sympathetically, as 'une recherche affectée dans le style, une grande subtilité dans les sentiments et une grande complication d'intrigues',[14] and bluntly explained in Chambers Twentieth Century Dictionary (1972 edn) as 'preciosity in writing'. All three could be applied to Finnegans Wake and there is a suggestion, too, of the marriage of many voices in the one continuous unfolding. The work is 'moodmoulded' presumably because the content of the chapters is shaped by and expressive of the varying moods of the dreaming mind, following each other in cyclic rise and fall. If it is a history, it is also a language with tense, voice, mood and accidence, and perhaps the description itself is meant to hint at a Viconian cycle in the succession of 'unfolded' (birth), marriage, 'mould' (death) and the 'wheeling' ricorso. Yet all of it is reflected by (not abstracted from) the writer's personal experience; it reflects 'life unlivable' because it is the essential life, which can be lived only by being translated into the accidents of space and time. This translation is performed by the consciousness which converts 'life' into living by projecting it into a world of things and people, and thus makes 'a dividual chaos' (that is to say, one distributed among a number of people or objects) out of the life within the individual. It is 'perilous', because always moving towards a fall, but 'potent', because always capable of re-creating itself. Since all creatures are involved in the physical cycle of birth-maturity-death-generation, it is 'common to allflesh', but, as the cycles exist only in the human consciousness of them, it is specifically and only human. It is 'mortal' because death is part of the cycle of living. The scheme attempts to relate the chaos of experience to its origins in the nature of 'life unlivable'; it is of the greatest possible generality but rooted in the writer's 'own individual person'.

The apprehension of general insights and the creation of the particulars of language, character and incident to express those insights are what engage all great novelists, and what Joyce had achieved in Dubliners, the Portrait and Ulysses. The method of Finnegans Wake most plainly derives from the 'Circe' chapter of Ulysses, where the movements of Bloom's unconscious are fantastically dramatized. There are hundreds of such dramatizations in Finnegans Wake: the difference is that there is no longer a sequence of events in the ordinary world of consciousness to which these dramatizations can be related. It is this absence of certain reference to

[13] Petit Larousse (Paris, Librairie Larousse 1967 edn), 1525.
[14] M-N. Bouillet, Dictionnaire Universel des Sciences, des Lettres et des Arts (Paris, Hachette 1854), 1005–6.

people, places and events outside the dream-world which causes most difficulty. It seems important to know who the dreamer is and what sort of life he is leading. Is he a Chapelizod publican, Humphrey Chimpden Earwicker, a man of many failures and fears, spending a troubled night, after a troubled day in the bar, with unconscious desire for his own young daughter as he turns away from his aging wife? Or is he the conformist son, Shaun, who certainly dominates several chapters, or the other son, Shem, the outcast artist? Is the dreamer, as Joyce is said to have told a friend, the legendary Irish hero, Finn McCool?[15] Or is he James Joyce himself? Or is the book a collection of dreams belonging to various members of the family? But, despite the differences about the identity of the dreamer, there is a general critical agreement about the incidents of the day leading up to the night of dreams: most critics agree that the scene is set in a Chapelizod public-house; that the Earwicker children are seen playing in the street before being called in to supper and then doing their homework together; that the evening in the bar is a somewhat rowdy one with stories and songs; that the publican, left in the bar, finishes the leavings and falls to the floor in a drunken doze; that when he has made his way to bed the sleep of him and his wife is disturbed by the crying of one of his twin sons; and that before dawn he and his wife make love together. This account is so frequently repeated that one hesitates to question it, but do dreams normally reflect so clearly the events immediately preceding sleep? No doubt, the story of Earwicker and his family is part of what is being presented in *Finnegans Wake*, but what is there to suggest that it refers to a 'real' world outside the dream? We must be careful not to require from the book rudimentary plot and individualized characters simply because we have come to expect such ingredients in novels. Joyce himself said, speaking of *Finnegans Wake*,

> One great part of every human existence is passed in a state which cannot be rendered sensible by the use of wideawake language, cutanddry grammar and goahead plot.[16]

He told a Danish journalist,

> There is . . . no connection between the people in *Ulysses* and the people in *Work in Progress*. There are in a way no characters. It's like a dream. The style is also changing and unrealistic, like the dream world. If one had to name a character, it would be just an old man. But his own connection with reality is doubtful.[17]

The last sentence again suggests Finn McCool, about whose historical existence there has been scholarly debate, and who, like the British Arthur, was supposed to be sleeping underground until the time should come for him to rise again. But Joyce, as in his book, seems to be avoiding specific identification – 'just an old man', – and even that phrase leaves it uncertain

[15] *Ellmann–JJ*, 557.
[16] *Letters* III, 146.
[17] *Ellmann–JJ*, 709.

whether he meant that the dream was an old man's dream, or that it was about an old man. If the dream were to encompass all human experience, it would have to be dreamed by an old man. Its forces and patterns would derive from our inheritance as men – basic human nature shaped by the whole of human history –, from our experiences since childhood, and from hopes and fears we take to sleep with us. These ingredients of every dream correspond, in historical and social terms, to the age of myth, the historical past, and the developing present, and, in all their forms, are at work in *Finnegans Wake*. In all of them H.C.E. and his family persist, but not as occupants of a public house. H.C.E. himself is sometimes a publican, but also a builder, a gardener, a politician, a viceroy, a producer, a proprietor of 'hotel and creamery establishments', and, at various times, is engaged in most other occupations; he appears as an Irishman, a Scandinavian, a Frenchman, a Turk, a Russian and is plainly an international figure. As 'Howth Castle and Environs' he is Dublin, as an early form of habitation 'a homelike cottage of elvanstone', as the builder of cities a man of 'hod, cement and edifices'; in the financial world he may be a prince of commerce ('Honour commercio's energy') or a despised tradesman ('He'll Cheat E'erawan'); as sinner he is 'human, erring and condonable', and as saint 'Ecce Hagios Chrisman'; he may be the 'High Church of England' or a chemical formula H_2CE_3; in his paternal role he is 'Haveth Childers Everywhere', and, by his universal title, 'Here Comes Everybody'. Why, out of all these roles, should that of the Chapelizod publican be singled out as the 'real' one? It seems more probable that the public-house and its occupants are no more than a contemporary image or symbol for the dreamer's somewhat confused sense of life – a place where the outer world surges in with its gossip, opinions, judgements and general rowdiness, where the private life of the family of man goes on upstairs and where Dublin's gifts to the living, the stout and whiskey flavoured by the waters and mud of the Liffey, are on tap.

This is, presumably, what Joyce meant by saying that 'there is no connection between the people in *Ulysses* and the people in *Work in Progress*'. There are, in fact, very obvious connections, both in terms of their inter-relationships and the nature of their experiences, but, in *Ulysses*, life is translated or subdivided into a number of individual selves in whom the universal forces are at work and the universal patterns displayed, whereas, in *Finnegans Wake*, the basic elements are the universal forces and patterns manifesting themselves in a kaleidoscope of 'one's thousand one nightinesses'. The psychic humiliations and recoveries of Bloom, Stephen's negations and sense of exile, Molly's uncritical acceptance of life as it is, all are subsumed in patterns implicit in man's nature and illustrated in the accidents of the life of each individual and society. We tend to explain the distresses of men like Bloom or Stephen in terms of their lives and situations, but *Finnegans Wake* goes beneath such particularities. All men experience psychological distress of one kind or another. We may attribute it to conscience, a divine discontent undermining our animal self-content; we may talk about Angst or guilt-complexes; or, if we are Christians, we may refer it to a sense of original sin. But whatever our explanations, we are all aware of the phenomenon and blame it on something that happened in the past, of ourselves or of our species. But, in *Finnegans Wake*, it is the universally recognized experience which is Joyce's concern, and our labels for it and explanations of it matter only because they are evidence of its universality – all the theories, religious, social and psychological, coexist because they are all human responses to the common human experience. In the dominant cyclic patterns, rise and fall is the fundamental movement, and consequently, from the first pages of the book, when Tim Finnegan climbs a ladder and falls off it, there are uncountable variations on the theme of falling – into sin, into crime, into bankruptcy, into loss of reputation, into social failure, falls due to drunkenness or to the physical law of falling bodies. Somewhere, at some time (or everywhere and always), Everybody has committed or feels that he has committed or is thought to have committed some quite unspecific offence. Or he has committed, in thought or deed, all offences, or, which amounts to the same thing, he is accused of all offences, for naturally, as Everybody, he is the accuser as well as the offender. There can be no end to it, no final verdict, for 'the unfacts, did we possess them, are too imprecisely few to warrant our certitude', and no two courts reach the same conclusion:

> Yet certes one is. Eher the following winter had overed the pages of nature's book and till Ceadurbar-atta-Cleath became Dablena Tertia, the shadow of the huge outlander, maladik, multvult, magnoperous, had bulked at the bar of a rota of tribunals in manor hall as in thieves' kitchen, mid pillow talk and chithouse chat, on Marlborough Green as through Molesworth Fields, here sentenced pro tried with Jedburgh justice, there acquitted contestimony with benefit of clergy. (*FW* 57–8)

The fact of the matter is that there are no facts, only 'unfacts' and they are few, imprecise and, in any case, unavailable, and verdicts, though innumerable, depend entirely on the mood of the court, *pro* or *con*. What is certain is that we are constantly on trial, in all the courts of our mind: the trials are not a consequence of a crime, real or imaginary; the supposed crimes are a consequence of the trials. The awareness of being tried is what is basic to human nature, and all the rest is projected from it into the worlds of consciousness and dreams.

Similarly, the conflict of artist and citizen becomes in *Finnegans Wake* merely a variety of a fundamental opposition within our nature, which may express itself in an allegorical debate between Justice and Mercy, in the cosmological myth of St Michael and Satan, in the legendary brother-conflict of Romulus and Remus, in the historical battles of Wellington and Napoleon, in the struggle for Irish independence, in a brawl at a wake, or in children's games. The fact of conflict is essential: its varying natures and the particular reasons offered for it are accidental. Like the sense of being on trial, the conflict is not something to be explained; it is elemental, irreducible, a source of explanations. Everything in our nature evolves its opposite in the process of defining itself, and without the opposition there would be no movement, no life, just as without a permanent principle of rising there could be no permanent principle of falling. Thus the writer who began by adopting the heroic pose of artist bravely facing the philistine mob ends by symbolizing literature as a letter dictated by the undiscriminating flux of life to the isolated artist, delivered by his opposite, the citizen (for without a society there would be no literature), and addressed to Everybody:

> Letter, carried of Shaun, son of Hek, written of Shem, brother of Shaun, uttered for Alp, mother of Shem, for Hek, father of Shaun. (*FW* 420)

The artist who had insisted on the *integritas* and *consonantia* of the apprehended image, requiring in the work of art the elimination of all that was irrelevant, or unrelated to the structural rhythm of the whole, was now trying to create an image so all-encompassing that theoretically nothing could be irrelevant or unrelated to it. By definition, nothing in human experience – however commonplace or esoteric, cosmic or minuscule – could not belong: the problem was to decide where it belonged and to invent ways of representing its relevance and relationship. To provide the multifarious patterns and connections, Joyce drew on all the religious, mythical, legendary, scientific, sociological, historical, psychological, linguistic, musical and numerical schemata that he could lay hands on, and supplemented them with every literary device and verbal trick he could bend to his purpose. The initials which link the hundreds of manifestations of H.C.E. and A.L.P. are only one example of the countless tricks of acrostic, anagram, paragram, logogriph, rebus, conundrum, Spoonerism, *double-entendre*, rhyming slang, parody and pun which are put to work, and carried to extremes as far beyond their normal usage as the functions they serve exceed their normal functions. Addison denied puns the name of 'true wit' because they were not translatable into other languages,[18] but Joyce, requiring a potential infinity of verbal links to match the potential infinity of his materials, punned in every language he knew and many which he plundered, creating multilingual and interlingual plays on words, as though all human languages were necessary to express all human experience. (Of course, English is the staple language of the book because it is from the dreaming mind of an English-speaking man that this universal vision emanates, but it is an English which, like the dreamer's mind, is subjected to pressures from a linguistic environment reaching all over the world.)

Given the length of the book and the variety of purposes for which Joyce employs his verbal devices – sometimes to mark the presence of a major theme or personage, sometimes to establish relationships between the parts, sometimes to give a general geographical or national colouring to a chapter or an episode, sometimes to suggest the coexistence of opposites, and sometimes to make a local point or joke – it seems unlikely that every detail of the work will be apprehended. Yet his management of the devices

[18] *The Spectator* LXI (10 May 1711).

is not merely surface embroidery: he is usually exploring meanings. For instance, the much-quoted phrase 'the flushpots of Euston and the hanging garments of Marylebone' (*FW* 192) seems at first sight merely a comical distortion of two familiar expressions, the kind of joke which one may laugh at once or twice, and regard as an attempt to belittle the sordid present by comparison with the glories of the past. But the phrase comes from the passage describing the nostalgic dreams of the exiled artist, Shem the Penman, and its allusions are specific. According to *Brewer's Dictionary of Phrase and Fable*[19] 'Sighing for the flesh-pots of Egypt' means

> Hankering for good things no longer at your command. The children of Israel said they wished they had died 'when they sat by the flesh-pots of Egypt' (*Exod.* xvi, 3) rather than embark on their long sojourn in the wilderness.

The same work of reference explains that the Hanging Gardens of Babylon

> according to tradition were constructed by Nebuchadnezzar, to gratify his wife Amytis, who felt weary of the flat plains of Babylon, and longed for something to remind her of her native Median hills.

Thus the joke unites two great images of the recurring theme of an exile's nostalgia, scales them down to the more mundane level appropriate to the 'low' Shem, and relates them to the more specifically Joycean sense of the artist's hankering after the commonplaces of the ordinary life of the citizen from which he is exiled by his vocation. (One is reminded of Mrs Piozzi's perceptive comment on Dr Johnson's recurrent turning to the poor friends of his early days – 'Ever sighing for the Tea & Bread & Butter of Life, when satiated with the Turtle & Burgundy of it'.)[20] Not all of Joyce's quibbles are as funny or as penetrating as that, but they are all, in various ways, similarly functional. They make the book very difficult (some would say impossible) to read, but it is hard to see how, without their aid, he could have condensed and integrated into a single work even his representative selection of the totality of human experience.

Assertions that *Finnegans Wake* was the product of a phenomenally ingenious talent with nothing to say, or of a mind turned in upon itself by partial blindness, or of a great writer spoiled by the adulation of an international literary clique are plainly wrong. With even a limited grasp of the book, one can see that it is the work of a searching and complex mind, exploring its own and human nature, and that its themes and attitudes and methods grew from Joyce's earlier work. Moreover, the view of Joyce as a man locked up in his own literary imagination ignores the greater part of his life and work: it naively reflects the portraits of the young Stephen Dedalus and Shem the Penman. The truth seems to be that, from early on, Joyce recognized and eventually learnt to live with and accept his dual

---

[19] 7th edn (London, Cassell 1963), 368 and 437.
[20] *The Life of Samuel Johnson LL.D.*, by *James Boswell, with marginal comments and markings from two copies annotated by Hester Lynch Thrale Piozzi*, ed. G. Fletcher, The Limited Editions Club: 1938: III, p. 343.

nature.[21] If as a youth, he sometimes felt cut off from his family and his fellows by his intelligence and talent, he was also the white-haired boy of the family, the prize-winner, the potential priest, and, according to report, a sociable and popular boy. He grew up to be Bloom as well as Stephen, Shaun as well as Shem; and, in his later years, the writer whose work was acclaimed as the product of high genius and denounced as obscene filth led a life of bourgeois respectability. Now that his private letters to his wife, with their mixture of high-flown spirituality and vulgar sexuality, can be read, they are referred to as evidence of an almost pathological inner torment deriving from

> Joyce's distaste for and disgust with his 'bestial' side and his *inability* to integrate polar traits in his personality.[22]

Anyone who claims to have achieved such an integration is deceiving himself. Sexual love is a mixture of the 'spiritual' and the 'bestial', though most men keep the latter from public gaze, and some even from their own. What the letters seem to show is that Joyce was so far from trying to integrate these 'polar traits' that he gave expression to each of them in extreme forms, as though he felt that life and development lay in their opposition and interaction.[23] It is not only the language of *Finnegans Wake* that is kaleidoscopic: every year of man's span brings new meanings to and discovers new meanings in his experience, and 'the book of Doublends Jined' combines these meanings; it tracks the orbit of the individual life returning to its starting-point; it traces the story of human society in the figure of the Dublin giant buried, but not dead, in the city's history and geography; it follows the 'cyclewheeling history' of humanity; and it presents the image of a human nature whose progression is dependent on the opposition of contrary forces. This view was not one that Joyce had grasped from the start, despite his long admiration for Giordano Bruno. In 1903, in reviewing a study of Bruno's philosophy, he remarked,

> Is it not strange, then, that Coleridge should have set him down a dualist, a later Heraclitus, and should have represented him as saying in effect: 'Every

---

[21] Cf. 'He was unwilling to give up either the spiritual idealism which had sustained him as a child, or the erotic drive which was agitating his adolescence. If debauchery was a part of his character, and he sometimes said it was, then it must be justified. The word 'artist', which in the late nineteenth century had been invested with a secular awe, offered a profession which would protect all his soul instead of only its idealistic side, and might yet give it a profane sanctity' (Richard Ellmann's Introduction, *Letters* II, xxxviii).

[22] Darcy O'Brien, *The Conscience of James Joyce* (Princeton University Press 1968), 51 n. 21.

[23] See, for instance, his letter to his wife on 2 December 1909: '*But*, side by side and inside this spiritual love I have for you there is also a wild beast-like craving for every inch of your body, for every secret and shameful part of it, for every odour and act of it' (*Letters* II, 269). Richard Ellmann's comment on Joyce's letters to his wife is perceptive: 'What was unusual about his attitude was not that he saw his wife as his mother or that he demanded inordinate fulfilment of either role. The novelty lay in his declining to confuse the two images and instead holding them remorsefully apart, opposing them to each other so that they became the poles of his mind' (*Ellmann–JJ*, 305).

power in nature or in spirit must evolve an opposite as the sole condition and means of its manifestation; and every opposition is, therefore, a tendency to reunion'?[24]

It no longer seemed strange in 1925, when he described Bruno's system in the very terms Coleridge used:

> His philosophy is a kind of dualism – every power in nature must evolve an opposite in order to realise itself and opposition brings reunion etc etc.[25]

The notion was one of those which, he was to say, 'have gradually forced themselves on me through circumstances of my own life',[26] and, in particular, it manifested itself in his career as a writer – from the initially separate images of the citizen in *Dubliners* and the evolved opposite, the isolated artist, in the *Portrait*, to their intersection in *Ulysses*, and, finally, to their conflicting union and identity in the everyman of *Finnegans Wake*.

As, in spirit, Joyce's writings drew nearer to the common man, so, in form, they drew farther away from the common man's notion of what fiction should be; as the artist learned to recognize and accept his identity with the citizen, so he was freed from citizen-like inhibitions on the practice of his art. The boy, Stephen Dedalus, had been humiliated when his father's cronies told him 'that he had a great look of his grandfather' and he felt that he was sundered from them and from his father by 'an abyss of fortune or of temperament'. Yet when Joyce's father, the original of Simon Dedalus, died, the mature artist was conscious mainly of his likeness to and inheritance from the old man:

> My father had an extraordinary affection for me. He was the silliest man I ever knew and yet cruelly shrewd. He thought and talked of me up to his last breath. I was very fond of him always, being a sinner myself, and even liked his faults. Hundreds of pages and scores of characters in my books came from him. His dry (or rather wet) wit and his expression of face convulsed me often with laughter. When he got the copy I sent him of *Tales Told* etc. (so they write me) he looked a long time at Brancusi's Portrait of J.J. and finally remarked: Jim has changed more than I thought. I got from him his portraits, a waistcoat, a good tenor voice, and an extravagant licentious disposition (out of which, however, the greater part of any talent I may have springs) but, apart from these, something else I cannot define. But if an observer thought of my father and myself and my son too physically, though we are all very different, he could perhaps define it.[27]

Although Joyce's concept of the role of the artist hardly changed, this letter shows how much his understanding of his own gifts and experiences had developed. The father who had unwittingly provided the material for the images of a venal and time-serving citizenry in 'Ivy Day in the Committee Room' and 'Grace', had served as model for the feckless and insensitive boaster of the *Portrait* and for the selfish old man of *Ulysses* whose failure

[24] *CW*, 133–4.
[25] *Letters* I, 224–5.
[26] *Ibid.*, 241.
[27] *Ibid.*, 312.

to understand his son had sent the young man elsewhere to find a spiritual father, now is acknowledged as the source of much of the artist's material and most of his talent. The confirmed egotist is seen to have had 'an extraordinary affection' for his eldest son; his inconsistency is attributed to opposed traits in his character – the 'silliest' of men is also 'cruelly shrewd'; the father's extravagance and licentiousness have been inherited by the son and have become the foundation of a dedicated and disciplined art; and a common nature, though indefinable, can be perceived in very different manifestations in the three generations. Even in the anecdote about Brancusi's drawing, one can perceive Joyce's satisfaction in his father's understanding of him – that beneath the idealized figure of the world-famous artist was 'Jim', at once more ordinary and more complex than any symbolic arrangement of straight lines and a spiral. At the end of the *Portrait*, Stephen had mockingly summed up his father's career as 'a medical student, an oarsman, a tenor, an amateur actor, a shouting politician, a small landlord, a small investor, a drinker, a good fellow, a storyteller, somebody's secretary, something in a distillery, a taxgatherer, a bankrupt and at present a praiser of his own past '(*P* 245). To the would-be artist, determined to pursue his vocation with single-minded constancy, the spectacle of his father's inconsequential and aimless metamorphoses was ridiculous and contemptible. But, later, that same Protean mutability was honoured in the figure of 'Here Comes Everybody', in whom Joyce united the natures of his father and himself.

It was this kind of maturing in his vision of himself, his family and his past life, and not aesthetic theories or the ideas of Vico, Bruno or Jung, that shaped Joyce's development as a writer and led to *Finnegans Wake*. It had been necessary for the young man to renounce his ties with others before he could re-establish them in a form where they were not only compatible with but necessary to his fulfilment as an artist; similarly, it was necessary for him to begin by emphasizing the irreconcilable conflict between the artist and the citizen in order to discover that that conflict raged inside himself and in all men, and was the necessary condition of anything he might achieve.

Index